THE MEANING OF RELIGION

THE MEANING OF RELIGION

LECTURES IN THE PHENOMENOLOGY OF RELIGION

By the late
PROF. W. BREDE KRISTENSEN

With an introduction by
PROF. HENDRIK KRAEMER

Translated by
JOHN B. CARMAN

MARTINUS NIJHOFF / THE HAGUE

Photomechanical reprint 1971

Published with a grant from the Netherlands Organization
for the Advancement of Pure Research

First printing 1960
Second printing 1968
Third printing 1971

ISBN 90 247 0084 1

PRINTED IN THE NETHERLANDS

TABLE OF CONTENTS

INTRODUCTION

by HENDRIK KRAEMER

*formerly Professor of the History and Phenomenology of
Religion at Leyden, and later Director of the Ecumenical
Institute of the World Council of Churches, Château de Bossey,
Switzerland*

This book needs a special introduction, for without it, its real significance and value cannot be grasped. This is particularly true because the author, W. Brede Kristensen, is entirely unknown in the Anglo-Saxon world. The writer of this Introduction counts it one of the great privileges of his life to have been one of his pupils and to have become, at the insistence of Kristensen himself, his successor in the famous Chair of the History and Phenomenology of Religion at the University of Leyden (Holland). Kristensen is not only unknown in the Anglo-Saxon world, but in nearly the whole world, except for Holland and the Scandinavian countries. Yet I do not hesitate to say that in the last fifty years, he was not only one of the most original and penetrating scholars in the field of religion, but also one of the greatest phenomenologists of religion, if not the greatest. In fact, even though I myself differ in a very marked degree from my teacher and friend Kristensen in my own approach to the subject of Religion, I am personally convinced that he is undoubtedly the greatest phenomenologist of religion in the first half of the twentieth century, not excepting G. van der Leeuw, whose name deservedly enjoys international fame.

That Kristensen has remained until his death internationally unknown, is entirely due to his characteristic personality. He was wholly absorbed in his field of study, and devoted to it as a lover to his beloved. It fascinated him to such a degree that he was not at all interested in publishing, nor in attending Congresses or Conferences on the Science of Religion, nor in creating a "school", but exclusively in pursuing the quest for understanding the phenomena of Religion as the believer in a given religion understood them. He was therefore entirely unconcerned as to whether or not he became well known. His life as a professor at Leyden (1901–1937) was entirely consonant with this wholehearted devotion and this rare unconcern. It is no exaggeration to say that in all these years he moved in four spheres: his study, the classroom, his daily walks, and his family, which included for him such intimate friends as the great historian J. Huizinga and the expert in International Law, C. van Vollenhoven. Most of his publications, which after all are rather numerous, came into being because he considered it his duty to present, if possible yearly, a communication to the Dutch "Royal Academy of Sciences", of which he was since 1911 a member and one of the most regular attendants of its monthly meetings. This form of publication suited his characteristic unconcern for all real publicity, because – as is well known – to publish only in the official transactions of a learned Society is often one of the best ways to self-burial, or, at least, not the best way to become known. For the rest, his writings appeared mainly in article form in Dutch and Norwegian magazines, and some in book form, either collections of special articles or longer treatments of one theme.*

Kristensen's lectures on phenomenology of Religion at Leyden University were as enthusiastically attended by the students as they were enthusiastically given by the master. What probably impressed his hearers the most was that Kristensen's evident and contagious enthusiasm was deeply rooted in an extraordinarily conscientious scholarship and grasp of the subject. The hours spent at his feet in the then rather unseemly lecture rooms of the University, or in his study in intense conversation, are among the most shining memories of my life as a student, in the years between 1910 and 1920.

During his lifetime I often tried to persuade Kristensen to publish especially his lectures on the phenomenology of Religion in order to leave them as a legacy and inspiring example to his pupils and the younger generation of scholars. He neither refused nor promised. After his death (1953) it appeared that, thanks to the faithful endeavours of Mrs. Kristensen and of one of his sons, the Rev. Bjarne Kristensen, there was available a coherent

* For a complete list of his publications see p. 497.

(though not complete) text of the various subjects he had treated
in his lectures on phenomenology. This circumstance induced
me to propose that this precious material be published in English,
because these lectures give an excellent impression of his way of
unearthing the inner meaning of religious rites, symbols and conceptions. Mrs. Kristensen was so kind as to agree with the idea,
lending moreover her indispensable assistance, and we were so
happy to find a young American student of Yale Divinity School,
Mr. John Carman, willing to do the work of translation. He was
fully qualified to do so, because he spent two years at Leyden
University studying especially phenomenology of religion, and
mastered in that time the Dutch language.

Having given account of why and how this book came into
being, it is now appropriate to give some facts about Kristensen's
life and career.

Kristensen was born in 1867, in Christiansand, Norway. His
father was the minister of the local church. His mother was a
sister of the famous dramatist and writer, Björnson. In 1884
he became a student in Oslo. His first choice was theology, but
after a year he switched to the study of the classical languages.
His deep conviction that religion is the profoundest thing in the
life of individuals and peoples led him to choose the History
of Religion as his special field. This choice in itself was already
an indication of the most marked feature of his personality,
that is to say, his independent individualism in the best sense
of the word. In those days the History of Religions as a special
field of study was hardly known. In many respects the tools
for applying oneself to it were still in their infancy. His friends
laughed at the idea, but his father understood his choice. This
decision became the starting point of a long and arduous course
of acquiring the tools for equipping himself for the task which
became his lifework to understand the ancient religions, or
better, to understand and interpret the believers in these
religions as they understood themselves and wished to be understood by others. In order to understand better Kristensen's
unusual power of intuition, one of the indispensable endow-
ments for a good phenomenologist, it is worthwhile to remark in
passing that he manifested in his student years his hidden artistic
nature, in a rather large production of poetry. His affinity

for art is, of course, easily explained by the fact that he was a nephew of Björnson, but appeared also in his student years in his friendships with artists or lovers of art. It seems to me that it may be said that no man can study in the field of the humanities, in which everything hinges upon the art of congenial interpretation based on solid knowledge, if he does not have something of the artist in his make-up, even if he does not practice in any field of art. This holds true specifically in regard to phenomenology.

To acquire the most essential tools, that is to say a competent knowledge of the ancient languages, Kristensen studied Sanskrit, Hebrew, Egyptian, Babylonic, Avestan, and Phoenecian. In order to master them he studied not only (till 1890) in Oslo, but in Leyden, under the famous C. P. Tiele and A. Kuenen, and in Paris with the not less famous Egyptologist, G. Maspero; at the same time, together with his friend, the later well known archbishop, Nathan Söderblom, continuing his study of the Avestan language. He also stayed a year in London, working particularly in the British Museum. For seven years, from 1890 till 1897, he assiduously pursued this apprenticeship, except for a break of two years back in Oslo. In those days this apprenticeship in mastering these ancient languages and in learning to read documents in them was a far more formidable performance than it is even today, because one often had singlehandedly to penetrate these languages, and the available documents, as for instance good grammars and dictionaries, were still nonexistent or rudimentary. Only irresistable passion, certain indispensable natural gifts and dogged perseverance, all combined, could lead in such a situation to satisfying results. Kristensen manifested the combination of these qualities, e.g. in his stay at Leyden (1890–1892) by locking himself in for about two weeks in order to master Babylonian cuneiform script. In 1896 he acquired his doctor's degree with a dissertation entitled, "Aegypternes forestillinger om livet efter döden i forbindelse med guderne Ra og Osiris." This first fruit of his scientific abilities already struck one of the grand themes which fascinated him his whole life: the mysterious interrelation of life and death as evident, for

* "Egyptian Ideas about Life after Death in Connection with Gods Re and Osiris".

instance, in the Egyptian myths of Light (Ra) and Vegetation
(Osiris). In these years of untiring study, it was not only language
and texts, but deep experiences of life which contributed to his
formation for understanding the mystery of life and death as
conceived in the religions to whose understandings he devoted
his powers of mind and heart. I am thinking here of his marriage
in 1896 with Anna Lunde, one of the first Norwegian woman-
graduates in Law, whom he lost by death in 1897, during their
stay in Paris.

From 1897 till 1901 Kristensen fulfilled a teaching assignment
at the University of Oslo, taking by preference as his subject
the Avesta religion, which remained a lifelong favourite with
him. In 1901 Leyden called him to become Tiele's successor.
He accepted and never regretted having done so. He appreciated
highly the free academic atmosphere in the theological faculty
of Leyden (in Holland the Chair of History and Phenomenology
of Religion is always in the theological faculty) and found ample
opportunity for his studies in Leyden's museums. This made
him decide to decline in 1912 a call to a professorship in his own
university Oslo. Drawing the logical conclusion from this decision
he applied for naturalization as a Dutch subject in 1913. He
acclimatized fully in Holland, and mastered the language in
such a way, that it is a delight to read his richly varied, pure and
virile Dutch style. In 1916 he married Jacoba Heldring, the
daughter of one of his best friends, a well-known minister of the
Church in Amsterdam, belonging to one of the outstanding
Christian families in Holland. So he became a fully integrated
Dutchman, finding it at his retirement in 1937 self-evident to
stay on in Holland till his death, which occurred in 1953.

Since Kristensen in 1901 became a professor in Leyden, he
led in general the uneventful life of the scholar, fully committed
to his field of study. Some special events need, however, to be
mentioned. In 1912 he stayed for reasons of research in Greece,
Egypt and Rome. In 1922 he delivered the well-known Olaus
Petri-lectures in Uppsala, which resulted in the publication of a
book, entitled *Livet fra döden* (Life out of death). In 1946, when
he was already nearly ten years professor emeritus, he acted for
some time as a guest professor at Oslo University. The lectures
there resulted in a book *Religionshistorisk Studium*, also transla-

ted into Dutch by Mrs. Kristensen under the title: *Inleiding tot de Godsdienstgeschiedenis* (Introduction to the History of Religion). This excellent little book, which treats in Kristensen's masterful and original fashion the Roman, Greek, Egyptian and Avestan religions, and adds some phenomenological chapters to this treatment, contains the ripe fruits of lifelong studying and thinking, and probably without intending it, makes many illuminating observations, fully relevant to the problem of religion today.

During the German occupation of Holland (1940–1945), Kristensen had occasion to show his true mettle, his imperturbable independence of mind, and his truly religious spirit. Although apparently he continued his ordinary life of quiet study, of non-participation in the events of the day, he was passionately interested in the fight for justice and fearless freedom of the mind. In those days, since I lived next door, I often visited him to inform him of all that was going on in this fight. He rejoiced always in every straightforward, fearless action, and encouraged us to go on without hesitation. He was obliged to leave with his family his house in Leyden and to live in a house which belonged to him, situated in a beautiful village near Arnhem, because there the food conditions were better than in Leyden. But it so happened that he and his family lived through the whole ordeal of the battle around Arnhem in 1944 after the famous British air-borne attack. The house was largely destroyed; the whole family had to flee. In spite of his 77 years Kristensen retained his customary cheerfulness and fearlessness. As always he had his moorings in eternity. One of the main losses in this catastrophe was the nearly total destruction of all his annotations and drawings, patiently brought together in an uninterrupted life of assiduous study during more than fifty years. We, his pupils, when in visiting him in his study, always looked with awe at this mighty battery, this rich arsenal for giving content, authenticity and colour to his fascinating ideas. Everybody who heard about this loss, thought this was not only irreparable, but certainly would be to Kristensen a stunning blow. One of the most impressive experiences of my life was my first meeting with him after this catastrophe. When I started talking about his loss, he cheerfully waved it aside, saying: "Let us not complain

about that. Let us rather begin again. The good side of it is
that I now have to try to look at things again with new eyes.''
With these remarks the whole matter was dismissed, and the
young old man of 77 took up another topic.

Till his death, on September 25, 1953, he continued his studies
with the same keen enthusiasm, evoking from many of his pupils,
now in high places of responsibility, moving and grateful articles
and adresses in which they expressed their deep indebtedness
to his inspiring teaching and personality.

This little had to be said about the man and the scholar
Kristensen, because it is a real help in understanding the peculiar
character of his work as it is [e.g.] evident from the phenomenological studies, contained in the book for which this introduction
is written. One of the items of Ancient Wisdom, which he had
made his own, was the belief of the Ancients-particularly the
Egyptians-that all script has a soul. The attentive reader of this
book will discover that what Kristensen writes does not merely
enlarge his knowledge and insight, but brings him into communication with the soul of an extraordinary man.

The book itself opens with an Introduction and then treats
extensively three great fields of Ancient Religion: Cosmology,
Anthropology (in the sense of: understanding of man), and
Cultus, subdivided in A. Concrete objectifications of the Cultus,
B. Cultic Acts. In A there were originally also two chapters on
"Holy men" and "Holy doctrines", but they were not incorporated into this book because the state in which they were left
behind by Kristensen was too incomplete. Out of respects for
Kristensen's original personality, those who with scrupulous
care prepared the text for print did not want to give on their
own account a more rounded version of these chapters. This
means by inference that the text contained in this book reflects
Kristensen's lectures on these subjects as they were given in the
course of the years of his academic activity. It should, however,
be noted that the field he actually treated was wider.

Originally Kristensen's mind roamed over wide spaces, as
appears from the languages he studied. But in the course of the
years he excercised a severe self-limitation. In his Phenomenology
as presented partially in this book, he occasionally alludes to

common concepts in the Mediterranean civilizations and India and China, but he expressed his self-imposed limitation often in the words: I stop at the Hindu Kush. During his professorate he lectured at different times on Egyptian, Babylonian-Assyrian, Avestan, Greek and Roman religion, but he concentrated in the long run mainly on Egypt, Greece and Rome, though the interpretation of the religion of the Avesta also remained a pet subject for him, just because of its peculiar character. His self-imposed limitation never meant a total abandonment of the fields accessible to him by his solid knowledge of their languages, and behind this self-limitation lay his high conception of the indispensability of the mastering of the "sources." In his lifetime the sources for the study of the fields with which he was familiar grew so rapidly and immensely that even a man of Kristensen's stature felt himself unable to keep fully abreast with them, and therefore he decided with characteristic scientific modesty in favour of greater concentration. His real centre of concentration was Egypt and its religion. Egypt's world of religious wisdom was the gate through which he entered into the whole range of the ancient Mediterranean civilizations and religions, among which he also counted the pre-prophetic religion of Israel. The great conclusion to which he came was that they all had in common a few all-pervading apprehensions. These common apprehensions were their cosmic orientation, their "religious sense of nature," by which term Kristensen tried to formulate the direct, intuitive apprehension by the Ancients of Cosmos and Nature as a spiritual, divine reality; the duality of death and life, transposed and harmonized in the oneness of the totality, whose mysterious ineffability nevertheless is magnificently suggested in the many myths and symbols of the Ancients. Other ways, peculiar to Kristensen, of expressing this was to call it the theme of the spontaneous, divine life, rising out of death, the ever recurring, truly miraculous resurrection of life, the supreme reality, the supreme wonder and the supreme mystery.

Terms like the "religious sense of nature" etc. recur over all the pages of what he has written. He rightly recurred constantly to them and to the interpretation of their meaning, because this ancient apprehension of Nature and Cosmos has become entirely alien to us, children of the modern Age. The need for true and effective interpretation requires repetition.

Kristensen moved with heart and mind in this world of elementary apprehensions and he applied himself with endless delight to the interpretation of their manifold concrete expressions in myth, cultus, speculation and attitude towards life, the world and the structure of Society and State. Everyone who studies his publications with inner understanding will be im-· pressed by the remarkable combination of a grand monotony with a colourful polyphony. He lived so intensely in this grandiose, vanished world of religious apprehension, and in his effort to understand and interpret it, that although his lucid mind remained wholly under the control of solid scholarship, his remarks in lecture or conservation had a rhapsodic quality. As a student when listening to him, I often had the feeling that not only did I hear an unusually gifted teacher, but that I was in the presence of a scholarly equipped mystagogue, who initiated us in a world of unsuspected mystery. He gripped us, because he himself was gripped. This was the secret of his never flagging enthusiasm. I had the privilege of knowing Kristensen from 1911 till his death. In the last years of his life his enthusiastic way of telling about a subject that occupied him for the time being was as bright as ever. Countless times he could return to his seemingly "monotonous" interpretation of the facts by integrating them into the great elementary apprehensions, but in doing so it was as if he made for the very first time an unexpected discovery. He certainly knew a great deal of the unspeakable joy of true discovery, which falls to the lot of truly great scholars. Kristensen, who rightly had a high regard for Schleiermacher's power of religious intuition, was in fact the man who spelled out in concrete interpretations Schleiermacher's famous definition of Religion as "Anschauung des Universums."

It needs to be mentioned that Kristensen worked hard for a while in the field of the so-called "primitive" religions. I remember very well a course on the famous books of Spencer and Gillen on the Australian Aborigines, on which Durkheim built his famous, but untenable theory of the origin of Religion. However Kristensen later entirely abandoned this field of study. He had the feeling that he was not able to enter into their inner reality, because he did not know the languages of these people.

Moreover, he distrusted more and more the reliability of the sources; that is to say the voluminous descriptions of tribes or of all kinds of customs and beliefs, by perhaps partly competent but in many cases patently incompetent people. I have often listened to his spirited denunciations of these anthropological studies, and could not always refrain from dissent, because my own experience in this field – particularly in Indonesia – inclined me to a more positive attitude. In Kristensen's case, however, his attitude was perfectly logical, because a man of his calibre and training could not but work first-hand, by direct and personal access to the sources. Work on the "primitive" religions was to him only possible at best second-hand, and that was to him "contra naturam." The consideration that the study of "primitive" religions and societies was since E. B. Tylor's *Primitive Culture* increasingly in fashion, did not impress his splendid independence of mind and judgment.

Phenomenology is at present the order of the day. Not only Phenomenology of Religion, but of Law. etc., of nearly everything. This is to a great extent due to the development of the philosophical phenomenology through Husserl, Scheler, Merleau-Ponty and others. There is justification for saying that it is nowadays fashionable to know about the phenomenological approach and its famous rule of "epochè," and to practise it; or, what is oftener the case, to pretend to practise it, because many take it – quite mistakenly – wholly as a new method for ascertaining objective knowledge. It is undeniable that the genuine inspiration behind the phenomenological vogue is the not less genuine scientific desire to have a new possibility of approximating the unattainable scientific objectivity, which has haunted the world in a peculiar way during the last century. Indeed, especially in regard to the various areas of culture, which are the creation of man, a well disciplined phenomenological approach is an indispensable and rewarding enterprise in the field of all social sciences or, to use the time-honoured German term, "die Geisteswissenschaften." This phenomenological approach is the effort to understand these areas of culture, e.g. religion, according to their *own* inner meaning and structure, leaving aside in the course of this endeavour all judgment upon them.

The great significance of Kristensen in this whole matter is that he, though not ignorant of all this clamour, quietly and determinedly went his way, unruffled by the preferences and pet theories of the day. He simply *was* a phenomenologist. He was a phenomenologist "avant la lettre." He did it "auf eigener Faust." He lived in it. In the field of Religion, as I have already said, I do not know one better. By studying his works, without necessarily becoming his disciple and the adherent of his ideas, one can better learn to *practice* the phenomenological approach than by studying the works of Husserl or Merleau-Ponty, valuable and epochal as they certainly are. For one who wants to be a phenomenologist, Kristensen is a splendid model to emulate. For from his example one can learn that good phenomenology – which really succeeds to a certain extent in making the subject of study speak, as it were, with its own authentic voice – is not primarily a method but an art, on the basis of a solid, critical knowledge of the facts involved. It is an art which demands the total personality, all the powers of intuition, divination and penetration. Phenomenology, to use a modern analogy, is the art of finding the key for decoding the secret code of the inner meaning of Religion. In the introductory part of his book Kristensen gives a clear account of how he conceives the phenomenology of Religion. He defines it as the systematically pursued, comparative endeavour to interpret and understand (not: explain) religious phenomena of the same category (sacrifice, prayer, sacraments, etc.), appearing in different religions, to get at their inner meaning. The requirement, he says, is a scrupulous reverence for the facts and genuinely sympathetic understanding. It is clear that this is something else than a new method of research, which automatically yields results. It is for the true phenomenologist the lifelong *education* in the *right* art of empathy (to use this clumsy translation of the German "Einfühlung") for the subject of his research.

Kristensen does not make extravagant claims for phenomenology, as if it can deliver all the goods we desire. He takes care to note that the phenomenological endeavour towards true understanding and adequate interpretation remains necessarily proximate, because we as detached observers always remain in the sphere of "imaginatively entering into." That is the limit of all empathy. The phenomenologist must not try to understand "the

essence of religion." That is a philosophical concern. His special
task is to enter into the mind of the believer. To understand a
religious phenomenon as the believer understands or understood it, is the true job of the phenomenologist. It testifies to
Kristensen's perspicacity and discernment that this understanding is, according to him, quite different from attaining to
the *faith* of the believer.

With this conception of the existence and activity of the
phenomenologist, it is wholly understandable that Kristensen
makes the striking statement that the student of religion
"grows himself religiously" with and by his work. It is sad to
say that this statement is not only striking, but unusual. The
impression one often gets is that many students of religion grow
sterile, detached, uncommitted or indifferent to religion. For
Kristensen religion was a sovereign entity, independent of all
finite entities. Religion was to him being rooted in eternity.
Although he held that religious language is entirely symbolic, he
had the fine spiritual tact to maintain that – in spite of this –
faith is oriented towards an immediate divine Reality and not
towards symbols of this Reality; a tact not always shown by
philosophers of Religion, who manoeuver so confidently with the
concept of Symbol.

When in 1901 Kristensen came as a young man to Leyden, he
had already practically lost all interest in the evolutionist explanation of Religion, which in those days was so dominant.
In that respect he was not following the path of his great prede-
cessor C. P. Tiele, who was one of the scions of this evolutionist
view. There were some important reasons for this choice to go
his solitary way. His real aim was to interpret and penetrate
the inner meaning and the reality of the religious phenomena as
understood by the believers themselves. These phenomena had
to be grasped in their own authentic significance and value.
The genetic, evolutionist explanation and grading of Religions
repelled him by their superficiality and artificiality. This approach to the mystery of Religion seemed to him a wasteful
occupation *about* Religion, but not a serious entering *into* the
reality of Religion. The book I introduce contains many utterances of impatience with the genetic and evolutionist dog-
maism of the day. His criticisms in this respect, made fifty

years ago, are now more and more accepted, but for a long time they were lonely deviations from the dominant thinking which revelled in explaining and construing grand tableaux of religious evolution, without having ever asked the preliminary fundamental question of what religion really is. It was taken for granted that one knew this, even if the scholar himself was religiously entirely uncommitted. Kristensen, on the contrary, affirmed – as is evident in this book – that no serious student of Religion could do so without being himself profoundly religious. By taking this line Kristensen showed himself a true phenomenologist, who does not measure and compare as to the stage of value, but whose sole aim is: to understand.

This independent attitude led him naturally to his own characteristic approach, which pervades his whole phenomenology. That is to say, to understand every religion in its own, inherent, characteristic value and meaning. Every religion takes itself as absolute, and the scholar has to take this attitude seriously in order to understand as the believers understood themselves. One of the most challenging results of this conception of his task is Kristensens interpretation of the Roman religion. One can have reservations and critical questions in regard to his intuitive interpretation, but I for one do not know any description of the religion of the Romans by any one of the great "authorities" in this field, which equals the brilliant, thought-provoking presentation of Kristensen's.

Kristensen was quite conscious of the relation that exists between Phenomenology and Philosophy of Religion. In the field of the Philosophy of Religion he lectured for a number of years on Kant, Schleiermacher, Hegel and Kierkegaard. He knew that all phenomenology operates, consciously or unconsciously, on the basis of some philosophical assumptions, and in its turn influences by its results the kind of religious Philosophy one upholds. Various remarks in this book testify to this awareness. Kristensen, however, was by nature not a philosophical thinker. Except for his solid and ever increasing scholarly equipment, his main instrument was the magic prospector of his intuition.

Here, it seems to me, lies, as so often, both Kristensen's strength and his weakness. His thesis of the absolute absoluteness of every religion for its serious believers, and their relative absoluteness on the plane of History, deserves full consideration and yields many profound insights in the meaning and reality of religious phenomena. It is exceedingly helpful for congenial understanding of wholly alien worlds and for recognizing the essential incompatibility of the inner sanctum of the different religions. He dwells in his phenomenology often on this strangeness of the Ancient Mediterranean Religions, utterly alien to us, children of the modern age, in so many respects moulded by quite a different religion, i.e. Christianity, and by the modern scientific approach, which is quite oblivious of the immediate religious sense of Nature and Cosmos, which was the spontaneous attitude of the Ancients. He considered himself called to try to be a faithful interpreter of these alien worlds, and combined this with being a convinced Christian. He found the justification for this combination in his thesis about the subjective absolute absoluteness and the objective relative absoluteness of every religion. Moreover, as a convinced Christian, he combined liberal and classical-orthodox traits.

Taking this fundamental view of his into account, it is quite understandable that he did not want to have anything to do with a theological approach to Religion. On this point, which is indeed a point of importance, he and I, his pupil and successor, went quite different ways. As I see it, the weakness in his strength is that, with his exclusive stress on the full right of the diverse religious intuitions, he is involuntarily driven towards a blurring of the majestic problem of Truth, which lies behind the undeniable reality of experience and value. One of the reasons that in my conversations with him I always defended the *ultimate* rightness of a theological approach, after having given all due attention and application to the phenomenological one, was a different conception of the relation of truth and experience. Kristensen accepted without question the absolutely basic character of experience in formulating the problem of Truth. For me, on the other hand, experience, as a chief element in the problem of Truth, is truly relevant, but not basic.

His brilliant phenomenological approach leaves the mind with an indelible impression of the seriousness and relevance of Reilgion, but it offers no way to uncover and tackle such a disturbing problem as that of the perennial ambiguity of Religion.

Such a problem can only be really and adequately tackled by a theological approach, which is nevertheless fully aware of the indispensable preparatory training given by phenomenology.

These few remarks must suffice to indicate where Kristensen and I differed. Our deep difference did not prevent him from wanting me to be his successor, showing thereby his generous broadmindedness. It does not prevent me from acknowledging myself his grateful and deeply indebted pupil. Therefore this Introduction to Kristensen's person and work has, without intending it, become an homage. Kristensen was one of those men who simply compel one to "rendre hommage."

This book is published in the hope that his original contributions to the Phenomenology of Religion may become a creative and inspiring element in the current international discussion.

TRANSLATOR'S FOREWORD

This translation of the posthumously edited lectures of Prof. Kristensen has been kept as close as possible to the wording of the original text. Occasionally, however, the wording has been slightly altered in order better to convey in English the author's actual intention in a given sentence or paragraph. Such slight deviations from the text, as well as other difficult points in translating, have been discussed with the author's wife, Mevrouw J. Kristensen-Heldring, and with his successors in the Chair of the History and Phenomenology of Religion at the University of Leiden, Prof. H. Kraemer and Prof. K. A. H. Hidding. This extensive consultation has been extremely valuable. Naturally the translator remains responsible for the final result attained. He was also asked to do any further editing which might be appropriate for publication in book form. An occasional repetitious reference has been deleted, but such editing has been kept to a minimum.

Dutch and Scandinavian readers who are already familiar with the author's monographs will recognize that all of Prof. Kristensen's detailed studies have been woven into the context of this, his most general treatment of religious phenomena. The book remains essentially a series of classroom lectures, and it can probably best be read and appreciated as such. It is my hope that this translation will enable readers to sit with me, as it were, in Prof. Kristensen's classroom, and listen there with me to this enthusiastic and original venture in the understanding of religion.

I wish to take this opportunity to express my gratitude to all those who have helped me. First of all, I should like to thank Mevrouw Kristensen and Prof. Kraemer for entrusting me with this first English translation of one of Prof. Kristensen's writings and for their generous cooperation all during the course of this work. With Mevrouw Kristensen I have discussed a number of difficult points, and Prof. Kraemer has made a critical reading of the entire manuscript. Secondly, I should like to acknowledge my very considerable debt to Prof. Hidding, who introduced me to the Phenomenology of Religion during my two years at Leiden. During the first and most difficult months of translating, he gave most generously of his time and advice, going over a large portion of the first draft with me, and he has remained a counselor during the entire course of the work. Two former colleagues of mine at Leiden have been of great assistance in checking the notes and putting them in the proper form for publication: Mr. J. Schoneveld, *theol. cand.*, assistant to Prof. Hidding, and Mr. J. Balkestein, *theol. drs.*, assistant to Prof. A. de Buck, Professor of the History of the Ancient Religions at Leiden. I should also like to thank members of my family for checking the English of a large part of the first draft: my grand-father, the Rev. Robert C. Hull; my mother, Mrs. Naomi H. Carman; and my sister, Mrs. Eleanor Macfarlane. My thanks are also due to Mrs. Frances Hopkins for typing over the much corrected first draft. Finally, I should like to state how grateful I am to my wife for her advice, assistance, and repeated encouragement throughout the preparation of this book.

November 1957   JOHN B. CARMAN

CHAPTER 1

GENERAL INTRODUCTION

A. PHENOMENOLOGY OF RELIGION

Phenomenology of Religion is the systematic treatment of
History of Religion. That is to say, its task is to classify and group
the numerous and widely divergent data in such a way that an
over-all view can be obtained of their religious content and the
religious values they contain. This general view is not a condensed
History of Religion, but a systematic survey of the data. The
different religions present a rich variety of facts. The ritual acts
and doctrinal tenets within each separate religion do indeed
exhibit a certain similarity; they bear the stamp of that particular religion, but the religions differ in character from one
another. The correspondences are only partial. History of Religion leads only to consideration of the particular; the over-all
view that it gives, which we call general History of Religion, is
not systematic or comparative. It is this systematic view that
Phenomenology of Religion attempts to provide.

Instead of "Phenomenology of Religion," we could use the
older and more familiar name, "Comparative Religion," if usage
had not given to the latter term a meaning which is scarcely
suitable for the scientific pursuit of this discipline. The term
"Comparative Religion," which has been in use since about 1880,
has always signified a comparison of religions for the purpose of
determining their value. During the nineteenth century, many
religions about which there was previously little knowledge
became much better known through the discovery and study
of the original documents. This was especially the case with the
ancient religions, such as the Avesta religion, and the ancient
Indian, Egyptian and Babylonian religions, but it was also true
of the so-called primitive religions, which do not possess any
written documents. When an over-all picture was thus obtained,

a picture taking in a large and varied terrain of mankind's religious life, the first question arousing general interest was this: what is the relative value of these religions? By comparing them with one another, it should be possible to determine the degree of each religion's development, to determine which religions were lower and which were higher. And most important, could not the comparative approach clearly demonstrate the superiority of Christianity? Thus the most important task of the comparison was to give a general view of the different degrees of religious development and to indicate the place of each religion in this line of development. In the minds of most people, "Comparative Religion" still continues to have this meaning. I shall have more to say about this later, but I should now like to proceed immediately to mention in addition to this first type of comparison a second one, completely different from the first and better characterized by the name "phenomenology." It is this second method of comparison which we shall apply in our study.

Phenomenology does not try to compare the religions with one another as large units, but it takes out of their historical setting the similar facts and phenomena which it encounters in different religions, brings them together, and studies them in groups. The corresponding data, which are sometimes nearly identical, bring us almost automatically to comparative study. The purpose of such study is to become acquainted with the religious thought, idea or need which underlies the group of corresponding data. Its purpose is not to determine their greater or lesser religious value. Certainly, it tries to determine their religious value, but this is the value that they have had for the believers themselves, and this has never been relative, but is always absolute. The comparative consideration of corresponding data often gives a deeper and more accurate insight than the consideration of each datum by itself, for considered as a group, the data shed light upon one another. Phenomenology tries to gain an over-all view of the ideas and motives which are of decisive importance in all of History of Religion.

The corresponding data in different religions are very numerous. Completely unique phenomena hardly ever occur. Here is an example. Sacrifices take place in almost all religions, although in different forms. This cannot be accidental. How is this fact to be explained? The sacrificial acts evidently issue from a religious need of a very universal nature. How are we to become acquainted with this need? In any given religion perhaps only one particular conception of sacrifice is expressed. We wish to know more: what religious need has caused men, in all times and places, to present offerings to the gods? To learn this, we must study the category "sacrifices" in the various religions; we must pay attention to that which in the actions and conceptions of the various peoples is common to the basic idea of sacrifice. Now to determine what is common is not so simple. It is certainly not to be sought in the outward traits which are held in common, in how the priests are clad and how the rites are divided among them. It is the common meaning of the sacrificial acts that is important, and that we must try to understand.

How do we come to see what the religious significance of a sacrifice is? Of the innumerable data, not all give equally clear indications. Sometimes the religious idea is indicated quite precisely by the accompanying texts or by other particulars which make its religious meaning clear. To such data we have to give special attention. It is not important in which religion we find them. We must then try to see whether they do not clarify other cases where the religious meaning comes less clearly to light. Thus data from one religion can shed light on data from another because the meaning of the former happens to be clearer than that of the latter. Current opinion holds that we must conceive of sacrifices as gifts to the gods similar to gifts offered to princes as evidence of respect and homage, gifts which sometimes meet real needs. But is that conception right? I think not. It is difficult to give an answer on the basis of data from one particular religion. We must have a general view based on observations gathered from as many religions as possible in order that we may achieve certainty. Therefore we must compare them with one another, and that is the research undertaken in Phenomenology; to consider the phenomena, not only in their historical context, but also in their ideal connection. We call this kind of study "phenomenological," because it is concerned with the systematic treatment of phenomena. Phenomenology is a systematic science, not just an historical discipline which considers the Greek, Roman, or Egyptian religion by itself. The problem is to determine what sacrifice itself is, not just what Greek, Roman, or Hebrew sacrifice is. It is clear that Phenomenology in this way makes an important contribution towards a better and deeper understanding of the separate historical data.

Take for example such a characteristic religious phenomenon as prayer. In every religion it has a different form and a different character, but there is no single religion that informs us completely about the religious need which has led to the practice of prayer. We are acquainted with "magic prayer," often connected with sacred rites (sacrifices, for example) which are intended to ensure the effectiveness of prayer or at least to strengthen the compelling power of prayer. But besides this first type there is "spiritual prayer" that signifies surrender to God's will and from this surrender draws spiritual power. But in both cases we speak of "prayer." Now it is the task of Phenomenology of Religion to answer the question of what we should understand by the concept "prayer" and what is common to its various forms.

Here is another example. "Ritual purification" is a practice which occurs in most religions. What is its religious significance? Only on the basis of comparative study of corresponding data is it possible to ascertain whether the purification has the positive effect of strengthening the one purified, or whether it has the negative aim of washing off spiritual stains.

Another instance is that of the oracle. What religious significance has been ascribed to the oracle? One particular case, such as that of the Delphic Oracle, does not give us sufficient information. The significance was self-evident to the believers, but just for that reason they often do not dwell upon it and thus leave us uncertain. They could suffice with hints, immediately comprehensible to them, but not sufficiently clear to us. We have to take great pains in order to try to understand that which was self-evident to them, for from our own religious experience we are either not acquainted with oracles, sacrifices, purifications and sacraments at all, or only incompletely. Our principal aid in learning to understand them is the comparative method of study. "Sacrifice," "purification" and the like are universal terms common to all religions; it is on the basis of a fairly complete knowledge of their application that they are to be understood.

Still another instance is the Greek and Roman concept of kingship. It is clear from certain ritual acts that in these nations not only was the king the high priest, but he was also conceived as a divine personage. What did that mean? What capacities were ascribed to him? What position did this god-man occupy among them? It has been thought that *dios*, "divine," should not be taken literally. Homer uses the term, not only for gods and princes, but also for other eminent men. The use of the term is thought to have arisen simply from an extravagantly great respect for the head of the people. Or the term is explained as survival from earlier primitive circumstances before the dawn of history.

It is, indeed, impossible to probe much more deeply into this question on the basis of the vague and meager literary materials of the Greeks and Romans: it is difficult to find a religious explanation. The notion strikes us as strange and "primitive"; that is to say, we don't understand it. Yet among other nations of Antiquity the notion of the divinity of the king is not only a fact, but a fact about which we are well informed. We cannot remain in doubt about the religious significance of this notion among the Egyptians and among some of the Semitic peoples, especially the Babylonians. God appears on earth as man (the king) to lead the people on the way of life, abiding life. He stands at the head of their social and political institutions, which are the divinely determined structures of the nation's life. Wars are the wars of the god with his enemies; treaties with other people are divine agreements, concluded not in the perceptible, finite world, but in the infinite, other world embodied in the organic order of the cosmos, in the divine order of the universe. The king who leads the people actualizes the abiding life of his people; that is, the continually repeated resurrection of that life. It is he who realizes for the people victory over death, who is responsible for the fertility of the soil and for triumphing over outside enemies who threaten destruction. Therefore he is repeatedly identified with the god of death and resurrection; and thus he represents among the Greeks and Romans Dionysus, Jupiter or Janus. The comparative approach enables us to understand the sacredness of kingship among the Greeks and Romans. The meager data, which by themselves are not readily under-

standable, gain a meaning, indeed a very deep meaning. Greek
and Roman society, too, were based upon that same religious
foundation which is clearly distinguishable among other peoples.
Indubitable certitude or clarity cannot be obtained and, indeed,
can never be reached when we are seeking understanding, but
we can come to the greatest attainable probability.

The divine world order is another subject about which there is
a group of related data; how has it been conceived in the various
religions? It has become clear that certain definite forms of
nature worship appear in a large number of religions, though
always in different forms. The worship of the earth (as god or
goddess) occurs in a great many religions. What religious idea
is the basis of this and what religious values does it represent?
Furthermore, just what did the sacredness of fire, water, etc.
mean for the adherents of so many religions? And what particular elaboration of the idea do we find in the particular cases of
fire worship or water worship? The answer is not precisely the
same in all religions, and no answer is complete. Only after
comparative analysis are we able to penetrate to the thoughts
which lie deeper, and more or less exactly to determine the
religious significance or value of each separate form of worship.

Comparative study is in numerous instances a quite necessary
aid to the understanding of alien religious ideas, but it is certainly not an ideal means. Every religion ought to be understood
from its own standpoint, for that is how it is understood by its
own adherents. The result of comparative research, and of every
kind of historical research, is likewise less than ideal; only
approximate knowledge is possible. Let us be completely aware
of the limited validity of historical research. This limitation is
imposed by the subject itself; namely, the absolute character of
all faith. Every believer looks upon his own religion as a unique,
autonomous and absolute reality. It is of absolute value and thus
incomparable. This is true not only for the Christian, but just
as surely for the adherent of a non-Christian religion. And it
is true not only for every religion conceived as a whole, but also
for every part and every particular of religious belief. Not only
"Christianity" or any other particular religion is unique, autonomous and incomparable; so too is every belief and each sacred
rite. The belief that Hades is the giver of all life and the sacred

act by means of which that belief is actualized in the ritual of the mystery religion are absolute truths for the believers. But the historian cannot understand the absolute character of the religious data in the same way that the believer understands them. The historian's standpoint is a different one. There is a distance between him and the object of the research, he cannot identify himself with it as the believer does. We cannot become Mohammedans when we try to understand Islam, and if we could, our study would be at an end: we should ourselves then directly experience the reality. The historian seeks to understand, and he is able to do that in an approximate way, approximate, but no more. By means of empathy he tries to relive in his own experience that which is "alien," and that, too, he can only approximate. This imaginative reexperiencing of a situation strange to us is a form of representation, and not reality itself, for that always asserts itself with sovereign authority. We can even assume such an outside position in respect to our own spiritual inheritance: we can form a more or less clear picture of our own national character, and we often do so. But then we always feel the shortcomings of our own formulation; the representation is always something else than the reality. The "existential" nature of the religious datum is never disclosed by research. That cannot be defined. Here we see the limit to the validity of historical research. But recognizing a limit of validity is not to deny the value of this research.

In order to understand particular (historical) data, we must frequently (and perhaps always) make use of the generalizations which are the results of comparative research. The sacredness of the Greek and Roman kings must be seen in the light of the ancient concept of kingship; particular sacrifices in the light of the religious essence of sacrifice. Now it is true the Ancient conception of kingship or the religious essence of sacrifice is a concept and not historical reality (only the particular applications are reality), but we cannot dispense with those concepts. In historical research they are virtually considered as realities: to an important extent they give the research direction and lead to the satisfying result of understanding the data. The limit of validity of scientific results, which is the consequence of using such fictitious realities, is not a phenomenon unique to historical science. Such fictitious realities and general formulations are assumed in all science, even in the natural science, where they are formulated as "natural laws." Research always anticipates the essence of the phenomena, which essence is nevertheless the goal of all scientific endeavour.

The relationship between history and phenomenology thus becomes clear. The one assumes the presence of the other, and vice versa. Phenomenology's way of working (the grouping of characteristic data) and its task (the illustration of man's religious disposition) make it a systematic discipline. But if we must group the phenomena according to characteristics which correspond as far as possible to the essential and typical elements of religion, how do we then determine which data typically illustrate men's religious disposition, and how do we determine what are the essential elements of religion? This question can not be answered on the basis of the phenomena themselves, although this has indeed been tried. There is a popular notion that that which all religions have in common must be religion's core. If we but set aside all that is peculiar to a particular religion, what we have left are the common ideas, feelings, and practices, and they express what is essentially religious. This is a method which seems so simple as to be almost mechanical, but it is impracticable. There are a great many elements which appear in all religions. Unessential and unimportant elements also occur in large numbers. On the other hand, none of all the facts which have been observed occurs in all religions. We do not even find the well known trio of "God, soul and immortality" everywhere. When we consider the idea, "God", even ignoring the fact that this is absent in Buddhism, we must conclude that there is no particular idea of deity which is everywhere applicable. And if we relinquish the given forms of particular ideas of deity in order to find that which is common behind them, we are then left with empty concepts. The common element that we find in this way is so vague and fleeting that it gives no guidance in the research of Phenomenology. It can be said just as truly that all religious data, seen more deeply, are held in common. If we but pay attention to their religious significance, they prove not to be alien to us, and certainly not to other believers. Consider, for instance, the many nature gods, such as Osiris, Demeter and Athene. As soon as we learn to understand their essence, the alient element disappears, and they correspond to feelings and insights which are echoed in ourselves. Just for this reason we can understand that which is alien. This is the case with all religious ideas and practices as soon as we comprehend them in their true significance. Seen more deeply, therefore, everything is held in common. Nothing and everything. It is clear that by following this path we do not learn to know the essence of religion.

That which is really essential is shown by philosophical investigation. Essence is a philosophical concept, and it is the chief task of Philosophy of Religion to formulate that essence. The principal ideas in Phenomenology are borrowed from Philosophy of Religion. Philosophy must furnish the guiding principle in the research of Phenomenology. In other words, a mutual relation exists between the two. Yes, Philosophy presupposes personal religious experience; the theory of religion presumes the practice of religion. Whoever seeks to know the essence of religion must possess a general picture of the different types of religious thinking and action, of ideas of deity and cultic acts; this is the material for his research. This material is precisely what Phenomenology provides.

Phenomenology of Religion and History of Religion also stand in this same mutual relation. Naturally History provides the material for the research of Phenomenology, but the reverse is also true.

Thus we see that anticipated concepts and principles are used in all the provinces of the general science of religion: history, typology and philosophy. We are continually anticipating the results of later research. That typifies the character and the "authority" of each of the three subdivisions of the science of religion. None of the three is independent; the value and the accuracy of the results of one of them depend on the value and accuracy of the results of the other two. The place which the research of Phenomenology occupies between history and philosophy makes it extraordinarily interesting and important. The particular and the universal interpenetrate again and again; Phenomenology is at once systematic History of Religion and applied Philosophy of Religion.

It is evident that in the philosophical determination of the essence of religion, we make use of data which lie outside the territory of philosophy, outside our knowledge. We make use of our own religious experience in order to understand the experience of others. We should never be able to describe the essence of religion if we did not know from our own experience what religion is (not: what the essence of religion is!). This experience forces itself upon us even in purely historical research. That has already been demonstrated by the mutual relation of the three areas of study. A rational and systematic structure in the science of religion is impossible. Again and again a certain amount of intuition is indispensible. We are certainly not confronted with a comparative science of religion (history-phenomenology-philosophy) systematically built up as a logical unity. The purely logical and rational does not indicate which way we must follow because in Phenomenology we are constantly working with presumptions and anticipations. But that is just what makes our labour important. This study does not take place outside our personality. And the reverse will also prove to be the case: the study exerts an influence on our personality. This gives a personal character and value to the research in the areas we have mentioned. An appeal is made to our feeling for the subjects which we want to understand, a feeling which gives us a sureness to our "touch." There is an appeal made to the indefinable sympathy we must have for religious data which sometimes appear so alien to us. But this sympathy is unthinkable without a intimate acquaintance with the historical facts – thus again an interaction, this time between feeling and factual knowledge. It is not true that our study is a theoretical activity with which our practical life is not concerned. There is simply no doubt that we grow during our scientific work; when religion is the subject of our work, we grow religiously. In saying this, we have indicated the highest significance of our scientific task. We believe that we work objectively and scientifically, but the fruitful labour, without any doubt, takes place by the illumination of a Spirit who extends above and beyond our spirit. Let us simply call it intuition – then at least no one will contradict us!

Now we must make a few remarks about the method which

Phenomenology applies. Phenomenology has as its objects to come as far as possible into contact with and to understand the extremely varied and divergent religious data, making use of comparative methods. Let me now contrast with this object the popular conception of the task of "Comparative Religion" to which I alluded in the beginning. According to that conception, it must determine the relative value of the data; it must provide us with the standard by means of which we can distinguish between the lower and the higher forms in the religious life of mankind. This comparison is worked out systematically in an evolutionary interpretation of the history of religion. This interpretation was held in high regard about the end of the last century, both in scholarly circles and elsewhere. At present, however, it has practically disappeared among scholars, but it still persists among large sections of the historically and religiously interested public. It is really popular, and therefore we cannot leave it outside our consideration. We shall be well advised to consider it carefully both in its strengths and in its weaknesses. The basis conviction is this, that the history of mankind has had just ourselves as its goal, and after frightfully great pains it has generated our civilization, as the result of all that which had preceded it. History has a meaning: it follows a continuous line from the primitive through the developed up to the highest. In religion as well as in the rest of our culture we stand on the apex of the historical pyramid. This is clearly shown, according to the evolutionary view, by comperative analysis of the historical types of religion. Such analysis leads to an evolutionary interpretation of the history of religion.

Evolutionary theory is of two types: historical and idealist. According to historical evolutionism, the results achieved in each historical period are handed down to the following generation by them and further developed. The values never disappear; they are always taken over by the succeeding generations. There is a historical contact between all periods of culture. That was the theory of Tiele, and many agreed with him. According to idealistic evolutionism, the idea of humanity and of the essence of religion has an existence of its own. It realizes itself by means of historical phenomena, even by those beyond observable historical relations. It detaches itself more and more from the undeveloped   reality which is clothed in primitive forms and comes to light in full clarity in the highest civilization and the highest religions. This idealistic evolutionism includes (among other views) the Hegelian conception of development; the history of religion is understood as the dialectical self development of the Idea of religion.

From a philosophical standpoint it must be recognized that a case can be made for this evolutionary type of comparative research. It is the task of Philosophy of Religion to describe the essence of religion by determining the relation of religion to other spiritual realities – the intellectual, moral and aesthetic factors in our spiritual life – and thus to arrive at a definition of religion's distinctive nature. Of course, when the essence is described, the unessential element in the religious phenomena has also a right to be shown. This is the indisputable right of Philosophy of Religion. Some religious forms, some formulations of belief and some sacred rites then prove to express this essential element better than others. Higher and lower forms are thus distinguished and pointed out in history. And religion is seen to be in its essence a living force, which maintains itself even when confronted with ignoble tendencies and obstructive circumstances. Such a conception of religion leads automatically to the notion of growth, a development of religion in the course of history. On philosophical grounds historical and idealistic evolutionism can both be defended. The philosophical method is deductive; by discerning how the phenomena develop from the essence, the historical data are understood.

It must be recognized, furthermore, that the essence of religion is a concept which not only the philosopher, but also the historian and the student of Phenomenology cannot neglect. The scholar must be able to separate the essentially religious from the unessential in all the given historical phenomena which are the object of his research. In order to reach the right conclusions he must have a feeling for religion, an awareness of what religion is, and this awareness is precisely what Philosophy of Religion attempts to formulate. Many historians are gravely lacking in this "feeling." But the reverse is just as true: the philosopher who wants to describe the essential element must work with historical data. He does not conjure them up by pure deduction.

He cannot decide that particular data must have existed. History and philosophy must work together; that is to say, the one may not lay down the law to the other. Each is equally autonomous in its own territory.

But the autonomy is denied if a particular pattern of development, the evolutionary pattern, is forced on history. History of Religion and Phenomenology do not have as their object the formulation of our conception of the essence of religious data. This is the task of the philosopher. They must, on the contrary, investigate what religious value the believers (Greeks, Babylonians, Egyptians, etc.) attached to their faith, what religion meant for them. It is *their* religion that we want to understand, and not our own, and we are therefore not concerned here with the essence of religion, for this is necessarely expressed for us in our own religion.

All evolutionary views and theories therefore mislead us from the start, if we let them set the pattern for our historical research. Believers have never conceived of their own religion as a link in a chain of development. Perhaps they have thought of it sometimes as the goal, but never as an intermediate link; yet in the evolutionary view, this is an indispensable concept. No believer considers his own faith to be somewhat primitive, and the moment we begin so to think of it, we have actually lost touch with it. We are then dealing only with our own ideas of religion, and we must not delude ourselves that we have also learned to know the ideas of others. The historian and the student of Phenomenology must therefore be able to forget themselves, to be able to surrender themselves to others. Only after that will they discover that others surrender themselves to them. If they bring their own idea with them, others shut themselves off from them. No justice is then done to the values which are alien to us, because they are not allowed to speak in their own language. If the historian tries to understand the religious data from a different viewpoint than that of the believers, he negates the religious reality. For there is no religious reality other than the faith of the believers.

The concepts, "primitive" and "highly developed" forms of religion, are therefore fatal for historical research. Religious ideas and sacred rites are degraded to a series of relative values, whereas in reality they have functioned as absolute values. We must understand the others as autonomous and spiritual individuals; we must not let our appraisal be determined by the degree of agreement or difference between them and ourselves. For the historian only one evaluation is possible: "the believers were completely right." Only after we have grasped this can we understand these people and their religion.

That does not imply, of course, that every passing religious tendency to be found in history can lay claim to such an evaluation. Of course, insignificant or superficial points of view appear again and again which are of such slight value that they scarcely merit our attention or respect. How can the one be separated from the other? That is no great problem. That which is insignificant always proves to have no lasting existence in history. Because of their slight value, these phenomena have only a brief existence. As far as the Ancient religions are concerned, most of the data of this sort have disappeared without leaving us any trace, or at least they are not longer visible because of their distance from us. The religious phenomena which primarily engage the attention of the historian and the phenomenologist, however, are the formulations of belief and cultic practices which have endured for centuries and sometimes for thousands of years. They have proved themselves able to bear the life of numerous generations, because they have accurately expressed the religious consciousness of an entire people. This is true of the very ancient forms of worship of nature and of spiritual beings (the two cannot be sharply separated) which have survived, even into our own time. It is also the case with the mythical images in which faith is formulated and with the sacred practices and usages, such as the numerous forms of sacrifices, divinations, etc. The enduring existence of all these religious data proves their religious value: they have been felt to be as essential values of life, and they have indeed been just that. The impressive civilizations of the Ancient peoples were founded upon them. That cannot be said of the passing movements and temporary phenomena. Just as insignificant individuals cannot command the same attention as outstanding personalities, so transient ideas cannot claim the same interest as convictions which have proved their inner power. In studying the Ancient religions, the great distance in time (between them and ourselves) offers this advantage: numerous passing fluctuations have undoubtedly disappeared from sight, and the principal lines indicating what is enduring and valuable come much more clearly into focus. That which has been carefully weighed and approved by generations and has been able to serve as the basis of life has proved its inner value. And we can understand that only in the same sense in which the believers have understood it – that this value is the absolute value of life.

The evolutionary point of view is therefore an unhistorical view-point. It is extraordinarily popular because a feeling for history is so extraordinarily rare. For most people it is a difficult task to do justice to the viewpoint of others when the spiritual issues of life are at stake. In historical research, we confront religious data as observers; most people find this attitude difficult to achieve, and so place themselves directly in the stream of life and adopt only those ideas which fit the realities of practical life. When this has been done, a condemnation of the other point of view on the basis of our own is inevitable. From a practical point of view these people are right, for in practice we show our disapproval of that which is alien by not adopting it ourselves. From a theoretical point of view, however, they are wrong.

B. THE 'HOLY'

Here in the Introduction I shall not give a list of the recent works in the field of Phenomenology of Religion. The most important are the monographs on particular subjects, such as initiation rites. Many of these will be noted in the appropriate chapters. I do want, however, to refer to one work, not so much because of its importance as because of its familiarity. This book is Rudolf Otto's *Das Heilige*; a book of two hundred pages when first published in 1917, but considerably enlarged in later editions. It is one of the most widely read books in the contemporary theological literature.

Otto quite rightly sees "the holy," the typical religious principle, in the often very involved complexes of ideas and feelings which characterize religious life. The holy is an element *sui generis* and cannot be expressed in intellectual, ethical, or aesthetic terms. First the "moments", which are the self-realizing content of the idea of the holy, are distinguished from one another. This is not done in Hegel's dialectical fashion, but is carried out psychologically, by analyzing the religious fact. The impossibility of this kind of endeavour is shown, however, by the fact that while the treatment is systematic in form, it is not so in content.

The most important contribution of Otto's book, though it is not particularly original, is the analysis of the concept "holiness." The different elements (also called components or moments) are provided with labels which are now familiar to every historian of religion. This study in Psychology of Religion is actually quite theoretical in nature and properly belongs to the field of Philosophy of Religion, which seeks to determine the essence of religion in general. But it is fatal for the rest of the exposition that Otto the philosopher and systematic theologian does not see that on this basis no transition is possible to the *historical* understanding which he sets as his goal. He makes the opposite mistake of Tiele and Pfleiderer, who on the basis of historical data try to ascend to the formulation of the essence of religion. Like Hegel, Otto believes that in the essence the germ of all phenomena is contained, that the phenomena have to be understood on the basis of the essence. "In the acorn the oak tree is present in germ." This statement has no connection with Botany. The analysis of the structure of acorns does not give us the slightest inkling of the nature of the growing tree. It is simply an illusion to think that even a partial understanding of the developed organism can be gained from its germinal form. So too, it is an illusion to suppose that there can be a systematic development of the science of religion from the essence to the phenomena, or vice versa, whatever notion of the essence of religion is employed.

The unity of the psychological study is disturbed by the evolutionary pattern of Otto's presentation. The *daimonion* becomes *theion;* the *numen* (in the Roman sense) becomes *deus;* worship of natural objects becomes worship of spiritual beings. This growth in a definite direction might at least be possible if human history were a kind of natural history, comparable to the acorn becoming an oak tree. But in human history, regular growth in a definite direction is entirely absent. Egyptian civilization and religion remained about the same for two thousand years and then disappeared. And how many thousand years has the culture of primitive peoples remained at the same level? Moreover, in most religions, those of Greece and Rome, for example, the *daimonion* continues to exist alongside the *theion;* the nature gods continue to exist alongside the spiritual gods, etc. Even the same individual gods can have both meanings. It is extremely probable, or even certain, that both types of deity have their own distinctive religious values. The evolutionary pattern is evidently forced upon the historical reality – for the sake of a certain conception of the "germinal forms" of the religious consciousness. Otto is wrong in thinking that history proves the correctness of his theory. His view is actually forced upon him by an historical fact: the difference between his own conception and what we call the "primitive" idea of the divine. To understand the other conception he wants to bridge the gap systematically. The idea of the divine which has no value or meaning for me must be the germinal form of my own. If a cultured Parsi priest wished to present an over-all view of the history of religion, he would undoubtedly say that his own religion was the crown of the historical development. Such statements come, not from an historian, but from a theologian. In the history of religion one can find no proof of the truth of his own faith; "evolution" proceeds in a hundred different directions. The believer finds the validation of his faith in quite a different realm. This validation comes, not in the comparative approach in which one's own religion is thought to be the purified form of the religious heritage of mankind, but in the actual practice of religious life. Any believer will say that he owes the certainty of his faith to God. That is the religious reality.

We must put the questions differently than Otto does. We should not take the concept "holiness" as our starting point, asking, for example, how the numinous is revealed in natural phenomena. On the contrary, we should ask how the believer conceives the phenomena he calls "holy." We do not need to make a particular application of the concept "holiness" to any object for holiness is the most essential element in reality itself.

The Ancients' perception of nature was different from ours, and it is *their* feelings and conceptions which we must try to understand. Then we shall recognize that the believers were right in holding such a view, and that this view is not primitive, as Otto maintains. If we come to understand them well, we shall see the truth of their ideas, the truth that natural phenomena are sacred or "holy." The startingpoint of Phenomenology is therefore the viewpoint of the believer, and not the concept "holiness" in its elements or moments.

If we apply this phenomenological method, all the theories about primitive, higher, and highest standpoints at once collapse. We come to know the absolute (namely what is absolute for the believer) in its various expressions, and what is absolute is never just relatively absolute!

Following this approach, we shall become acquainted with more and more different expressions of the holy, but we shall never arrive at a definition of the holy. It is indeed presupposed in historical and phenomenological study that holiness is also a reality for us, a reality *sui generis*. This is an *a priori* assumption in our research. Yet the historian who wishes to understand phenomena has a different attitude than the philosopher, who wants to understand the essence of a reality, and who tries to comprehend himself. It would be foolish to sacrifice one discipline to the other, or to deny the distinctive value of both. The historian cannot speak as a philosopher, or vice versa. Otto has tried to join the two in his evolutionary theory, and his argument therefore comes to grief. Naturally, Otto has more historical knowledge than Hegel, but nevertheless he remains a philosopher, and he is no more able than Hegel to do complete justice to the characteristic feature of alien religious ideas – their absolute character. The historian must refrain in his research from using a particular definition or philosophical analysis of religion.

C. THE TWO TYPES OF RELIGIOUS ORIENTATION

Phenomenology of Religion attempts to understand religious phenomena by classifying them into groups. These groups, which are the typical phenomena, are indefinite in number. We must restrict our study to the larger and more clearly outlined groups.

It is possible very roughly to speak of two types: the type represented by our European civilization, and especially by Christianity, and the "Ancient" type – I don't know any better name
for it – which the nations of Antiquity represent and also, at
least for the most part, those civilizations which are "foreign" to
our own. This distinction between our own and that which is
foreign to us is at least of practical importance in our work.
A difference comes to light which it is possible to formulate. I
shall not spend much time discussing it here, since the detailed
elaboration must be done when the special groups and types are
treated, but it is useful beforehand to indicate that the difference
exists.

It is a remarkable fact that the peoples of Antiquity very often
understood each other surprisingly well in religious matters,
in spite of all their differences in national character and religion.
Not only is this evident from the relatively few literary statements on this subject; it is especially clear from the agreement
of their basic religious ideas and institutions, notwithstanding
the different ways in which they are expressed. We modern
Europeans sometimes have very great difficulty in understanding these Ancient religious ideas. This is evident from the
numerous mistakes made, even in respect to what is most essential: the real character and the religious value of these strange
notions. These mistakes have been made even by serious students of the subject during the last few centuries – including the
twentieth – in spite of the great aids furnished by philology and
archaeology. It is quite certain that a greater distance lies between us and the nations of the Antiquity than between those
Ancient nations themselves. The difference in time is not the only
cause, for there were greater differences in time among the
Ancients themselves than between them and us. The cleavage,
moreover, existed even before the beginning of the Christian era.

What we really have to do with here are two types of "civilization" in the broadest sense, and these two types we term
Ancient and Modern. Our type of civilization came into being
early in Greek history with the classical enlightenment. This
rationalism in which the individual became conscious of his
abilities won the leading position in Greece and Rome, but the
Ancient type continued to live alongside it.

This rationalistic type was pushed rather into the background by Ancient Christianity right up to the thirteenth century. Then the mentality of the "Enlightenment" won back a great deal of lost ground by means of the Renaissance and especially by the revival of Aristotelian philosophy in Scholasticism. Since then it has characterized all of modern civilization. Our scientific and ethical orientation is preponderately Aristotelian, that is to say "enlightened-classical." * It is this orientation which makes it so difficult for us to understand the Ancients and to evaluate them justly.

That which is characteristic of the Ancient civilizations and religions is the vivid consciousness of the cooperation between, indeed a fusion of , the finite and infinite factors in all phenomena connected with the essentials of life. Modern man, too, is aware that all of what he knows and understands is based upon an unknown reality. What is force? What is energy? Are the basic principles of all mechanics – gravity and centrifugal force – mythical ideas? And above all, what is the simplest life process, life itself? Since the time of the Greeks, however, the conviction has dominated in Modern man that the unknown can and must be more and more limited and that it proves to be not essentially different from that which is already known. That which inspires this line of thinking is the sense of the autonomous and dominating activity of the human mind in subjecting nature to itself.

But every value is won at the cost of another value; here it is at the cost of the awareness of the mystical background of existence. In the man of Antiquity there was dominant just this sense of the mystery that surrounds us, a feeling of the spontaneous forces and energies whose meaning he always understood in the form of myth. He was, to be sure, also acquainted with rational relations of causality, but he attached primary significance to that which eluded conceptual understanding. It was this irrational factor which was most important for him. One might think that this should not be so difficult for us to under-

* Prof. Kristensen makes a sharp distinction between the terms "Ancient" and "Classical" with reference to the ancient civilizations, identifying "Classical" with "rationalistic" and "enlightened." When the author uses "Ancient" in this special sense, referring not so much to a period of time as to a state of mind, this is indicated by capitalization. The meaning of "enlightened," as the author uses the term, is: similar to the rationalism of the Eighteenth Century *Enlightenment* (Dutch, *verlichting;* German, *Aufklärung*). *Trans.*

stand, that we would acknowledge that the Ancients were completely right, and that we would think in just the same way. A great difference, however, remains. We comprehend the innumerable expressions of the mystery of being in one total view. The mystical ground of being is always the same. everywhere and in all its expressions: all that exists and all that happens witness to the reality and the activity of God. For the Ancients, on the contrary, the mystery of one phenomenon differed from that of another quite as much as the phenomena themselves differ; each case is new and special and points to a new "numen." According to this view, each phenomenon of life is unique; it is not to be reduced to anything else, and it possesses a unique quality of being. Autonomous substances differing from one another cannot be reduced to one and the same principle; otherwise they would not be autonomous. They point, therefore, to different gods. That is the realism in this view. Polytheism is the conception of the divine which corresponds to the infinite variety in the mystery of being. Rational differences (of size, weight, and force) are relative and can be comprehended in a generalization, but not so with irrational differences. It is just upon these facts that the religious value of polytheism is based. A different ultimate force works in the sprouting seed than in the stem which bears the leaf, and it is also different from the force present in the forming of the ear. This is what polytheism is. The ultimate and autonomous is seen as divine energy, even in events and objects which most certainly would not induce *us* to worship. Consider, for instance, animals, which for the Ancients were so often divine emblems or divine beings. It is very difficult for us to understand what special sanctity the nations of Antiquity and other peoples saw in animals and what significance they attributed to them. Our modern approach, using the method of generalization, gives us no answer to this question.

This pluralistic notion of the mystery of life's expressions is induced by the religious sense of nature, a sense which the Ancients had very strongly but which we have lost. This religious sense of nature was, however, not only related to "nature" which surrounds us (the basis of cosmology), but just as closely related to mankind. In our life, too, there are ultimate and autonomous (divine) energies at work – in growth and reproduction, in the creative power of body and mind. The awareness of these energies results in a conception of man (an anthropology) which strikes us as completely alien. The Ancients actually spoke of man's holiness, not in general, but in very definite respects; this we may call religious realism.

The same divine fact, the birth of a child, for instance, which is the mystery of origin of human life, is quite differently conceived by different peoples. The Greeks believed that birth took place through the work of powers of the realm of the dead, which they considered to be the home of absolute life. The Persians, on the other hand, believed that birth occurred in direct opposition to the powers of death. The same rite (in this case the "purification" of the young mother) can thus have quite different backgrounds in different religions. We do not penetrate religious reality if we go no further than formulating theories about sanctity in general, or even about the sanctity of the young mother; we simply remain on the surface. Each must be understood as far as possible on its own terms. Then it becomes evident that each religious fact, with all of its particulars, is grounded in a particular religious orientation, and that every one of these facts has an autonomous religious value. Sweeping explanations of religious data are always more or less superficial and frequently are even misleading.

From the viewpoint of Phenomenology, the sense of sanctity appears in all the instances in which the phenomena arouse the awareness of spontaneous factors which are infinite and absolute. Another world invades the world we know, and this other world is an incalculable world which makes all the calculations of ordinary life quite insignificant. In this other world is the mystery of all of life's foundations. By this invasion the entire society can be dislocated and lamed. The infinite and incomprehensible factors in the process of nature, whether they are constructive or destructive, take control and abolish the ordinary order of life with its purposeful expenditure of the forces at man's command. The various tabus which must be observed at such a time are only the recognition and acceptance of this extraordinary situation. The entire society is in a sphere of sanctity, surrounded by unfamiliar and spontaneous powers. No particular god confronts the religious community; the phenomena themselves are sacred and divine. *We* see nothing infinite in such phenomena, at least nothing but the infinite element which may be said to be present in all phenomena, but the believer really does see these particular phenomena as having a special quality of infinity. And we may not say that he is wrong. We like to think of eclipses (of the sun and the moon) as phenomena which can be completely explained, as completely explained as the shadow which the tree casts on the ground, but it is nevertheless a fact that an eclipse of the sun engenders a deep emotion in everyone who observes it. One may delude himself into thinking that this is completely natural, but the movement of the heavenly bodies, including the sunrise every morning, does not fail to arouse the feeling of the invading presence of infinite powers. It is simply foolish to call this feeling a primitive and naïve superstition.

We gain a different conception of the "holy" when we take the reality of the believers' faith as our starting point than when we choose to take the "essence" of religion in general as the starting point. This reality proves to be self-subsistent and absolute; it is beyond all our rational criticism. The only difficulty for us is to form an accurate conception of this reality and to understand it from within.

The subjects of Phenomenology of Religion may be classified into three groups: the conceptions or doctrines which we find in the various religions about the world, about man, and about the practice of worship. These three subdivisions are, in other words, religious cosmology, religious anthropology, and cultus.

PART I

COSMOLOGY

CHAPTER 2

INTRODUCTION TO COSMOLOGY

A. THE MEANING OF 'COSMOS'

Religious cosmology is the religious conception of the world and particular phenomena in the world.

The first question which arises is what religious meaning the term "cosmos" has had and with what religious ideas the term has been connected.

The Greek word *kosmos* means literally "beauty, regularity, order, being as it ought to be." Pythagoras (ca. 570–500 B.C.) was the first to use this term for the concept "entire world" or "universe," because of the order and harmony which he saw in the universe. He used the term, however, not on the basis of his aesthetic conception or of a sense impression; it was for him rather a philosophical or scientific term, but – as in all Ancient philosophy and science – closely akin to the religious view. Pythagoras' science was mathematics, and his doctrine of universal harmony was mathematically formulated. It is well known that Pythagoras discovered that the interval (distance) between two tones is determined by the length of the vibrating part of the string, and that the tone relation is thus at the same time a numerical relation. Musical harmony can be expressed in the figures of proportions of length. Music is thereby connected with mathematics. This became for Pythagoras the typical example of all "harmony"; musical harmony was for him the combination and cooperation of existing life in all its forms. Numbers express the cooperation in order in all relations. In this respect some numbers have special significance because they occur in a large number of relations and laws. These are the "sacred numbers," such as three (beginning, middle and end), and the like. Number is the objective principle of the universe and thus expresses its essential being; it is substance, but also *mimēsis*, the imitation of things. The even number represents infinity, because by the possibility of division it is a reality which can dissolve itself and disappear in another reality. The uneven number is finitude, because it resists division and disappearance. Now harmony is the cooperation of different magnitudes, not only in music, but also in other realms. "The unity of opposites" is the law of the world's life; it is the cosmos or world order determined by numerical relations, which contains both the finite and the infinite. The highest and all embracing harmony is according to Pythagoras "the harmony of the spheres," the cooperation of the heavenly circles, superterrestrial worlds. He calls it the celestial "music," even though it is not audible, but purely ideal.

This is the meaning of Pythagoras' statement that the universe is a "cosmos." It remains primarily a scientific theory, for it tries to explain the universe by reducing the multiplicity of phenomena to their unity. But it is theory which immediately relates itself to religion, for it contains an *Anschauung des Universums* ("beholding" or "contemplation" of the universe; the term is Schleiermacher's). It perceives the universe as an organic whole that displays a definite character – a cooperation bound to laws. "Harmony" as the cosmic principle was actually a religious term among the Greek long before Pythagoras. Harmonia was the name of a goddess of the Mysteries at Thebes and in Samothrace. She was not a goddess of music, but of the combination of opposites, of the cooperation of typical opposites, life and death, which together constitute absolute and divine life. Or her opposites were the finite and the infinite; the true infinity includes such finite realities as human life. Harmonia was closely akin to the goddess of the Eleusinian Mysteries, Kore. They are both goddesses who die in order to live again.

This idea of the cosmos as a harmonic, organic, living whole has also been given other religious formulations. In most of the Ancient religions there is present the idea of the "cosmic law" seen as the divine law of life. This is indeed a doctrine of central significance, characteristic of the picture of the world which the religious believers had in their minds, and characteristic of their *Anschauung des Universums*, in which the universe was not conceived in terms of numerous finitely determined phenomena, but was seen as a world full of miracles.

B. PARTICULAR RELIGIOUS CONCEPTIONS OF COSMIC ORDER

The concept *rita* in the Vedas and the concept *asha* in the Avesta both signify "stable, almighty and all determining order." *Rita* and *asha* are especially attributes of Varuna and Ahura Mazda respectively. They are the highest gods, whose activities are the most inclusive. These "Kings among the Gods" are the divinities of *rita* and *asha:* their essence *is rita* and *asha.* Thus the most characteristic phenomena of nature are subject to them.[1] "The rivers flow in accordance with *rita*" and "the breaking dawn appears to Aditi or rita." The sun, which typifies regularity, is called "the shining face of rita." But rita is nevertheless not the same as our natural law. Rita is the divine energy which maintains itself against disturbing forces. An eclipse of the sun is "against rita" because it is resistance to the divine order. But this order is supreme and thus is superior to such resistance. Therefore this is, more specifically, the order of life. It is the order of abiding life, which gains the victory over finitude and destruction. Rita reveals itself in the mystery of life's self-renewal. Agni, the energy of fire which lies hidden as vital energy in water and plants, is "the son of rita" or "born in rita." In accordance with rita the cow gives men their food, which is the basis of their enduring life. Rita is the order of life in the quite universal sense. Therefore it is usually conceived in the religio-ethical sense. Ethical action is then conceived as man's law of life; truth, honesty, and righteousness are rita. The religious man will try to live in accord with them, for he will be saved if he lives in accord with the universal cosmic order: this is the supra-ethical, religious meaning of rita. Ethical life is religiously determined; it is a particular expression of universal divine life. And of all human acts sacrifice is the most characteristic rita-act, because it is the most typical religious act. Sacrifice is rita itself, for by the means of the *sacri-ficium* divine life is actualized.

The term *asha* in the Avesta has exactly the same meaning, but with even more emphasis on the cosmic character of man. All good creatures are *"ashavan,"* possessing *asha;* the creations of Ahura Mazda are earth, fire, water, the cow, and the "righteous" (pious) man. Opposed to them as their enemies are the creations of Ahriman, drought, sickness, and deceit. The believers never lost sight of the cosmic significance of *asha;* they put nature and man on the same plane. The statement that Ahura Mazda has created "the ox and the righteous (*ashavan*) man" does not indicate a ranking which places the ox above man. But the prerequisite of human existence is mentioned before human existence itself. Yet both are equally sacred, because asha is equally sacred in everything. Asha is the essence of Ahura Mazda and as such equally sacred everywhere.

These are genuine religious conceptions of the world order. They are not "theories" which try to explain it, but rather what Schleiermacher calls *Anschauung des Universums*. This *Anschauung* sees the world itself as a divine reality. Man, who is a part of the world, is absolutely dependent on this world in its divine determination. In the universal asha of this universe he actualizes his absolute life and his victory over finitude. It is quite clear that this conception is not pantheistic .Struggle and victory do not belong in pantheism. The Avesta is dualistic.

The Egyptian idea of *ma-a-t* shows much similarity to but also much difference from these conceptions. It is the universal order by means of which gods and men live and triumph – thus again not pantheism. It is conceived cosmically and ethically as the pathway of life for nature and man. Yet it is different from rita and asha, for ma-a-t was originally an earth goddess. Her hieroglyphic and symbol, ☐, ▱, or ◿, signifies the earth's height, the place where the earth lives. Her essence is the mystery of the earth, which is at the same time the underworld and realm of the dead. Thus she contains both life and death in a harmonious unity of opposites. This is the Egyptian view of the divine order and law of life. Death is a friend, because only in death (in the other world) is absolute life attained and realized. But in another sense death is also an enemy; it is finitude and transiency, which, however, is the precondition for the infinite and imperishable. Now ma-a-t is the law of the earth, and that law holds for the entire universe. The earth also gives her life to the sky gods, the gods of light. And this law of the earth also holds for man. Everything which signifies for man the law and order of life is summed up in ma-a-t. Thus in ma-a-t the essence of Egyptian religion is expressed. It is the Egyptian *Anschauung des Universums.* Divine life is ma-a-t. This is the inscrutable cooperation of all that which is contradictory for human thought, of that which we understand by "life" and "death." The earth, with its realm of the dead, is the place where the two opposites are reconciled and brought into cooperation. The Egyptian symbol for ma-a-t, the scales, is not only the balance upon which the dead man is weighed to ascertain his merits, but it also signifies the two parts of the world. Cosmic life is the balance of the two opposites; neither one outweighs the other; they are both equally indispensable in absolute life. Not until death does man come to know absolute life, when he and ma-a-t come upon the scales of a balance. He is weighed against ma-a-t to see whether he is "righteous toward the world (heaven and earth)". It is thus tested whether he shares in the life of the universe, or rather, his accord with it is ascertained. In this respect the Egyptian conception of ma-a-t displays a character different from the Indian and Iranian conceptions of rita and asha, in which there is of course no question of a combination, but rather a struggle of opposites; no reconciliation, but a victory. Ahura Mazda's realm will triumph over Ahriman. This dualistic *Anschauung des Universums* (world view) is also the basis of the Indian conception of rita. In India and Iran the divine order is conceived dynamically. It is a force, an energy, which breaks resistance and destroys it. There is no thought of reconciliation. Ma-a-t, however, does not accord with a dynamic view, but rather with an ontological or static view. It is the doctrine of being, not of becoming. In the mystery of the continually existing world life – a mystery transcending human concepts – the "contradictions" work evenly and harmoniously together. This view agrees with the conception of the goddess of the Mysteries in Samothrace, Harmonia. The balanced scales is an especially illuminating symbol of this cosmic righteousness, this cosmic law of life. It is much less suitable as a symbol of Justitia administering justice, for here no balance is possible; the balance must tip in favor of one of the parties. Justitia's scales symbolize the just weighing of pro and contra by our judges. But that must of course result in the tipping of one scale – thus the same thought as that in the Indian rita and the Iranian asha. The Greek poets took over the Egyptian "*psycho-*

stasia," the "weighing of the soul"; for instance, in the judgment concerning Achilles and Hector. But the idea was not taken over. The poets gave it an ethical significance and let Hector fall. The Ancient Greek goddess Themis does correspond more to ma-a-t. Her law is the law of the earth, of life and death. And that is the law of man.

The Chinese notion of *tao* shows much similarity to ma-a-t, but it lays more stress on the mystical and inexpressible. The concept *tao* sums up the Ancient Chinese conception of the cosmic order and of the world's life. It is described at length particularly by Lao-tze in the Tao Te Ching, "the book of the world law and its activity." But the concept *tao* is older than Lao-tze, who lived at the beginning of the sixth century B.C. Tao means literally "way," and tao is the way of cosmic life; the way which life follows is the law of the world process. From ancient times tao, like the Egyptian ma-a-t, has been conceived as the cooperation of the two opposites in every area of the universe: light and darkness, warmth and cold, dryness and moisture. In tao both the spirit of earthly finitude and the spirit of heavenly infinity are working. There is the alternation between spring and autumn, and there is the alternation between the masculine and feminine element in the universal life, in which everything is yang or yin (masculine or feminine). This combination of opposites is, in China, as it is according to the Pythagorian and Samothracian ideas in Greece, the "Harmony." Lao-tze says expressly that this harmonious combination occurs in silence. Like the alternation of day and night, of the seasons, and the years, this takes place as an imperceptible process. No one sees or understands how it occurs. The life of the world, "the way of the world," includes all opposites but without perceptible clashes between them. This cooperation is prepared and actualized in the depths of the world. It is man's task to be in accord with it. In silence, in the depth of his heart, he must hold to this same balance in which all opposites are abolished. His passions and desires are then restrained; he no longer knows disappointment, unhappiness and grief; inner peace, happiness and modesty then constitute his essential being. The wise man withdraws into the spiritual foundation of his personality and ignores all externals. There no influence from outside can reach him. In close contact with the world-governing power, he draws from its inexhaustible spring. For man is a microcosm, the cosmic tao is also his life path, for in the imperceptible depth of his soul the cooperation of his life forces takes place.

In this Chinese conception there is a great similarity to the Egyptian conception of the universal world order but also great differences. The picture of the world is in the main the same, for both conceptions contain the idea of the balanced and harmonious cooperation of the typical opposites. But the religious attitude is completely different. He who follows the tao shares – in the midst of finitude – in infinity. The Egyptian believes that absolute life means death. But according to Chinese wisdom, divine life is the state of being elevated above the world of finitude; it is the combination of all finite influences into a harmonious whole – into a microcosm. This engenders a religio-ethical attitude which is alien to the Egyptian attitude and to the Indian renunciation of the world.

The Taoist is characterized by his retiring disposition, loftiness, dignity, and silence; he abhors all bustle, busy-ness and superficiality. "Tao does everything by doing nothing," that is to say, its activities cannot be noticed in anything external. Its work is imperceptible and thus inscrutable. The wise man must conduct himself in the same way. He does not maintain himself by reacting to the world, following a certain conduct, or seeking certain ethical goals, but by holding high the dignity of his personality; "while he practices doing nothing, everything is attended to." Such an attitude of doing nothing cannot be "ethical," but is religio-ethical or mystical-ethical, for it is based on an *Anschauung des Universums*. "One must be active as if one were not active, create as if one did not create; enjoy as if one did not enjoy; one must treat the little as something great." [2] In other words, one must not strive after finite goals; be busy, or be carried along by others, and one must see the apparently small in the light of eternity (*sub specie aeternitatis*). "Tao appears to be without (definite) content, yet he who makes use of Tao finds it to be inexhaustible." [3]

Now all these conceptions of the world order (rita, asha, ma-a-t, and tao) may be called "speculations," but they are not empty speculations or lifeless abstractions. A power has come forth from them. This is certainly proved by the fact that they maintained themselves for centuries, even for thousands of years, and could sustain countless generations. This power comes forth only from religion. They are not philosophical abstractions but religious doctrines and formulations of certain particular *Anschauungen des Universums*, in which the universe is conceived as a spiritual unity. Each of the concepts – rita, asha, ma-a-t and tao – correspond to a certain picture of the world and a certain attitude toward life, which together form the central fact in each of the various religions. They are striking illustrations of what Schleiermacher calls the individual character of the various religions; each religion has its own central *Anschauung*. Having discussed these entirely general and all-inclusive conceptions of the cosmic order, which encompasses both nature and man, we shall now take up the particular applications, especially those concerning nature.

C. THE WORSHIP OF NATURE (NATURE RELIGION)

May we really speak of "the worship of nature"? This expression sounds somewhat strange to us. Is it not rather the spirit of nature which is worshipped? This is indeed the case. But we shall see that the Ancients called "nature" that which we call spirit, and vice versa. Let us therefore keep the term "nature worship"; we shall see that the term originates with believers themselves.

Herodotus relates that "the Persians worship not only Zeus (Ahura Mazda); they also sacrifice to the sun, the moon, the earth fire, water, and the winds." [4] They thus worshipped all of nature. Herodotus finds this very strange, since he has long since departed from the Ancient nature religion – as had all educated Greeks of his time. Yet his report is accurate. In Vendidad 19 : 34–39, Mazda says to Zarathustra, "Invoke this creation, which is the creation of Ahura Mazda!" Zarathustra does this in the following words: "I worship Ahura Mazda, the creator of the creation; I worship the earth created by Ahura, the waters created by Mazda, the plants living according to the law of asha, the shining sky, infinite space," etc. He also names the different parts of the earth and the glory of the Arian lands. And in another passage (Yasna 35 : 1) he says," We worship Ahura Mazda and his spirits; we worship the entire world (or creation) of God, both the spiritual and the physical." Thus in all the Ancient religions, including that of ancient China, the sky and the earth, the clouds and the winds, the mountains, rivers, and seas, etc. are worshipped. They are thus quite certainly divine beings and real gods. We can justly speak of a "worship of nature." Now if we consider this phenomenon in the light of our own religious ideas and feelings, it seems to us to be the greatest possible degeneration of religious life. Or, to be more precise, practically this religious attitude is for us completely incomprehensible. For in practice no bridge can be built between the familiar and the alien. We cannot bring nature worship into accord with Christianity. There is no point of agreement. Seen in the light of Christianity, there is not a single value to be discovered in alien cultures. Thus it is stated in Romans 1 : 25 that the heathen have "exchanged the truth about God for a lie and worshipped and served the creature rather than the creator." From this standpoint there is not a single reason to speak of "nature religions," for this name implies that they are in accord with religion. As a dogmatic standpoint this view is certainly defensible.

For the historian, however, this is an impossible point of view! History shows convincingly that the nature religions posses real values. They have stood the test of time. Throughout countless generations they have supported the life of individuals and peoples. How they have been able to do this we can learn only from their adherents. It is to them that the historian must listen if he wants to understand the religious fact. Here our own opinions and experience don't help us at all.

Now when we allow the Ancients – and perhaps all non-Christian peoples – to speak, it becomes evident that they understand something different by "nature" than we do. In the first place, nature taken as a whole is for them a living being. In the cosmic order they recognize a universal order of life which is supreme in all the created world, including man and nature; there is thus a being with a will of its own which continues to sustain itself. They worshipped "plants, water, etc., which are ashavan "or "the world created by Mazda" or "the creatures which reveal

tao." These are thus the phenomena in which God's activity
reveals itself. But that is not to say that the phenomena differ
from God's activities, because the one is the result of the other.
We are always inclined to distinguish between cause and effect.
For the religious consciousness of the Ancients, however, the
phenomenon was a divine phenomenon, a revelation of a self-
subsistent life from God. In the case of every "phenomenon,"
we think of something finite, of which we then conceive God to
be the cause; we are ready immediately to analyze the phenomenon, to dissolve it into elements which are rationally related
to one another. But in the proces the phenomenon is broken
into pieces and destroyed. The unity of its essential being, which
is inaccessible to rational analysis, is set aside. The phenomenon
as such is then something finite; therefore we do not consider it
to be altogether a revelation of God. The Ancient's view of
nature was of a different sort, very unscientific, but entirely
spiritual. It was directed especially toward the essence of phenomena, and the essence determined all the constituent elements.
Thus the Ancients saw in the earth or in the fire in the first
instance energies or living beings. The essence of phenomena
was divine life. This is the religious view of nature. Nature was
thus essentially spirit, and God Himself was worshipped in the
phenomenon.

It is difficult for us to think in terms of this view of nature.
We feel ourselves much more at home with the conceptions of
the essential contrast between body and spirit, as in Plato's
doctrine of Ideas. We think in the forms of the "enlightened"
Greek philosophy and thus attach preponderate value to the
spiritual, in contradistinction to the physical. Even our various
modern monistic systems, such as spiritualism, psycho-physics,
and also materialism, do not bring us back the Ancient view.
They are of course philosophical, and not religious views. They
are theories, rational explanations of reality, and not *Anschauungen*, which see the living whole and translate the "vision" into
a religious attitude. Like all theory, monistic doctrine is wooden,
stiff and dead in comparison with reality. In this respect the
Platonic doctrine of Ideas, dualistic and "enlightened" though
it may be, is closer to the religious attitude than are modern
monistic systems: the Ideas too are beings, divine beings. But

Plato's doctrine does point in a direction which is the opposite
of that in nature worship.

Nature which is worshipped is spirit, but it nevertheless remains
nature. This last point is often forgotten in interpreting the nature religions. An illustration from Antiquity is the attitude of
Plutarch (who died 125 A.D.) in his book *De Iside et Osiride*,
towards the Egyptian religion. In many respects he understood
this religion well, but his difficulties are our difficulties. The
difference between his attitude toward foreign religions and our
own is that we, with our exact knowledge of those religions, are
more sharply aware of the difficulty than he. For there remain,
in the last analysis, insoluble difficulties, areas into which we
shall never fully penetrate. Plutarch begins quite correctly:

> It is a mistake to believe that Osiris or Isis is water [that is to say,
> what we and the "enlightened Greeks" call water], or the sun, or the
> earth, or the sky, and that Seth is consuming fire, drought, or the barren
> sea. But it is no mistake to ascribe all which is immoderate and disorderly
> (unordered) in these matters to Seth, and to consider and hold in honour
> all the good, ordered and beneficial as a work of Isis and as an image and
> replica (imitation) of Osiris.[5]

In other words, the nature of God is thus the order of life which
reveals itself by means of these objects. This is good so far, but
then in chapter 66 Plutarch continues along this line of thought.
He holds that Osiris may indeed be called the "Nile god" and Isis
the "earth goddess" provided that those gods are "not made into
special gods of the Egyptians" and provided they are not identified with the Egyptian Nile.

> For in so doing other men (who are not Egyptians) would be deprived
> of great gods. Those other men (among whom he counts himself) have no
> Nile, Buto, or Memphis, but nevertheless they are acquainted with Isis
> and her circle of gods. These men (we) have only known about those Egyp-
> tian names for a short time, whereas they have known and reverenced
> the power of those gods from of old.

And Plutarch states in chapter 67:

> Just as sun, moon, sky, earth, and sea are common for all, yet by some
> are called this and by others that, so of the one all-ordering reason and
> all-governing providence, there is among one people one kind, among
> another people a different kind of worship and nomenclature – in accor-
> dance with their religious tradition.

Plutarch thus wants to share the Egyptian gods even though he does not live on the Nile. He holds that the essence of these gods is the divine essence, which is not foreign to any believer.

Plutarch has here mixed together correct and incorrect viewpoints. He has stated the principle whereby we can at least approximately understand these alien gods and their worship. He has pointed to that side of our understanding which is closest to the Egyptian view. But it is certain that the Egyptians themselves did not so conceive their gods. For them the Nile was not an accidental expression of their idea. They could not dispense with that expression; in any case they did not do so. Plutarch thus sees empirical objects as religious symbols. But "symbol" is not a religious term. The symbol is an arbitrarily chosen image, used with an awareness of its metaphorical character. For the Egyptians the Nile was not a "symbol" of Osiris, but his image. And his image signifies his revealed essence. We may take our own conception as a starting point, but we must also try to go further. We must try to probe deeply into the ideas which linked the Egyptians with their concepts "Nile," "earth," "sun", and the like. Even when we have gained a general impression, we must not loose our grip on these objects in order to continue our thinking on the basis of our own feelings. If, however, we keep to the Egyptians ideas of these objects, then they prove to exhibit distinctive features which we cannot identify with our own notions. The Nile definitely remains an Egyptian river. Generalization does not bring us further into this subject matter; it does not give an accurate explanation, but points in just the wrong direction.

To put this in different terms, Plutarch remarks correctly that worshipped nature is spirit. But the opposite is also the case: spirit is perceptible nature. The Egyptians do not understand by spirit and nature what we call spirit and nature.

An example from the Avesta shows how little the spiritual content of faith in these religions can be coupled with the tangible natural phenomena. It is obvious that faith is most purely formulated in a creed or confession. Although few creeds have survived, we do indeed find one in the Avesta: "... the party which has chosen the waters, the plants, fire, the sacred cattle and the entire creation of Mazda, that is our party; that is our will and law." The believer feels himself sustained by a cosmic law of life, by asha. But what help are our concepts of "nature" and "spirit" here? They are modern concepts, which are pitfalls for us when we use them as the basis for understanding other religions.

When the "body" of a number of gods or divine beings is invoked (Yasna), what is meant is the visible revelation, the manifestation of those gods: the bodies of water, the earth, etc. Mithra, who reveals himself in the sun, is called "the embodiment of the sacred word" (*tanumanthra*) – that is to say, he is the word which has appeared in this world. This sun god is the revealed religion as a power in the empirical world and as founder of the empirical life of the believers. So it is also said that the whole creation created by Mazda at the end of time will be an embodiment of the Mazda religion; this is the Kingdom of God, on earth, about which the Avesta so frequently speaks.

This is the Ancient religious idea of the "resurrection of the flesh," not only the human body, but also the entire physical and living world. There is no essential difference between body and spirit. The Avesta teaches that at the termination of world history their unity will become complete reality. This idea is nothing else than a particular – and particularly clear – formulation of the thought which is the basis of all nature religions.

CHAPTER 3

THE WORSHIP OF THE SKY AND OF CELESTIAL BODIES

A. THE HEAVENS (THE SKY)

Why was the sky worshipped? How was the sky conceived, and what types of *Anschauung* do we encounter? How are the different conceptions worked out in detail?

In treating these questions we need first of all to pay attention to those instances of sky worship in which the believers themselves have formulated their conceptions. So we come to the literate religions from which sacred writings have been preserved or, as is the case with the Greeks and Romans, no sacred writings but other documents concerning their religion. The ethnographic material contains less trustworthy data because the information has been only indirectly procured. It comes from foreign informants, such as missionaries, or travelers who often have little understanding of religion. Ethnographic material can indeed show us how widespread "sky worship" is. But the term has little content if we are inadequately informed concerning the reasons for sky worship, for this can have so many meanings that we cannot understand it on the basis of the brief indication given by our informants. They do not arouse our sympathetic interest in the data, and without such interest we shall never understand that which someone else values. Tylor gives a broad survey of the phenomenon of sky worship, but this does little to orient us correctly.[1] He reports that the sky god is sometimes worshipped as chief of the gods or as the creator who regulates seasons, wind and weather, or as the guardian of compacts. This is the case, for example, among the Polynesians and many tribes in South Africa, among the Algonquin Indians on the Hudson Bay, the Huron Indians on Lake Huron, and among other peoples. All this, however, is too vague and too general. Even when he cites statements of religious believers – and these are always very short statements – the question remains as to how we should understand them. We hear that the Bonny tribe at the mouth of the Niger have, like the Babylonians, only one word for the concepts "sky" and "god." But we do not know whether for them the sky signifies the supreme god or how the sky is conceived. In a certain sense ethnographic material is easy to use. But that is only because it does not go into the real difficulties, namely the distinctive value of that which is alien to our experience. These difficulties remain untouched, although they prove to be present in every foreign religion with which we become well acquainted.

Therefore the literate religions come first in our inquiry. They enable us to gain at least an approximate understanding of a few forms of sky worship. That must be sufficient for us. He who wants to know everything abandons science.

Now sky worship in the literate religions does indeed exhibit traits which are held in common and may rightly be considered characteristic. They occur repeatedly, and they evidently concern that which is essential in the midst of all the difference in formulation. In the all-embracing sky the religious man saw an image of the highest and all-embracing principle of reality, the visible image of the cosmic order or law which brings unity in all variety.

The spirit of the sky is the governing will in the universe ruling both nature and man. Therefore the impenetrable sky is repeatedly called the place of divine wisdom, the wisdom of absolute life, of the ultimate and irrational law of life. This is among many, though not all, peoples the most important religious *Anschauung* of the sky. From perhaps no other form of nature worship do we become so clearly acquainted with what Max Müller calls "the perception of the Infinite." He means by this that an infinite, self-subsistent, or divine reality is sensed as the essence of the perceptible phenomenon. This is according to Schleiermacher the characteristic religious sense of absolute dependence, dependence on the law of abiding life, of the universal law of life.

Of all forms of nature worship sky worship is indeed the easiest for us to understand. The religious *Anschauung* which forms the basis of sky worship in the instances which are well known to us is excellently described by Immanuel Kant. He does this, however, without any connection with the Ancient sky worship, for that he never discussed.

> Two things fill me with a steadily increasing admiration and respect: the starry heavens above me and the [autonomous, absolute] ethical law within me. Neither is to be sought in what is hidden, nor are they fantastic [*überschwängliche*] magnitudes whose existence I can only surmise; I see them before me [perceptibility], and I relate them immediately to the consciousness of my own existence [subsistence].

Kant speaks here thus of a perception of the infinite without us and within us. The sky and the ethical law which takes no account of finite considerations, he conceives in immediate relation to his own existence. The sky is thus not only the image – in the ordinary sense of the word – of the absolute within us; that is the aesthetic view. No, the sky's infinity is also our infinity. The law of the sky and the law of man are essentially one. This is in accord with the Ancient religious conception of the sky. Thus Kant's prophetic and poetic intuition with his vivid sense of infinite values indicates the right point of view for understanding a religious phenomenon according to its spirit. With Kant we can really speak of a religious sense of nature. What is especially remarkable is the phrase: "I relate both immediately to the consciousness of my own existence." The idea of an ultimate universal law of life which embraces both nature and man was in Kant's mind; he knew that the natural law and the moral law were in essence one. It is the idea of the law of life including nature and man which is also formulated in a number of religions (asha, rita, tao). And it is quite noteworthy that all of these are related in a special sense to the sky god. Nothing is so characteristic of the sky god as the attributes of asha, rita, and tao, which likewise express the divine law of man. Kant himself did not and could not know how much religious facts would confirm his statement. Let us verify this briefly on the basis of the data at our disposal concerning the worship of the sky god.

Nowhere does sky worship seem to be so consistently elaborated as in the ancient Chinese religion. There the sky is the supreme god, the *ti* (lord, emperor) or *shang-ti* (supreme emperor). The earthly emperor is his "son"; he is the earthly representative of the supreme emperor, the mediator between deity and world through whom all earthly blessings arise. The yearly winter sacrifice from the emperor to his father, the sky, insures an undisturbed alternation of the seasons, for the sky governs the regular course of the world's life. This winter sacrifice took place in the night of the winter solstice. Frequently, as in the case here, the nocturnal side of the sky god is the most important. Other examples are the Greek Uranus, the Indian Varuna, and the Egyptian Nut. In general the sky was thought of as the starry sky at night; the conception was also widespread that night was more original than day. According to many cosmogonies, night was the original mother of universal life. The idea of night is always connected with that of the chaos, the material for creation. Night is the mystical source of light and life; therefore it is called the world principle of the supreme lord. The sky is called *Tien*, and conceived personally is called *Shang-ti*, "lord in the heights" or "supreme emperor." Under the sky is the whole hierarchy of gods, among them the earth, the imperial ancestors, and the god of fields and grain. But these are all animated by one spirit, by tao, the spirit of the sky god. The earth lives by means of the sky, and all other creatures live by means of the earth. In the silence of tao all vital energies work effortlessly together. The sky does not speak, but as the greatest world power and the highest wisdom it penetrates and determines everything which happens. This mystical character of Chinese sky worship is quite noticeable. When Confucius once refused to give instruction and information, he added, "Does the sky speak, then? Yet the seasons run their course, and all beings come into existence." The mysticism of the silence of the highest governance arises from the idea of the night sky.

Among other peoples the same basic conception concerning the sky gods prevails. But it is differently applied and differently elaborated and coloured in accordance with the particular nature of the people. The hierarchic depiction of the supreme power of the sky god in both society and nature is specifically Chinese. The one will of the sky becomes effective in the will of all the subordinate powers, also those in the social hierarchy. The sky is presenting them, although it is imperceptible and is not recognizable by any special features. According to this mystical conception, finite relations and goals are never essential. Other peoples describe the activities of the sky god in still different terms.

The sky god of India and in particular of the Vedic religion is Varuna. He too is the supreme god, who is called the "universal king" (*samrāj*). His exalted rest contrasts sharply with the industrious nature and display of power of the other Vedic gods, such as Indra. There are no myths about him, and he has little personification. His will and essence is the universal order rita. His activity does not take place with an outward display of power, as does that of Indra, but with *māyā*, a secret and magical power. This clearly sums up the religious significance of magic. Yet nevertheless Varuna is a different type of god than the Chinese god with his tao. The spiritual impulse of Indian imagination goes in a different direction. Varuna's law is not the silent power which does everything by doing nothing and which draws man out of active life. That conception of the law of life has existed in India, but it only came later, during the period of Brahmanism and the religious speculation which accompanied it. There, however, it was not connected with the idea of the sky god, and not even with any personal god. For man the law of Varuna was a law of actual daily life in which there is an alternation of the feelings of victory achieved by righteousness and of defeat caused by transgression or sin. The belief in the sky god Varuna brings the element of infinity in the consciousness of good and evil. The ethical consciousness thus acquires a predominantly religious character. These conceptions are therefore of a completely different type than that of the mystical in tao. The moral law is seen as a law of life, since it is ultimate and even a cosmic order of life. Thus man with his sense of responsibility is placed in a divine order of life. In the Varuna hymns conscious transgressions are mentioned, but also "unconscious transgressions." Although man is not aware of these sins, he nevertheless feels responsible for them. "Original sin" is also mentioned, and this notion implies that the transgressions of someone else are also our transgressions. With respect to such sins our individual conscience is not a trustworthy guide concerning good and evil. For man is ruled by the life law of the world governor, the sky god, and there is no one who knows, understands, or fathoms that law. "To fathom" is an individual capacity, but in essence man is not an individual; he is included in the infinite context of which the sky god is the ruler. The life of our ancestors is also our life – original sin is a consequence of this; the world's life is also our life – the unknown transgression is a consequence of this. This can be expressed as follows: our actions have results which we cannot foresee; their effects extend infinitely in space and time. Influences proceed from us into the infinite and inscrutable. We cannot judge our acts according to their essence. And on the other hand, the divine judgments of our actions fall outside our judgment. That is the element of infinity which is brought into the judgment of human acts along with the belief in the sky god. It is not only the recognition of irrefutable truth, but the sense of infinite responsibility for our action is connected with it. This sense points above and beyond the ethical, which presumes a knowledge of good and evil. We have here a religious attitude toward ethical problems and a religio-ethical sense. It is not "ethical-religious," because religion here determines ethics and sets its stamp on it, not vice versa.

So we too can understand the relation of the believers to this sky god. He invokes the grace and mercy of Varuna, because Varuna judges and determines man's fate on the basis of inscrutable considerations and unfathomable wisdom which we call "arbitrariness." Over against the world governor and lord of absolute life all human selfrighteousness is foolishness. The believer prays for grace: "free us from the sin which we have inherited from our ancestors" and ". . . and from unconscious sin." Grace is required, for the inherited and unconscious in the religious attitude also bring responsibility with them. This is not legal or ethical; we can never plead that we could not do otherwise because we were determined by previous generations or by circumstances. This attitude is quite different from that of the Chinese. Self-confidence has here been shaken.

We certainly sense here an affinity with Christianity, more so than in the case of the ideas concerning tao. Yet faith in Varuna is something entirely different from our faith. Every misfortune is proof of transgression and sin, for the law of Varuna is the universal, cosmic law. Divine life is as much natural life as spiritual life. Misfortune and disaster prove that man has deviated from the law of life. Here we meet again that which we discussed in the chapter on the nature religions: the spiritual significance which is ascribed to natural life.

In the Vedic religion the worship of the sky god is coupled with the recognition that man is not the measure of things, and this makes it evident that there is less self-confidence. But this recognition penetrated even more deeply in the Babylonian form of sky worship. There there are remarkably sharp formulations of the sense of disharmony and even of contradiction between human and divine considerations, goals, and judgments.

The Babylonian sky god is Anu, whose cuneiform ⟐ means *shamû* (sky), Anu, and *ilu* (god). The sign has developed from the sign for the north pole and the sky with its meridians; its threefold form ⟐ means "star." Sky and god are thus indicated with the same cuneiform sign, but with different words. From these ancient data it is quite certain that the sky, more than any other phenomenon or object, expresses the divine essence and the character of the divine power. The sky is "god" in general. It is sensed even more strongly than this, however, for the sky's divine nature determines the theological system, in which Anu is at the head of the gods. He is the typical Babylonian god.

There is abundant material at our disposal to inform us about the work of this god. It is quite noteworthy that the stress is put deliberately on the non-ethical character of this world governor and god above all gods. It can be said that Anu is just as ethically indifferent as a natural law. He is elevated above "good" and "evil"; both proceed from him. Indeed, there is even the tendency to put the emphasis on his evil and hostile attitude towards men. His sons ("messengers" or "servants") are the "seven evil gods" who bring misfortune, disaster, and sickness. They are repeatedly called *lemnûti*, which can have no other meaning than "evil." Yet that cannot have been their only quality, for seven is in Babylonia the number for totality. These seven sons of Anu include all the gods and all the factors in the world governance; they represent Anu's total world governance. And they are also the *Ilâni rabûti*, the "Great gods" (Greek *Megaloi theoi*). In Greece only the gods of the Mysteries, such as the Kabires, the Dioscuri, and Demeter-Kore, are thus named. These gods alone represent at once both death and life. In Babylonia, however, there is no mystery religion with its initiation into absolute life in connection with the Seven Gods. For there, such a systematic harmonization of opposites as is found in the mystery religions, with their conviction that death is absolute life, was never attempted. The spirit of the Babylonian religion, or of Anu, was a different one. What was connected with the totality was especially the idea of that which embraced and dominated dissimilar elements, namely the idea of a divine sovereignty and elevation above all human goals, desires, and insight. The difference between God and man was therefore always in the believer's mind. And especially in misfortune he was quite aware of this difference. This is the reason why he so often speaks of "the seven evil spirits of Anu." They are not "evil spirits" in the sense which we are inclined to read into that term, a meaning which has nothing to do with totality. Lamashtu, the demon of children's diseases, must be understood in the same way as "the seven evil spirits" who are the sons of Anu. She too is called "the daughter of Anu," the sky god and king of the gods. A superficial observer – someone who has not taken the pains to look through history – will call this a proof of the inferiority of the Babylonian idea of deity. The right evaluation, on the contrary, is to see this as an indication of the "demonic" character of the Babylonian sky god, and perhaps indeed of all the Babylonian gods. But as is well known, the term "demonic" indicates divine sovereignty and totality. (The evil gods were the seven great gods.) If we want to understand the Babylonians, then we shall do well to look at the idea of deity in the book of Job, which in our religious tradition comes the closest to the Babylonian conception. God does not justify his action. He does not act according to human norms of justice and fairness; He causes man's ill fortune just as surely as He causes his good fortune. Man does not fathom His decrees. Sickness, too, and even destruction, are the work of the sovereign god. And the believer accepts that destruction as the divine decree. The only thing from which he can expect good to come is the invocation of God's grace. The pious Babylonians also invoke that grace: the Babylonian Lamentations provide moving instances of this. It is not the demonic in the idea of god which is "inferior," but the lack of any understanding of it.

We repeatedly encounter instances which indicate that it is precisely the action of the supreme god, the sky god, in his world governance which has a demonic character. It is supra-ethical and, humanly speaking, arbitrary. Fatum and Moira, "fate" for the Greeks and Romans, is also the divine decree which does not accord with human desires. Man is thus bound and subjected to the divine will. But this divine will is the highest wisdom, for it is the objective wisdom which reveals itself as the universal order of life. Fatum and Moira, however, also mean "death," for the absolute absence of freedom and the abolition of all autonomous action is the state of death. This is the religious meaning of fate. It is not an impersonal concept of the natural sciences, not a determinism in the materialistic sense. According to the Ancient conception Moira is not above the gods; only Homer and other Greek rationalists so portray her. Moira represents the sovereign divine will, just as does Fatum. Fatum literally means that which is "dictated" (*fari*, "to speak" as the oracle speaks, inscrutably, "to dictate; *fas*, "justice," not as human law but as divinely determined law). Therefore Fatum and Moira also sometimes mean "death": they are the inexorable powers which abolish all human will and activity.

Towards the will of the highest world ruler two feelings prevail. They are the awe of God's majesty, "godly fear," and the sense of man's insignificance and shortcomings. These feelings are expressed again and again in the Babylonian religious texts. Schleiermacher calls this sense of absolute dependence the essence of religion and contrasts it with our effort to maintain ourselves by our own powers. By means of our thought and our will we try to subject the world to ourselves and our ideals. In religion, however, this egocentricity is denied; here man conceives himself as willed by the universe (a divinity) and individually formed with a special task to perform. Thus he listens in childlike passivity to the voice of the universe. In the Babylonian texts this sense of absolute dependence is religious reality in complete earnest. Hegel was alluding to this sorrow over man's finitude when he called the "Syrian" (Semitic) religion "the religion of sorrow." Nevertheless the world order of Anu is the order of abiding life, which is superior to all forces of destruction. According to the Babylonian account of Creation, Creation occurs through Marduk's slaying the demons of the Chaos and thereafter founding the world order. In doing this Marduk shows that he possesses *anūtu*, "the authority of Anu." This is the enduring and self-renewing life of the world; this is objective divine wisdom. Like the Hebrew, the Babylonian knows that he is taken up into this cosmic life. His eternal life lies in the permanent existence of his family and people. His wisdom is not his rational insight and capacity, but his obedience to the divine will and his subjection to God.

After all that we have already said, we do not need to enlarge on the character of the worship of the sky god in the Avesta religion or on Ahura Mazda and asha themselves. Here again we are struck with the religious profundity of the conceptions. The supreme power of absolute life is here found in the "wisdom" (which is life itself) of "Mazda," the sky god and the universal order of life; it also is found in *khshathra*, Mazda's kingdom (the heavens) which is to come. These conceptions accord with the particular nature or imaginative power of the Avesta people.

The Egyptian sky goddess Nut is also all-embracing. But she is so in a still different sense than the other gods mentioned; she includes both life and death in the resurrection of life. It is characteristic of her that she is called both the mother and the grave of Osiris. And Osiris is the prototype of the dead man. Both his mother and his grave (or casket) enable him to rise from the dead. The night sky, Nut, is the "other world" of the realm of the dead, that is to say, the world of divine life and man's eternal life. And in Christian usage, too, Gods' dwelling is called "the heavens." In the idea concerning Nut there lies an *Anschauung* of the starry heavens comparable to that of Kant. It is the visible infinity which Kant immediately connects with the consciousness of his own existence.

Akin to the Egyptian idea is the Greek notion of Uranus, the sky. According to Hesiod, this is "identical with (*isos*) the earth," the second home of absolute life; it is called "the safe dwelling place (*asphales hedos*, unaffected by any influence) of the blessed gods." [2] Since he "has brought himself forth" (*autolocheutos*), he is an original and self-sustaining cosmic power. He is the father of the Muses, the goddesses of the universal "harmony" or cooperation of opposites, and of the Moirai, the supra-rational and supra-ethical rulers of men and things.

In all these various forms of sky worship a certain definite idea of deity proves to be present, even though it is always worked out in a different spirit. The sky god represents the summation of divine attributes and activities. More than any other god he is the world governor and the representative of the cosmic law of life, the supra-ethical and supra-rational law of abiding life, in which calamity, destruction, and death are also included. Therefore he is always called the Highest, the King, of the gods. It is noteworthy, however, that these sky gods, such as Anu, Nut, and even Varuna, are not always the first and most important gods in practice, in the actual worship of the cultus. Their preëminent position is sometimes more theoretical than practical. In other words, the theoretical formulations of the divine essence have been primarily connected with the sky god. And in these views we have the best guide to orient us with respect to the religious attitude of the believers and the best indication of what the believers considered to be the essential and the central core of their religion. Part of that essential core is the sovereignty or demonic character of the gods, and the universal order of life (tao, rita, or ma-a-t) in which man is included but which extends far beyond man.

On the other hand, we should not underestimate the significance of these sometimes preponderately theoretical reflections. They have arisen solely and wholly through religious thinking. And sometimes they attest to that which has moved religious people most deeply. In sky worship, for instance, the negative element so frequently comes to the fore. In the eyes of the sovereign, "arbitrary" god, human values of ethical or intellectual nature are denied and abolished. It is then that we should not forget that the greatness of a great man or people, such as the Babylonian nation, is perhaps proved most emphatically and convincingly by its sense of its own littleness and insignificance as it stands before God.

B. HEAVENLY BODIES

The great significance of the worship of the heavenly bodies can be measured by the emphasis with which the Old Testament warns against it. "And beware lest you lift up your eyes to heaven, and when you see the sun and the moon, and the stars, all the host of heaven, you be drawn away and worship and serve them ..." (Deuteronomy 4 : 19). It is reported in II Kings 21 : 3 that Manasseh, King of Judah, sacrificed to the sun, the moon, the constellations of stars, and all the host of heaven. Even as early as Amos (5 : 26) the worship of heavenly bodies is reported. (Kaiwan is Saturn or Mars.) Aside from the worship of the *ashera*, the sacred tree trunks, the Hebrew prophets considered star worship the most important form of foreign religion. The fact that the prophets conceived the danger to be so great proves the power of these forms of worship. They evidently contained religious thoughts and motives which even such a remarkable "people of religion" as Israel could cling to and which could impress the rulers of that people. That would have been unthinkable if it had been a case of harmless and superficial worship, primitive idolatry without depth. It is becoming more and more clear that this worship was supported by the entire Ancient civilization, which on the whole was religiously determined, and especially by the civilization of the Babylonians and Egyptians, the teachers of Antiquity. There can thus be no question of superficiality or lack of seriousness and thorough consideration. We shall come later to the treatment of Ashera, the goddess of growth or fertility in death (death here meaning absolute life). So too Osiris and Dionysus had in the treetrunk with its religious mysticism an enormous power over the emotions, just as did the religious speculations to which this worship gave rise. And just for the Semitic peoples this cultus had a terrible earnestness; there was even self-mutilation connected with it. That can certainly not be explained on the basis of laxity or sloth. No, this is a case of the worship of the lord of the heavens.

C. THE 'SEVEN PLANETS'
(SUN, MOON, VENUS, JUPITER, MARS, MERCURY, SATURN)

The Religious Basis of Astrological Views

The age and point of origin of astrological views is of but slight significance for phenomenological inquiry. Like all origins, they probably cannot be completely traced. We continue, however, to want to speak about the origin, because we imagine that we there have the key to the understanding of the reality – sometimes so difficult to comprehend. What is really important however, is the fact that astrological views have been a powerful factor in the religious life of many peoples. The best known and most detailed data come not from the Babylonian period but from the beginning of the Christian era. And we find them right up into the sixteenth century (Tycho Brahe, who died in 1601), and even later. But then astrology becomes more and more a profane art, a "science."

The religious basis of astrology is quite clear. It is a particular form of worship of the sky god. The basic thought is that everything on earth occurs in accord with the law of the heavens, the sovereign will of God; that everything is a completely pure reflection of the heavenly order. God's will in the heavens also occurs on earth, all the way to the smallest details. This religious thought has been strong enough, in spite of all the contradiction of experience, to keep astrology in existence. It even continued for more than fifteen centuries within Christianity. Up through the Middle Ages it was an enormous power of radical significance.

The conformity was very early conceived in such a way that human institutions were only considered to be permanent and stable when their prototypes could be found in the sky, the home of true imperishability. According to a Babylonian or Assyrian text in the time of Sanherib, the city of Niniveh was drawn on the sky from the beginning of the world; "Niniveh, whose image has been formed since eternity and whose wall is brilliantly traced in the writing of the sky." (*itti* is "in" or "on.") [3] The temples, too are built "in accordance with the writing of the sky." The temple is the image of Anu's heaven, the real dwelling of the gods. Therefore the original architectural plan of the temple could never be changed later, for that would be human arbitrariness and an interference in the heavenly order. The true plan was drawn on the cornerstone. King Nabunaïd (ca. 550 B.C.) describes in a text his restoration of the Shamash temple in Sippar. This temple had fallen down, even though Nebuchadnezzar had repaired it shortly before. Nebuchadnezzar, however, had sought in vain for the cornerstone. Not finding it, he began on his own initiative (*ina ramānishu*) to build "anew." The result was that after forty-five years the temple again lay in ruins. Now Nabunaïd started to search, and eighteen el down he found the cornerstone, placed by Naram Sin, "3200 years before me." "The cornerstone was found and its lines (*uṣurāti*, "boundaries") were seen." On this basis Nabunaïd began to build "so that the temple did not diverge an inch from the plan towards the outside or the inside." This is a house of eternity! The Babylonian architect built in accordance "with the writing of the heavens." The priest-king Gudea had himself depicted as a temple architect. The task given to man is a divine commission. Its accomplishment is indeed human activity, but activity viewed *sub specie aeternitatis*.

This is the basic notion of astrology. From the alternating state of the stars, "the writing of the heavens," the alternating fate of Niniveh can be read, and likewise that of the Babylonian state and of all other affairs. The writing of the heavens expresses itself especially in the movement of the planets in the zodiac in their relation to one another and to the signs of the zodiac. The sun and the planets move within the zodiac. The other stars provide commentaries on this book of the heavens. We read repeatedly that this book, "the tables of the world's fate," is kept among the gods. These tables determine the course (*palakku*, circle, circulation?) of the heavens and the earth. Upon them "the commands of the gods" and "the life of men" is written. The art of interpreting this writing of the heavens has been revealed by Ea, the god of wisdom. The righteous (god fearing) king must pay attention to this writing of Ea. Everything is written in the stars.

Now we must not simply conceive of the term "writing of the heavens" in the sense which we unconsciously attach to it. It is

not a metaphorical expression for "a series of signs which have
a meaning." For the Ancient peoples there was something
mysterious about writing. It was the visible thought, just as
the word was the audible thought – the imperceptible become
perceptible. It is a thought which has entered the empirical
world and therewith become reality. Writing and word possess a
creative power. In the word the thought comes to the outside.
God spoke, and what was spoken stood before him. According
to the Egyptians, the divine word is the life of the world; the
world is created by the word and exists by its power. Or the
existing world is a thought created by God. God wrote, and that
which was written (that which was expressed by the writing)
became (perceptible) reality. The world order is called into
existence in and with the writing of the heavens, the constellations of the heavenly bodies. God's Word and Writing are the
mediators between God and the world. They are the executors,
the actualizers, of the divine thought and will. Ancient astrology
was based thus not only on a presupposed conformity between
sky and earth, but also on the belief that the existing world is
the thought of God made visible. This is also the belief of Tycho
Brahe. During the Hellenistic period and thereafter much less
was said about the writing of the heavens. But the basic religious
idea was preserved; the seven planet-gods continued to be called
the world governors. The view of conformity between sky and
earth was thus not a scientific one. The fact that there are seven
planet-gods points quite certainly to the notion of totality; in
Babylonia *kishshatu*, totality, is written with seven arrow-headed
characters: 𒀸. In the worship of the sky god totality is the
central thought. He is the inclusive deity, and therefore the
sovereign and demonic god. It is, however, not obvious that this
astrological view also explains the fact that seven signifies totality.
There is a writing about the number seven in the universe, *Peri
hebdomadōn*, which probably dates from even before Pythagoras.
It contains reflections on the seven-sided character, the totality,
of the universe. This expresses itself in various ways. The world
consists of seven parts: ether, stars, sun, moon, air, water, earth.
Furthermore, the agricultural year is divided into seven seasons
which together form a closed annual circle, a period. Man passes

through seven ages. In the head there are seven vital functions: inhalation and exhalation, sight, hearing, smell, taste, and the ability to swallow. The world consists of seven lands. In accordance with the notion in Babylonia, but also that in modern Britany and Russia, the writer counts seven points of the compass, and he does so because the atmosphere or *anima* (wind) is the invisible home of gods or spirits. Pythagoras, however, refers with his sevenfold conception of the heavens to the seven concentric planetary spheres. Their movement brings forth the cosmic music, the Harmony. For totality is harmony. The definition both of totality and harmony is: cooperation of the various elements in one whole. The world governance reveals itself as cosmic harmony, as the *mousikē technē*, "the divine music." Its mythical formulation is the idea of the seven or three Muses, the goddesses of the fine arts. These Muses belong in the other world, the world of absolute life where death and life are one, and for that reason there are seven Muses. At Troezen, the Muses and Hypnos were sacrificed to at the same time, "because it is said that Hypnos (sleep) is especially beloved by the Muses." (Pausanias 2. 31. 3.) Hypnos and Thanatos, death, are very closely akin. They both belong in another world, the world of divine life. In that sevenfold world opposites work together. From there the divine world order is revealed. This occurs by means of various kinds of oracles, such as the Delphic oracle and the dream oracle -- Hypnos is the god of sleep.

It is quite probable, however, that the fact that there were seven "planets" gave rise to the idea of seven as a symbol of totality.

The most extensive accounts of the worship of the planet-gods date from the Hellenistic era and thereafter. In the theater at Miletus the seven archangels are depicted in the seven niches, each with the sign of a planet. Near every image is written, "Protect, oh saint, the city of the Milesians and all those who dwell therein." Furthermore each of the images is marked by one of the seven vowels of the Greek alphabet (α, ε, η, ι, ο, υ, ω); the "vowels" are the elements of music. To be more accurate, they all had the whole series of vowels, but each had its own specific vowel at the front of the series. Thus they all had different chords. These archangels were identified with the seven Tychai and the seven Moirai. They too were determiners of fate and of the divine decree, of the "accidental," humanly speaking ,which religiously conceived signifies divine order. Therefore the Gnostics taught that the Moirai had discovered the seven vowels.

The names of the days of the week, formed in accordance with the names of the planet gods, prove the power of the belief in the dominion of the seven planets. In Babylonia and Asia Minor this nomenclature is very ancient; in Europe it has prevailed since the first century A.D., and it has remained even after Constantine the Great. According to Dio Cassius, each of the twenty-four hours of the day is named after one of the planet-gods: Saturn, Jupiter, Mars, the Sun, Venus, Mercury, the Moon. The day itself is then named its first hour.

Another remarkable application of the astrological idea is known from the Hellenistic era. It is the ancient idea of the descent of the human soul from heaven to earth in order to be born, followed by the ascent from earth back to God's heaven in order to attain eternal blessedness. This descent and ascent proceed through the seven spheres. In these planetary spheres the soul receives during its descent its various human qualities and during its ascent it gives them back. For every planet has its own special attribute, its own *archōn*. This idea of the heavenly journey through the different planetary spheres is probably very old. The zikkurats, the Babylonian temple towers with three, four, five, or seven stories, undoubtedly represent the cosmic spheres. These heavenly spheres form together the world mountain. The top story is "heaven," the home of the temple god. The tower of Babel was intended to extend up into heaven (Gen. 11 : 4), and according to the Babylonian texts, too, the temple towers extended "up into heaven." This should not be considered exaggeration, but religious theory and religious belief. And it was considered meritorious, a kind of initiation, to climb these towers. The number of spheres of the towers differed, however, for in addition to seven there were other numbers considered "sacred": three, four, and five. These all signified one "totality" – conceived in various ways. Thus too in Greece there was, in addition to seven the sacred number three (earth, air, and sky). The seven stories of some of the temple towers very probably represented the seven planetary spheres.

This doctrine of the heavenly journey of the soul attests to a majestic thought. It is set forth in various gnostic systems, and also in the Mithra Mysteries. The downward movement expresses the thought that the human soul originates in heaven. According to an idea in the Avesta, in the heavens infinite light prevails, light which splits up into the seven spectral colours, the properties of light. So too the infinite essence of the human soul is dissolved into finite qualities during its descent. Yet this "Fall" does not mean the surrendering of the divine implanted nature; only this is now split into contraries, with the result that the harmonious unity is lost. Within earthly finitude the soul receives a deeper content. In the midst of the life of contraries it wages war for the Kingdom of God. The Avesta describes in detail how the fravashis, the souls, descend from the heavens in order to dwell in human bodies and there to wage war for Mazda's heavenly kingdom against the spirit of death, the evil one. The victory is assured. The soul's return to heaven as it successively sheds its human attributes is the individual victory, the union with "infinite light." This return is dramatically portrayed in the Mithra Mysteries, whose starting point lies in the Ancient Avesta religion. The floor of the Mithra temple in Ostia consisted of seven terraces ascending towards the center. But it is especially in the cultus that this idea is carried out, actualized by the seven degrees (steps) of initiation. Few details are known to us, only the names of the degrees, and they do not enlighten us very much. "Pater," the name of the highest degree, meant according to the Ancient notion the self-subsistent and autonomous one – it was a title for God.

In the Hellenistic era ideas are also encountered which are indeed akin to these astrological notions, but which nevertheless diverge from them in another respect. For they contain a dualistic view which is foreign to astrology. A well known instance is the doctrine which appears in some Gnostic systems of *heimarmenē*, fate. Although fate is conceived in the astrological way as a divine determination and disposal, here it also has the meaning of a curse, a bondage from which man must with divine help liberate himself in order to attain infinite (eternal) life. This thought is not astrological. The seven planet gods are evil powers which enslave man. Man sighs under the dominion of "the Seven," the hostile gods; these are similar to and perhaps even the same as "the Seven evil gods," the sons of Anu. According to the gnostic sects these Seven gods are not only the powers of disaster and destruction active outside man, but also the inclinations at work within him which bring him to ruin. This is a religio-ethical dualism like that which is present in the Avesta religion. In Southern Babylonia the gnostic sect of Mandeans still exists, whose belief contains Babylonian, Persian, and Christian elements. According to this doctrine, man's heavenly journey proceeds upwards through the "seven prisons," the seven spheres. The journey is extensively described, each sphere separately. "Which prison is this, and which men does it contain?" is the question asked, and the answer given is: "Here are they who have shed blood and practised magic." The unbelievers, not the Mandeans, are purified there. The believer may go through when he has stated his name and the sign that he has received the water of life in baptism. Like the sign of the cross, this symbol is the sign of the divine power which has been received. It is remarkable that these divine enemies too, are called the lords of the Seven spheres and the "world rulers." Commissioned by the god who is enthroned in the highest heaven, "they rule and govern the course of the world." They too are the children of the *Pneuma hagion* (the Holy Spirit), the divine creator.

Here there is clearly the influence of the demonic god who creates both good and ill. The demonic is here seen even in human nature. According to this mystical monism the evil inclinations originate from God Himself, and the Seven gods work against men. Such ideas sometimes also occur in the Old Testament. According to II Samuel 24 : 1, God incited David against the people by having them counted; in the parallel account in I Chronicles 21 : 1, it is "Satan" who incites David. According to Exodus 4 : 21, God hardens the heart of Pharaoh. According to ethical judgment and rational thought these are contradictions in the idea of God, but evidently not for the religious consciousness. Man feels himself guilty, even when he cannot discover the cause of the divine wrath, when God himself has thus willed his guilt.

Then it is man's task to escape from the prison, the state of bondage to the powers of finitude, ruin, and destruction. This

conception denies the principle of astrology. The demonic character of the planet gods and the conception of fate as a curse indicate a different orientation than that of astrology. The statement that no one penetrates God's counsel is not an astrological
one, for the writing of the heavens gives insight into the divine
governance of the cosmos.

In Europe astrology attained its zenith in the fifteenth and
sixteenth century, under the influence of Arabic philosophy. It
was furthered by Melanchthon (died 1560), Tycho Brahe (died
1601), and Keppler (died 1630), and even Bacon (died 1626)
recognized it in principle in the New Logic, the *Novum Organum*,
which he revised twelve times. The ancient notion which is at the
basis of astrology remained the same. It is a majestic attempt
to comprehend universal life as a unity. God's heaven lies above
the stars, and thus universal life moves downwards through all
the planetary spheres until it reaches the material world, the
earth of men. Now astrology had the objective of ascending from
the ground of existence along the path of perception to the source
of all life, to God. This certainly shows us a religious world view.
Astrology achieved at least one result of a practical religious
nature; it aroused many groups in society to take part in the
battle against the belief in witches and broke the Medieval belief
in the almost universal dominion of the devil. According to the
Medieval conviction, through man's Fall Satan became the prince
of the world who is active everywhere. Fear and dread of diabolic
influences have certainly never been so universal and so radical
with respect to the spiritual attitude in general. The trials of
witches with their unwearying denunciation of victims graphically indicate the hardness of heart, the cruelty, and the love-
lessness in this situation in which the all important concern was
the struggle against the devil. It could even occur that all human
feelings were denied. Belief in the devil had become a terribly
serious reality. We have great difficulty in imagining the state
of mind of these folk; simply to condemn it as a degeneration
of feeling would be to fail to appreciate the seriousness of the
view and its real motives. Men had not become devils because of
evil impulses or a cruel lust for pleasure; they were concerned
to limit the power of the devil. And it is at this point that astrology successfully took up the battle. Not the devil, but the

wisdom of God rules the w ɔɪ ːd. The writing of the heavens – the fate of world and man – was of course the writing of God. God's almighty will proceeded from His dwellingplace there above in the heavens and disposed the most insignificant matters here below. Nothing accidental existed and nothing was caused by an unaccountable diabolic design. The assurance which the astrological world view provided must in comparison with earlier medieval belief indeed have been sensed as a revelation and as gospel (good news). Astrological theory and the belief in it meant for that time a new religious force. It did not lead to a deadening fatalism, passivity, and resignation to one's fate. For, in the first place, according to astrological theory everything was determined from above, especially at man's birth, but there were only very few able to interpret the signs. The cooperation of the decisive factors was extraordinarily intricate. In order to draw someone's horoscope not only knowledge of the state of the planets was necessary, but also the character of the hour and month of birth and their influence on each of the planets. For this the eye of a genius is requisite, and even then mistakes are continually possible. Even Tycho Brahe mentions the slight measure of reliability, even when there are the most precise observations and interpretations. And not everything is said with a particular notion; above this extends the general belief, which is the intention and the meaning of the entire system, that all things are placed in the hand of God. The will of God in the heavens is done on earth, the will which can indeed be seen in the heavens (if the signs can be understood). Moreover the individual will was not eliminated from the situation when the horoscope was deemed accurate. Frequently it had precisely the effect of strengthening the individual will and giving it a definite direction. According to the horoscope which Tycho Brahe drew in 1594 at the birth of Gustav Adolf for his father Duke Karl, Gustaf Adolf would one day become King of Sweden. This prediction was for his family, a branch of the royal house, certainly a motive in their organization of the insurrection which removed the reigning main line of royalty from the kingship. Thus the realization of the prediction was forced. In this way belief in astrology has repeatedly elicited the confirmation of a horoscope by giving force and direction to the individual will.

Predictions of disaster undoubtedly have a certain paralyzing effect, but even they do not abolish the religious attitude; even they do not lead to fatalism. For the astrological belief was that the influence of the planets – the divine world governance – is in itself always good. Evil lies only in man, and only in that impure matter does the influence of the planets become evil. Man is guilty when misfortune strikes him. He should have given another direction to the influence of the planets. If he had but had a good will, the prediction would really have become different. In his prediction the astrologist must take account of human impurity. Tycho Brahe says: "The astrologists do not bind man's will to the stars, but they admit that there is something in man which is elevated above the stars, whereby he can abolish the fatal influence of the stars." This conception of disaster is one which we repeatedly encounter in religions, from the Babylonian Lamentations to Christianity. Disaster arouses the sense of one's own guilt. And it is just this sense of guilt which proves here again to be the most fertile soil for religious life. Medieval religious astrology also worked in this direction. The central idea remained unchanged, that man in any case is called to actualize the divine will on earth, the will which reveals itself in the heavens, if only men are able and willing to understand it.

It may be thought inconsistent that the notion of free will should be connected with precisely the astrological view. But that inconsistency was a religious act whereby a sublime world view of the heavenly governance of earthly affairs could be rescued in the face of intellectual objections. The astrologists were confronted with a problem with which we too are acquainted and which will always remain a problem for man's thinking faculty. This problem is the position of the free will in relation to divine omnipotence and the divine governance of worldly affairs. The fascinating character of the astrological conception of the world governance lies in the lucidity of the formulation: "the divine will can be seen in the heavens." And this lucidity of the basic thought signified a great power and religious value.

D. THE SUN

When research into the history of religions arose about 1875, under the leadership of Max Müller, there was a tendency to ascribe an especially great significance to sun worship in the religious life of non-Christian peoples. "Sun gods" and "sun myths" were discovered everywhere. The sun gods among the Semites were Baälim; in Egypt there were Osiris and Ptah, and in Greece there were Apollo, Athene, and Hercules. The historical existence of Buddha in India was called into question; he too was seen as a sun god. Furthermore, the many myths of the dying and rising god were called sun myths; the "Christ myth" was explained in the same way as the "Buddha myth." Scholars believed that this central significance of the sun was based on a quite understandable view. No natural phenomenon was so impressive or so important for every form of life on earth as the sun. It was revered as the benevolent god, or feared as the harmful god of the scorching heat – and therefore placated. Naturally the sun had to assume first place among the natural objects which were worshipped. – The opponents of this school ridiculed this explanation by describing Napoleon as a sun god!

It has been proved that the religious conception of the rising and setting of the sun, "the sun myth," has indeed in countless cases exerted an influence on the religious notion of the attributes and activities of the gods. And some of the best known religious myths, for instance the accounts of Creation and Flood, prove to have been predominantly sun myths. By "myths" we understand, of course, not empty or false inventions, but expressions of religious belief in the form of visible images. There have, however, been far fewer "sun gods" than was first assumed. Most nature gods prove to be extremely composite beings. Not by chance, but by a real affinity in essence, the earth god can display traits or attributes of the sun god, or vice versa. In general this occurs because a "nature god" represents an idea just as much as it represents an empirical object. For the Ancients, nature which was worshipped was as much spirit, self-subsistent life as, on the other hand, deity was a natural being. Their religious interest was directed to the essence of the phenomenon, to its self-subsistent and spontaneous nature, and this could be in accord with the essence of an entirely different phenomenon. The sun, which rises out of the earth, has received its life from the earth. In the life of earth and in the growth of plants the same repeatedly arising energy reveals itself as in the life of the sun. The earth god and the sun god are thus essentially akin, and thus it is not surprising that such sun gods as Helios, Re, and the sphinx can also be earth gods. The god proves to be a "nature god," but not exclusively a sun god or an earth god. His essence (about which the believer does not speak) is a religious idea; it is self-subsistent life seen and portrayed in a particular way, and it is not what we call a certain definite phenomenon. The simplistic notion of "nature gods" which prevailed about 1875 is quite mistaken. There have been fewer sun gods, and perhaps more sun myths, than scholars then believed.

Nevertheless, there have indeed been gods which can rightly be called "sun gods." Helios, Shamash, and Re have this specific name. They are "personifications" of the sun. This is not a naïve conception of nature; for the believers' consciousness they represent primarily the divine energy of the sun. Naturally the *Anschauung* of the divine power of the sun is different for each people. But it is noteworthy that emphasis is usually not placed on that which we would automatically consider the chief characteristic of the sun. Two impressions come to the fore in our consciousness: the aesthetic impression of the splendour of sunrise and sunset, and the "physicist's" impression of warmth and sunlight as the sources of life and growth in the world. These properties are indeed often praised in the religious texts and hymns of Indians, Persians, Egyptians, and Greeks, but then they do not concern the sun god to whom sacrifices are offered in the cultus. They are only poetic outpourings, and not cultic hymns. The Homeric Hymn 31, to Helios, is characteristic. It glorifies the visible Helios who when he ascends his chariot shines for gods and men with his beaming eyes and his luminous head "like the immortal ones" (*epieikelon athanatoisin*) and as a demi-god (*hēmitheos*). The glorious beauty of the sun is thus here only in a figurative sense a divine attribute. In the Avesta, Yasht 6 is dedicated to Hvar, the immortal shining sun with the fast horses.

When the sun in the East lets its light be seen, then hundreds and
thousands of heavenly spirits arise, then they gather all the triumphant
lustre of the victorious light and divide it over the whole earth created
by God, in order to strengthen the good world. If the sun did not rise,
the gods could not resist the demons, the powers of the dark. Then the
entire world would be delivered over to death.

All these terms are borrowed from religious metaphors: the
"triumphant lustre" which "is divided over the entire world"
and the "purification", that is to say, the inclusion or re-in-
clusion in the order of life and the wresting away from finitude
and transiency. All these and other terms express the notion
that the whole world owes its enduring existence to the sun.
This is also our scientific conception. This description is so beautiful and so simple that everyone can understand it. It is really
a beautiful piece for an anthology of the sacred writings of foreign
religions! And yet the visible sun, the *hvar*, plays no special
role in the cultus or the practical life of the Avesta religion. It is
not more than one of the countless "creatures of Mazda"; it is
not a sun god. The hymn is written by a poet. It is a religious
theory, a reflection on the benevolent activity of this heavenly
body. The actual sun god who was worshipped in the Avesta
is Mithra, even though this name does not mean "sun," but
"compact," or "agreement." It was rather in this god that the
believers saw the divine essence of the sun.

Time after time a remarkable fact confronts us, a fact to
which too little attention has yet been paid; the invisible sun
is worshipped more than the visible sun, either as the nocturnal
sun or as the invisible spirit of the sun. It is as if the natural
phenomenon of the shining sun were too dominating to leave
scope for the creative imagination of the religious *Anschauung*.
It is evidently difficult to bring harsh sunlight into accord with
the mysticism which characterizes every form of nature religion.
The sun can be the symbol for our "enlightened" science, but it
is not the symbol for Ancient science. Whatever the explanation may be, the fact remains certain. The Helios worshipped
in Greece belonged in the realm of the dead. The gods together
with whom he is worshipped prove that sufficiently. Pausanias
relates that in the worship of the Mysteries at Hermione (Argolis)
there were a series of small temples standing next to one another
dedicated to Helios, Athene, the three Graces, Serapis, Isis, and

Demeter-Kore, respectively [4]; this was evidently a circle of the invisible, chthonic gods of the Mysteries. Pausanias also reports that on the Acrocorinthus dedicated to Helios, beside the altars for Helios, there also stood a sanctuary of Isis, two sanctuaries of Serapis, a temple for the daughters of Nyx (Ananke-Bia), one for the mother of the gods, the earth goddess, one for the Moirai, and one belonging to Demeter-Kore and Aphrodite.[5] An inscription at Smyrna reports an important worship of Helios there, with images of Pluto (Hades, the underworld)-Helios (the sun) and of Kore (the earth goddess)-Selene (the moon). Martin Nilsson believes that this is an Egyptian Helios, like Re in Amenti (the underworld). This is true, but the same idea appears in Greece concerning the Helios who was worshipped. The chthonic character of Helios is also indicated by his family. His son Aeëtes (von Wilamowitz-Moellendorff proved that this name is the same as Hades) is king of Aea, Gaea, or Ge, the earth. In the tenth book of the Odyssey, Odysseus and his comrades come to Aeaea where they meet Circe, the daughter of Helios. She is the sorceress who by means of her magic potion removes all memory of home and the world of the living, who transforms men into swine and directs them towards Hades. Helios' granddaughter is Medea, the sorceress with power over life and death. After completing her work she rides back in her chariot of snakes to her fatherland Colchis or Aea ,the underworld; yet this is not suicide on her part, for she belongs to death. This is thus the family of Helios. In contrast to the impression given by the Homeric Hymn, he is certainly not worshipped as the visible sun.

The cultus shows this, too. On the island of Rhodes a *quadriga*, a foursome of horses, was consecrated to Helios each year and then cast into the sea, "because he rides around the world with this team." Thus Helios dwells in the sea, out of which he rises and into which he descends. The (white) horse is well known in the cultus of the dead; Hades is called *Klytopōlos*, "he with the famous horses," and Demeter is sometimes depicted with a horse's head. In Athens and in Greece in general, the libation to Helios consists of a honey drink.[6,7] "On his altars no sacrifice of wine is offered, but *nēphalia* (wineless offerings) consisting of milk, honey, and water. These were the typical offerings to the dead which were also given to the chthonic Dionysus of the mysteries."[8]

We thus see that the nocturnal Helios in the realm of the dead was worshipped. This is because at night, in the realm of the dead, Helios receives his immortality, his divine nature. On the islands of the blessed his horses eat the magic herb consisting of *ambrosia*, the food of immortality. The realm of the dead is Helios' home. According to Strabo "the sunbeams lie in the gilded apartment of the city of Aeëtes (Hades), on the edge of Oceanus." Like many of his contemporaries, Julian the Apostate considered Helios to be the representative of all the gods. But he adds, "there are two kinds of Helios; the Helios which our eyes see is the image of *tou noētou kai mē phainomenou* (the spiritual and imperceptible one)." [9] This Platonic or Neoplatonic distinction between the visible and invisible sun is in accord with very ancient notions. It had great significance in the struggle with Christianity when Christianity started to battle against nature worship. The invisible god has his visible reflection in the world, and in this reflection he "reveals" his heavenly origin.

Now the question is what the believers from the most ancient times considered the activity of this sun god to be. For the Ancients he was Soter, the redeemer or saviour, the Eleutherios, the liberator. This is completely understandable when we note that Helios properly belonged in the realm of the dead and that there he received his divine life. He is the saviour who rescues from all distress and danger, above all from death itself, and he can do this because he knows the secret of the rising of life. In death he triumphs over death. At Troezen Helios was worshipped after the Greeks "had escaped from the Persians' slavery." The same thing is reported in the worshipping of the heroes. According to Xenophon the heroes, the great dead who are no longer in this life, saved Greece in the Persian War and made it invincible. The "Heros Soter "is indeed very closely akin to Helios Soter or Eleutherios. Therefore the bearers of the earth's blessing and the earth's life, the three Graces, were called either the daughters of Helios or of Asclepius, the god of healing and resurrection; the Graces were worshiped at Athens in a cult of the Mysteries. The sun god who possesses the earth's life also possesses the magic power of life, for life is a creating, magical

energy. Thus the sorceress Circe is the daughter of the sun god
and the sorceress Medea is his granddaughter. The visible sun
does indeed rise, but the real rising, the resurrection, has already
been fought out and won in death, for it is in death that the
mystery occurs.

The saviour is the battling and victorious god, just as Heros
Soter has gone through battle and victory. And here again as
in the case of the hero, the victory is achieved in death. This
battling sun god is well known in Egypt. In chapter 17 of the
Book of the Dead the activity of the sun god is described. He
gains the victory in "the arena of the gods," "which is Amenti,"
the realm of the dead; there "the sons of resistance," the enemies,
are destroyed. Time and again we encounter the notion that
death can only be defeated in the territory of death. The best
known portrayal of the Egyptian sun god is the winged disc of
the sun. He is inscribed with wings spread wide above the temple
gates and above the inscriptions on the grave steles. He represents
the Horus of Edfu. And it happens that this Horus is precisely
the battling sun god, as is proved by the many descriptions of
his meetings with his mythical enemies; his chief chamber in
the temple is called "the arena" (m'sn). This god is not the sun
who passes through the heavens by day. The wings as a divine
attribute always indicate the soul, the spirit, the invisible essence – just as they do in the portrayal of angels. The feather,
the wing, and the bird or "soul bird" are signs of air, *anima*, life.
The winged sun is thus not the visible, but rather the invisible,
the spiritual sun; that is to say, the sun is here thought of as a
soul which battles and triumphs. The realm of the dead is his
"arena." Therefore he is inscribed above on the grave steles,
which are – as is well known – images of the grave and the realm
of the dead. The winged sun god, (the) Horus of Edfu, achieves
in death the victory for the dead man.[10] For this reason Horus
of Edfu is very often depicted as a mummy (a man with a
falcon's head). Even though in these instances he has no wings,
the meaning is the same as that of a bird with a man's head,
the "soul bird."

The sun god as Saviour, in the first place, saves himself from
death, in which he is. This is the divine nature, the mystery, of
his essential being. The daytime sun is not a being of mystery;

whenever the Ancients speak of mystery, they always do so in connection with the realm of the dead. The mystery of the sun god is formulated in a remarkable way. The East is certainly the place from which the sun god rises, but then he has already gained the victory before his rising. To make this quite clear, it is said that the sun god rises in the West or on the Western horizon. When the gods of the South, the North, the East, and the West are listed, the sun god is indeed repeatedly, and that already in very ancient times, linked with the West as "the waxing one," Kheper (a beetle or bug). When this occurs, it is done quite deliberately, for as a rule Kheper belongs in the East. Furthermore, it becomes evident that the life of the rising sun god is the life of the earth situated in the underworld. In the East the sun rises in the form of a snake, "the son of the earth," and how can the snake be a creature of light. The life of the sun is identical with the life of the earth. Sometimes the sun rises in the east out of a tree; the tree of life is a well known symbol of the life of vegetation or of the earth. Then, at this tree the sun god defeats his enemy and saves himself. The vegetation myth and the light myth are here identical.

A different form of the sun god is the Sphinx, a lion with a human head. Re-Harakhti is his name and he is often depicted with wings, as a soul. Yet he is quite certainly a creature of earth, and he is the lord of magic power. The riddle of the sphinx − "Who walks in the morning on four legs, in the afternoon on two, and in the evening on three?" − (having as its answer, the child, the adult, and the old man), is certainly no ordinary children's riddle. It is the riddle of the rising and dying sun god − his own riddle − the riddle of the earth god or sun god who possesses spontaneous life. He who solves this riddle has discovered the secret of the sphinx and has defeated him.

But the sun god does not triumph over death simply for his own sake. It is for the whole world that he enables the life of the world to rise. He is the creator who in the beginning enabled cosmic life to rise. Not all creation myths are sun myths; for instance Creation may be ascribed to God's word, whereby the divine thought is transformed into an outward perceptible (first audible) reality. But one creation myth is very closely connected with the daily rising of the sun: the rising light of the sun is the energy creating the world. Nocturnal darkness is thus a chaos, the state of being before Creation, whereas the light makes the things of this world appear; it "creates" them. This is the Babylonian and Egyptian notion; according to the Egyptians, Creation takes place every morning. In Israel this notion is linked with that of the creating work: the light is the first thing created by the Word of God. This myth of the creation in the beginning is a formulation of the essential element, the idea of the daily repeated creation. What happens every morning is just as miraculous, it is the same miracle, as the creation of the world in the beginning. It is precisely the characteristic of the myth that it expresses the ideal form of a recurrent phenomenon as if it were a unique event. Every year Osiris, the god of the Nile and of the growth of vegetation, dies and rises again, and every year Kore is abducted by Hades and later given back; according to the myth this happened only once. Creation took place "in the beginning." The sun god is really the saviour of the world's life, which – according to the Egyptians – every day he enables to rise again out of the chaos of death. It is noteworthy that in both the Egyptian and the Babylonian myths a struggle precedes Creation. This "cosmogonic" struggle rages between the sun god and the demons of darkness or chaos. According to the Babylonians the struggle was between Marduk and Tiamat, according to the Egyptians between Re and the snake Apap, and the Greeks too recount the struggle between the gods and the titans and giants. Thus here again the notion is present of a struggle waged in the realm of the dead, "the arena of the gods." There the life of light asserts itself and victory and salvation is achieved. Here again it is evident that the sun god (like Helios) belongs more to the night and to the realm of the dead than to the day. The invisible sun god is the creator of the world.

Similar to the creation myth is the eschatological myth, which deals with the end of time, the moment when life will decisively rise in triumph and celebrate its victory. This myth too is sometimes very clearly elucidated as a light myth or sun myth, for instance in the Avesta. The last and decisive victory over death and over the finitude of this world takes place at the "rising" of the saviour (the sun god) out of the sea in the east. He then brings eternal life to the whole world; there is no more sickness, old age, or death – the kingdom of Ahura Mazda prevails. It is quite certain that also the last victory is, according to the religious conception, the same as the (sun's) rising which has taken place countless times, indeed every day. For every sunrise reveals absolute and spontaneous life. The eschatological myth appears to speak only of an eternity which begins at a particular point in time at the end of the world. This appearance is necessarily given by the form of the myth. But rightly understood, the myth refers to a timeless eternity which reveals itself every day, every year, and in all times. Again we see that the myth expresses the idea and the essence of that which continually repeats itself. It is "myth," but it contains the truth of the continually recurring phenomenon. It contains religious truth, even clothed in a mythical form which may seem strange to us. The religious myth is always an attempt to express the inexpressible and make it transparent.

Thus the sun god is the saviour of the world. This notion is given a specific application in the thought that the dead man is the rescuer from death. In the Egyptian grave texts for the king who had died, such as the Book of the Dead and the Pyramid Texts, the theme recurs repeatedly that the dead man identifies himself with the sun god and lives his life. "I am the sun god," reads the text in these cases. This is not audacious self-deification, for only the dead man, who has left all finitude behind him, can say this. There are not two kinds of immortals, one human, the other divine. In death man wins the same victory as does the sun god, and the victory of the dead man is no less a miracle than the victory of the god. Whereas the Greeks preferred to speak of the victory of the hero, for the Egyptians all the dead were heroes. The idea of a judgment is indeed present, but every believer is "righteous"; every believer recognizes the divine essence, the mystery of all that which is life – even of material life. Every Egyptian was convinced of this. It is the same judgment as that with which the hostile powers of darkness are condemned and destroyed. There is no question of an ethical judgment in our sense, even when ethical considerations are also taken into account before Osiris' judgment seat. Now this identification of the dead man with the sun god does not mean that the Egyptian belief in human immortality originates in the observed immortality of the sun. This is for the Egyptian not observation but a mystery. And only he speaks of a "mystery" who knows it or feels it active within himself.

The light myth of the sun is repeatedly linked with the vegetation myth of the earth. The most striking instance of this is probably the worship of Mithra in the Mithra mysteries of the Roman Empire during the second and third centuries A.D. Of course these Mithra mysteries depict in dramatic form the resurrection of the dead god. It was said that Mithra sacrificed himself, for he kills his own representative in this world, the sacred bull who even at Creation was the bearer of the entire life of the world. Mithra Tauroctonus ("the Bull slayer") is the chief dogma in the Mithra mysteries. In all the temple caves dedicated to Mithra his image occupies the central place, comparable to that of the cross in Christian churches. His face expresses the tragic notion that the pain of death is the prerequisite for resurrection. Divine dying is divine living, even though it is imperceptible and immortal – that is the mystery. Now Mithra is evidently both a sun god and a god of vegetation. Mithra is called Sol Invictus, "the undefeated sun," but his bull is the earth bull, god of the earth's fertility; the drops of blood from his wound are depected as grains of wheat and his tail as a stalk of grain. Mithra himself is also portrayed as Mithra Saxigenus, the one "born out of rock," who has spontaneously arisen out of the *petra genetrix*, "the creating stone." He rises as Sol Invictus, the sun, but his resurrection corresponds to the *anodos* (ascent) of the earth goddess Kore out of Hades. Is he then a sun god or an earth god? The most important thing for the believer is that Mithra's death and resurrection also has saving efficacy for man; in the initiation into Mithra's Mystery it is relived in the believer's experience. The religious meaning of all the Ancient Mysteries is that the mystery of natural life is likewise the mystery of human life.

All the ideas we have mentioned concerning the invisible nature of the life and essential being of the sun god could be called "mystery-ideas," even when the believers themselves do not use the term. The equating of the dead man with Re is for instance also related to the life of the sun in and out of death. But this description only partially indicates the religious meaning of the worship of the sun god. There is, in particular, one other important view of "religious *Anschauung*" which is repeatedly encountered. The sun god is the founder and the upholder of the stable order, regularity, or law which characterizes all abiding life of nature and man. For scientific thought, too, the regular rising and setting of the sun and its yearly movement correspond to a "natural law" in our sense of the word. For the Ancient way of thinking as well as our own, "order" or "law" signifies the unchangeable in all changeability, the imperishable in the midst of that which is perishable, the abiding essence of the changing phenomena. Nevertheless there is a great difference between our modern conception and the religious view of the sun's course. Natural science derives the law from the phenomena by formulating the point of agreement between a number of different phenomena. The religious view imposes the all governing law on the phenomena. The divine founder and upholder of order (law) puts an energy into the world, a living force, and his law is thus a law of life which sustains itself automatically – by the will of the creator. Natural law is not energy, but only the formulation of a factual correspondence between the phenomena. The law of gravity and of centrifugal force do not sustain themselves, whereas the "law of life" is indeed the law of self-sustaining life. "Law of life" is a completely unscientific concept, because "life" is undefinable. Religion conceives the regular course of the sun as "abiding life." This is not the result of sense perception but of an intuitive grasping or *Anschauung* which transforms the concept "life" into a universal idea, into a universal law including man and nature. This law is, in other words, the divine life which governs everything and extends its power over everything, and which constitutes the abiding and imperishable essence of the world.

The idea of divine life is linked with the sun god – it is the description of his divinity. The Babylonian god Marduk founds at Creation the stable order or law of the world; he creates the supreme divine power which abolishes all finitude, isolation, and arbitrariness. The image or symbol of this order is a fabric, "the world fabric;" the threads crossing one another represent the intricate yet regular connection of events – the universal world law. Marduk is the creator and the sovereign lord of this

law. At his word the law disappears and then reappears. He is
"the King of the Gods." The cosmic law of life is thus the divine
will. And although this god of the world order proves in other
respects to have a more inclusive nature, he is quite certainly a
sun god. As such he creates first the year, the twelve months,
and the days, the pattern of the entire world order; the regularly alternating periods impart their regularity to the whole
world process. But Shamash, the sun god, also founded the
stable order or law of human life, namely the social order and the individual law of life. His sons are Kettu and Mēsharu (cf. Hebrew
kūn and yāshar), "stability" and "righteousness," that is to say,
the divine law of human life. Shamash sees to it that men are
able to live in accordance with Kettu and Mēsharu and thus be
saved. Men cannot be saved on the basis of their own strength,
for they have not conceived their own laws of life or learned them
through experience. Thus the sun god creates the life force, a
divine energy in men, and he does this, for reasons which men
cannot understand, by creating and establishing the law for
them and communicating it to them. King Hammurabi receives
even his Civil Code from the hand of Shamash, the sun god.

According to the Egyptian notion, the sun god Re is the father
of Ma-a-t, the goddess of order or law and of the life of the world
which also includes man. The earth goddess Ma-a-t is at the same
time the daughter of the sun god. The ideas of order and stability
are essentially connected with the idea of the sun god. And as
the father of M-a-a-t, Re is as much the god of the cosmic as of
the human law. "Every day he puts Ma-a-t on the scales."
According to both the Egyptian and Greek conceptions, of
course, the divine law of life also includes death and destruction.
Now Re lets the destructive and constructive powers in the world
offset each other and keep each other in balance. This is the
religious conception of the order of life, and it is quite different
from all scientific and ethical concepts concerning the cosmic
order of life; this order sustains itself and extends far beyond
the scope of all such concepts. On these scales the dead man is
also weighed, and man is subjected to this verdict when he rises
with Re in the east. It is a cosmic verdict whose basic principle
rises above human comprehension and judgment, just as man's
resurrection with Re in the east remains a mystery for man.

The basic religious idea here is that the earthly life of man is weighed in order to determine his "righteousness," that is, his faith, his religious orientation which has an infinite meaning. His responsibility extends into the infinite because according to the law of the sun god man is bound up with God's whole creation, with the entire cosmos. The judge over man is the judge of the heavens and the earth – and that is the sun god. The mystical character of eternal life is maintained because the law of life is also valid for the whole creation around man.

In a very remarkable way the Avesta, in which Mithra is the "worshipped sun god," expresses the idea that the sun god has created and sustained the stable order (the self-sustaining law of abiding life), because the sun marks the daily and yearly regularity of continually changing cosmic life. The Avesta is not the book of a mystery religion; here death has no right to exist; it is purely and simply an enemy, the essence of Ahriman. Dualism cannot be combined with the religion of the Mysteries, because it not only contrasts an evil and a good spirit, but also, and most especially, contrasts life and death. Only about the beginning of the Christian era do the Mithra Mysteries develop, largely detached from the Avesta. The Mithra of the Avesta is thus indeed the god of the sun visible during the day. But he does not have the attributes which we automatically connect with the sun. In the Avesta the sun possesses something quite different from simply beauty, namely the power to produce and maintain the life of plants, animals, and men. The sun is the highest of all physical creatures, the closest to the heavenly and spiritual Ahura Mazda. Therefore he is the mediator between heaven and earth, between god (Ahura Mazda) and men. He reveals the divine law of life in human society and carries out the divine will. And it turns out that that which this sun god reveals and actualizes in our world is once again stability and order, conceived as the basic principle of abiding life. He brings agreement or "the compact" (Mithra), not so much in cosmic relationships as in human society. Mithra is the god of trust-worthiness in all agreements; the whole society is a *contrat social* of an absolute nature, that is to say, sacred and divine. He guards, protects, and upholds the cohesiveness of the larger and smaller groups within society, the unity of the nation, tribes, communities, families, and brothers (sisters); in short, of "all men who make an agreement with each other" and thereby bind and obligate themselves. This sun god thus represents the order which can be counted upon; his typical enemy is *druj* (deceit, death), Mithra-druj, "the compact-breakers," who is identical with Ahriman and with death. The Avesta is unique among the Ancient religions in ascribing a divine character to truth and sincerity, in which infinite life is believed to live. We discover, furthermore, that Mithra, the god of the visible sun, participates in earthly society as a warrior for Ahura Mazda. Armed with his weapons he leaves the high heaven, together with his countless satellites (among whom is the revealed word of Mazda), to do battle against Mazda's enemies, against druj. The stable order or law maintains itself by means of divine energy; this is the idea of the Ecclesia Militans in this finite world, and of the term in the Mysteries, *"miles* of Mithra." So this mediator brings, actualizes, and sustains divine life among men. Because truth and trustworthiness signify an absolute obligation, they make human life divine. In this respect the idea of Mithra in the Avesta is indeed the same as that of the Mithra of the Mysteries. In Yasht 10, the most important Mithra text, the natural phenomenon of the visible sun is, however, completely in the background. This is very characteristic of the spirit of the Avesta religion. In the Avesta ethical values are religious values, because the believer conceives the ethical in accordance with its absolute and all inclusive nature.   For although the idea of the law of society does stand very much to the fore, it should not be forgotten that this law is included in the view of the cosmos – even though not in the same way that it is in the Mysteries. The struggle which Mithra wages in society against druj is part of the world struggle. Druj is also the typical enemy of the cosmic ruler Ahura Mazda, and his name is the most frequently used term for the evil spirit, the arch-deceiver. *Druj nasu,* "the deceit which kills" brings death wherever it reveals itself in creation. The worshipper of Mithra takes part in the struggle between "the two spirits." According to the eschatology of the Avesta, the struggle will lead to a victory in which druj will be defeated for good. This religious factor in the ethics of the Avesta can nowhere be seen so clearly as in the conception of the sun god Mithra. In this way he is the mediator, the one who actualizes divine life in the finite world. And for this reason therefore he could become the god of the Mysteries.

We have now mentioned the most important types and forms of sun worship. There remains just one very well known histori- cal fact, the monotheistic sun worship of the Egyptian king Ikhnaton (*Akh-n-aton*, or Amenophis IV) in the middle of the fourteenth century B.C. Ikhnaton means the (life) lustre of the sun. It is questionable, however, whether this form of sun wor- ship is one of the most important types. It was conceived by Ichnaton and disappeared with him. It is a completely individual idea of deity, but not founded on prophetic individualism, such as we find in Mohammed, Zarathustra, and the Hebrew prophets. The prophet sets a new and lasting stamp on the religious life of his people because his inspiration is a religious one. Ichnaton, on the contrary, did not have such a lasting effect. He was certainly a poet and a great thinker in a time of high spiritual life. It is understandable that this conception of the sun god as his only god has greatly fascinated modern scholars. The hymns in honour of Aten are as easy for the modern reader to understand and admire as is the poetic glorification of Helios and Hvar. And probably they too should be considered more as religious poetry than as real religion. It is especially striking that except for Aten, the sun, all other gods are rejected and denied and the entire traditional cultus is abandoned. According to this "monotheism," Aten is the only god. This view is characteristic of the philosopher and poet. Aten, the creator and organizer of the world's life, is life in all that which lives. This thought is developed in the same mood which we might exhibit in saying that all life on earth has arisen and exists through the light and warmth of the sun, which as the source of all life is the only god. The sun creates the fruit in the mother's womb and causes it to grow: "Thou art far away (in the heavens), and yet thy rays are (active) on the earth." What is completely new is Ikhnaton's notion that the rays of the sun end in hands. These hands are a sign of the actively creating energy of the sun, or they represent the sun's life as "Absalom's hand" (II Samuel 18 : 18) represents Absalom's life. "Thou goest to rest in the west, and the world is in darkness like that in death; thou arisest, and men awake:

thou hast called them into life." We get the impression that the poet has here made use of the ancient religious idea – occurring in the pyramid texts, for example – of falling asleep and awaking in the sense of dying and rising again. Aten is seen not only as the god of Egypt, but as the lord of all peoples: "Their languages, their physique, and their skin colour differ; thou has created them all differently." "Thou art in my heart; it is (of course) thou who hast given me wisdom, thou who makes plans and art the power (in their realization)." "Thou art the continuance of life." Neither is there any trace to be found of religious myths and cultic acts. Everything is spiritualized, just as we might expect of a thinker and poet. The reformation of Ikhnaton is a temporary triumph of the spirit of "enlightenment." A monotheistic view suits this spirit precisely. Religious rationalism will always tend towards monotheism. The religious significance of Ichnaton has undoubtedly been overestimated. He was not a prophet or a religious genius, and he did not bring a new form of real sun worship. This also explains the fact that his activity left no trace behind it.

E. THE MOON

The worship of the moon as a divine being is one of the best known and widespread forms of nature worship. It is problematical which property of the moon really occasioned this. As in the case of the sun, the answer cannot be given on the basis of our impression of the natural phenomenon or on the basis of general historical views or speculations. This has indeed been tried. Moon worship belongs particularly among nomad peoples, who must journey at night because it is too hot to do so during the day. Thus the moon is worshipped the most by the Semitic peoples, the Babylonians for instance, among whose various peoples there are nomads even at the present time; probably in prehistoric times all the Semites led a wandering existence. This explanation is no more convincing than the corresponding explanation of sun worship, which would be very natural, since light and warmth are the sources of all life and since the sun has such a brilliant appearance. No, we also find worship of the moon by such peoples as the Egyptians, who certainly were never nomads, whereas sometimes there is no special moon worship even among peoples who certainly were wanderers in earlier times, such as the Iranian peoples. Why, moreover, does moon worship continue in historic times, that is, periods for which we have literary records, after the nomadic peoples had settled down, as had the Babylonians – even assuming that they were previously nomads? Then the assumed importance of this heavenly body must, of course, have completely disappeared. Since its worship nevertheless continues, the moon must have been quite differently conceived. And it is just this historical period which interests us most, for only then do we find the precise details which enable us to penetrate into the meaning of moon worship; only then have religious ideas acquired a fixed form, and sometimes they have become known far beyond the boundaries of particular peoples and thus have become part of the spiritual inheritance of many peoples. The assumed origins can at most only partially explain that which has arisen from them. Or more accurately, they really do not explain the new development at all.

We are brought much closer to real moon worship by the collections of folklore concerning the popular belief of the last fifty or sixty years and by modern popular conceptions of the activities and nature of the moon. We obtain these data from a large number of peoples, both within and outside Europe. It is interesting what a striking agreement in conception they show, an agreement which corresponds to the almost universal character of moon worship, which is really not at all restricted to nomad peoples. The modern conceptions also prove to have a large measure of agreement with the Ancient views, which we encounter both within and without the Ancient religions.

The phenomenon of the various shapes of the moon has attracted special attention. The moon successively waxes, wanes, and completely "dies." In this the heavenly example or prototype has been seen of all growth and all regress in earthly life. In the Avesta, Yasht 7 : 4, there is written: "When the moon shines (when the moon is waxing), the plants grow, and in the spring they sprout." This is the popular belief and the popular science of all the centuries. In his *Naturalis Historia* Pliny states:

The moon is the planet of life (*luna spiritus sidus*), for in its waxing phases it fills bodies, and it empties them in its waning forms. That is the reason why crustaceans (lobsters and oysters) increase in size during the waxing of the moon ... even men's blood increases and decreases according to the moonlight, likewise leaves and herbs, for the (moon) energy penetrates everything (*in omnia eadem penetrante vi*).[12]

Sometimes it was believed that the waning moon also provided a divine power of growth, namely for all that which belongs to the world of death, to the underworld. Plutarch states that onions are the only plants which grow contrary to the moon's influences. But they, too, do that by means of moon energy. Among French and German farmers the belief is prevalent that plants whose fruits grow above the ground must be sown during the waxing of the moon, but plants whose fruit is in their roots must be sown when the moon is waning. The idea of rising is thus linked to the waxing moon, and the idea of the descent of the upper world to the under world is linked with the waning moon. This belief is also given another practical application. Sowing, grafting and other activities which further the growth of vegetation are performed by the waxing moon; activities which hinder growth, such as felling or uprooting trees, are performed by the waning moon. In the eighteenth century in France this was even fixed by law, in the interest of the buyers of wood. Even today offers are made in the newspapers of "trees which have been felled by the waning moon."

According to another very widespread formulation of the moon's vital force, it is considered the residence of the liquid element. According to Ancient physiology, liquid was the element of growth; lack of moisture naturally stopped growth. Thus Melanchthon states in his *Initia Doctrinae Physicae:*

As a rule weak children and those who do not live long are born at the conjugation of the sun and moon, at the new moon, and this is especially the case when the moon moves toward the sun [waning moon]. This evil is sometimes indeed softened by other favorably disposed heavenly bodies, yet it always remains significant. Not only did Aristotle know this, but every experienced midwife knows it ... The cause [of this] is obvious: the moon controls the moist elements in man. If it does not cast its light into the body, then the bodily moistures dry up and the [favourable] sanguine element is lost. Consumption and leprosy are the results of this. It is quite understandable that it cannot be otherwise.[13]

All these views are important for understanding the religious conception of the moon; in any case they are much more im-

portant than conjectures about the significance of the moon
for nomads. Data from folklore and such views as Melanchthon's
concern "the quite understandable influence" of the moon on
all of nature. These views are formulated like natural laws,
in the style of natural science: they see a large number of phenomena as the results of an assumed rational cause. There is
however a mistake. A natural law is formulated which is the
precise inversion of the truth. It does not do as an explanation,
and it is rightly called superstition – not because of the intrinsic
falsity of the view, but because of the attempt to give scientific
validity to what was a religious idea. As is so often the case, here
too superstition is a survival from religious belief of earlier times
or a different spiritual atmosphere. We here confront an un-
prooted and dead belief which has acquired the semblance of
insight but which is evidently mistaken.

Religious belief speaks a different language. "The moon god
controls all the prosperity and all the decline in this world."
This standpoint differs essentially from the one we have just
considered. The religious view deliberately renounces every
rational explanation. The term "moon god" does not occur in
folklore or in Melanchthon's writings. The religious view concentrates attention on the inexplicable nature of the phenomena:
in that inexplicability the self-subsistent and spontaneous divine
energy at work in the phenomena reveals itself. That which
the self-subsistent god performs is irrational and remains inexplicable – such is the religious view. Growth and degeneration,
death and the rising of life which succeeds it are just as mysterious
as the god (in this case, the moon god) who causes life to arise
and to die. When the believer says that the moon god brings
about all growth and all death on earth, then in a certain sense
he has indeed formulated a natural law. As far as its form is
concerned his statement is superstition. But he has conceived this
natural law as an autonomous being with divine will and power,
a notion which has nothing in common with our concept of natural law. This is not a mistaken natural law; belief in this self-
subsistent law is not superstition. Religious belief is never superstition. Only an uprooted belief from which the god and his
worship have disappeared can be called "superstition." Religious
belief as such is always correct, because it is concerned with the

ultimate and irreducible nature of the event and because it sees that ultimate nature as its essence. Even modern natural science can have no objection to this.

It becomes evident from the historical data that the moon god is again and again linked and even identified with other gods who were also agents of growth and decline, death and renewal of life – and especially with the gods of the earth. From this it is evident how acutely the basic religious principle was sensed in moon worship. It would not occur to anyone to confuse the moon as an empirical object with the earth as an empirical object. They are totally dissimilar. But in both there is the same divine activity.

Osiris-Sokaris is a god of the earth and the growth of vegetation who was also believed to be a moon god. In the performance of the Osiris mysteries the priest fashions the image of Osiris from a mixture of moist, fertile earth and grains of wheat. First, however, he shapes this dough into the form of an egg [14] or of a crescent moon [15], and only later does he shape it into the human form of Osiris' mummy. The god of vegetation, depicted by an image made of fertile earth, is thus here conceived as a moon god, in particular as the god of the new moon. The spontaneous life of the moon god (who is also called Osiris) arising anew from his own death leads to the same symbolism as that of the egg.

Here is another application of this thought. The god of vegetation, Osiris, saves himself by journeying in his boat across the sea, that is, through the realm of the dead. This boat is sometimes depicted in the form of a crescent moon 〰️, or with a crescent moon placed within it. Osiris saves himself; he arises as the moon god. Thus according to Plutarch the chest in which the image is placed is also in the form of a crescent moon.[16] According to the usual conception the chest or box is the image of the earth itself. All this gives a good illustration of the concept "nature god." That a certain natural object is seen as a divine being is not the most important thing, for there are two objects of importance, earth and moon. The main thing is that an idea, an *Anschauung*, concerning cosmic and human life is expressed by one or more natural phenomena. In addition to being a moon god and an earth god, Osiris is also a Nile god and even a sun god. In literate

religions, such as the Egyptian, we can distinguish all these
attributes clearly, but in the illiterate religions, for instance
those of Asia Minor, there were probably also similar ideas.
In one case, namely that of the Cretan religion, this can be proved
by comparing Cretan symbols with those known to us from Greece and Egypt.

Another example of the affinity between moon god and earth
god is provided by the Babylonian and Egyptian notion of the
bull, the Babylonian *Nannaru-Sin*. (Sin means "moon.") It is
the powerful young bull with strong horns. The "horns of the
moon" certainly furnished occasion for the development of the
notion of this celestial bull, but they certainly did not cause it.
A bull does not grow from a pair of horns, and certainly not a
celestial bull. But there is on the contrary a very familiar notion
in all the Ancient religions from the Mediterranean to the Ganges,
that of "the bull of the earth," which is the mythical image of the
nutritive energy of the earth which creates and sustains life. The
horns of the terrestrial bull symbolize his power; in Crete they
were the most sacred sign, comparable to the Cross in Christianity. (Cf. the drawings ⌣⌐ and ⩔⩔.) This was also the
significance of bull and ram horns on Cretan, Roman, and Hebrew earth altars. The bull and the ram have the same symbolism; their sacrifices (*taurobolion* and *kriobolion*) alternate, and
the animal of the Egyptian Ammon-Min is similar to a ram or a
bull. A related idea is that of the "horn of plenty" in the hand of
Hades-Pluto, or Ge, or of the young Dionysus. This "cornu
copiae" or "cornucopia" is never depicted as a drinking horn
but is always full of the fruits of the earth. And the believers
also saw these horns in the crescent moon. The moon god is the
celestial bull; there is essential connection between the life of
the moon and the life of the earth. In Babylonian texts, too, the
moon is conceived as the fruit of a tree which grows by its own
power. The Egyptian earth bull Apis also represented a moon
god – we see this from the connection between the worship of
Apis and the different phases of the moon, and we also read
that the father of Apis is the moon god.

In Rome Juno Lucina was the goddess of the first visible
narrow crescent of the new moon. This moon goddess is the goddess of birth; she is the feminine "genius," the life spirit of all

women. Identified with the goddess of birth, Eileithyia, she bestows the mysterious beginning of life. But Juno is equally the earth goddess, the virgin mother goddess, like Athene. This is evident from her emblems, the snake and armour.

Such moon worship lies behind modern popular superstitions about the moon. All the emphasis was placed on the mystery of self-subsistent life, on the same mystery that was seen in the heavenly bodies and in the earth.

Moon worship is characterized by the fact that the moon god turns out repeatedly to be, not the god of the full moon, but of the first crescent or the new moon. (This new moon was of very little use to the nomads!) The divine character of the moon lies thus in its "resurrection." According to the Babylonian texts, the first light of the new moon, notwithstanding its weakness, is the most beautiful light there is; the splendour and glory of the temple is compared with the lustre of the new moon. We cannot explain this on the basis of a simple aesthetic perception of nature. It is a religious view, an expression of the religious sense of nature, like the worship of the invisible sun god in the underworld. The Babylonians also said that the light of the moon was the first light at Creation, and that it existed even before sunlight. It was the light of the world which generates itself and all that which lives. But it was also the divine self-sustaining and renascent life of the world, just as the Greek or early Christian *phōs* (light) can mean life.

In Greek religion and myth the idea of the new moon is peculiarly developed in the story of the two Dioscuri. Their sister Helena or Selene is portrayed standing between them with the crescent moon on her head. Theseus, Paris, or Hector abducts her: this is the disappearance of the new moon. After that her brothers the Dioscuri, bring her back again. The twin brothers, Castor being mortal and Pollux immortal, represent the double nature of the new moon, its death and its life. The relation between brothers and sister points quite certainly to affinity in nature, just as does the relation between father or mother and child. The Dioscuri live alternately on Mount Olympus or in the underworld; together they represent the alternation of death and life, the double essence of resurrection. Therefore they are Soteres, the "saviours," not only of Helena, but of anyone in mortal danger, especially at sea. The new moon, conceived as a double divinity, is the saviour of life because it is itself the risen one. Therefore the Dioscuri are also worshipped as gods of the Mysteries, together with the Kabires. Only gods of the Mysteries are called as they are: *Megaloi Theoi*, "Great gods." Through death they bestow immortality. The new moon has the nature of a mortal man and of an immortal god: the father of Castor was Tyndareus, a man, and the immortal father of Pollux was the god Zeus. The moon is the mediator between man and god; it possesses the nature of both.

This explains why the king is frequently conceived as a moon god. Especially in Babylonia he is much more the representative of the moon than of the sun, and his diadem has the form of moon horns. The king is the mediator; he is God appearing as man; he represents the order of life and sustains the abiding life of men. The Roman double-faced Janus was also a god of the new moon, "Janus Junonius." Indeed we read that he was the first king before the link between the heavens and the earth was broken. In historical times Janus was considered the divine prototype of the Roman king; during the Republic and the Empire the Rex Sacrorum was the special priest of Janus Junonius. Ancient Sparta was ruled by two kings at the same time. These kings represented the two Dioscuri, which were especially revered in Sparta. The nature of the god-man, the divine king, was thus divided between two persons. No modern scholar has been able to give a rational explanation (for instance, political or historical) of the double kingship.

It is evident from the Babylonian texts what a vivid awareness there was of the double nature of the moon, which was at once mortal and immortal, finite and infinite, man and god. The new moon was called a "twin god," thus a double god like the Dioscuri, "who reconcile the heavens and the earth" (the idea of the mediator). It is of divine and human nature. According to Babylonian speculation, both have divine significance: as finitude and death, and as infinity and resurrection, which presuppose each other – so too, both the Dioscuri are divine beings. "This new moon lets its light shine as the god who has been created in the heavens, the divine world, and on the earth, the human world; this new moon is the combination (*kishshatu*, "totality") of the heavens and the earth: as creature of the gods and a product of men, it is formed with care (wisdom)." This is one of the very remarkable statements in the Ancient religions which amazes us by its depth of thought and the audacious imagination in its formulation. It reminds us of the doctrine of the great medieval Christian mystics, such as Eckhart and Ruysbroeck. According to these mystics, man, too, is in a certain sense a creator, for his finitude and imperfection is a definite factor in the divine life of the world. In the divine wisdom man is indispensable and intended to be a finite and imperfect being. In man God has willed his own opposite, but in doing so He has nevertheless only willed Himself. Man performs a divine task. These thoughts are akin to the Greek, Roman, Egyptian, Babylonian and other Ancient ideas concerning the king as the godman, the god appearing on earth, the mediator who looks after the life of men. In the Babylonian texts religious speculation is given free play, and the writers were quite aware of the daring character of their statements, just as were the Christian mystics. In its application to men, this view is only true of the king. When ordinary men are under discussion, the idea of contrast between man and god comes much more to the fore, especially in Babylonia. This is also true in Greece. Pindar says, "There is one who is God; man is quite a different being." This is certainly inconsistent. But such inconsistencies and contradictions are present in all genuine piety; it is only in more or less rationalistic formulations that they are absent. Human experience attests to man's finitude and his difference from God. But it also testifies to affinity, which is the prerequisite of every religious relation. It is impossible to eliminate this contradiction. The Ancient conviction was that the king was essentially different from man. But when the king is called the "god-man," then this term also presupposes the awareness of an affinity between the human and the divine essence. The typical Babylonian hero Gilgamesh was "one-third man and two-thirds god." There are more expressions of this idea, even in the Babylonian religion. The Greeks believed that the man *par excellence*, the hero, is also divine.

Sometimes the moon god is the special god of wisdom, as was certainly the Egyptian moon god Thot. This god was identified by the Greeks with "Hermes Trismegistos." About the end of the third century A.D. the syncretistic speculation which conceived the world as matter ordered by God and brought to life viewed the mythical figure of Hermes Trismegistos as the bearer of all wisdom. He was the divine teacher who gave men information as to how by piety and self-knowledge they could enable their souls to return to their divine source. This is a syncretism composed of Pythagorean, Greek, and Egyptian ideas. Indeed it is quite certain that from the earliest times the moon god Thot was the Egyptian god of wisdom. Scholars have tried to explain this from the fact that the phases of the moon determine the calendar and chronology – the oldest form of science. This conjecture is not based upon factual data. In any case the wisdom of Thot is differently conceived in the historical period, and that goes back into very ancient times. Thot is called "the Lord of the divine Word" and "the Lord of Writing." This has nothing to do with the calendar. It means that he actualizes the divine essence, will, or life in the world and by audible or visible thought makes it perceptible. The productive Word and Writing are not only active in the beginning at Creation, but also in the entire world governance. All the emphasis is placed on the magical, that is the divine, power of word and writing. The moon god is the god of the magic power whereby the world was spoken and written in the beginning and whereby it has existed ever since. This is related to the nature of the new moon, whose god is Thot. He knows the secret of life, and especially of the life which is continually renewing itself. The Greeks understood his significance correctly when they identified him with Hermes Trismegistos: Thot is the god of the secret of the cosmic order – nothing is ever said about a calendar. His distinctive emblem is the net. The symbol of the net is well known; the net signifies the all embracing order from which nothing and no one escapes; it is itself the image of complex regularity and order. According to a Babylonian text, "the net of Marduk" (or of other gods) is "the divine Word." It is thus the thought of God which governs the world. "The net is the fate of the world"; "it spans sky and earth"; "it is the dwelling of the divine judges," that is, of the upholders of cosmic and human order. The moon god Thot also "dwells in the house of the net," in other words, where the world order is determined. We know that this is the meaning of the net because the believers themselves so described it. Thot is also called "the lord of fate," and he is the one "who makes the word (command) of the dead man a triumphant word," for he is the god of resurrection who in death makes potential life into actual life. The insight into and the power over the mystery of life is the wisdom of the moon god. Thot, "the writer of the *ma-a-t* of the gods (the order of life)," makes this ma-a-t into a visible and actual order by the magic power of writing. The pyramid texts testify to a belief in this magic power. Many of these grave texts, chiseled with great pains into the walls of dark and inaccessible rooms, were not designed to be spoken by the dead man. Just the description of the victories which the dead man had to achieve was enough to ensure that these victories would occur: the magic inscription is as effective as the magic formula which is recited.

Thot, the moon god, knows the secret of life. Indeed he is also called "the consort of the goddess Ma-a-t," who is the goddess of the cosmic order and especially of the life of the earth. These are not theoretical speculations about the essence of the moon god, but they are religious views with an intensely practical aim: the securing of immortality. Thus was the moon god worshipped in Egypt.

CHAPTER 4

THE WORSHIP OF EARTH GODS

A. THE SACRED EARTH

The earth has a very special place among the objects of worship in nature. No other object is so universally venerated. The earth is considered to be the bearer and revealer of divine life. It brings forth life, sustains it, and takes it back only to let it rise anew. Thus all peoples throughout all times have more or less consciously conceived the earth as the basis of life. They have linked ideas concerning the self-sustaining nature and mystery of life itself especially with the religious conception of the earth's life. And this view has been such a dominating one that it has drawn into its orbit many other forms of worship – of sun, moon, fire, water, and even of ancestors. Religious metaphor, too, is frequently derived from the phenomena of the earth's life.

This leads to a remarkable fact about the worship of the earth. The "earth god (or goddess)" is often conceived very impersonally, not with individual attributes and particular activities, such as are portrayed in religious myths. It is the earth itself which is worshipped, the earth which is seen with that religious sense of nature, that religious *Anschauung*, which comes into immediate contact with the perceived phenomenon. That sense of nature has never expressed itself so strongly and so purely as in the Ancient feeling about the earth. The entire Roman religion is characterized by a rather impersonal portrayal of the gods, just because in this religion the divine is directly seen in the phenomena of natural and human life. This same attitude which characterizes all of Roman religion is in other religions expressed especially with respect to the earth or the earth goddess. In the worship of the Greek goddess Ge (poetic form, Gaea), the earth as an object is not forgotten for a moment, in contrast to the

worship of other gods. Helios, for instance, does to be sure
appear as a god in the cosmos, but his essential being is hidden
behind his manifestation as the sun and he dwells in the invisible
world. He also possesses a complete personality. That he is
the Saviour and rescuer from danger cannot be immediately
deduced from his appearance. The same is true of the moon god.
On the other hand, Ge is the earth itself, individual but impersonal – she appears in very few myths – and she seldom participates
in the joys and cares and changing shifts of circumstances.
Albrecht Dieterich remarks in *Mutter Erde* that Ge is often
mentioned alongside or even in contrast to all other Greek gods.[1]
Thus Demosthenes repeatedly exclaims *ō Gē kai theoi* ,"O Ge
and gods." In general she is indeed the mother of gods and men,
the all-mother, but she is mother in the sense of the divine material of the visible and tangible earth, from which everything
can be derived. Ge is conceived not philosophically, but religiously, as the Romans thought of all their gods. She is the
hestia, "hearth," of gods as well as of men. At the point where
the hearth stands, the life of the family or state is connected with
absolute life. According to the Romans, *Vesta Terra est*, "Vesta
is the Earth," and in the hearth fire the ancestors continue to
live. But not only the family or the state, but also the gods live
the life of the earth.

The earth also plays a role in the myths of the world's origin,
at least in the myths concerning man's origin. Thus the Ancients
said that men "are formed from earth (clay or stones)." The
earth has sometimes been conceived as dust which is made alive
by the Spirit of God; however the earth's dust is the necessary
material for creating any living being. Sometimes it has been
conceived as the living divine substance or matter.

The Avesta apprehends the sacredness of the earth with that
intense religious sense of nature which is so distinctive of it.
This conception is differentiated from the Roman one by its
graphic and sometimes poetic formulation. The essence of the
earth is its strengthening of universal life. It has, according
to this dualistic view, chosen the side of Mazda, *ashavan*, in
order to battle against the powers of transiency and death,
druj. It abhors deformity and death. "The earth shudders whenever a corpse is buried in her." Since the same is said of fire,

water, and plants, corpses are placed in wide, open towers
(*dakhmas*), and are left to the vultures. This is very different
from the Greek and Egyptian view, according to which the
earth takes back life in order to actualize its divine essence.
Both conceptions are equally religious: the earth actualizes
divine life, either by struggle or by the mystical reconciliation
of life and death. Thus it is possible to have divergent religious
conceptions of the same phenomenon. There is another statement which is very characteristic of the Avesta. Zarathustra
asks where the earth feels the happiest, and Ahura Mazda
answers, "Most of all where a righteous man offers sacrifice and
invokes the gods of agriculture (namely Mithra with large fields
and Raman with extensive pastures). In the second place, where
the righteous man builds a house, with hearth and cattle, with
wife and children, and where everything in the house prospers,
where grain is sown and fruit trees are planted, where the dry
ground is sprinkled and the excess water is drained off. For the
earth is not happy when it must lie fallow a long time and must
wait for the good labourer. She is like a beautiful woman who
lives for a long time without children and desires a good husband."
(Vendidad 3 : 2 ff.) The earth is here indeed thought of in personal terms, but nevertheless it remains the earth. The religious
sense of nature plays a larger part here than does the personification of nature itself. Directly after this passage comes a remarkable reflection on the sacredness and triumphant power of grain.
"Holy Creator, how is the religion of Mazda best furthered?"
asks Zarathustra. And Ahura Mazda replies, "By sowing grain
with zeal. He who sows grain, sows the order of life (*asha*,
righteousness) ; he furthers and feeds the Mazda religion as much
as by a hundred, a thousand, or ten thousand sacrifices.
When grain is sown, the demons (the spirits of *druj*, death) are
afraid; when it comes up, their hearts shudder; when it is green,
they scream; and when the ear shoots up, they take flight ..."
    Here there is no mention of "earth gods" as individual de-
tached personalities, but rather of the earth itself and of the
divine energy which it possesses and reveals. It is as if we here
have before us the elements out of which the idea of a personal
earth god could be made. For this reason this elementary conception of the earth in the Avesta helps us better to understand

the religious meaning of a number of religious facts. In the first place, it is selfevident that the earth is sacred, because it is in the service of life, the universal life of Mazda. But its sacredness only becomes a reality when man cultivates it. It needs man's help. Man is thus God's co-worker. His religion consists of that cooperation, much more than of a thousand or ten thousand sacrifices. This idea of the actualization of and participation in divine life is present in all cultus – for agriculture is a cultic act. God demands that man further and extend the "Kingdom of God." (This term is from the Avesta.) Man's religious life is equated with an increase in the power of divine life in this world.

The conception of earth gods in the Avesta also helps us to understand something else. It makes clear to us the psychology of a particular cultic act, namely ritual purification. It is true that the word "purification" is not mentioned, but the essence of the concept is precisely indicated. The demons take flight before the grain which grows and brings life and prosperity. Here there is purification in both the negative and positive sense, that positive sense which has frequently been overlooked. "Ritual purification" means to bring something within the circle of divine life so that it is absorbed into that life. Thus the house in which grain is stored is a purified place because it has received divine power. And so too in purification by means of consecrated water, the life creating power of the water is imparted to the "purified" object.

According to these Avesta texts, agriculture *is* religion, and grain or food *is* the representative of the divine being. We are inclined to take this as an expression of a grossly sensual and materialistic world view. When this is called "religion," it sounds cynical to us. The reason for this is that our conception of agriculture is so materialistic. We tend to consider the raising of grain and the consumption of food as activities governed by the laws of physics and chemistry. We concentrate our attention on the natural side of our life, on that which is physical and not spiritual, and we take it as a matter of course that eating should lead to a renewal of vital power. We cannot help it that we so sharply distinguish the spiritual from the physical. We need not be ashamed of this fact, and we may rightly consider our conception to be of great value. Yet a completely different conception is possible, and it has indeed existed. According to this view, growth (the arising of life) which results from eating and drinking is no less a mystery than resurrection from death. The Ancients, and with them many peoples of a different mental type from our own, had a keen sense that food contains a creative power, a divine energy. The meal is in essence a sacrament, an imparting of divine power. The best known illustrations of this are the sacred meals, such as those eaten by the Athenian councilmen on the state table in the Prytaneum, and especially the sacrificial meals in which the believers partake of the divine substance, the body of God.

This spiritual or religious conception of foodstuffs is indeed very clearly formulated in Egypt. The special god of bread or food is Ptah of Memphis. But it is precisely Ptah who is also the god of the divine, creating word. In the beginning he created the world by his word: he spoke and it existed. As with Thot, the word is here conceived as the thought which has become perceptible. Creation testifies to and reveals the word of God, and by the power of that word everything continues to exist. But this Ptah of the divine word is the same as the Ptah of bread and of food. The Egyptian term for "word" or "command," *ḥw*, also means "foodstuffs." The underlying idea is quite clear. Foodstuffs are the special bearers of divine energy and of renascent life. Therefore they are seen as the "word" made "flesh." In a certain sense this seems to be a materialistic conception of the word of God, but actually this matter is spiritually conceived and understood. And we may safely say that the Ancients understood matter more profoundly than is possible for us as modern and "enlightened" men. For it offends us when they speak of "the divine essence of food."

In summary we may say that according to the Avesta, and also in the Eleusinian Mysteries in Greece, cultivation of the earth is a sacred act because man is God's co-worker. Man makes the earth live; as in every cultic act he actualizes divine life. The life of the earth reveals itself in grain and in other foodstuffs which the earth produces. Thus food is divine life made perceptible, and it possesses the creating and sustaining power of the earth because it enables life to rise and prosper. Thus does the meal become a sacred act.

The Egyptians linked this idea with that of the Word of God. God's word is God 's thought become a perceptible reality; it is the creative word which has created the earth. "By means of that word the world lives and continues to exist." [2] Now food is the perceptible basis of life and is therefore called the representative and bearer of the divine word. So it can be explained why according to the Shabaka stone, foodstuffs were the first things created, before all other things. This means that the mystery of creation is nowhere so clearly and so graphically present as in foodstuffs, which create and sustain themselves. In the life which they enable to rise there is the same mystery as in the beginning at Creation. According to the Egyptian view, bread is the incarnation of the divine word.

The earth's life proves then in a special sense to be the divine life of the cosmos. This conception is not only an Egyptian one; it is found in all Ancient religions. Life arises out of the earth and returns to it in order to rise again.

All these ideas are combined in the Egyptian god Ptah of Memphis. He is the god of the earth; except for Geb, no Egyptian god is so expressly described as the earth god. And he is the god of foodstuffs, and he is also the creator by the word. We sense clearly how spiritually matter is here conceived, quite differently than by Plato. Plato does not have the idea of creation by the word. For him the embodiment of the divine thought, which in Egypt is called Ptah's thought, means descent into a lower world. And we moderns prefer Greek and Platonic philosophy in its lower estimation of matter. But the prologue of the gospel of John approaches the Ancient notion of the creating word. All things are made by the word, in which there is life; that word has become flesh. The Egyptian expression, "food of eternity (i.e., of eternal life, food of the gods or ambrosia) and drink of eternity (drink of the gods)" is more than a figure of speech; it suggests the spontaneous, self-sustaining and creating power of food.

The religious idea of the riches of the earth is closely akin to this. We know that for the consciousness of the Ancient peoples, all that the earth brings forth and sustains is almost identical with riches in general. Grain and cattle constitute the typical riches. Now their conception of these "riches" proves to be so lar-

gely shaped by their religious view that we must take great
pains in this respect rightly to understand them. Our own traditional viewpoint puts very great obstacles in our way.

The basis of this notion is the view that possession of the earth's
products means a participation in the earth's life, that is to say,
in the divine power of growth and resurrection, in the mystery
of the earth. The mystery of the earth's life is transferred into
the riches of the earth. Plenty is the embodiment of resurrection
and therefore the sacred symbol of the mystery. A few facts are
sufficient to illustrate this. We know that in the Greek religion
Pluto was the god of "riches," just as was the Roman Dis Pater,
"Rich Father." But Pluto is identical with Hades, the god of
the dead and of the realm of the dead, who as the consort of the
virgin Kore, in a mystical way enables life to arise. This by itself
gives "riches" a peculiar content which does not belong to this
world. Hades, like Pluto, is portrayed with the horn of plenty.
This thought comes out even more sharply in the Eleusinian
Mysteries, in which Pluto, who is Riches personified, plays a
vital role. He is the "son of Demeter," the brother of Kore, and
he is always depicted as a child. In Eleusis the child – sometimes
too with other names – is the newly arising life and the immortality which initiation into the Mysteries bestows. The child
is the Saviour, whose birth is announced to all those present by
the leader of the Mysteries, the hiërophant. Pluto does indeed
represent the earth's products, but it is these products conceived
as the sacred gift to men. He is the mystery of the earth's life.

Another example is the notion of the treasury of the earth,
the Greek *thēsauros* or the Roman *aerarium* in the temple of
Saturn, the god of vegetation. Long before the seventh century
B.C. the Greeks had already named various sacred buildings
(temples and graves) *thēsauroi*, and sometimes they are also
called "heroes' graves." Frequently they are underground cham-
bres quarried with arches, for instance under the temple of
Asclepius in Lebena, near Gortyna in Crete. They were also
dug in a hill or built above the ground, but again, as a rule,
dome-shaped. The treasury or the grave of Atreus in Mycene
dates from the fourteenth century B.C. Why are they called
"treasuries"? This is naturally because of their connection with
Pluto; his dwelling is the underworld treasury which does not

belong to this world. And it is quite certain that the grave was
called a "treasury" because the treasury was the place of resurrection. It is the same thought as that present in the notion of
the child Pluto at Eleusis. The treasury is the place where life
arises – including the life of the man who has died. The notion
of the treasury therefore does not derive from the fact that various
silver and gold valuables were frequently placed in the graves
to accompany the dead; it comes rather from the belief that the
riches and blessings of the earth were resurrection. Asclepius'
temple at Lebena can only be explained as the treasury of Zeus,
the point where his lightning strikes. It was said that these
thēsauroi or heroes' graves were the same as the Egyptian
"thēsauroi," which were graves in the form of granaries, and
that in Egypt these were called "the life of the earth"; such is
the case with the grave of Ptah at Memphis. Thus the Greek
grave received the form of a granary. And behind this form is
really the notion of the earth's treasure chamber. The very
ancient and widespread custom of burial in the large *pithoi*
can also be understood along these lines. The *pithoi* were enormous vases or urns buried in the ground, in which grain or oil
were usually stored. These pithoi were thus also a kind of thēsauroi. The riches of the earth are its life and its resurrection.
And in these urns the dead were buried.

Because of this conception riches are called a "divine blessing"
and are comparable to the blessing of Jacob (Genesis 49, especially vs. 25 f.). "Blessing" is one of the many terms whose
Ancient meaning – which includes its meaning in the Old Testament – somewhat diverges from its Christian meaning. It takes
great pains and self-restraint for us to comprehend values which
are alien to us. Blessing in the Ancient sense meant heightened
vital power and enlarged energy, *Lebensfülle*, "fullness of life,"
with inseparable material as well as spiritual components, a
state which man cannot himself create without divine help.
Just as the meal is a sacrament, the impartation of divine life,
so too are riches a divine gift; this is the life of the earth, an impartation in material form but with a spiritual content. Men do
not create riches; they cannot create life. The only one who does
this is the god of the earth, Pluto or Hades. According to another
belief, riches are brought among men by Hermes *charidōtēs* or

dōtōr eaōn, the bestower of blessing, the mediator between the divine and the human world and the bringer of divine life among men (*kerdōios*). Hermes' immortal *rhabdos* is the branch of *olbou kai ploutou*, of prosperity and riches. [3] What do men do in order to obtain riches or the earth's blessing? The religious view of this is remarkable. Rational measures of insight or deliberation are of secondary importance. They concern only the outward side of what actually occurs in the accumulation of treasures. The most important means was naturally agriculture. But all peoples regarded agriculture as a mystery, taught by a divinity of the underworld – Ea, Osiris, or Demeter. The cultivation of the Rarian Plain is one of the sacred acts at Eleusis. This is certainly not a rational act, but rather a cultic act. The Roman words *opus*, "work" and *ops*, "power, ability, riches, help," both come from the Sanskrit *apas*, "work, rite." The semantic development here is not, as van Hamel believes, from "work" to "the capacity gained with work," in which sense the word is easily elevated to a religious sphere. Then "work" and "yield from work " would be the basic meaning; this would then lead to "riches," to "power," and so to "supernatural capacity." No, it is rather that in *opus*, "work," the magical factor is already present. The meaning of "magic power" is not the finishing point, but rather the starting point and the element which continues to be present in the semantic development of the word. The basis of all riches is a mystery. This notion is also formulated in the following way: riches are in essence an *heuresis*, a discovery. This "find" is not gained by one's own deliberation or exertion, but by the "chance" (Tyche, Fortuna) which simply comes upon one. There is in this attitude a denial of intentional effort, present both in Greek and Vedic religion. The Vedic god of riches, Pushan, "he who gives prosperity," displays great resemblance to Hermes. He is the mediator between the other, divine world and this human world; he is the one who knows and walks the "far ways," and who has even found in the other world (according to the Greek notion, stolen) and then brought to this world the hidden riches of Soma, the drink of life, and of Agni, the sacred fire. He makes men rich by " letting them find" treasures [4]; thus he bestows the divine blessing. And when men succeed in their strivings for good fortune, it is still Pushan who has brought them to the point where

they make their find. Hermes was likewise the god of every
chance discovery, which is the really typical form of his gifts to
men. The description of the "temple treasure," the thēsauros of
the temple, as *heuresis* is particularly significant. The sacred
riches of the temple treasure is a "find." Only in form was it
accumulated in a known and verifiable way by the "generous
gifts" of the pious; in essence and according to its true nature
it was a "find," that is to say, something put right into one's
path by God. The God of the temple treasures is called Zeus
Heuresios! This explains a remarkable regulation concerning
gifts to the temple. The law was that the amount of the gift
placed in the thēsauros had to remain secret and that no one
might see or know who the giver was. We cannot help but be
reminded of Matthew 6 : 1–4:

> Beware of practising your piety before men in order to be seen by
> them ... when you give alms, do not let your left hand know what your
> right hand is doing, so that your alms may be in secret (*en tōi kruptōi*) ...

The resemblance is striking, yet the meaning is totally different. We understand the statement in Matthew immediately:
the value of the ethical act – the giving of alms – lies in the
inner disposition and the purity of the ethical motive. Do good,
but not in order to be praised by others or by yourself. The
Greek regulation, however, concerns a religious act – sacrificing
to deity – and the value of this lies in the supra-human nature
of the sacred act. The thought which the believers thus tried
to express is that sacrifice is not a gift to God in the same sense
that alms are a gift to a man. The pious man hands over to God
that which is God's; he recognizes and actualizes the true
essence of the offering, in this instance the riches which are the
hidden life of the earth. The temple treasure is not "accumulated
by private contributions"; it is sacred, which means that it has
been created by God himself. Like sacrifices, gifts are wholly
irrational acts, for there are really no human givers; no one
knows how the gifts from the other world reach us. The mysterious and secret gifts correspond to this mysterious character
of the temple riches.

Now it would be quite natural to think that while the Ancient
conception of riches was perhaps of the sort which we have just
described, in the practical exigencies of life the notion of riches

was in any case quite a different one. Surely the Ancients conceived of earthly possessions just as we do, as material possessions
which are the source of power and enjoyment, for our conception
is, of course, original and self-evident! What we are here concerned to show, however, is that the religious conception of
riches as a "find" (a chance discovery or stroke of luck) really
was held and that it was quite emphatically maintained in the
cultus. The Ancients had a different view than we do; they
really saw in riches a mystical reality, just as they did in foodstuffs. In this connection we are not interested in whether this
view was shared by everyone or whether the believer was
conscious at each moment that riches had this character. We
know quite well from our own experience that our religious belief
is not always expressed in our conduct. Furthermore, the farther
we go back in history, the less does the state of affairs resemble
our own. It is an illusion to hold that origins are simple (by
"simple" we mean what appears simple to us). We see more and
more clearly that the whole life of the Ancient peoples was
determined by religious ideas. We don't know anything about
"original" states. If we think that we have found the origin of
kingship purely and simply in a strong man who with his stick
(scepter) as the first king was able to force his compatriots to
obedience, it is not history which we have come to know by
means of such "common sense," but only the less worthy side
of our own nature. This is the point to which our theories of development invariably bring us.

The mystical character of the earth's gifts, as we have seen
in Hades with the horn of plenty, has sometimes been depicted
in a remarkable way. They are good but also dangerous and fatal
for men. On the floor of Zeus's dwelling stand two jars, one filled
with good gifts and one with evil gifts [5]. And the two *pithoi* encircled with snakes are the emblems of the two Dioscuri, gods
of death and of life. According to the myth, Prometheus, the
free and highly gifted man, gains possession of the divine fire,
that is, of technical and intellectual capacity. He then tries to
build up his civilization according to his own ideals in technical,
intellectual, ethical, and social realms. But Zeus prevents him
from accomplishing this: because of his *hybris*, his presumption,
he is bound to the rock with brute force. The finite man who

aspires to the divine does indeed attain his goal, but at the cost of his finite life. This is the basic idea in tragedy. The myth of Pandora is similar; it is a variation on the theme of Prometheus. As punishment for man's presumption, Zeus has Hermes bring the beautiful woman "Pandora" (All Gifts) among men. When she has put all the earth's gifts in her vase, she causes disaster and destruction. Her vase is a pithos or thēsauros, and its contents, riches, are identical with ruin and death. The life of the earth is naturally self-sustaining and spontaneous; it is withdrawn from all finite relationships; it has no finite causes or effects. He who tries to live from Pandora's gifts comes to share in her absolute, self-sustaining, and infinite life. This means that he is removed from this finite world and thus dies. Men greet and receive Pandora (Riches) with joy, but it soon becomes evident that her sacredness is a terrible reality, a consuming fire. Just as in the myth of Prometheus, men gain the divine fire which they desired, but they receive it with horror and imagine themselves deceived. This idea is one which we repeatedly encounter. The special god of men is at once loved and feared. He protects and blesses by his mystery – as in food. But he also demands men for his absolute life. Death too is his "gift"; this is the divine irony which is fatal for men; this is the "deceit." But Pandora, who deceives men and leads them into death, is the beautiful earth goddess. The earth's life is beautiful. On the advice of Zeus the earth goddess Gaea made as a trap the enchanting flower, the narcissus, which delights gods and men. Narcissus is the beautiful youth who dies in the prime of life. Harmonia, who was quite certainly also the goddess of "harmony" and beauty, is a goddess of the Mysteries of the same type as Kore; here too the earth's beauty is thus linked with death. But beauty is connected not merely with the negative aspect of death (as the transiency of beauty might suggest). Like wisdom and every other human excellence, it also shares in the positive aspect of death, death which is part of the world of absolute life.

This double character of the earth's blessing and the sharing in the earth's life also leads to the idea of a double earth god or goddess. The well-disposed Eumenides and the Erinyes who rage against human interests are both goddesses of the earth's life and of fertility. Indeed they are identical in essence; in the cave

near Phigalia (Arcadia) Demeter-Erinyes was worshipped. However, in the period of the rationalistic "enlightened" and classical
civilization of Greece and Rome, the profound meaning of the
fear of God could not be understood. The deity had to fit human
ideals and desires: he had to be humane. Thus the "fatal"
character (for our finite existence) of the earth's gifts was denied.
According to Aeschylus the Erinyes became Eumenides when
Orestes' guilt was atoned on the Areopagus; henceforth they no
longer exist. Throughout all periods of "enlightenment," including our own, people have been inclined to misunderstand the
meaning of the fear of deity or even to deny it as unworthy.
Surely God is humane! – as Plutarch says when he discusses
deisidaimonia. Scholars so often expatiate on the great fear
which the so-called primitive peoples show toward divine powers
or spirits and see in this fear a sign of religious inferiority. But
the words "fear" or "dread" by themselves tell us so little. It is
hard enough at best to understand fear, and if we want to try
to do so, then we need much more precise descriptions. Sometimes
we hear that the same "primitives" also expect good fortune and
advantage from those same spirits. The Latin derivation of
religio is *religere:* to pay attention with all one's senses, to take
stock, to watch out, to look on anxiously, to note the divine in
ordinary phenomena, to be wary. This attitude is certainly
characteristic of Roman religion. But this religious attitude did
not detract from the greatness of the Romans. They were the
religiosissimi omnium gentium, the most religious of all peoples.

The double nature of various earth gods, their being both
favourable and hostile – a double nature corresponding to the
two-sided significance of death – is in many instances expressed
in the notion of the snake of the earth. No one doubts that the
snake was felt to be a creature of the earth: it was portrayed
in the grave hill; heroes sometimes have the form of a snake;
the snake is sometimes called "son of the earth" or "life of the
earth," etc. As a creature of the earth it is the symbol of resurrection and immortality. At Epidaurus the snake of Asclepius
was worshipped and Psyche married Eros when he was in the
form of a snake. Perhaps these ideas are related to the snake's
periodic acquiring of a new skin. But the snake also causes death
and is the archenemy, as in the Garden of Eden. Similarly, for the

Greeks, the snake guards the golden fruit of immortality in the garden of Hesperides and keeps it away from men. In Babylonia it is the snake who steals from Gilgamesh the herb of life, and in Egypt the snake is the archenemy Apap. It is not "good" or "evil" as we understand these terms, for to the lord of absolute life, which the snake of the earth represents, no human ethic is applicable. In the Ancient religions the dual nature of the snake corresponds completely to the dual nature of the Erinyes-Eumenides and of Pandora. It is, however, quite understandable that the mystery of death, represented by the snake, should have occassioned two kinds of conceptions even for the same people or the same individual. Death is the finitude and transiency of man, but it is also the actualization of man's eternal life. "Enemy" and "friend" are thus both conceived in the religious or the religio-ethical sense. In other words, the enemy as well as the friend is a divine being. In a large number of religions this is the conception of the snake of the earth.

Determination of Fate by the Gods of the Earth

In treating the astrological view in connection with the cosmic rule of the sky gods, we discussed the determination of fate by the celestial gods. But there are two types of religious conception of destiny, or more accurately, two kinds of conception about the way in which man becomes acquainted with divine decrees. One type is astrology, which is a more or less secret science, the art of interpreting signs on a religious basis, either the signs of heavenly bodies or other portents, such as omens, the casting of lots, or the condition of the entrails of the sacrificial animal. The attempt is made to discover in the apparently arbitrary, unordered, and accidental a supra-rational meaning, that is to say, divine destiny. All these religious practices are based on the majestic view that nothing happens accidentally. Everything finite occurs according to the eternal example; there is a conformity between empirical finite phenomena and the infinite reality of the divine world governance. But the divine order, the law of abiding life, cannot be discovered by ordinary perception, which is only concerned with finite relationships. The art or science of oracles points to the order of the other world in what is apparently accidental. Thus these practices are religious acts; they are not superstition, for in superstition there is no comprehensive "view" of the nature of the cosmic governance.

The second type is connected with the worship of earth gods. It does not interpret any signs or omens, and it does not seek a conformity between finite and infinite realities. There is a more intimate relationship between the finite and the infinite; in a certain sense there is identity. The basic idea and the majestic view of this identity is that man, and with him all animate creation, lives the life of the earth. The mystery of the earth is also the law of life, the lot of men. God imparts the law of life directly to His favoured elect, namely to His inspired prophets, or seers who in ecstasy sojourn in the divine world. They know the law coming from the earth, for instance by means of earth oracles, such as at Delphi through the mouth of the *maenad* Pythia, who receives her wisdom from the earth goddess Themis or Ge. The notion of a secret science or art is altogether absent.

The earth god or earth goddess determines fate, which proves to be the life of the earth itself. We find a remarkable illustration of this in Egypt. Among the various goddesses of fate which are mentioned there is one who can be especially well defined: Renenutet, the goddess of grain, from the earth's treasury. She is the "harvest goddess" and "the ruler of foodstuffs." The word *renent* also means riches, blessing, good fortune, and that in the Ancient sense of sharing in the life of the earth. For this goddess of grain and harvest proves to be the goddess of the increase of life among men. She is goddess of birth and proctectress of sucklings. Again and again she is portrayed as the divine wet-nurse with a child at her breast, and frequently she is depicted with a snake's head as a sign of her earthly nature. She is also the earth goddess of the fate of men, who is present when the human heart is weighed before the throne of Osiris to determine the man's eternal fate. It could not be said any more clearly than this that the life of the earth is men's destiny. This is life in the absolute sense which includes both increase and downfall.

In many remarkable and profound ways fate is formulated as the law of the earth. The earth god and harvest god Kronos, banished by Zeus to the underworld, "sleeps" on the island far in the West. According to Plutarch "there he dreams the fate of the world." '(Compare the Dream Oracles.) The fate of the world is a dream, a supersensory reality, that is to say, the reality of the other world, in relation to which our empirical world is only a transient reality. The Ancient religious myths, such as that of Kronos' sleep, appear to be the free play of poetic imagination. When we understand them, they prove to be the utterances of seers, and by no means products of a playful fancy which takes no account of reality.

Most of the oracles in Antiquity were earth oracles. The Babylonians believed that the oracle of Ea comes out of his dwelling *bīt-nēmeqi*, "House of Insight," situated in Apsu, the waters of the underworld. There in the depths of the earth absolute life is known, which is the universal and cosmic law of life, the fate of the world. The oracle is a revelation of this fate and this cosmic order. There in the depths is also the dwelling of the divine "word" which existed even before Creation, thus the word of the preexistent world order. But the best known is certainly the Delphic or Pythic earth oracle, so called because of the snake Python. At one time the (earth) snake must have been the oracle spirit there, just as among the Semitic peoples. From the Hebrew *nāḥāsh*, "snake," *nāḥash*, "soothsaying" is derived. As the earth's animal the snake is the "knowing one " or the cunning one; it knows the mystery of the earth's life, which is as much death as it is life. "As a child Apollo killed Python." The renascent young god consigned the snake to the place where it belongs. There are two elements present in this myth of resurrection, for Python did not cease to exist. In the historical period there is in Delphi "the oracle of the earth" of the earth goddess Ge or of Themis, who is identical with her. The Pythia receives the oracle out of the cleft in the earth (which perhaps did not even exist), above which she sits; it is only as a *maenad* and in ecstasy that she proclaims the earth's law received from Themis. This oracle does not so much have the purpose of gaining knowledge of the future as of learning the path of life when a great calamity has occurred. Rescue from death, the secret of resurrection, it is this which is the secret of the earth.

An oracle is conceived in the same way when it is asked and given at a spring. The spring forms the connection between the underworld and this world, and so brings us the knowledge of

the divine order of life or the law of abiding life. In Delphi the
Pythia received her inspiration by drinking water from the spring
Cassotis, which came up within the temple. The Zeus of the oracle at Dodona, who "dwells in the root of the oak tree" – thus
not in the rustling of the leaves – is called Zeus Naios, "from
the spring" (cf. the Naiads); there was thus a spring by the tree.
And therefore court was also held by the spring; the judge reveals the divine world order or law of life, just as does the dis-
penser of oracles. In Genesis 14 : 7 the En-Mishpat, the "spring
of justice" at Kadesh, is mentioned (cf. Exodus 18 : 13 ff.).

The notion of the earth's order, which is also men's order of
life, is sometimes very clearly formulated. It then often appears
to us as grossly materialistic, because we so largely lack the Ancient religious sense of nature. Thus at Eleusis the child Pluto
(Riches) was worshipped. This point of view is also very characteristically formulated in the vigorous language in which it is
expressed in some Avesta texts. The earth wants to be cultivated;
it fervently desires to enter the service of life. But then it is
also men's religious duty not to despise or obstruct the welfare
or progress of life. All kinds of asceticism and self-mutilation
are most strongly condemned: the ascetic plays into the hands
of the evil spirit Druj.

I Ahura Mazda declare that he who is married is superior to him who
lives in continence, that he who possesses a house stands higher than
he who has no house, that he who has children ..., that he who is rich
[i.e., possesses the earth's life] stands higher than the poor man. And
of two men, he who has eaten his fill is better able to take in the good
spirit [the spirit of Ahura Mazda] than he who is hungry. The latter is
like the true death, but the former battles with courage against the
attacks of the demons; he battles against the well directed arrow; he
battles against the winter; ... he battles against the godless heretic
who glorifies asceticism.

It is noteworthy that it is precisely in the Avesta religion that
this thought is to be found, in the religion in which – except for
Christianity – ethical ideals assume a more important place than
they do in any of the other Ancient religions. This is because the
ethic of the Avesta is a religious ethic; it is not based on senti-
ment or feelings of sympathy and love for men, but rather on the
consciousness of the universal order of life which for man, too,
is the law of abiding life. Thus *asha* is also righteousness in the

cosmic sense; plants, bodies of water, etc., are, like men, also
ashavan. And if we are rightly to understand the glorification of
prosperity and material fortune, then we must not forget that
the abhorrence of asceticism was by no means an expression of
self-indulgence or spiritual laxity. For these qualities are completely alien to the Avesta people. Seldom in a religious writing
are enterprise and daring, industry and active life so highly
praised as in the sacred scriptures of this people. Asceticism, on the
other hand, is here conceived as a flight from the world, a breaking of the bonds which link human life with cosmic life, especially with the life of the earth. And this is a denial of the spiritual
significance of the empirical and material world. What is characteristic of the Avesta religion is the enthusiasm with which the
believer accepts the battle for the kingdom of Ahura Mazda
against the powers of death in the spiritual and the physical
world; this shows the opposite of laxity. When the human souls
before the creation of the world had the choice of staying with
Ahura Mazda in the heavens or descending into the world and
struggling there, they chose the struggle. The passionate condemnation of asceticism in all realms of life has developed from
the religious conception of welfare and prosperity, whose ultimate
and essential being was sensed in immediate experience. This
gives a religious significance and a seriousness to these condem-
nations of asceticism which, at least in this context, is unknown
to us.

The best known symbol and the best known bearer of the
earth's life in most Ancient religions is the Bull of the earth.
For us this is a "mythical notion," but for the Ancients it was
a reality. The Egyptians believed that on the boundaries of the
earth in south, north, east, and west, were "the horns of the
earth"; bull and earth were evidently identical. The bull Apis
of the earth god Ptah was the bearer of the earth's order of life;
Apis was the earth's life and was worshipped as such. He was also
called "the living image of the soul of Osiris," Osiris here being
conceived as a supernatural being, as the repeatedly arising
life of earth. He is also called "Ptah's herald," meaning that he is
the one who brings and imparts Ptah's word (the life of the world);
he is the bringer of Ptah's food. In Crete the sacred horns of the
bull of the earth are the most important symbol in the cultus.

(Cf. the Minotaur in the Labyrinth which represented the realm of the dead.) At the Bouphonies, the Athenian festival in honour of Zeus, the bull of Zeus Chthonios was sacrificed. It is quite certain that by this act the bull of the earth was consecrated. In all the temples of the Mithra mysteries, the "altar piece" was the image done in relief of Mithra killing (i.e., sacrificing) his bull. The meaning of this is as clear as it can be. Mithra, the god of the earth's life, sacrifices himself in order to actualize through death his divine life. This was the mystery of Mithra, which was granted to his follower at his initiation.

Finally we should say something about the meaning of hills or the high places of the earth in the cultus of a great many peoples. The *bāmōth*, "heights," are among the Semites frequently the temple sites; in the Canaanite cultus they are the normal sites for altars. Among the Egyptians "the Height" was the name and the symbol of the temple; the dwelling of Osiris was called "the High Mountain," the earth mountain – the underworld. For the "height" is the place where the life of the earth reveals itself in vegetation; the underlying thought here is that rising or getting up is an image of life. *Cadaver*, the one lying down, is death; the earth lives where it is high. In Egypt ◁══▷ is the sign for high land (by being combined with ◢ it is also drawn as ◢══). This sign serves as base, foundation, and elevation for the earth gods Min, Ptah, and Osiris and indicates their ever newly arising life. Every Egyptian temple, as a matter of fact, is built on an artificial height (◞══◝). The sign for this hill, ◁══ , is also the sign for ma-a-t, who is the order of life in the universal sense. This is the background of the sacredness of the *bāmōth*. Related to this is the notion of the hill of Creation, where life arose in the beginning. The earth height which came up out of the primeval waters was the place where the earth began to live. There life arose and from there it spread. The life of the cosmos is thus conceived as the life of the earth. The light myth is also connected with this notion of the creation of the world; from the (sun) hill the sun arose in the beginning. The Egyptian texts call the day of Creation "the day of the elevation of the earth (Book of the Dead 1 : 19). The height or hill as a sacred place is thus the place where the life of the earth reveals itself, the place of divine revelation in general. Here the

altar was built, the altar which according to Ancient belief was
sacred because it represented the dwelling of God, the altar which
itself was the image of the high place. (Cf. the horned altar in
Israel, Greece, and Rome.)

This is also the religious meaning of the tumulus, the grave
hill. Burial is an impartation of divine life, a sacrament which
bestows the life of the earth on the dead man. Therefore the
grave is the earth hill. Like burial in the treasury of the earth,
this is an instance of the cosmic character of the grave.

Among all the Ancient peoples and even in Israel the notion
of the hill of Creation is formulated in a remarkable way as the
omphalos, the navel of the earth. The "navel" is the place where
new life begins and the point from which it spreads. Therefore
it is situated in the middle of the earth. Homer calls the island
Ogygia *Omphalos tēs thalassēs*, the hill of Creation in the midst of
the primeval waters. The omphalos is usually depicted as a hill,
thus as a high place, or else as in Delphi as a hill-shaped stone,
quite similar to the tumulus. The temple mountain in Zion and
other hills in the Holy Land are called "the navel of the earth."
The hill is the site of the temple because the divine powers of
the earth there reveal themselves. So it can be explained why
the omphalos is thought of as a microcosm. The dome-shaped
hill, ⌂, is also conceived as the image of the celestial dome
but is nevertheless still called the "navel." These ideas are
sufficient to explain certain connections in which the term
"navel of the earth" occurs. At Delphi the omphalos is the site
of the oracle, where Apollo resides as god of the oracle. At the
omphalos one can come to know the life of the earth and of the
cosmos. It is here that life arises – rising life is divine life. The
Delphic oracle is also called the universal hearth, *koinē hestia*,
the residence of Hestia or Vesta. The hearth fire is the life fire
of family and world; the hearth is the point of communication
between the underworld and this world (according to the Romans
the Lares, the spirits of the dead, live in the hearth), and it is
here that the resurrection of the family takes place. The hearth
is the site of the mystery of life. The earth mother Vesta or
Hestia is the virgin goddess out of whom life spontaneously
arises; the virgin Athene Parthenos is likewise goddess of the
earth.

Many mountains are worshipped as high places. Mt. Olympus
on the boundary between Macedonia and Thessaly, was considered to be the home of the gods. The same was believed of a
number of other "Olympoi." They existed in Mysia, Cilicia,
Elis, Arcadia, Laconia, Galatia, and in Cyprus there were actually two. It is not far from the truth to say that there was an
Olympus in each Greek state. The resemblance to the "navel
of the earth" or the high place is quite clear. Olympus is the
home of the gods. This is not because this ten thousand foot
high mountain in Macedonia and Thessaly "sticks into heaven"
with its peak and is surrounded by clouds; the small Olympoi
are also the homes of the gods. Neither is it because it indicates
the exalted nature of divine being. No, the mountain – here Mt.
Olympus – is, like the omphalos, the place where the earth lives
and therefore also the place where the cosmos lives. Just as
in our linguistic usage the earth is "the world." When the earth
came up out of the waters of chaos as the hill of Creation, the
life of the world began. The omphalos is the microcosm, the
world in miniature. On the world mountain dwell the gods;
that is the home of divine renascent life. In the Avesta the sacred
mountain Ushidarna is a mythical mountain far in the east, the
home of blessedness and of the divine wisdom. It is also called
"the fertile mountain." Babylonian texts often speak of fertility
in connection with mountains, because the high place is the place
where the earth lives. The notion that the home of cosmic life
is situated in the east relates to the rise of light in the east.
The mountain Ushidarna thus corresponds to the hill of Creation
which is also involved in the light myth. It is always mentioned
together with *khvarnah*, glory, the immortal nature of gods, men,
and all creatures of Ahura Mazda. It rises "up into heaven,"
as does Mt. Olympus and also the omphalos. In modern Greece,
an extraordinarily large number of peaks or high mountains
are called *Hagios Elias;* Baedeker lists more than twenty peaks
with that name. Naturally they owe their name to the ascen-
sion of Elijah, even though in II Kings 2 no mention is made of a
height or a mountain.

It can thus be explained why there is sometimes a close connection between "mountain" and "temple" as homes of divine
life. In Babylonia this thought is consistently carried through.

The Babylonian-Assyrian word *e-kur*, "mountainhouse," stands for the cosmic mountain, the "mountain of fertility" as the seat of the earth's life. It also means "temple"; the temple towers with their three, five, or seven steplike stories were the most important part of the temple. And then finally, this word also means "god." God reveals himself in his cosmic dwelling, that is to say, in the world process; it is in this that he is recognized. The temple is the image of God. How could God better be depicted than by means of the mountain, that part of the world in which His activity and life is most visible? The constructed temple is the image of the universe, God's real dwelling. Therefore it is called a "mountainhouse," *e-kur*. This "mountain-house" is not only the image of the living earth, but also of the celestial mountain, just as Olympus can mean "the heavens." The stories of the temple towers correspond to the different planetary spheres of the heavens and indeed represent them. So too, the building is an image of the celestial dome. The earth and the heavens are corresponding realities; they exist in mutual relation. This idea of correspondence between the earthly and the celestial process is at the basis of the astrological view of the world. Therefore earthly places are situated in accordance with cosmic examples; Niniveh was drawn in the writing of the heavens; the city of Uruk is the image of the realm of the dead, etc. At these places God's activity and being can be seen. The earthly temple is God's image. In Egypt too the temple, as image of God's real dwelling, was built according to cosmic example. The entirely dark holy of holies in the back of the temple was the image of the realm of the dead, which is the home of absolute life. The temple gate was the point of transition from the other world into this. This is the "gate of the world in the east" mentioned in Egyptian texts; it is there that God appears in our world. The temple of Solomon, on the other hand, like the Greek temples, was not built according to cosmic example at all. During the period of the prophets in Israel and the Greek "enlightenment" the Ancient idea of deity had disappeared: "Behold heaven and the highest heaven cannot contain thee; how much less this house which I have built." (I Kings 8 : 27).

B. TREE GODS AND PLANT GODS

The tree gods and plant gods are particular forms of earth gods. There is a voluminous literature on this subject. The two most important works are those of Wilhelm Mannhardt, *Wald- und Feldkulte* I–II, a work of lasting significance, and J. G. Frazer, *The Golden Bough*, 1911–1916. The third edition of this work is in twelve volumes with material from history, folklore, and ethnography, and an index which is certainly the best guide in the area of religio-magical ideas, especially with respect to their description; it is not surprising that the religious significance and value of the data are not always done justice.

Tree worship is one of the most widespread forms of worship, and in the various periods of history and among various peoples it has been remarkably constant in type. In all the alterations of form the same viewpoints and religious themes recur. And it is noteworthy that the customs linked with tree or plant worship prove to be practically ineradicable. Even in entirely new surroundings, such as in the Christian setting, many of them have continued to exist independently. This is true among the farm population of all European countries. There is, for example, the May pole, the May king or queen, the May fire, the bride of Whitsun, and the Wild Man or Wild Woman. But the religious character of these customs has indeed largely disappeared. The connection between the customs and the phenomena of vegetation in nature is still sensed, but the customs have become games and there is no longer the feeling that life and wellbeing depend upon them. Therefore it is as a rule a defective and fruitless method to explain religious ideas and customs by means of the corresponding material from folklore, for instance by calling Ancient tragedy ("goat drama") a simple parallel to our idea of the scapegoat. The explanation of a religious idea or act must lie in a religious theme, and it is just this which has disappeared in folklore. The data from folklore concern only the bare structure and the outward form from which the religious meaning and spirit have disappeared. Sometimes, indeed, the religious theme can be deduced with a large measure of certainty. This is the case with the custom of striking a person with green twigs while reciting the words, "fresh green – live long" or "now you'll be lucky"; this is a more or less conscious impartation of the plants' energy to men. But if these recited phrases had not been preserved with the act, then many would certainly have thought that this was an "apotropaeic act." The notion that a man should be beaten like a rug with a stick or a bundle of branches is much "simpler" than is the idea that branches are the conductors of vital energy.

But just as with the bringing in and decorating of the May pole, and with similar customs, so also even in the striking with "rod of life," the seriousness of the custom has disappeared, and it is just that seriousness which always characterizes the religious act. Life and prosperity are no longer at stake. The "Pharmakos sacrifice" at the Greek festival of Thargelia in honour of Apollo is a striking but also an extraordinarily sinister instance of the real religious act. After a crop failure or during a famine someone was chosen to be the *pharmakos*, "means of salvation, saviour," and fed for a period of time at the cost of the State. Then he was put to death at the festival of Thargelia, after he had been beaten with fruit-bearing plants or branches. The details of this ceremony prove that he represented the spirit of vegetation and by means of his death he was consecrated or sacrificed to that spirit. Therefore not only were the branches sacrificed; the absolute life of the plant god, his death and resurrection, was actualized. The striking with – and perhaps killing by – the plants was the striking with the "rod of life" which possessed divine life (the absolute life containing resurrection from death). "Death is caused by life"; where both death and life work together, there we find absolute life, the spontaneous, self-sustaining, divine life. Thus the *pharmakos* became the saviour who by his sacrificial death actualized divine life for men. We are amazed at such cruel cultic customs, but their religious character is unmistakable. The divine saviour must undergo death, because only in death is divine, self-sustaining life possible. Remarkably enough, this whole idea is encountered again in some spring and harvest customs in folklore. The May king or Maypole is also killed in effigy by burning or drowning. But the religious significance and seriousness of this have disappeared; they are found only in real cultic acts.

We here confront the cruelty which is characteristic of the

worship of the gods of vegetation. The all-mother (omniparens) Cybele was worshipped together with the Phrygian vegetation god Attis. Cybele was the *Dea Syria* en *Elementum omnium Domina*, who is at the origin of all things. Her lover Attis emasculates himself and dies, or, according to another reading, is killed by a boar. Now the swine is the special animal of the earth; this is the reason he was depicted on the Eleusinian coins. After his death Attis is transformed by the all-mother into a pine tree, so that he comes to life again. The priests of Attis undergo the fate of their god. In the first days of the annual Attis festival, during the mourning ceremonies accompanying the death and burial of the god, they mutilate (emasculate) themselves or let bloody wounds inflicted on their arms suffice. Unrestrained sensuality also occurs in which the women must sacrifice their chastity to the god; evidently all finite norms of life are rejected.

Why do the priests of Attis offer themselves as a sacrifice? They must actually undergo the god's fate because they represent him on earth; sometimes, for instance, they wear masks of the gods. But this explanation is not sufficient. In equal measure they represent men before the deity. In the name of the people and on its behalf they offer sacrifices, including this sacrifice of self-mutilation, to the gods of vegetation.

The complete answer is that their self-sacrifice is the initiation into the divine mystery, into the divine death which signifies absolute life. The meaning and intention is the same as that for every believer, who had to be initiated in order to obtain a share in divine life. The priests represent men. Initiation is always a dying, a renunciation of finitude. In the Eleusinian and other Mysteries, people had to die in effigy, but there, too, we can rightly speak of a "deadly seriousness" of the ceremonies. In the mysteries of Attis there is even more reason to speak of a "deadly seriousness." Divine life comes to finite man as a terrible revelation from outside. It does not thus raise our native disposition and our ideal capacities to their highest possible level. Ethical and intellectual ideals are erased and disappear; even the festive sense of participating in the life of nature and of vegetation, such as is present in the customs of folklore, disappears. Initiation is new life, rebirth. The self-mutilation in the

cultus of Attis graphically depicted the spontaneous life of the
god of fertility, in which men participate in the same way as does
the god: by the death of fertility. This is the mystery of the
cruel Attis cultus.

Thus was one initiated into the mystery of the god of vegetation. We modern men are also quite able to speak of the mystery of vegetation. The factors and causes in the unceasing and
regular resurrection of plant life from its annual death are not
understood; they lie beyond all perception. This is a mystery.
But this is not yet religion; the recognition of the mystery does
not touch us personally. It is only a question of the insufficiency
of our knowledge. The religious attitude towards this fact or
datum, on the other hand, arises as soon as we conceive the
mystery, not negatively, as beyond our knowledge, but positive-
ly, as the expression of an absolute and divine power. This does
not occur by means of perception, contemplation, or aesthetic
feeling, but by means of the absolute life outside us (vegetation)
which is to be conceived in accordance with the absolute within
us. Then we conceive nature to be, in essence, spirit; we see the
same power at work in nature as in man. In other words, the
religious attitude towards the phenomenon arises from the
"religious sense of nature," which was distinctive of the Ancient
peoples because they were not bound to the Greek and modern
type of understanding. The man with the religious sense of nature
does not stand simply as a spectator alongside that which he
perceives. His attitude is not passive, contemplative, objective,
or aesthetic; he feels that his own existence is very much concerned with the phenomenon. He cannot help but take a hand;
he is already involved in it. He takes part actively in divine life.
This intervention is the religio-magical cultic act ("magical"
because it is an act with overtones of infinity, aiming at a goal
which transcends our finite life). Worship of the god of vegetation and living and dying along with him is the human actualization of divine life. In his religion man is always the co-
worker of God; by means of his religion man possesses infinite
power.

Thus the priest of Attis who executes the divine death on
himself is in the first place the representative and co-worker of
God. In him God dies and lives again. But at the same time he is

humanity's representative before God. He is the mediator who acts in men's name and through whom men obtain a share in divine life. It is especially in the worship of the gods of vegetation that the seriousness of this relationship comes very clearly to light. These gods are the special gods of the Mystery; in their worship we frequently encounter human sacrifice, as in the Greek Pharmakos sacrifice.

The general Egyptian term for plants is "wood of life." The notion of the "tree of life" is almost universal. And it, too, proves to be so deeply grounded in man's feelings that it can continue to exist apart from religious surroundings. People continue to link the life of a people or individual with a tree. Such trees, for instance the "Queen's trees," * are then symbols with aesthetic value and nothing more. Such data shed little light on the religious idea of the tree of life, which is – quite obviously – related to the mystery of vegetation. The tree which grows up out of the underworld and there renews itself possesses and reveals a life withdrawn from all observation. It draws its power from the indestructible power of the earth. As a symbol of renewal and resurrection the sacred *ashd* or *shent* tree stood on the grave of Osiris [7] and the name of the king was written in an egg cartouche on its leaves.

A striking instance in the cultus is the sacred olive tree on the Athenian Acropolis, a gift from Athene Polias to the people. This olive tree was indeed the bearer of the people's imperishable life. Sophocles glorifies it as "the tree which never grows old and which is selfcreated (*autopoios*), the terror of enemies," because it is unconquerable.[8] After Xerxes had set fire to the tree along with the buildings on the Acropolis, "two days later fresh branches were seen to grow out of the trunk." According to Pausanias, "the tree which had been burned down grew up two el the same day." [9] The life of this olive tree was the life of the earth: under the trunk was depicted the snake, who represented Athene's nature as goddess of the earth, or the earth spirit Erichthonius, the original ancestor of the Athenians. The tree was not called *ho elaios*, the olive, but *Moria*, the tree of fate. "Fate" (*ho moros*) is the divine decree which can con-

---

* Dutch *Koninginnebomen:* memorial trees, planted on the occasion of the birth or coronation of a king or queen. *Trans.*

flict with human wishes but which is nevertheless the order of
absolute and eternal life, the cosmic order. For the Athenian
people was taken up into this order. The Moria on the Acropolis
was the guarantee of their enduring existence. This is a tree of life in
the religious sense, and one which plays a role in the cultus.

In the Avesta religion, the Haoma plant is the plant or tree
of life. A liquid pressed out of shrubs was the chief constituent
in the typical Avesta sacrifice, the Haoma sacrifice. The Haoma
juice was the drink of life, "ambrosia," the drink of immortality;
one drop of it was poured into the ear of a dying man, and the
blessed are brought to resurrection by drinking this white liquid.
Haoma is "the lord of all plants," that is to say, their genius,
their representative, and it is repeatedly called the "wise one"
(*hu-khratu*), that is, the one in whom the spirit of abiding life
(the cosmic order) dwells. It is also called *dūraosha,* "he who fends
off death." This is the tree of life in the cultus.

The meaning of the tree or plant of life becomes most evident
in myths. In myth, imagination has complete freedom to make
the mysterious character of the tree of life apparent. According
to the Babylonian myth, the spice of life grows in the depths
of the sea, that is, in the realm of the dead. The hero Gilgamesh
seeks eternal life; the hero of the Flood, Utnapishtim (Noah),
who himself has attained eternal life, tells him the secret: at the
bottom of the sea grows the "herb of the renewal of life." Gilgamesh dives under water, brings up the herb, and is just on the
point of taking it home when he is deprived of it by the snake –
who is thus its guardian. This religious myth says quite clearly
that the tree of life belongs in death. Only he who dies comes to
possess it.

This mythical tree of life also appears in Greek religion. In the
Garden of the Hesperides, the land of the dead or paradise,
stands the tree with golden fruit, the tree of immortality, guarded
by the snake Ladon. Helios rises out of this tree, for the sun receives its life and its power to rise in the east in and from the
earth. Thus it is also related that Helios' horses eat the magic
herb or spice of life on the isles of the blessed in order to be able
to rise again. Like the Babylonian spice of life, this too is guarded
by a snake. And Polyeidus makes Glaucus live again by this
same herb, which is brought to him by a snake.

Sometimes we hear of a double tree of life. According to the Egyptian notion, two trees stand far in the east, and between them the sun rises. In Babylonia the same thing is said of the new Moon, Nannaru. The Ancients speak repeatedly of the two differentiated elements, the two complementary factors, which together constitute absolute life: life and death, or the heavens and the earth – cf. Osiris and Seth, the two Dioscuri, Apollo and Python, etc. So we hear of a tree of life and a tree of death. In the Old Testament they are called "tree of life" and "tree of the knowledge of good and evil." "Knowledge" in the Ancient sense is identical with death; in the (Syriac) Odes of Solomon the tree is indeed also called "tree of bitterness." The snake in Paradise is essentially the same as Ladon at the tree in the Garden of the Hesperides, as the snake guarding the Babylonian spice of life, and as the snake at the Athenian olive tree.

The tree of life is repeatedly conceived as the "cosmic tree," the tree of the entire life of the world, of cosmic life. The idea here is that the self-sustaining and self-renewing energy of the earth, as it reveals itself in vegetation, is the basis of everything which lives and renews itself. Perhaps this can be expressed even more accurately by saying that in all that which lives, the mystery is at work which has its typical place of activity in the earth, and that everything occurs in accordance with the law of this life. This notion is elaborated in mythical form in the remarkable tradition related in the middle of the sixth century B.C. by Pherecydes of Syros (one of the Cyclades). He does this in a poetic manner, but not in the manner of profane poetry. Zeus or Zas, "life," bestows on the earth goddess Chthonia at her wedding a winged oak tree. And "he makes (*poiei*) a large and beautiful tapestry (*pharos*) in which he artistically weaves the earth and the houses of the sea (the cosmic chambers or parts of world and underworld). He spreads this tapestry out over the winged tree." "Out of this (*ek toutou*) arose the law for both gods and men (*ho nomos egeneto kai theoisi kai anthrōpoisin*)." There is no doubt about the meaning of this remarkable metaphor. What the "Living One" gives to the earth goddess is naturally her life – the tree of the earth's life. The wings or bird represent the *anima*, air, or soul and thus also life; therefore they are repeatedly used as an image of renascent life; for example, the "soul bird." This oak is thus the tree of the renascent life of the earth. The tapestry in which the world is woven is a well known symbol for cosmic order or "law." The goddess of the earth, Chthonia, thus obtains from the god of life at her marriage with him the tree of universal life as her attribute. In this myth the meaning of the "tree of life" is indicated in poetic philosophical terms; in no other way can it be put into words.

Zeus' tree of life also appears in an entirely different context. At Dodona in Epirus, Zeus gave the oracle by the rustling of the wind through the foliage of his oak. Yet the notion present here is not that the oracle-giving Zeus dwelled in the tree's foliage, but rather "in the root of the oak" [10]. He gave the oracle, which is fate or law, the world's law of life, out of the depths of the earth. The rustling of the leaves is only the way of communicating it. The tree knows the secret of the earth's law of life and can reveal this in the oracle. The idea of "the tree of knowledge and also of life" is here quite consciously worked out, just as it is in the Old Testament and in the notion of the wise Haoma plant in the Avesta. The oracle is given by the spring as well as by the tree of Dodona, for this Zeus is also called *Naios*, "from the spring." Like the tree, the water from the depths of the earth transmits the oracle, as at Delphi. The oracle-giving tree of knowledge is also a cosmic tree, for fate is universal.

The mythical tree of Yggdrasill displays entirely similar traits. The poetic imagination of the Ancients was very much occupied with this tree, but this was not profane poetry: because of the consciousness of the religious meaning of the tree of life, they remained religious myths. We shall here note only the best known myths in order to illustrate the universality of the tree of life. The branches of the tree extend over the entire earth, reaching into the heavens; its roots penetrate to the very depths of the earth. Like the winged oak tree of Zeus, Yggdrasill represents the world's life. Nor is it forgotten in the myth of the world' destruction; it shakes and burns down. And this is also a tree of knowledge: one of the three roots is nourished from the spring of wisdom. From this spring of "Mimir" Odin or Wodan also drank, as a result of which he came to possess insight in the secret of life. This runic insight was the same as the mystical insight that Hermes possessed; Odin too, god of death and resurrection, was the guide of the souls of the dead, and Ancient writers identify him with Mercurius (Wednesday-Mercredi). It is noteworthy that Yggdrasill not only appeared in the myth but also in the cultus. At the temple in Uppsala a sacred tree, the image of Yggdrasill, was worshipped, and just as at Dodona there was also a sacred spring alongside it. Thus there is an entire world view (*Weltbild*) in the religious *Anschauung* of a tree!

Modern scholars sometimes speak of a mythical celestial tree whose foliage forms the celestial dome; "myth" is here conceived as a poetic imagination dissociated from religion. The Egyptian sky goddess Nut is depicted in a tree while she passes food and drink to the soul of the dead man and gives him the breath of life. But here too what is meant is the tree of the other world or of the air, which is the realm of the souls. In Egypt the realm of the dead is also frequently conceived as the night sky. "The dead man is buried in Nut"; "she covers him as the grave," and causes him to live again. This is expressed in the image of food, drink, and breath. The tree of Nut is the universal tree of life with branches in the heavens and roots in the very depths of the realm of the dead, of the same type as the "tree of life" which has already been mentioned. There is no special "celestial tree."

Thus the sacred tree is the bearer of absolute life and of absolute wisdom – both connected in the mystery of the earth's life. As far as I know, in religion there have never been trees for individual human lives; these conceptions of sacred trees concern the mystery which is the same for all and which encompasses the entire universe. Everything which lives and renews itself is included within it. In religious views this is consciously thought through and expressed as clearly as possible, in each instance with different applications. We can sense how little data from folklore can serve to instruct us here. The ideas and customs of folklore have no religious content or background; on the contrary, they must be presupposed precisely as the probable explanation of the original. Even when a certain earnestness characterizes actions of this sort, this is still never of a religious nature. The disappointed father who in the Argau chops down the birth tree of his son intends and feels this act seriously, but nevertheless there is here no real religious seriousness; for him it is only an expression of anger and sorrow. Religion can indeed illuminate data from folklore and ethnography, but seldom vice versa.

In conclusion, a word about the symbolism of the golden fruit in connection with the tree of life. Gold frequently symbolizes imperishability or immortality. It is thus that the various myths of the golden branch or "the golden bough" (Frazer) are to be explained. Hermes wields the golden branch; with this "immortal branch of riches and prosperity" Hermes *Chrysorrapis* puts men to sleep and awakens them. According to Roman tradition, in order for Aeneas to descend into the underworld and return again, he must pluck a golden branch from the sacred tree in the forest of Diana and give this to Persephone in the underworld; with this branch in his hand, he has power over the mystery of death, and thus of resurrection [11]. The same golden branch from the forest of Diana was according to tradition the symbol of Roman kingship. For the king, the god-man, looked after the abiding life of the people; he continually bestowed on the people the life represented by the branch. (On this subject, see Frazer.) The prototype of the Roman king was the Rex Nemorensis, the King of the forest of Diana. He who succeeded in breaking off a branch of the sacred tree was allowed to duel with the Rex Nemorensis; if he then killed him, he took over the kingship. "The golden branch" is a novel formulation of the religious conception of the concept "tree of life." And there are many other different formulations.

C. GODS OF THE WATER

We find the notion of holy water in all the Ancient religions and in a large number of illiterate religions as well. Sometimes particular geographical waters, especially rivers, are considered sacred. These are then seen as divine beings, although the transformation into divine persons is somewhat obstructed; the empirical object is difficult to conceive as a complete personality, for instance such objects as the Nile, the Phoenecian rivers Belus and Adonis and in Greece the Aetolian Achelous and the Scamander. Moreover, a healing or predicting power was ascribed to numerous springs with their spirits or nymphs. These waters

are not conceived as mythical persons with a full personality;
all the attention is put on the element of water, which however
is something different and something more than simply the
phenomenon. The element contains divine energy. (This is the
Roman understanding of deity.) Sometimes, too, the religious
idea is dissociated from particular phenomena and the sacredness
of water is conceived more broadly and generally. This makes
possible a developed personification of gods in whom the divine
nature of water is more or less conceived as universal energy
and who leave room for the forming of myths without however
losing sight of the chief theme, sacred water. Examples of these
gods are Ea, Osiris, Anahita, Apām-Napāt, Poseidon, and Aegir-
Ran (Mimir). In these figures we see the expansive power of a
religious idea: all the most divergent phenomena can be related
to it as the expressions of a particular energy which is divine.
For phenomenological study both types are equally important.

Let us first try to indicate the universal element in the conception of sacred waters. Why is water sacred? It is certain that
in general it was worshipped because of the utility and indispensability of water for the sustenance of life. This is again and again
pointed out in discussions of this subject, usually, however,
without wholly understanding the religious meaning of "utility"
and "indispensability." Just as in connection with gods of vegetation, the meaning of "utility" was a different one than we
attach to it. According to the Ancient conception, water, which
is essential to the life of plants, animals, and men, and which
enables life to flourish, must possess a self-subsistent life energy, i.e. a divine power. In the nature and activity of water there
is revealed self-subsistent, divine life: God himself. Water is the
mysterious bearer of divine energy. Here again the Ancients'
religious sense of nature expresses itself; here again the concern
is with the religious view of growth as creation or as a series of
creative acts. The religious sense of nature discovers the creating,
self-subsistent, or spiritual energy in the manifestations of life
and in the essentials which are the bearers of life. The Avesta
expresses this divine character of water with special clarity and
almost theoretical abstractness. Water as such is one of the
most important of Mazda's creatures; it works along with Mazda
to achieve the final triumph over Ahriman, death, and to bring

Mazda's kingdom of eternal life on earth. Water is *ashavan;*
it is "righteous" – rightly on the path of life. "Can water kill?
No. When someone drowns, then it is not the water which has
killed him; it is the *Ashtōvidōtu* which binds the drowning
man – the water simply rocks him...'" (Vendidad 5 : 8.)What
is reported in Yasth 13 : 93 about the birth of Zarathustra is
characteristic: "The waters and the plants shouted for joy and
sprang up out of the earth; all the good creatures of nature exul-
ted: Zarathustra is born, he who will extend the religion of
Mazda over the earth (and lead it to triumph)." The prophet
of Mazda works in the spirit of all these good creatures of nature,
or vice versa. In the worship of the river goddess Anahita, the
Avesta also depicts water in mythical or personal terms. "She is
as great as all waters combined which flow over the earth; she is
all the waters." From the high mythical earth mountain Hu-
kairya she travels to the world sea, and from this one stream
branch off all the rivers through the sevenfold earth; at Mazda's
request she descends to earth. "Men long for your presence,"
says Mazda. And now the universal and spiritual nature of the
principle of life which she represents is developed and the natural
object disappears. "The warriors worship you because they desire
speed for their horses and triumphant energy for themselves,
the power which always has the upper hand. The priests worship
you because they desire wisdom, and young people because they
desire a loving spouse." "And all this thou must give them in
thy great power, O Anahita." What has here become of the
idea of visible water? – She descends and says to Zarathustra,
"To me has Ahura Mazda entrusted the task of protecting and
keeping alive the entire world which follows Mazda's law (which
is *ashavan*). It is by my glorious power that animals and men
move about the earth; I watch over the good creatures as does
the shepherd his flock." It is by invoking Anahita that Mazda's
warriors, the saints, perform their work for the victory of Mazda's
kingdom; they cause the work of the enemies to fail. It is even
said that they have caused the prophet Zarathustra to arise
according to *daena*, thinking, speaking, and acting. It might be
thought that the purely spiritual has here suppressed and
supplanted nature religion. But such is not the case; everyone
knew that Anahita was the water goddess. The contrast between

spirit and nature did not exist for the Ancients. They did not have our materialistic conception of nature.

We also find this conception of the sacredness of water in a widespread cultic act which occurs in practically all religions: ritual purification by means of water. This is usually conceived as a "washing off" of stains and evil influences. There are indeed ritual purifications which strongly give this impression, for instance in Brahmanism the purification after the *dīkshā*, whereby the man who has been made divine is divested of his sacredness, which is dangerous for the world. After other religious ceremonies as well, such as those which occur in Hebrew religion, water frequently washes off sanctity. The Romans sprinkle themselves with water after a funeral. The washing even removes sins and transgressions; thus the Creek Indians divest themselves of all transgressions committed in the previous year by bathing and washing during certain ceremonies. The negative, apotropaeic aim of removal is certainly the most important one. For this reason there is a tendency to call every purification a simple magic act, in which one can hardly speak of the sacredness of water. But it should not be forgotten that "the simple washing off of stains" is not an explanation. "Washing" rinses off that which is visible and outward, whereas the "stains" (*dīkshā*, for instance) are invisible and spiritual. Purification is indeed a magical act; evidently in these cases, too, a spiritual power is ascribed to water which is strong enough to remove all ill fortune. In this respect, a sacredness, a supernatural power, of water is presumed. Such purifications by means of water are repeatedly reported. When Babylonians were in danger of death because of a scorpion sting, they went down to the river and immersed themselves seven times; this number seven is enough to show clearly that this is not an ordinary washing. In II Kings 5, Elisha commands the leper Naaman to bathe or immerse himself seven times in the Jordan; then he will be clean. Thereupon Naaman asks whether the rivers of Damascus are not better than those of Israel. It is clear that the empirical element of water does not as such have a magically cleansing effect. What we find is particular water with particular power. The same principle, however, is just as conceivable in respect to water in general.

In these cases the negative aim, the removal of stains and ill fortune, certainly is in the foreground. But at the same time it is presupposed that a supernatural and entirely positive energy proceeds from water, that water possesses a vital power which is original and invincible in the whole cosmos. In many cases this notion is quite consciously linked to the ceremonies for the removal of impurity. A Babylonian inscription states: "Take up water at the mouths of the two rivers; recite above this water your sacred word, sanctify the water with the sacred formula, and with this water sprinkle man who is the son of his God." So too, divine power is deliberately put into the consecrated water of the Roman Catholic church. This water takes possession of everything which it touches and draws it within the range of its animating and vitalizing effects. There are two sides to the activity, and the positive effect is just as strong as the negative. But it is understandable that the rationalising explanation directs attention to the negative effect. According to the Avesta, infected grain, which has been in contact with *druj nasu* (death), must be sprinkled with water (Vendidad 7 : 33–35). Now it is just the Avesta which expresses the sacredness of the waters, or of Anahita, more clearly than any other religion. It is quite clear what is intended in sprinkling the grain: the sacredness of water maintains itself against all disaster and abolishes it. The element of life – for that is what sacredness means here – is naturally stronger than death, because spontaneous life includes victory over death. So it can be explained that the man who has touched a corpse must sprinkle himself with water from head to foot to remove *druj nasu* (Vendidad 8 : 35–72). Druj then flees before the water which takes possession of man. Most cases of ritual purification are certainly to be explained in this way. "May my sin depart with the water over my body," says a Babylonian text, "and may the evil influence flow away from me together with the water of purification"; "may the streaming water take away my sin." To say that this is simply the washing off of a certain state does not furnish any explanation here. In the same Babylonian texts, moreover, mention is made of "purification by butter, milk, and cream (copper, silver, and gold)." We find the religious explanation, that is to say the explanation of the believers, as soon as we understand the religious sense of nature with respect to water, with its spontaneous and vitalizing power. Thus according to the Avesta, Anahita "purifies" husband and wife in order that they may be fruitful. In Egypt the water of purification is written in the form of a series of signs for life. [12]

With this are naturally related the notions of the purifying and (re-) creative power of baptismal water. Tertullian says that water is the most ancient element, *divini spiritus sedes;* since water has brought forth all living beings, it is not surprising that baptismal water can "animate" (*animare*). The genus of the baptismal water is the same as that of the water of Creation; it differs only in species; let no one say that they are two different kinds of water.[13] Not until Tertullian did the practice begin of deliberately consecrating the baptismal water. The creative and renewing power of water is evident from Pausanias [14]. Hera bathes annually in the sacred spring at Nauplia and thereby "becomes a virgin" (*parthenon ginesthai*); that water thus gives her spontaneous and absolute life. "This is the secret doctrine (*logos tōn aporrētōn*) in the worship (*teletē*) of the Mysteries, which are there dedicated to Hera.

This leads us to the views, which are present in all religions, concerning the mystery of water in the realm of the dead. They agree completely with the notions of the spice of life which grows in the realm of the dead.

One of the best known formulations is the myth of the Babylonian fertility goddess Ishtar, who descends to the underworld and returns from it. On the way to her sister Allatu, the goddess of the realm of the dead, she passes seven gates; at each gate she must remove a piece of her clothing. When she appears before her sister she is struck with illnesses. The life of men and animals on earth pines away, and no more births take place. Then Ea comes to her rescue. He sends his messenger (herald) to Allatu and commands her to sprinkle Ishtar with the "water of life" and to allow her to return through the seven gates. This occurs; at every gate she gets back her piece of clothing; life arises once again. The water of life is found in the realm of the dead. The woven material of her clothing is a symbol of cosmic life; in Egypt, too, the images of the gods were thus ritually attired, and a net was placed over mummies. – Is the water of life in the realm of the dead then really water of life or water of death? The same ambiguity is the chief theme in the Babylonian myth of Adapa. When Adapa is summoned to appear by Anu in heaven, his father Ea warns him: in heaven you will be offered "food and water of death"; do not take them. But when he has come into heaven, Anu offers him "food and water of life." When Adapa refuses them, he is sent back to men. But both Ea and Anu have spoken the truth. Ea's "deceit" is the same as the deceit of Pandora and of the snake in Paradise.

We also find the notion of the water of life in the cultus. Instead of sprinkling the sick man with pure water from the two rivers, the prescription is sometimes given that he should be sprinkled with water from Apsu.

Quite similar notions are found among the Greeks: time and again we find proofs of the agreement between the religious ideas of the various Ancient peoples. According to Hesiod, Styx, the river in the realm of the dead, is the oldest of the three thousand daughters of Oceanus; that is to say, she is the most important of all flowing waters.[15] She is called *Styx aphthitos*, the "imperishable," who exists through her own power and can bestow imperishability.[16] Her essence is victory; the goddess of victory, Nike, is her daughter, and Kratos and Bia, irrepressible force, power, and violence, and also Zelos, "instinct," or "impulse," are her other children. These are peculiar names for a river. But Styx is the water of divine death: feared because she triumphs over all life and at the same time worshipped because she triumphs (*aphthitos*) over the mortal enemy. She is a victorious energy, an irresistable impulse, and she is imperishable, just as is Mazda's powerful helper, Anahita, who gives victory to the heroes. According to the well known myth, Thetis makes her son Achilles imperishable and unconquerable by holding him above fire and embalming him with ambrosia – or according to the Roman poet – by immersing him in the water of the Styx. This latter notion is not a classical one; it is based on more ancient tradition. In Arcadia there flowed a river which was called the Styx. Whereas Pausanias considers the water from this river fatal for men and animals,[17] the belief prevails at the present time that one becomes immortal if he drinks water from this river on a particular day; here again is the paradox which we find in the deceit of Pandora, Ea, or the snake. In the myth of Eros and Psyche, Psyche must fetch water from the Styx for Aphrodite in order to get back Eros; like the tree of life, the Styx is guarded by dragons and cannot be reached by the living. Naturally it is there that Psyche must fetch the water of divine life. This alone can satisfy Aphrodite. Rohde assumes that "Styx water" is a mistake of Apuleius, who has passed on the myth to us: "Wozu wäre das gut?" (What would that be good for?) [18] And then there is the remarkable statement in the *Iliad* that the gods swear by the Styx. [19] Virgil makes an even stronger statement in the *Aeneid* "swearing an oath by the Styx is the only *superstitio* which exists for the gods." [20] Only by this oath do the gods go out beyond themselves (the *ek-stasis* of the gods!). The Styx is the only being which is above and beyond the gods. She is thus conceived as the basis of the gods' life. – One always swears an oath by the basis of his own life. The notion is comparable with that of Moira, which exists above the gods; in reality Styx and Moira represent essential divine being.

The notion of the underworld water of life was evidently present in ancient Hebrew religion before the prophetic period. In Southern Canaan there is the place Beer-sheba, "Well of seven" (*be'ēr shebha'*). Although in Genesis 21 : 31 and 26 : 33 the etymological explanation of this name as "Well of the oath" (*shābha'*) is probably mistaken, the real significance of the well is nevertheless rightly grasped. Seven is "totality," in the sense of absolute, divine life, which combines both death and life; therefore "seven" is the number for the realm of the dead. People swore by the "Well of seven" just as they did by the Styx.

The best known of all the numerous notions of the water of life is certainly that of the water of Creation, the water of Chaos, out of which the world has come into being. Tertullian says quite rightly that it is the *sedes spiritus divini* and thus can "animate." The Egyptian god of the primeval waters, Nun, is the father of the gods and the creator of all things. The creating water existed even before life began; it is the "realm of the dead" itself, the realm of potential life, that is to say, of spontaneous and absolute life. The perceptible image of this mythical water was the sea, which in all Ancient religions represented the other world or the realm of the dead. The Sirens, the souls of the dead in the form of birds, are water birds and are portrayed on or near the sea; the sea is their dwellingplace, their realm of the dead. The appearance of Dionysus and Apollo in this world occurs when they arrive by sea, Dionysus in the ship and Apollo upon the winged stool (or sometimes both are portrayed riding dolphins). Plutarch relates that "at Argos, Dionysos is called up out of the water with the flourish of trumpets while a ram is thrown into the depths (*eis tēn abysson*) for the doorkeeper (of Hades)." [21] In Egypt the sacred boat was the most important and often the only cultic object in the holy of holies. The journey over water expresses the essentially divine, namely, resurrection from death; the water is death and the boat is the saviour.

This realm of the dead is the realm of absolute life and resurrection. In the Egyptian religion the water of the annual flooding of the Nile was identified with the water of Chaos or Creation; both were called Nun. The water of the Nile flood also covered the populated earth, like the water of the flood which exterminated all life, and out of this water, too, the earth appears again; it is water of death and resurrection. We find this theme in some drawings in the early Christian catacombs. Noah in the ark is there the prototype of resurrected man.

According to a widespread conception, the cosmogonic water was the seat of divine wisdom. This idea is comparable to the notion already mentioned, that wisdom dwells in the depths of the earth (oracles) or in the tree of knowledge and insight. Objective cosmic wisdom is the divine renascent life of the earth and it reveals itself in the order of abiding life, which is the only worthwhile object of knowledge. The water out of which the life of the world has arisen was necessarily the original location of cosmic wisdom; this was the world in the form of thought, before the thought became outward reality. The Babylonian formulation of this is especially clear. The water of Creation, Apsu, is called *bīt-nemeqi*, "house of wisdom" [22] and it is the house of Ea, the god of wisdom. In the account of Creation this thought is further developed in speaking of Apsu's messenger or herald, his servant Mummu. According to the Neo-Platonist

Damascius, who relates the Babylonian account of Creation
quite correctly, Mummu means *ho noētos kosmos*, that is to say,
the cosmos as a divine thought. In the main his interpretation
is correct. "Mummu," from the same root as the Assyrian
'āmaḥ, anu, amatu, means "word" (Böhl). Mummu is the spirit
of wisdom which existed before Creation and dwelled in the primeval waters. Thus it is precisely the god of wisdom Ea who is
called "Mummu who creates all things." Nabunaïd speaks of
"the wise men who dwell in Bet (house) -Mummu," which is
the name of the Babylonian university. Mummu means "word"
in the sense of the logos, which existed before Creation and by
whom all things have been created. This word is the objective
wisdom of the pre-existent world order. As the messenger or
servant of Apsu, Mummu carries out the divine will and thought.
This is creation by the word. In Babylonia as well as in Egypt
we find the notion of the double logos, which according to the
Platonic conception was formulated as the pre-existent and the
existent Idea.

Apsu and Mummu, and likewise Tiamat, are thus divine beings
of the primeval ocean of the waters of Creation. The account
of Creation is really quite remarkable. Apsu, the primeval waters, is disturbed by the bustle of the gods. A struggle develops
in which Apsu and Mummu are defeated by Ea; after this comes
the Creation, carried out by Marduk. This is the mythical
formulation of the notion that the original state has been over-
come and has ceased to exist, and that the present world has
taken its place. The arising of life, the "resurrection" at Creation,
is a victory over "death," which is here conceived as an enemy.
The whole story of this turmoil among the gods and of their
struggle and victory sounds like a fairy tale or a naïve myth.
Apsu and Mummu are water gods. But this story really formulates one of the most important thoughts in the history of religious speculation. And like the Egyptian story, it comes from
the most ancient historical period with which we are acquainted.

According to this account of Creation, Ea defeats Apsu and
Mummu; he is the creator in the cosmogony which Mummu
actualizes. Yet according to the usual conception, Ea, the underworld god of wisdom, dwells in the underworld waters of Apsu;
he is called "king of Apsu," and Apsu is called "house of wisdom.'

From this dwelling he has instructed men in all the arts and sciences. According to Berosus (275 B.C.), men originally lived without order, as animals; then a "wise being," the fish-man Oannes (Ea) arose out of the sea and taught them writing, the building of cities, science, laws, and agriculture (sowing and harvesting). But at night he went back to the sea, and since his time there is nothing new to learn. The order of abiding life and the wisdom of life are thus derived from the original element, water; in water they were potentially present. Like Apsu and Marduk, Ea too is called the creator. He caused the empirical world to arise out of the waters of Creation, in accordance with his wisdom, which acquires outward form in Creation. One of his names is *Mummu bān kalâ*, "the word which creates all things." As the craftsman who gives form to things he is also called the "potter" or "omniscient potter who knows everything" and also "carpenter," "smith," or "stone-mason"; the artisan practices a creative art. This water god is the artist who creates the cosmos with wisdom. The prayer is offered for the king: "May Ea, the Lord of the waters of Apsu, grant him wisdom." But above all he is the Bēl Balāṭi, "the Lord of Life"; in his stead the priest sprinkles water on the mouth of the image of the god; by this means the god lives. The gods must receive their life from their original element, water.

It is noteworthy that the ideas connected with this Babylonian water god have played such a central role in Greek philosophy and later on in Christology.

A number of religious notions concerning the nature and essence of the water gods becomes understandable for us in the light of the Ancient conception of water as the *primordia mundi*, seat of cosmic wisdom and order, with a creating energy. The daughter of Oceanus is called *Mētis*, "the Thinker," "the Wise One." She was the first wife of Zeus after he had defeated the Titans and had accepted the kingship of the world.[23] To this notion corresponds the Babylonian myth that Marduk as king after the cosmogonic struggle called into being a cosmically woven tapestry. Another example of the notion that water gods possess a mysterious insight are the Sirens. These spirits of the dead who belong in the realm of the dead are water birds and they are omniscient. According to the *Odyssey*, their enchanting songs say that they know everything which the Greeks and Trojans have had to endure in accordance with the decree of the gods, and that they know everything which goes on in all the wide world.[24] All this corresponds with the Babylonian conception of Apsu; Apsu means both the waters of insight and the waters of the realm of the dead (or the primeval waters out of which the entire cosmos has been created). Frequently it is the spring which is named instead of the waters of the underworld or the realm of the dead; at the spring the highest insight is attainable. According to Germanic mythology, the gods determine the world's fate at their daily court session beside the spring Mimir. So too is the ancient practice of law explained among the ancient Germans, Greeks, and Hebrews: judgments were rendered at a spring. (Grimm writes in detail concerning the springs of justice of the Germanic tribes.)

Another notion is that of the obtaining of divine inspiration, the suprahuman insight of seer or poet, at springs. According to the oldest data the Greek Muses are nymphs connected with springs. They are the goddesses of music, song, and poetry, the gift of vision, insight – in the order of the apparently disordered – and thus too of science in the Ancient sense, insight into the divine order of the cosmos. In general the Muses are the goddesses of that which is revealed and attained by divine inspiration. But inspiration is always an impartation from the supra-sensual world: the Muses belong in the other, the divine world. Their number of nine, three, or seven indicates that they are goddesses of totality in the religious sense, of that perfection (making perfect) in which apparently contradictory factors work together. The typical totality is the coming together of life and death in divine harmony; Harmonia is the same goddess as Kore. "Dionysus flees to the Muses and he keeps himself hidden among them." But according to another reading he flees into the water and is called up out of the water with a trumpet flourish. The Muses are the water goddesses or the nymphs of the springs, and water is here the home of that divine life which can be beheld only in inspiration. At Troezen, "the Muses and Hypnos are sacrificed to jointly because it is said that the Muses especially love Hypnos" [25]. Hypnos, too, is a god of the other world, of the realm of the dead. The "lym-

phaticus" (from Latin *lympha*, Greek *nymphē*, "water") means
insane, senseless, beside one's self from fright. *Nympholēptos*
has the same meaning, gripped by the Muse; this is also said
of a poet who possesses divine insight. Nymphs are reportedly
depicted as the enchanting singing goddesses of the spring water.
He who looks into this water becomes insane.

Closely connected with this notion is the practice of inquiring
from oracles at springs. Pausanias writes about the Delphic
Oracle.[26] Directly to the north of the temple was the spring,
Cassotis whose water flowed underground to the *adyton*. When
the Pythia drinks from it, she receives the gift of prophecy;
that is really where the spring comes up. Some call this water
"the water of the Styx," thus indeed the water of life and of
knowledge from the underworld. In his commentary on the *Aeneid*, Servius says in connection with "sacro fonte": "nullus enim
fons non sacer," "for there is no spring which is not sacred." [27]
Even at the present time Moravians bring food to the spring
on Christmas Eve with the words, "Little spring, little spring,
I bring you supper; tell me the truth, tell me what will happen."
These present day customs are "superstition," dead belief. The
real religious notion connected with them was once alive. But
now it has been forgotten that the water from the soothsaying
spring originates in the underworld, in the realm of the dead,
that it is identical with the water of Creation, the seat of all
wisdom and life.

It is in connection with this water of wisdom that we can understand the divine ordeals by water. A transgression is a departure
from the divine order, from the path of life which is represented
and revealed in the sacred water. The energy of the water is the
energy of life, and as such it will take cognizance only of the
truth; the water will show itself to be the representative and
upholder of life. According to the Avesta (Vendidad 4 : 54),
he who is accused of a lie against Mithra must attest his inno-
cence with "knowing" water. We are familiar with the divine
ordeal by means of "sacred water" (water of the curse) Numbers 5 : 11–31. The priest puts dust from the temple in the water
and utters the curse over it; the woman drinks it, and if she has
been unchaste, she gets dropsy and dies. A better known form
of ordeal by water is the one which we find among the Arabians

in Hadramaut [28]. If someone there is bewitched, he brings together the suspected women and pushes them under water;
the one who floats is the guilty one. In 1618 in Sweden a witch
was immersed who floated as easily as a goose.[29] In sight of the
tribunal and more than a hundred spectators she was twice
pushed under water, and both times she immediately rose again
above water; she didn't even have any water in her mouth,
nose, or ears, and when she came out of the water she was dry
immediately. King James I of England wrote: ' It appears that
God hath appointed for a supernatural signe of the monstrous
impietie of witches that the water shall refuse to receive them
in her bosom that have shaken off them the sacred water of
baptism." [30] Here there is a correspondence between the water
of the divine ordeal and the baptismal water. They are both
the water of life, but the former is evidently so in a preponderately
religio-ethical sense.

Similar data from a wide variety of sources provides striking
confirmation of our conclusion that divine ordeals by water can
be explained on the basis of the sacredness of water. In Egypt
the man who had drowned was considered a sacred being.[31]
Herodotus reports that when in Egypt the body of a drowned
man washed ashore, "the inhabitants must embalm the body
on the spot in the most careful manner and place it in a sacred
grave. No one may touch it, no relative or friend, except for the
priests of the Nile; these priests must bury the drowned man with
their own hands, as if it were the body of a superhuman being." [32]
It is precisely in Egypt that this very remarkable belief and
custom is completely understandable. The Nile is not only
"sacred" in general, but it represents Osiris, the god of death,
who like the flooding of the Nile again and again causes life to
rise anew. Now the Ancient tradition relates that Osiris has
been drowned in the Nile, just as Apis, too, was drowned in
effigy; his death is that of water, that is to say, eternal and
absolute life. The drowned man, more than any other dead
man, has become an Osiris, for he has been consecrated by water
and so removed into absolute life. Therefore he who is received
by water is sanctified and justified before God; he is on the
way of eternal life. The divine ordeal by means of water is entirely in accordance with this belief.

This correspondence between the Egyptian belief and the practice of divine ordeals by water could be accidental. But the belief in the sacredness of the drowned man received by water is too widespread for this to be possible. On the journey to Aea one of the Argonauts, Hylas, drowns near Cyzicus on the Phrygian coast of the Sea of Marmora; thereafter he is worshipped there as a divine being. Ino, who drowned with her son Melicertes, is worshipped at Megara on the Isthmus of Corinth. Medieval legends attest to the same notion; they are often very closely related to the divine ordeals. In Denmark three sisters were declared to be saints who drowned during a sea voyage and out of whose graves – according to the legend – a spring came up. Such Medieval accounts come to us from many countries. We also encounter this belief far outside Europe. In Mexico, the corpse of a drowned man is too sacred to be touched by anyone else than a priest; this is thus wholly identical with the Egyptian belief.

It is in this that we must see the religious essence of the water ordeal. But when the religious significance of the custom is no longer sensed, then rationalistic reflections and explanations appear, and they sometimes cause alterations in the custom itself. Thus he is considered the guilty one who drowns during the ordeal by water. This is a very understandable alteration of an irrational religious custom.

In conclusion a remark about the Ancient religious conception of water in Greek philosophy. The first of the Greek philosophers of nature and also the first representative of independent Greek philosophy is Thales of Milete, in the beginning of the sixth century B.C. It is indeed remarkable that it was precisely he who considered water as the *primordium*, in which all existence has its origin. Water contains the energy, the essential being, which reveals itself in all existence; in water is the unity of differences. His doctrine is rightly called a "scientific view" in our sense of the term: it attempts a rational formulation of the unity of phenomena. But it is just as certain that it draws from the traditional religious conception of the nature of water. That could be presumed of him *a priori*. But this assumption is confirmed by what Aristotle says about him. "Thales believed that all things were full of gods (*panta plērē theōn einai*)" [33]. He thus conceived

of the energy of water not only as material, but also as spiritual
energy. Just as in the religious view he saw the energy of water
as a revelation of divine life, indeed its most adequate revelation.
In other words, he saw water as the seat of creating and spontaneous life. What Cicero says about him is perhaps not altogether accurate, yet it is certainly not far from the truth.
"Thales says that water is the source of worldly reality, but that
the source of the gods is the spirit (mind, *eam mentem*) which
created all things from water (*quae ex aqua cuncta fingeret*)." [34]
This dualism of matter and spirit or material and form is, it is
true, foreign to Thales; Cicero has in mind the tradition according
to which the one spirit who develops into many gods is the spirit
of water. In any case, the Ionic philosophy of nature takes its
starting point in the religious conception of nature. We see this too
in Anaximenes' theory of air (pneuma, anima), and in the doctrine of Harmony (order, *kosmos*), which according to Pythagoras forms the unity of opposites.

D. SACRED FIRE

In the practice of religion, sacred fire as a principle of life is
equivalent to sacred plants and sacred waters. Fire is a prerequisite for life, specifically as bodily warmth and as warmth of
personality ("fire of youth," "to speak with fire"), and also in
nature as the prerequisite for growing and maturing. It is conceived as the cosmological principle, originally (and theoretically) imperishable; when it ceases to be perceived it has only
changed into another form. This imperishability reveals divine
life. Therefore fire is worshipped as mystical power, existing by
itself, and supporting man and the world. When the emphasis is
put on the utility of fire, it must not be forgotten that man does
not worship that which he can cause to serve himself. That
which is subjected has no autonomous existence, and man is its
superior. Man worships only that which can be conceived as the
basis of his existence. This basis as such extends far beyond
man's control and is therefore also of a living and spiritual
nature. The fact that a natural object such as fire can be viewed
as the bearer and revelation of the basis of existence can be
explained only on the grounds of the Ancients' religious sense of

nature, the sense of the absolute, self-subsistent energy at work in natural phenomena. Man is not superior to this energy, as he is to "the useful" in the ordinary sense of the term.

The sacredness of fire, like that of water, is of a positive as well as of a negative nature. Fire removes that which is evil, hostile, and destructive (this is its negative side), because fire is its active opponent (the positive side); its will and law is a different one, specifically, the law of self-subsistent and abiding life.

Here are a few of the significant data. Ancient physiology teaches that fire is the principle of life, or a revelation of this principle: *corpus est terra, animus ignis*, "the body is earth, the spirit fire." A large number of peoples in our part of the world and elsewhere identify bodily warmth with other kinds of "fire." In general fire is thought to be present even where it is not seen. Fire dwells as the soul of each object in wood and in plants, in the waters (Heraclitus: ". . . in all water that extinguishes fire"), in the stones of the earth, and in the heavens. In the Vedas we read of countless "births of Agni," that is to say, countless embodiments of this god of fire, especially in bodies of water (*apām napāt*). "Agni is the germ of everything which moves and which exists." The Avesta classifies fire into social fires and natural fires. There are three kinds of social fires: that of priests (wisdom), warriors (energy), and farmers (agricultural skill) – corresponding to the three *khvarnahs*, the three glories or victorious powers. Each of these three fires had its own temple at different places in Atropatene, "Land of Fire," where flames of gas came out of the earth, probably in connection with volcanoes or burning oil wells. "Each of these three burns without receiving fuel or being ignited, and they are not afraid of water." The nature-fires are subdivided into five or seven kinds: the Celestial Fire of Ahura Mazda, lightning, the plants' power of growth, men's power of growth, and, most important, Bahram (Vrthragh-na), the sacred fire of victory that burns for every province in the provincial temple. Another one of this group of fires is Nairyosanha, "the fire of the word (command) of men," the power of the word or the will. It is like Brahmanaspati, the spiritual power which in the invocation during the rite brings about a link between man and deity. In him is the same spiritua¹ energy as in the living word which expresses the infinite in man. This commanding word, which by its authority brings something to pass, is the creative word. This divine spirit in the man issuing commands, this fire-energy which has descended into him is handed down from one king to another. Thus is formed the magnificent epic of the Iranian kings. A king Yima, "who was filled with love for the untrue, false word," was "forsaken by this fire," and he died immediately. According to the myth, this fire was present for the last time in Zarathustra; thenceforth it has hidden itself in the sea in the East. At the end of time the fire will rise again out of that sea in the Saviour, and it will return as a god on earth to redeem the earth.

Atar, Fire, is called the son of Mazda, his beneficent spirit. But he is Ahura Mazda himself, worshipped in fire. Therefore the Avesta people are called a people of "fire worshippers"; a fire burns in the central chamber of every temple. In the chief temples – there are three in Bombay – the fire is found in its purest form; from these chief temples the smaller temples are provided with fire. This soul and essence of all the fires consists of sixteen different fires, and this is prepared once a year. The house fire is repeatedly renewed from the smaller temple fire, and this fire, in its turn, is renewed from the larger fire. Thus there arises an all-embracing hierarchy of all fires.

The notion is widespread that the life of the earth is a fire-energy. The Greek god Hephaestus and his dwarfs, the Cyclopes, are the smiths who dwell in the earth. They forge the wonders of earth, in the first place the life of plants in the spring. The earth spirit Erichthonius (the prime ancestor of the Athenians) was the son of Ge or Athene and of Hephaestus, who formed Pandora. Hephaestus also made the image of Dionysus, which was placed in a chest – the underworld – and was brought by Eurypylus (Hades) to Patrae, where Dionysus arose. In the Eleusinian mysteries the torch made of a bundle of plant stalks represents the fire-life of the earth; this symbol of Kore's divine life was thrown in her honour into a chasm in the earth. The torch is indeed the emblem of Demeter and Kore, the goddesses of the dying and freshly arising life of the earth. In the Greek *lampadēphoria*, the ritual contest with torches at funerals and weddings, the rescue of the fire had the significance of the arising of fire from its ashes, thus signifying its victory. In many respects the funeral and wedding ceremonies are the same; they are both concerned with the same mystery, namely that man lives and dies the life of the earth or the life of fire. Thus the torches were carried before the newlyweds, after which a struggle began for the possession of the torches. The ritual struggle in the cultus of the Mysteries in Greece and in Egypt dramatically portrayed victory over death.

In the Mithra Mysteries two *daidophoroi* were depicted; one carried the torch turned downwards and the other carried the torch turned upwards. Together they represented Mithra himself, who dies and lives again. When a torch turned downwards is sometimes depicted on our gravestones, it is only a sentimental symbol of death; only if two torches were depicted would this symbolism have a religious meaning.

The thought of the fire life of the earth also appears in the cosmogonic myth. In Egypt the site of cosmic arising at Creation is called "the fire island." The island is the first piece of earth which appeared out of the primeval waters; "fire island" therefore means "island of life." This is also the island of the blessed in the realm of the dead: it is here that the earth lives and the dead live the same life. In the cosmogonic myth fire thus alternates with light. The light of the sun first appeared on the hill of Creation or the island. It is known that the Gnostics identified light with "life" – (cf. John 1 : 4, "the life was the light of men"). This "life" is not only insight, but the entire spiritual life which the believer possesses. This corresponds with *khvarnah* ,"glory," in the Avesta, which constitutes the divine nature of life in nature and man; in man it is the triumphant power of the believers. "In the (creating) word was life, and this life was a triumphant splendour (*khvarnah*)." This need not necessarily mean that the Gnostic and early Christian term is borrowed from Persian religion. The idea was a familiar one everywhere. The Egyptian *akhu*, "the glorified one," is the spirit or soul of men and gods, and means "the one providing light." Justin Martyr calls Christian baptism a "light, enlightenment": *phōtismos*.[35] Gilles Wetter, calls this "light" the divine vital energy which reveals itself in the darkness: the light at Creation which is the life of the world.[36] Closely connected with this idea is the notion of the fire energy by means of which the life of the world exists.

This conception of fire makes it quite understandable that in many religions it was considered a sacred duty to insure there being a continually burning fire upon the altar. Among the Hebrews the fire is to burn continually upon the altar and not to be extinguished (Leviticus 6). We find the same notion in the Brahman religion, among the Greeks, Romans, and many other peoples. The continually burning fire is the enduring divine energy of the eternal life of the universe and especially of man. The idea of the fire of the earth by which men live is the clearest in the Greek and Roman notion of the hearth fire, *Hestia* and *Vesta*, respectively. The hearth stands in the middle of the house and is, so to speak, its center of gravity. From it the life of the family arises, and to it returns. Ancestor worship takes place at the hearth fire; the ancestors dwell in the hearth (Rohde assumes that in earlier times they were buried there), and they are the generating spirits of the family. A typical example of this conception is the myth that the first Roman king, Servius Tullius, was begotten by the Lar Familiaris in the hearth fire of the Vestal Virgin Ocresia: this is the religious conception of the origin of human life. It is quite clear that this fire of the ancestors is inseparably connected with the realm of the dead, the place of absolute life. Such is the explanation of the mysterious character of the hearth fire, and also of its role in the worship of Vesta, which took place chiefly at the hearth fire of the city. Vesta is the virgin goddess who ever anew causes the life of the people to flourish. In her temple the Romans kept the *pignus* (or the pignora) *imperii Romani*, sacred symbols and objects of unknown nature. Her consort was the god of the fire of the earth; her servants, the Vestal virgins, represented her and dressed as *matronae*. In case of infidelity towards her divine consort, the Vestal virgins were buried alive, that is to say, handed over to him, consecrated – not punished. In each Greek city the *Hestia* (hearth) of the city was the "navel of the city." It was there that life originated, and it was there that there was communication between the other world and this world. Thus, too, according to Greek belief, the self-renewing life of the realm of the dead revealed itself in the hearth fire. The exceptional significance of the worship of Hestia is made clear by the fact that at all their sacrifices the Greeks invoked Hestia both first and last. This can only mean that in her, the goddess of the earth's life which is active in the earth's fire, the essential being of all the gods is brought together. People were aware of the chthonic (underworld) character of the entire world of the gods. The earth goddess Ge was the mother of gods and men, the *terra mater*. And Vesta was also the *terra mater*.

Sometimes it is suggested that fire, which contains autonomous energy, must have originated autonomously and spontaneously, without any action of men. Pausanias declares that he has himself seen how the wood on the altars of two Lydian cities spontaneously springs into flame when the sacred texts are sung.[37] But as a rule the lighting and maintaining of the sacred fire is a sacred act in which man takes a hand in the divine life and actualizes it in religio-magical fashion. This is the distinctive mark of all cultic acts: in ritual fashion, i.e. with a mystical and supernatural effect, the divine activity is performed in image. The sacred fire of Hephaestus on Lemnos was extinguished every year for nine days while ships went to Delos to fetch new fire; when these ships came back, "a new life began." The fire in the temple of Vesta was also renewed each year, on the first of March.[38] The idea at the basis of this custom is that the yearly renewal of the life of nature is not a natural event that occurs automatically ; it is a miracle, the repetition of the miracle of the original Creation. Man is witness to this miracle, upon which his life depends, and which indeed constitutes his life. He cannot permanently confront this miracle of nature as a passive spectator. Such an attitude is indeed possible for us, because we think we are dealing with a Nature which is impersonal. Ancient man, however, felt himself taken up into this miracle; he shared in it. There arises personal contact between this cosmic event and man; spirit confronts spirit. Then the relation is of a practical nature. Man intervenes actively; he takes part in the divine mystery and actualizes it by his religio-magical, sacred act. This is Psychology of Religion's explanation of every cultic act. Man takes action as God's fellow worker. Thus he creates "the new life" of the world at the ritual renewal of the fire. In lighting and maintaining the sacred fire in the cultus, man performs not only a religious, but a divine act.

Nevertheless, he keeps the sense of dependence on this divine energy which he himself has helped to actualize. For the sacred fire is worshipped; it is thus a divine being, above human powers of attainment. The contradiction in this relation to the object of worship is clear – man performs a divine act, but is nevertheless not a god. This, however, does not trouble faith at all. Contradictions of this kind belong to the essence of the religious relationship; only in rational, finite relations are they excluded. When cultic acts are disapproved because they are superhuman, magic acts, as they were by the Hebrew prophets, then many and various motives may be operative, but one of these is certainly of a rationalistic nature, a view which fails to understand the religious psychology of the believer.

It is noteworthy that in one religion the idea of human activity in the fire sacrifice seems to have become completely dominant and to have done away with all sense of dependence. This is the case with the theory of sacrifice in later Brahmanism in India. According to it, the sacred fire is the life of the world itself, and the priest directs the life of the world by means of his activities with the sacrificial fire. There is no personal god at work in the rising and setting of the sun, the change of seasons, etc. It looks as if the priest himself is the god of the world, and not just his representative. But – he is an initiate, a man clad with divine power. We should keep in mind that in some sense this is true in every religion: each believer through his religious relationship possesses the superhuman capacity to triumph over finitude.

Myth and cultus give many examples of consecration by fire, sanctification through being consumed by fire. The best known form is the burning up of the offerings which characterizes all "burnt offerings." A well known Greek example are the Laphria of Artemis in Patrae. Artemis was the goddess of fertility in general, of the life of the earth conceived as an energy of fire. But she had a demonic nature; the mystery of fertility includes death as well as life. She was called the Deliveress, but it was also related that the livestock died and the harvest failed whenever the goddess was enraged. The saviour, the deliverer from death, is able to save just because he is also the god of death itself. This explains the cruel cultic customs in the service of

Artemis, which even included human sacrifices. At the festival of Laphria a large burnt offering of living animals and field crops was sacrificed to Artemis. Around the altar where the crops lay, an enormous fence of fresh wood was built; wild animals and edible birds were driven inside, and then everything was burnt up. This is undoubtedly a consecration; by death in fire the life of all of nature is sanctified. The holy belongs to the other world; this thought recurs wherever offerings of vegetable produce and animals – whether already slaughtered or not – are consumed on the altar.

It is still more remarkable when the god himself is consecrated. According to the myth, the Phoenician Hercules, Melkart, sacrificed himself in the fire, to rise again at "the awakening of Hercules." And the Hercules who on Oeta mounted the pyre and thereafter was taken up among the gods was worshipped as a *hērōs* (hero) who had triumphed over death. In the cultus the Phoenician colonists at Gades (Cadiz) burned Melkart's image in the yearly rite of the mysteries. Fire was actually the essential being and the nature of Melkart. In the temple there was no image of the god, but on his altar there burned a permanent fire, and in that fire he dwelt. Only for the annual festival was there an image made of him, and that was then burned. This is quite clearly consecration, the sacrificial death in which his essence is actualized. Thus in each sacrificial act the way in which the offering is consecrated manifests the nature of the god. The offering always represents the god himself. When the offering is consecrated, the nature of the god is actualized. In honour of Sandan a pyre was set up annually at Tarsus in Cilicia on which the god was burned in effigy. In this way the fire-essence of Sandan was actualized: like Melkart he was the god of vegetation in which the fire of the earth is at work.

European peoples of the present day are acquainted with a great many similar customs. In the Easter and St. John's Day fires the tallest and strongest tree is burned.[39] Sometimes a human figure of wood is put into it, or a straw man who represented the spirit of vegetation itself is burned with the woodpile. The ashes are scattered over the fields for the fertility of the land. The Roman Catholic clergy have often opposed the Easter fires because they quite rightly saw it to be an "idolatrous custom";

but sometimes they have "christened" this custom. During the singing of Easter hymns or during a procession around the church, "Judas" was burned in the Easter fire or "Judas fire."

Consecration also takes place in the baptism by fire, a rite which corresponds to water baptism. The Fifth Homeric Hymn (written in the middle of the seventh century B.C.) relates the myth of Demeter and Demophon at Eleusis. During the day the goddess anoints the young Demophon with ambrosia and at night she holds him in "the power of the fire." The boy grows up "looking like the celestials." In this way Demeter would have made him immortal, if his mother had not prevented it. For when she saw that the goddess held him in the fire, she ran to the fire and wrenched her child out of the hands of the goddess. "Foolish one!" cried the goddess, "I am Demeter ... I would have made your son immortal, but now he cannot escape death and Keres. Yet imperishable honour shall remain his, because he has rested on my knees and in my arms ..."

Cremation is quite especially a consecration. In Homer it serves to bring the dead person as soon as possible to rest in the other world, so that his spirit will not roam around on the earth. Here there is absolutely no thought of worshipping the dead. In Homer this is quite understandable. But for the Ancient peoples, still unaffected by the "enlightenment" of the Classical period, cremation was a sacrament, which bestowed on the soul the absolute life of fire; thus like burial it is a consecration. So the burning of the bodies of the Roman emperors on the *rogus* – depicted on coins – is quite certainly a "consecration." It is the same idea as that present in the burning of Melkart and Sandan and in the myth of Hercules who mounts the flaming pyre. In Rome cremation was connected with the idea of burial: the *rogus* was built like a tomb, with a door like that to the tomb. In Athens many examples have been found of cremation in the ordinary grave. In India, where both cremation and burial are practised, cremation is considered a sacrament. By means of Agni the dead person attains the heavenly world: "By means of this (dead) person Thou (Agni) art born, so through you may he now be born again." The fire of the funeral pyre is the special fire of the person who is being cremated. He who has only had to maintain the household fire is consumed by the household fire, and the priest is consumed by the temple fire. Agni is the *psychopomp*, the guide of souls.

Finally, fire also removes all evil influences. But just as with water, this negative effect is most closely connected with its positive activities. We find much data on this subject especially in connection with the conception of darkness and night as elements of evil beings. Fire disperses them and purifies. So it is in the Roman Catholic Church in the *benedictio candelarum* on the Candlemas of the Virgin Mary (February 2). The ancient ritual for it reads: May God bless the candless "so that in every place where they are lighted or placed, the princes of darkness will shudder and flee stricken with fear." It is thus that purification by fire occurs. In the incense sacrifice it is the smoke which purifies, as we see from the Egyptian custom and in the survivals of it in the Roman Catholic Church.

In the most ancient Greek philosophy fire is here also conceived as the universal principle of life, the *primordium* (first beginning). Ancient philosophy (including Greek) builds upon religious speculations; that is the psychological sequence of the conceptions. According to Pythagoras (sixth century B.C.), the world fire is in the middle of the universe. Around this central cosmic fire, this Hestia of the world, are ranged the heavenly bodies, including the earth. From this central fire all vital energy goes forth, energy which contains the mathematical relationships underlying the permanent order of life and the regular course of events. For the formal principle of the cosmos, on which in this philosophy the strongest emphasis falls, is the mathematical relationship; it is the essence of all things. Mathematics thus becomes the all-inclusive science, certainly the most abstract, but thereby also the most fundamental. The harmony of numbers, which is the harmony of the spheres, expresses the permanent mutual relationship of all things. Nevertheless, fire remains the actually effective principle and the moving force. Heraclitus (fifth century B.C.) is one of the Ionian physicists or philosophers of nature, although he can rightly be called the Hegel of Antiquity. According to him, fire is the eternal life of the world, just as for Thales, water was this life; here fire is as much spirit as it is matter. This is the same conception as that in the Avesta, in which life is also conceived as the cosmic logos. According to the dialectical conception, each concept presupposes its contrary, and the fusion of opposites is the characteristic of life. In the whole realm of becoming, the fire is present which makes everything come alive and which consumes everything, working constantly without even any appearance of rest. On the *katabasis*, the downward road, the fire fumes when extinguished turn into water, and when congealed turn into earth. But then by its own motion and its own energy it turns again along the *anabasis*, the upward road, back to its original state: when melted the solid substance of earth again becomes water, and through evaporating this once again becomes the celestial fire. This construction, destruction, and new construction is the eternal cycle away from fire and back to it again. Everything flows, becomes, turns into its opposite. Even invisible movements "upwards" or "downwards" are assumed; the smallest particles are also in continuous motion. Everything consists in opposites and exists because of them (Hegel!). Fire is the eternal unrest, the living energy in all things. This philosophy of nature is in its essence religious, because it is built on the religious sense of nature, on the recognition of the absolute, the divine, in the phenomenon of nature.

CHAPTER 5

PARTICULAR GODS AND GODS PERSONIFYING CONCEPTS

A. PARTICULAR GODS

The objects of worship which we have so far considered have been solely nature gods. Many particular gods and gods representing the personification of certain concepts are also nature gods, but they are of a quite different character from the preceding ones. They do not represent any universal principles; the area of their activity is always limited, sometimes to the smallest possible scope. And even within these limits they are often not of a permanent nature. They do not pretend to be powers controlling the world or men in any universal sense.

Thus they do not tend to widen their sphere of influence. On the contrary, they express only the peculiar mystery of a particular phenomenon. In the case of natural phenomena, we meet with a remarkably realistic conception of deity, but that realism testifies to spiritual power. In the case of the "concept gods," we find the same realism, but here in the scholastic sense. The concepts are not *nomina*, but *realia*.

Although we have known about the worship of particular gods for a long time, we have usually not properly appreciated their great religious significance. These gods actually appear in all Ancient religions. But they are "smaller" gods, and scholars have therefore frequently overlooked them. It has been supposed that they arose because of "artificial theory, poetic license, individual arbitrariness," etc. Usener for the first time brought to light the *Sondergötter* (particular gods) and *Augenblicksgötter* (momentary gods), but he did not grasp their religious significance!

Beside the great central divine figures stand a multitude of *dii minores*, minor gods. Sometimes these are just as important as, or even more important than, the great gods, but each one is concerned with a very limited area. In China there are in addition to the two main gods – of heaven and earth – countless other gods of clouds, rain, winds, particular mountains and rivers, seas, city walls, etc. The Avesta mentions in addition to the omnipresent gods scores of gods of mountains and rivers. This is not pantheism; these are all autonomous gods who maintain their individuality. The creatures of Mazda owe their sacredness not only to the universal principle of world order or world life; because of its own nature each one is in a limited sense a sacred creature. We sometimes get the impression that among the Greeks each tree and forest, each stream and spring, and each field has an autonomous existence as a spiritual and divine being, and that every one has its own nymph, dryad, or spirit, which is worshipped only there and nowhere else. The rage of the river Scamander, described in Book 21 of the *Iliad*, proves how vividly this was conceived.

It is peculiar that there are clearly no bounds to the forming of new gods. Anything, large or small, perceived in the environment can be conceived as a "god." It is characteristic of this religious need that people try to engross themselves as deeply as possible in the particularities of phenomena, without forgetting a single one. It is understandable that the Avesta views time as a divine being who encompasses all beginning and ending, all waxing and waning. But we discover that various periods of time are also invoked separately; the five parts of the day are worshipped in separate litanies, each with its own area of protection and divine activity: cattle and horses, small domestic animals, men, fruit, and grain; or the five circles of society: household, region, province, country, and congregation of Zarathustra. Furthermore, the gods of "the four seasons" and of "the years" are all separately invoked.

Perhaps the Roman agricultural gods show this specialization most characteristically. They mark off the various moments in the growth of the grain. *Seia* is the goddess of sowing, of the sprouting seed in the earth. *Segesta* is for the shoots which have come up above ground, *Proserpina* for the stalks. *Nodotus* forms the sections of the stem; *Volutina* forms the protective sheath around the ear; and *Patelana* later removes it. *Lacturnus* and *Matuta* take care of the different ages of ripening, and *Flora* makes the plant blossom. The Church Fathers ridiculed this "*plebs* of gods" – in Rome there were more gods than men, they said. And yet these were not sham gods, arising out of artificial theories. They were living, powerful beings who were worshipped. Proserpina, Flora, and Pomona were among the most important Roman gods. In the Circus Maximus there were statues of Seia and Segesta. That they were conceived quite personally is made clear by what Herodotus relates. When the Athenians wanted to remove the images of Damia and Auxesia (goddesses of growth and prosperity) on Aegina, these images knelt down and begged .... Herodotus adds that he himself does not believe the story, but perhaps others do.[2]

The need of gods for all kinds of moments and aspects of experience is universal, and this fact proves that these gods are by no means artificial. Even in Christianity the saints of the Roman Catholic Church represent all kinds of particular needs and activities. In addition to universal saints there are local saints, and not infrequently new "popular saints" are created to meet new needs. Usener lists forty saints invoked in the French Vosges as guardians of livestock and protectors from all kinds of sickness, such as gout, toothache, and burns (St. Augustine, for instance, protects one from warts), as protectors in storms and against fleas.[3] This is certainly a direct continuation of the pre-Christian religion.

Yet alongside these minor deities were the great gods, Ahura Mazda, Jupiter, Zeus, and the Christian Trinity. One would think that these great gods would be sufficient. In them is expressed the longing to see the connection and unity in the cosmos, the world-governing power which, like the gods of sun and moon, is detached from particular natural phenomena and elevated above them. But alongside of this desire remains the other desire to conceive of each separate entity in its own particular and autonomous nature, and thus according to its divine nature. For in every phenomenon about us there is also the element of that autonomous and spontaneous nature in which the divine reveals itself. The life of the world continues through the change of times, but every period of time with its content has a new meaning and signifies a new beginning in the organic process of historical development. One period of time cannot be explained causally on the basis of another. Each period of time contains something spontaneous, something autonomous, which cannot be derived from the preceding period (the Greek *Hōrai*). In its saints the Roman Catholic Church sees the inexplicable nature of divine aid; in every separate instance the miracle is of a different kind. With a religious sense of nature it thus penetrates deeply into reality.

Now the character of the particular gods also determines the corresponding character of the worship of these gods, for example in the case of the gods of agriculture. When the farmer grows grain, he accomplishes something which actually exceeds the powers of a finite being. When he causes life and growth to arise, he takes a hand in the divine process and sets in motion the secret forces of the divine activities, forces which he does not know or understand. These are cultic acts, and in the cultus there is always an element of magic. Everything the farmer does has results which extend far beyond his capacities. It is thus understandable that every one of his (sacred) acts is guided by a god. Therefore in each act he invokes the divine power which represents what really happens. This religious act is a long way from all speculation, from the mythology in which the Greeks so frequently engulfed their gods, and from all art. It is thoroughly realistic religion, which takes as its starting point the particularities of life, and it is applied to the realities of life. Common daily acts become sacred and religious acts; this conception of religion certainly contains depth and value. What comes to light very clearly here is the special meaning of polytheism in comparison with monotheism. The latter generalizes and sees in "everything" the activity of God. But this "everything" diverts attention from the characteristic features of the various elements and moments, and it weakens the sense of the individual. (Kierkegaard ironically calls "everything" and "always" practical words.) Here is an example of a value which – in exchange for other values – has been lost. The Ancients had deeper insight into the character of Nature, and in this respect they had a wiser understanding and a greater sensitivity than we.

B. MOMENTARY GODS

Closely akin to the "particular gods" are the "momentary gods." [4] They are not permanent, but exist only for a particular instance – and so too are realistically conceived. The divinity of the last sheaf of grain, invoked at the ceremonies for blessing the grain, lives for a year at most, and there are as many of them as there are fields. The separate lightning flash which was considered a god, Keraunos (without connection with Zeus), was worshipped where the lightning had struck; he came into being at one particular instant. The Greeks saw a special divine being, a *daimōn*, in each piece of fortune or misfortune. The tragedians speak repeatedly of *ton paronta daimona*, the god who dominates someone at a particular moment, for instance during mourning over a dead person or on being shamed. The personal god of the individual, the *genius*, is also a momentary god, who disappears when that person passes off the scene. In Babylonia man is called the son of his god. The Romans believed that the individual's genius or Juno was active from the time of his birth in shaping his tendencies and personality, and a Roman worshipped this god on his birthday.

C. GODS PERSONIFYING ATTRIBUTES OR CONCEPTS

Another related group is that of gods of attributes or concepts. Here an attribute expressing the originality of a spiritual being is personified as a self-subsistent being. Such is the case in the Avesta with Vohu-manah, wisdom, and with Asha, righteousness, and Khshathra, dominion, who besides Ahura Mazda are the principal gods. The same is true of Angra Mainyu, the evil spirit, who is portrayed in as personal terms as possible. The former three do not differ essentially in nature. In Yasna 1, they are invoked as the "beautifully formed power," the "conqueror of the enemy" (Sanskrit *vritrahan*) or the "triumphing superiority." They have thus been conceived as the impulses and drives toward lasting and eternal life which are active in every man created by Mazda, not as powers originating from us who are finite individuals, but as divine energies which are at work in the religious man to assure him of eternal life. Although they are present within the righteous man, these divine powers extend far beyond human capacities. Khshathra is the power which represents faith, the dominion of the Mazda religion, actually the kingdom of God. They are not thought of in "ethical-religious" terms, but rather in "religio-ethical" terms, and are even conceived as vital energy in general. They are the élan, the self-renewing power of life, the triumph over everything which undermines life. Here too, in this clear awareness of the superhuman nature of the impulses and forces which enable us to make progress, the especially realistic character of this idea of deity is expressed. The forces are self-subsistent, and therefore can also be at work outside man. Thus *asha* is also Nature's law of life, because it is the basic principle of that life.

In Egypt, too, these "attribute gods" tend to come down to particulars. Sometimes in this way an entire system of religious psychology or physiology is built up. There are fourteen *ka's* ("souls") of man: the personified psychic and physical attributes which keep man alive, the irreducible foundations of individual existence. This personification does not indicate an artificial production of speculation; these were real gods. Among them are *Hu*, "the power of the word"; *Shepsu*, "riches," *Nekht*, "victory," and *User*, "influence"; *Akhu*, "the splendor of being initiated," and *Djed*, "stability"; *Sia*, "wisdom" or "insight," and *Heka*, "the magical capacity of the vital force." Many of the nuances largely escape us. The Egyptians make other distinctions than we do; in this respect they are finer and more precise, and they have a keener eye for particulars than we have. Where we suffice with one word, they use three or four. And these attributes are for them divine beings, because they are vital energies. Living man is the bearer of an infinitely large number of powers and energies, even more than are present in the growing seed. Because of their tendency to descend to particulars, the Egyptians could have multiplied the fourteen souls any number of times, and indeed they have doubled that number by putting a feminine being with a separate name beside each masculine one. Each expression of the life process is impenetrable and inexplicable; the religious value of this kind of idea of deity is related precisely to its sharp perception and its deliberate antithesis to any notion of mutual connection and causal relation. Thus the religious value of these "attribute gods" can in a sense be measured by their numbers.

In the Avesta we also find the personification of "religion," the Mazda religion, as an attribute of man. She is portrayed in very personal terms as a beautiful young woman. When the spirit of the dead man meets her in the hereafter and asks who she is, she replies that she is his religion. She was already beautiful, but through his life he has made her even more beautiful; she was beloved, but he has made her even more beloved. Then she gives him paradise. The religion of the individual is a self-subsistent divine power, independent of the individual and superhuman. "The word of God;" "the holy law" against the *daevas* (namely the *Vendidad*) is given the same kind of personified nature, and so are all the separately revealed books of the *Avesta*. In the sacrificial rites they are all invoked as self-subsistent divine beings.

Other "concept gods" are the powers and feelings which can dominate a human individual or community. On the *aigis*, the tapestry of Pallas Athene, there are depicted Force, Strife, and Terror. For the Greeks these were not merely the artistic symbols which they would be for us. It is related for instance, how Eris (Strife) alone was present during the battle, while all the other gods remained in their houses on Mt. Olympus.[5] Eris is thus conceived as a personal goddess. The same is true in other places of Deimos, Fear, and Phobos, Fright. The Roman "concept gods" also provide countless examples of this.

The significance of "concept gods" has been extremely great. And it is noteworthy that they have formed a link between the better known "nature gods" and the "primitive ideas of deity." In them men have conceived the divine power in the common but inexplicable phenomena of life. They are closely related to other ideas of divine power which for some reason have attracted more attention, those in animism, fetishism, and the belief in *mana*.

CHAPTER 6

THE WORSHIP OF ANIMALS

We have seen that religious cosmology is concerned with the relation between man and the world around him, and in particular with the way he is determined by that world. The fact that he is determined by the phenomena of the world is, seen from the religious point of view, not a mechanical determination, for that would make of man a mechanical product. He is himself spirit, and he can only be determined by spirit. In the natural event there are spiritual factors at work; these are the ultimate factors, which cannot be reduced to anything else. There are not two forms of spirit; one life or one spiritual reality encompasses both man and nature. Nature, the cosmos, to which man is related, is thus essentially spirit. The visible emerges from the invisible; what can be perceived is finite and rational; it can be defined. On the other hand, what cannot be perceived is self-subsistent or divine (self-subsistence is a definition for the divine). So the religious man always looks beyond the rational towards the irrational. Even visible phenomena have an irrational essence, for the self-subsistent element must always be the essential and sovereign factor.

Religious cosmology is concerned with understanding the divine life of the cosmos. This living world includes animals which men have considered as beings just as self-subsistent or divine as certain plants, bodies of water, etc. In most religions there are "sacred animals," which are themselves worshipped as divine beings, or are conceived as emblems of the gods. These emblems are symbols or images of gods, usually portrayed in human form. This human form of the gods is, however, only a symbol or indication of what transcends man. The thought of a god in human form is not strange to us, and it is quite possible for us to enter sympathetically into this kind of thinking. But the idea that an animal is sacred is really very difficult for us to understand. In other objects, such as heavenly bodies, plants, fire, and water, it is much easier for us to perceive the universal principle of life which believers have seen in them and which reveals itself in our own existence. The reason why it is much more difficult for us to conceive of this universal principle in an animal is clearly that we unconsciously feel spiritually superior to the animal. A comparison of the animal with man suggests itself ver yreadily because the two show such similarity in much of what they do. But his comparison can easily become an evaluation in which man is the standard and the animal therefore shows up unfavorably in comparison. If, however, we start with the realization that man lives the life of the earth, then we cannot engage in an evaluative comparison. When we are concerned with the observation of animals, the ideal human norm is precisely what we do *not* see in them. Animal worship brings us close to a "primitive" sphere which is far away from us. Yet this idea of deity is also one which we must try to approach as closely as possible if we want to understand religions with which we are in other respects well acquainted. There are a large number of sacred animals even in Greek religion, not to mention all those in Indian, Persian, Egyptian, and other religions.

In some cases the belief in the sacredness of animals is actually based on the recognition of a universal principle of life. This is made especially clear by certain myths about sacred animals. Myth is not bound to the perception of external realities and therefore offers the opportunity for unrestrained speculation about the phenomena. In the *Avesta* (*Bundahishn*) there is the myth of the *Gaush aevodāta*, the "Bull created alone." When this first of all living creatures of Mazda had been killed by Ahriman, there arose from his body all the plants and animals on the earth. The spirit of death has by his activity at the same time caused eternal life to develop. The bull, which recurs in the Mithra religion, represents the generating power which has called everything into life and the nourishing power which repeatedly renews life. Man is dependent on the ox in the same sense that he is on water, fire, and similar elements; the vital nature of the bull is in everything that lives. Thus here there is really a universal principle formulated. There is nothing conceivable which is comparable to *aevodāta*, just as it is said that the Logos that is *monogenēs* (only, unique, or only-begotten; the term is used in John 3 : 16 and I John 4 : 9, as well as in non-Christian references to the Logos). The source of life is divine. In the power of the bull men have seen an "image" of that vital energy. It is thus that we are to understand the sacredness of the bull in the Avesta, a conception which is to be found not only in the creation myth, but throughout. It is remarkable that in the decidedly ethically oriented Avesta, even in the *Gathas*, all the religious duties toward cattle and other livestock, including the duty of good treatment, are enumerated right alongside the duty of striving for the ideal of truth, trustworthiness and a regular order of life, and the duty of living in accord with *asha*, the cosmic law whereby nature and man exist. We must not suppose that this was a sentimental notion like the modern concern for protecting animals; the animal represented the universal life created by Mazda. Mazda creates "the cow and the righteous man" (Y. 37.1) – a remarkable sequence! "We worship Ahura Mazda, who created the bull and *asha*, who created the waters and the good plants, the celestial lights, the earth and all good things." Thus many times it is the bull (or cow) that is mentioned first, as the special and most important creation of Mazda. The connection with the ethical ideas is clear. In principle the cosmic pathway of life and the ethical pathway are one; the will of God is eternal life. Sometimes instead of "bull" we find the expression *Geush urvan*, "the bull's capacity to choose." The bull has chosen life, just as has the righteous man. *Geush urvan* and the *urvan* (capacity to choose) of the righteous man are, indeed, interchangeable terms, and *Geush urvan* is even mentioned along with the spiritual being (*khratu*) which is called the will and wisdom of Mazda.

In Egypt we find ideas of the same type. There the cosmic bull is the bull of the earth, which is the earth itself. He brings forth life and maintains it; bulls are sacrificed to the earth. He even gives life to the god of light. He is also called "bull of the heavens," but hardly with the significance of fertility. The bull of Memphis, Apis, which is called "the life of the (earth) god Geb," or "the (visible) image of Osiris' (invisible) soul," thus represents universal life; he is also called "the soul of the House of Generation (the temple at Memphis)." Similar notions to express the "soul" or spontaneous life are connected with the ram of Mendes. The horned altar and the sacrifices of bulls or rams are also based on these ideas.

In all these ideas the bull or ram is a symbol of life, of the foundation of human existence. Now one can ridicule the notion of such a material foundation of life, yet it is no more explicable or less mysterious than a spiritual foundation. The material foundation is spiritual because it is truly the foundation; it is self-subsistent and possesses spontaneous life, which is eternal life.

These cases of real animal worship are still somewhat understandable. The religious sense of nature has conceived of the animal as a universal principle of life, and just this universality makes the conception understandable for us. There are other and more numerous cases which are more difficult for us; the details often make them entirely incomprehensible. Many Greek writers mention the worship of animals in Egypt and the notion of their sacredness as something quite remarkable and incomprehensible. It should not surprise us that this has occasioned much misunderstanding; thus a Roman lawyer of the second century A.D., Polyaenus, relates that Cambyses conquered the city of Pelusium by having sheep, dogs, cats, and ibises walk ahead of his troops.[1] Herodotus however, has what is on the whole an accurate conception in saying that "all tame and wild animals are sacred there." [2] He means by this that there is no kind of animal which is not considered sacred somewhere in Egypt as a symbol of the local gods. The dead animal is often embalmed, and we have found many of these animal mummies. Yet the impression which these writers give us cannot be entirely accurate. It is clear from the many original documents that animal worship had quite a different character. Animals were sacred more as symbols of gods than in themselves. Not the empirical individual animal, but the different kinds of animals are sacred, for they posses divine energies and attributes. In the Egyptian texts and cultus there is little to be seen of "animal worship"; the animal was evidently conceived as a symbol, and less significance was ascribed to the outward ap-

pearance than the accounts of the Greek writers would lead us
to assume. Nevertheless, the actual relation between the animal
and the god remains unclear to us. In many temples there was
probably one example, a live animal of the species which represented the god, and it was maintained as a sacred animal, for
example, the bull Apis. This also occurred in Greece, where we
hear especially of sacred snakes: of Zeus Sosipolis at Olympia
and the snake Erichthonius of Athene in the Erechtheum on
the Acropolis. And the animals representing the Greek gods are
conceived in essentially the same way: the owl of Athene, the
dog of Hecate, the eagle of Zeus, the wolf of Apollo, and the
bull of Dionysus, etc. In Rome too, the snake was conceived as
the genius of a place or house (the *Agathos daimōn* often portrayed on or near the altar), and there, too, there was Juno's
goat, etc.

How are such notions of deity to be explained, when there is
no idea of a universal principle of life such as is present in the
conception of the earth bull? As a rule these ideas are called
survivals of earlier and extremely primitive notions. But it does
not make the fact any more understandable to label it a "primitive" notion from ancient times. And how are we to explain
"survival"? If men in the historical period had been unable
to form some idea of a sacred animal, they would have abandoned
the notion entirely.

One thing is certain; the animal which was worshipped was
quite differently conceived than we conceive of animals. In one
respect or another the sacred animal of the god was the embodiment of a self-subsistent power or attribute, of a spontaneous
energy not derived from any other source. Men saw in the animal something inexplicable and enigmatic, something inscrutable.
They naturally noted the special capacities of the animals, so
often of superhuman proportions: the keen nose of the dog, the
sharp sight of the bird (according to Horapollo, the vulture
sees carrion at an incredibly great distance; it even sees where
there will be carrion at some time in the future, after a battle),
the capacity of the skin-shedding snake to renew itself, and the
powers of so many other animals. In all these things men certainly saw mysterious and divine attributes, not to be derived
from any other source. These animals belong to a different world

than the one we know; they reveal a different order than the
finite order of nature. Such capacities as mysteriously sharp
sight do not differ from human capacities only in degree, any
more than the divine power differs from the human only in
degree. That which is inexplicable does not belong in the empirical world. Mystery is always a spiritual reality. The sacred
animal is conceived as a spiritual being.

The sacred animal is conceived as spirit. The widespread
conception of the birdlike form of the human soul illustrates
this in a striking way. We do not see anything supra-empirical
in a bird, but other peoples must have regarded a bird differently.
Greeks, Egyptians, and a number of other peoples have represented the human soul in the shape of a bird. Kruyt relates that the
soul or vital power of animals, and even plants, is also thought of
as a kind of crow.[3] But although it is called a "kind of crow,"
or, as by the Greeks, a web-footed bird, it is not viewed in accordance with biology. The believer sees in it quite a different
being from what we see. It is indeed an atmospheric being (anima means both air and soul), but it is definitely a kind of atmospheric being with which we are not acquainted. Neither
is it a "materialistic conception of the soul," for such a soul
bird shows an incredible contempt for "matter." In Greece and
Egypt it is depicted with a human head – which is indeed
the best proof of how unhampered people's conceptions were by
empirical observation. In Middle Celebes people say that when
a man dies, or even sneezes, the soul in the form of a bird flies
out of the nose, which is the organ of breathing.[4] How is this
possible for the "matter" of this bird? And nevertheless it is
called "a bird." Among these people "matter" is not, in the
last analysis, thought of more materially than spiritually. These
people have noted peculiarities of matter to which we pay no
attention, just as we too must express what is spiritual in words
and images which are borrowed from material things. Thus
idea comes from idein; it is "that which can be seen in something,"
thus the spiritually seen, the essence, the idea.

When the soul is conceived as a bird, the idea of an atmospheric being is certainly present. But any animal, of whatever
kind, can in itself be a soul or the bearer of someone's spiritual
essence. It is well known that the (were-) wolf was thought by

the Greeks and the Germanic tribes to be the soul of a man who had died, but we should also realize that the horse, and among many peoples the snake, were thought of in the same way. This is strikingly illustrated in the Egyptian religion. The sacred animals of the various gods are there called "souls": Apis is the "soul" of Ptah, the Phoenix is the "soul" of Re, the ram of Mendes is the "soul" of Osiris. Thus it is precisely the spiritual essence of the god of which the animal is the bearer. This can only mean that the animal represents the supra-empirical, invisible nature of a living being, not the finite and perceptible, but the infinite and imperceptible, the other world. This is in accord with the mysterious essence of animal attributes which we noted above, qualities which differ not in degree but in essence from finite human qualities.

Special emphasis was laid on the essential difference between human and animal activities and capacities. The Ancient peoples among whom we encounter animal worship were accustomed to the idea that all human qualities and capacities are finite and limited, and are even turned against the divine. Men's sensory capacities are finite, because they correspond to the observed finite world; the intellect is finite, just as is that which a man has come to understand; man's power is finite. The infinite and the divine, the absolute, begins on the other side, beyond human capacities; it begins where all humanly limited qualities are transformed. The world which is different from the one known to us is the divine world. To attain its imperishable and absolute life, man must get outside himself and must rise above his finite thinking, his normal judgment, and all his ordinary human characteristics. This, at least among the peoples whom we know the best from authentic documents, is certainly one of the most important motives which have led to animal worship. It is a religious requirement to abandon the human when the absolute must be grasped or portrayed. But that which is above and beyond the human must turn into that which is like the animal. This is a necessity, though it is one which does not necessarily signify the fatal and unwilled consequence of a high aim. The animal is quite consciously chosen as the bearer of superhuman, absolute life, and it is with complete conviction that it is considered as such. The animal represents the uncomprehended mystery of life, and therefore it is called the "soul" of men and gods. It is precisely in the strange behaviour of the animal, its irrational and unethical actions, that the believer sees something that lies beyond human finitude: the superhuman in the religious sense, the absolute. The superhuman is the inhuman, for the sublimation of what is normally human is still not an essential change. The highest human aspirations and ideals do not lead man beyond his finitude – except in those cases when they really shatter him, so that they abolish his human existence (Prometheus).

It is in this light that we should see the close connection between animal worship and the mystery religions, which also grasped absolute life and made it a reality for man. It is noteworthy that there is a close connection between religious ecstasy and animal worship. In the worship of Dionysus, the Thyiads or maenads, the "raving women," went about dressed in the skins of young deer and held snakes in their arms. They were animals, or at least they wanted to be. In ecstasy (*hiera mania*) they dashed over the slopes of the Cithaeron and partook of the god by tearing to bits the living sacrificial animal and eating it raw. In the most ancient times the bull of Dionysus was that sacrificial animal. The leading women participated in this rite. The Delphic priestess Clea, who was so highly esteemed by Plutarch and to whom he dedicated his *De Iside et Osiride*, was herself a maenad. The priests of Dionysus were also identified with the sacred animal of their god and they were called *tauroi*, bulls. And it is noteworthy that this animal ecstasy was also conceived as the highest wisdom, in Greece, of all places! When Pentheus refuses himself and forbids his people to take part in these rites, the seer Tiresias and the old Cadmus participate "as the only wise men among all these foolish folk (namely Pentheus and his people)," "for," says Tiresias, "Dionysus is the seer and he grants the gifts of the seer." Ecstatic madness is precisely to sojourn in the non-finite absolute world. In this sense the animal is mad. Documents of the Germanic religion speak of the wisdom of the raven, the bird of Wodan.

This at the same time explains why Artemis, *Potnia Thērōn*, "mistress of the animals," also had an orgiastic cultus. In Greece this was just as old as the rite of Dionysus. In her worship, the stress rests again on the extrahuman; she is often depicted, not as a human figure, but as a pillar or a navel stone, and she is connected with the Land of the Hyperboreans, the land of bliss, without old age or sickness, from which she came to Delos.

Among the most varied peoples it is the priests and other initiates who are repeatedly identified with some kind of animal. The initiates in the service of Bacchus were called *hippoi*, "horses," those of Demeter-Kore, *pōloi*, "colts," those of Dionysus, *tauroi*, "bulls" or *boes*, "cattle." The Attic priests of Artemis were called *arktoi*, "bears," and Mithra's initiates were *korakes*, "ravens" and *leontes*, "lions." In Rome the Hirpi Sosani were the wolf priests of Dis Pater [5]. This notion has reference not only to priests, for all who wish to perform a superhuman feat can do this by acquiring the capacities of an animal, or by identifying themselves with an animal. In stories about medicine men or sorcerers, we read repeatedly that they assume the shape of a horse, a cat, a frog, or another animal, but each sorcerer can only turn into a particular kind of animal.[6] To be a sorcerer is to possess the *manitu*, the spirit or *mana* power of a particular animal. The power of the sorcerer is derived from the animal. Jamblichus, about 300 A.D., speaks of *magoi leontōn* and *magoi opheōn*, "lion and snake magicians," who likewise possess the power of these animals. In Egypt we find a number of religious texts whose intent is to transform the dead man into some animal, and thereby let him attain that which is impossible for the ordinary human soul: finding the way in the underworld, conquering all sorts of enemies, coming to life again with the sun god, etc.

Usually animal worship is based on the need to get outside human limitations. This explains why animals so often symbolize the realm of the dead or the underworld, the other world, and serve as emblems of various gods. The dog belongs to Hades and Hecate (Cf. the dog's name, Pluto); it is really depicted as a symbol on funeral reliefs, and at certain ritual purifications a dog is sacrificed. The horse belongs to Demeter with the horse-head, to Hades *klytopōlos*, and to Poseidon; white horses are used for funeral sacrifices. The ram's skin belongs to Zeus, *Dios kōidion*. The boar is sacrificed in the grotto to Demeter. The ass of the Hyperboreans is also the symbol of Hephaestus and of Seth. The rooster was considered to be a funeral offering and a "soul bird." The owl was the symbol of Athene. The fish is a funeral offering, etc. It is a difficult question as to why one animal is worshipped more than another. It is clear to us in the case of the snake, the owl and the fish, but much less so with the dog, the horse, the ass, or the ram.

Related to this is the idea of the animal as the saviour, the rescuer from death. As rulers of the realm of the dead and of absolute life, they cause absolute life to arise in the midst of death; it is precisely in this act that their absolute life is revealed. Thus the snake is often considered to be the image of continually self-renewing eternal life (and of eternity). It is also held to be *sōsipolis*, the liberator of the city of Elis. The fish, which knows the way in the sea, which is the underworld, is the saviour from death, as is also the dolphin, who rescues Dionysus, Eros, and the hero Theseus, and so too *ichthys*, is the symbol of Christ the Messiah. The snake of Asclepius and Hygieia, and the Centaur (the horse of Cheiron) are also "saviours" in the sense that they are healers. But because of their great powers as soothsayers, animals are also worshipped as beings connected with the oracles. The Hebrew word for soothsaying, *nāḥash*, is related to the word for snake, *nāḥāsh*. The snake Python bestows absolute insight, that is to say, madness. Seeing Dionysus depicted as a snake makes Eurypylus mad; it takes him out of the world of finitude. Oracles are received from birds by means of *oiōnizesthai* or *auspicere*. The bull Apis made predictions by eating or refusing to eat from the hand of the questioner; by bellowing and shedding tears he predicted the fall of Egypt in 30 B.C. "In nature the highest wisdom reigns everywhere and always" [7]. But that wisdom of the cosmos is infinite and superhuman; its revelation must occur beyond human reason.

These, however, are still only general explanations of the very widespread belief in the sacredness of animals. In general, animal nature is conceived as above and beyond human nature, as a divine nature. This conception is certainly the basis of the religious ideas concerning animals as "symbols" of gods or as themselves divine beings. But as soon as we turn from the general idea of the animal as such to particular cases, we confront greater difficulties. The animal as such or all animals collectively

are never considered sacred; if they were, we could understand
animal worship better. The general aspect of a subject is as a
rule more understandable than the particulars of which the reality itself actually consists. For this reason psychology provides
little help in historical research; it touches only the formal
problems and not the concrete difficulties. We wonder why
particular kinds of animals are considered sacred, why Wodan's
bird was thought to be wise, why the wolf in Greece and in Egypt
was thought to be the guide of souls, and the werewolf was
considered the human soul itself, and why Hecate, the goddess of
the spirits and the dead, had the dog as her sacred animal. The
established facts about these matters are indisputable and sometimes they are elaborately, even excessively, explained. Nevertheless, in many cases they remain inexplicable, and they cannot
be derived from a definite general idea of the animal. Take,
for instance, the significance which is ascribed to the horse in a
great many religions. In the funeral cultus the "soul horse" and
the horse appear very frequently. Numerous Greek reliefs depict
how the dead man at the funeral meal lies on a couch at a
table covered with food, while his wife lies at the foot of the table
and others bring offerings; in one of the upper corners a horsehead is drawn, as in a painting. Sometimes the dead man is
sitting on it, yet this horsehead is not the hero's battle horse,
since it is also depicted in the reliefs of women. A possible explanation is that the horse, which as the animal of the distant
roads (the realm of the dead) brings his rider's journey to a
successful conclusion, represents the saviour in death. The
Dioscuri with their horses are indeed "Saviours." Thus the
horse saves from the realm of the dead. But the god of the realm
of the dead, Hades, is called *Klytopōlos*, renowned for his mares,
and Poseidon is called *Hippios*. The water of the sea, the spring
and the rain are frequently represented by the horse. The rain
god Tishtrya of the Avesta is depicted as a white horse; the
Vedic *Apām napāt* (son of the waters) is called *aurvat-aspa*,
"with the swift horses." These connections usually point to a
definite idea: the horse represents in these cases the life-bringing
energy of water. (Poseidon is *Phytalmios*, the Generating One.)
The horse is sometimes conceived as the divine generator of life.
During the Vedic *ashvamedha*, the horse sacrifice, the sacred horse

after his sacrificial death must be the consort of the queen, and thus be the mysterious procreator of life, just as Dionysus on Chios is the consort of *Basilinna* (the Queen). It has been asked, then, whether a special vital power, a resurrecting energy, has been ascribed to the horse, and whether this is the explanation of the well known *Totenpferd* (death horse) and *Seelenross* (steed of the soul). With familiar Homeric and German admiration for aristocratic knighthood, von Wilamowitz-Moellendorff believes it is, since "the steed is for the Greeks the noblest and most soul-filled animal." With this sort of reasoning we can explain many riddles! We do better to recognize that in spite of abundant and very precise data, we do not understand the symbolism of the horse. In concrete cases the sacredness of animals remains an enigma for us. We are dealing here with "primitive" ideas. This does not mean that they are inferior ideas; they are rather ideas which we do not understand.

CHAPTER 7

TOTEMISM

"Totem" is a word from the Algonquin language, and it means the object, whether animal or plant or something else, which is viewed as the divine representative and bearer of the life of a particular group of people (a tribe or clan). The relationship is of such a kind that the group takes for its name the name of the totem. Totemism was first observed among the American Indians at the end of the eighteenth century; later, about the middle of the nineteenth century, similar ideas were found among the Australian aborigines. In the decade between 1870 and 1880, these ideas were also discovered among other peoples. Whether it is also demonstrable among the Indo-European peoples depends on what one understands by totemism. The most abundant and trustworthy material comes from Australia and America. In 1887 Frazer wrote the first comprehensive survey, *Totemism*. This book is solely descriptive, and the same is true of the four volume work in which it was later included (*Totemism and Exogamy*, 1910).[1] This too is only a collection of data. The first one who tried to penetrate to the heart of the phenomenon was Robertson Smith in his classic *Lectures on the Religion of the Semites* (1889).[2] He relates totemism to the Semitic sacrificial practices, especially with the communal sacrificial meals. According to his theory, the original offering is the sacred animal, which was ritually slaughtered and whose meat was eaten in the sacramental meal. The burnt offering, the actual burning up of the animal, is thus in this view a later practice. This sacred animal is the totem of the tribe, which means that it is related to the tribe while at the same time it represents deity. Man originally sacrifices the god, in the form of the sacred animal, after which by means of the sacral meal he takes the god into himself as divine power. This does not happen, however, because of an individual religious need, for the totem represents the life of the tribe and gives to the tribe its name ("Antelope," "Fish," "Cow," etc.). The sacrificial meal is thus intended to strengthen the tribe's life, and it achieves this by actualizing the unity of the god or totem and man. Sacrifice is then essentially – and originally – social, like the Roman *sacra gentilia* and the Greek *phratria* sacrifices. No one from outside the state can participate in the sacrifice or in the sacrificial meal. It is always very deeply sensed that to eat together means to be taken up into a family relationship. The tribe has originated from the totem, which is an animal species, and there is thus the same relationship between the tribe and the totem as between the various members of the tribe. Tribe, totem, and deity are of one blood. It is natural that the totem sacrifice is the characteristic religious act, as indeed is any sacrifice. The killing of the sacrificial animal was done during certain religious ceremonies. Therefore in Israel the slaughtering of livestock had to be done ritually, for every meal of meat was originally a sacrificial meal: the animal (in this case the ox) was a totem animal, a sacred animal. Thus sacrifice, the sacrifice of the totem, is the characteristic religious act – the believer thereby unites himself with his god. Rites which are clearly totem sacrifices have survived into the historical period, especially the sacrifice of "unclean" animals. That animal is "unclean" which ordinarily may not be eaten because it is "sacred," because it is a totem. But at the sacrifice, and then only, it is indeed eaten. The Cypriotes and the Syrians offered the pig sacrifice to Aphrodite or Adonis; the priests of Atargatis offer daily a sacrifice of fish, which otherwise is forbidden food; Hecate is offered her animal, the dog, etc. At the *Bouphonia* in Athens, there took place the sacrifice of a bull, symbol of vegetation and the growth of grain. Sopatros, who had sacrificed the first bull there and had afterwards fled to Crete, had required all citizens to take part in the sacrificial meal and to accept him as a citizen; thus citizenship was obtained by means of the communal sacral meal.

This is the gist of Robertson Smith's totemistic theory of sacrifice. It is the best known theory of his book, but probably not the most important. The theory has quite rightly been

sharply criticized, especially its generalization that all sacrifices
were originally totem sacrifices. There are certainly other types
of sacrifices, such as the libation, and, moreover, the origin of
something is a dubious explanation of the meaning of the Semitic
tribal consciousness. The tribe possesses a mystical personality
which lives in every member. (This is the basis of blood revenge.)
This tribal consciousness is in any case closely related to ideas
concerning life in the totem. Robertson Smith was certainly
the first to understand the basic idea of totem belief. But it has
become clear since the appearance of his book that the basic
idea provides only a very much simplified abstraction from the
actual data.

Since the time of Robertson Smith's work, the amount of
collected material on this subject has been enormously increased,
and many facts have been more precisely established. The results
of a series of investigations in America have been published in the
Annual Report of the Bureau of American Ethnology. Spencer and
Gillen wrote about totemism in Australia in *The Native Tribes of
Central Australia* and *The Northern Tribes of Central Australia*,
and Howitt has written *The Native Tribes of Southern Australia*.[3] The Australian aborigines are perhaps further removed
from us, because, spread out as they are in the desert, the necessities of life are harder come by than they are in the organized
society of the American Indians.

The central fact in totemistic society is the conception of a
mystical group kinship which forms the basis of each individual
life. It is mystical, because the tribal unity is not only supra-
individual, but also supra-human, grounded in an animal species
or some other non-human being. The life of the tribe is absolute
and divine, not finite and human. Blood kinship plays absolutely
no role here; the concept is not even considered. Only group
kinship is of account. In general, every tribe is divided into two
exogamous groups, each of which is split up into two or four
subgroups, and actually there are even further subdivisions. The
members of a particular subgroup may marry only the members
of one particular subgroup of the other moiety of the tribe. A
man calls all women whom he would have been permitted to marry
– but to whom he is actually not married – by the same term
of relationship as he does his real wife. It is clear from the many

regulations to which he is subject that he is even ritually married to all these other women. All the women whom his father might have married he therefore calls "mother." All the sons of the brothers of his real father he calls "brother." He does not know any other terms of relationship. These relationships also determine all sorts of duties. If one of his many fathers-in-law dies, he must observe various duties of mourning. If he does not do this, all the other fathers-in-law, may give his wife to another husband whom she is permitted to marry, because he has insulted the collective father-in-law group.

Finally, the totem determines the mystical "kinship." The two exogamous groups and their subgroups are divided into a large number of totem groups. Someone from a particular totem group is usually permitted to marry only someone from one other particular totem group. The child belongs to the totem of the father or of the mother or of that totem group within whose territory the mother first noticed that she was pregnant. In any case the most important units of the tribe are determined not by blood relationship, but by the totem, and these are the totem groups. Those who bear the same totem name are "akin" and feel themselves to be of the same blood. This blood relationship actually exists with only one of a man's parents, and in some cases with neither. Individuals are united in very large groups by bounds of a social nature (duties of assistance, vengeance, mourning, and marriage) and of a religious nature (religious festivals, initiations, etc.).

Thus every individual belongs by birth to a particular totem. As a rule the totem, is a plant or animal; in exceptional cases, the wind, sun, moon, water, rain, or fire. But practically all kinds of living or lifeless objects present in the surroundings can serve as totem names. There is an identity between the individual and the totem. A native of Central Australia, whose totem is the kangaroo, sees a photograph of himself and says, "This picture is exactly the same as I – and so too is the kangaroo." [4] Australian totemists of the present day believe that at birth the spirit of one of the ancestors passes into the child. Through the reincarnation of that totem ancestor the child belongs to that totem, or he *is* that totem. Here perhaps we may appropriately use the term, "essential identity," the identity of the essential element, like

that which exists between the symbol and that which is symbolized (for instance between a flag and the nation of which the
flag is a symbol). The contradiction in the term "essential identity" exists only for our logic, which considers that nothing more
is possible than an essential "similarity." Large and small stones
at the totem's home site can represent all kinds of totem animals
or plants, and thus together form the whole species. A large
stone is, for instance, a mature larva, a smaller stone is a pupa,
and other small stones represent the eggs. In keeping with the
notion of essential identity, these stones are used in performing
the ceremonies to cause the species to grow.

The *intichiuma* ceremonies prove that the totem is quite
consciously viewed as the basis of the totem group's life. These
ceremonies are intended to further the life and growth of the
totem. They are performed in the season of the luxuriant growth
and flowering of the young totem animals or plants, usually
at the sacred spot of the totem, where for instance the different
stones represent the totem. While songs are sung in which the
totem is urged to increase in numbers, these symbols are rubbed
and beaten with branches. The life of the totem is strengthened
by all this in order thus to assure the life of one's own tribe in the
absolute and mystical sense. The totem represents the absolute
life of the tribe; the manifold data make this quite clear. The
performers in these ceremonies repeatedly identify themselves
with the totem in quite unmistakable fashion. They play the
part of the totem: in a peculiar fashion they are attired as the
totem, and – while they sing the ancient sacred songs – they
walk or creep in a manner appropriate to the totem animal. They
depict the totem symbol on their bodies; they spill their own
blood on the ground and then draw the totem symbol in it when
it has dried; they walk along the same trail as that taken by the
totem ancestors; they rub the totem symbol into the skin of
their abdomens, etc.[5]

The totemistic ceremonies are actually religious Mysteries in
the ordinary sense of the word. They are concerned with the
mystical basis of the totem group's life. Whereas ordinary rain
magic can be performed or attained by anyone, only the initiates
of the water totem perform the *intichiuma* ceremonies; neither
women, children, or anyone else may be present.

This mystical character of the totem is especially clear in the long drawn out and very complicated initiation rites undergone by the young man until he is thirty. The last rite lasts more than four months and is divided into sixty to seventy sections.[6] The almost exclusive concern of all these rites is the totem mystery: the young man is initiated into the secrets of the tribe. He learns the songs which have been handed down from the totem ancestors; he learns their animal dances (*quabaras*) and their routes of travel; he sees the sacred objects (*churingas*) and learns to understand them; he becomes acquainted with his secret name, which is used only at the ceremonies, and then in a whisper, and repeatedly it is impressed upon him that he must impart nothing of all this to the uninitiated. He begins a new life; at first he may not speak, and he lives three days in the wilderness to symbolize his transition to this new life. A break occurs in his life, similar to that experienced in the initiation into the Mysteries. The mystical basis of his life is imparted to him in connection with the totem secret. He comes to know that he is the incarnation of one of the spirits of his totem ancestors.

The *churingas*, the sacred objects of the Aruntas, represent the totem beings of the past. These pieces of wood or stone, usually oval in shape, about half a yard long and inscribed with the totem symbol, have been left behind by one of the ancestors as his spiritual legacy when he disappeared into the ground, and they are sought and found whenever a child is born. Only at the final initiation are the young men allowed to see this object, and then the totem symbol upon it is inscribed on their bodies. "This evening we want to take you along and let you see your ancestor" is the formula which announces the revelation of this central mystery. The *churingas* are kept in a communal storehouse of the totem group, and are brought out from there during the sacred ceremonies, at which time they are looked over and polished. (Through this repeated polishing the oldest ones have entirely lost their drawing.) The life of the individual is closely related to them, although not in the sense that his life dwells in them. Yet he mourns deeply and fears misfortune if his *churinga* is lost. The word itself means "bull-roarer," the name of an Australian variety of bumble-bee, whose sound discloses the presence of the spirit.

The respect toward the *churingas* is striking, and this respect is shown not only by members of their own totem group, but also by others. Sometimes they are even lent out in a remarkable ceremonial fashion, which certainly attests to much fine sensitivity.[7] The group which wants to borrow the *churingas* first sends an emissary to the other group. When he has arrived, he remains standing outside the camp until he is noticed and it is understood that he comes with a message. The visitor has brought along a few of his own *churingas:* would this tribe keep them for him? The chief understands the intent of his query. If, after consultation with his advisers, he is inclined to part with a larger number of *churingas*, he accepts the objects in a friendly manner without saying anything about them; otherwise he refuses politely. After this the messenger returns home, and shortly afterwards he comes back with a large number of followers. Without speaking of the loan, the parties hold a great feast with dancing, and only in the evening are the *churingas* first brought out. They are inspected by both parties with the utmost interest and then lent: "we are glad to lend them to you; don't hurry to bring them back." The excellence of the *churingas* is then discussed in whispers, after which the emissaries take them along. Their return occurs two years later in equally ceremonious fashion. After the messengers have been sent ahead, the chiefs pay their respects to one another. All sing except the chief of the totem, who is too moved by the occasion and holds his head bowed. The bundle is brought forward and laid on the knees of the totem chief, who then passes it back to its bearers. They then untie the bundle and inspect each piece. "We return your great *churingas*, which have made us glad; we bring you as a gift these fifty cords (of human hair or leather belts), sad that we cannot bring you more," say the emissaries. The totem chief answers them: "we gladly accept these gifts, and we give you these (about fifteen cords). We are sorry not to be able to give you more." Then the visitors are given a meal, and the *churingas* are again carefully inspected.

In all these acts and ceremonies in which the totem symbol stands at the center, that which is of prime religious importance is the actualizing of the identity between the totem and the totem group of human beings. In the ceremonies the totem sign is repea-

tedly inscribed on the body, or dances are done in figures corresponding to the totem sign. This sign makes a man holy; women and
children may not see it. As a rule tattoos are of a totemistic
character, and the American Indians decorate themselves with
parts of the totem animal, for instance feathers as a head
decoration.

Now we must ask the question: what is the religious meaning
of the totem plant or totem animal with which a person is united
and in which he finds the absolute basis of his life? What is this
mysterious guardian and healer? And what conception does a
person have of this totem god? The totem god is certainly not
thought of as a personal being, for it represents the species of
animal or plant. It must be the mysterious mana power which
appears in these groups of objects. This may seem vague and
tenuous to us, but for the believer it is something very real and
tangible, able to arouse the deepest emotions and to regulate
an entire society. The data indicate that there is here a remarkable sense of close connection between man and nature surrounding him, a nature worship in the broadest sense. These people
are aware of a cosmic context which includes man and most
profoundly determines him. The idea of the mysterious power
of the objects in the surroundings corresponds to the consciousness of being determined by the infinite, and this is a genuine
religious feeling. The general sense of connection with the surroundings is accentuated with respect to the objects which constitute the totem. It is remarkable how the Australians consider
all the particulars of the land, such as rocks, crevices, trees, and
pools of water, as signs of the life and activity of the mythical
ancestors. The ancestors have made the crevices and the passes
in the mountain ranges in order to get through them. The rocks
and trees have sprung up where they set down their sacred objects on the ground, or their spirit went immediately into a rock
or tree. An individual still living can thus have his *nanya* stone
or tree. At least Spencer and Gillen relate an instance of an abo-
rigine who earnestly requested them not to chop down a particular tree. Thus does nature reflect human activity. But the
human spirit has also taken on the colour of the nature surrounding
him and thereby identified himself with his totem being. The
mystery of absolute life lies just in this connection between

man's spirit, on the one hand, and on the other hand, the powers surrounding him, mysterious forces which reveal themselves in nature outside man and are localized in a species of animal or plant.

CHAPTER 8

ANIMISTIC AND DYNAMISTIC IDEAS

Until 1867 all especially strange forms of worship and every expression of "primitive" religion or cultus was called "fetishism." But in 1867 in a lecture to the Royal Society in London, Edward Tylor pointed out the existence of a large number of similar religious facts for which he considered a new name necessary: "animism." By this he meant, "the child-like conception of the animation of all of nature" and the belief in "countless spiritual beings who are at work in the whole process of nature." The term "animism" really signifies an important discovery in the field of ethnology, and it was maintained until increasing insight into the character of the phenomena made the necessity of a second division apparent. The term "animism" also proved to be covering data which were too dissimilar. The belief in the activity of countless spiritual beings is undeniable, but "spirits" is in many cases an inaccurate term. A "spirit" is an individual, personal being with a definite will, confronting men as a friend or foe, but in many forms of belief this individual element is absent. The objects or phenomena themselves are spiritually determined, and there is no distinction between "spirit" and "nature." This is thus a step still further away from our thinking. This new group of data contained "manifestations of power" and "dynamistic" ideas. The first one to point this out was the English missionary Codrington in *The Melanesians, Studies in their Anthropology and Folklore* (1891).[1] He gives no theory concerning the characteristic religious phenomena, but solely a description of the Melanesians. Back in 1878 he had already written letters to Max Müller about these phenomena, and the latter immediately understood their importance and set them forth, giving Codrington the credit for discovering them. "Power" is called "mana" in Melanesia; among the Bataks it is called "tondi," and the North American Indians refer to it as "orenda," "manitu," or "wakonda."

The terms fetishism, animism, and dynamism have continued to be used alongside one another to designate different groups of data. The distinctions among these groups are certainly an important result of modern ethnography and ethnology.

We do not need to stop here to consider typical animism; it has frequently been described more or less accurately in travelogues and missionary literature. There are spirits of the dead in many forms, spirits of natural phenomena such as rain, wind and sea, and spirits of sickness. And sometimes there are spirits unrelated to particular natural phenomena: "evil spirits" who can exercise a fatal influence at critical moments in life. It is by means of cultic acts (sacrifices, and the like) or magic practices that all of them are called upon for assistance, appeased, and kept at a safe distance.

The boundary between animistic and dynamistic ideas is quite fluid. Codrington tells of a Melanesian who is very much feared because out of affection for his dead brother he has made arrowheads from his bones; he no longer speaks of "I" but of "we both." According to the Melanesian explanation "he has the mana of his brother," which in our terminology comes close to saying that he possesses his brother's spirit. The idea of the "rice soul" in Indonesia is very well known. The nutritive power ascribed to the "soul" of the rice is sometimes conceived quite personally as a being with an autonomous will. Kruyt lists various measures to keep her alive: she is fead, not only by fertilizing the field, but also by touching the heads of rice with food; otherwise the rice would rot. Strangers can attract the rice soul to themselves and take her along with them; therefore during the harvest no stranger is allowed in the village. Nor may one frighten the rice soul by making noise or insulting her with improper language. All this attests to genuine "animism." But at the same time people also worship the rice mother who represents the rice soul of the whole field and who bears and holds together the separate souls. She consists of a sheaf of large and powerful rice stalks that is brought home with care and kept in a storehouse – it must definitely not be eaten. She is the but slightly personal power of the rice, the power whereby the rice soul exists and is identified with the sheaf of rice. European peoples also treat "the last sheaf of grain" with respect and keep it in order to assure the nutritive power of the grain. Kruyt speaks of the "soul stuff" of rice and of various other objects. This conception is indeed suitable for indicating a transitional form between animism and dynamism, but his terms "soul" and "stuff" are hardly adequate. It is true that the "soul" of the rice is the same word as the "soul" of man, yet the concept "rice soul" is also very close to "power" or "fluid." By a given act, for instance by touching, it can be transferred from one object to another; it is thus a spiritual energy, not a "soul" or "material."

Tylor is mistaken in his opinion that each living object, or just any object at all can be conceived "animistically." Only those objects can be so conceived which are believed to possess a self-subsistent energy on which man is dependent. Animism is thus not a "primitive natural philosophy" of universal validity. Foodstuffs (rice, cocoanuts and cloves) possess this spontaneous power in a high degree; they bring forth life. Other "useful" objects, such as wood for huts or boats and stones for tools, are also believed to possess this spontaneous power. They are not merely "means" which man uses, for he does not control them. He does not understand why they are necessities for his life. In general this attitude is also understandable to us. Yet these similar general feelings do not take away the distance between our thinking and theirs; our scientific conception is diametrically opposed to animism and dynamism. The difference is based not so much on different epistemological axioms as on the feelings which accompany them. Dayak men will not eat deer meat because deer meat would make them become timid. They believe that the soul of the meat passes into them or (thinking dynamistically) that the meat affects them in keeping with its assumed nature. We see no truth at all in such a notion. Deer meat simply contains certain nutritive elements which necessarily have a certain effect after they are digested. According to both conceptions the "dynamis," the power, of the meat which is eaten is transferred to man, and in both views this happens through an inexplicable process. The difference between these views lies clearly in the conception of the "dynamis" and its effect. We consider it to be a non-spiritual energy, a consequence of the consumption of foodstuffs, a process which is set in motion by the non-spiritual cause of appetite, the instinct of hunger. The Dayak sees in this "dynamis" a spiritual energy of fear or courage, which is based on a spiritual motive – the horror of cowardice. He does not see himself in this situation as being determined by circumstances lying outside his grasp; neither is he determined as courageous or fearful by his character or inheritance. No, he develops himself in accord with his wish, will and need. He wants to be courageous and is convinced that he can indeed make himself courageous, for he knows the means to realize his will. He has his fate in his own hands. The Dayak differs from us in his conception of the nutritive process; his attitude is active while ours is passive. Now this dynamistic world view can, it is true, be coupled with fear ("it is dangerous to eat deer meat"), yet it clearly springs from a wider notion of man's sustaining himself than our minds can entertain. Man is "spiritual," determined by spirits, "dynameis," but he is also himself a spirit and not the passive object of all manner of influences; he knows the magic means to protect himself. "Nothing happens to us because it just has to happen." Man confronts other spirits as one who is himself a spirit. For this reason the difference between animism or dynamism and our rationalistic attitude is not an epistemological difference respecting causes and effects, but a psychic difference.

The animistic and dynamistic world views are clearly not explicable solely on the basis of a deficient knowledge of nature. Something positive, a practical need of man, is a contributing factor; his own interests take control. In this respect the relations are the same as in the case of mythical ideas. The religious nature myth is not to be explained simply on the basis of a mistaken or deficient view of nature. There are certain positive religious needs behind it, and it has a certain definite purport. The deficient view of nature is only the other side of the belief in the spiritual character of the natural phenomena on which we are dependent. For this view is solely concerned with these natural phenomena, not with a theoretical explanation of nature such as is given by natural philosophy.

Here we are in the area in which agreement with our point of view comes to light. We, too, are not determined by "natural laws." We are not essentially dependent on non-spiritual influences and energies; "non-spiritual energies" is a term which is itself a contradiction. "Natural laws" are not "energies" and are not even objective realities. They are solely the formulations of the observed (not essential) similarities between phenomena. And when animistic or dynamistic views are formulated in the same way as our rationalistic cause and effect theories, if for instance it is said that feeding the rice soul *causes* the growth of the rice, these views are certainly false natural laws, but they are true laws of the spirit; the irrational act corresponds to the really irrational character of the process.

The world view of astrology is a good example of how false natural laws can be true spiritual laws. It has been a conception containing great spiritual power and important truth, which has such value as to balance its objective (one might even say, evident) lack of value. That truth is this: the Kingdom of Heaven also possesses sovereign power on earth.

Scholars have often failed to appreciate the spiritual significance of false natural laws which have continued to be held for many generations. The evolutionist philosopher Herbert Spencer contends in his *First Principles* that the animistic conception cannot possibly be original; it must be secondary, the result of a partially understandable view. He claims that even a dog does not make such mistakes in distinguishing the "living" from the "lifeless." A dog would not think that a living power is present in a peculiarly shaped stone or in an arrowhead. Man must have been brought to this madness by considerations of a quite different kind. According to Spencer's theory, what is primary is the belief in the freedom of man's soul in sleep or death. This soul can then take up residence in various objects and thus make them living, and so animism originates.[2] A. Réville challenges this theory: animals do not make mistakes of this kind, but it is man's privilege to be mistaken – more so than less intelligent beings. That is correct. Animal instinct includes no hesitation and no freedom for interpretation. Man, with his sense of responsibility, confronts numerous possibilities, among which he must choose, and he confronts various considerations of an intellectual and ethical nature. The possibility of deviating from his spiritual destiny is the condition of spiritual life. No creature can sink deeper or climb higher than he. The impersonal accurate apprehension, which is most important for the animal, is not always most important for him. He strives after other more imaginative and subjective goals in order to maintain his spiritual superiority. This is true also in the purely intellectual realm: the scientists who have never made any serious mistakes, such as the collectors of documents, who catalog, register and state facts, have not been the greatest scientists – they have not realized the spiritual value of their research. It is fair to say that the nebulous animistic idea that phenomena have a spiritual significance is more valuable for man's world view and self-consciousness as a spiritual being than is an unimaginative observation of objects. Animism is mistaken, but its mistake is full of promise.

The general and basic agreement between the animistic way of thinking and our own lies in the active character of man's relation to his environment, in his maintaining himself against the world. Man is not essentially determined by "natural laws" or circumstances; he determines himself in keeping with his own desire and will. The spiritual, personal factor, which is an active factor, is operative whenever man rises above the natural determination. In principle, therefore, the animistic and dynamistic ways of thinking do not differ from our own. Even when we think we are describing the impersonal and non-spiritual in the natural process, we do so in terms borrowed from the realm of will and spirit: gravitational "force," centrifugal "force," "energies" which for instance are set in motion by combustion. Even "natural law" is as a rule conceived animistically or dynamistically as the regular and stable will of phenomena and objects. Man is essentially spiritual and free. It is for this reason that there are so many "false natural laws" which correspond to true spiritual laws. Moreover, the possibility of making serious mistakes is the privilege of spiritual man.

We see that the principle of the superiority of spirit to nature is unconditionally maintained. All of nature is put entirely at the service of human goals: the magical act gives practical expression to the omnipotence of the human will. The absoluteness of this goal requires absolute means, and therefore inscrutable factors are put to work. Household animals and plants are among the necessary conditions for human life; thus they must prosper. This is achieved by applying rational means with care and diligence, but the greatest and deepest result is achieved in different fashion, by using pieces of stone or wood which are full of mana power for animals and plants. A tree will grow without this added power, but not rapidly. Without it a net will not catch many fish, and a boat will not go as swiftly and safely as possible. If someone finds a peculiarly shaped stone, he sees that this stone is certainly not an ordinary one; it displays an autonomous nature – there must be power in it. Then he tests it by putting it on the ground at the root of a tree; the result shows whether he was right. A bunch of leaves on his waistband or a tooth tied to the finger which draws the bow brings success in warfare or hunting. And there are numerous similar customs. The strength and hardness which constitute the power of iron are viewed not as objective properties, but as images, symbols, bearers of human power, will and life. It is for this reason that iron can heal. Man attaches his desires to this object in order to gain a share in its power. The mysterious energy imparts itself through touch, or simply through the intention of the act. This is the living nature of this energy; a relation exists like that between two people. According to Codrington, the prosperous Ambonese "sacrifices" a pig in order to increase his own power. He sacrifices it not to a god or spirit, and without an intermediary. Human sacrifice also strengthens the household, not through the mediation of a household god or spirit, but through the directly transferred power. The same idea lies behind head hunting. A similar act, but more easily performed, is the borrowing of someone else's sacred objects, such as the borrowing of *churingas* among the totemistic Australians.

All magical practices attest more or less clearly to the belief in the superiority of spirit to nature. Castrén (Roskoff, 132), who was better acquainted with shamanism than anyone else, asks rhetorically, "Who will not immediately concede that all of shamanism is a protest against the blind violence of the powers of nature against the human spirit?"

All these expressions of belief in man's unlimited capacity

to maintain himself belong to a realm which is not altogether strange to us. But it is wrong to pay attention exclusively to the subjective factor in this mental attitude. The believer himself does not feel that he has personally created these spirits or powers and actualized them according to his own capacity. And we do not understand him if we say that that is actually all he has done. The "rice mother" is not a creation of his own mind; for his consciousness she has an objective existence. The same is the case with all the other powers which he puts in his service; they nevertheless remain independently existing powers. His attitude toward spirits and powers is not an attitude of subjective caprice. He is also dependent on these powers. It is true his dependence is spiritual and not natural, yet he is by no means simply their master. This is the actual situation, difficult perhaps for us to understand, but it is the religious reality.

The superiority of spirit to nature is maintained unconditionally. But "spirit" is in this connection an ambiguous term. It is not identical with "man"; the sense of the finite nature of man's capacity is also essential. As a spiritual being man can exercise absolute and infinite power, but this clearly is sensed to be something extraordinary. The primitive man, too, knows that his magical act belongs to an order of things different from his ordinary activities. When he is practising magic he must observe all sorts of special rules and regulations. The mysterious power which under certain conditions he can command is in the last analysis stronger than his own power. It has an autonomous reality, and if man is careless, it can turn against him. The same objective factor is here operative which is present in every religious act. Man performs magical-religious acts with awe, because he is in contact with powers which extend beyond him. In other words, he is himself finite spirit, but the basis of his existence is infinite. And this basis is one he does not himself control. Thus the rice mother has an autonomous and objective existence outside man; she constitutes the basis of his existence, a basis which is not dependent on him. The autonomous existence outside him makes him dependent and constitutes his religious attitude of respect, awe, and reverence. Only in and through his religious relation is he omnipotent; i.e., only so does he win the rice mother for himself.

It is not true that man creates his gods, or that the gods are reflections of his wishes, and thus actually his equals (Feuerbach). In reality, namely in his own evaluation, equals are precisely what they are not; they are rather his superiors. The element of transcendence is essential here, and it appears in all primitive forms of religion, as well as in other forms. Indeed it can be said with a certain justice that man prescribes laws to nature on the basis of his own needs – true spiritual laws, but untrue natural laws – and impresses them upon it. In astrology he does this consistently. He does it to a lesser degree when he assumes a causal relation between the growth of a tree and the power of a little stone. But this still does not mean a denial of the objective factor in the religious relation. It does prove that he has not thought of nature as matter. "Prescribing laws" is an effort to grasp the spiritual character and essence of nature. And the religious element in this activity is man's coming into a practical relationship with nature so conceived, which thus possesses objective reality, and this relationship is, more specifically, that of absolute dependence (as for instance in the relation to the rice mother). By means of these spiritual laws, this relationship of friendship on the basis of vital interest, a personal contact is brought about between man and cosmos. But in this context, too, the absolute spirit extending beyond us continues to stand over against our spirit. This religious relationship exists in worship.

This is the religious significance of the external and sensory nature of those objects which according to animism and preanimism contain spiritual powers. These objects have an objective existence. God reveals himself in the objective world (whether material or spiritual); He stands beyond and over against us.

In the animistic and pre-animistic religions, too, the religious man is at the same time both spiritually free and spiritually bound. We find this characteristic combination of freedom and dependence in all religions.

We sense, however, that the riddles of these forms of religion have not yet been solved, not even when we understand all this in general terms. The difficulty lies in this concept of nature, which is alien to our way of thinking. As modern men we work with

categories (matter and spirit, personal and impersonal) which
are quite unsuited for application to these data. Only he is able
to give the right explanation who through personal contact
with the believers has really learned their way of thinking and
feeling. But if he then came back to explain it to us, we should
not be able to understand him either; we might just as well
have a Papuan come to talk to us!

What is most difficult for us to understand in these forms of
religion are the expressions of the sense of an uncomprehended
and passive dependence on the spirits and powers which determine the life of man. We are speaking in particular of that sense
of fear which according to the reports of missionaries and other
observers dominates the life of the primitives – certainly not
the only feeling, but indeed a very real and concrete one. The
Roman concept "religio" is close to this and can help us to gain
some understanding of this sense of fear. Cicero derives *religio*
from *re-lego*, meaning to keep together, to ponder, to be attentive
and cautious; thus *religio* is awe and fear. But it also indicates
the object of this awe: the supernatural, mystical, magical
nature of something, the "mana" (for example, *fani religio*, the
sacred nature of the temple, the awe which the temple arouses).
The *fascinus*, a phallic symbol, protects the child *religione* by
its "sacredness" or the mystical-magical effect which it has.[3]
The *prodigia*, the portents, are *religiones*, supernatural revelations.[4] And the notion of *religiosus* is quite similar to that of
tabu. According to Festus, the sepulcre is *religiosum;* days on
which nothing can be done but that which is quite necessary are
religiosi.[5] "That is *religiosum* which one is not permitted to do;
if one does it anyway, it happens contrary to the divine will."
Man's *religio* is the attitude which corresponds to the objective
religio, this entirely mystical or magical sphere which surrounds
him. The *religiosus* acts circumspectly, sensing the secret and
supernatural powers which are present round about him. *Religio*
is thus fear, but it is fear containing the mystical element of
awe towards that which is inscrutable and sovereign. This is the
psychological explanation of *religiosus* as well as of *tabu*. *Religiosum est, quod propter sanctitatem aliquam remotum ac sepositum
a nobis est"* [6]: "*religiosus* is that which is removed and separated
from us by any sort of sanctity." The holy repels and inspires

fear, but its positive side is that it is also the source of the greatest power.

Sometimes tabu regulations have a quite general purport and are not connected with particular objects. An entire area can be tabu, just as it can possess a mana property, a sanctity. An instance of this is the ceremonious way of speaking and acting during the performance of magic, which sometimes includes the use of peculiar language especially learned for the occasions. In Assam, the spiritual headman can decree a *genna*, a state of general abstinence, whenever something abnormal has happened such as an earthquake, eclipse, attack by enemies or wild animals, or an epidemic; or if something important and difficult must take place, like sowing, or bringing the souls of the dead to rest. Then the village gates are closed; men and women eat apart; food tabus become effective, and commerce, fishing, and hunting are forbidden. The state of dread makes caution imperative: any activity can cause a dangerous discharge of mana. More than at any other time people feel themselves surrounded by the unknown and the unaccountable. Who is able, in the last analysis, to trace the effects of our actions, and who knows the course and control of events? Superhuman powers are at work, so caution dictates a general tabu.

It is especially the mana power of the king which by any number of primitive peoples is a factor of the highest importance for the life of the people. Many ethnographers have treated this subject, and a whole literature has developed about it, of which Frazer's *Lectures on the Early History of Kingship* is especially worth mentioning.[7] The king is a divine man or a man-god, a god among men on earth, the revealed god who has become man, the son of the invisible god in the heavens. Such was the conception in Egypt and Babylonia, and this is also the character of the ancient Greek and Roman kingship. By means of his mana power the king bestows life on the people, and he looks after fertility and prosperity. According to a Norwegian royal saga, the rivalry of the different sections of the country for the body of King Halvdan the Black was met by giving each section a portion of the corpse. Worship of the king is the most important religious and social principle among a great many peoples; social life is entirely determined by it. A great role is played in this worship by the collective will to live, the law of the society's life. This law is supra-individual and therefore is but slightly subject to rational criticism. It is supported by the communal tradition and exists independently of individual insights. The authority of the king and the kingship is undoubtedly based in part on the requirements of the collective consciousness embodied in custom and tradition, for which no one can give a rational explanation. A power is ascribed to the king which is closely akin to the mysterious mana power. For us this is a hint as to how we can gain some kind of understanding of the character of the belief in mana.

A prince is also tabu, too sacred to be touched. The Malayan annals relate how difficult it was to find a wife for the founder of the Malayan dynasties; there was too great a difference in the quality and quantity of mana power. What the king touches is also tabu.[8] Until two hundred years ago the food of the Mikado always had to be cooked in new pots, which were broken after they were used. The food which the Mikado had eaten continued to be linked with the rest of the food in the cooking pots; the part is an image of the whole (*loi de la participation mystique:* "the law of mystical participation). This belief has frequently elicited its own proof. Frazer tells of a case in New Zealand. A slave came along the same road which the prince had taken a little while before. He found some food left over from the royal meal and he ate it. "I knew that unfortunate man well," says Frazer's informant, "– he was a strong, courageous fellow in the prime of life." But no sooner had the man heard that he had eaten the prince's food than he was stricken with a severe cramp, which continued until he died, on the same day.[9]

Strangers are also tabu.[10] They belong to strange gods and bring with them strange, supernatural power. Nieuwenhuis tells how in Borneo during the visit of men from a distant tribe, no woman had left her house without taking along a little bundle of smouldering bark.[11] Embassies are frequently received only after ceremonial purifications. The emissaries must in such cases stand with their gifts between fires; they are sprinkled with water or they and their vehicles are brushed off with branches. The Australians burn little sticks "to cleanse the air" when they are in foreign territory or come back home from a journey.

It is very common for women to be tabu. They too are laden with super-natural power. Psychology explains this as arising in the last analysis from a certain natural nervousness of one sex towards the other. Often every woman is considered a potential witch. Especially just after the birth of a baby, she is stringently separated and must subject herself to all sorts of purifications. The Avesta praises all that which brings forth life as divine and belonging to Mazda, considers agriculture the highest religious duty, and believes barrenness to be a serious sin. It is quite noteworthy, therefore, that it is the Avesta which prescribes the most stringent measures of purification for the woman who has just borne a child. Similar purifications are prescribed in one other case, after touching a corpse. The woman is tabu just because she is sacred; she is just as dangerous as the corpse, and actually for the same reason, because of the supernatural element, her mana. Naturally it is just the ordinary and everyday things that possess no mana power which are tabu for the sacred one. All the negative prescriptions of fasting, continence, and other special actions during preparation for sacred rites are a consequence of this.

Remarkably enough, it is just the objects and persons most highly provided with mana and most strictly tabu who are themselves most accessible to the dangerous influence of alien mana. The king may never be seen eating or drinking, lest he be affected by the dangerous influence of the evil mouth and the evil eye. At Loango, in the French Congo, all those present prostrate themselves, and if a dog is present in the room when the king sits down to eat, it is killed on the spot. We frequently hear of kingdoms in which the king may never be seen by the people. Herodotus describes how in Media an imposter took advantage of this fact by pretending to be the king.[12] Warriors, too, are subject to all sorts of tabus. Sometimes they are not permitted to walk on the beaten paths, etc. It is understandable that he who is himself laden with mana lives in a permanent state of tension in which it is difficult to keep his balance. He stands outside the earthly order, and this state of sanctity causes a lasting disquietude of the most painful caution and watchfulness.

The Roman concept *religio* undoubtedly formulates a religious

attitude which is very difficult for us to understand in the forms
it takes among peoples who are culturally far removed from us.
However, we can also discover the idea of a mysterious, magical
power ("mana") in particular objects and acts in religions which
are in many respects closer to our own. The credit for having
pointed this out belongs to Nathan Söderblom.[13] He directs our
attention to the concept Brahman in Vedic religion and especially in later Brahmanism. The oldest meaning of Brahman is
Sacred Formula, the Sacrificial hymn, which by the power of
the word made the offering effective. It possesses the same
autonomous power as the creative power of the word whereby
the gods perform their activities. Brahman in the neuter is the
term for the divine power in general; Brahman in the masculine
is the designation of the priest who controls this power by means
of the sacred sacrificial rites, and who is himself called "a god."
In the philosophical elaboration of Brahmanism, Brahman is
the divine essence of all existence, the impersonal "soul" of the
cosmos. This "soul" or "self" ($\bar{A}tman$) transcends all outward
forms; "I myself" is the comprehensive principle of all the expressions of my being. The Brahman is indeed the theoretical
formulation of the mystical and magical power which reveals
itself in man and nature. There is an unmistakable affinity
between this conception and the Melanesian conception of mana.

In the Avesta, the *khvarnah* is the splendour and glory created
from Mazda, which is in everything belonging to Mazda's kingdom. It is the power of the gods and of everything which permanently exists. It does to be sure have a different character
than that of Brahman. Brahman eludes all expression in words;
it is eternal and unchangeable. *Khvarnah* reveals itself in the
triumph of life and in the glorious deeds of gods and men. The
people of India have not produced any history, whereas the
people of the Avesta have done so. The Avesta religion was
directed towards an historical goal: the actualizing of the Kingdom of Mazda, which will be realized at the end of time. *Khvarnah*
is the same energy that is present in mana.

PART II

ANTHROPOLOGY

CHAPTER 9

MAN'S ORIGIN

Most of the religions which we know contain theories and doctrines in mythological form concerning the origin of the human race or the creation of the first man. Thus we read in Genesis 2 : 7 that God formed Adam from the dust of the earth. Such theories are important, especially because the believer also expresses in them his conception of the essence of man. And this is a subject which greatly interests us. Time and again it becomes evident that ideas concerning origins are determined by the total impression on man of all that which exists. Myths about origins are formulations of what man considers to be the foundation and the essence of existence.

In Babylonia, Rome and Egypt, there are religious myths about the origin of human civilization, with all its laws, social institutions, and arts, such as agriculture, etc. They give an explanation of what exists by tracing it back to a divine revelation. The god of the underworld, Ea, Saturn or Osiris, as the case may be, has in the beginning granted or revealed to men the structures of civilization. It is quite clear what these myths signify. An irreducible factor was sensed in the existing civilization and was conceived as the constitutive law of society (the basis of its life). But such constitutive laws are not thought up by human insight. As the foundations of life they are divine realities with which men are always confronted. The existing civilization is felt to be a divine reality, and therefore the origin of the civilization has been ascribed to a divine revelation. The myth of the origin is only a projection into the past of what exists in the present. Although the form of the myth is historical – "Once upon a time..." –, the content is ideal.

Such myths are still formed at the present time, even by those who believe they are thinking scientifically and rationally. This is the case when, for example, it is assumed that the origin of human civilization must be sought in the simplest material and organic needs of "primitive" man to assure individual and collective existence, and that therefore the struggle for physical existence is the origin of all civilization. This too is a mythical projection of that which is conceived at present as the foundation of life. It is the expression of a materialistic and sense-bound conception of the basis of life. No one has observed the origin; the idea of the origin therefore always remains a theory. It can be a religious or a materialistic theory, but in religions as well as in so-called rational sciences it is a myth, a projection into the past of what one in the present sees or thinks he sees. Those who do this believe that they can give a genetic explanation of a given reality, but they only project into an historical past what they consider to be the essential element of that reality, and then they speak of its "origin." Such myths never explain what exists, but they do inform us about the conceptions of those who have formulated the myths. It is for that reason that the religious myths about the origin of man are so important. They teach us what has been thought about the essence of man.

In most of the religions with which we are acquainted, there is the sense or conscious notion of an organic connection between man and the natural world surrounding him which comes to the fore in the myths dealing with man's origin. This is the feeling or consciousness of participating in cosmic life. But this connection is conceived, not in general terms, but always in relation to particular, cosmic manifestations of life. If we limit ourselves to the religions of Antiquity, which can inform us the most accurately because they give extensive literary descriptions, then we are struck by the noticeable agreement in the conception that the life of man is organically bound up with the life of the earth. Man has originated from the earth. In this religious doctrine concerning the origin of man, the conception of the whole essence of man is expressed. Man lives the life of earth and dies the death of earth.

He is created from the earth, from clay or loam. This is not because soft clay has been the modeling material most used for

vases, statues and bricks in all known periods of history, but
because man is earth and a possessor of the properties of earth.
It may be uncertain whether "Adam" is etymologically related
to "Adama," "clay earth," but it is certain that the writer of
Genesis 2 : 7 believed that the two words essentially corresponded
in meaning. The typical Babylonian man, though not expressly
called the first man, is Enkidu, or in Akkadian, Eabāni, "creature of Ea." Now this Enkidu was modeled by the goddess
Aruru from the clay of the earth. The Greek term *auto-chthōn*,
"from the land itself "or "native," probably also contains the
idea, "from that part of the earth where he later continued to
live." Prometheus forms men from moist earth; he is the Titan,
born from the earth, the enemy of the gods, but the special
protector of men. This myth indicates a contrast between mortal
men and the divine powers which is very characteristic for the
conception of man's nature. In this respect the myth of the son
of Prometheus and the earth goddess Pandora, Deucalion, and
his wife Pyrrha is especially clear. After their rescue from the
Flood, they inquire in Delphi from Themis (or Ge) how mankind
can again come into being. The answer of Themis is, "Throw the
bones of the Great Mother (Mother Earth) behind you." They
throw the stones of the earth behind them, and these become
dust, from which men come into being. In Athens, the earth
demon in the form of a snake, Erechtheus, was the progenitor
of the citizens; he was worshipped on the Acropolis as an earth
spirit.

A variation of this conception is the notion that men originally
grew up as trees. According to Bundahishn 15 : 1–5, the first
human couple, Mashya and Mashyana or Mashyoi, "the mortals,"
consisted of trees which had grown together, in which Mazda
created human life so that they changed into man and woman.
According to Phrygian tradition, too, men grew up as trees;
they were *dendrophyseis*. Among the Germanic tribes, the ancestors of men were called Askr and Embla, ash and elm. This
is related to the frequently occurring idea that the life of an
individual or a people is dependent on the existence of a tree.
The sacred olive tree on the Acropolis in Athens represented the
life of the Athenian nation. We are also acquainted with life
trees for particular individuals. (Cf. the Dutch *Koninginnebo-*

men, "Queen's trees." * They are trees of fate, of "moira"-mo-
res, that is to say, of the life determined in the underworld.

The tree is in this and many other myths the bearer of the life
of the earth which reveals itself in the growth of vegetation.
Created from the tree, therefore, means the same thing as created from the earth. But the life of the earth has an ambiguous
nature; it contains death as well as life. Man's subjection to
death is already determined by his origin. "The origin" expresses the essence. The special god of the human race, the protector
and friend – often against the other gods – is actually the earth
god, the god of the underworld. The Babylonian "god of that
which is below," thus of the underworld, Ea, is called in a special
sense, "the lord of mankind." He is also the rescuer or saviour
of mankind in the Flood; "rescuer" because as god of the kingdom of the dead and of the underworld he causes life to rise from
death; he "rescues." The snake in Paradise (Genesis 3) was
probably formerly a special god of men. In any case, according
to that account, men have chosen the side of the snake, with
the civilization and knowledge belonging to the snake. Hermes
Chthonios, the earth god, is also the special friend of men:
Philanthrōpos or *Philandros*.

This is the significance of the religious myths about the origin
of man. He is essentially from earth, and he absorbs the earth's
life as he uses the earth's products to live. We are here confronted
with a characteristic expression, not of the aesthetic, but of the
religious sense of nature, a sense that is encountered in all Ancient religions. It conceives of nature spiritually and not "materially." The life of the earth can be the life of man because the
life of the earth, too, is a self-subsistent, that is to say, a spontaneous and spiritual reality; that which is material is not self-
subsistent, it is finite and finally reducible to a more ultimate
substance. In all these religions the life of the earth is conceived
as the typical mystery; it is that which exists from its own power
and by itself, the imperishable and constantly self-renewing. In
the life of the earth a divine and self-subsistent life was seen.
That life was absolute because it also included death. It characterized the life of man. The Ancients conceived the mystery

---

* Memorial trees, planted on the occasion of the birth or coronation of a king or
queen. *Trans.*

of the manifestations of life in nature and in man more vividly and clearly than we with our orientation towards the natural sciences are able to do. For that reason they could say that man is organically connected with the earth and originated from the earth. That was the way that the divine nature of their life was expressed. Man is thus included in the mystery of the earth and shares in it. In particular, he knows the mystery of death, which at the same time is life; he knows the victory over death, just as the earth knows it. It is man's glory that he in this sense lives the life of the earth and dies the death of the earth.

It was said in Egypt that man originated from the tears of the sun god. Now the Egyptian word for "man" is *rmt*, and *rmj.t* is "tears," but this play on words does not by itself give a sufficient explanation of the idea. According to the Egyptians, life was situated in the eye, so that "come forth from Re's eye" is the same as "originated from Re's life." The myth relates that it was in this way that man originated, just when Shu and Tephnut had brought to Re the eye which he had lost and when he had thereupon collected his organs, that is to say, had restored himself from death. We thus have to do with an idea well known in Egypt, that the life of men is the resurrected life of the sun god. This conception of the origin of human life, however, does not diverge very far from the idea familiar in other religions of his origin from the earth. For the life of the sun god Re is the life of the earth. Re lives by the power of the earth, and he has communicated that power to man.

CHAPTER 10

MAN'S 'VITAL PRINCIPLE'

How in the various religions, has life been conceived as the opposite of death, and in particular, how has human life been conceived?

We do not, of course, encounter any attempts expressly to define "life," and we do not find any theoretical reflections about it. Even we modern men, who are rather eager to define concept and essence, do not venture to do so. The adherents of the non-Christian religions were even less so inclined. They were much more deeply filled than we are with a sense of the mystery of life. But in what context did they see human life, and what did they consider to be its universal and characteristic expressions?

It is certain that the Ancients thought differently about life than we do. In the first place, they applied the term "life" more widely, not only to men, animals and plants, but also to cosmic beings in the broadest sense. Nature in its entirety was, to their way of thinking, a living being. "Natura" is derived from *nascor*, "to be born," and the Greek word *physis* from *phyō* "to cause to come into being, to generate, to grow." Life is the eternal element in things, that which is always renewing itself. For that reason it is conceived as a revelation from deity, from the god who reveals himself in the universe. The nature gods, such as the sky and the heavenly bodies, earth and water, are facets of cosmic life. The divine activity is visible in the enduring life, in the governing of the whole cosmos. Included in that context, human life is equally imperishable; it stands in a special connection with the life of the earth.

There are also statements of universal purport. They amount to this: man and world are animated by one and the same energy or will. Indian Brahmanism sees in brahman the self-subsistent, divine power which animates everything and which is active in man in prayer and in the cultus. Man knows brahman in his religious experience, which lifts him above finitude to his true, imperishable life. But in the formulations of this knowledge, philosophical reflection has at least as important a part as the religious sense. In the Avesta, where the religious sense of nature has found such a striking formulation, a statement appears which gains a special significance because it is encountered in the creed. It goes as follows:

I declare myself a worshipper of Mazda, a follower of Zarathustra and adherent of Ahura's law.

and then:

what the waters have chosen (the "faith" of the waters), what the plants and the cattle and Ahura Mazda, the creator of cattle and of the righteous man, have chosen, what Zarathustra and the sacred heroes of the religion have chosen, that is my choice and my faith. As worshipper of Mazda and adherent of Zarathustra, I confess my faith.

This is a religious and not a philosophical pronouncement. The believer follows the same way of life and chooses the same life as the entire world created by Mazda. Coupled with this is the statement: "I repudiate the daevas (the spirits of the dead)." The life of man was for the Zoroastrian the divine imperishable energy which in the entire creation had gained a triumph over death. Man is organically connected with the divine nature of the entire creation, of water, plants and cattle. His life is the life of creation.

The idea of choice expressed the religious (not the metaphysical) significance of this. The cosmic nature of human life does not imply that it has a neutral character. There is here no pantheistic conception of life, no abolition of all contrasts. According to this Avesta conception, which may be called typically religious, life is not a static condition, but a process of becoming and of striving. It is not the condition which exists as long as the heart beats and breathing occurs; that condition is passive, independent of our will and our impulses. Life is growth, conceived as activity, an impulse constantly pressing to the fore and triumphing over resistance. It is a movement in a definite direction, at once a "choice," and a continually repeated victory. According to the religious conception, it is the life of the spirit of victory, called in the Avesta, *uparatāt vainaintī*, "the triumphing superiority," which is itself thought of and invoked as a divine being and is connected with the divinity Vrthraghna, the defensibility or victory. This certainly does not indicate a neutral condition of a pantheistic sort, but the maintenance of oneself in the face of destruction and death. Life is a continually repeated resurrection. At the *anodos*, (resurrection) of the earth goddess Kore, *Nike* (victory) is pictured in the hand of Demeter. In the Avesta, *khvarnah*, "glittering, glory, power of soul," is another term for life. It is the energy which animates the heroes and which flew away from the ideal man Yima when he was filled with a love of the deceitful word and thereby met his fall and brought death among men. The saviour will come, the resurrected Zarathustra, by his *khvarnah* will cause eternal life to triumph for good. But the rain, too, is called "the *khvarnah* created by Mazda"! These are mythical definitions of the vital energy, and although they are expressed in metaphor, they tell us a great deal.

This "life" moves in a rising line (*uparatāt vainaintī*). Therefore only health is "life"; sickness, which signifies descending life, broken spirit and a passive state, is in essence death. According to the conception of the Ancient peoples, healing is a resurrection and a triumph over death. The Epidaurian games in honour of Asclepius, who is also depicted with Nike on his hand, dramatize healing. They are cultic acts with magical results, by which resurrection is actualized. All of life is a continually repeated ascent and resurrection. Therefore the life of the god or of the man who has died is represented and realized by setting his image or symbol upright. The stones and posts which are set up, whether they are Greek *hermai* or the Israelite *massebas* and *asheras*, signify resurrection ("arising"). In resurrection, self-subsistent divine life manifests itself. Health therefore signifies immortality as well as resurrection. In the Avesta, the two spirits or attributes of Mazda, Haurvatat and Amrtat, "health and immortality," are usually mentioned together as a pair of gods. They are represented by water and plants respectively, which are the food and drink of Mazda and of eternal life. This "ambrosia" characterizes all food and drink in the Ancient religions.

Life, that is to say, victory, is thus in essence imperishability and immortality; healing is life's victory. But when a sick person fails to get well, what has happened to the imperishability of life? The Ancient conception is that even when death occurs, healing or resurrection must be possible. The resurrection of the dead, in the sense of victory over death, is universally accepted, although represented in different ways. The victory over death is expressly proclaimed when the idea of mystery comes to the foreground (in the worship of Demeter, Attis, or Osiris). Death was there identical with spontaneous, absolute life that contained resurrection and victory. But outside the mystery religions, too, everywhere where the dead were worshipped with sacrifices, the victory of the man who had died was assumed, because death cannot abolish life. The victory was also represented and realized by the contest in the funeral games. Help was even expected from the dead in the most important matters, for instance, in those concerning the fertility of earth and of man; the dead were evidently primarily spirits of life. But then the question still arises what sort of notion existed in religions such as the Babylonian, Israelite, and Homeric, in which the dead were not worshipped and their lot was represented as the saddest possible. Was it not then believed in these religions that life had been worsted by death?

No. In these religions, however, the notion of immortality and victory over death is differently formulated; it takes a different direction. Immortality is here seen as the carrying on of a family line in its descendents. Life, then, is not an individual energy or function, but the family line continues to live on in the continually repeated victory over the threatening powers of destruction. Every individual must renew and strenghten that life; he stands in the service of the higher and more inclusive life, by means of which he himself also lives, because he has come forth from the family. Nothing is said about a life in the other world. There is no life there; men live only in this world. But man's life is still imperishable because of its continuing existence in the family, tribe and nation. It is true for all these peoples that "my life is the life of my family." When a relative is murdered, "our blood," the blood of the family, is shed. The individual continues to live in his descendents.

The highest and most characteristic of man's expressions of life is his fertility. The Israelite term for this vital energy is *berākhā*, the "blessing" of man.[1] This "blessing" is the vital power given to someone or something by means of which he is able to maintain himself and make his presence felt in the world outside. Like the *khvarnah* in the Avesta, it differs for every family. Each of the twelve tribes of Israel has its individual blessing: Judah is the ruler and warrior, Levi has the priestly blessing, etc. The blessing or vital energy of the king consists of the counsel given to him by God, by which he can lead his people on the right way and can give them good counsel, in which prosperity and power are included. For good counsel is power; he who follows the counsel will discover that he has obtained the alliance of a new power, by means of which he gains success. That power goes out from the king, because it is his blessing. "A spirit of counsel and power must animate the king." (Isaiah 11 : 2) One person has more blessing or vital energy than another; thus David has more than Saul, who had lost his blessing, just as Yima had lost his *khvarnah*. In I Samuel 26 : 25 Saul says to David, "You are blessed; you shall perform great deeds, and you shall be able to accomplish much." Jacob's blessing was his deceit, which enabled him to maintain himself. In the Hebrew and Avesta religions, furthermore, prosperity and riches are a blessing in the religious sense; they testify to a heightened vital energy. Prosperity is just as much a result and expression of that energy as it is its source. According to Pedersen there is no distinction between the power which works in the soul, the soul's ability, and the result of that power which reveals itself in the world outside.[2] It can thus be explained that in the Avesta, riches are valued above poverty and the married state above the unmarried. The satisfied man is better able than the hungry to appropriate the spirit of Mazda. He possesses (as a divine gift) a greater vital power. However the greatest blessing is fertility, for that is equal to imperishable life. When Yahweh had created the animals He blessed them, that is to say, He gave them the ability to perpetuate their kind and – especially – to multiply. After the creation of man, too, He blessed him: "Be fruitful and multiply and rule over all creatures." The good luck implied in the blessing given to children meant for the Israelites something else than it means

for us. That blessing gave a man the good luck of imperishable
life, not in death, but in this life. He felt himself more than simply
an individual; he lived in and by means of his family, his
tribe and his nation. So too in the Avesta: only the married man who has children fulfills the law of Mazda, the god
whose typical opponent was death and who gained the victory
over death.

It can thus be explained why in Rome, Greece and Babylonia,
adoption was a religious duty in a childless marriage. The worship of the ancestors had to be assured, and thereby the life of
the family assured and its own absolute and divine life realized.
The same is true of the levirate marriage among the Israelites:
if someone died childless then his brother, by marrying his widow,
must see to it that the man who has died can continue to live
in and by means of his family.[3] According to II Samuel 18 : 18,
Absalom had no son to keep his name in remembrance; therefore
he set up a stone pillar, a *masseba*, before him and gave it his
name. "And the stone is called Absalom's Hand up to this
very day." The story is noteworthy in various respects. The name
is man's spiritual image or his essence, independent of all circumstances. The individual continues to live in his name; we
should say in the "renown" of his name. Absalom wishes this
not so much from a thirst for honour, but simply because he feels
himself bound up with the enduring life of his people and his
family. Normally the name and thereby the soul is taken over
by the descendents, as a rule by the grandchildren. Absalom,
who has no descendents, sets up the *masseba* and gives it his
name; in this way he continues to live in the world. The *masseba*
is as a rule the image of the resurrected earth god. And the
possibility is not excluded that as a name pillar it indicated the
identity of the man who had died with the god of the resurrected
life of earth. At least the grave stone which was set up had that
significance for the Greeks and Egyptians. And even among the
Israelites, who otherwise paid so little attention to the fate of the
dead in the hereafter, perhaps it once had that significance.
The story of Absalom's pillar could then have been a survival
from that belief.

In all these cases there is a belief in enduring life, whether in
or outside the family. In other cases the emphasis falls not so

much on the length of life as on its autonomous essence, which just as much includes imperishability.

"The stone is called Absalom's Hand up to this very day." The hand is a new description of life or the vital principle. It symbolizes not so much physical power as the acting, forming, and creative ability which is the secret of the vital energy. Life is a spontaneous, creative activity; it is therefore portrayed by the hand, which possesses a magic power. The Babylonian god of the underworld, Ea, is the wise god who creates life and causes it to rise. Among the gods he is the wise one and the artist, who breathes life into the rough material and gives it form. He is therefore called "the god with the large hand" or even "with the wise hand." His wisdom lies in his insight into the origin of life, that life which he actualizes by the artistry of his hand. According to the Ancient conception, but one which was also held in later time, in the work of the hand the idea of magical, mystical "creation-activity" is implied. The word for amulet or talisman, "fetish," is derived from *feitico, factitius,* "made," but in the sense of bewitched, enchanted. Otto Weinreich discusses *Theou Cheir,* God's Hand ,and shows that the creative hand of God is also the healing hand (*paiōnia cheir*).[4] The god, in this case Asclepius, or his priest, heals by laying his hand upon the sick man or moving his hand above him. The Centaur Cheiron possesses knowledge of all means of healing. We have already seen that healing is equated with resurrection; in the same way the creating hand becomes the symbol of resurrected life. The stone which is set up is called "the hand of Absalom" because it represents and realizes his enduring life.

The same symbolic value is shared by the finger, the *digitus medicus.* The Daktyloi on the island of Crete were conceived at least by the Greeks as "finger spirits"; they were earth spirits and "discoverers of smithcraft." They hammered out or created the life of earth, just as Hephaestus and the Cyclops hammered out in their underground workshop their master piece, the life of earth, or Pandora. For the same reason they were spirits of healing and of rescue from death. They can be compared with the creating Babylonian earth god, the "smith" Ea, and with the little earth spirits, the dwarfs, who are also gifted with smithcraft and with magic and wisdom.

Other parts of the body, too, are special possessors of the autonomous vital energy. This is the case with the hair, for example. Samson is strong because of his hair. In the Greek myths, the lock of golden hair represents the life (conceived as the immortality) of its possessor. Nisus, the first king of Megara and Eleusis, received a golden or purple lock of hair on his head from Kore-Persephone. If this were removed, he had to die. The golden apples on the tree in the garden of the Hesperides are immortal fruit from that tree of life. In Egypt, the "Golden House" is a name of the kingdom of the dead conceived as the place of eternal life. The hair sacrifice is a sacrifice of life. Before sacrificing a bull the Romans cut off the hair between his horns. At Troezen in Argolis, just before marriage the bride offered to Hippolytus the hair sacrifice, that is to say, her life. For to marry is to die; it is an initiation into the absolute life which is the secret of the resurrected life; the prototype of marriage was the abduction of Kore by Hades, thus at the same time the death of Kore. In many other cases the hair proves to be the seat of life, that is to say, of the absolute, the resurrected and immortal life. Why? The data are here by no means so clear as the data concerning the hand or the finger, in which the idea of the magical ability to create, which is the divine craft and wisdom, certainly gives the explanation.

Then, again, life may be situated in the eye. "The eye of Horus" signifies divine life. (Horus is in this case deity in general.) The eyes too, portrayed on a sarcophagus or grave stele, represent the life of the man who has to die. Based on the same conception of the eye is the widely spread belief in the magical power of "the evil eye."

The emphasis here is always placed on the supernatural, magical character of the vital function, because it is inaccessible to every causal explanation. It is self-subsistent and creative. The Egyptian sign for life, ♀, is a knot or loop, the sign of magical activity. For all peoples in all ages, the primary bearer of magical power is the word or spell. The inspired orator had at his command, just as Hermes did, the magic power of the word. The religious formula gave a magical effect to the cultic act. Creation occurred by the power of the divine word, which was the word of life.

In the beginning was the word ... by the same have all things been made ... in the word was life, and the life was the light of men.

The word in Creation is identical with the life of all that which is created. For the word is not only a sound made in order to say something; it is animated by the personality of the speaker and weighted with his power. It is a "command" which continues to exort itself. Everything which lives lives by the "word" situated within it; the word is the vital principle itself. This conception of the essence of life is actually one of the oldest of which history can tell us. It is clearly elaborated in the Shabaka text, an Egyptian document from the third millennium B.C.

That which is most characteristic of the Ancient conception of human life, however, is really the cosmic relationship in which, to the minds of the Ancients, this life is found, especially the relationship with the earth's life and its products, with fire and water and other cosmic principles of life. This has been treated in the various chapters on Cosmology, in which the religious conceptions of these natural phenomena were discussed.

CHAPTER 11

THE SOUL

We have considered the conception of life as mystical energy and creative power. Now we shall be discussing, not the conception of life in general, but the depiction of that conception in the idea of a personal being: the "soul" as spiritual individuality in some way connected with the body. It is natural that there are innumerable formulations of this idea, for the reality intended by the conception cannot be contained in any rational definition. A self-subsistent reality is inexpressible and can be indicated only by metaphor or symbol. For us the formulations are often practically meaningless. What, for example, do "primitive" peoples mean when they call the soul an insect or a moist substance? We just do not know. Let us keep our attention on the data in those religions in which the believers themselves have indeed elucidated their idea: the literate religions.*

Our primary concern is the relation between body and soul. In many cases this relation is the same as that between matter and spirit. We distinguish between soul, the more or less personally conceived vital principle, and spirit, the divine or cosmic nature of created things. In the non-Christian religions, both ideas repeatedly shade off into one another. It is noteworthy that in these religions one seldom encounters a dualistic conception of body and soul. In Plato, however, we do find this dualistic conception. For him the body is the prison of the soul, which tries to free itself; the immaterial soul has come at birth from the realm of ideas. The notion most similar to this is that of the Vedanta, the dogmatic theology of Brahmanism, a notion set forth particularly in the Upanishads. Here the soul or the "self," Atman, is identical with Brahman, which is the principle of all

* i.e., religious which have produced written documents. Trans.

existence or of the force which creates and maintains the world and later takes it back to itself. Through the soul, Atman, we know our true being, our real self, which is not a part or an emanation of Brahman, but is Brahman itself. The empirical world and empirical man, named with "name" and represented with form (*nāma-rūpa*) is pure illusion. But both the doctrine of Plato and that of the Vedanta is much more philosophical speculation and theory than it is religion.

It is otherwise with the conception in the Avesta. The physical and the spiritual world, body and soul, are both created by Mazda. There are both "physical" (nature) and "spiritual" gods, and they are expressions of the religious sense of nature found in the Avesta, for which religious sense a dualistic conception is quite unsuitable. We first meet dualism in the contrast between life and death, in other words, between good and evil, stable order and deceit. The ideas in the Avesta do attest to a contrast, but not to a dualism of body and spirit. Preeminence is granted to the spiritual world: first the soul is created and only after that the body.

In Greece, the religious conception of the soul, unlike the philosophical one, is very vague. In Homer and in later writings, the soul is not contrasted with the body; it is rather a double of man, of body and spirit together. In the ordinary expressions of man's life it is not active; it dwells as an autonomous being in man. As is clear from the myth of Eros and Psyche, it also represents the immortal essence of man – an idea which naturally does not appear in Homer. Yet the conception of the "soul" is strikingly vague and little developed. In the ancestor worship at the hearth, the "psychē" of the dead is never worshipped. Likewise the Eleusinian Mysteries were not concerned with the immortality of the psyche, but of the whole man. Only the Sirens were pictured in somewhat personal terms, but about them little is known.

The essential unity of body and soul is expressed in the Israelite concept *nephesh*.[1] Nephesh is to be conceived as a peculiar formulation of the idea of "life"; the Babylonian *napishtu* means "life." Man does not possess a nephesh; rather he is a nephesh; with body and soul. According to Genesis 2 : 7, God fashions man from earth, and He breathes into this image His breath "whereby man becomes a living nephesh"; matter is thus made into a nephesh. Therefore it is said in Genesis 12 : 5 that Abram and Sarah journey to Canaan "with all their possessions and all the 'souls' which they had gained." "Souls" means here, not "slaves," but "men." Souls are also attributed to animals. "The earth brings forth a swarm of living nephesh." (Genesis 1 : 20f). Here nephesh means not "beings" but "animals." Nephesh is the organized and specifically determined totality in man or animal. The total impression which one receives of a man, by spiritual as well as sensory perception, is the impression of his "soul." This is the totality, the background of every particular impression. This totality of body and spirit is revealed especially in the will. It is characteristic that the Israelite has no separate word that corresponds to "will" in our sense of the word. For him the will is not an autonomous expression or ability of soul or spirit, but the total direction of the soul. In Genesis 23 : 8, Abraham says to the Hittites, "If it is according to your soul (will or consent) that I bring my dead Sarah from my house in order to bury her, then ... give me the cave of Machpelah." All spiritual activities come forth from the nephesh, the total being of man, and they witness to its presence. Forces from outside can also strike that totality of man or exert influence upon it. Therefore thinking has a different significance for the Israelite than it does for us. Theoretical and objective thinking without action and practical interest is alien to him; it is an aberration from normal thinking. That which is taken into the soul and assimilated by means of thinking must contribute something to the development of the totality of the "soul" and must exert its influence on the will. Thinking is practical activity. *Zākhar*, "to remember," also includes the meaning of undergoing influence from that which one remembers. "To remember the deeds of Yahweh" means to seek Yahweh and to allow one's self to be determined by his will. Our word "to think" has no equivalent in Hebrew. "Will" and "thought" are the particular expressions of the nephesh, which man does not possess, but which is the man himself. There are few abstract concepts in Hebrew; *tōb* means "good person" as well as "to be good," the realizer and bearer of goodness as well as goodness itself.

Wisdom, too, is an attribute of the nephesh. Wisdom means more than just "wise thought." It is the determining of the path of life in particular situations and the realization of enduring life. The Ancient peoples all shared the Israelite view of wisdom. They knew no other wisdom than practical insight, the art of life and the wisdom of life.

When the soul is conceived as the indivisible totality of the human personality, we come close to our concept "instinct." Instinct presupposes a real – though uncomprehended – correspondence between man and world. It is wisdom in the Ancient sense of the word; it finds the way of life in the world of phenomena and proves to know the world better than our intellect or our reason; its activity excludes any sort of contemplative attitude towards the world. The "soul," conceived as nephesh, reveals itself in the practice of life. It can be compared with Vohu-Manah, the term in the Avesta for "good disposition," the right insight or the tact which can relate itself to universal life. This tact is determined as much by ethical as by intellectual factors. The conception of the '·soul" as the totality of our being is the intuitive understanding of the unity of our spiritual and bodily nature, and just for this reason it is an extremely practical notion. The soul is a mystery possessing mysterious magical powers.

Idea and reality, the spiritual and the physical, are here undifferentiated, just as in our concept "life." The *masseba*, a stone set upright to serve as a grave stone, in Aramaic and other Hebrew dialects is called a nephesh and conceived in both physical and spiritual terms. The courageous man risks his "soul," that is to say, his life. (Judges 9 : 17.)

With respect to its extent and power, the nephesh is then a mysterious reality: no one knows what possibilities lie concealed within it. The "seer" (the old title of the prophet) sees more deeply than others into the connection of objects and events in space and time. His ecstasy is the most extreme development of his spiritual faculties, and it reveals other than ordinary forces in the soul. This extraordinary soul force is divine. God fills the soul of the prophet with His soul, "God's hand grasps him." The seer has received a new soul, "God speaks through him."

A strong soul makes the spoken word strong; it transforms it into a word with mysterious or magical effect. The entire energy of the soul can be present in the word. This is the case with the blessing, which is a communication of life force, and it is likewise true of the curse. If someone says, "You are blessed (cursed)," then this word or command creates the blessing (curse) and puts this into another person. The magic word is the direct revelation of the energy of the soul.

In Hebrew thought, the nephesh is not a particular part of man; it is the man himself. Therefore we hear little or nothing of its divine nature, for man, of course, is not divine. Other peoples, on the contrary, have conceived of the mystery of this life energy as a self-sustaining, divine power, which has come to dwell in man. The idea of a soul is then indeed present, although not that of our concept "soul." What is meant here is a divine being, which can even be worshipped as a god. In such a case, man does not worship himself, but this divine being within him.

This is true of the Romans and of the Avesta people, two peoples who in particular had a strong religious sense of nature, even with respect to the phenomena of human life. The Genius (the word is related to *gignere*, "to generate") is the soul of the living man. Paulus Diaconus, who in the time of Charlemagne made excerpts from the grammarian Festus (third century A.D.), writes, "Genius meus nominatur quia me genuit," and Censorinus, also in the third century A.D., says, "Genius is the god under whose protection every person lives." The feminine form of the Genius is called Juno, plural Junones, or the Fortuna Muliebris. Fortuna is the obscure background of events, the background which gives rise to and determines the events. Fortune is the good luck whereby along hidden paths a way out of the difficulty is found and a solution is reached. Life finds its way. The Fortuna Muliebris or the Juno of a woman is the spirit which guides and preserves her life. Like the Genius of the man, she is the religious formulation of the individual reality which we call the "soul" of a person, conceived with a deep sense of the ultimate and self-subsistent, that is to say, the divine nature of that reality. The festival of Fortuna Muliebris was celebrated on July 6, the day on which in 489 B.C., during the war against the Volsci, the woman Veturia saved Rome, because she persuaded Coriolanus, the leader of the Volsci, to withdraw. This "soul," Genius or Juno, represents the spontaneous factor pre-

sent in every expression of life; it is thus a divine force or a divine
being, conceived in personal and individual terms. It dwells and
works within us, for life triumphs over obstacles and again and
again sets itself aright, without our knowing how this process
occurs. Compared with this idea, our modern concept "soul" is
colourless and impotent. On the *dies natalis*, the festival of the
Genius or Juno, a sacrifice was offered to the spirit. This is not
self-deification, for the Genius is not the self whom we know.
It is rather an infinite "self," which as such is above and beyond
the reach of us who are finite beings, and therefore this infinite
"self" can be worshipped. The soul is, then, an infinite spirit and
is indeed conceived as a god. This is an instance of the religious
sense of nature, applied to our perception of ourselves. The
Genius proves furthermore to be the self-subsistent power in
everything which reveals self-subsistent life. There are just as
many genii as there are human beings, families, nations, and
even cities (*Genius loci*). They are in every place where the divine
reveals itself and is active according to its own nature. For the
religious consciousness the Genius is, nevertheless, not a "world
soul." Here too the religious idea has that pluralistic nature
characteristic of the Romans. The Greek educated Varro, living
in the first century B.C., does refer to the Genius of universal
life, or Deus, as Mundi Animus, but that is only an alternation
of the old Roman idea to bring it in line with the Stoic conception.

The Genius shows much similarity to the Egyptian Ka, the
"double" or the "image" of the person, particularly of the dead
person. The "image" is in this instance precisely the self-subsistent, imperceptible, and spiritual part of the person. The Ka
is a person's "life spirit" which works in the heart and which
fills food with the energy that enables life to continue. *Ka.u*, in
the plural, is even used as a word meaning "food." The Ka of the
dead person is a divine being, to whom sacrifices are offered.
It is remarkable that it is an offering consisting precisely of
ka.u which is presented to Ka. It is a striking illustration of the
religious conception of sacrifice: the sacred act which actualizes
the divine essence of the offering. Through his religious relation
man possesses superhuman power whereby he can accomplish
the religio-magical act of sacrifice; he actualizes the divine energy in the foodstuffs which keep him alive.

Closely related to the Genius and to the Ka is "my god" or "my gods" in the Babylonian religion and probably also in the Hebrew Psalms (Eerdmans). When misfortune strikes, it is said that "my god is angry with me" or "my god must be reconciled." It is the god of the individual person who is meant here, the *Il ameli*, "god of the man," or, corresponding to Juno, *Ishtar ameli;* every man is "the son of his god." In the Hymns of Lamentation we read, "God of man, may the life of this man become established," and "may the god who has created me (cf. "Genius quia me genuit") remain standing at my side." When different gods are addressed in succession, "the god of man" is at the end of the series. He is the divine soul and like the Genius a god who is worshipped.

The Fravashi in the Avesta shows similarity to the Genius and to the individual tutelary deity. But in the case of the Fravashi, the accent is put still more sharply upon the divine and cosmic character of the "soul" and upon the ultimate, self-subsistent, that is to say, the divine nature of that which we call our life, although we are anything but gods. When the human soul is invoked to help as a wise god and worshipped as a superhuman being, we must again insist that this is not to be taken as self-deification or any form of pantheism. The idea is rather that we do not know our soul, which extends infinitely further than our conscious self, and that our life is a gift of God which continues to belong to God and to dwell with Him. The etymology of the word *fravashi* is unknown, but in the historical times of the Avesta and later it was derived from *fra-var*, "to promote, maintain, feed," which was identified with Sanskrit *vriddhi*, "growth." This possibly mistaken etymology is nevertheless particularly important for our knowledge of the fravashi. The spirit of spontaneous life was evidently seen in the fravashi; growth and creation are related concepts (*crescere – creare*). The Fravashi is indeed the imperishable and eternal part of man. According to the Avesta, the Fravashis of the ancestors are worshipped, but also the Fravashis of the righteous among the living, and finally also the Fravashis of those who are yet to come: "we worship the Fravashi of these who triumph and who have triumphed and who shall triumph." (Yasht 13 : 154.) Thus this is not only a worship of the ancestors or of heroes, but worship of a holy spirit

which works in man and gives him power and growth. It is a
conception which can be compared to that of the Christian.

Much emphasis is placed on the cosmic activity of the Fravashis. In verse 65:

When water is taken up from the world sea (in order to fall as rain),
then the strong Fravashis of the righteous by hundreds, thousands, and
ten thousands hasten thereto to seek water, every one for his own family,
village, district, or land: "should our own land languish and perish from
thirst?"

According to verse 15, they make the families prosper, for by
"their power and glory (*khvarnah*), the woman are rich in children,
the leader of the people is born, and the wise man, who combats
and triumphs over heretics in debate." They are the rescuers
from all dangers:

When you are in mortal danger, oh Zarathustra, repeat this prayer:
I praise the Fravashis and invoke them, all who are, were and shall come,
the Fravashis of all peoples, the most friendly (?) of the friendly peoples,
(Verse 20.)

It is clear from verse 17 how far distant we are here from the
worship of the forefathers, who also bestow prosperity and pro-
geny: "the Fravashis of the believers (the righteous) who are
now living are stronger than those of the believers who have
died," – this is true because they participate more in real life –
"but the strongest of all are the Fravashis of the first and of the
last believers." These are those who were present at Creation
and those who will be at the final triumph, the Genii of the Mazda
religion and thus of eternal and immortal life.

This last quotation already indicates that the self-subsistent
life of these souls is the same as the life which animates the
world and world history. This thought is quite certainly expressed
in the remarkable beginning of Yasht 13.

Thus spoke Ahura Mazda to Zarathustra: I shall speak to you about
the power and the glory (*khvarnah*) and the help of the triumphant Fravashis
of the righteous, how they have stood by me. By their power and glory
I raised (in Creation) the heavens on high as a roof over the earth ...
established the earth in its width and breadth, this holder of the innumerable beautiful creatures, rivers, plants, animals ,and men; by their
power and glory I sustained the children in their mother's womb so that
they would not die, and by the great resurrection I shall again put together
their bones and hair and flesh. By their power and glory flow the waters
from the springs, grow the plants from the earth, the clouds blow in the
wind, and the sun, moon, and stars go along their lofty paths.

It is clear from verse 76 that the Fravashis were indeed present
at Creation: "they stood there on high when the two spirits
(the good and the evil) created the world." And in Bundahishn
2 : 10 it is told how before Creation Ahura Mazda let the Fravashis choose if they would remain in the heavenly rest or descend into the world, assume bodily form and participate in the
struggle against the evil powers. They chose the struggle, knowing
that it would end with victory over the evil spirit. This joy in the
conflict and confidence in the victory is characteristic of the
Avesta religion. It is a religion of the deed and of the practice of
life, no dreamy speculation about the essence of God, the world,
and the soul, such as is found in the Indian religions.

It is very remarkable that these "souls," as we see, represent
the power and wisdom, the vital energy of Ahura Mazda himself.
They are cosmic powers. "The Fravashi of Mazda" stands for
Mazda himself. (Vendidad 19 : 14.) We must not see in this
any artificial theory or playful mythology, but rather the formulation of a purely religious thought and belief. The reference
is always to the Fravashi of the faithful, righteous man. In other
words, in and through his religion man is a being who extends
beyond all finitude and who is able to triumph over finitude;
faith is a cosmic power. This is the power of man, but it does
not come from himself. We definitely encounter here, not a
philosophical, but a religious conception of the soul. Although
the formulation seems strange to us, we can nevertheless succeed
in understanding it. The Fravashis have sometimes been compared with the ideas of Plato because of the preexistence of the
spiritual reality, but the comparison is not very accurate. The
Fravashis are beings who are worshipped and thus belong, not in
philosophy, but in religion.

Another term in the Avesta for soul is *Urvan*, the faculty to
will and to choose (root *var* in "to will," "volo," "wählen"),
the free will and the responsible element in man. Unlike the
Fravashi, the Urvan can be good or evil; after death he is judged
and sent to heaven or hell. We must conceive of this willing and
choosing faculty, however, not in the strictly ethical, but in the
religio-ethical sense. The strictly ethical factor, which is naturally
autonomous and finds its rule in the conscience, appears in
every religion to have surrendered its autonomy. The ethical

will is thus subordinate to the divine will, which is concerned with the world as much as it is with man, and is the law of both. The Urvan or choice determines which way man must take. The result is welfare or disaster, fortune or misfortune, in both material and spiritual respects, both in this world and the other world. This is the religious element in the concept Urvan. It is the abrogation of the strictly ethical, which wills the good just because it is good, aside from any reward. By means of his Urvan man is able to bring himself into accordance with the world order, with the order of cosmic life which is as much material as it is spiritual, the good order in the religio-ethical sense. The nonethical aspect appears clearly when there is reference to the Urvan (choice) of animals. Thus in Yasna 39 : 1: "We worship the Urvans [the Nephesh is not worshipped] of ourselves and of the household animals which nourish us, they who exist for us and for whom we exist." Men and animals created by Mazda work together by means of their Urvan for the maintenance of the life which is the essence of Ahura Mazda. It is also noteworthy that "men exist for the animals." Thus even with respect to the conception of the soul as the choosing faculty and the responsible being, the concern is not just with human life, but with life in the cosmic sense, the divine life. In this way the remarkable meaning can be explained which the Urvan of cattle, *Geush Urvan*, has even in the Gathas. This is worshipped as a divine being who makes demands of man. He requires good treatment of cattle as a religious duty. – This was one of the main points in the reform of Zarathustra.

These are examples of the formulations of the concept of the human soul. They differ very widely. Yet they do display traces of similarity, even if *the* common religious apprehension (Schleiermacher's *Anschauung*) is difficult to indicate. They agree especially in this, that they see a cosmic being in the "soul" of man. That which "animates" man is also active outside of him: the Nephesh and the Urvan in animals, and the Genius and Fravashi in what appears to us modern men as lifeless nature. Yet there is no question here of a pantheistic conception; pantheism can only be a philosophical theory. The idea of the soul is extremely characteristic for the religious orientation of the Ancients. Human life exists in a more profound relation to the universal and divine life of the cosmos than can be accepted by our modern dualistic conception of matter and spirit. We do know a connection between man and cosmos which extends just as widely. It is not foreign to our thinking to believe that man is infinitely determined by spiritual and material influences; all of our science proceeds on that assumption and strives to demonstrate it. But the sense of relationship, in the deeper sense of spiritual correspondence, was much stronger among the Ancients than it is among ourselves. We simply do not sense that the soul of man is the same as the soul present in nature. We can indeed say that "the Spirit of God is active in man," and we can worship that Spirit. But we do not worship "our soul." He who does do that demonstrates a religious sense of nature in the form which this takes in man's apprehension of himself. The inscrutability of human life is then conceived, not simply as a riddle, but as a divine reality.

We should mention finally a formulation of "soul" which seems to be very close to our own conception, but which is nevertheless in essence entirely Ancient, because it maintains the self-subsistence and the divine nature of the soul. I am referring to the conception of man's religion, his religious life, as his soul or as his life in the infinite sense, the *Daena* in the Avesta.

The Daena is represented as a feminine being. She signifies religion or the religious faith of man. She is the guide through life, an insight and power not originating from man. She is the spirit of God. This is the good Daena, revealed by Zarathustra. There is however also a bad Daena, false and mistaken faith. The "Daena" is a "soul" because men are dominated by their good or bad Daena. Sometimes she is thought of in wholly personal terms, with the significance of a soul. This is the case in the statement about her at the last judgment, immediately after man's death. (Yasht 22). The righteous man is led to a region where he breathes the most fragrant scents. There his own Daena ("soul") comes to meet him as a beautiful young woman, who is like the most glorious creatures of Mazda. The dead man asks her, "Who are you, most beautiful of all the woman I have ever seen?" She answers, "I am your own Daena. You have loved me in all your life and work. I was beloved of men; you have made me more beloved. I was beautiful; by your thoughts, words, and

deeds you have made me even more beautiful." Then the dead
man enters paradise. The unrighteous man, on the contrary,
meets an ugly woman in the midst of the most disagreeable
odors, who blames him for having made her even uglier and more
hated than she had been. In different places in the Avesta, the
Daena corresponds to the "I," with concrete individuality, and
with the soul. (Bartholomae ad Yasna 44 : 8; 7 : 24.) She is
the particular life direction of man. But in Vendidad 3, for example, she is conceived in the typically Ancient manner as the life
of the world. "He who sows grain, sows righteousness (*asha*, life
as the will and essence of Mazda), and he causes the religion of
Mazda (*Daena Mazdayasni*) to progress and prosper." That
is to say, he strengthens the Daena, which is conceived as cosmic
reality, specifically the life of the world. Therefore Daena,
religion, is inseparably bound to both spiritual and material
prosperity. Even Zarathustra says, "The Daena, religion, is
attached to the best reward," (Yasna 49 : 9) both in this and
in the other world. We who are ethically oriented find the thought
of a reward an inferior one. Nevertheless, it is truly a religious
thought, because it can also signify a cosmic orientation. This
idea was not even foreign to Kant: reward may indeed not be
the mainspring of ethical life, yet it does remain a fact within it.

All these ideas have kept within a compass of thoughts which
is not altogether alien to us. Other data are further removed
from our thinking. In these cases our understanding is very likely
to be inadequate, and for convenience' sake we speak of primitive
or even of inferior, ideas. I shall not go into this area at length,
but simply indicate with a few examples what I mean. I
think of the ideas of the soul which having left the body
assumes the form of some animal. The most well known example, the one which it is easiest for us to understand, is the
soul bird: in Greece tne Siren and the Psyche, in Rome the imperial eagle, in Egypt the *ba*. As an aerial being the bird represents the *anima* or *animus*, air, breath, or spirit, and thus invisible life. It is comparable to the winged angels, which are
also sometimes conceived as the souls of the dead. Bird, wing, and
feather interchange with one another. The wings have even for
our consciousness a certain symbolic significance, the bird much
less so. For the Greeks and for many other European peoples the

werewolf (*lykanthrōpos*) was really the soul of the dead person, a "man (*were-vir*) -wolf." In Egypt various animals were called the "souls" of particular gods. The bull Apis was the soul of Osiris, the crocodile was the soul of Sebak, etc. In general it can be said that the animal is a being with a soul because it belongs to another world than this one, to the realm of the dead.

CHAPTER 12

ATTRIBUTES AND CAPACITIES OF MAN

The religious conception of human attributes and capacities is that each is in its own way an expression of the mysterious and self-subsistent vital principle or soul. In this way it is possible to understand the autonomous and spontaneous character of these capacities; one is aware of his own creative activity, just as he is aware of life in general as a creative energy. We are dealing with a religious conception, especially where there is an awareness that the faculties – for example, wisdom as sacred science – are directed toward infinite goals. This is, in other words, a feeling that these faculties serve to orient man in the life of the world and to bring him into harmony with it, to lead him into divine life and to enable him to participate in it. The finite intellectual or moral capacities are not able to do this. The capacities directed to infinite goals are themselves infinite, and an awareness of this lies at the heart of the religious conception of their essence.

Even bodily attributes are sometimes conceived as expressions of a self-subsistent and divine soul energy. David's handsome appearance attested to the life force granted to him, to the blessing which rested upon him.[1] He is described to Saul as "a forceful man, a warrior, an experienced orator, a man of handsome build, whom Yahweh assists." His ruddy complexion and his beautiful eyes were renowned. This outward appearance is not something accidental or inconsequential in David's appearance. It is understandable that a spiritual significance is ascribed to a man's appearance; the appearance, the posture, and the glance are external revelations of the soul. Thus the possibility is presented for a religious conception about man's appearance. The Greeks too conceived of beauty of appearance as a sign of divine nature. According to Herodotus, the athlete Philip of Croton was considered the most beautiful man in all Greece, and at Segesta in Sicily he was worshipped as a hero "on account of his beauty." [2] We must undoubtedly take account of this conception if we want to understand the religious character of such institutions as the Greek Games. People were quite aware of the symbolism of the religious games. Especially the oldest games, those held at Eleusis, clearly showed that the effect intended was the victory over the enemy of enemies, death. But the aesthetic impression of youthful energy and luster certainly worked in the same direction. Religious and aesthetic feelings shaded off into one another; neither was of a kind familiar to us. The beauty of bodily skill was conceived in religious terms. Thus we must explain the almost divine honour which was accorded the victors in the pan-hellenic games. Pindar composed his *Epinikia* in their honour. In these most beautiful religious hymns of Greek literature, the victor is the favorite of the gods and his victory is a proof of divine grace toward him, his family, and his city. Therefore, says Pindar, the victor has achieved the highest human honour. This is quite different from the modern custom of lavishing praise on a sports champion. The mythical ideal of the Greek athlete was Hercules, who in twelve battles had defeated the representatives of death, including the hound of hell and Thanatos himself. His divine nature was sealed by his being taken up among the gods. All Greeks worshipped him as the great protector against any kind of disaster. Thy myth here clearly indicates the religio-aesthetic motif of the Greek games. In the "enlightened" circles of Graeco-Roman civilization the consciousness of the divine character of the bodily energy disappeared rather completely, but this proves only that the Ancient religion had been undermined in these circles. These "enlightened" folk thought about games and contests in the same way that we do.

Here we must also note the conception of the attributes of living men which is at the foundation of hero worship. The hero is always one who has already died, and he is worshipped as one who had accomplished something unusual before his death; he had been a rescuer from distress – for example, a general, a celebrated wise man, a law giver, or the founder of a city. He

might be either an historical or a mythical figure, but in any
case the divine character of his special attributes was assumed.
It is in this respect that hero worship differed from ancestor worship. Only the hero possesses divine gifts even before his death.
That which excells the average and cannot be explained from
the context or from special circumstances, that is something
ultimate, a self-subsistent and divine reality. But for that reason
it is dangerous to the finite existence of its possessor. The greatness of man proves his undoing, for it does not rest before it
reaches its infinite goal. This is the underlying idea of Greek
tragedy. "Be unassuming and average, and you will be spared."
This is the sensible but hardly heroic advice of the Chorus in
Agamemnon. The great and ideal king Agamemnon, on the
contrary, compelled by his high calling, denied his ordinary
human feelings and even stepped across his daughter's corpse,
and he must pay for this act with death. But he has reached the
divine and is worshipped as a hero. His *hybris*, that is, his presumption, has crushed him, but it is at the same time his real
glory.

The Greek deification of human qualities has nothing in common with vain self-exaltation. The religious Greek was fully
aware that divine qualities and infinite aspirations lead outside
this life. The glory of the martyr awaits the great man. This is
an entirely religious conception of human greatness, which is
quite akin to the ideas about saints in the Roman Catholic
Church. Euripides formulates this conception especially clearly.
"Hercules causes his own downfall." But his destruction itself
implies his being taken up among the gods.

The hero is always one already dead. Notwithstanding any
number of excellent qualities, no one is worshipped during his
lifetime. In the preeminent human qualities, the Greeks saw
ultimate and thus divine forces, but their possessor could not
pride or exalt himself on that account, for they were not from
himself. Empirical man remained a finite being. Only after he
had undergone the initiation of death was he worshipped, and then
not simply as dead ancestors were, but as a hero in whom divine
energy had revealed itself. The superhuman nature of his gifts
is proved most clearly in the fate of such tragic heroes as Agamemnon, Hippolytus, Hercules, and Prometheus: the hero's

infinite and superhuman impulse (his hybris) leads him into death. He will not exalt himself because of his divine nature, for of all men he is the most unfortunate, hounded to death by the disfavour of the gods. Hercules, who had triumphed over the greatest enemy, death, becomes insane and kills his own children.

The Greek conception of the divinity of the king will be treated in connection with the religious conception of society. I want here to refer to just one particular. Beside the generally prevailing conception in both Greece and the Orient which connected divinity with kingship, we encounter the specifically Greek formulation, which Aeschylus indicates in his *Agamemnon*, that of the individual and personal greatness of the king. In the Hellenistic era kings, especially the Syrian *diadochoi*, were worshipped even during their lifetime because of their (presumed) personal qualities of courage, wisdom, and goodness. That does not occur in Egypt or Babylonia. In the Hellenistic era, however, the tragedy and martyrdom originally connected with this notion were abandoned. Perhaps this can justifiably be described as vain self-exaltation and self-deification, but it is difficult to say to what extent this apotheosis can be attributed to the true Ancient conception of kingship.

The religious conception of human abilities and qualities is especially evident in the case of particular expressions of man's artistic and intellectual aptitudes.

Free poetry, which treats of the joys and sorrows of daily life, has naturally existed at all times, whether as lyrical outpourings which come and go or as epic poetry with a longer life span. These forms of poetry have no essential relation to religion, and there are therefore no religious theories about them, or at least we are not acquainted with any. Free poetry knows no other norm than that which the creative imagination prescribes. Even when the subject matter is divine or religious life, the poetry can still be predominantly free. Homer and even Job are examples of this. While they may be among the greatest works of religious poetry, their form of expression is freely chosen and not prescribed by tradition or cultus. When, on the contrary, poetry is in the service of worship or cultus, we are dealing with an entirely different art and with different artists. The poet is a hallowed one if his word contains a revelation of the divine or has the superhuman, magical effect of a prayer or oath, such that he not simply describes the holy but actualizes it. Then he is "inspired," illuminated and guided by a divine spirit. His art is not free and cannot be judged by an aesthetic standard.

The monotonous litanies and the philosophical or theological reflections which we encounter in the Avesta, for example, are inferior, considered as art but important as religious data. The more than a thousand hymns of the Rig Veda, the oldest Indian poetry, were recited at the offering of the Soma sacrifice in order to invite the gods. In the earliest period the singer was also the one who sacrificed. (Oldenberg) The hymn possessed the same magic power as the act. To us it often sounds extremely artificial and consciously enigmatic, for it is sung by one who knows the mystery (the priest) to another who knows that mystery (the god). "The gods love that which is hidden, but hate that which is clear." For that reason these hymns, although containing many points of poetic interest, are not poetry which appeals to our aesthetic sense. They were composed by the Rishis, who were "singers," mythical priest-heroes who have "seen" the Vedas, and thus also "seers" who had attained the divine state and had penetrated into the secrets of the gods. They were also called the wise men, for they beheld the life structure actualized by sacrifice and hymn, that set the divine forces in motion. Through his superhuman relationship man has come into possession of superhuman ability and insight, which give to both the hymns and the sacrificial act a magical effect. It is significant that the recluse, the pious or holy man who has triumphed over the world, is sometimes called a rishi. Here we have a "poetry" which extends beyond finite capacities. Such a notion is almost completely alien to us. The Ancient "inspiration" is the divine wisdom and power at work in the singer.

Therefore the art of these poets is not only religious poetry like that which we find in Job, but divine poetry as well. Hesiod, who is not a mythical figure as are the Rishis, knows when he recites his *Theogonia* that it is not by his own power that he describes the divine order. "The Muses inspired me with divine song in order that I should proclaim the state of things in the future and in the past." [3] And the Muses gave him the branch as symbol, or more accurately as bearer, of his inspiration. This scepter represents the growth of vegetation and the life of the earth, and thus the divine life of the world which the poet reveals. The artistic value of Hesiod's art is not comparable to that of Homer. A contrast has quite rightly been drawn between "the Boeotian farmer" and the Ionian nobleman. Hesiod is not free with respect to his subject. Because he is inspired in the religious sense, like the inspired Pythia with the branch in her hand, he is as much soothsayer as poet.

This inspired art moves in an entirely different direction than free art and tends to abolish such artistic forms as balance, harmony, and meter. The absolute violates the normal standards of beauty. Pythia was a *maenad*, raving and insane. This is true of all forms of art of which the Ancient religions made use. In the dance the ecstatic element came to the fore, for example, in the Bacchantic worship of Dionysus, which orgiastic rite Pentheus vainly fought in Thebes, and in the "danced" Mysteries at Eleusis. The same thing is true of music. What we call "sacred music" is free art which has taken a religious theme and is comparable to Homer and Job. It originates in a religious mood, but it is not "inspired" in the Ancient sense of being revealed. The cymbals and flutes were the instruments of sacred music in worship, but they probably provided little artistic enjoyment.

The Romans recognized a god in whose cultus all these forms of art, dance, and music were united. This was the god Faunus, related to Pan. His worship was characterized by ecstasy. The preclassic meters which had fallen completely into disuse in Roman poetry were called the "Faunic" and the "Saturnic." Faunus was the soothsayer and the founder of one of the oldest Roman religious institutions, wherein the *vates*, the prophet and singer, when in ecstasy sang Faunic or Saturnic verses. According to the Ancients the name Faunus was derived from *fanaticus* (*a fando*). They added, "qui futura praecinit" – *praecino* is "to accompany with the flute," but also "to tell fortunes" – the wise *vates*, who declares the future.

It is known that Greek sculpture from the golden age and later was never conceived by the Greeks themselves as religious art. It was free and profane art, even when the subject was a religious theme, as in the case of Phidias' statues of Athene and

Zeus. The goddess Athene was, to be sure, goddess of "arts and sciences," yet she was not the goddess of the art of Phidias or of the wisdom of Socrates, Plato, and Aristotle. Creative art in the literal sense, on the other hand, was the art of Hephaestus, who brings forth the earth's life and fashions Pandora. And the science of Athene was the faculty of mystical knowledge and creative ability, which was expressed by her nature of *parthenos*, virgin. Of Egyptian art, we admire most of all the statues from the time of the Old Kingdom and later, and the art of Tel el Amarna from the time of Tutank-Amon. Most of this, too, is not religious, but free art. Religious art was called by the Egyptians a "mystery." This was the making of images of the gods in the temple workshop. The images were figures of but little artistry covered with attributes and symbols. The Greeks honoured the *xoana* as sacred images even when the technique of sculpture had long since improved. These objects were roughly fashioned wooden or stone figures of somewhat human form, though without clearly recognizable arms, legs, or head. They were clothed and adorned with flowers. In the Erechtheum, or perhaps in the Hekatompedon, stood the *xoanon* of Athene Polias, made of olive wood, which object was supposed to have fallen from heaven. According to Pausanias, it was "the most sacred image of Athene," even after Phidias' statue had been placed in the Parthenon. The *xoanon* was a work of restricted religious art, whereas the statue of Phidias was a magnificent votive offering, but the latter was probably not an image used in the cultus.

In all these cases the Ancient religious concept of "art" has a character which seems very strange to us. But with respect to one kind of art, the Ancient religious conception agrees to a large extent with our own. That art is eloquence. The great orator does not rely exclusively on logically convincing arguments; his eloquence is an autonomous power with which he exerts an inexplicable and spell-binding effect on his listeners. The impelling word can even acquire a demonic quality, a magical force which brings about a new state of affairs and new orientations and convictions. All eloquence contains this mysterious element, the "inspiration" which eludes all rational or psychological explanation. In this form of art we do at least gain some understanding of the Ancient meaning of "inspiration.'

The Latin peoples, among whom the tradition of oratory still continues from classical antiquity, understand this perhaps even better than we do. Viviani was one of the greatest French orators of the later period. According to his contemporaries, his words could act as a magic power; he had the word less in his power than had the word him in its power. His gift could even cause him to become terrified. It was as if he did not dare to take upon himself the responsibility for the effect of his words. In such a case the word possesses the creative power which is so often ascribed to it in the Ancient religions.

The Ancient orator was closely associated with the divine singer or poet. Everyone who stood up to speak in the Greek *agora*, the people's assembly, received from the herald a staff or branch to hold in his hand, the same staff as that of the magician. Both were bearers of the creative word of God, the imperative word of absolute authority, the word which actualizes itself. The orator in the Greek assembly determined the course of affairs and thus the fate of men; that was his task, that was expected of him, and that was what he himself believed he was doing. He led the people with a divine authority and with the wisdom which according to the Ancient conception extended above any kind of rational insight. The orator gives good advice, which means strong advice, drawn from his own spiritual power. Thus he paves the way which men can confidently follow in the conviction that it is the path of life. It is in this light that we must come to an understanding of the Greek Sophists. The Sophists laid emphasis on rhetoric because they saw in it the highest expression of human ingenuity, the highest power and the true wisdom (sophism) which cannot be expressed in syllogisms or rational expositions, but which reveals itself as a creative force. According to Plato, Gorgias had said that he had more success than a physician in the treatment of a sick man, for he could persuade the patient to do things which the physician could not get done. The *rhētōr* is the true leader of the people, and he determines the course of history. The Sophists considered his power as the greatest power given to man; in the spoken word spiritual power is revealed in the most brilliant way. Since they believed this, it is understandable that they were the sworn enemies of the ethical rationalism which they saw in Socrates.

The Ancient conception of eloquence shows much agreement with ours. Nevertheless, it differs in important respects from the modern view, of which the doctrine of the Sophists should be considered one form. We do not know a single representative of Ancient oratory. Like the great Ancient thinkers and poets, the Ancient orators are all anonymous. But we know that the orator in the assembly performed a sacred act, which can be compared with the act of sacrifice performed by the priest. The scepter or plant stalk in the orator's hand represents the life of the earth and thus the divine structure of life. Just like the Pythia, the speaker is inspired by it. The personality of the orator retires to the background, like the Pythia; he is simply the bearer of the revealed divine word. The *kēryx* (herald), too, performs a sacred task. He is the representative or "descendent" of Hermes, and Hermes is the mediator or *angelos* (messenger) between gods and men, between the other world and this one. With his magic staff and his word he brings the earth's life from the other world to this world; he is the generator of that life and is represented in the form of ithyphallic stones or wooden posts. The word of the herald is equipped with the same insight and the same force: it brings the divine energies to this world, and in the sacrifice it actualizes the divine nature of the offerings. The staff of the herald is the magically empowered staff of Hermes.

Nike, too, had the herald's staff in her hand. She not only brings victory, but she *is* victory, that victory which is resurrection from death. The eloquence of every speaker in the assembly is the eloquence of Hermes. It is a divine capacity, it is Nike.

The Avesta religion is also familiar with the mythical messenger of the gods, whose power lies in the word. Here he is the messenger of Ahura Mazda and is called *Nairyosanha*, "the human command" (cf. Greek *anēr*, man, and Latin *carmen* or *casmen*, magic formula). In the assemblies he is the "eloquent one," and his task is the bringing of divine aid, sometimes in the form of "healing," to men and to the entire world. The "human" command is in this case a "divine" command; in and by the power of eloquence divine aid is brought among men. Nairyosanha is also called *vyākhana*, "the leader of the assemblies"; by means of his word he has men in his power. (Darmest. Zend-

Avesta II, 290, n. 13). He is the eloquent one in the same sense as the Greek speaker, who cannot do without the herald's staff in his hand. Nairyosanha represents, in particular, royal authority. The Greek kings, too, carried as leaders – or more exactly, as creators – of the nation's life the scepter of Hermes as a sign of their divine power and function. Nairyosanha is a mythical figure, a divine being who is now and will always continue to be active in men, in the leaders of the people.

The Greek goddess Peitho, "persuasion," the power and leadership which come forth from the word, expresses the same idea. It is characteristic that this goddess is time and time again connected with Aphrodite and Eros: the word spoken in love has more persuasive power than any other word. But it is even more remarkable that Peitho is repeatedly linked with Tyche, Chance, as the goddesses of divine guidance of individuals and peoples. In "chance" there is divine leading, but men also allow themselves to be guided by the persuasion which comes forth from the traditional institutions, the *themistes* or divine commands. Peitho is the quiet and inscrutable power exercised on men by the divine order, the persuasion by which men are brought on to the ways of salvation.

The "magical," mysterious power of the spoken word is, as we have said, a reality which is not alien even to us. But to this reality with which we are indeed acquainted, the Ancients ascribed a divine nature. The word of man is creative, and the word of God is world creating; according to Egyptian and Hebrew belief, the world is created by the word. But the same power is meant in thinking both of the human and the divine word. The Greek orator with the scepter in his hand represents Hermes, who conjures up life with his *rhabdos*. The power of the word was for the Ancients a cosmic power, and the orator, like Hermes and the Pythia, drew his inspiration from the house of cosmic wisdom, the underworld. The staff shows this clearly. This is the religious conception of the word. The word was a cosmic and divine energy, which also existed outside man but which could reveal itself in man. In Egypt the same idea is present: the "command" or the authoritative spoken word is life as such. "The command of Osiris," of Re, etc., signifies their resurrection and their absolute life.

Much more recently, in the middle of the nineteenth century, this Ancient conception of the orally transmitted word was formulated in an almost theological way by the brilliant Danish bishop, Grundtvig. This poet and seer has exerted a permanent influence on the Danish people. He and his many followers in his own time and at the present day consider the oral tradition, and not the Scriptures, as the true bearer of the foundations of the Christian revelation through all the centuries. He considered the tradition to be formulated in the Symbolum Apostolicum (the three articles of the Apostles' Creed), in the Lord's Prayer, and in the words of institution of Baptism and the Lord's Supper. His opinion, which was vigorously and probably satisfactorily contested by his orthodox opponents, was that these words come from Jesus himself, but they are words which have come to us through oral tradition because the early church stood too much in awe of them even to write them down. Not the "Scriptures," the Bible, but rather the living spoken word was able to bring divine life; it was a divine capacity of man. What is important is thus not the divinely inspired word, but the word of tradition, the spoken word which as vital principle has been throughout all history the only suitable bearer of divine life among men. This conception has, as we have seen, deep roots in the history of mankind, certainly deeper than Grundtvig knew. His doctrine is a remarkable formulation of the very ancient idea concerning the word which is itself only by means of the word. "In the word was life." All eloquence points in this direction. Among the Ancients eloquence is conceived as a divine capacity of man. Grundtvig goes a step further by eliminating the variable individual factor and concentrating exclusively on the religious idea. When God reveals Himself, He does it exclusively by means of the spoken word which endures throughout history. Writing is a dead word.

This appeal to the spiritual nature of religious life made a deep impression in the Scandinavian countries. Among many people the old dogmatic differences sank away; the spirit, and not the letter, was the chief consideration. Organizations and schools were established. The schools were the so-called "folk high schools." A high spirited life with fresh impulses prevailed, and there was a sphere of animation by song, poetry, and religious enthusiasm. These schools were especially influential among the farm population and led to new zeal in many areas.

Finally, we must examine the religious conception of another group of human capacities: the ability to think, as it reveals itself in human insight, science, and wisdom. Here the difference between Ancient and Modern ideals proves to be very great. In the one case we find a religious, in the other case a rational orientation of intellectual activities. The meaning of the rational orientation is familiar enough to us. It investigates the finite relations between the perceived phenomena, ascending from the particular to the general, from simple to complex relations. Systematic inquiry of this kind was first undertaken by the Greeks. It is free science, in which the intellectual faculty seeks its own ends and formulates its own goals. Systematic inquiry was indeed sometimes pursued before the time of the Greeks, but it was prompted by religion.

Religious thinking takes its start in a given idea concerning the essence of the phenomena, which are then grouped around that essence and comprehended in their relation to it. This essence is given by religious faith. It is the phenomenon conceived in its absolute context, that is to say, as a phenomenon willed and determined by God. Thus welfare is a blessing which in the last analysis cannot be explained on the basis of finite causes, and calamity (sickness, etc.) is just as inexplicable as death. The absolute factor in the event, that which cannot be reduced to anything else, is seen as the factor which determines everything. Not all phenomena lend themselves to such reflection: why for example is one object so heavy and another which is just as large so light? No one sought an explanation; the subject was outside the area of "scientific" interest. It was otherwise with the organic phenomena, where the absolute reality formed the starting point for the religious view and gave the explanation of it. But many of these phenomena, too, such as the structure of organisms, the similarities and differences between living beings, etc., did not receive the interest of the Ancients. The urge for knowledge was only stimulated by what were conceived as the important issues of life. Therefore the mystery of human life as such and in its cosmic relationship was the primary object of inquiry. In the last analysis, the concern was always for man for his life history from birth to death and for his place in the largest context of the living universe. Man was the center of the created world.

The great power and spiritual value of this science lay in its vivid sense of that which is characteristic in the phenomena of life, their autonomous, irreducible, and therefore mystical nature. Ancient science is subject to destructive criticism in almost all respects, but not in this one and most important respect. Modern science prefers not to speak about the essence of things; it sees in that essence the unattainable goal of its inquiry. For the Ancients, this essence was precisely the basis for their reflections. The growth of the human individual is a series of creative activities. The fact that someone becomes an "adult" at a certain time in his life is a new birth, likewise the acquiring of ordinary human skills, such as insight and mature judgment, and the entrance into society. It cannot be reduced to anything else; it cannot be explained by circumstances; it occurs in a person through the action of divine powers. Ancient science wanted to formulate that which was characteristic about these phenomena themselves, to grasp and establish the many nuances of the mystery. According to the Roman viewpoint, there is therefore one god who teaches the child to walk, and another who teaches him to speak, and still others who give the child street directions, awaken love and hate, etc. This large number of gods corresponds to a realistic apprehension of the individual determinateness of phenomena. Instead of reflections on the mystery of life in general, there appears an intuitive perception of the forms of this mystery, which are so totally different from one another. As we study these phenomena, we gain something of an understanding of the religious value of polytheism.

But we also meet really systematic and comprehensive science of this type, especially concerning the life of the world or the activity of the world in which man is involved. Here too, the essence of the occurrence is in the foreground – and that which is essential in the phenomena of life is always a mystical reality. The essence is the divine governance, will, or law which contains the divergent phenomena and forms their totality and their unity. We meet repeatedly the idea of an ultimate and all-inclusive cosmic order of life undefinable, but nevertheless reality. This is indeed a majestic synthetic view, a systematic religious science or wisdom. Cicero speaks of "the divine law which existed before all laws, the eternal law of the world." [4] In Greek religion Moira, Fate, and the other gods are not dependent on one another. They are the inscrutable law of the world process, seen from different viewpoints. (von Wilamowitz-Moellendorff.) Other forms of the world law in Greece are the Themistes, the divine institutions of Themis-Ge or of Zeus; in the Vedas and the Avesta *rita* and *asha*, respectively, etc.

Although it is not the most important, the best known form of this Ancient science is the religious astrology which was practiced by the Babylonians and many other peoples. It starts with the assumption that all events on earth are determined by a heavenly will. There is a parallelism between heaven and earth: the heavenly bodies, the planets, guide the earthly events, and God guides the heavenly bodies. Thus unity of basic principle is seen in phenomena. And thus unity is not only conceived in the general sense of "all that occurs is willed by God," but the religious theory of a parallelism between heavenly and earthly events is worked out in a natural philosophy and natural science which applies this theory to particular events. The earthly phenomena were understood and explained in the particular cosmic context in which they appeared. Even events of apparently slight significance and fortuitous nature such as chance happenings in individual lives were understood as reflections of a world process which was indicated in the motion of the heavenly bodies. Every particular is determined by the whole; it is an organic part of the world which has been willed by God. The essence, the true significance, of the smallest *is* the greatest; it is not only "caused" by the greatest. What then is "small" and what is "great"? That distinction is completely transcended. It cannot be denied that a sublime idea is expressed here and that the central idea of this science cannot be affected by criticism. It can even be said that modern natural science has again brought to the fore the idea of the correspondence between the smallest and the greatest. The smallest reflects the greatest. In the structure of the atom with its core and planets of electrons, every atom is an entire world with its heavenly bodies. In the infinite variety of reality nothing is "small" or "great"; the world process reveals itself even in the smallest occurrence. It will perhaps be said that the thought lying at the foundation of astrology may have been quite right, but that it in any case has been wrongly applied. That would be true if astrology sought the same objective and impersonal knowledge as modern science. The Ancients knew, however, that the application of astrology could not be rational, because astrological science was at the same time the highest art, a priestly, religious art, which could be carried out only through divine inspiration. About 1600 the famous Danish astrologer, Tycho Brahe, thus expressed it. Because of the religious character of astrology, even its application eludes our criticism. It is not rational knowledge which is sought.

The difference between the Ancient science, which was religious, and modern science, which is rational, comes very clearly to light when we look carefully at the two types of Ancient philosophy of nature which have already been referred to: the notion of organic growth and the idea of the world process. Where the one relates, the other separates. Where modern science tries to conceive the phenomena of the growth process in their causal connection, there the religious point of view sees a division which cannot be bridged. But at the point where modern science sees no possibility of mutually relating phenomena to a single unity of cosmic process, in which human interests are included, there the religious view sees mutual relation and connection. Ancient science always asked the question: where is the essence, that is to say, the mystery, of the phenomenon? It directed all its attention to this question, whereas it is from just this question that modern science turns away. In some cases Ancient science saw the essence in the autonomy and spontaneity of the phenomena, in other cases in their cooperation.

The Ancient ideal of knowledge was not a theoretical or contemplative insight, but an insight of a very practical nature. Its goal was to assure the success of human life, outwardly as well as inwardly. Insight meant a mystical and magical (irrational) power over the basic conditions of human existence. It was a matter of vital importance that the many gods of the different stages of individual life, from birth right through to death, should not only be recognized but actually worshipped. In that worship was spiritual power. Very real and immediate interests were also served by the astrological insight into the cosmic process. And if one thinks that that power was in any event an illusion, he is confusing the Ancient type of science with the modern type and assuming that the Ancients saw as reality what we think of as reality, or, in other words, that they sought our goals. Our criteria of illusion or truth in scientific inquiry are different from theirs. The fact that their science disappointed them just as little as our science disappoints us proves that different goals were kept in view. With as little (or as much) justice it can be said that prayer is an illusion, because "reality" shows that ... etc. For what is reality? For the religious man it is certainly something different from what it is for the rationalist. Our natural science is rational and rationalistic, and that is what it wants to be, but the science of the Ancients was not. The science of the Ancients was at the same time religion and actually gave them the power which they desired, the power which we also desire and reach through our religion. Not every one understands the same thing by "power." It is the old question of historical understanding: if we want to understand reliligious astrology, then we must understand its own right to exist.

Astrology was indeed a striking example of mystical science. There are, however, also other types, but because of a lack of clear data we are too little acquainted with most of them and understand them even less. This is the case with soothsaying by means of omens, for example the observation of the behaviour of animals (especially of birds in flight), or the examination of the entrails of animals which had been sacrificed. Neither the principal idea nor the particulars are known. The examination of the liver in Babylonia and the so called "haruspicium" in Rome were evidently altered forms of astrology; the liver was an image of the sky. Perhaps the basic idea in every case was the assumed correspondence between apparently accidental earthly phenomena and phenomena of cosmic nature in which divine destiny (often mentioned in this connection) was revealed. In any case all these forms of mystical science sought insight and power over the basic conditions of human life. They were therefore usually communications or revelations from the gods of the secret of life, the gods of the underworld or realm of the dead: in Babylonia Ea, in Etruria Tages, in Greece probably Athene and certainly Demeter Thesmophoros, the bearer of the Themistes, the rules of human social life.

In many cases where it seems to us to be a matter of purely rational insight, the Ancients speak of revealed insight, because it is insight concerned with the important issues of life. This is the case when they are dealing with agriculture. For them agricultural knowledge is a mystery which is communicated to men by the god of the earth or of the underworld, by Ea, Osiris, Triptolemus, or Saturn-Kronos. It is understandable that this knowledge is called "revealed" knowledge. How could men by their own power have obtained power over the earth's life in plowing, sowing, and harvesting? Agriculture was a religio-magical act. Part of the sacred legend connected with the Eleusinian Mysteries, and probably also found in Egypt, was the story of the divine instruction in methods of agriculture, and the performance of typical agricultural activities was among the sacred acts. Thus on the Rarian Plain in Eleusis whenever the Mysteries were celebrated, the first plowing, sowing, and harvesting were repeated as a sacred act. In this way divine activities are performed, for such a finite act as the plowing of the field has results which go beyond any rational expectations; it has infinite results. The religio-magical act presupposes a mystical insight. One may ask whether each farmer who went out plowing was aware that he performed a sacred act and practiced a magical science. That is quite possible. Even we still sense somewhat the religious character of the meal. One may think of many old ideas and usages which are still held by certain groups up to the present day. Certain peasants still believe that when in the spring the plow is put into the earth for the first time, the spirit of plant growth then returns and wards off calamity from men and animals. In any case this was the religious conception of the art of agriculture, and it was not solely philosophical or theoretical reflection. It was expressed in the practice of worship, the cultus.

Medical science, too, which had as its aim the mystery of healing, that is to say, the resurrection of life from death, had

been revealed by the same gods of the underworld; it was practiced by the priests, often utilizing some magical means, such
as purification with elements considered essential to life (water,
oil, or honey), or purification through the touch of the priest
(the god). Naturally very rational means were also applied, but
their effectiveness was considered to be just as much a"mystery."
The "healthful herb" was certainly used in many cases with
good results, but it also served as a magic herb to compell
Circe's cooperation.[5] Plowing, harrowing, and watering, etc.,
were rational activities and nevertheless magical acts, because
growth resulted from them. Medicine was a sacred science because it was concerned with the important issues of life and with
the basic condition for life, irrespective of its applying "rational"
or magical methods. The systematic experimental research of the
Greeks was the first to eliminate the consciousness of the magical
character of medicine.

All Ancient science was mystical science. Its subject was the
mystery of life; its practice was the religious rite. Modern science
condemns all this because on principle it does not admit the
essence of the phenomena. But it too, as "strict science," has
often failed to escape "narrow-mindedness."

The ideal of wisdom is directly connected with the Ancient
conception of the goal of all insight and all science. True wisdom
and true insight are not of a theoretical but of a practical nature.
Completely in the spirit of the Ancients, the Stoic Seneca, called
the wise man an "artifex vivendi." The Roman sense of reality
and the feeling for the characteristic element in every phenomenon is closer to the religious sense of nature in the Ancient peoples
than is the Greek rationalism from the time of the "enlightenment." In Rome there is not such a deep cleft between old and
new as there is in Greece. Again and again we read that the wise
man is he who knows the path of life, the way of spiritual
preservation and of prosperity. Theoretical insight is of secondary importance. Thus *prudentia* is the practical tact necessary
to save spiritual values; it is a recourse to the universe and to
one's own soul. According to Wagenvoort, the emphasis in
prudentia is on the intuitive sensing, "seeing," and "viewing" of
what man should do.

In the Avesta this notion of wisdom found numerous ex-

pressions. The name Ahura Mazda means the "Wise Lord";
wisdom is religion, and religion is wisdom. Both concepts are
united in Daena, "religion," and "the soul" of man, derived
from *di* (*dhi*), "to see, to have insight, to think". Vohu-Manah,
one of the seven spirits of Ahura Mazda, corresponds almost
completely to the Roman *prudentia*. When Zarathustra comes
before his listeners, he appeals to their "understanding" and
proclaims to them what "wisdom" is: "I want to proclaim what
wisdom is for every one who possesses insight, to proclaim which
of you is the well considered (wise) man and what joy he will
finally enjoy. Hear with your ears the best things and note with
clear understanding the decision which every one must make."
(Yasna 30 : 1–2.) The two spirits which existed in the beginning
were the one who with good insight chose the right and the one
who with bad insight chose evil. Or it is expressed thus: "the
false teacher kills the understanding of life" – the right instinct
(Yasna 32 : 9). The godless man is a fool; compare with this
Proverbs 1–9 and also Psalm 14: "The fool says in his heart:
there is no God"; likewise Matthew 5 : 22: "... he who says,
you fool, will be punishable by hell fire." Divine wisdom lives
as an instinct in the faithful and pious man, and originates, not
from man, but from God. That is the religious character of this
Ancient wisdom. Vistaspa at his conversion attains wisdom,
which the giver of salvation (Spenta) Mazda Ahura has conceived
in agreement with the spirit of cosmic and human order or stability, *asha*, and the spirit of the right tact, Vohu-Manah (Yasna
51 : 16). Compare too, Job 28 : 28: "And he said to man,
'Behold, the fear of the Lord, that is wisdom; and to depart
from evil is understanding.' " Wisdom is religion and is therefore
conceived as infinite and mystical, and as a superhuman capacity.

Ancient science was a mystical knowledge and a magical
capacity, not only religious, but also divine, just as is "sancta
theologia." According to the Egyptian formulation of this
science, it was revealed to the wise men in "the House of Life,"
that is to say, in the realm of the dead. For this science was
always concerned with the mystery of life. That means, furthermore, that it existed objectively and autonomously, independent
of man. It was the law, or the life, of the cosmos and was actually worshipped by various Ancient peoples as a divine being.

One of the seven spirits of Ahura Mazda was Armaiti, "Wisdom." She is also a nature goddess. Even in the Gathas she is already mentioned in connection with the earth; later Armaiti became a name for "earth." The life of earth proves repeatedly to represent the life of the universe, and also the life of men; the resurrected life of the earth is the type of the life of the cosmos. Therefore the earth goddess or the earth is "the wise one." Wisdom is then the divine life which is identified with the world's life. The idea is related to the Greek "Holy Wisdom," *Hagia Sophia*, and to the Israelite "Wisdom," *Chokma* – the wisdom which existed before the creation and brought forth the life of the world. For it is the life of the world itself. Compare Proverbs 8 : 22–31 and Job 28, where it is described how the poet has sought everywhere for wisdom without finding it. God knows its place and searched it out when He created the world order. But He said to man: "Behold, to fear the Lord is wisdom, and to depart from evil is discernment." As soon as "wisdom" obtains this cosmic significance, the essential connection is therewith established between the human wisdom attained in piety on the one hand, and prosperity on the other. Agreement with the cosmic order is, of course, prosperity. The earth goddess Armaiti gives riches and welfare. We find the same thought in Proverbs 8 :18, where Chokma says, "Riches and honour are with me, enduring wealth and prosperity." We are likely to take such statements simply as metaphors, but such is not the case. In Yasht 16, Zarathustra sacrifices to *Daena* (Religion) and to "richly provided (with foodstuffs)" *Cista*, (Insight and Wisdom), in order to receive spiritual and bodily strength. The practical significance of insight and wisdom is in this instance especially clear. Through their religious sense the Ancients were able to relate spirit and nature more closely to each other than we can do; they even identified them. The thought that piety and righteousness, or wisdom and religion, must necessarily bring prosperity along with them is deeply rooted in the religious consciousness that man shares in the divine life of the cosmos. I shall have more to say about this later.

It might be asked whether this description of divine wisdom in the Ancient religions is not idealized and whether we have not one sidedly paid attention to formulations of an especially sublime nature. In answer to this question let me simply say that there are also other aspects which could be mentioned which seem less attractive to us. Divine wisdom, for instance, is again and again described as cunning. Kronos is called, "He with the crooked (crafty, sly) plans," just as is Prometheus, and the cunning of Hermes is well known; he even tricks his fellow gods. The Indic Varuna, the highest ruler of the world order and the wise one par excellence, is crafty and deceitful. Ea, the wisest of the Babylonian gods, is also crafty and deceitful. For the religious man the divine cunning or crookedness does not, however, signify an inferior wisdom, but just the opposite. The sense of the inscrutability of divine insight and capacity made itself felt again and again. The mystery remained a mystery, beyond all human inspection or verification; it was beyond human standards and norms, because absolute insight is not an extension of finite and human insight. Divine insight is, humanly speaking, madness. They who possessed it, such persons as the ecstatic worshippers of Dionysus and the first Hebrew prophets, were mad. The superhuman assumes forms which seem to be subhuman; nevertheless the religious person knows the true significance of these forms, just as he does when worshipping gods in the form of animals. Humanly speaking, divine wisdom is deceitful cunning and crookedness, because the rational and ethical element in it is abrogated and denied. Hermes is able by his cunning to make off with the spoils of Hades and thus to enable life to a rise; this is divine wisdom. The same is true of Kronos, the god of the underworld, and of Prometheus, who brings the divine life of fire among men. This is likewise true of Ea, who saves the life of the Babylonian Flood Hero, and of Varuna. Men do not understand how these works have taken place and therefore speak of "cunning." But this cunning is completely in line with the Ancient conception of wisdom.

Finally we would mention still another type of the religious conception of wisdom. The Vedanta, the philosophy of Brahmanism, teaches that the knowledge of Brahman releases man from finitude and transiency. Brahman is the divine essence of all existence, the soul of the universe. It cannot be known in the external, empirical world; only "by turning the eyes (within)" is immediate understanding possible of the eternal which can be attained in one's own self, of the enduring self (Atman), the spiritual unity behind all consciousness. This is expressed negatively in the finitude, determinateness, and relativity of *nāma-rūpa*, that which has "name and form." Wisdom is the tracing back of everything to the one enduring and real substance, which is attained by meditation, and later, in Buddhism, by asceticism. In this instance, too, the thought is present of man's participation in the divine life of the cosmos, but in another sense than for instance in the Avesta. Every relation between man and God is abolished, for there is complete identity. In the Avesta and in all other Ancient religions, "cosmic wisdom," man's participation in the divine life of the world, signifies a gift which has been made to man, an impartation of divine life. The religious relation is unaffected. But the wisdom of the Vedanta is not a divine revelation, as are astrology and insight in agriculture and medicine; it is not a divine gift to man connected with earthly blessing. The wisdom does not impart itself to man, as Armaiti imparts herself, but it is attained by man's own power; by means of meditation and reflection one comes to knowledge of reality, to the imperishable and the unchangeable. To say this more accurately, by means of Brahman or Atman in himself, by means of Brahman who thinks himself, man attains self knowledge and imperishability. Because this takes place through man's own power the religious character of the Vedanta has sometimes been denied, and it has been called "free science" or "metaphysics" in the sense of those terms familiar to us and to the Greeks. But it is certainly not that. In Greek science and philosophy the unity of the variety is formulated; the laws of the natural sciences and the essence of the humanities are always a definite unity, a definite universal. In the Vedanta, on the contrary, that which is determined and determinable, the *nāma-rūpa* is illusion. The difference between the one who perceives and that which is perceived is abolished, so that consciousness is abolished and the personality obliterated as "in a dreamless sleep." The resultant state is comparable to Nirvana in Buddhism. This is certainly not the Greek type of science or philosophy. The Vedanta might be called a religious metaphysics – not a metaphysical religion, for that is an impossibility – indeed it is religious thought of a pantheistic type. The goal of this metaphysics is, as we would expect, formulated in religious terms: release from finitude and the attainment of eternal life. The Vedanta is a theoretical doctrine of salvation intended for a small and elite circle of people. Buddhism, which contains no positive metaphysics or doctrine concerning the essence of phenomena, is a practical doctrine of salvation, and its asceticism is a method open to everyone.

CHAPTER 13

SIMILARITY AND DIFFERENCE BETWEEN MAN AND GOD

A. SIMILARITY TO GOD

The religious idea concerning the similarity or affinity between man and deity has already been mentioned briefly a number of times: divine energies reveal themselves in the fact of life, in the existence of the human soul, in the qualities and abilities of man. The sense of affinity was especially evident in the different ideas concerning man's origin from the earth, whether from trees or stones; man lives the divine life of the earth. But all this touches the subject only obliquely. Now we must pay attention to the instances where the question concerning affinity or difference between man and deity is deliberately asked and answered.

The totemistic conception of individual and society is quite rightly often mentioned as a clear formulation of the sense of affinity between man and deity. But it is regrettable that too restricted a meaning is usually given to "totemism" (a word from the language of the Algonquin Indians). Usually one has in mind only the belief that man has originated from a certain kind of animal or plant, sometimes also from another object in the realm of nature, such as the sun, the moon, water, and the like. The totem was the common tribal ancestor of a group and was therefore worshipped as a divine being. "Totemism" is, however, not only a form of belief concerning the origin of the race; it is as much concerned with the nature of the present living descendents of the totem ancestor. In the historical religions totem belief is seldom if ever met with in connection with man's origin, but rather in connection with man's kinship with a "totem object" considered as a divine being. Thus a vital link is assumed to exist between man and certain natural objects (considered to be divine beings); man is akin to the divine being.

It was particularly the work of Robertson Smith, *The Religion of the Semites* (first edition, 1889), which directed the attention of historians of religion to "totemism," especially to totem animals. The facts which he cites give little indication of definite ideas concerning the origin of man, but they do indicate some very remarkable notions concerning the affinity between deity and man. What Robertson Smith calls the "totemistic sacrifice" sheds the most light on this subject. Not every animal can serve as an offering, but only the "sacred" animal, the empirical bearer of the divine essence. In being slaughtered, the animal through his death becomes identical with the god. Death consecrates and brings life from the finite world into the infinite, divine world. In the sacrificial meal, at which all those present partake of the meat from the sacrificed animal, men take into themselves the divine substance. The sacrificial food gives divine life and actualizes the relationship between man and deity. In the first place, the participants in the sacrificial meal are mutually united by the same divine energy; a fellowship of believers is founded and the enduring supra-individual life of one's fellow tribesmen is actualized. In the second place, a communion or sharing of life is instituted between the god and men. The sacrifice with the sacrificial meal actualizes ever afresh the divine character of society, and thus the affinity or similarity between man and deity.

Such is the "totemistic" sacrifice in the historical religions. Striking parallels can be indicated in the primitive religions – for example, when the members of the tribe may eat the totem animal only on ceremonial occasions – but the religious meaning does not become clearer through these data. We understand the primitive totem sacrifices only on the basis of data which are much closer to us. Robertson Smith draws his examples from the well known religions of the Semites and the Greeks. Even closer to us is the Roman Catholic sacrifice of the mass, Holy Communion, in which the priest partakes of the Sacred Host on behalf of the faithful. Holy Communion, too, as it is understood by the Roman Catholic Church and by many other groups, is an actualizing of one's own absolute life by assimilating the divine substance. The central thought is that God imparts Himself to men, so that a communion of life comes into being which is more than a bond between man and God. In spite of his finitude man shares in divine life.

Not only the sacrificial meal, however, but also every other sacrificial act witnesses to the belief in man's participation in divine life. Every offering is for the believer a bearer of divine life: the plant sacrifice, the libation, the sacrifice for the dead, and even the sacrifice in the form of funeral games. The sacrificial act, the *sacrificium*, actualizes the divine nature of the offering and of the whole genus to which the offering belongs and assures the continuance of these divine energies in the world. It can be said with a certain justice that the deity lives by means of the sacrifice which is offered to him, by partaking of the food and drink offerings. But it is more accurate to say that the divinity or absolute life of the offering is actualized and assured by being offered to him from whom it has originated. In this sense the sacrifice assures divine life and the deity lives from the sacrifice. The first fruits of the field are sacrificed in order to conform and continue the blessing of this prerequisite to man's life or in order to actualize the divine life which reveals itself in the fruits of the field. By means of this sacrifice man recognizes that the god reveals himself in the produce of the ground which he sees not only as a divine gift, but as a self-revelation of the deity. Thus the sacrificer raises the finite phenomenon of the offering into the sphere of the infinite; he creates the foundation of his own existence. The consecration of the offering often takes place by killing it; in every sacrifice the chief element is the consecration.

Thus every sacrifice is a religio-magical act in which man cooperates with the deity. His similarity or affinity to god has become a fact. This idea proves in most if not all religions to be extremely important. It finds expression not only in sacrifice, but also in numerous formulations of man's general task in life.

This is especially clear in the Avesta. We find one of the main ideas here to be the thought that man participates in the cosmic world struggle between the good spirit of Ahura Mazda and the evil spirit of Ahriman, for or against the divine plan, and thus for or against the life of the world and mankind. The dualism of the Avesta is as much cosmic as ethical. Every act of man has infinite significance and contributes to the outcome of the world struggle. Man is the fellow worker of God. In Vendidad 3 : 30,

Zarathustra asks, "How does one advance the religion of Mazda?"
and Mazda answers, "By sowing grain with zeal. He who sows
grain sows righteousness (the path of life); when the grain comes
up, the demons are afraid; when it is ripe, they shudder; when
it is made into bread, they take flight." Thus even in ordinary
natural life, man performs in and by his religion a divine activity.
He "advances the Mazda religion," he helps it to victory. Every
"righteous man" who proclaims the true doctrine, every believer, is *ahum-bish*, "world healing," – a term which is also
applied to Mazda himself. Every unrighteous man is *ahum-mrnc*,
"world murderer." Later this idea is expressed in the thought
that the believer is in the god's army. In the Mithra mystery
religion, *Miles* is an expression for him who fights the battle of
Mithra; among the Egyptian gnostics he is called *Stratiōtikos*,
soldier. Christians speak of the *Ecclesia Militans* and of the
milites Christi. In all these instances the thought is expressed
that religious faith is also a cosmic power. The idea is certainly
present of an affinity between man and god and of a cooperation
of man with deity.

Sometimes the statements concerning the help which men give
to the gods are very remarkable: the god is dependent on that
help. This is the case in the myth in the Avesta about the
struggle of Tishtrya against Apaosha. Tishtrya appeals to men,
"Who will offer me sacrifices of *haoma*, milk, horses, purity
of soul? The world now owes me a sacrifice of prayer and piety."
After having fought three days against Apaosha, he retreats:
"Woe is me, oh Ahura Mazda; woe is me ye waters and plants,
thou religion of Mazda. Men have offered me no sacrifice. If
they had done that, then my strength would have been that of
ten horses, of ten camels, of mountains, and of rivers!" Then
Ahura Mazda offers the sacrifice, and Tishtrya triumphs. Thus
in this myth the god is dependent on man, and man is the superior. Yet there is no possibility that this is an irreligious idea.
Something in the Avesta which was felt to be irreligious would
not have found a permanent place. The writer of this passage
wanted to say only that when religion is lacking and worship
with sacrifices ceases, the evil power has the upper hand. Divine
omnipotence reveals itself above all in piety and religious faith
and bestows its omnipotence on them. When the struggle against

death is accepted and fought in the true religion, the victory is assured.

The religio-ethical application of this thought is certainly not alien to our own experience. What is striking in this story of Tishtrya's struggle is that this thought has a cosmic application. The god of the world's life, the rain god, is worsted by his enemy because the piety of man is lacking: piety is also a cosmic power. That sounds strange to us, but it is certainly religious, and, in the last analysis, it will prove, even for us, not to be altogether strange. It might be said that this passage about Tishtrya was composed by priests who found the believers too negligent in offering sacrifices, naturally to the priests' own disadvantage. That is possible. But even then it remains true that the formulation which is given would not serve as an incentive if it conflicted with the religious sense. For us, too, the problem exists that God's cause can lose through men's unfaithfulness; only in this story this problem is put in an unusual and paradoxical way, certainly unusual even to the thinking of the Mazda worshippers. Basically it is the same difficulty that arises whenever man's cooperation with God is presupposed, as it is in each cultic act – especially in the sacrifice.

Let us now fix our attention on the instances where the belief in the divine essence of man and his affinity to deity is expressly formulated.

According to Genesis 1 : 26, man is an "image of God, made in His likeness." According to the Babylonian myth (Berosus, third century B.C.) Bel or Marduk forms man from clay and earth, mixed with the blood of the gods. "Therefore men are rational beings and have a part in the divine intelligence." That they are of divine blood is evident from their insight, their mystical insight into basic essentials for life agriculture, medicine, and soothsaying, which together constituted Ancient science. The genuine hero and representative of man, Gilgamesh, corresponds completely to the idea which we find in Berosos. He is two-thirds god and one-third man, thus of predominantly divine nature.

What this means can be shown on the basis of numerous unambiguous data. Life in general, including human life, was for the Ancients a divine reality, a self-subsistent and creative power. Human life was inseparably bound up with cosmic life;

man lives the earth's life, and all human expressions of life from
birth to death form an unbroken series of revelations of divine
forces. Nevertheless every man has felt the finitude and limitation
of his capacities, something which does not indicate autonomy
or divinity. Inscrutable life was a reality extending above and
beyond the reach and the conception of man; he was not the
master of it, as was the god who was that life itself. Man must
die in order to be released from finitude, but during his earthly
existence he is not the same as a dead man. He is even afraid
of death, which proves that he is not a god. Indeed, Gilgamesh's
fear of death is the chief theme of the Gilgamesh Epic. His finitude
is his humanity, but nevertheless his divinity is that which constitutes his essential being; therefore he is one-third man and
two-thirds god. Personal names such as *"Shamash-abūni"* and
"Ishtar-ummisha" express his sonship. All Babylonian gods can be
called the "parents" of men, sometimes also "brother" or "uncle,"
as in *A ḫum-kīnum,* "the Brother (God) is faithful." In general
every man is *amēlu mār ilishu,* "a man son of his god," namely
of his particular tutelary deity or genius. Similar personal names
also occur in Egypt, for example, "son of strong Father Ptah."
In Rome every god is the "pater" of men; Jupiter is the best
known example.

This sense of affinity has developed in the mystical forms of
various religions into a sense of identity, of complete unity with
deity. The Sufi movement in Islam is especially characteristic.[1]
The Sufis derive their name from the woolen cloth, the *suf,* which
they wear as a sign of their asceticism and simplicity. There
are also other names for these mystics: "fakirs" and "dervishes," the "poor" who have separated themselves from any sort
of earthly possession. In the Sufi movement a conscious and
determined protest is expressed against the idea of God as lord
and master and judge of men and against the service of God
consisting of prescribed religious acts, such as recital of the
creed, fasts, and pilgrimages. The whole emphasis is on man's
disposition, on love for God, on being absorbed and hidden in
God. Sometimes the religious metaphor is completely borrowed
from the language of human love, the eros. The mood, furthermore, is often achieved in an artificial way – especially by means
of narcotic stupor, but also by singing and instrumental music

and by dancing (the dervish dance), and sometimes also by the strictest asceticism. The heroes of this movement, who lived in the ninth and tenth centuries A.D., were true saints in character and religious earnestness. They actually realized the *unio mystica*, and they described their union with God as the only true religion. "I am thou, and thou art I," "I am the absolute reality." In many respects they remind us of Brahmans of the Vedanta, but there is this difference, that as true prophets they stand in opposition to the orthodox religion. Although they sometimes deliberately tried to induce scorn and disdain from people, their unquestionable seriousness and integrity always finally compelled respect. It is a remarkable fact and an important one in forming a judgment about them, that the Sufi movement has remained in existence through the centuries, though divided indeed into a large number of sects. We must accept the Sufi conviction of unity between man and deity as a religious fact of great significance; we cannot pass it by as if it were a morbid phenomenon of one peculiar formulation of the divine relation. It has been thought that mysticism penetrated Islam from India and Greece, from the Neoplatonism of Plotinus and from Gnosticism. The possible foreign influences do not, however, explain the fact that the Sufi movement was able to put down such deep roots into the soil of Islam. Mysticism must have lain in the nature of Islam itself, and modern investigators quite rightly call attention to the many starting points for mysticism in the earliest stage of Mohammedanism, in which the whole emphasis was often placed on the inner disposition.

In a certain sense the Ancient "mystery religions" also represent the idea of unity between God and man. The best known are the Egyptian and Greek Mysteries and those of the Mithra religion. Their goal was release from finitude and transiency and the attainment of absolute life, even during this earthly existence. The difference from Islamic, Indian, Jewish, and Christian mysticism lies in the fact that the former have a sacramental initiation which is not restricted to certain classes or groups. The initiation took place in Eleusis by means of the *epopteia*, the gazing at stalks of grain which had been ceremonially cut. In the Mithra religion it took place through the bull sacrifice, the dramatic representation of the self-sacrifice of

Mithra in man's behalf, who thereby is "reborn for eternity."
In Egypt the initiation is "by following Osiris (or Sokaris),"
undergoing the sacramental death of the god. By this act man
breaks the bonds of fate and abolishes his finitude. As in all
sacraments, a new, divine life is granted to man through this
initiation.

Up to now we have treated only the different types of religious
ideas which attest to man's divine essence and likeness to deity.
But with respect to the similarity of man and God, another group
of data are important, namely those concerning the human essence of deity. Anthropomorphic ideas of deity signify theomorphic ideas of man, and the similarity which is then assumed
to exist between man and God is a subject which must be
investigated as much from the anthropological as from the
theological side.

"Anthropomorphic ideas of deity" is a term which has repeatedly occasioned, and still does occasion, misunderstanding, one-
sided application, and mistaken judgments. Ludwig Feuerbach
gave a systematic but certainly very one-sided exposition in
Das Wesen des Christentums and *Das Wesen der Religion*.[2] According to him theology is anthropology; he calls the wish, need
and hope of man the theogonic principle. What man extols and
glorifies is for him "god"; what he rejects is demonic power.
From this the anthropomorphic idea of deity originates. God is a
projection of the human mind, created according to the image
of man, and not vice versa. The gods are "wish beings (*Wünschwesen*), the wishes (of men) which are thought to be real" or
"wishes changed into real beings." Religion is therefore "a worthless illusion," and man loses nothing when he loses his religion.
This is really a remarkable example of a psychological explanation
which is extraordinarily unpsychological, and of theorizing which
is in flat contradiction to all experience. But here we can leave
that aside. What interests us is the element of truth undoubtedly
contained in the thesis that "theology is anthropology." In
numerous myths deity is represented more or less in conformity
with man's likeness, and the religious character of the anthropomorphic idea of deity deserves more attention than is usually
accorded it.

We must immediately exclude from consideration a series

of "myths" which are not genuine myths. This is the case, for instance, when a poet guided by aesthetic motives makes free use of divine figures. Homer provides many examples when he describes ordinary human quarrels and rivalries among the gods, or very commonplace scenes with the gods as the persons acting in the scenes. Such stories have nothing in common with true myth or with religion. The mythical idea of deity in which the believers express their faith is completely different. It is often "completely human," but is is nevertheless differently meant and is to be understood differently; the divine character of the mythical figures is not lost sight of. In the myth of Demeter who seeks Kore, the wanderings and encounters of the goddess are represented in a completely human form, yet everything is recited and heard in a very different mood than would prevail if it were a story about men. The background of everything is the consciousness that Demeter is a divine being. The myth moves freely in ideas borrowed from human life, but nevertheless the whole atmosphere is altogether different from that of the profane realm. Here poetic fantasy is in the service of religion. (In Homer it is just the reverse.) Everything breathes the spirit and reflects the cultus of Eleusis. Not the human idea, but the idea of deity dominates the story. The Egyptians myth relates that Osiris, while he was a guest at a meal given by Seth, was ambushed and killed. Not every aspect or particular of the story has a religious or symbolic meaning, but the whole is religiously felt and thought, quite differently than if it were concerned with men. The chief theme is of a religious nature. This is true of even the more or less incidental depictions of divine beings. Yahweh walks in the evening in the Garden of Eden; He comes in the form of three men to Abram in Hebron. Yet these human traits do not make Yahweh a man. If we want to understand the myth, then we need to take account of the apprehension of the author, and of the listener to whom it is directed, and we must not apply an alien rationalistic standard to it.

The religious man in his mythical ideas of deity makes use of human experiences and observations. He could not possibly do otherwise. Every idea of deity is a "mythical" idea; it represents the divine essence according to a human model. But what then is the fault in Feuerbach's thesis that the reproduction of man cannot yield anything superhuman? The anthropomorphic god is actually not a man; every religious person would affirm this, and only his testimony is of any value here. The explanation of this fact can be attained only on the basis of a precise observation of the historical data. The question is how the religious man who recounts the myth thinks about the human qualities which he ascribes to his god. The question is not how we modern, unbelieving men think about what the Ancients relate to us. We have already pointed out that the "human" qualities were for the ancient reciters of these myths not purely and simply human. In the human qualities uncomprehended factors are revealed. In love and hate, in growth, and in the chance happenings of life, spontaneous forces are active. In the generation of life, in triumphing over enemies, in the founding of cities, and even in the most commonplace events such as the consumption of food, and sleeping and waking – in all these things the human element proves to be not simply human finitude. And when the gods fight among themselves or against their enemies, or marry and generate children, or eat and drink, all these activities are for the Ancient man who recounts them as much divine as they are human, because even that which is human is an uncomprehended reality, a revelation of self-subsistent energy, and as such it is divine. This makes myth possible. We are inclined to see pure finitude in mythical tales because we lack an eye for what the Ancients succeeded in seeing. To the Ancient mind, the myth moves in a religious sphere. We do not notice this sphere, or do so with great difficulty, because the terminology is so foreign to us. Often it is too difficult, and we abandon the attempt. Then we say that "the anthropomorphic ideas of deity fail to do justice to the divine," and that they are "inferior." But we have as little right to say this as we would have to say that the Ancient languages are too difficult to learn but that everyone can hear and understand that they are barbaric languages!

Perhaps we understand better the religious meaning of anthropomorphic ideas of deity which testify to a similarity between God and man, when the concern is with spiritual rather than with bodily attributes and capacities. Man, too, possesses the wisdom of insight into the order of life ascribed to deity, and the spiritual power which is revealed in the magical power of the command, in the force of the word. But for the religious person, these are quite clearly irrational capacities and irreducible qualities. The divine power and wisdom does not become less divine because man possesses suprarational power and insight. It was taken as a matter of course that man does not derive from himself what he has and is; he draws on an infinite and divine reality. The similarity between man and God is therefore a wholly uncomprehended and incomprehensible fact, a religious fact. The human character of deity lies in the religious sphere; it is not rational. This is what Feuerbach overlooked, and on this fact his negative judgment of religion has run aground.

It is often difficult for us to project ourselves into the Ancients' anthropomorphic ideas of deity; we are inclined to see in them something quite unspiritual. Even in Antiquity this objection was felt by those who had wandered away from the Ancient orientation. Well known examples can be found in Plato, Philo, and the Stoics. They believed that what was accidental to human nature and all that which conflicted with ethical or physical laws was unacceptable in the idea of God. Their effort was to formulate the nature of divine being along the lines of human ideals. According to the Jew Philo, it is naïve to believe that God was sorry to have created man, or that Eve was fashioned from Adam's rib. In order to escape anthropomorphism, he interprets such ideas allegorically, in line with his own ideals and in agreement with the Platonic and Stoic viewpoint. He calls Adam and Eve the two-sided manifestation of spiritual being; Adam is the spirit as intellect, and Eve signifies the activity arising from that intellect. "Rib" stands for the force which slumbers in the spiritual activity and is already potentially present. God does not accomplish His will, according to Philo, by instrumental acts which can lead only to material results. God is spirit, and He actualizes His essential being in a spiritual way, being which is identical with absolute reason, beauty, and goodness. It is thus that the account of Creation in Genesis 1 is to be understood: Creation can have been only a purely spiritual event. The material creation of earth, water, animals and plants, thus the coming into being of matter from non-matter, is, considered by itself, an irrationality and impossibility which doesn't belong anywhere in reality. It serves only as the outward expression or image of the spiritual creation, which is indeed possible and which we know; man knows creative spiritual activity from his own experience. All of this is a systematic rejection of the mythical-sensual anthropomorphic traits in the idea of God. It does indeed seem that Philo with his allegorical interpretation has removed anthropomorphism from the idea of deity. But actually he has only accepted it in a new guise, in the form of intellectual ethical ideals, which are just as much humanly determined as are mechanical acts. It might be said that this is, nevertheless, an anthropomorphism less than that present in the myth, and from the philosophical standpoint this is indeed the case. But the question remains as to whether it is less naïve from the religious standpoint. Living religion always expresses itself in "images", "symbols," which however, are sensed to be not images but divine reality. The outsider calls this "metaphor"; the believer does not. There are as many kinds of religious formulation as there are religions.

One example will make clear that it is very doubtful whether religious interests are served by such ideal ethical formulations as Philo advanced. One of Philo's followers was Plutarch. He also wants to remove from the idea of God that which is ethically unworthy, for example a god who for inexplicable or silly reasons rages and wreaks vengeance. Plutarch's argument is the following:

> Is not the one who believes that there are no gods a more pious man than he who ascribes unworthy acts to God? I myself should prefer that it were said, there is no Plutarch and there has never been one, than that it were said, Plutarch is an undependable, irritable, vindictive, and narrow minded person. If you invite friends but do not invite Plutarch (do not invite a god to the sacrifice), then he is offended with you. If you are busy and do not think of Plutarch (God), then he becomes furious, he bites you, hits your child, and turns his animals loose to destroy your harvest. . . . [3]

God must thus be at least as ethical as this schoolmaster in Chaeronea. It has however, been forgotten in this argument that the creator of the world might possibly follow a different code of conduct than does the good Plutarch in his dealings with his fellow men. Human ideals can be obstacles to religious faith, and the difference between religious and irreligious anthropomorphism cannot be determined with the standard of human ideals. Divine arbitrariness or uncomprehended wrath does not

necessarily detract from the value of a particular understanding
of deity.

Anthropomorphic ideas of God are, as we have said, present in
all religions. They witness to the belief in affinity of man to
God, as affinity not of a finite but of an infinite nature. Yet there
is one religion known to us which appears to be an exception to
the rule – the Roman religion before is was subject to Greek
influence. This religion has no myths, or stories of deeds in which
a divine personality speaks; it has no images and no temples.
Here, it might be thought, no anthropomorphic notion of deity
is possible. It is indeed a remarkable type of religion; not a
unique example, it is true, but nowhere else so purely developed.
Divine activity expresses itself predominantly, if indeed not
exclusively, in particular instances, in the concrete phenomena
of nature, man, and state. The innumerable phenomena of life
are seen as expressions of divine activity. Vesta was the divine
energy of the fire in the state hearth, that is to say, in the self-
renewing life of the nation, the fire energy which was also present
in the earth ("Vesta Terra est"). The countless particular gods
of agricultural produce, of events, and of particulars, such as
Bona Fortuna, Fortuna Muliebris, etc., are of the same type.
This is almost always called a proof of "Roman unsentimental
common sense," which has been taken to indicate spiritual
poverty and "lack of imagination on the part of the Romans."
But this conclusion is quite unjustly drawn. The Roman conception testifies precisely to a deep sense for reality, reality
which also contains infinite elements. Schleiermacher defines
"miracle" as the "religious term for an event." No religion better
illustrates this understanding than does the Roman, although
the Avesta is also familiar with many "concept gods" of the
Roman type. This is certainly not an expression of spiritual or
religious poverty. It is true it does not indicate the artistic
imagination which anthropomorphism in the usual sense of the
word produces, but it does evince creative imagination, namely
the ability to conceive the reality beyond or behind rational
reality, to see the divine background and foundation of phenomena and to act in accordance with them. It was just this action
which was creative reality for the Romans. They were men more
of action than of reflection. But action presupposes just as much

imagination as does reflection, namely an intervention in the
course of affairs with an accurate insight into the nature of the
phenomena, for otherwise the action would end in failure. The
Romans had an extraordinarily keen insight into reality's essential element, that is to say, reality including its irrational factor. That was expressed in their religion and determined all
their behaviour. They possessed the creative imagination whereby
the gifted statesman, farmer, or merchant produces something
new. This imagination did not lead to anthropomorphic ideas
of God in the usual sense of the word, but they saw in the ordinary expressions of life, which included their own life, more
clearly and vividly than most Ancient peoples the activity of
divine forces. And thus they represented their gods. The mysterious, divine energies in their own life they also saw in the
phenomena of society and nature. In the Roman notion of deity
we do indeed find anthropomorphism, the idea of affinity of man
to God.

Nevertheless we must say that here a wholly new meaning
has been given to "anthropomorphism." The Romans gave no
thought to perceptible similarity, expressed in image and myth,
or indeed to any definable similarity, for the divine energies
cannot be described, though they lie at the foundation of all
reality. The difference has been discerned between all that which
can be called human on the one hand, and deity on the other,
but the human attributes of deity are not thereby denied. God
is the inexpressible in every phenomenon and relation of life.
This is not pantheism, because it is always a particular reality
that is kept in mind. There were in the Ancient Roman religion,
however, no myths concerning family relationships between
different gods, no divine images, and no temples; the divine
manifestation in the natural phenomenon was itself the god's
image and temple.

I believe that in this way we can gain at least some measure
of understanding of the meaning of a large number of anthropomorphic ideas of deity. The religious myth may ascribe accidental and external human qualities to the gods, but it is a
fact that for those who so represent their god, the god does
not because of those traits become a man in the finite sense.
That is because the "human" is according to the religious con-

ception not purely and simply human. Man exists and lives by means of the life which originates from God. That means affinity; God can be conceived according to the image of man, because man is created according to the image of God. The victorious power of Athene-Nike was a quality which man knew from his own experience, but his own triumph was a divine capacity. The divine herald who was worshipped was just as human as the human herald was divine. We have just as much right to speak of a theomorphic idea of man as of an anthropomorphic idea of God; man is created according to the image of God, or vice versa.

B. DIFFERENCE FROM GOD

The fact that even with the extensive humanization of deity in religious myth the consciousness of the difference between man and deity has never disappeared, shows that for the religious consciousness there is no contradiction felt between the types of ideas about God stressing the similarity of man to God and the types stressing the difference. The sense of essential difference is above all a sense of dependence. It may be true that human qualities and capacities contain elements of an ultimate and infinite nature (which elements give rise to anthropomorphic ideas of deity), but it is just as true that these ultimate factors are autonomous powers which man does not have at his command and on which he is dependent. These factors, which constitute the basis of his life, naturally extend beyond himself. The experience of every moment teaches man to recognize his finitude in both power and insight: he does not understand that which he would like so much to understand; he is not able to do that which he would like so much to be able to do. The divine forces which are active within him and without him transcend him; they exceed his powers of comprehension and control. They cannot be measured or judged with any human standard: that which is self-subsistent is beyond human attainment. The difference between God and man is fundamental and essential.

The expressions of this sense of difference are innumerable. They are formulated in all religions. That is even true with respect to the concrete form in which the deity is represented. It

does not agree with the human ideal, as it does for Plato and
Plutarch; the aesthetically beautiful proves to be something
totally different from the religiously sublime. Human form and
human mores are sometimes deliberately rejected.

This is the case when divine images show as little likeness
as possible to a human figure. The great sacredness of the Greek
xoana is well known; they were considered to be very sacred
even at the time when the art of sculpture had reached its zenith.
Yet they were simply pieces of wood or stone, almost wholly
without human form. The true image of Athene was the *palladion*
of Athene in the Erechtheum on the Acropolis and not the other
statue in the Parthenon made by Phidias, which was rather a
"votive offering." These Greek *xoana* are comparable to the
Egyptian images of a god represented as a mummy, without
arms or legs, a post with a human face. They signify a being
from the other world, as do the *hermai*, the stone posts, and the
figures of Dionysus or Osiris also represented as posts. Neither
is the god's dwelling a human house, but an image of his real
dwelling: the sky, the earth, or the underworld. Hermes dwells in
the (sacred) cave, Artemis in the (sacred) woods or tree. This is
exactly the type of dwelling which the Roman gods have. It is
always possible to see from at least one particular feature of the
temple that something other than a human dwelling is intended.
It is not only larger and more beautiful, but of a completely
different type. This is the case with the Babylonian temple towers, with the Egyptian temple base in the form of steps, and
even with the Greek triangular temple facade, the so called
tympanon. The essential element in the architectural form of a
temple is precisely its difference from a human dwelling.

But this sense of the difference in essence is most clearly evident in the conviction of human finitude and divine infinity. In
spite of his infinite aspirations man remains a finite being.
Neither his intellectual nor his ethical ideals are realized; they
remain aspirations; frequently they are utterly disavowed and
confounded by divine wisdom or divine will. In spite of man's
strivings with insight and will towards the infinite, peoples
throughout history have sensed the essential difference between
God and man. In his *Reden über die Religion* Schleiermacher has
devoted a few noteworthy reflections to this contrast.[4] He calls

intellectual and ethical strivings the most characteristic spiritual activities of man; here if anywhere pure humanity is present. But according to him it is just these faculties which are the greatest and most dangerous enemies of religion; in a certain sense the religious attitude is diametrically opposed to the ethical and intellectual attitudes. For intellect and will are under our own control and originate in ourselves. By comprehension and action we try to subject the world to us; these are our means to make life possible in nature and society, which we thereby try to subject to the ideal laws of our thought and action. Religion, however, is just the opposite attitude: the sense of infinite dependance concerning the basis of our existence. Religion is "Anschauung" (beholding), the intuitive grasping of divine reality and activity in the world and in man. In this act, human intellect and will lose all their autonomy; they are both in principle transformed. The religious attitude means the grasping in both areas of that which does not originate in man, namely the divine reality on which man is dependent. The active intellectual and ethical attitude is thus just the opposite of the religious attitude, which gives no priority to human initiative.

This is certainly a profound thought. That of which man is most proud is conceived in religion not only as insignificant but even as the opposite of the religious principle. And indeed in all religions only a relative value is ascribed to ethical and rational capacities. Self-subsistence is not an attribute of man's essential being; man is finite and in every moment this fact is experienced. That which is self-subsistent lies beyond him: self-subsistence is divinity. According to Schleiermacher, religion is the sense of absolute dependence, for by religious *Anschauung* of himself man sees himself as completely willed and determined by God. Our civilization, classical and "enlightened, "is just the type that brings with it the danger of forgetting this; it has the tendency to ascribe absolute value to human ideals and capacities. Thus arises the rivalry between civilization and religion of which Schleiermacher was thinking when he called intellectual and ethical values the greatest enemies of religion.

In a few cases men have not been satisfied with denying the absolute value of those ideals; their complete denial has been taken as the proof of divine inspiration. It lies outside the scope of our task here to focus attention on the mistaken character of those phenomena and to condemn them as a degeneration of the religious sense. That would only mean that we – undoubtedly with considerable justice – take a different point of view toward them. But we must learn to understand them as pure expressions of religious faith, even as heroic expressions of faith, because they conflict with the considerations of daily life. Thus it is sometimes flatly stated with respect to rational thought that just its opposite, the deliberate denial of all thought forms, signifies divine insight and divine wisdom. This is most clearly evident when madness is conceived as divine possession. This is the case with numerous prophetic phenomena. The first prophets in Israel, the Greek Pythia (*maenad*, "raving"), and the raving or mad dervishes in Islam, who attain union with deity by the complete abolition of human finitude, are all examples of this. But magical insight or power also belongs in this class. The magician sets forces in motion on which he is himself dependent, cosmic forces which originate not from himself, but from the depths of reality outside himself. And as far as ethical values are concerned, their insignificance is repeatedly sensed and recognized in the various religions in quite unforgettable fashion. Religio-ethical values prove to be different from secular ethical values; religious ethics speaks another language than profane ethics. In the further treatment of that subject we shall see that Schleiermacher's judgment that ethics is the enemy of religion has lost nothing in contemporary relevance.

The sense of conflict between human ideals and divine governance is expressed with special clarity in tragic poetry. The basic thought is universally human and recurs in every era; as a form of art, however, it has been developed especially by the Greeks.

In religious tragedy the notion of sin (departure from the divinely instituted law) is present, but it is sin in a very peculiar sense. The principal thought is that it is precisely man's noblest aspect, his infinite striving and yearning, which is judged by God as departure from his law. Man strives for an autonomy which is not given to any living man. When this effort is persisted in, it brings him necessarily to ruin. This is the condemnation of the man who cherishes infinite or absolute ideals of humanity. God tolerates no competitor among men; he does not tolerate anyone's reaching out for autonomous life. The divine "disfavour" (*phthonos*) is not a narrowminded impulse, but the maintenance of divine absoluteness over against human finitude, for the striving, too, is as such finite. In Aeschylus' "Prometheus Bound," this notion is developed in its most fundamental terms, fundamental because Prometheus is the representative of mankind, and he may even be considered man's creator, for he conceived Deucalion with Pandora (Demeter), and Deucalion was the primal ancestor of men; his daughter was Protogeneia. Prometheus takes up men's cause unconditionally; he is permeated through and through with love of man and love of neighbour. He is also the one who has put the highest aspirations in man and has taught him all the arts and crafts. As the greatest, but also the most dangerous, gift he gave man the divine fire, which according to the Ancient conception was a cosmic and divine energy. Man has thus obtained a means for creative labour which he cannot manage, though he should like to do so. Prometheus is punished as the ideal man who aspires beyond human finitude, and with him, naturally, the whole human race is punished; the gods send men Pandora with her fatal gifts. Prometheus is brought to ruin, and with him every human striving towards the ideal is condemned. He has willed only the good, but all justice is stamped under foot by the gods. "See what injustice I suffer!" are the last words of the ideal man. The only explanation of the poet is the warning of the Chorus, "the wise deliberation of men is no match for the divine Harmonia (the order in life in the mystical sense)." There is an enmity between god and men, between infinite and finite beings. Prometheus, the representative and advocate of men, was one of the Titans, the enemies of the gods. The difference between man and deity can certainly not be expressed more sharply. The divine fire which Prometheus brings to men is also the "divine fire" of enthusiam. But being divinely inspired is condemned as *hybris*, presumption. That is man's tragedy. His noblest strivings, those directed toward infinite goals, abolish his humanity and destroy him.

In the *Bacchantes* of Euripedes the theme is the same: enthusiasm turns the Bacchantes into bestial and inhuman beings. The only difference is that in this drama no divine condemnation follows the human presumption.

The principal idea in these tragedies has its source in the per-
plexing fact that the man of this world cannot bear the weight
of divine life. Prometheus is ruined. But his ruin is at the same
time his triumph; it is precisely here that his heroic essence comes
to light. He remains faithful to his high impulse and resists even
Hermes efforts to bring him to repentance. The description of his
high-spiritedness, prompted by a fine sense of the purity of his
motives, is the climax of this tragedy. Prometheus attains the
infinite, precisely in and by his destruction. This is not expressly
stated in Greek tragedy, for any theoretical reflection would
detract from the perfection of the poetic work. But the thought
is latent in the keen sense of sublimity in tragedy.

Death and destruction have here gained a different character
than that which they have as the typical expressions of finitude;
death is precisely man's glory. That is the view of the Mysteries
regarding the difference between the gods and men. Prometheus
was worshipped at Thebes as one of the gods of the Mysteries
there; Demeter communicated her mysteries (*gnōsis*) to him and
his son. It might then be said that man's destruction expresses
his affinity to deity just as strongly as it does his difference
from deity. In Egypt this is plainly stated; there even more than
in Greece death characterizes the affinity of man to God. According to the view of the Mysteries, death is nothing but absolute life. The Egyptian saw the difference between man and
deity exclusively in the finitude of the man of experience, in
the actual limitation of his insight, power, and will. This sort of
conception, however, provides no material for tragedy.

The chief theme of Greek tragedy is of a religious nature,
namely the Greek conception of the difference and the affinity
of man to deity, and only the hero, the man *par excellence*, can
be the leading character. There is nothing tragic about the ordinary and commonplace man; his sorrow or disaster has no exal-
ting effect. Apart from the Avesta, in no religion is the figure of
the hero so sharply drawn as in Greek religion. It is true that
Christianity also has an extensive "hero cult" in the veneration
of saints by the Roman Catholic Church. But no tragedy has
arisen from this, for the Roman Catholic ideal of man is poles
apart from the Ancient ideal. The Christian saints do not strive
for human autonomy. Like the Greek hero, the Christian hero

is venerated and worshipped; yet the Christian hero is completely different from the Ancient hero. The saint knows the struggle between man and God, between the finite and the infinite, but from the very beginning he has denied and surrendered his humanity. For this reason he lacks the trait which constitutes the tragic hero.

CHAPTER 14

RELIGIOUS SPECULATION CONCERNING MAN'S ESSENCE

In many religions including Christianity, philosophical-theological attempts have been made to determine the place and the significance of man in the totality of creation. They have led to speculations which were sometimes of a very theoretical nature, but in any case were closely related to religious faith, for they were prompted by the consciousness or sense of the infinite context in which man lives and by which he is determined. The concern was thus with relationships of a suprarational nature whose reality was unquestioned. The modern "enlightenment" is characterized by an agnostic attitude towards this subject (Huxley), which does not take into consideration an irrational but recognized reality. For the religious man of any era such an attitude is unthinkable; for him the infinite relations are all determining.

In the various religions, or in close relation to them, we frequently encounter theoretical speculations concerning man as a cosmic being, concerning the infinite relations in which he is involved, and concerning his own essential being. They sometimes have a remarkable profundity. Religious speculations prove here, as in other cases, to have furnished the impulse for important philosophical formulations. Ionic natural philosophy the precursor of Greek philosophy, was inspired by religious speculations about nature. Pythagorean philosophy, with its doctrine of the cosmic Harmonia and its theory of numbers, was directed as much along religious as along philosophical lines and perpetuated very ancient religious views; the same can be said of Plato's doctrine of the Ideas and of the Stoic and Neoplatonic doctrine of the Logos.

Characteristic of this speculation is the theory which has arisen independently among completely different peoples, containing the notion that man is a microcosm. In India the sky and the earth were called the two parts of the cosmos; man's head is the sky and the lower part of his body is the earth, and the part in between, the chest containing the breath of the mouth, is the atmosphere. The three cosmic lights are evidently present in man: in his face, in the beating of his heart, and in his power to reproduce. Or "man is the year," or he consists of the five elements of the universe: he is the totality of universal life.

According to de Groot, such ideas are well known among the Chinese. Man derives his vital power from the two world souls, sky and earth. Lao-tze and Confucius therefore teach that the human soul is a double soul; it consists of warmth (the power of sexual generation and life in general) from the sky, and of cold (barrenness and death) from the earth; man is like both sky and earth. It is remarkable that the same formulation appears in Egypt, but there is applied only to the dead man. He has a double soul: the soul of Osiris and the soul of Re, the gods of death and of resurrection. Lao-tze teaches furthermore that the human body is a mixture of five elements. Man is a microcosm spontaneously arising from and in the macrocosm and just as self-subsistent as the latter; the law of his life is that of the universe, the *tao*.

It is known that similar forms of thought appear in Medieval astrology; man makes an organic and harmonious whole with the universe, with the sky (or the stars) and the earth. The different temperaments originate through the predominating influence of particular heavenly bodies, which represent parts of the universe. Melancholy is, for example, the earth's temperament, originating through the influence of Saturn. Now Saturn is the Ancient god of the seed which lies in the earth and is the god of the depths of the earth. Another of his attributes is intelligence: the ability to concentrate deeply on objects. He gives "growth from the depths and from quiet reflection (self-concentration); hidden treasures (both material and spiritual) everything which can be obtained only with much difficulty." It is said that the dreams of a melancholic, thus the intuition of the earth man, always turn out to be true: insight dwells in the depths of the earth. The word "influenza" points to a very ancient thought. Like the Indian and the Chinese philosopher, the western medieval astrologist believed that the human body was a mixture of the constitutive elements of the universe. From top to toe it consisted of sky, air, water, and earth. Another form of classification was to assign the parts of the body to the twelve signs of the zodiac: the head to the ram, the neck to the bull, etc. The classification was depicted on all calendars, in order that people could know, for instance, when a blood letting should be performed. No operation could be performed on a part of the body when the moon was in the particular part of the sky to which it was related; at such times the moon's moisture would cause rheumatism. Some people, including the astronomer Tycho Brahe, divided the spiritual faculties with their respective organs among the seven planets: the heart, as the source of warmth, belonged to the sun, the intellect to the moon, etc. Plants and herbs were sought as medicines which stood under the same planet or the same sign of the zodiac as the ailing part of the body. All these ideas are governed by the majestic conception that the forces of the universe flow through man and that man is organically and harmoniously bound up with the universe. He may, indeed he must, take part in the divine contest of which the Avesta speaks.

In Babylonian speculation man does not appear as microcosm. But there are nevertheless remarkable expressions of the cosmic significance of human life. Man's finitude and mortality is conceived as a factor in the cosmos, as a necessary moment in eternal life. We read concerning the new moon, which binds together death and life, that she is a goddess "created in the sky and on earth, created in the totality (*kishshatu*) of sky and earth, formed with care as the creature of God and of men." [1] Gods and men, sky and earth together create the resurrected life of the dead moon. Human transiency is a necessary factor in cosmic life.

These are academic theories, yet the religious element in these theoretical reflections is extremely clear. The sense of unity with the universe is, when seen from the other side, equally a sense of absolute dependence (Schleiermacher's definition of religion), for man has no voice in or authority over the infinite relationships which constitute his essential being.

In the Avesta we encounter a religious formulation of this majestic view. In the lengthy creed (Yasna 12) this statement appears:

The side which the waters have chosen, which the plants and the well created (or well acting) cattle have chosen, which Ahura Mazda, the creator of cattle and of the righteous man, and Zarathustra have chosen, that side I choose; that is my law as Mazda's servant.

In other words, the creed of the waters, etc., is my creed; the waters, etc., have ranged themselves on the side of universal life. The waters, plants and cattle are named before Ahura Mazda and Zarathustra; the emphasis is deliberately put on man's cosmic relationship. Nevertheless man is a servant of God, a *Mazdayasna*, "worshipper of Mazda."

In various religions the myths about the "primeval man" also form a part of the religious speculation about man's essential being. It is a remarkable fact that he is called the first created being. All beings in the whole world have originated from him, and he has determined the character of the entire creation. This thought has been preserved even in the doctrine of Adam's fall. Adam's fate has become the world's fate; with him transiency, but also the promise of victory over transiency, has become reality for the whole world. According to the Avesta, the primeval man Gayomart (*gaya martan*, mortal life), the first creation of Mazda, was killed by Ahriman or had fallen because of his own guilt. With this act world history begins, the struggle between the two factors which together constitute the essential being of the primeval man, life and death .The idea of the primeval man also appears in various gnostic systems; Protanthropos is even conceived as a god, or as God the Father, as the god who first was simply undifferentiated, spiritual-material in essence. But then he imparted himself to matter as Logos and Zōē, Word and Life, and as Anthropos, Man, and he became immersed in matter in order to rise again out of matter. Thus is the world history and "salvation history" determined by "man." Cosmic factors of finitude and infinity, penetrating and conflicting with one another, are active in man. The Naässenes, a gnostic sect in the third century, also call the Archanthropos, the primeval man who is the essence of everything, "the uncharacterized Logos," that is to say, the Logos not yet differentiated into particular beings, while the "characterized Logos" or primeval man, immersed in matter, is the "son of man" and is identified with the Christ. (Compare the prologue of the Gospel of John).

Here we encounter the well known idea of the "son of man," the typical man, the Idea of man. He is a divine being, who, however, reveals himself in the world. As the prototype of empirical man, he is the possessor and the representative of what religious speculation considers to be man's essential being. His characteristics are of two kinds: he belongs to the finite world and is thus mortal, but at the same time he possesses the capacity to raise himself above finitude, because he shares in the divine insight into the secret of life and death. "Son" means the revealer of the hidden father who has appeared in this world; in this sense Hercules was the son of Zeus, and the Egyptian king was the son of Re.

In Babylonia the idea of the son of man is depicted in an impressive way. Here Adapa is the first and the typical man, the *zēr amelūti* – the seed (or the son) of mankind (probably thought of as a divine being). He is the protégé of Ea, the wise lord of the underworld and the divine representative of mankind ("lord of mankind") and is also called Ea's son. Adapa is also "the wise one" and to him "the innermost part of the heavens and the earth has been revealed," but he must die. According to the myth he was summoned to heaven by Anu, the king of the gods, and there the food and drink of life were offered to him, but because he had been deceived by Ea he refused to accept them, and therefore he had to return to earth. The attributes of wisdom and mortality are inseparably bound together, for in the Ancient religions wisdom always signifies the mystical-magical insight into the secret of life's growth, growth which presupposes the fact of death, and which can only be known in death. In practice this amounts to the interpretation of oracles (knowing the law of the world's life), healing (resurrection from death), and in general a somewhat mystical insight into – and therewith a power over – such essentials for life as agriculture, the building of cities, and the like. Adapa is also granted "everlasting rule." (Compare Genesis 1 : 26ff where man is created to rule over the earth and all the animals which live upon it.) Adapa is the man who fulfills the idea of man and his divine destiny; he is man as man is designed to be. He is a mythical figure who corresponds to the religious conception of man's essential being. The *zēr amelūti*, "son of mankind," must die, but he knows the secret of resurrection, and he is the lord of creation because his knowledge of life's secret gives him power over it. He who has mystical insight has divine power at his command.

We shall suffice with the following comment concerning the use of the term "son of man" in the Old Testament, New Testament, and Pseudepigrapha. According to Enoch 60 : 10ff, the son of man is above all the wise man to whom God "has shown the hidden (life) and has revealed the beginnings of all things in the high heavens and in the depths of the earth, even to the ends of the heavens and the foundations thereof." Like Adapa he knows the mystery of risen and abiding life. It is remarkable that at this point in the book of Enoch, it is Noah and not the Messiah who is the son of man: Noah was able to rescue himself from death; he is the risen one. In the catacombs, too, Noah in the ark is one of the oldest and most used symbols to indicate the resurrection of one who has died. Noah's wisdom is shown by his deliverance from death, which gives him a right to the title, "son of man." Utnapishtim, the Babylonian Noah, "knows the secret (mystery) of the gods," has thus attained eternal life, and like Adapa is "full of wisdom." He too is the protégé of Ea, "the lord of mankind." Enoch is also identified with "the son of man (of mankind)." (Enoch 71 : 14.) According to Genesis 5 : 22, Enoch walked with God, therefore God took him to Himself. In the Jewish tradition Enoch was the possessor of all human wisdom which later through Abraham penetrated to the West, and thus we understand why the apocalyptic book of Enoch is ascribed to this "wise man" and "son of man." In the Babylonian story of the first ten kings or patriarchs up to Utnapishtim, he is called *En-me-dur-an-ki*, "the prophet of the link between (or the oracle of) heaven and earth," "the wise one who knows the secrets of heaven and earth." Like Enoch in Genesis 5 : 24 and like Utnapishtim, he is taken up to live with the gods of the world's fate, Shamash and Hadad. He is the Babylonian "son of man."

Late Jewish literature also contains other reflections about man's essential being (his divine nature), which imply the transformation of his finite nature. He was pre-existent, present before creation as Logos or Archanthropos, one with God. As Messiah he is conceived eschatologically, but as one who belongs to this world he must die. Furthermore, he is the Soter, the Saviour; in the gnostic systems the Soter is sometimes called Christos and sometimes Anthropos, the idea of man.

The notion of pre-existent man is probably also present in Job 15 : 7, man full of wisdom and present before the creation in the council of God. Eliphas reproves Job for pleading his cause before Yahweh, for Job is of course not omniscient. "Were you then born as the first man and were you brought into the world earlier than the hills? Did you listen in the council of God and take wisdom along with you?" According to Gunkel and Dillmann, the "first man" was a hero who took part in the council of God before the creation. He is thus the mythical prototype of man, different from all men living at the present time.

Perhaps the Egyptian *sa-s* is also related to this idea. The ordinary meaning of the term is noble, free man, man who possesses all human capacities. There is a text known from the Middle Kingdom, about 2000 B.C., which states that after times of starvation and oppression a king will arise who will bring liberation and good fortune, and in his time the people will rejoice; this "son of man will make his name (that is to say, his life or his power) endure eternally." This then is the king as the ideal man, who brings deliverance from distress.

CHAPTER 15

MAN'S LAW OF LIFE

A. GENERAL REMARKS

The concept "man's law of life" can be understood in two senses. It can be conceived in the ethical sense as the moral law based on the conscience, on the moral consciousness in the Kantian sense. Then it is the autonomous law of practical life, the "practical Reason" (*praktische Vernunft*). It concerns all human behaviour; all its aspects are subjected to a moral law. But in the religious sense the law of life is determined heteronomously (from outside man); it is founded on the divine will. Now the question is what relation these different conceptions of man's law of life have to each other. What is the judgment of religion concerning the moral law? What place is granted to it in religious life – central, less important, or no place at all? It is important for our knowledge of man's religious disposition that we become familiar with these types, for they very largely determine the religious attitude or the character of every religion. There is much evidence that this subject has again and again occupied the attention of the adherents of the most diverse religions. And the phenomenological analysis of the relation between religion and ethics is made especially interesting by the fact that in this respect Christianity also represents a special type.

The great significance of the phenomena relating to this subject has led many modern scholars to adopt as their guiding principle in the classification of religions the conceptions concerning the relation between religion and moral law, or between the religious and the ethical law of life. Thus religions have been divided into two main groups: the ethical religions, represented by Christianity, Judaism, Buddhism, Hinduism, the Avesta religion, and Islam; and the non-ethical or nature religions, with all sorts of in between forms of more or less ethical types. The various religions have even been so arranged that the first group contained the higher religions; Christianity, as "pure ethical religion" assumed then the highest place. This classification, however, may unquestionably be kept outside our consideration. Phenomenology does not aim to give a comparative evaluation; it uses comparative observation or study only as a means towards better understanding of the distinctive nature and value of the various religions. In order to obtain a comprehensive view of all religious values and types it clarifies the meaning of that about which little is known with the help of that which is better known. However, we may not leave outside our consideration the question of whether we can effectually classify religions according to the criterion of ethics. Can this criterion actually inform us about the essentials of the various religions? It seems to me that such a classification meets with very serious difficulties.

The advocates of this classification place in the first main group the religions which consider moral consciousness as the central area of God's revelation and which believe that God is essentially ethical in nature. God wishes to be served "in spirit and in truth," not by means of outward acts. In this main group are the monotheistic religions, proclaimed by the Old Testament prophets, by Christ, Buddha, and Mohammed, and also the religions which tend in this direction. Included in the second group are the religions which, regardless of ethical values, consider cosmic life as the central area of divine revelation. This cosmic life is the life of the heavens and the earth, the energy of water and fire, and also the various phenomena of man's life. In these polytheistic religions man serves the gods by means of sacrifices and ceremonial acts whereby he confesses and actualizes his dependence and his unity with the cosmos.

Classification according to this principle, however, cannot possibly be carried out. In the first place, the same religion can change sharply in this respect in the course of centuries, for example the Avesta religion before and after Zarathustra and the religion of Israel before and after the prophets. In any case a religion could be typified only in a particular period, and the different periods would have to be considered as different religions. But even such a step does not remedy the situation. In one religion, at a particular time, both types sometimes exist alongside one another. Thus during the Vedic period in India there were numerous nature gods: the mighty Indra who slays the demon of drought, Rudra who protects the cattle, the fire god, Agni, the god of the sacrifice, Soma, and others. Besides these gods there is also Varuna, the god of cosmic order and human order, who in this life and in the life to come protects the righteous (all who follow his ethical law). In Greece, Themis, goddess of ethical order, is to be found along with a number of nature gods such as Hermes, Poseidon, and Hades.

Since this is the case, perhaps it would be better to speak of "ethical gods" and "nature gods" – at least in a particular period. But even the same god can display different sides. Zeus is the upholder of the *themistes*, but he is also the god of rain and of the earth's fertility, worshipped by the bull sacrifice and the vegetation sacrifice, and Themis herself is identical with the earth goddess Ge. Osiris, before whom man after his death attests his righteousness in order to obtain eternal life, is also the god of the water of the Nile flood and of the earth's life.

It cannot even be said that a particular god at a particular moment was worshipped by some believers as an ethical god and by others as a nature god, that there were thus two essentially different gods who had only the name in common. Even in the same invocation both sides can appear. According to the great hymn of praise to Anahita (Yasht 5 of the Avesta), she, the watergoddess, descends from the heavens to men, and with the thousand seas, canals, and rivers, she brings fertility and enables men to live in prosperity, "great as all the waters flowing over the earth put together." Yet in the same hymn all the gods and heroes ask for her gifts, and they request her to grant them the power which will enable them to perform great deeds; thus Mazda says, "make sure that the holy Zarathustra speaks, thinks, and acts in accordance with my religion." She agrees and lets Zarathustra be born in order that he may preach the ("ethical") Mazda religion. Thus she cares not only for cosmic life, but equally for spiritual life: good thinking, speaking, and acting. And Shamash, who communicates the law to Hammurabi as does Yahweh to Moses, is depicted upon the stele on which the law is engraved as a sun god.

It is evident from the examples we have just mentioned that
the nature religions or nature gods and the ethical religions or
gods are closer to one another than is assumed in the classification of religions according to the criterion of ethics. The explanation of this lies in the meaning which the believers have
given to "nature" and "spirit." These concepts have a different
meaning for us than for them. Cosmic life, which is central in the
so-called "nature religions," also contains man as a total being.
This means that moral law, too, is more or less determined by
the law of cosmic life. This conception is possible because "cosmic life" is experienced as a self-subsistent reality. "Nature"
means for these believers not only the realm of finite relations;
life in nature just as in the spiritual world of man reveals for
them a self-subsistent divine reality. All life, spiritual as well as
natural, contains the element of self-subsistence; for this religious consciousness, life is an ultimate and self-subsistent
reality. Our concept "natural law" has no place in these ideas.
It is indeed wholly unknown, or perhaps it would be better to
say that in their way of thinking, it can only relate to the external and unessential side of natural life. It is concerned with the
form but not with the content of natural reality. Therefore no
great value is attached to it. Naturally the religious man derives
this idea of the spontaneity and self-subsistence of cosmic life
from his own individual and collective sense of life, his impulses,
passions, and natural disposition. The "cosmic law of life" is
thus a mystical reality, in contrast with the "natural law" and
the "ethical law," which can indeed be formulated in rational
terms. It is only from his practical experience of life that the
religious man knows that the cosmic law exists. The starting
point of knowledge about it is thus the religious consciousness
of man himself, man as uncomprehended reality. The Ancient
religious sense of nature is rooted in the religious self-consciousness of the believer. It is from this starting point that ethical
norms are approached; or, to put it the other way round, in
religion ethical norms have a cosmic significance. For all the
emphasis is put on life's uncomprehended reality and infinite
divine nature. The sense of kinship (not identity) between nature
and man is made possible by the sense of life's mystery. And that
sense was more immediate for the Ancients than it is for us.

The separation between "ethical" and "cosmic" or "nature" religions is thus based on a criterion which, because it is derived from our own religion and the other ethical religions akin to our own, does not bring to the fore that which is essential in the religions foreign to our own experience. It is only our own group of religions which is characterized by the conviction that religion is a purely spiritual and not a cosmic orientation. In the other religions, on the contrary, one cannot speak either of a purely "natural" or of a purely "ethical" or "spiritual" orientation. Osiris, Varuna, Shamash, and Themis teach us that there are all sorts of forms in between.

What other criterion would then better serve as a principle of classification? Probably none. It is obvious that it is not possible to find a characteristic which indicates the different types. Grouping religions according to a particular characteristic is not a task for historical or phenomenological inquiry, but rather for philosophical inquiry concerning the essence of religion. For philosophical inquiry does not aim to determine the autonomous value and significance of the divergent types, but attempts to give normative generalizations. It is impossible for the phenomenologist to make such normative distinctions.

The religious conception of ethical values corresponds in general to the conception of intellectual and aesthetic values. The conscience, which is the basis of moral life, is one of the typical and essential human attributes, and all these attributes, according to the Ancient conception, testify to forces which extend above and beyond the finite; they testify to divine capacities in man. In religion the emphasis is always placed on this element of infinitude and ultimacy. The mystical insight and the magical capacity of the wise man, or the ecstacy of the poet or artist, is directed towards the order and the beauty of the cosmos, or towards the infinite impulse in human capacities; these abilities, too, contain a divine element. This is the attitude of religion toward ethical values and norms. There can be two kinds of result stemming from this attitude. Either a sublime height is attained or injury is done to the inspirations of mind and heart; in the latter case religion can have a disturbing and sometimes a destructive effect in all the areas just mentioned. As a rule, there is indeed no conscious conflict, but a latent antithesis is frequently perceptible. It is the antithesis between man's effort to subject the world to himself and the recognition of man's absolute dependence. A rational synthesis of both orientations is not possible. It was for this reason that Schleiermacher could call the intellectual and ethical dispositions the enemies of religion.

B. THE RELIGIO-ETHICAL LAW OF LIFE
(A PHENOMENOLOGICAL DESCRIPTION)

The term "religio-ethical" law of life is chosen to indicate that religion determines ethics. If the term were "ethical-religious," then ethics would be the autonomous and determining factor, but this conception is possible only in a philosophical ethic, and not in religion. Our task is to describe phenomenologically how ethical values are seen in religion, what position they assume in religion, and what value is attached to them.

It is a fact that religion in many cases transforms ethical norms into divine norms and makes them an essential part of religion. The first decalogue (Exodus 20) contains in part purely ethical laws which are then declared to be man's laws of life ("that you may long abide in the land that God has given you"). These laws are given by God and are thus religious laws. Besides these there are commandments which are often ritual in character, such as the Sabbath commandment. From this we may conclude that the viewpoint even of the first decalogue is different from the purely ethical point of view. But it is evident that no conflict exists. In the Babylonian code of Hammurabi there are likewise civil and moral laws alongside ritual commandments. Most Ancient legislation concerning moral and political life possesses divine authority; the laws are given by God. Thus the religious character of these laws lies especially in the fact that as divine commandments they are detached from the human conscience; they have been established by the cosmic ruler and creator. Moreover, there are promises of prosperity and good fortune connected with them, and also threats of disaster and destruction, in the external and physical as well as the internal and spiritual realms. They display the character of the cosmic law of life to the extent that man is cosmically determined

and organically bound up with the life of the universe. Yet in the
Hebrew prophets this thought recedes to the background, although it never entirely disappears; of course the good fortune
and the continued existence of Israel depends on its "righteousness." Reward and punishment are not purely ethical motives,
but they are certainly religious ones.

The formulation of religious ethics in the Avesta is very
enlightening for our understanding of this subject. Asha in the
Avesta means "righteousness," but has just as definitely the
meaning of cosmic life, the universal order which signifies eternal
life, in contrast with *"druj,"* the lie or deceit, which implies death
and finitude. Therefore it is especially the farmer or cattle tender
who is *"ashavan,"* righteous, because he is the man of regular
life and the man who cares for the earth's life. The meaning
of *ashavan* is most clearly evident when it is said that waters,
plants, fire, and cattle are also *ashavan*. Even the most ethical
commandments acquire this cosmic character: good towards
the good man and evil towards the evil man. Roughness and
murder are condemned, but only when they are directed against
a "righteous one." Only the killing of a believer is punished,
because the righteous man – that is, he who helps to realize the
divine world plan – stands on the side of Mazda in the universal
struggle. The godless, the followers of Ahriman, must be destroyed. The utilitarian motive and the thought of reward is
sometimes particularly strong in this religious ethic; *Ashi* means
"good fortune." Thus is the religious element indicated, for the
triumph of life over death and transiency concerns Mazda's
entire world, in its physical as well as its spiritual aspects. The
purely ethical feelings of sympathy, love and self-denial were
naturally just as well known among the Avesta people as among
all other peoples, but there is little or no mention of them in the
religion. With its self-interest and its intolerance the religion in this
respect is rather destructive of ethical requirements. The religious
principle differs from the ethical: the religious orientation proves
here to be cosmic, whereas the ethical orientation is human.

But it can also occur that both impulses, though different
from each other, aim at the same goal, and that the different
motives complement each other. Then a new value comes into
being which belongs as much in religion as it does in ethics. The

best example of this is a phenomenon so characteristic of the
Avesta people: the love of truth and the high esteem of the
reliability of a man's word once it has been given. Even more
decidedly than any other Ancient people, the Avesta people
sensed and proclaimed the sacredness and inviolability of agreements or alliances and saw in them a matter of both religious and
ethical importance. The religious principle involved here was the
stability of the universal order of life, in contrast to the arbitrariness and undependability of *druj* (deceit), which signified
death and transiency. The sun god Mithra represents in the
Avesta cosmic regularity and reliability. He is the god of treaties
and agreements, the upholder of stable order, who reveals himself
in faithfulness to agreements; he guards over them and avenges
deceit. "Sacred is every covenant between father and son,
between two friends, between any two parties which have concluded a covenant, even between two nations," so we read in the
hymn dedicated to Mithra (Yasht 10). At the very beginning of
the hymn are the following words: "Do not break an agreement,
Zarathustra, neither one you have made with a godless man
(*drugvant*, follower of *druj*), nor one you have made with a
righteous man, for the agreement is valid for both, for the godless
as well as for the righteous." This is really a remarkable statement
and one which is as much religiously as ethically inspired. The
view that everything is included in the world plan and that evil
too is bound up with the cosmic order is not an ethical one. This
state of being bound to the world order is the universal law of
life in the religious sense. The human act which corresponds to it
is to bind and obligate one's self by an agreement. It is thus that
the sacredness of truth is to be understood; the true word is the
undeceiving and unerring word which corresponds to the stable
order of the universe. It cannot be denied that the religious view
contains contradictions; the absolute validity of agreements and
the absoluteness of the love of truth harmonize poorly with
another requirement, "do good to the good and evil to the evil."
Such inconsistencies, which appear repeatedly when absolute
values are involved, must be allowed to stand as facts. Religious
motives and formulations are often contradictory (must holiness
be sought or avoided?), whereas ethical principles do not conflict with one another.

Thus ethical ideals, in particular the ideal of sincerity and faithfulness, can be complemented by religious views and raised to a remarkable height. We have already noticed the same phenomenon in the realm of art: Greek poetry reached its zenith in tragedy, which is as much religion as art. But if new values arise in this way, it may be asked whether this is not at least as much due to ethical and aesthetic impulses as to religious insights. Isn't the idea of the sacredness of every treaty simply an expression of an ethical ideal, and can it not just as well be called ethical-religious as religio-ethical? We do not have to consider here the normative side of the question, the answer to which would require an exposition of our own conception of the relation between religion and ethics, and this lies in the realm of Philosophy of Religion. We are concerned here rather with the phenomenological question of how the religious believers have conceived it. And in answer to this question we can say this: when the sacredness, the absolute validity, of the ethical requirement is recognized, then its religious character is entirely in the foreground. The ethical requirement is "holy" or sacred because it corresponds to the divine will or to divine being and is accepted and maintained by God. That is its sanction. If we restrict our attention specifically to the requirement of absolute trustworthiness, of keeping an agreement, then its religious character proves to be especially clear when the swearing of an oath is connected with the agreement or treaty, which is usually the case among all religiously oriented peoples, and thus among all the Ancient peoples. The Roman *fetiales*, who concluded the treaty with another people, made an agreement of absolute validity by the oath they swore on Jupiter. The idea implied was that a treaty was sanctified by being taken up into the divine order of the earth's life. Before their departure from Roman territory, the *fetiales* were consecrated for their sacred task by being symbolically buried. (Their heads were touched with a piece of grass sod.) They descended into the underworld or the realm of the dead, the home of the earth's life, for the treaty was concluded in the world of absolute life. Its absolute validity, which is its sanction and sanctification, in this way was actualized. ("Sanction" in the sense of punishment for breaking a treaty rests upon a misunderstanding of the religious meaning of sanction.)

Here again the religious conception of human qualities comes to light, in this case specifically the conception of the moral sense. The yearning for stability in agreements is an infinite impulse, a spontaneous expression of life, and is in its ultimate ground and essential being divine. The "holiness" or sacredness of the commandments means that religion has set its stamp upon the commandments and bestowed its own character to them. The ethical autonomy of the commandments is thus abolished. Autonomy or self-subsistence is always a religious concept; God alone is self-subsistent. This phenomenological analysis is in agreement with Schleiermacher's conception of the essential difference between ethical striving and religious feeling. The former is active; it is freedom; the latter is passive; it is dependence. By means of religious *"Anschauung,"* ethical freedom is seen as nature; the agreement is embodied in the law of the earth, in the cosmic law of life. "Nature" is then that which is independent of us and exists as the will and essential being of God. This cosmic moment on which Schleiermacher puts such emphasis is, indeed, just that which we encounter in religious reality, especially clearly in the Roman and the Avesta religions. The cosmic moment characterizes the religious orientation in the ethical realm; even the waters, plants, and cattle are "righteous," *ashavan.*

In the Ancient religions this type of view is encountered again and again, closely connected with that religious sense of nature which we moderns have so largely lost. The Indian *rita*, and *asha* in the Avesta signify the divine order of life in its universal sense. The Egyptian *ma-a-t* is the "righteousness" of the earth goddess, the righteousness of life which renews itself regularly and according to a stable order ("agreement"), in contrast with arbitrariness and undependability. Themis, the typical representative of moral life, is also an earth goddess. He who sacrifices to Fides or Jupiter Fidius wraps a white woollen cloth around his right hand – one delivers a blow with his right hand – as a sign that trustworthiness is a mystical reality. The Chinese conception of *tao*, "the way" or the path of life, is well known, and the *tao* is as much the world's way as it is man's way. In all these ideas the autonomy of the ethical principle, which is founded in the conscience, is recognized only in its connection with the cosmic law of life, of which it is a particular expression. Moral "freedom" is sublimated in absolute dependence on God.

According to this conception, the "righteous man" lives an infinite and enduring life; "infinite" and "enduring" are the characteristics of cosmic life. This thought comes repeatedly to expression in the belief in immortality. Immortality is not an ethical concept, and for this reason belief in immortality is primarily encountered and developed in connection with religio-ethical forms of thought. The religious man knows the way or the law of enduring and immortal life and can order his life in accord with it. In Egypt Osiris is the god of life in the hereafter and is the lord of *ma-a-t*. The dead man reaches eternal life with him after and by means of the *psychostasia* (the weighing of the heart, that is to say, of the thoughts and the disposition) and a negative confession of predominantly ethical content. The other type of immortality in Egypt is being connected with the sun god Re in his resurrection. The sun god's immortality is then imparted to the righteous man, provided that he possesses the stable order and righteousness of Ma-a-t, the mother or daughter of Re. In the Vedic religion immortality is attained with Varuna and Yama. Varuna is precisely the god of *rita;* the pious man "follows the commandments of Varuna," which are known both to the righteous and the unrighteous. According to the Greeks, the divine judges, Minos, Aeacus, and Rhadaman-thys, dwell in the land of the blessed. Here it is quite clearly evident that divine justice is concerned with the relationships not of finite but rather of infinite life. For Minos, Aeacus, and Rhadamanthys are indeed judges, but they are evidently repre-sentatives of the idea of justice in a purely abstract sense. They are not "judges of the dead" as are Osiris and Varuna; we do not hear that dead men are justified or condemned by Minos and his colleagues. No one appears before their court to hear their verdict. They are nothing but the divine embodiment of the idea of justice and its administration, and for that reason they belong in the land of absolute life, in the realm of the dead. There are three of them, because the number three indicates to-tality and absoluteness. The religious conception of justice is that it is the law of eternal life; justice is to act in accord-ance with the religio-ethical law of life. As soon as an absolute

significance is given to moral life, we are within the realm
of religion.

These conceptions and formulations of the law of life display
an unmistakably optimistic character; the ethical requirement
is sanctioned by God and is in line with divine life. It is possible
for man to walk the path of life, the way of abiding life, and thus
to be guarded against permanent disaster. According to this
type of thinking, religious life means good fortune and prosperity
in the external and physical realm as well as in the internal and
spiritual sphere, for the same law of life applies to nature as to
man. Water, plants, cattle, and everything else on which prosperity depends are *ashavan*, "righteous," they are the good part
of creation. This is "optimistic," even with respect to the external circumstances of life. This optimistic element is indeed
always present in religious faith; it even suggests the essential
character of religious relationships. That essential is trust in
divine governance, even when the conflict between that governance and human ideals is not only a fact, but is consciously
conceived as a problem.

It is easy to see that this conflict can arise. The ethical terms,
with which the Ancients were just as familiar as we are, have
in these religions received an altered content. The law which
is here conceived extends further than the human realm; it
concerns a greater reality, namely a cosmic reality. What the
law thus gains in extent and universality, it loses in ethical force
and inwardness. Notwithstanding all its agreement with the
moral law, the universal law of life, the divine order, is inscrutable.
Rita, asha, tao, ma-a-t remain mystical realities. How can natural
law and ethical law be one law of life? In some religions the
impersonal character of the law of life is indeed painfully felt.
But not in all religions, not in the Avesta or in Egypt, and usually not in the Indian or Greek religion. Yet even here a characteristic must be mentioned which attests in a peculiar way to
the distance between ethical feeling and religious faith: the
emphasis which is repeatedly put on the insight which is necessary in order really to know the law of life. A broad view is
necessary, directed not only towards man, but also towards the
world. "Goodness" and "righteousness" in the religious sense
are the same thing as wisdom, also taken in its religious sense.

This definitely means an altering of pure ethical consciousness.

What great power and spiritual value this Ancient religious conception of the law of life possessed is evident from many things, among them the fact that it again and again recurred in different forms among the Greek thinkers who had altogether departed from the old religious orientation. Plato's well known theory about the essence of the good, "virtue is insight" (thus containing a cosmic factor), is strongly reminiscent of the religio-ethical views. The idea of the good is the highest idea, in accordance with which the world is ordered. The good is the path of life and the law of life for man and world, and it is therefore also the highest wisdom. In its essential being the human soul is in accord with the world soul; the world soul is spirit, and its nature is *logistikon*, the "rational" (in a very exalted sense, not the "rational" which can be understood in a finite way). Virtue is "insight" or arises from "insight": it can be learned. But the science which teaches it is not a modern science but a very ideal science, somewhat similar to the *"Anschauung"* of the universe of which Schleiermacher speaks. Plato's doctrine of the Ideas is indeed closely related to Ancient religious speculation. The "pre-existent idea" was already a familiar thought in Babylonian and Egyptian religion, thousands of years before Plato.

This religio-ethical orientation in the Ancient sense also prevailed among the Stoics. The Stoic, such a man as Epictetus, Seneca, or Marcus Aurelius, is a free man, not in the individual, but in the universal sense – as a world citizen, in harmony with world spirit and world law. "Live in accord with yourself, with your 'nature' or basic disposition, that which is unchangeable and stable in you, and in accord with nature around you; there is accord between the human and the divine will, about which our rationality instructs us." "Natura" or *physis* is the opposite of sense experience; it is the world order of which man is a part, and it is formulated in *nomoi*, laws, just as the "law of life," *asha*, *rita*, *ma-a-t*, or *tao*. The life order does not exist as a visible or definable reality, but as a mystical reality. Yet the obligation remains to live "as if it existed." It does indeed exist, but in a transcendental sense. This philosophy is definitely more akin to Ancient than to modern philosophy, because it does not concern itself with finite relationships. The attitude of the Stoics

and of Plato differs from the Ancient religious attitude in this
respect, however, that it turns away with disdain and even with
abhorrence from the finite world of experience, and thus advocates a kind of escape religion. Stoic and Platonic philosophers
have separated the ethical good from all empirical finitude and
changed it into a union with the spirit of the universe. They did
this because the religious sense of nature present in their culture
was already greatly weakened. That religious sense was still
present among the Ionian philosophers and in the middle of the
sixth century B.C. in Pythagoras and in Phericydes of Syros.

C. THE CONFLICT BETWEEN HETERONOMY AND AUTONOMY

It has already been stated that the divine law or order of life,
which is spoken of in all religions which we know from written
sources, embraces all creatures including man. The awareness
of this character of the law of life is the basis of the religious
attitude. Thus it is believed that the religious man does indeed
"know" the divine commandments, for they have been revealed
to him: the commandments of Shamash through Hammurabi,
those of Yahweh through Moses, those of Ahura Mazda through
Zarathustra, etc. Even when no prophet is mentioned, the social
institutions and commandments are based on a divine communication or revelation at the beginning of history, whether by Ea,
Demeter Thesmophoros, or by other divinities. But all "revelation" is an authoritarian communication from the outside.
God does not explain the reason for his commandments; their
principle or basic idea remains unknown. The religious man often
gives as a principle "God's holiness"; such is the case in the Old
Testament. But this is only a formal principle; it does not provide
any governing thought or norm. For what is the result of this
holiness? It is solely absolute obedience, without respect to the
meaning or intention of the commandment. For the moral
consciousness, obedience is a purely formal principle. That which
is revealed is in its essential being not revealed; the essence – the
divine will – remains impenetrable, for no man penetrates the
counsel of God. It is only when the starting point for moral
action is found in human ideals or is written in the heart that the

moral consciousness contains the presence of a genuine moral principle, a directive norm.

This difference between the moral conscience and man's real law of life has repeatedly made itself felt and has led to conflicts in which human values, material as well as spiritual, must be denied, and it is accompanied by a mood of self-denial and sorrow. Hegel characterizes the "Syrian" (Semitic) religions as "religions of sorrow". Their adherents give up their finite ideals, and even life itself; they wish to die in order to rise and live with the deity. Such is the case with the worshippers of Adonis-Attis. The conflict on a grand scale has never led to an abandonment of the religious relationship; quite the contrary, it has made that relationship stronger and more conscious. Here if anywhere it is evident that just by means of the difficulties the greatest and deepest forces are summoned and set to work. This is religious growth. In this case we may speak of the "gospel of suffering" or "gospel of sorrow" – terms which no one will use without an inward shudder. It is especially among the Semites that the conflict between heteronomy and autonomy to which we have just referred has led to a remarkable elevation of religious life and consciousness and has created religious values which are among the greatest in history.

The best known and most moving example is the religious drama of the Book of Job. Here we want to point out only how profoundly in that powerful piece of literature the difference is conceived between human ideals and the cosmic or divine law of life, and how clearly and sharply the problem is formulated: what is the value of the moral law in the religious relationship or in the eyes of God?

We must begin by recognizing that Job is righteous in the full sense of the word; even in the eyes of God he is irreproachable. Thus God says to Satan, "Have you observed my servant Job? For no one on earth is so pious and upright as he, so God fearing and abhorrent of evil." This man is struck with the worst possible calamity. He meets not only with physical suffering but with degradation in the eyes of his neighbours (Job 19 : 9 and 30 : 9–15), for they believe in a divine righteousness which seems to exclude the possibility of Job's righteousness. Job, on the contrary, is brought to the point of doubting the divine righteousness; indeed he flatly denies it. And he has the complete right to do this, because he knows what righteousness is. Even Yahweh acknowledges that he has practised righteousness his entire life. With complete conviction and great authority he says that what he is now undergoing is not justice. He himself could not thus treat someone who had desired only good. It is clear that if God's righteousness is maintained in this case, "righteousness" or "justice" is an ambiguous term, with one meaning for men and another for God. The thought occurs to Job that "righteousness" is a problem about which we cannot easily speak. He replies to his friends, "Yes, indeed, I know that it is so (namely that God is righteous), and how should a man have a right before God? If He wished to dispute with him, he could not give Him the answer to one of a thousand questions." And Job elaborates on the "great and inscrutable things, miracles without number," which are done by the cosmic ruler. (Job 9: 1–10.) These are remarkable words to come from the lips of Job, for they make us aware how intense is the struggle in his soul. He has in mind not only the absolute power, but also the wisdom of God: in his sense of human insignificance and limitation of insight he admits for a moment that human righteousness must bow before divine righteousness. But the conclusion that there therefore must be two kinds of righteousness is ultimately an impossible thought for both him and his friends. He does not pursue this line of thought further, but lets the problem rest, and thereafter concentrates his attention on that fact which has now become an offense which evokes his protest, that "God destroys the good with the bad and ridicules the despair of the innocent." The moral law written in the heart is not the law of God, the Lord of the universe. "The earth has been surrendered into the hands of the godless." (Job 9 : 22–24.) These words arise from the depth of Job's moral conviction, and, as he himself says, he utters them without fear. His conviction and courage reach their zenith when he challenges God (Job 13 : 3 and 14 : 2) to tell him why God has made him – Job – His enemy.

> How many are my iniquities and my sins?
> Make me know my transgression and my sin.
> Why dost thou hide thy face,

and count me as thy enemy?
Wilt thou frighten a driven leaf
and pursue dry chaff?   (Job 13 : 23–25).

Yahweh does not hide his countenance. He gives answer,
and we know what that answer amounts to.

Then Yahweh answered Job out of the whirlwind:
"Who is this that darkens counsel by words
                              [without knowledge?
Gird up your loins like a man,
I will question you, and you shall declare to me."
                              (Job 38 : 1–3.)

And now come the questions, as blow after blow.

Where were you when I laid the foundation of the earth? . . .
Who determined its measurements . . .
Or who stretched the line upon it?   (38 : 4–5)
Do you give the horse his might?   (39 : 19)
Is it by your wisdom that the hawk soars,
and spreads his wings toward the south?   (39 : 26)

And the first speech ends with these words:

Shall a faultfinder contend with the Almighty?
He who argues with God, let him answer it.

Then Job answered Yahweh:

Behold, I am of small account;
what shall I answer thee?
I lay my hand on my mouth.
I have spoken once, and I will not answer;
twice, but I will proceed no further.

It is noteworthy that the word "righteousness" does not appear
once. Only wisdom, which is realized by the divine omnipotence,
gives expression to the essence of divine being. When righteousness is excluded from consideration, Job no longer has an answer.
And how would he dare to bring in righteousness when the
Omniscient God does not recognize it?

Nevertheless in the following speech (40 : 1–9) the word does
appear in a remarkable context:

Will you even put me in the wrong?
Will you condemn me that you may be justified?
Have you an arm like God, and can you thunder with a
[voice like his?
Deck yourself with majesty and dignity;
clothe yourself with glory and splendour ...
... tread down the wicked were they stand ...
Then will I also acknowledge to you, that your own right
[hand can give you victory.

Yahweh's right to act as he acts rests upon his power and majesty, or is at least inseparably connected with them. Divine
right is here equated with the interest of universal life, which
rises above man.

This is something other than moral right or justice. It is that,
but it is supra-moral justice. What God does is right, but only
because He, the World Governor, does it. He is not bound to a
principle above Him. Only man is bound; not God. The governing
of the world is God's work, not God's norm. Now we see what
the Book of Job is about. The question is not why God lets
righteous men suffer. To that question there are satisfying answers, such as "suffering serves as the touchstone of righteousness," or "in order to raise the level of religious life and to purify
it from finite elements." These are good answers but the Book
of Job is not concerned with them. It is concerned with the
validity of righteousness itself. The answer which Yahweh gives
to this problem is along the same line as the answer Job sought
when in piety and in humility he confessed: I know that God
is righteous, even though His righteousness is different from
my own.

The conception of the author of Job is sufficiently clear.
Man's moral conduct is indeed of value in the eyes of God.
Yahweh praises Job for his righteousness. This righteousness
is the path of life which God has prescribed for man. Man is
not a supra-ethical being, but God is indeed supra-ethical.

This is especially evident in the hymn of praise to divine
wisdom in Job 28. It dwells on the sublimity and the inscrutability of divine wisdom, whose place no man and no creature
knows. Even death and the abyss do not know where it is located.

(This last would probably not have been said by any Babylonian, Egyptian, Greek, or Roman of the Ancient stamp.) Only God knows its place and the way which leads to it, for His glance reaches to the ends of the world. And then suddenly the hymn concludes on a new tone with this one verse, "And to man He said: See, the fear of the Lord, that is wisdom, and to depart from evil is understanding." Nothing more is said. The genuineness of this verse has been denied because "wisdom" has another meaning here than in the foregoing verses and because this verse is written in prose. Perhaps it is really not genuine. But in that case the interpolator has inserted a very striking remark, for which we may well be thankful to him. For the verse illustrates in an excellent way the purport of the entire book. Man is not initiated in divine wisdom. But he knows all that he needs to know, namely that true human wisdom consists of godly fear and righteousness. That is *his* law of life. The law which God follows is an inscrutable mystery for man, and he does not need to concern himself with it.

It is in any case clear that if God accepts human righteousness as pleasing to Him, this is not because ethical conduct or moral law have autonomous value. Moral law has absolute authority because God has ordained it and ascribes value to it. That is the cardinal point: the belief of the pious man in the value of righteousness is subordinate to his belief in the sovereign, almighty, and omniscient god. This thought also occurs to Job, but he does not keep it to the end. When he challenges God, he ascribes to moral conduct an autonomous value. Whereupon Yahweh asks him to show the power of his righteousness. "Then I shall also praise you because your right hand gives the victory." Is might then right? Not in the finite sense, according to the author of Job, but might is indeed right understood in the infinite sense of cosmic power. Human power is at once impotence and injustice. But divine power is absolute wisdom, extending above and beyond human understanding, not theoretical wisdom, but the objective wisdom to which the world governance and world order attest. That wisdom is divine justice, which rises above human rules and principles. For the religious consciousness the concept "power" is just as ambigious a term as "righteousness."

Thus the religious orientation in the Book of Job is at the same time a cosmic orientation which abolishes man's central position. In this respect it is the same orientation expressed in the concepts *asha*, *rita*, and *ma-a-t* in the so called "nature religions." But besides the similarity there is also a noticeable difference. In Job the consciousness of a conflict between human ideals and divine being has been awakened. The solution of this conflict can be found only in an absolute subjection to the counsel and the will of God, and in a humble attitude towards God. This self-denial is the sorrow which Hegel considered to be the chief characteristic of the pessimistic "Syrian" religions. Schleiermacher is pointing to the same characteristic in defining religion as the "sense of absolute dependence," in which moral consciousness and intellectual endeavour are deprived of their autonomy and have become "nature" (that is to say, they have been put beyond the attainment or authority of man).

This point of view is not in accord with a humane, anthropocentric, and ethical view of life. But it cannot be inferior. It is responsible for the creation of the greatest poetic work in the Old Testament – some say, the greatest piece of poetry in all of mankind's religious literature – the Book of Job. And when we look through the history of religion, we find that this attitude toward the problem of the relation of religion and ethics recurs a number of times, and that it has led to the high points in religious literature. This is attested in Babylonia by a remarkable group of writings, the Lamentations.

These Lamentations are occasioned, like the Book of Job, by a disaster which has struck the poet or his people. The writer proves again and again to be unaware of any transgression which could explain his fate. The question is therefore: how can the righteous god thus treat the righteous man? Here too, there is no effort to soften the sharpness of the problem or to evade the question by engaging in reflections about "the educative significance of suffering" or "the divine testing of faith." These thoughts, in themselves quite religious, were certainly not strange to the pious Babylonian. But he did not use them as an explanation of the simple and undeniable fact which he could not overlook, the fact that this divine act could not be made to accord with what the pious man considers righteousness to be, which righteousness he tries in complete earnest to practice. He himself would never want to educate or test anyone in the way that God does; his moral sense would forbid him to do so. Does God then have a different conception of righteousness and goodness than man? Evidently He does, and the writer states this plainly. An instance of this are the well known utterances in the lamentation of the pious old man. These are simple words which – in spite of all the time separating us from them – have lost nothing of their force:

> I thought continually on prayer and invocation; prayer was my rule and sacrifice my daily order; the day for worshipping God was my joy ... to honour the king was my delight, and to be pleasing to him was my satisfaction. I taught my country to respect God's name; I gave lessons in revering the name of the goddess. Could I but know if all this was pleasing to God! But what a man thinks to be good is bad for God, and that which a man finds bad is for God good. Who is there who comprehends the counsel of gods in the heavens or who sees through into the plan of God, which is full of darkness![1]

This pious man does not challenge the deity as Job did. For he himself gives the answer which destroys every ethical world view, the answer which Yahweh gave when he brought Job to repentance. The moral law which is valid for men's actions, and which indeed has absolute validity for men, that moral law is not a valid norm for God's actions. It has thus no autonomous value. God alone is self-subsistent; his law is his wisdom and his omnipotence – two identical concepts. God's righteousness consists in His maintaining the world's law of life. Man does not know on what norm this righteousness is based.

Like the author of Job, the Babylonian poet was convinced that God had ordained the ethical law for man as his law of life. Hammurabi received his law from the hand of Shamash, the god who watches over justice among men and punishes injustice. But that law has absolute validity only because it expresses the will of God, and not because it agrees with the human sense of justice. For only then can it be explained why in the Babylonian religion, too, transgression of what we would call purely ethical commandments is put in the same category with transgression of ritual ordinances. The Babylonian considers as transgressions such things as sowing discord between relatives or friends, disrespect toward parents, violence and robbery, and especially all kinds of deceit, such as "saying both yes and no at the same time" (sincerely with the mouth but falsely in the heart), falsity in business, robbing an heir of his inheritance, moving boundary stones, not keeping promises, giving false instruction, etc. But besides these and between them the ritual transgressions are listed: touching impure objects, taking upon one's self the "spell" of a house, door, or hearth, and the like. This is a proof that the legislating gods cannot be conceived as purely ethical. But this does not mean that the religious stand-point of these people was undeveloped or "primitive," any more than the standpoint of the author of Job was primitive. These gods are not ethical beings because they are not human beings. The ritual ordinances indicate just as much as do the ethical commandments what men's path of life is. Both groups of re-gulations have absolute validity, not because man thinks they are good, but because God in His inscrutable wisdom and om-nipotence (objective wisdom) has declared them valid for man. Just the fact that ritual and ethical regulations are put on the same plane shows quite clearly the heteronomous character of the ethical ordinance. The believers considered even the ethical commandments to be of supra-ethical origin. They were religio-ethical, not ethical-religious; religion was the sovereign factor and had set its stamp on the ethic. In this sense it can be said that there is a religious ethic but not an ethical religion; there is a Christian ethic, but there is no ethical Christianity.

In this context we can understand the term, "unknown sin," which occurs repeatedly in Babylonian religion and also in the Indian worship of Varuna. "I do not know my sins; I do not know what impurity I have eaten (or touched)." Or differently stated: "I wish to tell you what I have done, but I am unable to tell you the deed; I wish to tell you what I have said, but I can not mention the word." In the moral sense the transgression of the sinner is always known, but it is not always known in the religious sense. God has indeed in many respects revealed His will to man, but because the basis of that will is not the moral principle but divine wisdom, with respect to his life-path man gropes in many cases in darkness. Without wishing it or knowing it he sins by his transgressions against the divine will. This is stated quite directly: "Men do not know anything by their own understanding; who has not sinned, who has not acted badly? The way of God, who knows it?" And in another place: "Men are deaf and understand nothing; whether they do evil or good – they understand nothing." [2]

This certainly conflicts with all ethical notions. But we also feel the greatness of this humility. It was the greatness of these believers to dare to recognize their human insignificance. They too knew that man is akin to God (Adapa, Gilgamesh); in spite of his mortality and transiency he shares in the divine essence. But kinship is not identity, and religious experience had taught them the terrible truth of man's finitude and insignificance in relation to God. In the Babylonian psalms the belief in God's mercy comes more to the fore than it does in the Book of Job. In the midst of all the suffering that belief is expressed again and again. Humility has no power in itself; it only indicates impotence. But humility towards God is the sphere in which divine power reveals itself as mercy and comforts man. And what of the "unknown sin"? That notion, too, is not so wholly alien to us. We need only to think of the words spoken on the Cross: "Forgive them (that is to say, be merciful), for they know not what they do."

Greek tragedy furnishes a second example of the conflict between heteronomy and autonomy outside Hebrew religion. This conflict takes its sharpest forms in "Prometheus Bound," which is perhaps the greatest of all Greek tragedies. In Greek religion, too, Job's problem proves to have stirred the religious consciousness to the very depths. There too the only solution which is indicated is this: no human considerations (*boulai*) are a match for the Harmonia of Zeus. For the religious meaning of Harmonia is objective, divine wisdom; it is the combination of that which is, humanly speaking, contradictory, the combination of the finite and the infinite, of life and death. This harmony provides no usable norm, for being divine wisdom and power it remains an enigma. Humility is the only possible human attitude towards it. Prometheus does not give it due consideration and is destroyed in the conflict. But by means of the Chorus the poet indicates this harmony.

D. THE DEMONIC GOD

We have seen that the religious apprehension of the heteronomy of moral life is coupled with the idea that righteousness is
a gift of God. The Babylonian god bestows *kettu* and *mēsharu* (stability and righteousness). This is in accord with the religious
conception of transgression which we repeatedly encounter.
It is a curse laid by God upon man, outside man's moral responsibility. God himself keeps man off the path of life and makes
him a sinner; man goes to his destruction. No one knows the
cause of God's hostile disposition, for the ground of the divine
will is unknown. This is the demonic god, who is also encountered
in other religions besides those of the Semites. Sin becomes
evident only in man's disaster and destruction. Nevertheless
the believer calls this disaster „divine punishment." God vents
his wrath and "punishes." It might seem that here the sense of
guilt, in any event, would be lacking, but such is not the case.
The sense of "guilt" proves to be connected with the conviction
of one's own insignificance or nothingness compared to God.
If man cannot appeal to anything because his ideals do not have
absolute validity and his capacities are finite and defective, then
he feels himself to be guilty, even when he is not aware of any
particular transgression; guilty not to men but to God. We saw
that Job and Prometheus, who declared themselves to be "not
guilty" before God, have judgment rendered against them by
God, and that the pious writer agrees with this judgment.
These terms, "transgression," "punishment," and "guilt" thus
have besides their ethical meaning a religious meaning.

This explains a peculiar linguistic usage: words for "transgression" and sin can also mean "punishment." The Babylonian
shertu or *annu* means transgression, sin, but the "shertu of God"
is the punishment of God. The Egyptian *isf.t* means "sin," but
we also read; "God gives 'sin' (thus punishment) to him who
has 'sin'." Transgression is punishment. It might be thought
that there was one word for these two concepts because the transgression, according to the Ancient idea, was placed on the guilty
one as disaster or punishment. It was indeed probably sometimes
so conceived in Antiquity, but such a conception is itself purely
naturalistic, and not religious: a self-subsistent god has no place

in this view. But there was also a different and more ancient conception according to which the transgression itself is a punishment
from God. Then the transgression or sin is in the literal sense the
will of God, namely God's punishment. God makes man sin and
"punishes" him in that way. This means that God declares
someone guilty and makes him guilty, just as he declares someone
righteous, not on account of some human act, but simply in his
sovereignty, in his inscrutable wisdom and omnipotence.
"Transgression" and "punishment" are then one and the same
fact willed by God. God vents his wrath for an inscrutable reason
and he makes someone guilty, that is to say, he punishes. In
this sense he is a "demonic god."

In the Old Testament there are some striking instances of
this demonic way of acting on God's part. Yahweh hardens
Pharaoh's heart (Exodus 4 : 21); he sends a lying spirit among
the prophets of Ahab (I Kings 22 : 22); he "incited David
against them" by telling him to count the people (II Samuel
24 : 1). (According to I Chronicles 21 : 1 it was Satan who
incited David to this – a proof that the older account from II
Samuel is referring to the demonic god.) The transgression itself,
and not only that which follows it, is the divine "punishment,"
the expression of divine wrath and hostile disposition. According
to the Vedas, Varuna sets a "trap" for man; that is to say, he
makes him become a sinner, declares or makes him guilty according to his unfathomable and all-wise decree. In a Babylonian
oracle text we read, "Shall the enemies succeed in their siege
of the city of Kishshatu...? O Shamash, let something be lacking
in their sacrifice; make sure there is impurity in the questions
they put to the oracle [so that they are wrongly informed, as
was Ahab by the lying spirit among the prophets], that something
impure is eaten, that the sacrificial lamb has blemishes ..."
In other words, the god must punish them and bring about their
downfall by making them guilty.

These gods do not explain or justify their way of acting. The
Babylonian Flood story is introduced as follows:-"It occurred
to the Great Gods (as the cosmic governors were called) to produce a great flood." No reason is mentioned. But the Babylonians believed that this disaster is inseparable from transgression and punishment. The Old Testament does give a motivation:

"And God saw the earth, and behold, it was corrupt; for all flesh had corrupted their way upon the earth." (Genesis 6 : 12.) So God decided to blot out men. Nevertheless it is doubtful whether this motivation indicates an essentially different conception from the Babylonian one.

We should not forget that the expression, "demonic powers" has acquired a meaning in our language which diverges to some extent from the Greek *daimonios*, the concept with which these religions are concerned. The essential character of the demonic god is not his terrifying or pitiless aspect, but his sovereign and ultimate nature. The daimon does not justify his actions, which are just as likely to be good as to be evil. Like divine wisdom they are unpredictable and "arbitrary." Greek religion provides striking illustrations of this. This type of conception certainly did not agree with the classical idea of deity, yet it was definitely present, as a survival of the Ancient belief which continued to exist alongside the "enlightenment" and indeed was the most important factor in the cultus. As an example let me mention the well known form of worship of Zeus about which there has been much dispute, just because of the misunderstanding of the Ancient concept *daimōn*. Alongside the worship of Zeus Meilichios (the friendly and generous Zeus) was the worship of Zeus Maimaktes (the cruel and wrathful Zeus). According to Plutarch and the lexicographer Hesychius, that was the same Zeus. Neither Plutarch nor Hesychius (especially Plutarch) would say this if it were not generally known, for this must have been completely incomprehensible for Plutarch, the man who believed that he who ascribed unworthy acts to God is less pious than he who says that God does not exist. Neither do modern scholars doubt the accuracy of their report that these two forms of Zeus are the same god. Zeus Meilichios, too, was a god of the realm of the dead; he had the form of a snake and was worshipped with nocturnal wine-offerings as Zeus Chthonios, the god of the underworld. It might be thought that there is a contradiction between these names which the believers could not possibly have seriously intended. One or the other must thus be eliminated. Most scholars are of the opinion that Zeus Maimaktes did indeed exist, but that Zeus "Meilichios" was a euphemism, prompted by the desire to dispose the god favourably, just as a dangerous dog is spoken to as "good dog." According to other scholars, there was a Zeus Meilichios, and his demonic character was added to his original nature when barbaric ideas from the popular religion penetrated into the civilized social groups.

If this were a unique case in Greek religion, it might remain uncertain how it should be explained. But there is another example, and its meaning is quite clear. The "friendly" and "blessed" Eumenides are the same as the Erinyes, the avenging demons for whom all considerations of an ethical nature are utterly foreign. Here no elimination is possible; both are equally deeply established in Greek belief and Greek cultus. Like Zeus Meilichios and Maimaktes they too are chthonic beings, depicted with snakes in their hands; they bring all good and evil; the earth or the underworld brings death as surely as life. (Consider "Pandora" and Dis Pater, who brought both good and ill.) They do not justify their friendly or hostile behaviour. Their demonic character consists in the fact that they act as sovereigns, like the god in the Babylonian Lamentations, like Yahweh with respect to Job, and like Varuna. We see how strongly this idea of god conflicted with the "enlightened" ethical concepts of the classical mind in the attempt made in the fifth century B.C. to exclude the Erinyes from religious worship. It is related by Aeschylus in the *Eumenides* that after their reconciliation with Orestes they became Eumenides and obligated themselves to look after the prosperity of Attica on condition that all the welfare of land and people should be ascribed to them. This is thus an old attempt to remove the contradictory element in this type of deity.

It is, however, just this type of deity which is characterized by contradictory attributes. All the powerful gods of the underworld, of whom Zeus Meilichios or Maimaktes was one, show more or less clearly this double, demonic nature. Likewise the name Hecate Calliste, "the most beautiful one" is not a euphemism. The contradictory names do not indicate insincerity on the part of the believers, but rather the belief in the mercy of these gods, just as in the Babylonian Lamentations. The cruel god was also a gracious god; good fortune and ill both came from him, and the good fortune revealed his graciousness and his mercy. The demonic gods were worshipped, not out of fear, but

out of awe. Their "arbitrariness" was divine justice. They were
the upholders of the universal law of life, the "harmonia of Zeus."
And they were especially the gods of the underworld, the home of
absolute life. The invisible "heavens," too, were that other
world, either as paradise or as realm of the dead – in any case
known only in or after death.

It is remarkable that the gods of this supra-ethical or demonic
type are usually the most exalted in rank of all the gods in the
pantheon; they are the universal gods. Thus in addition to Zeus
and to Varuna, there is also the Babylonian supreme god, the
"celestial" Anu. His children are the "Seven Evil Spirits" who
are repeatedly called the "Sons of Anu," and his daughter is
Lamashtu, the demon of the children's diseases. The "Seven Evil
Spirits" prove to be closely related to the "Seven Gods" or "Great
Gods" (*Ilāni Rabûti*). Seven is namely the totality, the summation
of all divine attributes. The Seven gods are the cosmic rulers
also conceived as the seven gods of the planets, who in their
demonic sovereignty impose the spell and determine the fate
which takes no account of human wishes or ideals. It is in connection with gods of this type that we encounter the most
majestic and most profound conceptions of the Ancient religions.
But all this completely escaped someone like Plutarch.

The Romans created a distinctive term to indicate the absolute character of these gods and the relation in which man stood
toward them, namely "sacer," being sacred or holy. The double
meaning of the term is noteworthy; it signifies divine disapproval as well as divine approval; if we look more deeply, we see,
however, that the same reality is meant. Everything and every
person which has come into contact with the divine is "sacer."
The Sacra Via is sacred in the good sense; so too is the Pontifex
Maximus, who is sacer. But he too is sacer who has left the human
path of life, has departed from human relationships within
which he could be punished, and has broken the divine commandments. Human measures, which are always of relative nature,
stop at this point. He who touches the Ark of Yahweh goes
outside the human sphere of life and becomes sacer; he dies.
He who touches the king dies. Such a "homo sacer" has put himself outside the *jus humanum* and can be killed without punishment. According to Dionysius, the client who behaves unfittingly

toward his patron by breaking the family bond is sacer and is "consecrated to some god or other – usually a god of the underworld." [3] His execution is here a sacrifice, not a punishment. He who steals crops standing in the field or lets his animals graze in someone else's field is consecrated by death to the earth and grain goddess Ceres. His offence is no ordinary thievery, but transgression of the order of Ceres. She has determined in which way men can without danger make use of the divine gift of the riches of the earth; he who does it otherwise comes into direct contact with the holy without taking the necessary measures to prevent the fatal results of this contact. He who is consecrated or sanctified in this way is considered to be the sacrificial offering; that is to say, he is considered to be the representative of the absolute, divine life of the earth. His death is thus certainly not a punishment.

The unfaithful Vestal Virgin, who is buried alive, has not committed a "transgression." She represents Vesta as Terra Mater; her consort is the god of the underworld (of the earth). By her death she has realized her mystical essence, with the result that she also becomes in reality the consort of the god of the realm of the dead. Her being buried alive signifies that she is identified for good with her goddess Vesta. Thus we even hear that the unfaithful Vestal Virgin Tarpeia was worshipped after her death. The Ancients always worshipped those who were killed because of religious transgressions. The Tarentine citizens, who had transgressed the divine institutions, were killed by the lightning of Zeus Kataibates; later their grave stones were placed before the houses of many Tarentine citizens and were worshipped with sacrifices to Zeus Kataibates. The death inflicted by Zeus was their consecration. Death by lightning always sanctifies. The oath breaker will be struck by Jupiter's lightning and be made sacred; being made sacred is never simply punishment. The divine "punishment" is destruction in this sense, that one is made sacred; he is removed to the divine sphere.

The sense of the absoluteness of the consecration also makes itself felt when men execute the death sentence. It is an infinite punishment, without any possibility of difference in degree, and therefore not comparable to other punishments. This fact has always forced its way into man's consciousness. When the death

sentence is executed, moral indignation disappears as a matter
of course and makes way for the prayer, "May God have mercy
on your soul." The appearence of death, even without God's
intervention, is always a sanctification, a making sacred,
because death ends life's finitude. God does not "punish" when
He brings disaster or destruction. It could better be said that
he who transgresses a divine reality thereby moves into the
sphere of infinite existence, into the divine sphere. Like the
unfaithful Vestal Virgin he offers himself for sacrifice. It is
hybris, presumption, which also brings the downfall of the hero
in Greek Tragedy, such as Prometheus or Agamemnon, who is
killed by Clytaemnestra. A higher world order than the finite one
with which one reckons in daily life then becomes effective, for
the transgression and its unavoidable consequence form a whole
which lies outside the area of moral life. Sometimes the Ancients
left a person who had transgressed the divine decrees to God's
disposal; when they did, however, remove him from finite society,
they performed a religious act, and not a judicial one. He who
is sacer, as the murderer is, may be executed, but it is not necessary. The awareness of this slumbers in our modern consciousness,
too; it is understandable that the opinions concerning the per-
missability of the death penalty diverge so widely. It is sensed
that the character of "punishment" has disappeared, but what
is less generally sensed is the religious character of the "death
penalty."

In short, it can be said that belief in the sovereign, demonic
god is coupled with a particular conception of man, with a certain religious anthropology, and that conception is this: it is
no credit to man that God declares him righteous, but neither
does it indicate wickedness in the ethical sense when God declares man unrighteous. Man does not know his own law of life –
he cannot know the infinite foundation of his own existence
stretching beyond him. If he lives and prospers, that is a gift
from God. If he is destroyed, then that is God's decree. Rescue
from misfortune or disaster, a restoration of the relation to God
in order to make life possible, is only attainable by the utilization
of the sacramental means which express the divine activity and
intervention. In a divine condemnation, man feels himself
guilty towards God, but not towards men. This consciousness

of guilt is very closely akin to the consciousness of human finitude, insignificance, and unworthiness. But the fact that a consciousness of guilt exists presumes potential righteousness; this potential, that is to say, that which has not been realized, explains the sense of guilt.

E. CONCLUDING REMARKS

Religious doctrines concerning man's law of life prove to diverge very widely. Besides a great optimism that sees man as God's co-worker, we encounter a deep pessimism which considers human insight and ability to be of no essential value. We must try to understand the religious meaning and value of the different types. The divergent conceptions prove to arise from the impossibility of combining human finitude and divine infinity in a concept having universal validity. "Man's law of life" is such a concept; its content can only be indicated in contradictory statements. It is worth while to notice how this problem also recurs in modern philosophy, for in so doing we are brought considerably closer to the problem, and we are rightly impressed with the permanent nature of the problems which the religious man confronts.

The most striking agreement with the material we have been discussing is shown by the religious philosophy of Kant. We can suffice with noting the well known points which are really the chief features of his thought. We shall see that the principal idea of the religious conception of the law of life is met with again in Kant's thought: man's participation in an infinite life extending beyond the individual in harmony with the divine law of the universe. And the unavoidable religious consequences also appear: deep-lying and theoretically insoluble conflicts between the human and the divine law.

Kant brought together his views on this subject in his book, *Die Religion innerhalb der Grenzen der blossen Vernunft* (*Religion within the Limits of Pure Reason*).[4] This is not a work which one discusses in order to decide whether or not one agrees with it. Whoever reads it and understands it must confess that it is one of those rare works which inspire such great respect that the desire or the courage to criticize it simply disappears. One is sometimes deeply stirred by reading it, and no one will escape the impression of being gripped in the depths of his soul. For it is just in this book, whose title gives such a strangely rationalistic impression, that this sober philosopher proves also to be a seer, and a seer of such a stature as we meet only in the great works of religious poetry. It is wholly in accord with the spirit of those religious works that Kant gives no satisfactory solution to the questions which he raises. His philosophy is not a rash attempt to attain the unattainable. We can hardly be anything but grateful to its author.

It is well known that Kant sees a close connection between ethics and religion. The central ethical fact is the consciousness of the "categorical imperative," the unconditional requirement to act in accord with the moral law, independent of such finite considerations as desire, experience, and utilitarian motives. It is the requirement to uphold our deepest being over against the phenomena of the world. In the "du sollst" (thou shalt) speaks the absolute, something of absolute validity and truth, a "Ding an sich," not dependent on any experience. In the ethical law an absolute divine reality reveals itself. This is the "praktische Vernunft" (practical reason), reason in the area of the practical affairs of life. Ethics is thus in its essence religion. That means that we are in our deepest being autonomous, for the ethical faculty "postulates" man's freedom. The absolute requirement is that we must actualize the moral law. The subjective condition for this is human immortality, for the ethical requirement cannot possibly be fulfilled in empirical life. The ethical requirement is of course concerned precisely to abolish the condition of being determined by experience, and it must therefore be fulfilled in an infinite life; this is the postulate of immortality. But the absolute requirement to fulfill the law also has an objective condition, and that is a world which is based on an ethical foundation, which is governed by God and not by the laws of the finite relationships of things. The empirical world is ethically indifferent; in this world the ethical, "the best world" for which we strive, cannot be realized. If the ethical law, which is directed toward the world, is not a vain reality and an unrealizable requirement, but actually does contain truth, then that law must be valid for the world in its essential being, for the world cannot basically

be in contradiction with that requirement. From this there follows the identity of the ethical sense and religious faith. Thus a
religio-ethical anthropology is postulated. The ethical law is the
intelligible (not found in experience) ground of the universe;
it is ultimate and absolute.

The religious character of Kant's ethic is thus at the same time
its cosmic character. Kant's ethic is removed as far as possible
from eudaemonistic motives. It is diametrically opposed to
considerations of prosperity, utility, and reward, but it, too,
assumes that in the last analysis a harmony must exist between
ethical action and the world process. The world must finally
be conducive and favourable, to the ethical man, so that happiness
is the result of ethical action. This does not need to occur in this
finite empirical world; it can also occur in the infinite life, in
eternity. For when faith is postulated, nature and freedom
(ethical action) are finally in accord. The combination of righteousness with good fortune and of unrighteousness with misfortune
is a basic feature of Kant's view.

When the cosmic element is introduced into ethical life, a
religious relation arises, a relation to the power governing the
world. The ethical requirement becomes an act of faith, namely
the faith in the objective truth of ethical law. Human centrality
is thus ended. As soon as ethical law in its absoluteness and
infinity takes cosmic law into itself, conflicts begin to appear.
No particular ethical law, inspired by sympathy or love of truth
is absolutely valid; that which is valid is purely formal, *du sollst*,
without particular application. The conflict between divine order and human aims, even the most sublime, is an unavoidable
one. Man is "autonomous," but in the mystical sense, according
to the mind of God; all his conscious thinking and acting conflict
with the divine law of life, which he knows but repeatedly dis-
regards. A pessimistic attitude is unavoidable in evaluating
human capacities, for they are diametrically opposed to the
conception of harmony between man and world. The cleft between
intelligible nature and man's experience is unbridgeable.

This pessimistic attitude comes to light again and again in
Kant's works on religion and ethics. Kant is the philosophical
preacher of radical sin, of original sin. His conception of sin
corresponds completely to the absolute and infinite character

of the ethical disposition: thou must, regardless of all considera-
ations and circumstances. The ethical transgression in the strict
sense of the word is not a particular action. Every particular
action is limited, ethically as well as otherwise; every transgression is of a particular and thus of a limited evil nature. Evil
itself must be sought at a deeper level and must include more than
particular instances. Yet it is not our empirical nature, for that
is given to us; it is something natural. We have not produced it
and are therefore not responsible for the fact that we are empirical beings. Evil consists in man's diverging from the moral
law, from *du sollst*, and choosing another norm than the law of
obligation – and that he does this of his own free will. Therefore
it is not men's sensory nature but his basic disposition which is
evil, that is to say, wrong or perverse; an "Umkehrung der
Triebfedern" has taken place. The source of the evil inclination
is just as inexplicable as the disposition towards the good. Man
knows the law, namely to act in accord with his obligation and
without regard for all finite considerations. This knowledge of
the law presumes a free will, but we use that freedom "to reverse
the motives." The bad or evil inclination has not originated in
time from a particular occasion; like the ethical law it is radical;
it is a radical sin. And just as the moral law is one and universal,
since the absolute "thou must" contains no particular instances,
so too is the transgression, the reversal of the motives of conduct,
not a matter of degree. Even the "smallest" and most innocent
transgression is radical sin, "mortal sin" in the literal sense,
because it shows up the reversal of the motives.

Kant's ethic has indeed become religion; "religious ethics" is
always religion. The absolute and infinite is introduced into
ethics as the all-decisive factor, and thus all judgment of circumstances, all gradation in good and evil, is abandoned. Our
self condemnation and self disapproval is absolute with respect
to our actual willing and doing. The highest is present in man,
namely the absolute, the supreme, and the divine. That man
nevertheless does not will that which is highest in him, condemns
him and brings him to destruction. Here there is an unmistakable
kinship with the central idea in Greek tragedy. There, too, the
highest and noblest in man condemns his actual life and leads
him to death. The difference is that Kant puts all the emphasis

on the will or lack of will, and tragedy puts the emphasis on man's incapacity. But in both cases the mood is pessimistic. "We are a lazy, cowardly, and false race," wrote Kant in a letter; "my dear Sulzer, you do not know what an accursed race we are." Nevertheless the idea of lack of will or incapacity is not the only one. In the midst of downfall in tragedy sounds the cry of victory, that the divine inheritance in man has nevertheless maintained itself. And in Kant we read that in spite of the Fall (that is to say, the primordial Fall, which concerns not one but all men) and just because of the consciousness of that Fall the absolute moral law responds in us. That voice is never silenced; the disposition towards the good is never blotted out. That is proved precisely by our self condemnation. And it is in this, according to Kant, that the possibility of restoration lies. "The Knower of the hearts" sees by whom the voice resounds and in whom the yearning towards perfection lives. He, and He alone knows where conversion has taken place – for conversion cannot be seen in an external act or a particular expression of will. If it takes place, then the "Knower of the hearts" accounts that to man as righteousness and declares him righteous. This is the redemption from sin (death) by God's grace. Kant uses all these terms, and indeed uses them in their religious meaning. His ethic is a religious ethic, even though his terminology sometimes makes this less than clear; *Religion innerhalb der Grenzen der blossen Vernunft* actually means the absolute moral law.

It is indeed remarkable that even when man's law of life is sought and found in man himself, in his autonomy, as we see occurring in Kant and the tragedians, the greatest dissonance is also possible, with struggle, tension and disintegration. Indeed it is necessarily so, since the absolute and infinite is introduced as a factor (and then naturally as the all-determining factor). The absolute necessarily brings disharmony into finitude. The harmony exists only for religious faith, or as Kant says, for faith in redemption from sin – death – by God's grace. We find in his reflections very divergent historical types of religious anthropology, both optimistic and pessimistic types. He has tried to define the essential relation between religion and ethics. No religion does that. Religion does not speak about the "essence" of phenomena, but about their concrete reality.

To the term "sin" Kant gives a meaning which is certainly not alien to the Ancient religions, even though they never formulate it as clearly as does Kant. "Sin," not "guilt." According to ordinary linguistic usage, and also for Kant's consciousness, guilt is related to breaking particular moral laws; it is a typically ethical term. The sense of sin arises, however, when man departs from his communion with God, or, as Kant expresses it, from the absolute in our own being. Sin is a religious term. Thus one and the same transgression can be conceived both as guilt and as sin; guilt is related to a fact which stands by itself; sin is related to a denial of the foundation of our existence. Sin is therefore the "evil inclination" which has a universal purport. But the sense of guilt towards God is always a sense of sin. Sin is therefore always radical. Kant also speaks of original sin, and just in connection with essential human nature, not with empirical man. Here again he is thinking completely in the spirit of Christian theology.

We do not need to pursue Kant's views any further. This much at least is clear, that he has furnished us with a document of religio-ethical anthropology which takes its place alongside the works of prophets and religious thinkers and poets among the Greeks, Babylonians, Indians, and Hebrews.

I repeat what I wrote at the beginning of this section – let others try their powers of critical judgment on these works, with partial approval and partial disapproval. I believe that we have more to gain from them when we try to let these views simmer down into our thinking. They are great enough to continue to instruct us.

In treating the phenomenology of religious ethics the standpoint of the Sermon on the Mount (Matthew 5–7) could have been included. But this subject is too important to be brought into a summary view of different types. Therefore I shall make only the following remark. The concept, "religious ethics," is nowhere so clearly illustrated in all of its mystical purport as in the Sermon on the Mount.

> You have heard that it was said, "An eye for an eye and a tooth for a tooth." But I say to you, Do not resist one who is evil. But if any one strikes you on the right cheek, turn to him the other also; and if any one would sue you and take your coat, let him have your cloak as well .... Love your enemies and pray for those who persecute you. (Matthew 5 : 38–40, 44).

We are far too inclined to interpret such words so that they can be reduced to a more ordinary stature, in order that they may be usable in ethical life. It would be mistaken to disapprove of this. But we also sense that the element of absoluteness and infinity has been introduced here which transcends all finite relations. "You, therefore, must be perfect, as your heavenly Father is perfect." (5 : 48). This is an ethical commandment which immediately implies condemnation. Here there comes to the fore the whole sphere of religious ideas concerning justification (being declared righteous) by God (by divine grace).

CHAPTER 16

THE COURSE OF THE INDIVIDUAL'S LIFE

We shall now discuss the religious conception of man's growth, and in particular the conception of the critical points in life when a new form is assumed and life is directed to new goals, the moments of transition from one period into the following one.

The usual religious conception which appears repeatedly in various forms is that growth is not a gradual process of becoming whereby one period arises or springs forth from the previous one; it is not a series of causes and effects. The idea that every life period "in germ," as potential reality, is already present in the previous period, is a thought which is alien to the religious view. The appearance of the various life functions, which come to the fore one after another in the course of life, is quite inexplicable; the changes or transitions are all metamorphoses, results of the forces in life which are always creating anew, and thus are spontaneous and divine forces. That which is new in each stage is new in the full sense of the word. The conception that it was already present in germ beforehand strikes the religious man as an attempt to give a rationalistic explanation of the mystery of life.

This religious conception of growth is expressed with remarkable force in Roman religion and there is given an extraordinarily clear formulation. There we find the conviction that the properties of growth as well as its stages cannot be reduced to anything else. This conviction and the belief that no rational connection exists between the stages explain the worship of the innumerable indigitamenta gods, which represent the successive stages in the life process and the various expressions of life in one particular moment. Thus the Romans are familiar with about eighty-two different gods concerned with the course of individual life. Each stage of growth and each property reveals the wholly unique divine activity of a particular god. Neither does one god perform any other task than his own; otherwise a connection could be seen between the different activities (expressions of life).

Religious ideas of this type occur much more frequently than is usually believed, even among the most different peoples. The basic thought, that each stage is a new creation, is so easy to recognize that in many cases we can make use of data from the so-called primitive religions, whose thought is so far removed from our own, without running the risk of making bad mistakes. The phenomena display a remarkable similarity in type.

Let me mention an example from one of those very strange religions, that of the coastal inhabitants of New Guinea, the Mayo Mysteries.[1] On attaining maturity boys and girls are initiated in the Mysteries. This initiation consists in the presentation in dramatic form of the "history of growth" of the human race. The novices are smeared with white clay from head to foot and even get clay in their mouths; man originated from earth. Then it is portrayed how they awake from the earth and obtain clothes of palm leaves, which according to this people were the original clothes. Then there follow the ceremonies of the fetching of the coconut from the tree, the catching of crabs, shrimps, and mussels, the fetching of sweet water, sago, vegetables dug out of the earth, etc. After that moment they may eat these fruits freely. Finally the customs of engagement and marriage are impressed upon them, and likewise the mutual obligations of husband and wife and the division of work in society. Thus the history of growth in human life is depicted as a series of mysteries and ceremonially imparted as a supernatural event, a series of sacred acts. The idea which is here acted out is that in the individual life the same ultimate, mysterious forces are at work as in the human race as a whole. The fact that the most necessary individual and social usages are always taught by parents to their children does not make them less mysterious. There are divine forces at work in the origin and growth of life.

The religious conception of the different stages of life is further characterized by the religio-magical ceremonies which take place at the transition from one period of life to another. It is not simply religious reflections and theories which are important; these are expressed in genuine religio-magical cultic acts. This is quite understandable. When men see divine forces, they are not content simply to recognize them. A contemplative attitude is appropriate to scientific insight, but it is impossible if one is to gain religious insight. The insight or religious apprehension underlying the *rites de passage* (ceremonies marking the transition from one stage of life to another) is of an extremely practical nature; it is not an increase of theoretical knowledge, but a becoming aware of a phenomenon of life. It is thus an awareness or insight, and the attitude connected with it is of a practical sort; in the sacred magical ceremonies the divine order which has been recognized and comprehended is actualized. This is always the case in the cultus. The religious form of insight and knowledge is human intervention and participation in the divine process; its effect is magical, that is to say, supra-rational. The individual's life itself contains the basis of that divine process. In the cultus man quite consciously sets the divine forces in motion which are always present within him. The sacred act of the religious ceremony at every point of transition in life is man's insight into the divine process; it is his conscious recognition of this. Among the Romans, worship (also a cultic act) of the gods of the indigitamenta was the practical side of their insight – we know this for sure about many of these gods. By means of sacrifices and the like the Romans shared in the divine process and actualized it.

The most important moments in life are birth, transition from childhood to adulthood, marriage, and death. We shall now note certain characteristic aspects of these moments of transition.

A. BIRTH

What divine, creative forces are active in birth? The most diverse peoples have again and again given one and the same answer to this question, that the forces present are those of the Magna Mater, the great mother. And Terra Mater, mother earth, is identical with her. Not only the Romans but all the Ancient peoples saw in the mother the superhuman, the divine. They considered the mystery of the origin of human life to be in the same sphere as the mystery of the awakening of cosmic life, particularly the life of the earth. This is expressed and realized in many customs, such as laying the newborn child on the earth and then picking him up again.[2] The Roman goddess of birth was called Levana: "Levat de terra"; she lifts up the child from the earth. The earth gives life; it enables the human race to come into being. The baby is brought into contact with the earth, and thus with life, in order to make him strong. Dieterich tells about a Hessian woman who had been weak and sickly as a child – for she was not laid down on the earth at her birth but only later was laid on fresh earth which was brought in.[3] There it is said of a sturdy fellow, "Yes, he was laid down directly on good earth," preferably on black forest earth from Ortenberg. In Norwegian the midwife is called *jordmor*, "earth mother," and the German word *Hebamme* also indicates that she enables the child to be born from the earth.

"The earth gives life to the child." This is only a particular formulation of the universal idea that all men live the life of the earth; by means of the food which is brought forth by the earth they receive the "power" of the life of the earth. God is not anthropomorphic, made in the image of man, but man is made in the image of God; in this case, Deity conceived as the Divine Earth.

All sorts of remarkable popular customs can be understood on the basis of the idea that the earth is the ever fruitful and continually productive mother. Thus Dieterich relates that sick persons are sometimes ritually buried by placing them in an open grave, from which they can then be lifted out alive.[4] The earth has given them new life, by means of which they are born again – each healing is a resurrection. A Danish prescription reads, "Place the sick man in the earth, plow and sow over him, and then take him up again." This is especially intended for someone who is "bewitched" (possessed) and thus wrested from this world. For he who lives in the other world must be born anew. Among various peoples where cremation is customary, such as the Romans and Hindus, children who die before they reach the age of two are buried and not cremated. They return to Terra Mater in order to be born anew; the baby still belongs completely to the earth from which he came.

This is similar to the conception of the goddess of birth among the Greeks and Egyptians, and among other Ancient peoples as well. It might be thought that birth has little in common with death and the realm of death, but nevertheless it is entirely certain that the Greek birth goddess Eileithyia was a goddess of the realm of the dead. She was worshipped with the dog sacrifice, and no one questions the underworld character of the dog (cf. the dogs of Hades). The dog sacrifice is the well known sacrifice to Hekate; the dog was sacrificed "only on those two goddesses." Eileithyia comes from the island of the Hyperboreans (the other world) to Delos in order to assist Leto there at the birth of her child Apollo or Artemis. Homer relates that she is worshipped in Crete in a cave – an earth temple.[5] In Olympia she was called the mother of the snake god Sosipolis; this "saviour" was an earth god, for the snake is the bearer of the life of the earth, the power of the rescuer or saviour. In Egypt Nekhbet corresponds to the Greek Eileithyia. She is "the ruler of the hidden land." [6] In all the Ancient religions this conception is related to that of the "navel (or navelstring) of the earth." This is the place where this world is connected with the other world, the underworld or the realm of the dead. That is the spot at which all life originated; therefore it is situated in the middle of the world. All vital energy goes out from this point, and it is therefore the seat of the Oracle, where divine insight, insight into the secret or law of life, can be attained. The cosmic place of birth the "navel," is thus the place where the powers of the realm of the dead reveal themselves. In Delphi the Omphalos stone (the navel stone) was very near by the cleft in the earth, which was the entrance to the underworld. The form of this stone was precisely the form of a grave mound or tumulus; this represented the earth hill or height, where the life of the earth arises. Thus the idea of the rising of life or birth was inseparably connected with the realm of the dead. And thus the goddesses of birth could be goddesses of death in the mystical sense. The typical mother goddess in Egypt, Hathor, is the goddess of foreign countries: the Sudan, Nubia, the Sinaitic peninsula, Pempt on the Somali coast, and Byblos in Phoenicia. According to Sethe she is "gleichsam vom Beruf die Göttin der fremden Länder." Why? – Because foreign territory is precisely the earthly image of the other world. In Egypt itself she is the goddess of the nocturnal sky, Duat, the realm of the dead, and is also the mother of the sun god. The night bears the day – that was for the Ancients a great mystery. That light can come forth from darkness is the same mystery as the arising of life from death. The mother is the goddess of death. Hathor is called "the healthy eye" of the sun god, that is to say, his healthy life. Life is healthy in death; the life of the god of light is healthy in the night.

In Rome there was a different but equally remarkable formulation of the mystery of motherhood: the divine mother, the prototype of the human mother, is the virgin Vesta Mater, and according to Varro, Vesta is the earth ("Vesta terra est"). She is represented by her priestesses, the Vestal Virgins. They too are mothers in the mystical sense, for they represent the mystery of motherhood. They dressed as *matronae* (married women) and they wore their hair as married women: braids around the head. Roman legends prove beyond a shadow of a doubt that the divine consort of Vesta and the Vestal Virgins was the generating fire (the god of fire) in the hearth: this fire was the life of the earth.

The religious idea of the virgin mother is to be found among various peoples; Athene Parthenos was also such a goddess. We discover more and more how widespread this idea was.

The idea of the "sacredness" of motherhood has been given still another remarkable formulation, namely that the act of birth makes the mother ritually unclean. This uncleanness sometimes lasts a long time; Leviticus states that in Israel the mother was unclean for seven days after the birth of a son, and after that she must stay away from the temple for thirty-three days. These periods are twice as long in the case of the birth of a daughter. Even among the Zoroastrians strict prescriptions are in effect concerning separation or abstention from all sorts of activities. In this instance it is indeed very remarkable, for everything which furthers or serves life and works against death is in the service of Ahura Mazda; cultivating the ground and founding a family are here synonymous with religion. Nevertheless there are extremely strict laws respecting the young mother; no one and no thing may touch her for fourteen days, not even fire, water, or household effects. The explanation of

this is that "uncleanness" is conceived as sacredness. The same
sort of sacredness or uncleanness, only in a higher degree,
occurs through direct contact with the divine, when the priest
performs sacred acts. He too must take a ritual bath of purification after forty days, like the woman who has given birth to a
child. Such is the case among many peoples, where the woman
in childbirth is "tabu," dangerous for her surroundings.[7] In
Silesia she (or actually, her demon) is warded off with a broom.
The Brazilian Indians shut up both parents with the newborn
baby for five days; in this period the parents may not do any
work and they live under strict dietary laws.[8] The sacredness of
the young mother and the baby is, however, not only dangerous
for others; the mother and child themselves are susceptible to
all sorts of dangerous influences, both bodily (illnesses) and
spiritual (magic). It is then stated that "this is on the basis of
considerations and experiences of a hygienic nature." It quite
probably is related to this. But we need to keep in mind the religious conception that sickness and susceptibility to sickness
is the situation of death. This is made evident by the conviction
that healing is a resurrection from death. Here we see again how
difficult it is for us to form an accurate notion of the considerations which lie at the basis of magical practices and have caused
them to develop. It is certainly mistaken to say that rational
hygienic considerations *explain* these practices, which are extremely irrational. The Brazilian Indians, however, shut up the
father, too. The mystery and the sacredness of fatherhood we
find indeed to be formulated in a similar way. That man is
Pater who possesses the generating power of the earth; pater
patratus is the title of the Roman ambassador with extraordinary powers, and the highest degree of initiation in the
Mithra Mysteries was the degree of Pater.

The Babylonians and Egyptians believed that a man's fate
was determined at his birth. That is also the significance of the
fairies at the cradle; it doesn't sound too strange, but like a
pretty fairy tale. But "fate" does not mean for the believers
what we understand by it: that which must occur to man willy-
nilly through the combination of circumstances. For them it is
that which lies in the sphere of universal life, that which accords
with the cosmic order. Through fate man's life is taken up,

right from the start, into the order of cosmic life. This is thus not a state of passivity, but rather of activity (life) in the infinite sense, directed towards the infinite goal of abiding cosmic life. This is also the Ancient religious meaning of Moira, which is not an impersonal power or natural law above all the gods, but the divine order of the world's life, thus the divine order of permanent life conceived in its greatest universality; in Moira the divine governance of the universe is expressed. The way in which the fate of a child is determined at his birth corresponds to these conceptions. In Egypt there are seven Hathors present to determine the child's fate. They are the goddesses of music, and they have tambourines in their hands, but their music is cosmic. Pythagoras, too, spoke about this cosmic music, referring to it as the Seven Heavenly Spheres (seven is totality); Hathor is also the goddess of the nocturnal sky. Her music is the cosmic harmony which contains all that happens, in all its conflict and contradiction: growth as well as decline, life as well as death. The life of the child is now taken up into that divine organic order of the cosmos. The child shares in the absolute life which includes both good and ill.

But fate is not only conceived as the heavenly order of music and harmony; it is likewise the earthly order. Another Egyptian formulation illustrates this. The goddess Renenutet, who determines in particular the fate of man and of the child, is the divine nursing mother – she is repeatedly portrayed with a baby at her breast – and along with Ma-a-t, Meskhent, and others she is the goddess of fate. But she is also the goddess of the granary, of the *thēsauros*, the store house, and thus of the riches of the earth. Just her appearance, which is that of a snake or of a woman with a snake's head, is enough to show that she is an earth goddess. Now it is she who determines the fate of the child; that is the life order of the earth which includes life and death. The Ancient religious meaning of "fate" is always: divine life.

These Egyptian and Greek data are very clear, but even clearer are the ideas of fate concerning the Babylonian Marduk, the god of the cosmic law, and the Roman Fatum. Fate proves not to be a finite dependence, determined by circumstances ("determinism"), for cosmic determination is infinite determination. It was thus a departure from the Ancient belief in fate

when in the late Greek-Roman period release from *heimarmenē*
was considered the goal of religious life and fate was considered
in the deterministic sense as finite bondage, and not as the universal order of life. Moira stands above all determinate divine
beings, because in Moira the religious principle is maintained
against the danger of poetic anthropomorphism respecting the
gods. So too the characteristics of Tyche and Ananke are what
we call "chance," but which seen more deeply is not chance – and
what we call "necessity," which however, is nevertheless a divine
activity. All rational terms fall short when it is necessary to
indicate infinite determinations.

If fate is determined at birth, then the child is essentially and
fundamentally raised above all happenstance and finite necessity.
Necessity is then only the universal order of life, the divine
organic law of the universe. This is Ananke (Necessity).

B. BAPTISM AND INFANT BAPTISM

Among the most diverse peoples, baptism has two meanings:
negative or apotropaeic, and positive or sacramental. (Heitmüller, speaks of exorcism, incantation, and sanctification.[9])
Sometimes the negative meaning is in the foreground, sometimes
the positive, and sometimes there is equal stress on both. But
in many cases, especially in the illiterate so-called "primitive"
religions it is impossible to say which goal is more important,
because only the external act has been described. When the
ethnographers do give an explanation, then there is often reason
to accept it with considerable reservation. For what happens is
that in such doubtful cases the traditional negative explanation
is given for magical or religio-magical practices in general.
Baptism is thus considered to have a repellent, apotropaeic
effect; the newborn child is tabu; he still belongs to another
order than that of our world, and that is a dangerous state of
affairs for the child and his surroundings out of which he must
be delivered as soon as possible. Baptism serves to remove that
danger; it is thus a ritual purification by means of water and is
indeed a "washing." [10] What is completely unsatisfying about
this conception, however, is that it remains unexplained how
an entirely external and bodily act employing ordinary water

can have a spiritual effect, for "tabu" can only be conceived as the "spiritual" state of impurity. The means must of course – for the "primitive" consciousness as well as our own – correspond to the goal; the water must be spiritual in the same sense as the goal. This is not the place to pursue this point further. Here we are concerned with the question whether it can be shown that infant baptism is ever actually performed as an exclusively repellent act. And the only possible answer to this question is that the instances which are well illustrated because the believers themselves have described their significance usually show that baptism in the first place has a decidedly positive significance of a sacramental addition of a divine energy – namely the power possessed by the means of baptism (as a rule, water).

The ancient Christian conception is well known and extraordinarily instructive. Tertullian writes in *De Baptismo:*

Water is the oldest and most venerable element, for it was in the beginning *Divini Spiritus sedes* (it was before the creation the dwelling of the Spirit of God), elected above all other elements by God's Spirit as His dwelling. The waters in the beginning brought forth all living beings (*animae*) – it is not surprising that water in baptism can make living (*animare*). The baptismal water *is* the water of Creation (the genus or kind is the same; only the species or appearance differs). Let no one say that they are two different waters.[11]

This is entirely in the spirit of the Ancient conception. The Church Fathers also compared the baptismal water with "the water of Osiris," the water of the Nile flood which is Egypt's source of life. According to the Egyptian conception Osiris has died in that water in order to rise in it or from it. Sprinkling with water is initiation into the divine death, corresponding to "dying with Christ" in order to attain eternal life. The dead man rises with Osiris.

In the earliest Christian era the baptismal water was not expressly consecrated. The water worked by its own power, just as Tertullian believed. Only in a later time does the ritual consecration of the baptismal water come into use, in order that the divine word pronounced at the consecration might descend into the water as God's Spirit did at Creation, or, according to the Roman Catholic formulation, "in order that the Holy Spirit with His light might penetrate the water and might recreate man to new life." The term "with His light" occurs because baptism was conceived as *phōtismos*, "enlightenment" [12]. Thus even as early as the middle of the second century A.D. Justin (who died in 165) reports that "a fire burst into flame in the Jordan when Jesus descended into the water." This idea is also related to the account of Creation, that life rose as light from water. Compare with this John 1 :4: "the life was the light of men."

The sacramental significance of baptism is set forth here as clearly as possible. The large measure of agreement with the Ancient religious ideas concerning the sacred nature of water is indisputable. This is also the case when – as often happens – baptism is conceived as a rebirth into divine life, the life which is present in all water. An example of this is the conception of Jesus' baptism which already existed in the earliest Christian church. At his baptism in the Jordan a voice was heard from heaven which said, "Thou art my beloved Son; today I have begotten thee." (Luke 3 : 22 in some manuscripts, Plooy).[13] This baptism is thus the divine birth or rebirth. Therefore on the sixth of January, the Feast of the Epiphany or the "appearance" (of God on earth, in Jesus) was sometimes celebrated in the Ancient Church as the feast of Jesus' birth (later December 25) and sometimes as the feast of Jesus' baptism by John. In Syria and Egypt the dates of both birth and baptism are set on January sixth. To this we must add that this sixth of January was conceived as the day of light; on this day the yearly triumph and resurrection of light took place, an event which corresponded to the original Creation. It was the well known comparison between the Creation in the beginning and that of every day of every year. In the Lutheran Church, at least according to Luther's baptismal rite, Christian baptism is still conceived as rebirth in or from death. The idea that water baptism signifies a rebirth is so deeply rooted in the religious consciousness of men that even ethnographic data with respect to it can be cited. Prescott reports that the Mexican Aztecs of the sixteenth and seventeenth centuries sprinkled water on the heads of their children, and that the women who performed the ceremony recited this formula: "Receive the water of the Lord of the world, the water which is our life ... for we are all children of the goddess of water." After baptism she says, "Now he lives anew and is born anew; now he is clean and spotless, and our divine mother, water, brings him again into the world." [14]

Another striking example of water baptism aiming thereby to give man divine and abiding life, thus baptism with positive effect, is the baptism of the ancient Germanic tribes and especially of the Norsemen.[15] In the Havamaal of the Edda, Odin says, "This magic act I know; if I sprinkle a young man with water, then he will not perish in war; he will not fall before any sword." Among the ancient Norsemen baptism was indeed performed in order to preserve life when it would otherwise be lost. Baptism rescues from death. Boniface, the missionary among the ancient Germans, reports this in 732 to Pope Gregory III. In his answer the Pope instructs him to perform the same baptism that the heathen do, but to do it in the name of the triune God.

Greek myth also tells about water baptism which protects the life of the baptized. Thetis immersed her son Achilles in the water of the Styx and thereby made him impregnable. However she held him by his heel, so that he could be wounded there, and there he was indeed fatally struck. According to another reading she held him in fire with the same effect. Fire baptism does indeed correspond to water baptism. When the queen of Eleusis, who had entrusted her son Demophon to Demeter for his education, sees that the goddess is holding her child in the fire, she rushes to her and grasps her son away from the goddess. Then Demeter says, "You fool, you do not know what you have done! I wanted to make him immortal, but now you have prevented it." He who has been baptized will be saved. It is also stated in Mark 16 : 16: "He who believes and is baptized will be saved (salvus erit)." We can understand that Boniface was struck by the agreement between the pagan and the Christian practice.

Many peoples relate the naming of the child to water baptism, for example in ancient India, in the Indonesian Archipelago, and among American tribes.[16] In these instances we find the notion that the name contains the personality of the individual; it is his spiritual image, and every image, including the visible image, is the spiritual double of the person. Sometimes the name is conceived as an autonomous being, as a person's soul and life: "Hallowed be Thy name." The naming of the child is thus

another religio-magical act which actualizes the self-subsistent
energy of the mystery of life. Naming someone provides him with
a supernatural protective power. Therefore much care is often
given in discovering the right and proper name for a child. Frequently it is the name of one of the ancestors, who then dwells
in the child and protects him. In ancient India there was the
notion of the true but secret name. This was given at the *nāma-
dheya*, the naming ceremony ten or twelve days after birth, in
addition to the ordinary name. Rome, too, had such a secret
name, in order that not everyone who knew the name of the city
could make his power over the city effective. The Aztecs in
Mexico gave a baby the name of one of his ancestors who would
watch over him until the second naming with baptism in later
life – thus until the transition at the new birth. This is the central
thought in Heitmüller's work, *Im Namen Jesu*.[17] To be baptized
"in Jesus' name" signifies "with the utterance of the holy name,"
with impartation of Jesus' divine power, or it signifies "to the
holy name" or to communion of life with Jesus.

C. TRANSITION TO ADULTHOOD

The ceremonies of puberty on the occasion of the transition
to adulthood are ceremonies of initiation, comparable to those
at birth. A person thereby attains his full personality. They
possess a creative activity having new effects; therefore they are
different ceremonies from those at birth. The concept of "growth"
as a gradual coming into being or as an inclusive principle and
idea is radically denied. Bergson too maintains that the concept
"durée" (unity of successive states) is the great mystery for our
thinking. The mystery of becoming or of growth is actually
not better comprehended by focussing on its unity than by
focussing in polytheistic fashion on its manifoldness.

These *rites de passage* have a very immediate significance for
those involved: the change really occurs as a result of the ceremonies. Bodily maturity is the external and nonessential phenomenon; the essential is a spiritual, a supernatural and mystical reality.[18] In a great many cases there is evidently no distinction between "children" and "the uninitiated." From the standpoint of society, the ceremonies make the boy an adult man.

Before these rites have taken place, the young man may not marry, participate in tribal deliberations or in war. The requirements for initiation are often very hard. For a long time the neophyte must refrain from sleep and food; he is subjected to chastisements, blood lettings, smoke and fire ordeals, etc. It seems entirely certain that all this does not serve in the first place to prove his courage and perseverance, but that it is done in order to give him a new soul. The former personality must be killed, destroyed, indeed utterly annihilated. The ceremonies try to push the hardships to the extreme, to unconsciousness and "death." The women and children are told that the male novices have died. They themselves are also taught this conviction. "The colour of death is white, and the novices are painted white," we read. They are thus transformed into a different life; they are born into a new life. And what is new is this, that now for the first time their tribal life, their social life, is imparted to them; only now may they marry, etc. It is evident that in a state of ecstacy they regularly attain the new mystical reality and are bound together with the tribal life of the ancestors. The secrets are now revealed to them.

It is indeed very remarkable that this dying in order to be reborn in a new life is to be found among the most diverse peoples spread over the whole earth. This is really an important religious fact which has been brought to light by ethnographic research, for the meaning of these ceremonies is unambiguous. As an illustration let me mention the ceremonies of the natives of West Ceram in Indonesia, which have been repeatedly described, but almost exclusively by Dutchmen.[19] Every village has an entirely dark hut in the forest for the initiation ceremonies. The boy is led before the hut, and the priest invokes the spirits. Soon a terrifying noise is heard from the hut, the sound of trumpets made out of bamboo. This noise comes from the spirits. The priest and the boy go into the hut; those standing around hear a loud yell and a dull blow, and they see that a bloody sword is thrust through the roof. The boy has been beheaded and the spirits take him along with them; the women looking on walk away crying. From five to nine days the young man remains in the hut, from which the same din and clatter of weapons repeatedly resounds. His entire body is painted yellow, in the

colour of the spirits, and a few crosses are tattooed on his chest
and arms. The priests address him as spirits, accompanying
themselves with strange sounds on the trumpet: they instruct
him in the laws, institutions and secret traditions of the tribe,
and they forbid him on penalty of death ever to tell anything
of what has been taught him in the hut. Heralds who are covered
with mud – they come from the realm of the dead – hasten to the
village with the news that they have been able to get the boy
back. Then the young man himself comes, carrying a staff with
feathers on both ends in his hand, as well as all sorts of signs of his
sojourn in the other world. He limps and walks backwards,
because he has forgotten how to walk, and he must make himself understood with signs, because he has forgotten how to
speak. Like a little child he must learn from the very simplest
beginnings to walk, speak, eat, etc., again. After twenty to
thirty days he goes once again to the forest for the ceremony of the
hair cut. After this has been completed, he has become a man.
Now he may marry, and he is completely adult.

This type of rite is reported in innumerable variations. Sometimes the ceremonies take place at new moon; elsewhere the
rebirth is really portrayed by having the mother play the role
of the childbearing women – if the mother has died, another
woman takes her place and from that time on really continues
as the man's mother. The forgetting of the past is taken so
seriously that when the novice accidentally gives evidence of
having remembered something, he must go through the entire
experience of suffering again. Thus there are any number of
variations. The ethnographers overwhelm us with their monotonous reports and with numerous strange or even bizarre particulars which they themselves evidently do not understand.
They have written down everything; one receives a dreary impression from all the unassimilated material. It proves to be
unfeasible to penetrate deeply enough into the minds of these
peoples so that all the bizarre elements so far removed from our
own experience can take on life. This is the curse which rests on
religious ethnography. Only the chief point of all this material
is clear: the boy awakes to new life.

In reading the extensive reports of these initiation ceremonies
(for example, those of Gillen and Spencer concerning the natives

of Central Australia), one does indeed gain a strong impression, not only of the seriousness of the persons taking part, but also of the reality of the experiences which are communicated to us. The novices do indeed experience something which makes new men of them. Even where it seems obvious for us to speak of tricks and displays for effect, there for those involved without any doubt sacred acts take place with a mystical but very real effect. In many and perhaps in most of these instances we rather have a vague notion of the meaning than any clear idea. The distance is too great. But I am convinced that only by having a respect- ful attitude toward these data do we have any chance to pene- trate to some extent into this reality. All too often it is forgotten that the experience of countless generations – the ceremonies are certainly very old – always has a claim to our respect, and that the result of a superficial judgment is meaningless.

In various historical and literate religions such initiatory practices as these are also known, although in other forms. In India the initiation consists in instruction in the sacred wri- tings; with this one really begins an entirely new stage of life, that of the adult youth. Even clearer are the Greek customs for admitting young men of 16 and 17 into the state. Before this admission to the state the child is made a member of religious communities of successively larger extent. Ten days after his birth he comes into the family (*genos*), a few years after that into the tribe (*phratria*), and finally into the *polis* as a citizen. Led before the altar of the city, the young man swears an oath which binds him to the religion of the city or state and gives him the life of the Hestia of the city. Only then does he have the right to take part in worship (*meteinai tou hierou*); by this religious act he has become an adult. Only this initiation qualifies him for marriage and for public activities, especially military service; all these things are regulated by religion. The new life is a new religious life, namely an admission into the divine order of so- ciety. That is a rebirth. The religio-magical act corresponds to the mystery of becoming adult – a mystery to which we modern men scarcely give our attention.

D. THE WEDDING

Among various peoples marriage is a religious duty. Thus in China throughout its entire history, or at least after Confucius (500 B.C.), even children who have died are married, with wedding ceremonies after their death. In Korea an unmarried man who is thirty years old may not complain about disrespectful treatment from anyone whomsoever. Likewise the Jewish Talmud prescribes marriage, and Mohammed says, "the believer who marries fulfills half of religion." According to Zarathustra the bridge to paradise is closed to the childless. In Greece similar conceptions prevailed; in Sparta not only was the unmarried man penalized, but he who married late did not escape a penalty either. In Rome the adoption of children is obligatory in families which remain childless. The explanation frequently given for all of this is that children are necessary for service to the dead. According to Greek belief the unmarried state signified godlessness by its lack of respect toward the ancestors, and eternal ill fortune for the person himself, since his own soul would be neglected after his death. The Romans and the Chinese also give this explanation. Nevertheless the deeper reason for the obligatory marriage is probably a different one. For while the Hebrews in historical times did not have any ancestor worship, it is nevertheless stated in the Talmud: "He who does not marry is like a murderer and he mutilates (violates) the image of God"; he is thus not fully man. Even if this belief was originally prompted by ancestor worship, the sharp posing of the problem nevertheless remains strange. There also is stated in the first account of Creation: "So God created man in his own image, in the image of God he created him; male and female he created them." (Genesis 1 : 27.) Thus only together are they human beings. This was certainly also the conviction of the Avesta religion ("The man who is married stands above him who is not married.") and of Islam. Now it becomes evident that the peoples who give ancestor worship as the reason for this belief definitely understand that the obligation to marry is not exclusively in the interests of the dead. For the ancestors live along with the living. Not only that they help the family in all its difficulties, but they share in the family in an essential and most important respect;

their life is the imperishable life of the family and of the individuals within it. They are worshipped at the hearth, where the permanent fire, the permanent life of the family is. Their life is the life of the earth; the goddess of the hearth is the earth (Vesta terra est). The fire of Vesta is the generating power of every generation, and in the bringing of many children, the ancestors enable life to flourish. The ancestors are taken up into everyone's life; the individual is only fully a human being in his family relationship. The worship of the ancestors is evidently rooted in the natural sense of solidarity with those who have departed this life. The religious duty to marry is in all instances probably ultimately grounded in the consciousness of the immortal renewing of life which is actualized in the family relationship. In this relationship the individual limitation which causes death is removed. Every member of a family is subjected to a higher unity; he who does not serve and preserve that higher life by his marriage is unfaithful to it; he insults his life instinct. So too is the thought in Israel. There is thus present far more than just the notion of duties to the ancestors. As is always the case, religion proves here too to be a desire for self preservation, taken in the broadest sense; we are more than "ourselves."

We shall here mention only a few of the most characteristic of all the many religious customs and ideas relating to the wedding ceremonies. According to the Greek conception there was a close connection between the wedding and the performance of the religious Mysteries. That is expressed in the term *telos gamou*, which we translate by "marriage celebration." The concept *telos* has no equivalent in modern languages. It certainly can be translated as "end, goal, completion," but nevertheless *telos gamou* does not mean the same thing as our "marriage celebration.'" The fact that *teletē* means "initiation" proves that *telos*, "end," was connected with the idea of "conclusion" in the sense of "summation, totality." In the concept of the "concluded" the parts are brought together, while "the end, goal" points to activities which have come to rest after having worked. "Conclusion, completion" in general obtains the sense of totality, the all-embracing. According to this "teleological" view, this means the end, not only in the negative, but also in the positive sense. This totality is thus the fullness of being. The attainment of this totality is the meaning of *telos* and *teletē* in the Mysteries. For the totality of being is not an empirical or a finite reality. It is "perfection," not in the ethical but in the metaphysical sense, absolute being, which only exists in the world of infinity. The *teletē* is removal into absolute, self-subsistent, divine life; that is "initiation." By means of *teletē* the resurrection of absolute life is attained.

Telos gamou is the "conclusion, completion" in this mystical sense, which is actualized by marriage. Marriage is an initiation into absolute life. *Telos* is the same as marriage (*gamos*); this is the cause of the remarkable similarity between marriage and funeral customs.[20] The best illustration of this is the abduction, "the robbery" of Kore by Hades. This is indeed considered to be the mystical prototype of the wedding. When Kore marries Hades, she enters the bridal chamber of the god of death. The mystical doctrine was that everyone who died married Hades, Persephone, or Kore. Death is the only initiation for newly arising life; therefore marriage is identical with death, and death is identical with marriage. The myth of Psyche (the human soul) and Eros is also the depiction of this thought in a myth about marriage. Although Psyche is more beautiful than any of her sisters, no one asks her hand in marriage. An oracle states that she will not marry any living man, but the god of the underworld (Eros). It advises that she be adorned with the bridal array of the sepulchre, be led to the top of a mountain, and there left alone. When she is brought there and left, truly as a "living corpse," a West wind carries the weeping Psyche downwards, down into the dephts of the underworld. There Eros receives her. But he is in the form of a snake; she is not permitted to see him in his own form. Once, however, Psyche disobeys this injunction, and the result is that Eros disappears, since she has removed his mystery. Only after many hardships are they again united in eternity. As in the myth of Hades and Kore, here too the divine nature of the wedding is described. The wedding is an initiation into absolute life. In Troezen brides offered hair sacrifice to Hippolytus just before the wedding. Hippolytus was the hero who had disdained earthly love and was therefore brought to destruction by Aphrodite. This hair sacrifice to him is remarkable just because it is reported as something quite ordinary, although without any sort of connection with the mystery religions, such as that of Eleusis. One would think that Hippolytus was the enemy of brides; the fact is just the reverse. He does not marry any living woman, as does Eros, but in his death he provides the initiation to marriage, as does Hades to Kore. This apotheosis of chastity in its mystical significance corresponds to the idea of the Virgin Mother. In Patrae in Achaia a boy and a girl as bridal pair were sacrificed each year to Artemis. Artemis, the chaste, virgin goddess, is the protectress of marriage, because the wedding is an initiation into death. Vesta the virgin is the typical mother in the religious sense; she is Mater above all Roman gods and is therefore portrayed dressed as a *matrona*. The Vestal Virgins are called *amata*, beloved. Their initiation formula reads: *Te amata capio* ("I take thee, beloved"). There is every reason to believe that the bride's veil, among the Greeks for example, had the same significance as the veil worn for the initiation into the Mysteries. The initiate is depicted with a veil; the earth goddess is also veiled: Persephone, the consort of Hades, keeps a large veil before her, and the wrathful Demeter is likewise veiled. Certainly the idea here is that of being hidden in a religious sense, of finding one's self at the (hidden) spring and source of life. But to this must be added the idea of being hidden in the world of absolute life, for the veil represents that world. As the god of life, Zas, Zeus gives his bride, the earth goddess Chthonia, the great and beautiful *peplos*. This cloth or veil represents the earth's life. Cloth, net, and veil were in Antiquity symbols of cosmic order and of cosmic wisdom. Thus Athene has the well known *peplos* as a sign of her wisdom. This cosmic order is the order of absolute life and of the absolute wisdom which dwells in the inscrutable and hidden realm of the dead.

Outside the Mysteries there were also other widely followed customs of the same purport, for example the crowning of the bridal pair with wreaths. Those who have died are wreathed; the wreath is always the sign of consecration and victory over finitude. Another example is the solemnizing of a marriage with a chthonic peace-offering, by slaughtering a hog or sheep. Or the bridal pair may sit down on a sheepskin, just as when an oracle is consulted. The explanation given of these customs is that they serve "to reconcile the powers of the underworld (the ancestors)." That is really the case. But the remarkable thing is just that the powers of the realm of the dead, such as Eros, the snake, and Hades, protect marriage. Samter reports that among many European peoples the young wife is led to the places where the ancestors are worshipped. At the hearth, on the door sills – on which she must step –, at the spring, and at forks in the path she must bring grain, peas, and coins as a death sacrifice to the "lares." During the offering her head must be wrapped up, or she must turn around and throw the gifts behind her in order that she may not see the spirits.[21] Comparable to this is the myth of the earth spirit Erichthonius, the progenitor of the Athenians. He grew up in a chest guarded by snakes, which was in the charge of Cecrops' daughters. When these girls opened the chest and saw Erichthonius, in spite of having been forbidden to do so, they went mad and threw themselves over a precipice. According to the Ancient conception, the wedding is an initiation into the mystery of newly arising life, like the initiation in the Eleusinian Mysteries.

Samter describes the custom of *katachusmata*, in which grain, figs, and the like are sprinkled over the young pair or over a newborn child. He sees in this custom an act which actualizes the conformity between human life and natural life, and thus gives men a more inclusive life.[22] One is inclined to wonder whether this is not reading too much into such an act and whether this is not an act which needs no profound explanation, just as little as does the sprinkling of flowers on the casket in the grave. *Katachusma* is of course an understandable symbol of fertility. But this custom begins to seem less simple when we read that the *katachusma* is also sprinkled over the newly purchased slave who is admitted into the family and – even stranger – over the ambassador who is sent out by the state to conclude a pact or to declare war. It is indeed an initiation into a mystery. At the initiation of the new slave into the family cultus, the dead are the chief figures because they rule over that life. When the ambassador must make an absolutely binding pact under oath, or must declare the absolute and divine right of his people, he represents its divine order of life; therefore he is initiated into that order of life which is the order of the re-

peatedly arising life of the earth. The *katachusma* does indeed
have a cosmic significance. When a person receives it, this fresh
life of the earth is imparted to him, just as it is imparted by
the Mysteries at Eleusis.

We attach our own significance to all these wedding customs,
such as the veil, crowning with wreaths, and scattering grain
and fruit, when we observe them. That meaning is usually es-
thetic, or sometimes sentimental. But if we want to know the
Ancient conception of marriage – and that was remarkable
enough – then we must not bring along our own interpretation
when we study the Ancient custom.

As far as the initiation of the ambassador is concerned, the
Roman form of initiation, not by the *katachusma* but by placing
a piece of grass sod on his head (as a sign of burial) shows in
quite another way the correspondence with the wedding initiation. The leader of the embassy received the title of pater;
he was made *pater patratus*, the father made father. According
to the Ancient conception the father, who generates new life,
possesses absolute and newly arising life. The ambassador, who
is "pater," represents the absolute life of his people; he is sacred
– his person is inviolate – and his word or oath has absolute
validity. The Ancients believed that the *pater familias* also
possessed that sacredness. He commands over life and death
("vitae necisque dominus"); as *pater* he is initiated into death.
His divine prototype is Hades, just as the divine prototype of
the mother is the virgin mother Persephone or Vesta, mother
in the absolute sense. Thus it can be explained that in the Mithra
Mysteries pater is the highest of the seven initiations. In this
highest step there is imparted the absolute life of Mithra, the
god of newly arising life. The divine title "Pater" for Zeus or
Ju-piter must certainly not be conceived in the Christian sense,
but in the sense of "lord of the development of life," divine
representative of all life.

This is the Ancient conception of the generating capacity of
the father. It is in this light that we must see the Ancient wedding ceremonies. In marriage the mystery of mysteries was
actualized. It is also noteworthy that according to Genesis
Adam and Eve come into contact with the snake when they
begin their marriage. According to the Babylonian myth the

primeval man Enkidu and his wife come to the home of the earth god Ea.

The wedding is the most characteristic family festival, and in all probability the Mystery cultus at Eleusis was once a family cultus in a closed group, in which no strangers could participate. (Rohde, Stengel, Samter.) In that case the mystery cultus was connected from beginning to end with the wedding ceremonies. The *hieros gamos* always remained an act of the Mysteries in Eleusis, performed in a sphere of mystery from which all desecration was excluded.

E. DEATH

It has been shown in the previous sections that according to the religious conception of many non-Christian peoples, life in its successive stages and periods is a mystical reality – or rather a series of mutually independent mysteries. Naturally death is one of these mysteries. For even for us "the mystery of death" is a well known and common idea, more common than that of the "mystery of life." It would seem obvious that here at last we are finally in agreement with the Ancient non-Christian peoples. Yet here too there is a great difference in spiritual orientation. In spite of the same terms, however, this difference is no surprise. For although the Ancients and we both speak of "mystery," the understandings of this concept diverge widely. It is precisely the greatest enigma which is susceptible to such divergent interpretations. We too call death the archenemy, but also the entrance to eternal life.

We consider "death" as the end of this earthly life and the beginning of a new life. The Ancients believed that all expressions of life contained "death." In all the decisive moments of life they speak of death. Birth occurs out of death (the birth goddess Eileithyia is an earth goddess), and even baptism sometimes symbolizes a dying; the transition to adulthood is a dying and coming to life again in a new state of being; the wedding is an initiation into death. It is obvious that the end of life contains the same mystery as the whole life which has preceded it. It is as if death is placed in the middle of life. This does not, however, have the result that the sense of the mystery of death has disappeared; it is probably not even weakened by it. It is only brought closer by, because death can be conceived as an experienced reality.

Especially in the Ancient Greek religion many striking formulations of this sense of death can be found – in addition to those already mentioned in connection with birth and marriage. But as a rule modern scholars understand them poorly. According to the Homeric Epic, Thanatos is death, and he is the twin brother of Hypnos, sleep [23]; according to Virgil, Hesiod, and others they are "brothers," *kasignētoi*. They are thus very closely akin. We are inclined directly to bring our own conceptions into the consideration of these data: like our own term "fall asleep" for dying, the Ancient formulations are very understandable euphemisms or metaphors – the resemblance is clear. Probably that was also the opinion of the "enlightened" Greeks of the classical type, Homer himself, for example. But it can be proved that the Ancient expression had a different meaning. Not only is the dead man one who has fallen asleep, but everyone who is sleeping is really a dead person. The proofs of this are convincing. With his magic staff (*rhabdos*) Hermes wakes men from their sleep and charms them into sleep. This same Hermes charms the *kēres* with his staff in and out of the realm of the dead. It is quite certain that awaking from sleep is actually conceived as a resurrection from death. The idea must have been that the sleeping man sojourned in the other world, the realm of the dead. The Ancients saw the resemblance between sleep and death with other eyes than we do. Here again death proves to be drawn into the middle of life and life into death in a way which is completely alien to us, namely as a daily experience and discovery.

This is no euphemism or metaphor. This is further proved by the fact that the identification of sleep and death occasioned cultic acts, specifically the incubation or dream oracle. This was a religious institution to attain practical goals of great importance. The dream oracle has essentially the same character as the earth oracle, such as the one in Delphi. It comes from the underworld or the realm of the dead, which is the home of divine insight. The sleeping person really sojourns in another world, where the secret of resurrection is found – in the dream oracle, healing. It is clear that in reality and not only in metaphor, sleep contains the same mystery as death. The dream sports with finite relations and rational thought, and just for that reason the Ancients saw in it the characteristic of infinite and divine relations. The supra-sensual reality of the divine world governance is movingly formulated in the myth that Kronos "sleeps" on the island of the earth (*gaia*) and there "dreams" the fate of the world.

Another cultic custom is the joint worship of Hypnos and the Muses. The Muses are the goddesses of the fine arts, which really do not engender sleep! Among the "fine arts" are included all the arts which reveal the divine order, for instance the art of the poet-seer. Music too was divine art, ecstatic music in the cultus and cosmic harmony in the myth. Sculpture was also a creative activity. (The Egyptian *ms* meant to sculpture as well as to bear offspring.) The Muses belong in the other world, in the world of sleep. A cultic usage in the religion of Dionysus was the search for the god by his worshippers, for "he has fled to the Muses." Dionysus is then "sought" as Kore and Harmonia are "sought" when they have disappeared to the other world of Hades (or the Muses), and are then called back. The Muses are thus worshipped jointly with Hypnos, because Hypnos is the god of the realm of the dead.

In this connection it must be noted that we too must admit that sleep is an uncomprehended and inexplicable reality. But because it is such a well known fact, we usually forget the mysterious element in its essential being. For the same reason we usually forget the mystery in the growth process of the individual and of the plant, in which the Ancients saw a creative process. The conception of sleep as temporary death is certainly not a "primitive" notion.

The Ancients also often call every sickness a state of death and every healing a resurrection from death. Death certainly signifies a mysterious transition, but it is of the same magnitude as all other transitions in life, such as sickness and healing. Thus there is nothing special about death wherein it differs from life. This is not so absurd as it appears. The living man can only think and speak in images which are borrowed from "life." Even when he says "death'," he must connect it with an idea of life if his word is not to be an empty sound. Only from experience does he know "real life." This life in the world of experience does not, however, need to be identical with "finite" life, because man experiences himself as an infinite being. For he exists in a communion of life with the infinite creation, and he is taken up into the infinity of family and state. Moreover, he who speaks of death in the negative sense is guilty of a glaring inconsistency: he suddenly forgets the law of inertia. Bodies naturally possess the property of continuing in the state of rest or motion in which they are. It is said that "the energy disappears." But energy cannot be lost. How can that which is spontaneous cease to be spontaneous and work against itself? Death must thus indeed be of the same magnitude as all other transitions in life. This primitive conception is here certainly quite logical. But that this logic has been accepted in complete seriousness, with all its consequences, is difficult for us to understand; perhaps we can only explain it.

It is in this context too that the numerous well known customs can be explained, such as the provisions made for the dead by giving them food, implements, and household effects to take along.[24] The smith is given his hammer to take along, the carpenter his axe, the housewife her spinningwheel, and the soldier his lance. Life continues in death. That does not mean that when this is recognized the mystery of death disappears. It is obvious that these acts have nevertheless been sensed as something irrational and paradoxical. The intention cannot be the same as that present in gifts to living persons. Thus the death feasts of the living with the dead are not ordinary meals; they are fettered by all sorts of tabu restrictions, such as not speaking too loudly, not using knives, etc. The tabu corresponds to the mystery, for both are outside the ordinary order. Contact with the dead is, of course, contact with another world. And this enables us to explain many irrational customs of mourning [25]. Thus in China at the death of the emperor all kinds of activity in social life were stopped, and this practice was observed right up to the revolution of 1912. Even when people have maintained that life continues in death, the mystery of death has thus by no means disappeared. Dying is similar to the other radical transitions in life.

Other characteristic expressions can be cited of the sense that life is not dependent on finite causes, outside of life itself. It is essentially spontaneous and self-sustaining, and cannot be placed in a finite causal connection. It can thus not be abolished by particular finite causes. Some peoples therefore consider the state of death simply as the result of the intervention of a power which is just as mysterious as the power of life. There are unambiguous ethnographic data which illustrate and prove this.[26] When someone dies of snakebite in the Torres Strait near New Guinea, it is believed there that the snake was influenced by a magician. It was the business of the next of kin to find the magician and take vengeance. According to Dobritzhofer the American Indians of the Abiponen tribe do not consider even the most mortal wounds, drowning, or the like, to be the real cause of death of one who has had such an accident. The next of kin are not satisfied with knowing the external or accidental cause, which is only the outward means through which the mystical cause works; they seek this deeper mystical cause. The spear which causes death was laden with evil magic power. He who is convinced that he has been struck by such a magically laden spear lies down to die – even if he is but lightly wounded. Even the Avesta states that the man who drowns does not die because of the water; the water is innocent, and the death is the work of the evil spirit (*druj nasu*).

He who speaks in this way takes the conviction seriously that death is in its source and essence a mysterious reality, and that death is as little dependent as life on finite causes. We speak of a "natural" death, in contrast to a violent death. We think it "natural" that the human organism ceases to function after a certain length of time or under certain conditions. But not one of us can say what "death" is. For the scientific physiologist, too, the arrival of death is just as incomprehensible as the origin of life. When we take note of this, the conviction of a mystical cause of death, a death by magical power, proves not to be so entirely absurd. That conviction does make a strange impression on us, because we are accustomed to be satisfied with popular – superficial – science. The observation of a certain external connection between certain phenomena prompts us to make the assumption that it is "natural"; we see no reason to think about a mystery.

There are, however, different types of religious attitude toward the mystery of death. The most important are the two types which have already been mentioned. One idea is that the demonic element (divine arbitrariness) can come to the fore; a power which is just as autonomous and inscrutable as life itself comes up against life as an enemy. The other idea is of a transition of life into a new state of being, like all transitions in life, but in this case a change to the state of infinite life, or of life in an infinite world. In this second idea the divine character of death is expressed; it is considered the attainment of that which has always been pursued.

Striking examples of the first conception are to be found among the Semitic peoples (the Babylonians and the Hebrews). According to them the finite life of experience completely includes the infinity of life. God reveals himself in individual and in social life, and gives it an infinite significance and value; thus every believer is taken up into the all-embracing divine order. Religious astrology is indeed a conscious formulation of the idea of man's cosmic life. The entire religious relation concerns the life of experience. Death, on the other hand, is the inexplicable and therefore terrible fate to which no one can be reconciled. Death is the tragic contradiction and rejection by the Higher Power of that which man feels to be his essential being and nature. Death is unnatural. "Why must man die?" This is asked again and again because of the feeling that death cannot belong to our true and original being. A special explanation is necessary for this enigma; that explanation is given by the various mythical and historical accounts.

Sometimes the answer is given that man is led astray by his own creator. Ea, the snake, as demonic god of the realm of the dead, thus sees to it that the food of immortality which was laid away for man and lay within his reach is taken away from man. So man is deceived by his creator with a trick and with lies – the snake in paradise was also undoubtedly man's special god. Man protests against this fate, which does not accord with his essential being. It is not against his lot in life but against death, that man's sense of his own finitude so despairingly rebels; for it is just in despair that the instinctive urge for life becomes dominant. In the Babylonian epic, Gilgamesh says at the death of Enkidu,

"My friend whom I loved has become dust – must I lie down
like him, never in eternity to rise again? ... Fear of death has
overpowered me; therefore I wander restlessly through the desert." When Gilgamesh seeks immortal life, the goddess of wisdom and the guardian of the realm of the dead, Siduri-Sabitu,
says to him, "You shall not find it. When the gods created men,
they instituted death for him; life they kept in their own hands."
It is proved that she is right when Gilgamesh has brought up
the spice of life from the very depths of the primeval waters:
just when he is safe on the shore with the spice, he drops it.
A snake catches hold of it and disappears with it for good.
Sometimes it is by his own blindness, by his demonic disposition
and inexplicable will, that man chooses the way of ruin. According
to the Avesta, the first man, Yima, was immortal; in his land
(paradise) there was no sickness, old age, etc. But he developed a
love for the false word, not that spoken by others, but that spoken by himself. Untruth or lie is the unreal, the denial of that
which is and abides, and only the truth or the constant word
stands firm. The result of this love is that his *khvarnah*, immortality,
immediately disappears. The Greek *Atē*, "infatuation," is a
demonic power – even for Zeus.

Yet a onesided emphasis must not be put on the notion that
death "does not belong to man's distinctive essence." That
thought would elevate man above his fate and remove his
anguish, pain, and fear. Death exists; it is the characteristic mark
of the real finitude and transiency of all that which is human,
outside divine aid and grace. This is a fact which is as evident
for the religious consciousness as its awareness of that other
central fact: the autonomy of life. The one is just as inexplicable
as the other. The fact of death is coupled in all religions with the
humble consciousness of distance between man and God; this is
everywhere a central religious thought. And when the inexplicable will of man has caused this distance from God, then the
separation has been brought about by a radical and original sin.
In later Judaism the snake is completely identified with the
evil power.

It is obvious that death as the denial of human autonomy is
conceived as lack of freedom and bondage. A good example of
this is the fact that the Greeks and Romans identified death with

Fatum, fate. "Fatum" is the state of being determined by the
divine world order, and not by man's own individual or collective
will. How can the order of absolute and abiding life gain the
meaning of death, ruin, and destruction? Like all formulations
of cosmic or infinite determination, this idea of the divine fate
seems to us ambiguous. The positive significance of the Fatum
is that the belief in determination by a divine order gives an
eternal meaning to finitude and to the life of experience; things
are then conceived *sub specie aeterni(tatis)*, in the light of eternity.
But Fatum also has a negative side. When God disposes, then
man's proposal is without significance. So all finite relationships
are as such without essential value, and all human interests and
aspirations are thus opposed and denied. This divine denial of
all values of life which can be thought of in the spheres of intellect, ethics, and aesthetics springs from the fact that the divine
governance of *Fatum* occurs in accordance with infinite, cosmic
considerations. And the divine denial of the life of experience
means death. That is the ambiguous and contradictory element
in the idea of *Fatum*. Being taken up into the divine world
order, or being determined by *Fatum*, signify absolute freedom
and participation in sacred life (thus activity) but at the same
time absolute lack of freedom by denying the will's life (or its
value); it is also the denial of everything that we know and
experience as life; it is death. It is noteworthy that both conceptions are equally religious for the latter conception, too, is
based on the conviction of rule by the divine order of life. "Determinism," the rationalistic conception of *Fatum*, does not
appear here. Ambiguity and contradiction naturally occur in
each religious relationship.

Death is thus Fatum, conceived as man's passive state and
lack of freedom. It is that which is inhuman, which is a denial
of what is human, and which nevertheless is part of man. With
respect to death the ambiguity of man's "infinite determination"
does indeed come to the fore with a terrible gravity. It is understandable that Fatum or Moira is especially spoken of in connection with an untimely death. This is most strongly expressed
in tragedy, as for example in the myths of Meleager and of
Adonis, the handsome youth who was killed by wild boars.
Moira is the "share" or "allotment," allotted rather than chosen.

Moira spins man's thread of life; she determines everything that
will happen to him. That means passivity and lack of freedom
for man. Moira is often identified with Thanatos, death (in
Homer and Hesiod); only later in Greek history does determinism appear. According to Hesiod, Moros, Ker, and Thanatos
(fate, the spirit of the dead, and death itself) are the sons of
Nyx, the goddess of the night from the underworld or the realm
of the dead.[27] They are thus thought to be genuine "demons,"
outside all rational norms.

The characteristically religious element in the Babylonian
conception of death should certainly not be lost sight of. Death
and fate, which are effective for all life do not give man a self-
evident finitude or a natural limitation in which no spiritual
elements are involved. Such a conception would definitely obstruct spiritual and religious life in all respects; it would give
welcome aid to the argument for the annulment of man's ethical
endeavour, and it would destroy the power of a religious attitude.
The dull sense of being bound is no power at all. Quite the contrary. According to this type of thought, too, death is an uncomprehended and incomprehensible reality, because it is the
denial of life, the only evident reality. Death is that inhuman
reality which can only be explained by the fact that man has
been deceived or led astray. The reality of this death, which is
a state of passivity, cannot be accepted by man without protest.
The Romans and Greeks have given an especially clear religious
formulation to this state. Fatum and Moira signify death; they
are the divine determination of life in which human determination is abolished. Thus Moira, that which is allotted, is
sometimes identical with Thanatos, Death, who is indeed a
demon, but is nevertheless also a god. On the other hand, the
"deterministic" conception of Moira or the "fatalistic" conception of Fatum is not an Ancient, but a rationalistic concept
which is not religious. It tries to dissociate itself from *heimarmenē*
(etymologically related to *moira* and *moros*), from the influence
of stars, etc. This idea of natural limitation prevails, for example,
in Stoic circles. When the religious type of passive idea of death
is encountered, however, then it is linked with the consciousness
that finitude caused by death is not a natural limitation. Moreover humility towards God and the divine determination is

always connected with a sense of guilt, as at the fall of Yima and Adam. The sense of lowliness or humility is certainly not caused by the deity's superior physical power, but rather by the sense of one's own shortcomings: "it should have been and could have been otherwise – death is our fault." This does not prompt, as does natural determination, the vague sense of being bound; this conviction brings a permanent tension in life, a tension of a spiritual nature. In this humility towards God lies a spiritual depth and height, because the consciousness is present that man is nevertheless created for an infinite life.

The second type of religious attitude towards the mystery of death is predominantly affirmative; it accepts the transition to a new life, which is absolute life. Death is then the true manifestation of life, which in essence is self-subsistent but only in death becomes truly self-subsistent.

The Egyptians have quite consciously exchanged the terms here in the most paradoxical manner imaginable. They call the underworld "the land of life" and the funeral casket "the lord of life" – the lord who gives life. Death is life, not in a nonsensical euphemistic sense, for "life," too, has acquired a corresponding meaning, because life and death contain one and the same mystery. Death means divine life. The majority of the Egyptian gods were depicted in the form of mummies; in that form they are gods. But also before his death man knows this absolute, divine life – there is no other life – as a divine gift. For a divine power or a god imparts himself in the food which man consumes. By his death, however, man himself becomes a god. How the concepts of life and death merge into one another becomes evident in the description of the royal palace. The Egyptian king, who in reality leads an earthly life, lives in a "grave"; his palace is repeatedly referred to as "the grave" and his name is written in the sign for grave.

This type of conception of death also occurs among other peoples. Thus there is the Indian idea that Buddha enters Nirvana at his "death." There he is in absolute life, without name or form, because he has departed from finitude. And every man who has really died to the world attains that same absolute life. According to the Greeks, death is initiation into absolute life, an initiation, however, which can also be attained before natural

death. The corpse is wreathed as the victor in the battle of life.
The wreath or crown (*corona*), twined with twigs and leaves,
always "hallows" (makes sacred), whether at sacrifices, festivals,
or triumphs, for it imparts to the one enwreathed the divine life
of the earth – of vegetation – and thereby gives victory over
death. Herodotus relates that among certain Thracian tribes the
newborn child is received with wailing, but the dead man is
buried with a display of joy, "because he has escaped all suffering
(all finitude) and lives in complete bliss." "Dying is beautiful
for them." This reversal in the meaning of concepts is sometimes
just as consciously paradoxical among the Greeks as among the
Egyptians. It is not a euphemism when the Greek says that the
Erinyes (the spirits of death) are identical with the well meaning
Eumenides, or that the underworld god Hades is the same as the
god of riches, Pluto.

It is this actual identification of "death" and "life" which
is meant by the term "mystery." It is almost a technical term;
all sorts of religious ideas and doctrines which to our minds are
mysterious–for instance the Vedanta doctrine of unity between the
absolute subject and the absolute object (Atman and Brahman),
and similar ideas in other religions – are not to be called "mysteries." In Eleusis the mystery is the state of death, *teleutan
teleisthai;* in an inscription we read, "Thanks to these beautiful
mysteries, given to us by the gods, dying is no longer a misfortune for men, but good fortune." The mysteries are thus given
to us as a reality, and not taught to us as a theory. The sacred
acts of the ceremonial initiation are thus imparted and granted
as gifts; no doctrine or theoretical commentary can give information concerning the essence of the Mysteries. The mystery
cannot be expressed by a verbal formulation, but exclusively by
the religious-magic act. Thus the Mysteries at Eleusis, in Egypt,
and in the Mithra religion have no doctrine of their own, but only
the sacred acts of *horan kai orcheisthai*, "seeing and dancing."
Comparable to the doctrine of transubstantiation in the Roman
Catholic Church is the mystery of transubstantiation in the
Ancient religions. Transubstantiation is a sacrificial act (Compare the term, "sacrifice of the mass"), a religio-magical sacred
act performed by the priest which at a certain moment actualizes
the death and resurrection of the Saviour. The same mystery is

also present in the acts of the Greek wedding ceremonies, which aim at initiation into absolute life, into divine death. The doctrine corresponding to these cultic practices is the myth of Psyche and Eros. But that is not a "mystery," for it is only the legend of a mystery. It is like the myth of Osiris, which had to be played or performed in order to be a "mystery." The mystery is the absolutely unutterable essence of life – that is to say, of death.

Now it must not be forgotten that the awe for death is not eliminated by this complete affirmation of death as the only true life. It is difficult to analyze and define "awe," but in religious life it is always the feeling or mood present in meeting the absolute, the holy. There are certainly two elements to be distinguished within it. Confronting the absolute man feels himself, his insight, ability, and willing condemned. This engenders dread in every meeting with God; to see God is to die. But it is just in this situation that man seeks and finds at the same time his salvation and release from the passivity of finitude. The Eleusinian Mysteries signify initiation into "the most terrible, but at the same time the most joyous state that man knows." These are the terrors of the realm of the dead and the joy at the rebirth to a new life. Plutarch speaks of "the joy which the initiates know, linked with fear and consternation, but also with the most glorious hope." That is the fear of death, in which the fulfilment of life is seen.

When death is conceived as the completion of life, it is repeatedly linked with the idea of totality – of the all-inclusive, the completed, in which beginning and end merge. For various reasons, some numbers have the meaning of "all" or totality. In Babylonia, Egypt, and elsewhere in the Ancient world, the number seven was totality (in Babylonia, *kishshatu*). And seven also proves to be the number representing the realm of the dead. The realm of the dead is surrounded by seven concentric walls; the domain of Osiris is sometimes called the Seven houses (districts), and the Babylonians, Egyptians, and Greeks believed that the realm of the dead had seven gates. In Babylonia and Greece there are also earthly cities known with seven gates, walls, etc., in order to identify them with the realm of the dead, which is the home of the absolute life of the divine totality. The Egyptians – and perhaps also the Hebrews in front of Jericho –

make the ritual procession (which in itself expresses totality) seven times around a city, by which means they gain power over it. By means of this sevenfold round they have actualized its secret and have triumphed over death (here conceived as an enemy). He who knows the secret has it in his power. In Greece and Babylonia the totality is expressed especially by the number three. The mystery gods in Samothrace are the three Kabires; these "Great gods" (*megaloi theoi*) have their home as mystery gods in the realm of the dead. The three Greek goddesses, the Moirai, also hail from the underworld, just as do the Tria Fata, Tres Fortunae, the three judges of the dead who represent the threefold Hades, and many others. Totality is always linked with death and the realm of the dead. Hesiod speaks only of the three winds: Boreas, Zephyros, and Notos; North, West, and South, respectively – East he skips. As chthonic beings or *animae*, souls, the winds also belong in the other world. The Babylonians distinguish seven winds. Besides seven and three, two, four, nine and twelve can also be "sacred numbers" and express totality; as such they are therefore connected in the cultus with the realm of the dead. All this is certainly very characteristic of the conception of death.

Akin to this "totality" is the religious concept of *harmonia*. Etymologically the word means "junction," *harmozō*, putting together so that the parts form a completed whole. Philolaus, a contemporary of Socrates, put special emphasis on the meaning of the "working together of opposites," *dicha phroneontōn symphronēsis* or "accord out of discord." The fullness of being, existence, or life is only reality in the other world. Death is, then, not the opposite of life; it is on the contrary precisely the goal towards which all empirical life strives in order to attain its fullness and completion (*teletē*). This is the central reflection in all mystery religions.

How deeply this thought is rooted in the religious consciousness becomes evident from the fact that we even find it where man has not dared to apply it to himself and to human life. The Babylonians considered man's death as a curse which was laid upon him, as divine confirmation of human insignificance. Nevertheless they too believed that death as cosmic reality is the completion and fullness of life – wholly in accord with the Greek and Egyptian conception. In Babylonia, *kishshatu*, totality, is the characteristic of the realm of the dead; Uruk, the "Seven-city," was the realm of the dead, and there are other examples. And in Hebrew *nishba*[c] is the *niphal* of *shābha*[c] "to swear," "to say seven (*shebha*[c]) times." "To say seven times" and "to swear" are undoubtedly identical just because they both signify a statement of absolute validity, accuracy, and truth, a statement which is withdrawn from finite relationships and is placed in the divine world order. Without any doubt, in Israel the number seven also meant totality, and thus death, in the positive sense of fullness, completion. But because of the religious conviction of man's insignificance and guilt, this is not applied to man's death.

Another expression of the conviction that totality, fullness, and completion – thus divine being – belong in death is present among many peoples, including the Semites. They conceive the realm of the dead specifically as the place of absolute insight or absolute wisdom, that is, insight into the order of life and the law of life, which is revealed by earth oracles. This idea was also known in Israel: the word *nāḥash* (Piël *niḥesh*), "soothsaying," has the same root as *nāḥāsh*, the snake. The snake, which according to Genesis 3 was a shrewd animal, full of insight, corresponds to the snake Python at the oracle of Delphi. The gods of wisdom belong in the realm of the dead; the Babylonian wise god Ea dwells in the primeval waters of the realm of the dead, Apsu. Only in the realm of the dead is the order of life really known. According to this conception, death is entirely positive: the completion and perfection of life, as divine life. But the Semite did not dare to ascribe that life to man, since for him death was not a completion, but a curse which had been laid upon him. According to the Greek view, man, too, either at his death or at his initiation into the Mysteries, was taken up into that absoluteness; the omniscient Sirens were dead persons. Plato's derivation of "Hades" from *eidenai* (to know) is indeed an impossible one, but it is not so artificial as it obviously appears to us. It is really an etymology which corresponds with the Greek conception of death and which is worth far more to us than the (probably) correct derivation from *a-idēs*, "the invisible, hidden."

Finally a brief word about the ritual treatment of the corpse
and about the religious significance of burial and cremation.
It is certain that they are both sacraments whereby divine life
is imparted to the dead person. When the body is placed in the
earth, it is given back to Mother Earth, wo gave it life at birth.
Burial is thus a *sacrificium*, a sacrificial act, in which man is the
offering. All living men live the life of the earth which they receive in food as a gift, and they die the death of the earth. In
Athens and also in India the cemetery is plowed and sowed;
the corpse is layed upon a layer of thyme or vines or olive tree
branches, to some extent with an apotropaeic intention. Modern
scholars put all the emphasis on this purpose. But how can the
branches accomplish this? The answer to this is to be found in
the fact that the branches possess the power of the earth's life
and can impart that power; they thus triumph over all forces
of destruction. The same custom in Egypt proves this. There in
the cultus of the Mysteries, the dead Osiris is placed on the
branches of his sacred tree. And from his grave the plants grow
up as expressions of his distinctive life as god of vegetation. The
grave itself is the place where the earth lives; the grave hill or
tumulus cannot be distinguished from the *omphalos*. The Ancient
Greek *pithos* grave (before burial) is the *thēsauros*, the earth's
storehouse. The ancient dome-shaped grave had the same significance, such as the "grave of Atreus" at Mycene. The Egyptian
mastaba is also probably the image of the grain storehouse, which
in Memphis was called "the life of the earth." That was the
religious significance of burial.

Cremation has exactly the same significance. In burning the
body was delivered to the fire, which was as much an element of
man's life as it was of the life of the universe. Two well known
examples of fire as man's vital element may be noted: the fire
baptism in the myth of Demeter, who hid the young prince "in
the power of the fire" in order to make him immortal, and the
fact that Hestia or Vesta, the goddess of fire, was also the goddess
of abiding life in the family. In addition to these gods there is
Hephaestus (the god of fire), the craftsman who forges the life
of the world. In India the fire god Agni in the sacrificial fire is
the life of the world; the pyre on which the corpse is placed
there has the significance of the dead person's "place of birth."

In cremation, as in burial, rising life is thus seen in death. So it can be explained why in Greece and in India burial and cremation could continue side by side. They are evidently not sensed to be contradictory customs. Sometimes they are even linked together, as when the corpse is burned and after that the ashes are buried, or when the corpse is placed in the grave and there burnt. The god of fire works in the earth, and the smiths of Hephaestus are the dwarfs who live and work in the earth.

CHAPTER 17

LIFE IN SOCIETY

Religious anthropology also contains the religious conception and doctrine of the different forms of social life. Social life is an integral part of individual life. Sometimes it is felt to be the most important factor in it; that is in the cases when the full personality of an individual is only acknowledged when he is a member of a particular community. Social life is in these instances a higher form of individual life and determines it in various respects. This is the most characteristic part of religious anthropology. We are here not so much concerned with the different forms of religious communities (in the stricter sense) belonging to the cultus, as with the anthropological significance which religious believers ascribe to community life. It was known that the individual was more than simply an individual, and that this supra-individual aspect was part of man's essential being.

In most religions a religious theory or doctrine concerning social life is to be found. It is then recognized as an irreducible factor and as a basic principle of human existence; it is self-subsistent and thus of divine nature. That means that the social community is a sacred community. The concept "agreement," or "covenant" – the basic principle of social life – proves again and again to contain the religious idea of the unbreakable order, the stability of relationships, independent of fortuitous phenomena or occurrences. This character of absoluteness is frequently called "ethical." That is all right, provided it is not forgotten that the word "ethical" has the meaning Kant ascribed to it: it is actually religious. The conception of absoluteness implies that the relation between man and man has the same character as the relation between man and God. Thus there is also one sacred relation between men which is binding under all circum-

stances. The ceremonially concluded agreement in the establish-
ment of a convenant proves repeatedly to have been a sacred
act, because it was sensed as a form of life, a form of life's mystery. In the *Iliad*, we find the words, *philothēta kai horkia pista
tamontes*,[1] "offering (sacrificing for) a friendship and a trustworthy treaty"; in the proper sense this is the *foedus ferire* and
kārath berīth, "to strike (slaughter or sacrifice) the treaty."
The agreement itself is thus sacrificed. Thereby it is made a
divine reality; by sacrificial death it is brought from the world
of finitude into the world of absolute life. Thus the *horkion* is the
oath sacrifice that is offered to the gods of the oath, such as
Zeus Horkios. These gods are always chthonic gods, because
unconditional life lies hidden in death. In the treaty this positive
aspect is primary. The negative aspect, the vengeance occurring
if the oath is broken, remains secondary.

The religious conception of the treaty or agreement is nowhere
so clearly elaborated as in the Avesta. Mithra (literally "covenant") is the god of all compacts, compacts in the broadest sense,
also in the cosmic sense. For the cosmic element is the religious side
of the agreement. The entire cosmic order is a "compact"; it is an
agreement which is entirely dominated and determined by one
principle: the absolute validity and trustworthiness of the order,
the order of life, which maintains itself under all circumstances.
The typical opponent of the convenant god Mithra is druj, "deceit," which does not uphold itself but arbitrarily diverges from
the norm; it is the unprincipled power which cannot be counted
upon. Therefore druj is also death, transiency, and finitude – the
mystical sense of death is unknown in the Avesta. This Mithra
of the cosmic life is also the upholder of "truth," as the trustworthiness which can be built upon in the human agreements
which form society. Every union of a social nature is under
Mithra's protection. For society and people are as such naturally
sacred, just as the land where one lives is a "sacred land." The
lord of the house, of the village, of the district, and of the country is
repeatedly seen as the representative of the sacred compact
which is organically connected with cosmic order. All these
groups are conceived as religious communities; the religious
idea of the group is akin to the idea of the bundle or collection,
"the bundle of life"; the whole consists of the working together

of its fixed and ordered parts. But there is a gradation in this social cohesiveness of a wholly religious nature, and its measure is the significance of the interests of life. The Mithra (or compact) of members from the same district is binding twentyfold, within the town thirtyfold, within the house fortyfold, in one apartment fiftyfold; the "Mithra" between brothers binds ninetyfold, and that between parents and children one hundredfold, but then there follows – remarkably enough – that the Mithra between two countries binds a thousand times and that between two countries who both adhere to the service of Mazda ten thousand times. This is indeed a very remarkable scale. The bond between two countries is thus even more sacred than the covenant between parents and children. And the most sacred covenant of all is the fellowship of the believers, who will bring the kingdom of God to triumph. The religious character of every compact is hereby expressly indicated. Related to this is a statement of a quite universal purport: "Where two men make an agreement, there Mithra is present as the third."

In various religions, but again most clearly formulated in the Avesta, a classification of another type of social cohesiveness is encountered: division into classes. The Avesta distinguishes between priests, warriors, and farmers; each of these classes is a religious community of a supernatural nature and is animated with its own particular "fire," a spiritual capacity and energy. The activities or vocation of every class is a particular, distinctively determined revelation of divine energy and forces; therefore every class is a religious and even a divine unity. The communal life of society is the result of powers – "the divine fire" – which are indeed active in men, but which do not originate from them. Society is not the result of human ingenuity in organizing. It is a divine institution.

This religious or even divine character of the various groups in society comes again and again into conflict with what we call the humane element in society. Greek religion provides well known instances of this conflict. According to the Ancient conception, the family was not based upon blood relationship, but upon cultus community. According to the laws of Gortyna (Crete, fifth century B.C.) slaves are real members of the family, who share in the family cultus. The family was founded by means of the mystical and religious wedding ceremony; because of its religious character the Roman *pater familias* was lord over life and death. Of course he represented the ancestors, who possessed absolute life. This implied that he himself had power over life and death.

The larger communities were also autonomous religious organizations, animated by divine life. The founding of a city was a religious act. All inhabitants of the city shared in the same divine life. The laws of the state were never abrogated; the most that could happen was that new laws were added to them. And this had to be the case, for they were not human arrangements, but divine laws of life, with sacred formulas, prayers, and proverbs. According to Aristotle, in ancient times the laws were not spoken but sung. This is supposed to be the explanation of the words *carmina* (verses) and *nomoi* (songs). And therefore most significance was attached to the words and the letter of the law, and little attention was given to its intention or spirit. It is noteworthy that Demeter-Kore is the *thesmophoros*, the law giver, and that the *themistes* are inspired by Themis or the earth goddess Ge. It is the gods of cosmic order who give laws to men: Shamash, Re, Ma-a-t, and Mithra; asha, rita, and Ma-a-t, moreover, determine the cosmic order just as completely as they do the moral order.

The religious significance of the serving class, the slaves, is a remarkable one. In many religions there are data available concerning the religious conception of servitude in general, thus of serving in contradistinction to ruling. Information has been preserved especially from Greek and Roman Antiquity concerning the religious conception of slaves as a social class. These data are very remarkable and very characteristic of the religious nature of Ancient society.

In the first place it is striking that in the Graeco-Roman world slaves in the most ancient period were more highly respected than later. In the earliest period Greek and Roman slaves were members of the family. They participated in the ancestor worship at the hearth – later they were excluded from it. The master was the protector of his slave; he considered him as a helper and a co-worker, especially in work in the field, the most important activity in those times. There was indeed a patriarchal relation

between master and slave, just like that between the master
and the other members of the family. There is nothing to indicate the presence of the contemptuous and cruel treatment
which was so common in Rome at the end of the Republic and
in the time of the Empire. As the civilization developed, the
position of slaves became steadily worse; one need only to think
of the gladiatorial games in the time of the Roman Empire. The
altered conception was already in vogue in Aristotle's time;
Aristotle even asserts that the slave is a *ktēma empsychon*, a
piece of live property or an implement, and that he can be treated
like any other implement. That conception continued to prevail
until both Christianity and Stoicism caused it to change. The
cause of this increasing depreciation was without any doubt just
the victory of the classical type of mind, such as that of Aristotle's.
The Ancient religious character of society, represented especially
by the kingship, was abandoned. And thus the religious conception of slaves as a class (which like each class had a sacred religious significance) also fell into disregard. After that slaves
were only considered as "possessions." The republic and de-
mocracy brought very great suffering for slaves.

But what was the Ancient religious viewpoint and doctrine
concerning slavery? The characteristic of the slave has always
been his lack of freedom. *"Servus"* means the one who is locked
up; *servare* is to be kept in custody by being locked up. What
kind of religious character was seen in this lack of freedom?
What divine reality was recognized in it? Finite, empirical
servitude was seen as an image or symbol of an infinite, cosmically determined servitude; therefore a certain sacredness
was ascribed to the social class of slaves, just as it was to other
social classes. This is most evident in the way in which a person
is made a slave and also in the way in which a slave is set free.

Among all peoples, slaves are drawn from among prisoners
of war and their descendants. According to the Ancient conception, all wars were waged that the people might maintain
itself, specifically that the divine order which sustained the
people's life might be maintained. As threatener of the order
of life, the enemy was thus the "mortal enemy." Therefore
prisoners of war had to die. Their execution was not a penalty,
but a matter of course: as enemies they belonged to the other

world. For foreign territory also represented the other world; therefore exile was equivalent to death. The buyer thus brought a dead man into society. Naturally this introducing of a dead person was a sacred act. In Rome the slave was sold (*vendere, venire, venundari, emere*) *sub corona*, with the wreath on his head. Roman authors have as little explanation for this as they have for other Ancient customs. But it is certain that among the Greeks and Romans the wreath always indicates a "sacredness" and "involvement in the sphere of the divine." Therefore the sacrificer also wears the wreath, and so too does the victor who in war or contest has enabled life to arise ,and likewise the participants in a feast for some god, Dionysus for instance. Because of this absoluteness and sacredness of death, the corpse is wreathed, and the wreath is used at many other occasions. The leaves and twigs of the wreath represent the divine life of the earth. By the wreath the slave is undoubtedly indicated to be a sacred being or is made into such a being. As the son of hostile foreign territory he continued to be someone from the other world; Roman authors with the classical mentality could not possibly understand this, or even recognize it. And as the wreath indicates, the slave was in particular a person who was animated by the life of the earth. We shall see shortly that the slaves' religion among the Romans confirms our conclusion.

The ceremony when a slave was given his freedom is in complete accord with this conception. The lictor touches the slave with his *vindicta*, a thin stick or stalk, with which he advocates (*vindicat*) the slave's freedom, or with his *festuca* (stalk or blade of grass). On this occasion he holds the fasces over his left shoulder and the vindicta or festuca in his right hand. The meaning of the ceremony must be related to that of the fasces, which symbolized the earth's life and order, imperishable and newly arising life; the fasces is the scepter, like the one which Hermes uses. Being touched with the vindicta is a magical act corresponding to the contact with the *rhabdos* in Hermes' hand. For this stalk is the magic staff which gives Hermes power over life and death and enables him to charm men in and out of death. The lictor with his fasces also has power over life and death. Thus the touch of the vindicta brings the slave from the other world into this world.

Now the most remarkable thing is that at the sale of the slave
– thus when the prisoner is made a slave – the same religious act
takes place as at the slave's liberation. The *pileus*, a round cap,
is then put on the slave's head. He is sold *pileatus* (with the cap
on), and he is set free *pileatus*. The pileus is a high cap which
especially among the lower classes, such as manual labourers,
farm help, and fishers, is the ordinary headgear. But it is also
certain that it had a special significance in the cultus. The Roman
priests (flamines, pontifices, and salii) performed the sacred
acts *capite velato*, with their heads covered by the pileus. The
pileus was, furthermore, sometimes adorned with small wings,
the characteristic mark of some gods and heroes, such as Hades,
Hermes, and Perseus, but it was above all the symbol of the
Dioscuri and of Mithra. It was also very well known among the
Romans as the *pileus libertatis*, the "hat of freedom" – or "cap"
in the form in which it was taken over by Jacobins in the French
Revolution. According to the usual explanation it is called the
pileus libertatis "because the slave received it when he was
freed." But the ordinary headgear of the lower classes in Rome
did not have that significance. And the explanation is quite
satisfactorily refuted by the fact that the prisoner also received
the pileus when he was made a slave and was sold. It is quite
clear that the pileus of the slave, just like that of the priests,
had a sacred meaning identical with that of the corona on his
head.

It seems to me not at all doubtful what meaning was intended.
The Ancients were acquainted with the idea of the "hat which
makes invisible," the *Tarnkappe*. Hades possessed it, and Perseus used it in his fight against Medusa. The pileus could be
drawn down far over the head so that the whole head was
covered. Then it had put darkness around the person or made
the person invisible. Therefore the invisible Hades and Perseus
wore the pileus, and so too did Hermes, who accompanied the
shades through the realm of the dead. The Germanic mythology
called the thunder god, Wodan, the god "with the deep hat"
(*os pileo obnubens* or *obnuptus*). And the ancient emblem of dwarfs
and gnomes, the elf's cap, is a genuine pileus. The idea also
occurs in German mythology of the *Tarnkappe*, which makes
one invisible. The pileus is the symbol of Hades, the realm of the

dead, conceived as the other, divine world, and it is the symbol of darkness, not so much the darkness of the underworld as that of the realm of the dead and of the night sky; the two wings on the pileus represent the atmosphere. For that reason the Roman priests wore the pileus; by the sacred act of sacrifice they were removed to the divine world. And so too the mystery gods, who in this instance as in many others acquaint us most clearly with the religious conceptions of the other world. Like Mithra, the *Megaloi theoi*, the Dioscuri, are gods of death and resurrection; Castor is mortal and Pollux is immortal. Both Mithra and these Dioscuri wear the pileus.

This explains the sacred meaning of the slaves' pileus. Together with the corona it symbolizes his becoming a slave, and together with the vindicta it symbolizes his being set free. With the corona it indicates that the slave belongs to the invisible world (foreign territory); the slave should have been killed. At his manumission the slave is *pileatus*, because he rises from the invisible world, just as do the Dioscuri, whose most important task is rescue and liberation from death. Therefore the pileus is the symbol of freedom, in the sense of rescue from death, and it is the symbol of resurrection.

Just the ceremonies of enslavement and manumission are enough to prove that slaves had a sacred significance in society. They were sacred because they belonged to the other world – from which, indeed, they had come.

In Rome the slaves were the "priests" in the worship of the Lares, the spirits of the realm of the dead. These lares were worshipped at the *compita*, the crossroads inside and outside the city; there Hekate *Enodia* and Hermes *Enodios* were also worshipped. The crossroad is, in fact, the place where the spirits of the dead come together, for the road is that which lies outside – in the other world. And in addition it is reported by Dionysius of Halicarnassus, as well as others, that "no free men but only slaves may participate in the sacrifices to the lares at the crossroads, for the lares prefer to be served by slaves." [2] This is certainly very striking, but yet completely understandable if slaves actually had a sacred significance. The Lares (or heroes), spirits of the dead, want to be worshipped by those among the living who belong to the other world – thus by slaves. It is for this reason, too, that tradition relates that the compitalia, the festival of the lares, "was instituted by Servius Tullius." Servius was of course the Roman king who was a slave, and furthermore, according to the myth, the son of the slave Ocresia and the Lar familiaris of the house of Tarquinius Priscus. It is evident from all this that the slave has the nature of the lar (familiaris), and therefore the lar has the nature of the slave. This indicates most clearly the religious significance of the slave.

The lar is of course not so much the family's ancestor as he is its special helper and protector; he keeps the family alive. He is the generating spirit of the family and of that part of the natural world which the family owns (Cf. Jordan-Preller, *Die guten Geister der Erde.*) He is the divine servant of the family, for a servant is he who looks after the well being of others and leads them to victory in life. The lar is invisible and the slave the visible servant, but they both have the divine task of enabling the life of others to flourish. Thus servitude possessed a religious significance. Now it can be understood why in Ancient times when the Ancient belief was still held, slaves were more respected than later, when they were considered live property, whereas earlier they could even be members of the family. They had an autonomous religious significance. They had to serve and toil, and as servants they were not free. But they were in the service of the gods of the ascendance and resurrection of life, that is to say, the gods of the realm of the dead. They themselves could also rise from death; that occurred at their manumission, which also signified their deliverance. The pileus on the head of the freed slave was the same as the pileus of the *Sōtēres*, saviours, the Dioscuri.

This close connection, so frequently confirmed, between the concepts of "servitude" and "belonging to the other world," "having died or dying" is indeed remarkable. The idea which we find here is that the servant or slave has the task of performing the heaviest and most difficult work in the vital interest of the living. The prototype of his work is the victory over death, which according to the Ancient conception had to be achieved continuously every day and every moment of life maintaining itself. Therefore the dead man is the prototype of the servant or slave. When Varro speaks of the yearly sacrifice to Acca

Larentia, "the Mother of the Lares," on the Velabrum, he also relates that right next to it a sacrifice was offered to the *Diis manibus servilibus*.[3] These are not the "divine spirits of slaves," but the "divine spirits of the dead, who are now slaves." Varro also adds that both places of sacrifice lie outside the city – thus outside the known world and in the other world. And among the Greeks it is precisely Hercules, the toiling servant, who is the greatest of all heroes or lares. It is he who triumphs over disaster for men, but also for the gods. In his poem on the Shield of Hercules, Hesiod says that "Zeus has generated Hercules to ward off disaster from gods and men." [4] And in the struggle against the Titans Zeus will defeat his enemies if a mortal fights alongside the gods; Hercules is elected for the task. In Greece there are also many other myths about gods and men who go to serve in foreign lands to atone a murder, and thus triumph over their own death. Those myths also make evident the religious idea of the typical nature of the servant or slave.

We find the same idea concerning servitude in the Egyptian religion. Thus there "the servants of Horus" are the dead, who triumph over death for gods and men.

In the *'Ebed-Yahweh*, the "servant of the Lord" of Isaiah 40–55, a similar figure is to be seen. He is represented as one who has died and is buried, but who is raised and glorified. He is the tireless, toiling servant, a man of sorrows, who takes our sorrows upon him. He is the Saviour, who will gain the victory for the people and will lead it out of darkness. Sometimes he is represented as the entire people of Israel, which must know death in order to be able to come to resurrection. Sometimes he is represented as the typical mythical figure of the servant, who brings resurrection for others – the people. He is a figure like the Messiah.

PART III

CULTUS

CHAPTER 18

INTRODUCTION

Cultus is objectively determined by the general circumstances under which it is performed and by the means which it utilizes. This is in contrast to the kind of sacred acts in which the human subject is the determining factor. Among the most important objective data are the places where, the times when, and the images with which the cultus is performed. These are, in other words, the sacred places, the sacred times, and the sacred images which play a role in the practice of worship. Our question is: how are we to understand this sacredness or holiness of cultic places, times, and images?

The concept sacredness or holiness as such is not a subject for phenomenological investigation, precisely because it characterizes *all* religious ideas and acts. Our relation to the holy or sacred* is our relation to the absolute; it is our religious relation. All parts of History and Phenomenology of Religion have the holy as their subject; holiness is a central religious concept; the holy is the divine. The essence of holiness is the essence of religion, so that it is a subject for Philosophy of Religion and not for Phenomenology. In his well known book, *Das Heilige* (English title: *The Idea of the Holy*), Rudolf Otto has tried to analyze this concept. He distinguishes between *mysterium fascinosum* and *mysterium tremendum;* the holy attracts, but it also arouses fear and awe. The two qualities are joined in the concept *majestas*. This is certainly quite rightly stated, but it is anything but new. *Das Heilige* (the holy) is "the divine," the object of *die Religion*, or of *das religiöse Gefühl* (the religious sense), which manifests itself equally in love (*fascinosum*) and in pious fear (*tremendum*). This book has been considered ex-

* Both English words are covered by the Dutch *heilig*. Tr.

tremely important, and Otto has been called "the discoverer of
the Holy." But it would be just as true to say that he is the
discoverer of the divine, or of religion, and this is simply absurd.
People have been too impressed by the title of *Das Heilige*.

Thus in beginning to investigate the idea of sacred places,
times and images, we do not take the concept "holiness" as our
starting point. On the contrary, we shall try on the basis of the
historical data to understand what the believers have understood
by the holiness or sacredness of these objects. Why have they
called certain particular places, times and images sacred or holy?

CHAPTER 19

SACRED PLACES

A. PLACES NATURALLY SACRED

We find sacred places in all the Ancient religions. Some places are dedicated to God and therefore withdrawn from ordinary intercourse and ordinary activities. They are thus inaccessible ground, *abaton* (sc. *pedon*). The Greeks even gave this as a name to the sacred place including Osiris' grave at Philae. Here is another instance, given by Pausanias.[1] In Phocis was a temple which might only be entered by those who had been invited by the goddess in a dream. Once a man attended the sacred rites who had no right to be there, but no sooner had he returned home and told what he had done than he died. In II Samuel 6 : 6–7, we read that Uzzah touched the ark of Yahweh and died immediately. He was not authorized to do so, and only those initiated, like the priests, may walk in sacred places or touch sacred objects. The ark was the place where Yahweh revealed himself; it was His sanctuary, His temple. For "holy" places do not belong to the finite world, but to the infinite, divine world. Whoever stays there unauthorized and unitiated, dies. This is not a "punishment," but simply a necessary consequence of the act. To die is to be torn loose from the finite world. He who touches the sacred place is by his death initiated into absolute, divine life. Only the "initiate," that is, he who has observed the ritual prescriptions, can even before his death come into direct contact with or possession of absolute life. Thus the initiates of the Eleusinian Mysteries were even during this earthly life in possession of an infinite existence. Whoever attends the Mysteries without authorization, dies!

But what is it, then, that makes a place "holy" or "sacred"? It is certainly not the fact that a sacred act is performed there, such as the utterance of a prayer, the swearing of an oath, or the

performance of a ritual purification. It is rather that this is the
place where God dwells and where He reveals Himself. On the
abaton at Philae was the grave of Osiris; that is to say, the place
where he caused life to rise again. The ark of Yahweh was God's
dwellingplace. The question then becomes: in what sense does
God "dwell" in a place? When his "sacredness" is transferred
to that place, what is the special relation between God and his
dwellingplace or "temple"? How can the dwellingplace share
in the attributes of its inhabitant? We must not be satisfied
with sentimental explanations using the analogy of the impressions aroused by visiting a place where a well known or
beloved personage has stayed and where his spirit is still present.
These impressions are really memories of the past. But religion
is concerned, not with a memory of what used to be, but with
the present reality.

The clearest data point in quite a different direction than that
of sentimentality; they direct us to the Ancient conception of
divine nature, or the nature god. In ancient Rome there were no
constructed temples, but many sacred places. Thus the spot
on the ground which had been struck by the lightning or meteo-
rite of Jupiter was fenced in by a low fence (*bidental, puteal*) and
made an *abaton*, a sacred place. Sacrifices were offered there to
Jupiter Fulgur, the god of lightning and rain, and consequently
god of vegetation. The earth lives by means of rain; the *puteal*
is the special site of this life of the earth. The place where the
lightning and the rain have driven into the ground is the seat
of divine power, buried by the lightning in order to rise again,
fulgur conditum. It is impossible to make a separation between
the place and the activity of the god, because the god only
reveals himself in the life of the earth, and thus at this place.
The *puteal* reveals the holiness of Jupiter; it represents the life
of the earth, which is self-subsistent, divine life. On the basis
of the Ancient conception of divine nature and the nature god,
it is quite understandable that such a place is sacred. Another
instance is the *nemus*, the sacred grove of Diana Nemorensis
at Aricia on the Sea of Nemi. Diana is the goddess of the trees
in the forest, of vegetation, and thus of the earth's life. Now in
this sacred grove one tree was the most important, and a branch
of this tree was the official staff of the priests of Diana Nemoren-

sis. In Virgil's *Aeneid*,[2] the myth relates that on the advice of
Circe, Aeneas had broken off a golden branch of that tree before
he descended into the underworld, and with it in his hand he
went safely through the underworld. The "Golden Bough," the
golden branch, is the branch of immortality; gold is imperishable.
Aeneas held a branch of this tree because it represented the renascent life of the earth: the tree was the tree of life, a familiar idea in
the Ancient religions of Greece, Egypt, Babylonia, and Israel. The
grove of Diana with the tree of life in its midst was, like the
"garden of the Hesperides," a "paradise," that is, the seat of the
repeatedly arising and immortal life of the earth. Diana Nemorensis was its goddess. The grove was sacred because her divine
life was revealed in and through it. The earth's life, that is to
say, vegetation in general, was represented by paradise, a sacred
grove. The grove was represented by a "tree of life" and the
tree by a particular branch. In the third Homeric Hymn,[3]
Hermes is celebrated, he with the golden branch, prosperity
and riches, the immortal one: *"rhabdos olbou kai ploutou chru-
seiē akērios."* The conception is quite clear and is quite similar
to that of the sacredness of the *bidental* and *puteal*. It fits ad-
mirably in the Ancient view of nature; here the earth's life was
localized, the life which repeatedly renewed itself by death and
resurrection. But just because of this Ancient spirit, the sacred
grove was not understood in rationalistic Roman circles, nor
is it usually understood among our modern classicists, who
blindly follow the classical writers. Otto Kern has written about
the Roman sacred places: "How powerfully the dim light of a
grove works upon the feelings of a religiously sensitive soul!" [4]
And he quotes Seneca, ". . . the slim lines and the height of the
trees, the mysterious gloom of the place, the wonder at the
shadows, so thick and unbroken, calls forth in you belief in a
divinity." Kern adds on his own initiative that at the founding
of temples, therefore ,"beautiful trees were immediately planted
around them," – and what is more, for the benefit of the priest –
"namely fruit trees." With such sentimental and aesthetic
tirades we come not a step closer to the religious reality. But
this is a good example to illustrate the difference between the
Ancient religious sense of nature and the modern aesthetic
sense of nature. According to the former, the place is sacred and

thus divine, because through the manifestation there, the divine activity is seen which is inseparable from the sacredness of the place. According to the latter, the mysterious gloom causes a mood which could, to be sure, lead to a religious view, but certainly would not lead one to use the expression, "sacred place." All the Ancient, non-Classical peoples had this religious sense of nature. The nature gods are the beings who correspond to this religious sense. The plural of this polytheism is a consequence of the plurality of natural phenomena manifesting divine power. We of the modern age have almost entirely lost that sense and that religious view. The concept "nature" meant something different to the Ancients than it means to us. With our aesthetic view, even when sometimes religiously coloured, we confront natural phenomena as free and detached beings, but we make a distinction between nature and God, and confronting God we are not free.

Sacred places of this Ancient type are to be found in all Ancient religions. The sacred place of the West Semitic Baal was each naturally fertile spot, whether an oasis or the vicinity of a spring, and it was called "Baal's land".[5] There were likewise in the Canaanite and ancient Hebrew religion the "high places," the sacred sites of the cultus on which sacrifices were made. They were sacred, not because they were widely visible or would strengthen the impression of the elevated sacrificial rite, but because the height is the place where the earth lives and repeatedly comes to life again. It is there that sacrifices are made to the gods of the earth's life, the gods of fertility.

It is thus not correct to say that God's holiness is transferred to His dwellingplace; that idea would be entirely incomprehensible. The holiness of the place *is* the holiness of the god who is worshipped there; the god reveals himself in the nature of this place. It is true that the site is the "dwellingplace" of deity, the sacred grove, for instance, being the dwellingplace of Diana, but here "dwellingplace" and "deity" are very closely related concepts, with quite a different relation to one another than the relation between man and his dwelling.

Another group of sacred places which in this sense constitute "dwellingplaces" of gods are the many sacred grottoes, especially found in Greece, Asia Minor, and Crete. Why are they sacred and places of worship? Once again the classicist essays an explanation which is based on aesthetic feeling. Otto Kern inquires as to the cause of this striking fact, and he thinks that he has found it and thereby come to understand the grotto cultus.[6] When once at Vari he had clambered up Mount Hymettos and reached the grotto dedicated to the nymphs, he came under the spell of "this loneliness of a grotto." He "was able to relive in this romantic solitude the magic of such a cultus." (This quotation is not from a travelogue but from *Die Religion der Griechen*, the chapter on "Religion and Locality.") It is demonstrable that grottoes were not sacred because of their romantic appeal. For in the Mithra cult a grotto was sometimes artificially constructed when no genuine grotto was to be found in the vicinity. A cultic room was built against the face of a rock wall. The two or three other walls were made by piling up boulders, and the "grotto" was finished. This proves that the mood was not the important thing. If scholars would only keep in mind that religion is not a mood; it is rather a vital concern! A grotto, or something which could pass for that, was necessary for the cultus, because a religious meaning was attached to it. What this meaning was we must learn from the believers themselves.

Which gods were worshipped there? In Greece especially the three Nymphs, and also Pan and Demeter; on the island of Crete the chthonic Zeus and Eileithyia, a chthonic goddess of birth; in Asia Minor Cybele, the *Magna Mater* (Great Mother). All of them are gods of the mystery of the underworld; they are the earth gods who cause life to rise ever anew. It is quite certain that the grotto represents the actual dwellingplace of these gods, which is the underworld, where the mystery of these gods is enacted. The sacred grottoes on Mt. Ida and Mt. Dikte in Crete were deep hollows. Numerous reliefs portray the three Nymphs, Charites, or Korai, with Hermes leading them out of the grotto. This is Hermes *Charidōtēs*, the mediator, the guide from the other world. Pan, the son of Hermes and Nymphe, is also the god of the earth's life. Demeter withdraws in a rage into her (sacred) grotto near Phigalia in Arcadia; this grotto too is the underworld. There she is found by Pan and brought back to earth, just as the three Nymphs are led out of their grotto. It is for this reason that the typical sanctuary of the Mithra of the Mysteries was the *spēlaion* or *spelaeum*, the grotto, artificially constructed if necessary. For this Mithra was the god of the resurrection of the earth's life, and thus of human life. Sometimes the *spēlaion* is actually a room under the ground, as it is in Rome and Ostia. This certainly does not suggest any peculiar "loneliness of a grotto." Moreover the large grottoes were as a rule extremely damp, so that water seeped through the walls and the ceiling. Therefore it was the Nymphs who were especially worshipped there. They were water spirits; Aeschylus calls them *biodōroi:* by means of water the earth lives and comes to life anew. (Cf. the rain god Jupiter Fulgur, who was an earth god.)

The sacredness, and that is the divinity, of the grottoes proves to be the same as the sacredness or divinity of the underworld, conceived as the realm of the dead. How could the underworld better be involved in the cultus than by representing it as a grotto? In the underworld the mystery of resurrection takes place; spontaneous and absolute life makes the grotto the sacred place where divine energy reveals itself. If the grotto represents the underworld, the Ancients were right in considering it sacred.

B. SACRED CITIES AND COUNTRIES

So far we have considered instances of naturally sacred places of worship (not: places which were worshipped!). There are other similar categories, sacred islands, for example. All of them were places which because of their peculiar character and qualities revealed divine life. The category we now turn to, sacred or holy cities, is apparently quite different from the categories just discussed, but actually it is closely akin to them. They are not naturally sacred, yet their sacredness is represented in the same way.

There are a great many sacred cities. Perhaps the Ancient peoples considered every city to be sacred. This is certainly the case with all the cities of Greece and Italy, and, at the very least, for a large number of other cities as well; the data we have show this quite clearly. In Greece and Italy the cities were sacred because they had been founded with special ceremonial rites appropriate to the occasion, and thereafter they were governed in accord with divine prescriptions. In this way the life and continuing existence of the city were brought into harmony with the universal and permanent divine order and removed from the transiency and finitude of this empirical world. Thus its continuing existence was as much assured as that of self-renewing cosmic life. That was the theory, and that is what we are concerned with here; the believers' faith is the religious reality. After the destruction of Rome by the Gauls in 390 B.C., the people shouted that they wanted to move to Veji and settle there, but Camillus argued that the city had been founded in accord with the divine order, that the gods had chosen the place and taken up residence there – with their ancestors. Although the city had been destroyed, it nevertheless remained the dwellingplace of the Roman gods.

If the ceremonial rites were neglected when a city was founded, it would necessarily perish, and people believed that history bore this out. This is what Pausanias writes about the experience of Epaminondas with Messene and what Herodotus writes about Dorieus, who without consulting the Delphic oracle and without performing the ceremonies founded a city with a Spartan colony in the most favorable region of Libya; shortly thereafter the city was destroyed.[7]

Therefore the city was in general a place in which self-subsistent, divine life revealed itself, as in the case of the *puteal*, the high ground, and the grotto; it was a sacred place. In Babylonia and Assyria this conception was expressed in different terms, in keeping with the Babylonian conception of divine order. Sennacherib says, "The plan of Nineveh was at its founding drawn in the celestial script, where its firm construction shines forth." The city is thus included in the eternal cosmic order to the extent that it is an image of the eternal order which embraces both progress and decay; it is imperishable, a sacred institution. The believers believed that practical considerations were not decisive in a city's construction; human insight is finite and does not lead to a permanent existence.

Among a number of peoples of Antiquity, this Ancient conception of the divine life and sacredness of the city was given a very striking and characteristic form. A large number of cities are quite unambiguously identified with the realm of the dead. They are thus considered as images of the realm of the dead, i.e., of the other world, where divine life has its seat, or of the site of renascent life. The city name "Kutha" (a place near Babylon) is also one of the names of the realm of the dead. The chief god there was Nergal, a god of the underworld and Lord of the realm of the dead. The city is thus the earthly image of the actual dwellingplace of the god; it is the place where his divine nature reveals itself. The city of course possessed divine life; the inhabitants were safe there. In the South of Babylonia is Uruk, the city of Ishtar, built according to the model of the realm of the dead. With its "seven walls" and "seven districts" it is the site of totality, *kishshatu* ⟨⟨⟨. A number of Greek and Egyptian cities also had this significance. This was the case with Megara in Corinthia, to the west of Eleusis. The derivation of the name from the Hebrew *me'ārā*, grotto, is improbable. Presumably it comes from *megaron*, large hall or palace, whose plural form, "the large dwellingplaces," is the familiar term for the underground sanctuary of Demeter, and thus of the underworld or realm of the dead where the mystery was enacted. It is clear from Pausanias that Demeter was indeed worshipped in the city of Megara.[8] The inhabitants there were thus in a sense initiated into the mysteries; there they shared in resurrection and immortality. In this sacred city par excellence, the laws of imperishable life were in force. Another instance is the city of Thebes in Boeotia, with the legendary Seven Gates. (Cf. the land of Osiris, and Uruk.) The chief goddess here was again Demeter. The citadel of Cadmeia was called *Makarōn nēsos*, "the island of the blessed." In the citadel was the sacred spot where Semele had been struck by the lightning of Zeus, an *abaton pedon* (flat piece of ground). This is the place where the earth's absolute life is situated, an *ēlysion*, and that is *makarōn nēsos*. All these cities are sacred places in which divine life is revealed, just as in such naturally sacred places as groves, grottoes, etc. This is also true of the various cities in Elis and Sicily which have the name Pylos (gate), and where Hades was especially worshipped. It is clear from the myths that the gate quite certainly signifies the cosmic gate of Hades. These cities represent the point of transition between the two worlds, the coming together of finite and infinite life, especially conceived as resurrection from death. Everywhere in Antiquity the symbolism of the gate had this meaning. There was the gate of Janus, the god with two faces, one turned towards this world and the other towards the other world. In Egypt the gate was one of the most familiar symbols of eternal life, appearing, for example, in the upright gravestone with the shape of a gate. Whoever lives in the Pylos, on the cosmic boundary, shares in the life of two worlds; finite and infinite life meet one another in resurrection. Babylon is *Bāb-ilāni*, the gate of the gods; it is *markas shamê u erṣeti*, the link between sky and earth.[9] In Genesis 28 : 17 we read the following: "And he was afraid, and said, 'How awesome is this place! This is none other than the house of God, and this is the gate of heaven.'" Beth-el itself is the link between heaven and earth.

But this "religious geography," whereby places are conceived to be sacred places, is not limited to cities. It also extends to rivers and mountains. The different terms for the water in the realm of the dead, the "water of life," are also given to earthly rivers: Lethe (*Lādōn*, *Lēthaios*) and Styx. Lethe flows in Elis along Pylos, through Boeotia alongside Thebes (the Ismenos, but "it used to be called Ladon") and through Thessaly alongside Trikka, where the chthonic god Asclepius was worshipped. The only thing that is known about the Styx is that the Pythia at Delphi drinks from the spring of the Cassotis, or, according to some, from the spring of the Styx. The power of the realm of the dead can also be brought among men by the water of springs. The sacred and thus divine places which represent the gate or the realm of the dead lie on sacred streams, on the water of life from the realm of the dead. Finite life is thus taken up into infinite life and thereby sacramentally made sacred. The religious value of this is quite clear.

Furthermore, it is sometimes very apparent that an entire country is a "holy land." In contrast with the "holy land" of Palestine, these regions are holy or sacred because the divine and self-subsistent power of imperishable life and resurrection is revealed in the land itself. In the Ancient view, the concept *Patria* (Fatherland) was entirely religiously determined. The "enlightened" Classical conception of *Patria*, which is also our own, does indeed contain much feeling, but it is not religious. The term did not mean for the Ancients, "where our forefathers have lived," but rather, "where they live," were they are worshipped and still active. But above all, it was for them, "the land which possesses the character of the father." This only becomes understandable after we have become acquainted with the Ancient meaning of *pater*. It is an Indo-European word, but its etymology is unknown. But other data inform us about the idea and it is an idea which is quite remarkable. For the Ancient mind, the concept *pater* is linked with the idea of the life of the earth and soil, and therefore the *pater* possesses the earth, land, or soil. This is proven by the ceremonies (the *fetiales*) with which the leader of an embassy which had come to Rome to conclude an alliance was consecrated as *pater patratus* (i.e., *pater factus*, one who had been made a father). This was done by touching his head with *sagmina* or *herba pura*, the sacred grass taken from *locus sacer* the "sacred place" of the Capitol. In concluding the alliance he wore as his insignia a grass clump of *herbae purae*. These plants represent vegetation; by touching them he is buried: he obtains the earth's life, the nature of the land. Thus he becomes *pater* "*patratus*." He is thus the "father" who possesses the generative power of the earth; the energy in both is the same. And so *patria* is the land which, like the father, creates or generates life. Its sacredness is to be understood as a consequence of this creative and thus divine nature. This is also the activity and the religious significance of the forefathers who live in the soil of the *patria*. They are worshipped at the hearth because the hearthfire is also the life of the earth; the mystical consort of Vesta is Vulcan, just as Hephaestus is the consort of Athene. It is not only among human beings that the forefathers are generators of life; they do this in nature, too, by looking after the fertility of the soil. The grass sod was the insignia of the *pater*, but also of the *Penates*, the Greek *Kēres*. These gods of the mysteries are also called *Patrōioi* (father gods) by the Greeks, or alternatively *Genethlioi* (begetters) or *Ktēsioi* (dispensers of riches, which is the earth's blessing). Thus the father gods are also nature gods, and *patria* in its Ancient meaning is the generating land, the living land, the divine land, which reveals its power in the life of nature and men. Not in the sentimental sense, but in the religious sense, the soil of the fatherland is "sacred"; it is *locus sacer*. The mystery of the Fatherland was also actualized at Eleusis, during the ritual plowing and sowing of the piece of land called Rarian Plain; this was thought to be the same sort of action as that of the conception of a child. And the conception of the mother corresponding to this conception of the father we find in the figure of the *Vesta Mater*. *"Vesta Terra est* (Vesta is the Earth)," it was said in Rome.

The Egyptians conceived of their fatherland in terms of this same idea of the "holy land" or sacred country. Egypt possessed and revealed a creative energy, a creative and spontaneous divine life. But this idea was elaborated in quite different terms than it was in Greece and Rome; it is not connected with the concept "father." Egypt is the "double country," the "twin lands"; the valley of the Nile and the delta together form "Upper and Lower Egypt." In the "religio-geographical" sense, Egypt represents, and exists by virtue of, the two contrary and yet cooperating factors in absolute life: death and life. In Egypt, two is the number standing for totality. Again and again we read in the texts of the "unification or reconciliation of the two lands," and we see this idea embodied in the Egyptian coat of arms. From the time of the first king, at every coronation, i.e., at the beginning of every new period, there occurred a renewing and resurrection of life. "Double Egypt" is Egypt which possesses absolute, divine life. It can be asked whether the geographical or the religious meaning of the division is older; probably one is exactly as old as the other. In the natural formation of the land is revealed the divine life which is the "reconciliation" of death and life. In the historical period the entire geography of Egypt is based on this division into two. There are many twin cities, such as the two lands of Heliopolis and the real "twin cities" which have two names, and there is the double Nile, etc. The eastern and western horizons are also conceived in terms of this division into two. Therefore Egypt is the sacred, divine land in which the gods reveal themselves; Egypt is the sacred place of worship.

Closely linked with the idea of the "holy land" is that of the "holy people," which we cannot consider here. Its basic idea is

that in the divine land the life of the people is regulated in accord
with the divine life of the land. The laws and norms of society
reflect the order of the country's life and that of the earth in
general. Themis (the goddess of social order) is equated with
Ge (the goddess of the earth). The term "holy people" or
sacred nation implies that a divine reality or activity is revealed
in the life of the people, just as it is revealed in the "holy land."
The nation is then taken up into the divine order and will continually renew itself; its newly arising life is identical with divine
life. Like Osiris, Ea, and Saturn, Demeter has imparted to the
people the law of eternal life.

The religious value of this notion of the sacred (holy) city,
land, and people is quite understandable. Ancient society was,
indeed, in a wider sense than we can imagine, built on a religious
foundation, which formed the basis of state and family life, of
all business, including the business of war, and of all the arts
and sciences. Its basic idea was that even in daily life men walk
in a world which is the Kingdom of God on earth. This is what
gave such stability to Ancient institutions; they were religious
communities. The "holy city" and the "holy land" were ideas
which expressed religious power.

C. TEMPLES AS SACRED PLACES

One might think that the religious significance of a building
would have to differ sharply from that of places which are sacred
by nature. God can perhaps reveal himself within a building, but
surely not in the building itself. Any essential correspondence
between the place and the divine activity here seems unthinkable.
Nevertheless, the difference between these two types of sacred
places, in the Ancient view at least, is not an essential one. This
is because the temple was conceived as an image of the actual
dwellingplace of God, the place which is sacred by nature. And
in this world of thought, the image possesses the nature of that
which it images. This is not the conception of the temple in the
"enlightened" or rationalistic circles of classical Antiquity. In
the Classical Graeco-Roman period the conception of the temple
as the image of God's cosmic dwellingplace has almost entirely
disappeared. (The same thing could be said of the conception

of church buildings in our own time.) In the Classical view, the temple is then only in an unreal and metaphorical sense a "holy place." This is also the view of prophetic Yahwism. Solomon's prayer at the dedication of the temple is characteristic. (I Kings 8 : 12–53.) Yahweh is enthroned in heaven and not in the temple. It is stated repeatedly that the temple "has been built for the name of Yahweh," i.e., for the divine power which is revealed at the invocation or utterance of his mysterious name (Judges 13 : 18). There is not a thought of any sacredness of the building as such; it is only a place of prayer.

But now let us return to the Ancient conception of the temple. There are cases where the line between the naturally sacred place and the human construction is quite obscure, as with the grotto temples of Mithra, two or three of whose walls were built. These temples, too, represent the actual underground grotto dwelling of the god. This was also true when the temple of Mithra was a room built underground. It thus becomes clear that in the Ancient conception of the temple, the difference between constructed and naturally sacred places was never essential.

The Ancient temple is always built or furnished so that it is the image of the actual cosmic dwellingplace of God. Even the word *templum* itself indicates this. The Greek word *temenos* (from *temnō*) is a piece which has been cut out or marked out. Its first meaning is that of a particular (demarcated) section of the sky within which the god reveals himself in the flight of birds or in lightning flashes. This part corresponds to the whole sky, in which omens are seen. And then projected upon the earth, it means a corresponding section on earth, the so-called *templum minus*, which first becomes *locus consecratus* by means of the *locum effari*. There the augurs observe the signs and perform other sacred acts. The actual *templum* is in the sky in which and through which God reveals Himself. The idea is very old indeed that all earthly events occur according to the example of the divine order in the sky. The earthly *templum* is the image of the celestial one. Therefore it is a suitable place to receive divine insight by means of omens, and to actualize divine life by offering sacrifices – in short, to participate in divine life. In this sense the *templum* is a cosmic locality, a sacred place; in the full sense of this term God is at work here.

There are instances of this among all the Ancient peoples. Among the Semites we think first of all of the "house of God," *Beth-el* (*baitulos*), with its upright stone, the *masseba*. The earth god is present in it; it is there that the earth lives and that there is a link or gate between this world and the other world. In Babylon the temple is *E-kur*, "house of the mountain," which represents the earth mountain, the cosmic mountain, or even the cosmos. This temple is the image of the cosmic dwellingplace of God; "*Ellil* is the living essence of *Ekur*." But *E-kur* is also a term for deity, especially when it occurs in the plural, *ekurrāti*, meaning "gods." Nabopolassar prays for the "temple's" blessing. The most important part of the Babylonian temple complex is the *zikkuratu*, the temple tower, a building which by its three, five, or seven terraces represents the cosmic mountain; "it extends to the heavens," God dwells at its top. It is conceived as a cosmic symbol. The architectural plan of these temples, consisting of maps and measurements, was not devised by human beings, but was revealed by God; man by himself did not know the dwellingplace of God. The document of this revelation, the building plan, was inscribed on a stone, which was set in the foundation of the building as the cornerstone. Even if the building were later enlarged, this original plan might not be departed from.

The revelation of the building plan was probably the result of astrological observations and calculations, or other observations of a mystical-scientific nature. The governing principle of these calculations was to make the temple the image of some particular cosmic locality. There is an image of Gudea as an architect, sitting down with the floor plan on a stone resting on his knees, with this the inscription, "he has built the temple and made everything in it as it ought to be, faithfully following all the words from the mouth of Ninib." [10] Unlike the classical Greek temple architecture, Ancient temple architecture was not free art, but a sacred imitation and image making; it was anonymous art bound to a religious theory. This sacred character influenced the art and often adversely affected its artistic quality, which, as a matter of fact, was not aimed at all. The architect's lack of freedom was the prerequisite for the sacredness or divine power in his work: with his temple he brought divine life among men.

It turns out time and again that religious and artistic interests diverge and sometimes even conflict. The religious factor makes itself felt as a factor which is not of this world. This does not mean that because of their conflict they must necessarily exclude one another; the hierarchic forms of art can also be very impressive. The Egyptian pyramids, graves which also must be thought of as "temples" (symbolizing "high places"), impress us because of their lines and their size, and the Sphinx of Gizeh (built about 2500 B.C.) is also in our modern judgment a remarkable masterpiece. But when there is an actual clash of religious and aesthetic values, we must nevertheless try to understand the architectural work as the believers understood it, even when their conception differs entirely from our own. A conception of the holy is not primitive because it diverges from the one we hold.

The Babylonian temple was the image of God's actual cosmic dwellingplace, and so too, was the Egyptian temple. The oldest (known) temples in Egypt are those of the god Re, and they go back to the third millennium B.C. The most important building of the entire temple complex lying within the enclosure was comparable in form to the Babylonian temple towers; it provided no space for cultic rites. These took place, as they did in Babylonia, under the open sky within the temple grounds. This building mounted by the obelisk constitutes during the Old Kingdom the familiar tomb which represents the sun god's realm of the dead. The obelisk, like the masseba, is the sign of resurrection. Like the Babylonian temple towers, this building represents the cosmic mountain. The idea of the tomb, however, is broadly interpreted. One of these temples is called, remarkably enough, *sp*, "corn stack" or "grain pile," and another is called *sḫt*, "the fertile field." The explanation of this is that these names are representatives of the earth's life, and thus of the underworld, by means of which Re lives. Compare the Greek word *thēsauros*, which means "hero's grave" (*taphoi thēsaurōdeis*) as well as "treasury." It is from the earth, that is, from Pluto, that all the abundance of agricultural produce (and thus all riches) come forth. Riches are equated with the earth's life. Now if the earth's life is bestowed on the dead man, his grave, too, is the *thēsauros*. Thus the temple of Re stands for the realm of the dead. This is the place where the earth's life is situated, and where Re re-

ceives his divine power. This place has reason to be sacred!
The temple of the earth god Ptah at Memphis is also called "the
grain storehouse of Egypt," a name which has furnished outsiders a welcome opportunity for contempt and ridicule. But the
temple was also called "the grain storehouse of God"; its meaning
was the same as that of the *thēsauros*. This tomb type of temple
with an obelisk or pyramid recurs in the later Theban temples
of the dead after 1400 B.C. These buildings, where the dead were
worshipped, had the shape of a grave with a roof in the form of a
pyramid or obelisk, , representing the hill of Creation.
They were thus the cosmic site of the rising of the life of the
dead man. The same building in miniature, a single stone from
one to two meters high, is in an even later time, during the Greek
and Roman periods, placed in the holy of holies, and the idol
stands beneath the gate. This is the site of the god's renascent
life; the stone is the earth itself.

   This same idea of "sacred place" is also frequently applied
to the tomb and to the sarcophagus, the coffin, which are, then,
thought to be images of the realm of the dead as the site of resurrection. The sacred places (tomb and sacrophagus) bring about
the resurrection of the dead man. In the Sakkara pyramid the
chamber for the sarcophagi has a black ceiling with yellow stars,
representing the night sky or the realm of the dead. Such representations are found in the New Kingdom, for instance in the
royal tombs at Thebes. Like the *cella* of the temple, the
sacrophagus is an image of the realm of the dead. The goddesses
of the night sky, Nut and Amenti, are depicted on the cover of
the coffin; there is even written, "Nut is the coffin." The coffin,
too, is oriented toward east and west, the regions of the sky
which stand for death and life. The mummy chest is called the
"chest of the mysteries" (*kistē mystikē*), which means that it is the
image of the living earth which causes life to arise. The ideas
concerning the coffin or the "chest of life" correspond entirely
to those about the tomb. In other Ancient religions the religio-
magical nature (sacredness) of the grave is actualized in different
fashion. At Athens, and also in India, the area of the grave was
plowed, sown, and watered in order to give the renascent power
of the earth to the grave, and thereby to the dead person. This

is the sanctifying or "making sacred" of the grave. In the most literal sense it is consecration (or initiation) and is quite different from the consecration of a church by a bishop, in which the building receives no divine power. In this latter case the term "consecration" is only used metaphorically.

Another form of temple which presumably is present among all the peoples of Antiquity is the arbor booth, the chapel for the gods of vegetation, who are the gods of the earth's life. It too, in the Ancient sense, is the image of the actual dwellingplace of these gods. In Egypt the arbor booth was from time immemorial the sign of religious festivals in general, but especially of the festival of Osiris' resurrection. Probably it was set up anew for every celebration of the festival, although permanent "bowers" are also known, made of woven reeds, among them the sanctuary of the South. Among the Greek and Romans, too, the arbor booth was frequently the place for worshipping the gods of the earth. We know of the festivals at Rome on *Nonae Caprotinae* in honour of Juno, and the oldest temple of Vesta was an arbor, the roof covered with stalks and the walls woven with reeds. According to Ovid the temple of Vesta has always remained an image of her dwelling in the earth,[11] for *"Vesta eadem quae terra"* (Vesta is the same as the earth).[12]

Very probably the Hebrew arbor booths of the Feast of Booths (Tabernacles) once had the same significance.[13] In Exodus 34 : 22 it is said of the Feast of Booths that "it is a harvest feast at the turn of the year"; that is to say, on New Year's Day, which the Jews celebrate in the autumn. The festival lasted seven days, and during that time people went "outside to dwell in booths." It is said to be "in remembrance of the journey through the wilderness," but this explanation is impossible. It always remained the chief Hebrew festival. I Kings 8 : 2, 12 : 32, etc. speak of "the feast." This corresponds to the Egyptian 𓅓𓆄, which means feast in general as well as the Feast of Booths. According to Leviticus 23 : 40, the participants carry "palm branches" and "branches of leafy trees" in their hands; in later Judaism they carried the *lūlābh*, a bundle of plants or a bouquet. Plutarch calls it a "feast of Dionysus": [14] Dionysus was the god of vegetation and the earth's life.

This bundle of plants was also well known in Antiquity in the worship of gods of vegetation. In Egypt it is depicted countless times in the hands of the participants in the cultic rites in which the vegetation gods are worshipped, sometimes as a simple bouquet, sometimes as an extremely complicated flower arrangement. It also appears in the arbor booth; its name is "life."

The libation which was offered on each of the seven days of the Feast of Booths is intended, according to the tradition, to assure rain at the time of sowing and to bring a fertile year. We may compare this with the Roman *fasces*, a bundle of plants with the symbol of lightning, the axe.

The shape of all these temples was determined by the essence or activity of the god who was worshipped there.

But even where the temples are large buildings with many chambers, they represent cosmic localities. Thus the colossal Egyptian temples at Karnak, Luxor, etc., some of them dating from the Middle Kingdom, but most of them from the New Kingdom (about 1250 B.C.) are different from the temples of the Old Kingdom, but they too, represent the actual dwellingplace of the Egyptian god. The temple gate, the *pylōn*, is the gate of the world, which means the place of contact and transition from this world to the other world; it represents the eastern horizon as the place of exit. "The sun rises between the two obelisks" which flank the gate, it is said. But it is also the place of entrance, of the western horizon. Behind this *pylōn* lies the peristyle, an enclosed gallery of pillars under the open sky. Further into the temple comes the hypostyle, the covered hall of pillars, which is darker. At the very back of the temple is the holy of holies. That is entirely dark: it is the image of the realm of the dead, where the god dwells, and only the king or high priest is permitted to enter it. It is also called *akhet*, the horizon as the place of resurrection. The Greeks, too, knew this meaning of Egyptian temple architecture. In *De Iside et Osiride*, Plutarch says the following about the construction of the temple: "They extend on the one hand in chambers and wings open to the light, while on the other hand they contain dark 'underground' areas which are like trenches for coffins." [15] This is entirely correct. But the notion of the cosmic prototype is expressed in still another way. For the entire temple constitutes a "high place": the floors of the temple are laid out in three terraces. High ground was the site of the earth's life; it is also called the hill of Creation, conceived as the place where life arose at Creation.

As far as the Greek temples are concerned, to the mind of the "enlightened" Greek authors they had no other significance than Solomon's temple or our presentday churches. They were places where the name and thus the power of the gods are invoked. But it is quite possible (and the data we have seem to prove it) that the triangular *fronton*, the *tympanon*, was not originally set up for some such practical reason as keeping out the rain, but rather had the significance of the Egyptian

, the high ground on the earth or the night sky as the place of resurrection. In ancient times it certainly did not belong on ordinary houses, but Caesar was permitted to use it as a mark of divine honour.

The temple was made an image of a cosmic locality in still another way, through its orientation.[16] The building faced the point of the rising of certain celestial bodies, either the sun or certain stars on a particular day. This was true in Egypt, Greece, and Rome. In Egypt Seshat and the king mark off the lines of the temple with stakes and a measuring line in accord with astronomical observations. The particular features of these plans are often difficult to reconstruct, but the main idea is clear: the orientation takes the temple up into the divine order. Nissen believes that some early Christian churches were definitely built in corresponding fashion. But in these cases the Ancient significance of orienting the building was only vaguely felt.

D. THE THRONE OF KINGS AND GODS

According to the Ancient conception the king is God, who has appeared on earth to guide men on the road of abiding life. He belongs in the other, divine world; his palace is, like the temple, the image of the divine dwellingplace, of the realm of the dead, conceived as the seat of absolute life. Now the throne is the place where he appears to the nation, and thus to our world, and where he receives people, and as such it is the place of resurrection. In Egypt "the king arises"; he rises anew ($\underline{h}$') to his throne just as the sun god rises (anew every morning). The armrests of the throne are formed by two lions, just as the sun rises between the two lions of the earth. So too is the throne of Solomon in I Kings 10 : 19.

Sometimes the throne of a king or god has the traditional hieroglyph for a house, palace, or temple. Not that the king or god is thought to sit on the roof; no, he arises from his palace or temple, where he dwells in hidden mystery; this temple is the realm of the dead. He rises from death when he appears on the throne, and therefore the throne is sacred, as the image of the site of his resurrection. In the throne the king reveals his power of resurrection.

The throne is also indicated with the sign of the *pylōn* or gate described above.

CHAPTER 20

SACRED TIMES

A sacred or religious place is the place in which God reveals Himself. It is the same way with sacred or divine time: at certain particular moments the divine activities are revealed. What happens at those moments not only corresponds to the essence of the god who is worshipped, but it *is* itself a self-subsistent, divine event. In the stream of events certain periods or moments are distinguished as new starting points, characteristic of divine activity. The spring, as a sacred time, corresponds to "Baal's land," as a sacred land, because of its divine nature or self-subsistent life.

Yet there is also an essential difference between sacred place and sacred time, corresponding to the difference between the character of the categories of space and time. Time is not an empirical reality, whereas what exists in space is. Even light and darkness are perceptible, but "daytime" and "nighttime" are ideal realities. For by every duration or computation of time, countless events are brought into a mutual relation and seen from a single point of view, namely the viewpoint of a particular event. "At twelve o'clock noon" is not a particular empirical phenomenon, but a link between the highest position of the sun on the one hand and countless other contemporaneous events on the other. A point of time includes and determines all that which is contemporaneous. The nature of this particular event, such as the sun at its zenith, is more or less imparted to all the other contemporaneous events. To give an example borrowed from religious speculation: the moment of transition between phases of the moon. The empirical side of this transition explains the worship of the moon as a divine being possessing self-subsistent life. Now the period of this transition is all-embracing;

the moment is sacred because the moon imparts itself to all
that which is contemporaneous. When the moon is waxing, all
things increase; when the moon is waning, they diminish. Waxing
and growth thus lie in an all-embracing time; it is time – an
ideal reality – which is waxing. The same energy flows through
all that is contemporaneous; everything is seen from a single
viewpoint. Waxing and waning moon correspond to the life and
death of all things. The Indian (and Indo-European) sacrifice
for the dead takes place under the winter sun and the waning
moon.

These religious ideas and rites in connection with sacred times
make a strange impression on us. There is a great distance between that world of thought and our own. It is, nonetheless, at
least partially understandable. We too believe that certain
events make their imprint on all contemporaneous phenomena.
This can also be expressed as follows: our "mood" imparts itself
to all our perceptions. During an especially joyful or sorrowful
event, one factor of our consciousness dominates a whole complex of impressions. In such cases our perceptions are emotionally
rather than rationally determined. There is then a peculiar unity
brought into the phenomena. This is, it is true, irrational, but
it is nevertheless very real, and sometimes it even has a higher
or more commanding validity than any rational unity. In such
a case rational considerations are set aside as being a reality of a
lower order. Yet for our modern consciousness this is a more
or less passing mood. It is not a conscious idea or a well formulated belief concerning a power which dominates all that is contemporaneous in the world and among men. But a conception
of this nature is found again and again in the various religions.
This is a conception of, or a belief concerning, the objective
reality which corresponds to the subjective reality of mood and
feeling. Here the state of the world at a given moment is a unity,
an organic whole which is individually characterized and is
different from the state of affairs before or after that moment.
At every separate moment the world is a peculiarly determined
organism, a living whole which is determined by a single soul
(like the determination by our mood). Considered by itself,
leaving aside for the moment any religious applications, the
conception of a mutual connection between all contemporaneous

events is no absurdity even for the modern mind. Undoubtedly the world reveals at every moment a particular constellation which is different from that of the following moment. The idea of the mutual connection of contemporaneous events is one with which, especially in certain fields, we are well acquainted. According to the religious conception of contemporaneity, the moment is dominated by a spiritual, indeed a divine energy, which does, it is true, reveal itself in a particular phenomenon, but which nevertheless is self-subsistent and encompasses all empirical reality. The particular moment is therefore also an infinite reality.

This conception of time as an all-encompassing and self-subsistent reality is opposed by rational thought. It is rightly called superstition if we devote our attention to the rational and causal connections of phenomena, for in such causality there is no occasion for arriving at the conceptions just described. This "superstition" is, however, religious faith as soon as the religious sense of nature apprehends the self-subsistent and thus non-causal factor. Such factors are present at every moment in the entire creation, in cosmic as well as in organic life, but they elude causal, rational, or finite definitions. When an absolute, self-subsistent factor is conceived (in the course of the heavenly bodies or the change of seasons, for example), this is a reality of a higher order than all empirical, finite realities. For it is then the basis of the whole, conceived as creative power, or as the divine energy which has an infinite significance and an all-embracing effect. And just as inevitably as our mood brought about by certain events influences our conception of the phenomena we perceive, so do the striking revelations of divine activity affect our conception of the world we see. Everything is then seen and understood in the light of those revelations; this influence cannot be abolished even by rationalistic arguments. With respect to the time of natural phenomena, this point of view is almost impossible for us to imagine. For us, therefore, it is really superstition when this view continues to exist in our culture in ancient beliefs, about the influence of the waxing or waning moon, for example. The Ancients were often mistaken regarding the material course of events, but with respect to the spiritual side of events, they often saw more deeply than we.

It is true here as always in the study of alien religions that psychologically and theoretically we can understand the strange conceptions, but psychology and theory fall short when we are concerned with the facts of the alien faith. There is no other way to make the alien come alive for us than to immerse ourselves in the concrete facts about it.

In considering the particular conceptions of belief in sacred times, it will be best first to note the formulations of general purport. In these cases the divine governance of the world is expressed in terms of sacred times or divine periods (of time). All periods and epochs "must surely be sacred" as such, because within them continually different particular expressions of divine will are recognizable, and this proves to be true, not only in theory, but also in fact. The religious science of the calendar all through Antiquity attests to this. Every period had a particular religious mark or characteristic. This was true of day and night, and of the seasons; it was also true of the hours, which were determined by the moon (the twelve months) according to the twelve signs of the zodiac. Thus the passage of time in general was religiously conceived. The task of the religious science of the calendar was to set down the different factors determining the time with the character of each: sun, moon, stars and planets, light and darkness, heat and cold, etc. Each particular time, whether morning, noon, evening or a particular date, had its own definite character. Each hour of the day and each day of the month was dedicated to particular gods or was itself considered to be a divine being. In Egypt the sacredness and divinity of the twenty-four hours is clear from the fact that each hour has its own goddess with a distinctive name. The first hour of the day is "the hour of the newly arising world of the sun god," and the second is, "the hour which puts darkness to flight." The twelfth is "the hour that is united with (absolute) life," and the twelfth hour of the night is "the hour which beholds the splendour of the sun god Re." Each time plays its role in the divine governance, and each time is characterized by a particular divine activity. This is a genuine religious idea.

In the Avesta religion, the five parts of the day are divine beings.

The Romans gave the days of the week the names of the plane-

tary gods, names which we still use. As early as the time of the
Babylonians there were seven planetary gods: Saturn, Jupiter,
Mars, the sun, Venus, Mercury, and the moon; there was an hour
of the day dedicated to each of these gods. The days were named
according to the divinity of the first hour of the day.[1] The Roman
Catholic calendar is comparable to this, in that it has a saint
for each day. And the religious meaning of lucky and unlucky
days for various activities should be similarly conceived. Hesiod
wrote about this in his *Erga kai Hēmerai*. Much of this book is
explicable, for instance the interpretation relating to the changes
in the phases of the moon, but most of it is still inexplicable,
including such instructions as that the ship's keel should be laid
on the fourth day after the new moon. All such customs have a
religious origin, to be sure, but this origin has often been forgotten, by Hesiod as well as by others. Yet the religious meaning
remains, even if the origin is long since forgotten. "The days of
Zeus should be observed according to the universal order (*kata
kosmon*)." By means of the periods of time, human activities are
thus brought into accord with the cosmic order, with the divine
order of the universe's life. It is as if people thought in personal
terms of the various periods of time which dominate the world.
Man does not stand isolated and powerless over against an impersonal nature, but he knows that he is included in the omnipotent and universal order.

The Romans divided all the days of the year into two kinds:
sacred and profane days. On the sacred *Nefasti* all ordinary activities are forbidden; it is *nefas* (against the divine order) to
perform such ordinary activities. These "feast days" belong exclusively to the gods, because they are special days or periods
of divine activity, which has set its own stamp on these particular days and has given its own character to all contemporaneous
events, to everything which happens on these days. Thus the
Nefasti have obtained the character of divine life, and are for
this reason, since they are outside the matrix of finite relationships, unsuitable and forbidden for ordinary activities. These
are "feast days," and are therefore called *Nefasti* or *Nefasti
Publici*, a term which probably comes from *Nefasti Feriae Pu-
blicae*. The derivation from this *feriae*, etymologically related
to our "feast," is uncertain. Our word "vacation" comes, how-

ever, only from *dies vacantes*, vacant days. According to the regulation of Numa, one hundred nine days in the year were dedicated to the gods, and on these days all work therefore had to be stopped, but according to the *Flamen Dialis*, "*quotidie feriatus est*," each day is thus completely dedicated to the service of a god. Sacred festivals (holidays) are days of rest upon which and through which the various gods reveal their particular activities, especially in connection with the change of seasons; February, for example, had twenty holidays. The *dies fasti* are *profanum*, lying before the *fanum;* they belong to ordinary life. Because the religious holidays are days on which the particular activity of a god is revealed, the character of the festivals differs as much as does the nature of the gods. Yet it is possible to speak of typical holidays, of days which display with special clarity their festival character, because in some religions this typical element is expressly indicated. Thus in Egypt the festival of resurrection and epiphany is the typical one. There are various Egyptian words for "festival," and all of them also mean "resurrection." 𓎛𓃀 *ḥb*, "festival," is the image of the underworld, the depth or cavity of the earth, above which the god (for instance the newly arising Osiris) is portrayed. The "festival" is indeed linked with resurrection from the realm of the dead. Another word "festival" is 𓎛 , *ḫ'* (corresponding to *panēgyris* or *agora*, general gathering) is rising, appearance, especially of the sun, or the epiphany of the god. 𓉐 is "the exit" of a god, when he is carried by the priests from his dark dwellingplace in the temple and shows himself to men – here again there is epiphany; *pr.t* also means the maturing of a seed or the rising of a star. For these reasons the festival of a god in Egypt and Greece was also frequently his "birthday"; it is the day on which he appeared in our world (epiphany). Thus the "birthday" of Apollo is the day of his return from the land of the Hyperboreans.

It is known that in the fourth century the Christian festival of Epiphany was celebrated on January 6, sometimes in memory of Jesus' birth, and sometimes in memory of his baptism, his rebirth, with the idea that life arises from water. The ordinary Greek name of this festival was *hē hēmera tōn phōtōn*, the day of light. The meaning of *phōs* is the light whereby one finds the way, the pathway of life. "In the creative Word was life, and that life was the light of men" (John 1 : 14). The annually renewed and newly arising light remained the image of the spiritual light which shines for the believer. In any case, the birthday of God, conceived as the appearance of God in our world, was and remained the most important festival of Christianity.

Another important type of sacred time is the period, in the Ancient sense of the term *periodos*, cycle or "rotation," in both the spatial and the temporal sense. The circle or ring is that which is closed in itself, or the totality of a movement, the coming together of beginning and end, of falling and rising; every point on the ring is at once end and beginning. The period is therefore a religious concept. All that which is contained in a period of time or space has received the character of absolute, divine life. An example of the spatial period is the well known Roman *Lustratio*, the rotation whereby that which is encircled is made sacred; i.e., drawn into the divine order of abiding life. The temple of Jupiter was lustrated, and thus purified in the positive sense, so that its sacredness was actualized anew, because the team of Jupiter's wagon ran around the temple (three times, also indicating by the number the idea of totality). The nation was lustrated, thus constituted anew as a sacred community, by the five yearly (temporal period) rotation (spatial period) of the priests of Mars with the *su-ove-taurilia*, the offering to the chthonic god. After each *saeculum*, a five or four year period, came this lustrum festival, celebrating a period of both time and space. This religious conception of the period as self-renewing time was probably also operative in the pre-prophetic period in the celebration of the last day of the Hebrew week, the Sabbath. It is presumably also the basis of the planetary days of later Antiquity. The seven days form a closed whole, a closed circle, and thus a period. In Babylonian totality is both ꙷꙷ and ꙷꙷ; both stand for *kishshatu*. The day of the closing of the cycle is – as in the case of the *saeculum* – also the day of the new arising. The resurrection in which setting and rising, decline and advance, are brought together is divine life. Totality is completeness or per-fection (being made full), the combination and cooperation of beginning, middle, and end, of rising and falling, in a closed whole. This is the mystery of resurrection. The coming together of beginning and end is sacred; therefore it is a day of rest for men, the Roman Nefasti. According to Genesis 2 : 3 it is a day of rest for man, and even for God. In Babylonia the last month of the year, the month Adar in the spring, was dedicated to the "Seven gods, the Great gods." This number seven clearly indicates totality, the totality of the year conceived as a "period" (in the Ancient sense). So this agrees completely with the conception of the last day of the week. Among various peoples, such as the Persians, Romans, and Greeks, this last month of the year is the time for the festivals of the dead, not because it constitutes the end of the year in the sentimental sense, but because it is the moment of the closing of the cycle. The dead are in the mystical sense the bestowers of the life and fertility of nature and men. The dead, the *Lares familiares*, live in the hearth; it is from there that life arises. The *Lar* is the *hērōs*, the *sōtēr*, and the hearth belongs to Vesta or Hestia.

But the beginning of the year is naturally also a sacred time and a distinct religious idea. In Egypt it is depicted as a young stalk with a bud on it, ⌒ ◻ ⫯ . This suggests its self-renewing character, its becoming young and fresh again at a certain time, and it is said of heavenly bodies, plants, bodies of water (the Nile) and of human resurrection from the dead (which is a cycle, as is clear from the sign ⫯ above the grave). The New Year's festival, which is celebrated by all peoples, is the moment of selfrenewal. At this moment, which determines all contemporaneous events, the absolute and eternal divine life is revealed in and through finite time. Besides New Year's Day there are also other days of transition on which a climax is reached and the descent from the zenith begins, Midsummer's Night, for example. According to Troels Lund, the water from ("sacred") springs has its greatest power of healing on Midsummer's Night; it is then that in Norway the pilgrimages to the church of Röldal are made.[2] On that night the hills where underground beings dwell are open. At the moment that death and life touch one another, there is communication between this world and the other world. At that moment soothsaying and similar practices are possible. Divine powers reveal themselves in that moment and impart themselves to all that which is contemporaneous. That is a sacred time.

The Greek *Hōrai* and the related ideas in other religions are worthy of note. These should not be thought of simply as "seasons," but as "time" or "times" in the sense of the thought in Ecclesiastes 3 : 1–8: "For everything there is a season, and a time for every matter under heaven: a time to be born, and a time to die . . ." All things have their time, namely the time in which their essence is revealed. They are determined by fate, by the divine will.[3] The *hōra* of a person or object is the moment in which some one (something) achieves his (its) goal, and thus unfolds and reveals its essence. As a religious concept the *hōra* is the moment in which the self-subsistent, individual energy which is at work in all growth reveals itself in course of development and growth; it is "the fullness of time." This is a teleological idea, with the thought of a *telos* ("goal") which is pursued in history, of the coming to pass of the right moment for an event. The *hōra* of a year is when the year is filled and closed off. But the three *Hōrai* are also the three seasons: each of the three has its fullness as a self-subsistent being. And because each one thus reveals the divine energy of the life process, each is conceived as divine time, imperceptible but real. This time, the fullness of time, is sacred, for a particular moment naturally reveals what was present potentially. The human body also has its *hōra*, the time when it has attained its complete development. But there are also separate *Hōrai* of childhood, youth, and adulthood. The combining factor which always lies in the concept "time" thus concerns all the various factors or elements which constitute the fullness of the phenomenon. "Youth" is an indefinable combination of a series of phenomena, all controlled by one single combining divine energy. That energy is divine because it is autonomously active in all growth and development, or, to say it more accurately, in the various stages of growth, for growth is not one continuing reality, but rather a series of distinct creative acts. The *Hōrai* of the various ages in life were sacred for the Greeks, and this sacredness was seen in the self-subsistent phenomena of those different ages. The *Hōrai* are thus the salient

moments of the total phenomenon of life. Even repeatedly
recurring expressions of life have "their time." Eating, sleeping,
harvesting, and indeed all other activities are controlled and
animated (made living) by the developing time which makes
particular moments arise for all expressions of life and sees to it
that everything attains its goal (and thus its autonomous being).
The *Hōrai* are therefore closely akin to the three *Moirai*, the
goddesses of "fate" in the Ancient sense of divine determination
and governance. The *Hōrai* are the daughters of Zeus and Themis
(or Ge), the goddess of cosmic order; they actualize the all-
encompassing order of life of the earth, the cosmos, and man.
They are the cosmic order expressed in terms of time.

The belief in the *Hōrai* is the religious form of (scientific)
evolutionism. A goal is posed for every being which must be
attained or is attained; what is potential in everything becomes
actuality. But we should not lose sight of the difference between
religious and scientific evolutionism. The latter conceives the
phenomenon in its causal context and tries to explain it on the
basis of preceding causes by analyzing the phenomenon. It thus
tries to derive the phenomenon from something else and does
not even consider the possibility that this phenomenon might
have its own autonomous existence. Every stage of the process
of growth is considered to be the result of a number of preceding
factors, whose effect is distinguishable in this stage. According
to the religious conception, however, divine growth is an inscrutable process which can be seen in two ways. The first is
"teleological becoming" in which the "divine will' (the goal)
is actualized. This factor is autonomous, not to be derived from
anything else and is thus called "fate." Seen in the second way,
growth is mysterious and divine because conflicting factors
cooperate. The finite and the infinite, good and evil, life and
death are united within it into an absolute and divine being.

Thus *Zervan*, time, unites all opposites in himself; he is the
saviour of men because he transforms the finitude of their temporal existence into infinite life and eternal existence. In other
words, the religious view conceives the phenomenon as an attained goal – the concept of goal presupposes autonomy, for
a goal or end does not point beyond itself – or, in contrast to the
analytical method, views the phenomenon as an organic whole

of all that which is contemporaneous and included in the same moment. In this way the phenomenon is seen in its autonomy, and not as a result or effect in a causal process. Scientific evolutionism and divine determinism are here opposed. The latter is certainly not a rational historical concept. Its teleological view sees a meaning in all becoming. Time is the divine energy, the all-determining cosmic law. Time is divine growth, an active divine being.

In other religions, too, the cosmic order or fate is a divine determination beyond rational and ethical norms, and is conceived as divine "time." [4] In Hindu literature, especially in the epics, we meet with *Kāla*, "sublime Time, the determinations created by the god of fate." Here too history is conceived as divine will: "Existence and non-existence, joy and sorrow, all things are rooted in (the) *Kāla*. It creates all things and destroys them; it brings forth all forms of existence, both good and evil." Just like Moira, *Kāla* is the divine "caprice," since it is supra-rational and supra-ethical, and demonic. This is not a blind "natural law" but a supreme divine will. When astrology came into India, *Kāla*, because it determines all things, became the power of the heavenly bodies. The astrologist was given the name *kālajna*, "he who knows the time." For the astrologist determined the character of a particular moment or a particular time. The moment dominates all that which is contemporaneous (the synthetic, non-analytic conception), and it recognizes its character in the stars. There was only one god above *Kāla*, and that was Brahman, the unchangeable, who stands above all change, without a recognizable will and without an active governance. Here is the synthetic view in the absolute sense; every distinction is abolished and transcended.

This conception of time also appears in the later Avesta in the form of *Zervan*, the Greek Chronos or Kronos. *Zervan* was worshipped as the perfect image of God, as the highest god, as the divine meaning of all becoming and occurrence. He unites all opposites in himself, or he makes everything serviceable to himself, even life and death. Therefore he is conceived as the saviour of men, who transforms their temporal existence into eternal life. In the Roman Mithra Mysteries he is called *Zervan akarana* (the infinite). In his totality he is the father of Ormuzd and Ahriman. He is the god who imposes peace, for he conquers death by and in his own death. He is portrayed with a grimacing lion's head which suggests the wildness and the demonic in the government of the cosmos. A snake is wound around him three times or seven times and sticks its head out above the lion's head of *Zervan* himself. Destruction by the lion and renewal by the snake together express eternity. Sometimes the snake sticks its head even farther out, right into the lion's mouth: that which is destroyed renews itself. *Zervan* has four wings, four being the number of the principal directions and of the seasons, and two keys, which are perhaps his original insignia. They have the same meaning as the keys of Janus, *initium* and *exitus*, the divine changes, the transition. They are the Keys of Heaven, which Peter carries.

CHAPTER 21

SACRED IMAGES

A. THE RELIGIOUS MEANING OF THE IMAGE

What did the image mean in worship? Quite obviously something different from our modern "image." It is known that among the Ancient peoples, and also among modern peoples outside our civilization, a mysterious relation is assumed to exist between the image and the original; sometimes we should be inclined to say that the image replaces the original. In Egyptian tombs the dead man is depicted upon the walls, sitting before a sacrificial table. By means of the image he thus really has food and drink. This is identity, or in any case an irrational, mystical, or magical relation between the image and the original. Thus the temple is the image of the cosmic location at which and in which God reveals Himself; therefore the temple is sacred, just as the location itself is. The altar is the image of the high ground in which God reveals Himself. The image possesses the properties of the original and replaces it. All "sympathetic magic" is based on this conception of the image. One does the same things to the image that he wishes to do to the original; the effect is the same. The image of an enemy is injured or killed; the image of a god is fed and worshipped with ceremonial rites. Sacred history is often brought into an image; that is, it is played as a drama. The image of Osiris is made, buried, and raised again, and as such it is an image of vegetation, which manifests life. Greece, too, had such a "rite," the *drōmenon* or the *mimēsis*, for instance that of Demeter, Kore, and Hades, which was performed at Eleusis. It was a play, an image of the myth, but nevertheless it had entirely the same effect as that which it imaged. It is, at least with respect to spiritual reality, a repetition, a "reproduction" of that which has once happened. Of such a nature is the doctrine in the Roman Catholic liturgy

that at every holy mass the Lord Himself descends to the altar
and that by means of the consecration of the bread complete
transubstantiation takes place. This is therefore more than an
image of an event which once occurred; it is truly a repetition
of the original reality, for the sacrifice of the mass is the sacrifice
that Christ accomplished. All the Ancient divine images which
play a role in the cultus have this character. They are the divine
beings themselves. They are solely votive offerings, *anathēmata*,
and not works of art and imagination, as are the images of the
gods made by the Greek artists Phidias, Praxiteles, Lysippus,
etc.

All these facts are very well known. But that we are able to
describe them does not mean that we understand the Ancient
meaning of the image. It seems to us "superstition" to suppose
that the image of the dead man in the Egyptian tomb, the play
at Eleusis, the repetition of the mystery of salvation in the mass,
and all the Ancient images of the gods could completely replace
the original realities which they imaged. But to call such a belief
"superstition" does not explain it at all. It only means that that
way of feeling and thinking is not valid for us. We must ask
what validity and religious value it had for the believers. Only
after answering this question shall we be able to understand
the facts, yet this question is almost never asked.

It is obvious that for the Ancients as well as ourselves the
imaged and the image were not simply identical. Material identity is quite obviously impossible. The physical fact is unique,
just as an historical event – as an observed fact – is unique.
Naturally the material image is something else than, and thus
not identical with, the reality which it images. And yet the
two were conceived to be in some sense identical. In what sense?
The answer must be: in a spiritual sense. We can at least partially reconstruct how this identity should be conceived. The image
is a deliberate repetition which can occur again and again, ever
anew. This continual repetition presupposes the continuing
reality of that which is repeated. The repetition thus expresses
the permanent significance of that which, temporally considered,
is an unique instance, which means that it expresses, not its
material, but its spiritual reality. This agrees, too, with the religious meaning of the repeatedly presented image in the cultus.

On the one hand, the sacred history of Osiris, although it is unique, is imaged again and again; also the Mysteries at Eleusis, and the sacred history of Christ is similarly repeated in image by the mass or by the passion play at Oberammergau. This occurs because of the believers' need to perpetuate and confirm the real spiritual significance of what has once occurred, and thus to give an altered significance to the historically unique event by abolishing its material character. On the other hand, the sacred images of a god, which are thus repetitions of him, are placed everywhere where his presence is desired or assumed to be; this too is a denial and abolition of his material or physical being, which of course must be unique, and the actualization of his omnipresence, of his spiritual being.

The psychological meaning of the image in the cultus proves not to be its material significance, as has always been thought. It is rather that the spiritual significance of the divine fact is accentuated and actualized by the image, which can be repeated or reproduced again and again. "Idolatry" is thus not a materialization of worship; the believer would certainly not call it this, and he is the only one who has a right to speak about the religious meaning of the worship of images. No, "idolatry" or image worship is one of the ways in which the believer becomes aware of the spiritual meaning of divine reality. Naturally there are also many other ways, as for instance the creedal formulation of Christ's sacrificial death in Protestant churches. The cultus image should not be confused with a "fetish," for the fetish is always unique, and its spiritual power is inseparable from the single object. There is no possibility of repetition with a fetish, whereas every religious Greek or Egyptian knew that there were countless sacred images of Apollo and Osiris. The image of the Holy Virgin with the Child is the perpetuation and confirmation of historical fact: what was, is also present here and now.

The conception of the spiritual meaning of the image appears to have been present among all peoples outside our civilization, that is to say, among all peoples whose civilization does not manifest the Greek type of "enlightenment." The image contains precisely the spiritual essence or the soul of that which has been imaged. It is a well known fact that among many peoples there is a fear of being painted or photographed, and it

frequently becomes clear that this is because of a belief that
man's soul would thereby be taken away.[1] It is not a satisfactory explanation to say that these peoples are afraid that the
person will be harmed by magic performed with his image in the
painting or photograph. It is also related that among certain
tribes where it was believed that women did not possess a "soul,"
this belief was successfully refuted by showing photographs of
women. The soul is thus present in the image.

The image in the cultus has a distinctive value and fulfills a
special function. It serves to make conscious the spiritual nature
of that which is imaged. This still does not mean that it is identical with what is imaged; it is rather its double. This term suggests precisely that which is less material or entirely immaterial.
If a person sees his own "double," that is a fatal omen, for then
he has seen his own spirit or shade. There is in the Egyptian
religion a well known example of what the image of a person
signifies. This is the *Ka*, 𝖴 or Ω. Its ordinary meaning is
that of the "soul" which represents the vital power or the autonomous spiritual essence of that which is imaged. The plural
form *Ka.u* also means "food" or "foodstuffs." The *Ka* is the
life of man that as living soul, as homunculus, is at work in us,
like the heart. After death a man's *Ka* lives in the grave and is
fed there. But *Ka* also means the image of the individual, the
"double." A newly born child is sometimes depicted twice, as
two completely identical children, original and image. The original is the child that we see and know empirically; the other is
his *Ka*, his "alter ego," who is conceived spiritually. It is his
invisible life and at the same time his image, his double. The
image thus represents the invisible, spiritual man, and the concept *Ka* is therefore quite identical with our concept "soul."
Frequently a statue of the dead man is placed in the grave. This
image is the *Ka* of the one who is depicted; it is his life itself;
thus the image "lives" in a very special sense. The mummy, too,
was conceived as the image of the dead man. It is noteworthy
that all the emphasis falls precisely on the life of the mummy:
its mouth and eyes are opened and sprinkled. Naturally people
knew very well that the visible image, the material mummy, did
not live nor could it be made to come alive, but the image which
can be multiplied represents the spiritual, living part of man.

We find an even more familiar example in the Greek concept *eidōlon*, from the word *eidon, horaō:* to see, become visible. This means both the image or statue of a man or woman, and the soul, the immaterial and thus invisible shade of the dead person, a little creature hovering about.[2] The *eidōlon*, here meaning the spirit, is also revealed in dreams. This indicates the religious meaning of image worship, or, as the New Testament calls it, *eidōlolatria*, idolatry. This means the worship of spirits, and it is used in the New Testament to mean the worship of false gods, especially the apostasy involved in syncretism and gnosticism. The image is a spirit, and it represents the spiritual part of that which is imaged. This was clearly also the Hebrew conception. At least it appears to me that the general prohibition of making images in the Ten Commandments presupposes this notion of the concept "image." Exodus 20 has in verse 3: "You shall have no other gods before me (or "besides me")," and in verse 4: "You shall not make yourself a graven image (*pesel*) or any likeness (*tᵉmūnā*) of anything that is in heaven above, or that is in the earth beneath, or that is in the water under the earth," and in verse 5: "you shall not bow down to them or serve them; for I Yahweh your God am a jealous God ..." This is thus a general prohibition of making images of men or animals, either portraits or statues (and they were actually never made in Israel), and now comes the special feature: "because "Israel may serve no other gods than Yahweh. Quite clearly any portrayal, including that of a man, even of such common activities as hunting, is the image of another god. Every image is an image of a false god, an *eidōlon*, a "double," a spiritual being, a spirit (*'ᵉlōhīm*). Images of any objects whatsoever, in the sky, on earth or in the sea are *'ᵉlōhīm 'ᵃhērīm*, "other gods," which Israel may not tolerate in its midst. In this context the general prohibition of images in verse 4 is quite understandable; it need not be a later addition, as Eerdmans assumes.[3] But even if it had been interpolated, it still presented the conception of the interpolater. Every *eidōlon* or image, including that of a man, signifies a spirit, a *'ᵉlōhīm*, and the spirits had to be banished from Israel.

Let us now look more closely at the psychology of image worship in order to gain at least a partial understanding of the believer's attitude toward it. If the image in the cultus is the per-

ceptible – not the materialized – representation of a spiritual
reality, whether of a god or a sacred history, we are actually
dealing with a form of metaphor, which is a "figure of speech."
Metaphor is the language in which we are aware of the spiritual
meaning of the terms used. All our representations and ideas,
even those which are most sublime, must be expressed in terms
of sensory perception, and thus in metaphor. This is no hindrance
to thought, no "despiritualizing of the spiritual"; the visible
image is often precisely the most suitable form for bringing out
the spiritual content. Hamlet gives a classical instance of this
when he tells the actors what the task of drama is: it teaches
us what man is by showing us man's image. "The purpose of
playing ... was and is, to hold, as 'twere, the mirror up to nature (which is thus that which is imaged); to show virtue her
own feature, scorn her own image, and the very age and body
of the time his form and pressure". 4 Plastic art is therefore
not only "re-productive." It possesses and manifests an autonomous, spiritual value. According to a historian of Shakespeare's
time, "the actor Yorick told Queen Elizabeth more truths than
did all her chaplains." The image is thus the clothing of a value,
quite a necessary clothing in order to bring out its spiritual
content.

   Thus the *eidōlon*, the image or visible likeness, can also acquire
the meaning of "spirit." While *to eidos* or *ta eidea* signify on the
one hand the outward and physical form of something (to be
clearly distinguished from *hylē*, matter), it signifies in addition
the Platonic Idea, a purely spiritual essence. From our analysis
of the concept "image," we have learned that the emphasis is
placed on the spiritual reality, because the image, as the repetition
of the original, has no real material reality; the material object
is unique and can of course not be repeated. The image is thus
the ideal reality, bound to neither time nor space. This idea is
closely connected with that of the permanent spiritual essence,
the "Idea."

   And now as to image worship in the cultus. We have to deal
here with a conception about the relation of matter and spirit
which diverges so radically from the one we hold that it is extremely difficult for us to understand image worship in its religious reality. As a rule it is not properly evaluated. For the

instances are often very striking and at the same time amazingly
well suited for leading us astray. It frequently turns out that
even when the emphasis seems to lie very strongly on the material
nature of the sacred image, awareness of its material character
has almost entirely disappeared, and the consciousness of its
spiritual nature is completely dominant. In Egypt, for instance,
the image of the god in the temple, which is only about one meter
high, is taken care of every day. With much ceremony it is cleansed with water, dressed with various types of cloth and ribbons of
different colours, fed with bread and milk, and given incense, etc.
Apparently everything has been taken into the sphere of the
material and finite, of the most familiar human activities. Man
has made the image and causes it to live; the image is entirely
helpless. We should think that the priest, whatever he may think
of the god, must consider himself superior to this image. Yet
that is not the case. For in this material image God is present;
the material nature of the object or the rite has completely disappeared from his consciousness. The various ritual acts are not
finite and ordinary, but rather mystical acts, superhuman and
"magical," just as is every cultic act, which is, of course, the
repeated and thus abiding reality of divine life. In all this material
reality the infinite spiritual reality is never for an instant lost
sight of. How can an image eat, and why must it be clothed?
Just the evident nonsense of these acts, when they are taken
as finite actions, was a permanent pointer to their spiritual
meaning. The water and fire with which the image was cleansed
pointed to the ultimate, self-subsistent, and divine energy of
life; the act of dressing the image was related to the idea of
awaking, and thus also of a new arising or resurrection. Thus the
feeding, for instance, was not only a religious, but also a divine
act. In the cultus man was endowed with divine power; he was
the fellow worker of deity. The rites performed with the divine
image are never ordinary acts; they all have an infinite meaning.
A familiar form of religious metaphor in image worship is setting
an object upright, particularly an aniconic image, a pillar such
as the *masseba* in Israel or the *djed* pillar of Osiris after Osiris'
death in the Mysteries. This expresses resurrection and actualizes
it. How can the mystery of resurrection be otherwise expressed
than in an image? The idea of resurrection cannot possibly be

precisely formulated, and if we try to do so in abstract or philosophical language, the resulting concept has in any case nothing
to do with religion. Neither should we forget that we use such
"religious metaphor" precisely in order to bring out the spiritual
meaning of such expressions or cultic acts as "resurrection",
"the Lord's Supper," etc. The metaphor is, however, not felt to
be a metaphor, because it has become the only possible manner
of expression. The image and the spiritual reality have become
one. It is in this sphere that all religion lives. It is as if the infinite, divine, or spiritual reality must reveal itself in and through
the finite in order to manifest its true nature. In cultic acts, matter,
world, and finitude are conquered, denied, and transcended.

B. THE RELATION OF THE SACRED IMAGE TO ART

It is understandable that a great difference exists between the
interests of religion and those of art. With the sacred image the
consciousness of its spiritual character completely prevails and
that of its material character has practically disappeared. It
frequently turns out that little attention is given to what we
would call "the artistic requirements"; perfection of form or
fashioning is not a religious requirement. The anthropomorphic
form of sacred images is often quite defective, and sometimes is
entirely neglected. There is indeed a tendency to make the image
"free" from the requirements of naturalistic art. It is then
overladen with "symbols" in order to bring out its spiritual
nature, whereas the material reality, or even the possibilities
of the material, is hardly considered. So on Roman Catholic
images of the Sacred Heart of Jesus, this heart is depicted with
all kinds of symbols on the breast. In Egypt the pillars of the
canopy above the king were also images designed to bring out
the king's spiritual essence as god of vegetation. Such images
are not at all bound by the material or by empirical observation:
they represent spiritual realities. This tendency characterizes
all "sacred images." Greek sculpture was in its prime in the fourth
and fifth centuries B.C., but it did not contribute any new value
to Greek religion, no new cultic monuments, though it did make
a number of magnificent votive offerings. The great religious
significance ascribed to the *xoana* is characteristic. They were

crudely worked wooden sticks, stones, or pillars with somewhat
human lines, but without any clear arms, legs, or head. They
remained the most sacred images of the gods, even when sculpture had achieved great heights. The statue of Athene in
the Parthenon which Phidias made was not a cultic image,
but a votive offering, an *anathēma*, but the *xoanon* or palladion of Athene in the Erechtheum was a cultic image.
Sometimes a *xoanon* was even made of marble, perhaps after
the model of an original wooden object, in order to make it more
durable. "Religious conservatism" is not a satisfactory explanation for this, for even in prehistoric times people were able to
make very good images. We should conceive the *xoanon* in the
same way that a believer in the historical period conceived it:
it is precisely in the crude or faulty image that the god who is
represented is most free. It is just when there is no attempt to
limit the divine empirically, by representing the rational in
forms familiar to us, that the infinite, spiritual, and supernatural
essence of the god is done justice. The sacred tree-pole, whether of
Dionysus or the Semitic *ashera*, was such a *xoanon*. No one could
say what activity would proceed from this superhuman object,
and since this was so, the image perfectly expressed the spontaneity and the untraceable and mysterious activity of the god.
The divine is not subject to any human norm of aesthetics or
rationality. The concerns of religion diverge widely from those
of art and science. Art and science are but little concerned with
religion – and vice versa. The Homeric gods are drawn as magnificent artistic images, but religiously they are farther away from
man than the artistically crude pole or pillar gods. The impression
of the strange and uncommon is essentially religious; it is thus
that the superhuman is best expressed. Perhaps the present interest in and admiration for the "primitive" ecclesiastical art
with stiff and crude images of saints with staring eyes (if this
admiration is not affectation) signifies an awakening sense of the
mystical or spiritual meaning of the sacred image and a realization of the truth of the Ancient conception that the image is a
spiritual being. The Second Commandment also presupposes
this notion of the image, but in the Ten Commandments, polytheism – the worship of the many gods and spirits identified with
all such images – is completely rejected.

We may indeed say that for us, too, the "image" in its essence
possesses the spiritual nature of that which is imaged. It follows
from this that the more observable correspondence with the
depicted model or with the outward likeness of the image disappears from one's mind, the more the spiritual meaning comes
to the fore. A striking illustration of this is given by an Arab
historian. The story goes as follows: There were five esteemed
and upright men (whose names are given) who all died within
the same month. Their relatives were hopelessly bereaved. Then
someone said to them, "I shall make you five images, although
I cannot thereby give life to these dead." He fashioned five images
and set them up so that each one of the mourners could visit
his dead brother, father, or relative and could do him honour.
This went on until the whole generation had died out. But the
following generation did them even greater honour, while the
third generation said, "our fathers have reverenced these images,
because they trusted in the intercession of these dead with God,"
and they began to worship them. It was thus that image worship
arose, says the historian. But God became enraged at this and
sent the Flood over the earth.

In this story the psychology of the origin of sacred images
is certainly correctly described. In the first generation the spiritual significance of the image was slight, because the spirit of the
dead man still had its natural point of support in the thought,
remembrance, and love of those still living; the visible image only
served to call up the memory image. In the second and third
generation there was no longer any memory, but the spirit of the
dead man continued to live through the reports about him in the
tradition and now found its suppport in the image. Yet this image
is not a second body; it is an *eidōlon*, the "form" in contradistinction to the matter. "The forms of things" are of a purely
ideal nature; they are the *eidea*, the Ideas, non-material and
invisible beings. The image is always, but most of all in religion,
an ideal image – even a photograph is something else than its
unique, physical model. Even when the image is regarded as a
repetition of the original, it still is only a repetition of a spiritual
kind; thus the repetition of sacred history is a continuation
and confirmation of its spiritual significance. For matter can
obviously not be repeated. The worship of the five h uman images

illustrates the prohibition of images in the Decalogue, which is also directed against human images. Every image is a spiritual reality. So we see that the psychology of the concept "image" also helps to understand the psychology of image worship. Yet even here we cannot say that it is General Psychology which has helped us out; I don't know of any textbook in Psychology which treats the psychology of the image. It is rather the other way around; the religious data can here be very enlightening for Psychology. Here again we see that to understand a religious phenomenon which constitutes an element in the religious life of any number of peoples means at the same time to understand its right to exist, and it is the right which believers have ascribed to the very basis of their life. To understand the right of phenomena to exist is the only form of historical understanding which is worthy of the name.

Let me recall a statement of Kierkegaard about the concept "repetition," an idea which is equally remarkable, and for the same reason, as the concept "image." Intentional repetition, he says, always brings forth a new, and indeed a spiritual reality. He gives among other illustrations the following one: Prof. Ussing, a great and impressive personality, gave a speech in which a certain passage aroused disapproval. As soon as he noticed this, he pounded his fist on the table and said, "I repeat it!" The effect was startling – everyone was impressed. In reality he had said something new, and something which this time made an impression. Intentional repetition produces a new spiritual value. Repetition is the characteristic ethical act; it is the maintenance of a decision, the faithfulness to an intention. The intentional repetition is no more a mechanical reproduction than is the making of an image; it is only unintentional repetition which is simply mechanical. As an example of this Kierkegaard tells the story of the dignified chamberlain who was very deaf, but would not admit it. Once when he was sitting at a dinner and a joke was told, he laughed along with the rest, although he had not understood it at all. But then he stood up and said, "Now I shall tell a joke." Then he began to repeat the story which had just been told. That was a repetition which impressed no one.

C. RELIGIOUS SYMBOLS

The question arises in connection with sacred images: what do we mean by religious symbols?

There is much misunderstanding about this subject, just as there is about the image. Like the image, the symbol indicates the essence of a reality. Nevertheless, there is an important difference between the symbol and the image. In general the symbol is more loosely connected with that which it symbolizes than is the image with its original model. The "symbols of justice," for instance, are the scales and the sword of the blindfolded goddess of justice. The symbol is a more or less conscious sign, sometimes rather arbitrarily chosen or invented, of a spiritual reality, for example the tricolour (the flag) of the Dutch nation. It is thus not a "double" as is the image. And because the symbol is a consciously chosen image, it is not a religious concept. It may indeed be a theological term, as for instance in the *Symbolum Apostolicum* (the Apostles' Creed), meaning a "watchword" or "motto," besides which other symbols are also possible. The word is also used in the expression, "Symbolic Writings (Books)," the formulations of faith recognized by the church, and sometimes *Symboliek* is used to mean Dogmatics, which is a systematic explication of the content of faith, but one done with the awareness that the formulation is not adequate to the reality. Yet this usage of the language is frequently misleading. What we as observers must call a symbol will be called something else by the believer. Protestants like to call the Cross and the Crucifix "Christian symbols," but the Roman Catholic believer will choose other terms which bring out better the sacred nature of these objects and better express the essential connection between the symbol and that which is symbolized. Truly sacred images are not symbols. The image of the fish in the Catacombs and elsewhere is indeed the image of Christ, the Saviour, of the spiritual being conceived as divine reality. The "symbol of Zeus" was lightning, and the symbol of Athene was the owl or the snake, yet these symbols, which were at the same time emblematic signs, were also for the believer the actual images of these gods, images of their divine essence and activity.

In the Egyptian religion, the sacred boat, which actually

represents the god of the temple, is the saviour in death over the
waters of death. The temple boat is called *sshm.w*, of the god. The
Dictionary says (4.291): "the cultic image of a god and his
portable boat, image of a god (as a statue or a drawing)."[5] We
would say that the boat is not the image but the symbol of the
god. But the boat is a sacred being and therefore not a symbol.
It is indeed a *sshm.w*, an image, of the god or king, but it is an
"image" which reflects the spiritual essence of the person, his
soul, just as the Apis bull is "the soul" (the image) of Ptah. The
concept "image" is here thus entirely separated from the observable phenomenon.

In the Ancient texts there is no equivalent for our word
"symbol." Indeed, the whole concept of a religious symbol was
unknown to the Ancients. Nowhere is it indicated that myths,
sacred rites, or sacred objects have a deeper meaning than the
obvious one, that they have a symbolic meaning. It is true that
in the Mysteries names and expressions sometimes appear which
are more precisely explained, but that is not symbolism. There
is no Ancient instance to show that ideas or myths must be symbolically interpreted, and this fact has always been the strongest
argument of classical philologians against such symbolic interpretations. It was with this argument that the brilliant work of
Friedrich Creuzer was convincingly refuted.[6] Since that time
the generally prevailing opinion among philologians and historians of Antiquity is that all religious data must be understood
as literally as possible. This conflicts with our notion of reason-
ableness and reality, as for instance when the identification of
Athene with the owl or the snake has to be taken as a survival
from primitive conceptions in which anything is possible. Symbolic explanations are called unhistorical, modern fantasies to
embellish the facts and give them a deeper meaning ... "For
the Ancients evidently conceived everything quite simply and
literally, and they nowhere indicated a symbolic or esoteric
meaning." This is an *argumentum e silentio*, but in this instance,
considering the quantity and extent of our data about the
Ancient world, it is not without force. The result is a sober
"common sense" treatment and explanation of the religious data,
with a literal and sometimes incredibly primitive conception of
Ancient utterances – a stone could represent a goddess –, and an

utterly simple explanation of rites – "they are in accord with
Ancient thought." This conception is simple and naive, and often
primitive. Creuzer and all "symbolists" were called fantasts.

But neither can this conception possibly be the right one.
Although it is certain that the religious Ancients never speak of
a symbolic meaning of their religious ideas and rites, we, nevertheless, are sometimes forced to speak of "symbols" because we
have discovered the "real" meaning of the sacred object, rite, or
myth, and now know it, yet must express its meaning differently
than by the traditional symbol. For in this task we cannot
dispense with the "term" symbolism. The sacred boat is a "symbol" of divine life, not an image of it, and the same is true of
the two sacred signs of Cretan religion, comparable to the Cross
in Christianity: the horns and the double edged axe. Every one
now admits that the horns are quite evidently the horns of the
earth or of the bull of the earth and that they suggest the fertility of the earth or of the earth god. They are related in meaning
to the axe, the "axe of lightning" or the axe of rain. The horns
often appear in pictures and reliefs, sometimes in a peculiar
connection – placed on the altar and joined with plants. This
forces us to speak of "the symbolism of the horns"; we know
what they mean. It is the only suitable term, for we cannot
possibly imagine the earth as a bull. The same is true with
myths. No one will suggest that the myth of Eros and Psyche
is an ordinary fairy tale. It agrees completely with the notions
of divine marriage, such as the one we know from Eleusis of the
marriage of Hades and Kore. The myth has, to be sure, the form
of a fairy tale, but what we know about Eros and Psyche in
Ancient Greek religion proves that in reality it has a very serious
meaning and a "symbolic" significance. Nevertheless, the Ancients did not find it necessary to expatiate on the real, the secret
and esoteric meaning of this myth or of the horns and the axe.
We must take a great deal of pains to make clear the meaning
of such seemingly simple data, and frequently we have to proceed in a very roundabout way. What is the cause of our difficulty?

The answer to this question is simple enough. Our categories
"symbolic" and "esoteric" are aids which we need to understand the Ancients. We can only imperfectly put ourselves back

into the thought world of the Ancient religions, even when a great many literary documents are at our service. The ideas of an alien religion are comparable to the words of a foreign language. These, too, are sometimes extremely difficult to translate because they have no equivalent. Only by roundabout and subtle paraphrasing can their meaning be accurately reproduced; literal translation leads to nonsense. With great pains we try to ascertain the meaning which is so hidden from us, whereas the Ancients, in their own languages, sensed that meaning immediately. They did not need any interpretation. It is precisely the same with foreign or alien religious ideas. It is sometimes extremely difficult for us to indicate their real meaning, because we have no equivalents. The terms and the signs in which they are expressed sometimes give us the impression of being mysterious metaphors, whose real meaning we must try to unravel. The "literal sense" gives us only a hint as to the real sense. Sometimes there just is no "literal sense" and what is taken for it is a pure fiction. Symbols of ideas which are more or less alien to us correspond to words in foreign languages which are signs of concepts not formulated in our own language. Every alien religion represents for us an alien world of thought. We see signs (or symbols) of thoughts and must interpret them. For the believers, in this case the Ancient peoples, this was naturally not the case. They understood their own language directly and lived in the ideas of their own religion. Therefore the concept "symbol" was unknown to them. This word did not appear in their religious vocabulary, but for us it is a necessary aid to escape the delusion of the literal and obvious meaning.

But all too often we forget this great difference between the Ancients and ourselves in the conception of religious ideas. Creuzer, too, forgot it. He ascribed his own conception of myth and other religious notions to the Ancients themselves. He believed that myths are the conscious and simple expressions of spiritual reality; they were conceived and composed in verse by the spiritual leaders of the people. The inaccuracy of this thesis has been proved by his critics. But this does not prove that his "symbolic interpretation "is valueless. His interpretation is in many cases very acute. Sometimes he saw the data with the eye of genius; in other cases he missed the mark, because the know-

ledge of Antiquity in his day was almost entirely confined to
Greece and Rome.

The great difference between the Ancients and ourselves can
be put as follows: what we must call "symbols" were for them
reality. All alien beliefs, including the Ancient ones, were to the
believers not signs or "symbols" of something else which lay
hidden behind the signs, but rather the only accurate and completely adequate expressions of the reality which was meant.
The startling thing is that the reality which they meant is no
longer a reality for us. The myth of Eros and Psyche is, for
example, an entirely adequate explication of the Greek conception of marriage. Marriage, from which, of course, new life
arises, is an initiation into absolute life – and that means: into
death. The marriage of Hades and Kore is the prototype of
every marriage. Therefore the myth relates that the bride Psyche
is attired as a living corpse, brought to a lonely place in the
mountains and deserted by her neighbours. Then ghosts bring
her to the deep valley (the realm of the dead), where she is
received by Eros, whom she, however, is not permitted to see.
During the day he disappears, and only at night does he come
to her. For the Ancients this myth expressed the mystical
reality of marriage in a quite adequate way. For it was, of course,
concerned with the idea of newly arising life, which is always a
mystery. Thus at Eleusis the prototype of marriage was celebrated, the marriage between Hades and Kore. But the reality
in the myth is no longer a reality for us. We have the greatest
difficulty in seeing in the myth of Eros and Psyche the description of every marriage. For us it is a charmingly simple
description of a profound thought in the form of a fairy tale, a
poetic symbolization of a religious idea which we can understand, to be sure, or at least we have gained some idea of its
meaning, but it no longer *lives* for us, and therefore for us it is
no longer a reality.

This is true of all myths. To our minds they always have the
form of a fairy tale, yet we understand very well that they are
not simply fairy tales. Therefore we try to understand the
meaning, the "symbolism." But this is only a proof that we have
become far removed from these myths. Our faith and our view
of the world have become quite different. It is therefore quite

natural that a symbolic interpretation of myths and other religious ideas is first advanced in the circles of the Greek enlightenment, in the time when the Ancient religion was becoming in the leading circles a more and more alien and uncomprehended religion. Plutarch (who died about 120 A.D.) is a zealous proponent of symbolic interpretation. He is deeply impressed by the wisdom of the ancient tradition in myths and cultic rites, but for him they are "symbols" of truths which are valid for himself and, so he believed, for all right thinking men. He tries to set forth the meaning of the Egyptian myths, and sometimes he does that quite accurately.[7] In this way he believes he can make the ancient ideas live again for his contemporaries. "The Egyptian religion is also true for us," he says. "The Nile is not only an Egyptian river ..." In the various Greek and foreign gods he saw sacred symbols of a providence which he believed governed all things. Polytheism was only a means to represent in a visible way eternal truths, which had already been recognized in hoary Antiquity. It should now be clear to everyone that in holding this conception, he was far removed from the faith of the Ancients. It turned out that the enlightenment of Plutarch and his contemporaries did not cause the Ancient faith to rise again in new glory, as they had expected. On the contrary, everywhere it penetrated, it undermined the Ancient faith and hastened its downfall. The spirit of symbolism proved to be the death of the Ancient faith. Actually the new interpretation was simply a confirmation of the fact that the Ancient spirit had already died. The new spirit brought in its stead religious philosophy which no believer had ever consciously held. Plutarch thought he would save the essential core of Ancient religion, but the essential element of his doctrine was his own religion, not that of the Egyptians.

This always happens when a person deliberately starts using alien ideas in order to learn something from them for himself. He who does this perhaps becomes wiser in so doing, but he has shattered the alien conception. Such a person thinks he has respect for the alien, but he really does not. Above all, he wants to be himself. There is also a different kind of respect: that respect which does not allow us to forget the distance between others and ourselves.

The believers do not have any symbolic interpretation of their myths. What we understand by the concept "religious myth" – a story with another and deeper sense than is immediately evident from the story – simply does not exist for the believer. He himself does not speak of his "myths," but rather of his "sacred traditions," for instance the *hieros logos* at Eleusis. To an outsider, Christianity also has many myths; we need but think of the second article of the Apostles' Creed:

And in Jesus Christ his only Son our Lord; who was conceived by the Holy Ghost, born of the Virgin Mary, suffered under Pontius Pilate, was crucified, dead, and buried; he descended into hell, the third day he rose again from the dead; he ascended into heaven. ...

For the believer this is not a myth, but the adequate formulation of divine reality. So much of what is written about "mythical thinking" is based on a deficient insight into the meaning of "myth" for the believer.

"Symbols" of the creative and thus divine life of the earth are especially numerous. For us the sacred horns are symbols of the fertility of the earth, because for us the idea of the earth in the form of a bull has no meaning or reality. But for the Ancients the power of the bull was present in his horns, while the "bull of the earth" corresponded entirely to the mystical reality of the earth's life. The sacred horns were not the "symbols" but the images of the earth's life; that is to say, they were the visible bearers of the spiritual reality or of the divine power and energy of the earth. But this Ancient conception of the "image ' is not alive in our consciousness, and so we shall just have to continue to use the terms "symbol of the earth's life" and "symbolism of the sacred horns."

Most of the symbols of the earth's life are borrowed from plant life, and particularly from the growing of grain. A familiar term for eternal or absolute life is "the bread of life," *ho artos tēs zōēs* (John 6 : 35) or even (verse 51) "the living bread," *ho artos ho zōn*. It is difficult for us to conceive of "bread" in this context as anything else than a conscious religious metaphor, comparable to the "water of life" or "the living water" (John 4 : 10), of which we shall speak in a moment. It is quite difficult to make out how the writer of John 6 : 35 conceived this expression. But it can be said with certainty that among the Ancient peoples the idea of the "bread of li'e" has a non-symbolic meaning. Bread, and food in general, were conceived as the typical representatives and bearers of observable divine life. Bread, or food, was a divine being, and it was therefore not a symbol, but a divine reality. No one in our moder 1 civilization could say that. The Egyptian data on this subject are extremely clear. "In bread and in all foodstuffs," we read "is situated the divine word which created the world (i.e., made it perceptible), and whereby the whole world lives." "Food" (hw) also means in Egyptian, "the commanding word," or "the command": it is the word of the Creator. Bread, which in our opinion simply sustains life, was thus not a symbol of divine power or life, but the revealed divine life itself; it was the bread of life. If we call this a materialistic conception of the divine, we show that we have even less understanding of Ancient thought than the little of which we *are* capable. Matter and spirit are "enlightened" Greek and modern concepts, and they do not help us to understand Ancient conceptions. We really have no equivalent of the Ancient conception of "food." Not even in the Lord's Supper, for there we have consecrated bread, and not bread in general, and the idea of the transformation of the bread indicates precisely the non-Ancient character of this belief. The Ancients presupposed no transformation, but an original and permanent identity of all food. We cannot approach the Ancient conception of "food of life" more closely than by calling food a symbol of divine life. This use of the concept "symbol" is an aid which we need in order even partially to understand the Ancients. But for the Ancients the head of grain in the Eleusinian Mysteries is not a symbol, and neither is the cultivation of the Rarian Plain.

The various scepters of gods or kings and high officials are other symbols of plant life. We call them symbols of divine or royal authority. But for the Ancients, they were objects in which the divine or magical power of the bearer of the scepter was present. For the scepters are the stalks of plants, which have in them the divine, creative power of the earth. This is strikingly illustrated in an Egyptian representation of a number of scepter bearers, one of whom bears before him as his scepter a whole tree. We are acquainted with the scepter with magic power in the "magic wand," for to perform magic is to create. It is im-

possible for us to put ourselves in such a train of thought as the
Greek idea that the speaker in the assembly can only be well
inspired if he holds the scepter in his hand. When he does this,
he has the magic power of the word and proclaims divine truth,
that which is in accord with Themis, the divine order of life in
the earth. The scepter is thus not a symbol of divine or royal
power and authority, but its reality.

One more instance: the meaning of the "living water," the
water of life, in the story of the Samaritan woman (John 4 : 10).
In this case it is quite certain that the writer deliberately used
a metaphor in which water is the symbol of life. For us, too,
that is the only conception possible. But for the Ancient peoples
water was a divine being, because of its renewing power. In
Egyptian texts the water of the Nile, and in particular its flooding
is frequently called "Osiris," and sometimes Osiris is called
"water." Thus he is not called "the god of the water"; we use
this expression for our convenience, but, in my opinion, it occurs
nowhere in the texts. This divine water, also called "the living
water" [8] "purifies and divinizes" the person.[9] This is the Ancient
water baptism. Water baptism is thus not a symbolic act representing regeneration, but a religio-magical means to actualize
regeneration. It is well known that baptism still has this meaning
in some Christian churches, which teach that in and by means
of the water, the Spirit creates new life. But to the minds of the
Ancients, no Spirit was necessary for this: the water itself performed the miracle. Water was conceived as a living being, as a
god. It is quite clear that this conception or perception of water
is one which we do not have at all. The Ancients thought neither
of a material nor of a spiritual being. What they beheld as the
reality of water is no longer a reality for us, because we think
and perceive in the enlightened Greek way, not in the Ancient
way. To be sure, we can agree in a metaphorical sense with
John 4 : 10 that water creates life, but for us this is a figure of
speech. If we really believed it in all seriousness the way the
Ancients did, we too should have to worship water as a divine
being, for of course it is only God who creates. It is impossible
for us to believe this. We can go no further than to call water a
symbol of divine life, but a symbol is not reality. We must
suffice with saying that the Ancient peoples saw in water and

in food symbols of the inexpressible divine reality. But this is
not wholly correct.

There are some instances where Ancient sacred objects or
"symbols" have remained in use, apparently quite unaltered,
right down to our time. Actually, however, they have been strip-
ped of their sacredness and have become real symbols. Among
these are the symbols of kingship, the royal insignia: the scepter,
the orb, the crown, and, to a certain extent, the throne. They
were sacred because the king was a divine person. He was the
god who appeared among men to cause the people to live, for
he looked after the prosperity and well being of the people; he
brought the gifts of earth, such as good harvests, and the blessing
of an ordered life – peace, well being, and justice. So the "regalia"
were the various bearers of the earth's life. The scepter or the
branch was vegetation; the golden orb was the golden fruit from
the tree of life in the garden of Hesperides, and so was the cross
on top of it, for in ancient Christianity the cross was thought of
as the tree of life. The crown had the significance of the wreath,
the *"corona."* The wreath of the victor in war, the winner in
the games, or the dead man is "the wreath of victory" or "the
wreath of life," a plant symbol that represents the resurrection
of the earth's life. Therefore the rescuer of an army or a city
received the *corona graminea*, the wreath of grass. All these
symbols and insignia of kingship represented the divine nature
of the king. For us they are only "symbols," because their sacred
nature is as impossible for us to conceive as is the Ancient significance of kingship.

There are a number of other symbols of the same kind still
extant. They very probably are directly related to Ancient sacred
objects, but their Ancient significance is no longer felt, even
when it is known what it once was. Many symbols of such secret
societies as the Free Masons are probably of this kind. They
have now become mystical symbols, and thus something else
than sacred objects and rites.

D. IMMATERIAL IMAGES

"Immaterial images" are images which represent both ideas and ideals. In this connection we think especially of the shadow and the name. In religious thought and in the cultus both are closely akin to the sacred image. Both represent the immaterial essence, the spirit of a person or of a god, and that is just what the sacred image essentially is.

The Shadow

It is understandable that the shadow is thought of as the visible but immaterial image. It is remarkable, however, that it is often considered to be the form of someone's soul or life, namely as his visible and yet spiritual "double." Many instances in ethnography indicate this quite unambiguously – something which ethnographic examples but rarely do. Kruyt relates that the Javanese takes care that his shadow does not fall on another shadow, for that could weaken him; the other shadow could carry off something of his energy or spirit.[10] This is comparable with the fear of allowing an image, portrait or model to be made. In New Guinea, anyone who steps on the prince's shadow is killed.[11] The shadow is evidently the spiritual essence of the person; is his ideal image, comparable with *eidōlon* in the sense of "spirit." This is made clear by ideas of such a kind as "the dead man casts no shadow." This notion is not based on the fact that the dead man lying flat on the ground casts no shadow,[12] but rather on the belief that the dead man is entirely spirit; he has no spirit or shadow, because he *is* such a spirit or shadow. Neither does a magician cast a shadow for he is a supernatural being who does supernatural things; he belongs to the other world.[13] According to Kruyt,[14] in Malaya everyone who wants to be a magician must first grasp his own shadow and eat it up; then he is a spirit.

The data from ethnography and folklore are countless but monotonous, because the nuances elude us. But that is not the case with the data from the literate religions. Particularly in Egypt the ideas about the shadow had been developed in a very special way. First of all, the familiar sign for shadow, ⌐,

the sun-shade, is one of the many forms for the concept "soul."
Moreover, an image or symbol, as for instance the winged disc
of the sun engraved over the temple gate, is called a "god's
shadow." This is evidently to lay the stress on the spiritual
character or divine soul of this image, in order to indicate that
it belongs in the other, divine world ,and in Egypt that other
world is the realm of the dead. Now we would think that there
could only be a shadow when there is light, but in Egypt the
shadow signifies the nocturnal aspect of the god, his invisible
and mysterious essence. The holy of holies, the *cella*, of every
Egyptian temple can be called "the shadow of Re (the sun god)."
The holy of holies, where the god dwells, is the image of the realm
of the dead, where he really resides. The "shadow of Re" is thus
in a sense nocturnal space, which is the same as the realm of the
dead; we may compare with this our term "shadow of death."
But the shadow is the soul or life, and so here, too, it is the site
of spontaneous life. By a drawing of the hieroglyphic of the
shadow, the sun disc, which frequently appears among the religious symbols, we read: "the life of every day (*ᶜnḫ n hrw nb*).
This precisely formulates the religious meaning of the shadow.
It can only mean that the shadow is the nocturnal aspect of a
god or sacred place, meaning its spontaneous life. Thus whenever ⵁ is drawn above the prostrate and dead Osiris, it signifies
his resurrection and life in death. Inscribed above the sphinx it
also signifies the life of the earth god, or of the sun god conceived
as an earth god. It is thus his "soul," conceived as his self-subsistent, divine being. In a portrayal of the throne of Queen Hatsep-
sut, it is not the queen who is depicted sitting on the throne,
but her shadow, ⵁ, who leans against it. The shadow is her
ideal image, her invisible, divine essence. So the shadow is the
spiritual double of the person, god, or place, but especially
emphasizes the divine character, the magical-creative ability of
the double. The shadow is the spiritual image, the divine essence
which is worshipped.

The Name

The name, too, is a spiritual "image" or double of the person.
It is not an abstract formulation of the essence, not a "concept"

whereby one becomes aware of the content, or a means for communicating an idea to someone else. Someone's name contains his living essence, his power and greatness, his mystical vital energy. This is its religious meaning. The name is therefore the "image" in which the person lives and maintains himself; it is the self-sustaining spirit. The name can also become a kind of talisman. In Babylonia it is said, for instance, that "Assur protects the king." But on the other hand, people give their children ugly names in order to ward off evil "spirits" or influences from the creature which is so ugly.[15] The ethnographic data agree entirely with what is known from the literary remains of historical religions. For they report that the life of an enemy can be trapped by using his name (which is his life, soul, and power) in magic formulae. It is a very common phenomenon that a man will not tell strangers his name.[16] Sometimes people prefer not to reveal their names to one another but speak to each other using various other designations. In these cases the name is uttered only at very ceremonial occasions. Rome had a secret name, which was used "only at mysterious cultic rites." The same was true of Ops Consiva, the mysterious goddess of germinating life. There are similar ideas held by quite various peoples. The names of the Dahomey kings known to the outside world were not their real names. In China and Korea the names of princes were only circumscribed, with such designations as "the perfect one" and "the descendent of angels." For the same reason the name of the dead person might not be mentioned: people should not call up the spirits of the dead, who are dangerous in this world. People should not even accidentally mention this name. Frazer reports that if the word of an animal, a plant, water, or fire was contained in the name, the designations of these objects or materials were changed, which naturally led to a ceaseless changing of the language. Sometimes the name is only of real significance if it is spoken by the person himself. Only then is it an expression of the person.[17]

Re, too, had a secret name.[18] Re had many names, but the true name which gave him power over the gods was known to no one. Isis knows everything – except the true name of Re. The myth relates, however, how she was nevertheless able to discover it. Re, who is old, once lets a bit of his saliva fall on the ground.

Isis mixes this with earth and causes a poisonous snake to arise
from this mixture. This snake thus shares in Re's essence, – and
is therefore a match for him. While on a walk Re is bitten by this
animal. When Re is suffering severe pain from the wound, the
omniscient Isis comes to offer her help. She can do this on condition that she learn his name, and thus his true and supreme
essence. Then Re answers:

> I am he who made sky and earth, who formed mountains and created
> all that is upon them ... who created the horizon, where the souls of
> the gods have their home ... I am he on whose command the Nile flows,
> but whose name the gods do not know [who is thus superior to the gods];
> ... who opens the year and causes the flood to take place.

But the effect of the poison does not abate. Then Isis presses
her demand again. "Your name is not in what you have said. Tell
me what it is and then the poison will leave you." In his suffering Re gives in, saying, "My name will pass from me to you,
and you shall keep it hidden [She is only to reveal it to Horus]."
So we do not get to know the name, but Re recovered.

In a sense every name is a secret name. For it expresses the
mystery of the imperceptible, spiritual reality of its bearer, of
his vital energy and power. Everywhere the idea is encountered
that the divine name is holy, just as God Himself is holy. We
can at least partially understand this, for uttering that name
signifies the causing of God Himself to be present. And this can
be dangerous for man, specifically when the holiness is primarily
conceived as the opposite of finite existence, just as the gaze of
God is thought to abolish finite existence. This is true of the
typical gods of the Mysteries, who are closely akin to the demonic gods. Herodotus does not dare to use the name "Osiris,"
but says, "the god whom I may not name." For Osiris is the god
of spontaneous life and of the other, absolute world – of death.
In Egyptian texts, too, Osiris is often called something else in
order to avoid the sacred name: "this great god," or some similar
designation. For the same reason the sun god Re on his way
through the realm of the dead is designated as "this god." The
Greeks referred to all the gods of the Mysteries in this way; the
Kabires, the Dioscuri, Demeter-Kore, etc., all were called *theoi
megaloi* or *theai megalai*. The seven Babylonian gods of a demonic
nature are also called the "great gods."

Similar ideas appear in the Old Testament and in the Rab-
binic writings.[19] It is said repeatedly that Solomon built his
temple for the name of Yahweh, which means, for his spiritual
image that here in our world is the bearer of His divine power
and essence: everywhere and always when God's name is uttered,
He is present. So we read in Psalm 33: 21 that Israel trusts in
His name – thus not only in the power, but also in the presence
of that power. And in Deuteronomy 25 : 58, we find the following:
"If you are not careful to do all the words of this law which are
written in this book, that you may fear this glorious and awful
name, Yahweh your God," then Yahweh will punish you severely.
Everywhere in our world where His name is uttered God is thus
present in His majesty and power.

And now an example from later Judaism.[20] In a commentary
on Deuteronomy 34, the death of Moses, the following tradition is
recorded:

> While Moses struggles with God for his life, God calls to the angels,
> "Close all the gates of every heaven, for the voice of prayer (of Moses)
> presses up powerfully!" They try to do so, but they cannot because of the
> voice of prayer. His prayer is like a sword that rends and cleaves in twain
> and is held back by nothing, for his prayer contains something of the
> unutterable name of God.

In this bit of magnificent Jewish imagination, in which power
struggles against power, God orders the doors to be closed so
that He will not have to listen to Moses' prayer, but the prayer
still penetrates, because it is laden with the unutterable name.
Like the image, the name contains the spiritual potency of its
bearer. He who utters the name has drawn this potency to himself and thereby caused God to be present. According to Heitmüller,[21] the goal of all Jewish Gnosticism was to become
acquainted with the true name of God and to use it in the right
way. The name was sought in a fantastic combination of twelve,
twenty-four, forty-two, or seventy-two letters. By the right use
of this name one could rule the world just as God rules the world.
It is in this context, too, that we should see the unutterability
of the sacred tetragrammaton *YHVH*, which was spoken as
adonai or, by the Hellenistic Jews, as *kyrios*.

This Ancient meaning of the name as spiritual essence, power
or authority is still alive – at least in part – in our expression,

"to speak or act in someone's name." This is an extremely old expression. It had not only the current worn down meaning of "by order of ...," but also meant originally, "with the spiritual power (soul) present of ...." He who thus speaks in someone's name is animated by the spirit and power of that person. In Deuteronomy 18 : 19 the prophet speaks "in the name of Yahweh." What he says therefore has the power of the utterance of Yahweh's name; God's spiritual power is present in his speech. In Jeremiah 26 : 20 it is said of Uriah the prophet that he prophesied in the name of Yahweh, which thus means, with the omniscience of Yahweh. In Micah 4 : 5 we read, "For all the peoples walk, each in the name of its god (therefore meaning, acts and lives in his presence), but we will walk in the name of Yahweh our God ...." Comparable to this is the phrase from Isaiah 2 : 5, "in the light (or law) of Yahweh"; this is the revelation of God in our world. And Christianity baptizes *eis to onoma Iēsou,* "into Jesus' name." [22] By this formula the goal and the effect of baptism is indicated: the baptized is brought into the power of the Jesus who is here present. The performance of baptism is described as occurring *en (epi) tōi onomati Iēsou,* during the naming of the name of Jesus: this is thus, once again, with the effect of the power which the Jesus who is here present possesses.

Origen holds to the idea that the name is the metaphysical designation of the essence, and says that names are not *thesei,* but *physei.*[23] They are thus not conventional designations of persons, but sharers and bearers of the essence. Whereas Celsus believes that it makes no difference whether the supreme god is called Zeus or given an Indian or an Egyptian name (thus putting our ideas above the names), Origen holds that we are dealing here with a profound and mysterious subject: the nature and essence of the name. The Stoics had earlier maintained the same position in criticising Aristotle. Origen considers it a fact that there are powerful names, for instance, among the Egyptians, Persians, and Indians. He does not see in so-called magic, as do the Greek philosophers, an art without a real basis, but rather a system which uses words which are only known by a very few people. When these names are spoken in accord with their essence, they possess a great power, which can also be used against evil spirits and evil influences. Origen then applies this understanding of the name to the names "Jesus," "God," and "angels." It is quite remarkable that Origen here advances against Greek enlightenment the Ancient viewpoint, which was also the ancient Christian view.

It is clear from all this that the name was conceived as the audible and spoken image of the person, which was taken to be his spiritual essence. In this last respect it is similar to every image. The idea of the magical power of the word makes itself felt in the conception of the name.

CHAPTER 22

PRAYER

Prayer is the most characteristic expression of religious life and the only religious act which takes place in all religions. In prayer man ceases all outward activity and enters into immediate relation to God: here the essence of religion comes to its purest expression. But just this central place of prayer in religious life raises peculiar difficulties for the phenomenological approach. Phenomenology has set itself the task of so grouping phenomena that they shed light upon one another and lead to a deeper insight into the essence of a whole group of similar phenomena. But prayer is not a phenomenon which can be easily observed. No religious act is so hidden and so difficult to evaluate as is prayer. The phenomena, which are the set forms in prayer, do not permit the motivating impulse to come so clearly to light, and they give more occasion for mistaken explanations than do the forms of sacraments, sacrifices, and consecrations.

The data are numerous enough, and they have been collected and classified by modern authors in overwhelming numbers. This is the case with Fr. Heiler.[1] The first edition, which appeared in 1918, was 475 pages long, and later editions were still longer. His work is certainly an amazing accomplishment, and it is one, moreover, in which the reverent attitude of the writer towards so many alien ideas makes a very favourable impression. Nevertheless, the overwhelming quantity of data sometimes causes more confusion than clarification. In such a quantity the material cannot be analyzed with any prospect of success. We want to know the spiritual factors which are active in all prayer, but faced with such extensive material, we must also have the courage, relying on a certain amount of intuition, to separate what is important from what is not. Then we must give our attention exclusively to the data which can reasonably well be approached and understood, and which therefore hold out promise of yielding positive results. In any case, we must avoid that besetting sin of ethnographic literature, the recital of dozens of similar instances where a single example is sufficiently clear.

Most writers in assessing and arranging the facts make a comparison based on their evaluation of those facts, and they classify the data according to the degree of development which they see indicated in them. That which is considered the least developed prayer is "the naïve prayer of primitive man" (Heiler), which is concerned only with security and outward prosperity. The highest type is that which is met within our own culture, which is generally called spiritual prayer. We must object to this kind of classification. All phenomenology is indeed based upon comparative observation. Phenomenology of Religion is the comparative study of the history of religion. But evaluative comparison does not come within its domain; that belongs in the provinces of philosophy and dogmatic theology. Phenomenology makes use of comparison only in order to gain a deeper insight into the self-subsistent, not the relative, meaning of each of the historical data. It wishes only to learn to understand the conception of the believers themselves, who always ascribe an absolute value to their faith. The construction of a history of prayer is obstructed by the fact that a separation between an unspiritual and a spiritual type of prayer cannot consistently be made; it is based solely upon external characteristics.

This fact is usually forgotten. We often consider prayer concerned with material desires to be simple and easy to understand. He who prays for good hunting, an abundant harvest, or a calm sea must surely have discovered that his prayer is often unfulfilled. Would not even primitive man come to realize in the long run that prayer is a useless means for exerting influence upon the course of nature? But it is nevertheless a fact that those discoveries do not cause him to abandon prayer; his conviction of its effectiveness always remains quite undisturbed. How is this to be explained if he is concerned only with the outward fulfillment of his wishes? This is evidently not the only important concern.

Prayer, even in its "primitive" form, cannot be compared to

a request addressed to a human being. Such a request is meaning-ful only if one can reasonably count on its being granted. Every prayer, on the contrary, is a religious act, in which probability is not calculated, because the external data are conceived in an infinite relation. Ed. Tylor gives many interesting examples of this.[2] In addition to the simple, "give me bread for today," which is surely not an unusual prayer even for us, there is also this other type (among the Algonquins): "Thou, you Great Spirit, have made this lake, and you have made us your children; you can now cause that the water shall remain smooth while we pass over in safety." Prayer is thus based upon the conviction that nature is subjected to spirit, the conviction of the spiritual source of outward phenomena. This type of prayer is found among the Incas in Peru: "Thou who gavest life and valour to man and woman, watch over them that they may live in health and peace." Human existence is traced back to its spiritual source; it is there that man's salvation must be found. The Zulus furnish another example. It is sufficient for them to pray to the spirits of their ancestors without stating what it is they want; the spirits know. Their prayer is simply, "People of our house," or "You know what is good for us, give it to us!" Socrates has said that we only have to pray that the gods will give us good gifts, for they know best what is good.

In all these cases, the basic attitude is one of surrender to and trust in the leading of the Spirit, who created and governs man and cosmos. Must this be called "primitive"? It is in any case clear how different this is from a request made of a human being. Even the denial of a prayer's petition has a mystical character.

Even in the simplest prayer present situations and possible future occurrences are conceived *sub specie aeterni*. They are understood not in their finite and causal determination but in their absolute determination; that is to say, as they have been willed and directed by an independent spirit. The man in prayer has won a victory over the world, and has realized in prayer his dependence on God alone. It is rightly said that prayer is born out of life's distress, out of man's sense of dependence as a finite being, and that its goal is liberation from this finite dependence. And, indeed, the dependence as a finite being is taken up in prayer into a new dimension: a dependence on the infinite, which contains all the finiteness of man and cosmos. Man withdraws to his spiritual foundation and there attains his true freedom; the world has lost its hold on him. This is the answer given to prayer; it is no problem for the man who is praying, but a reality which he actually experiences. It sounds paradoxical, but it is nevertheless true that prayer, even the "primitive" and most simple prayer, gives the one who is praying that power which enables him to be indifferent as to whether the calm sea or good harvest for which he prays actually results or fails to materialize. Definite favours are asked, but the observable fulfillment is not more miraculous than the lack of fulfillment, for in both cases the crucial point is the divine decision. This is the infinite, not the finite, determination of the event. The definite thing which prayer is about is really not "defined" or "determined," for it is conceived in its infinite determination. Thus prayer is always answered, but perhaps in another way than we would conclude from the words with which it is uttered. This explains why "primitive" man will never abandon prayer.

It is clear that at this point we touch upon the essential element in the religious relationship. Man does not resign himself to the superiority of brute force; in a deeper sense he is not dependent upon it. In all adversity he remains the innate victor. In the proud words of Pascal,

> Man is only a reed, the weakest in nature, but he is a thinking reed. If the world destroys him, he remains nevertheless its superior; for he knows that he will die, and the world does not know how it has triumphed over him.

Spirit is dependent only on spirit. And there are not two kinds of spirit. The absolute spirit who rules the universe is not a power confronting man from outside, but forms the foundation of his existence, stretching far beyond him and yet recognized as his own essential being. Recognized, but not known, for no one knows his own essence. This is the meaning of the thought which can be found in every prayer, even the simplest: we know not what we must pray.

In prayer man engages in his highest spiritual activity, for in prayer he realizes his infinite being. We must, to be sure, remember that the terms in which we express the mystery of the religious relationship can never be adequate (for example, if we say that the man in prayer asks for something definite, which is nevertheless not "definite"). But provided we keep this in mind, we may also say that man in prayer possesses supernatural power and divine strength. Everything, we read, which rises from man to God, prayers, thoughts and deeds, have a divine origin; it is not the human self but the divine in man which prays.

Thou, my Righteousness (which yet is not my own), praise through me (divine) Righteousness; Thou Truth, praise Truth (through me).

Thy Logos (spiritual essence) praise Thee through me; receive from me through the Logos the universe as a spiritual sacrifice (*logikē thusia*). Thus do the Powers (*Dynameis*) in me cry out.

The Logos, the divine wisdom and regulating power active in the one who prays, thus bring to God the universe which He has created as a sacrifice. The basic idea implicit in sacrifice (which is also the essence of prayer) cannot be more accurately expressed. Every sacrificial act is a realization and perpetuation of the sacredness of the offering; therefore the perfect offering is the universe, which reveals divine life in the broadest sense. This sacrifice cannot be made in an external way, but it occurs in a spiritual sense in prayer, because in prayer the divine determination of all events is, in principle, established, and in this way the sacredness of the entire creation is firmly inducated. The bond between God and man in prayer is also represented as a circular path: rays of divine light come down into man and rise above as prayers. "Thou life and light, from Thee comes the hymn of praise, and to Thee it returns. Prayer is not of ourselves, and yet it passes through us." With this we may compare Romans 8 : 26 f.:

Likewise the Spirit helps us in our weakness; for we do not know how to pray as we ought, but the Spirit himself intercedes for us with sighs too deep for words. And he who searches the hearts of men knows what is in the mind of the Spirit.

We have thus considered a few examples both of simple prayer for material favours and of preeminently spiritual prayer, in which prayer itself is a divine gift to man. As we consider the widely divergent forms, the question returns as to whether prayer has not gone through a great many stages and does not show a process of growth.

To ask this question, one need not have in mind an historical connection between the stages, with influences radiating from particular centers or persons. But cannot an ideal development be observed, in which we are fully aware of the creative but inexplicable power of religious life? Is it not true that the lasting significance and value of this religious act comes more clearly to light and is more clearly expressed in some forms than in others? The believer always takes refuge in the spiritual foundation on which both man and the world rest. Can the ideal development not be measured according to the degree in which this is recognized? Hegel answers these questions in the affirmative: history, including religious history, is a process of growth governed and determined by spirit. He speaks of the dialectical development of the religious self-consciousness, and this growth is reflected in the many stages about which history teaches us.

But there are also important objections to such a history of prayer. If only it could be stated in which forms the spiritual content revealed itself more or less independently and consciously! The spirit (or the idea) must always have a body; only in theoretical reflection can the two be distinguished. If we speak of the essence or the religious idea of prayer, we must nevertheless not forget that the essence or the idea is always hidden in a form. It is certain that where all attention is devoted to the essential core, as is the case in Hellenistic mysticism, reflection about practical life displaces practical life itself. There may be a one-sided "spiritualization" of religious life, which attests to religious poverty, although it may signify philosophical riches. Prayer for "daily bread" is never antiquated, and we should not say that it is a primitive or selfish prayer in one religion and a spiritual prayer in another. With equal justice it might be maintained that it is precisely the simple prayer for material goods which shows most clearly the superiority of spirit to matter. We cannot decide on the basis of the words which a man prays what is occurring within him; even he himself can give no explanation of it. The religious relationship is an inexpressible reality; no psychology or philosophy can penetrate the secret of the man in prayer. It is true that not every prayer is suitable for everyone, but in every prayer a miracle is prayed for or a miracle is assumed, and a miracle is, according to Schleiermacher's striking definition, only the religious term for an event which means an infinitely (i.e., spiritually) determined occurrence. Miracle is just as miraculous in the spiritual as in the material world.

The study of Phenomenology, therefore, provides no criterion for determining by comparison the religious value of the different forms of prayer. We must always try in our study to put ourselves in the position of the believer, because it is there alone that the religious reality is to be found which we wish to understand. But in that reality, prayer, or the trust which expresses itself in prayer, always has absolute validity, and absolute values are not subject to comparison with one another. Obviously the follower of one religion will always reject the prayer of adherents of other faiths. When that occurs, we are confronted with a religious reality which cannot be considered invalid. But it is just as certain that the believer does not see the true – namely the absolute – character of the alien faith, and this indeed is proved by his rejection of it. His rejection is a religious act and must be understood as such by the investigator. It is even true that in practice every religious man is always rejecting alien positions and points of view simply by virtue of the fact that he does not follow them. But the research of Phenomenology is not the practice of religion. The attempt to understand religious phenomena historically and psychologically is a reflective and intellectual activity, not a religious one. We can come to see the absolute character of particular religious data in an approximate way, but never more than approximately. And the absolute character of the data offers resistance to the construction of an "ideal history" of prayer.

There are numerous data which warn us against any evolutionary classification, whether historical or ideal, and against patterns which are forced on history and distort it. To mention only one point: in the realm of prayer the "highly" developed and the "primitive" repeatedly appear side by side. In hymns to such gods as Mazda, Ushas, Shamash, Marduk, etc., we sometimes see a glorification of wisdom, power and faithfulness, and protection of righteousness and truth – prayers which we would consider to be genuinely pious. Yet such hymns frequently turn into the most "primitive" prayers for material goods: "give us power, riches, swift horses, and all kinds of splendour" or "break the sorcerer's spell." Or consider this example in a Babylonian text: "May the tables of my sins and foolishness be broken, may I be pure for Shamash and live!" [3] Immediately following this, however, come the prescriptions for all manner of magical ceremonies, such as smearing sacrificial blood on the door and pouring out all sorts of objects for the gods into water basins.

O Shamash, King of heaven and earth, ruler of all above and below, Thou who makest the dead to live again, who loosest the bound [the sick, for example], unbribeable judge, leader of men, creator of everything in heaven and earth, break the spell by which the sorcerer binds my head, my right and left side, break the spell over my house, door, hearth, chair, ... etc.

All sorts of religious thought are expressed in symbolic word and gesture: reconciliation for the house, and similar matters. This is magic, but undoubtedly of religious content and essence. It is difficult and sometimes almost impossible to understand such facts, but we do better to recognize this difficulty than to judge the data with standards which are alien to the believer himself.

There is a kind of "magic prayer," namely the invocation of God in different religious acts, in which a certain compulsion is exerted on the god. It is usually in connection with a sacrifice or another religious rite, such as purification, whose external appearance exhibits magical traits; it is not a favour which is asked. No, "man has done his part – now God must do His part too." God must do it in order not to endanger His own existence, or in order not to deny Himself. The world would perish if God's word, His will and law, did not remain effective. To help us to understand this coercion in prayer, we may compare what Luther said after a crisis of deep personal significance: "God could do nothing else; the pass was cut off for Him." This religious assurance is also to be found in magical coercion.

But this "coercion" of deity sometimes goes even further: if the god is not benevolent, he is punished. In China such gods are degraded. Augustine mentions that in the first circus games

after the loss of their fleet, the Romans did not carry around
the statue of Neptune. After the death of Germanicus temples
were stoned and images overthrown. Fetishes are sometimes
chastised. It is difficult to understand such cases; the term
"primitive" by itself explains nothing. One wonders how anyone,
while maintaining his faith in the deity, can treat him so con-
temptuously; how does he then imagine his god? The remarkable
fact is that he does not doubt the god's existence, yet for an
instant he feels himself his superior. He believes that he is right,
religiously, in the conviction that the power of the spirit must
maintain itself and may not give way to the wicked and the
accidental. In a surge of religious self-assurance he corrects the
god. This type is pictured in such a vivid way in the Old Testament that we should hardly wish to call it "primitive." When
Job in his despair challenged God to justify himself concerning
his way of acting, he undoubtedly felt himself the superior. He
is brought to repentance, not by his friends, but by God. His
friends are not his superiors, and perhaps neither are we.

This step between feeling one's superiority and administering
punishment is not so very great. In the latter we see so easily
a grotesque element, but the matter undoubtedly has another
aspect, even though we are not able to fathom it. The remarkable fact is that the faith in a god who is so treated does not
disappear. Man comes to repentance and will propitiate his
god, as Augustus propitiated Neptune.

We find personification of prayer in Brahmanaspati, "the
lord of prayer" or of the holy word. He represents the infinite
power of prayer, because prayer is a divine word. He sings the
sacrificial hymns, repeats the prayers and pronounces the in-
cantations "in which Indra, Varuna and Mitra find pleasure."
Here there is really the conception that the government of the
cosmos takes place by means of "divine prayer." Brahmanaspati
places the "shining word" in the mouth of the sacrificial priest
who sacrifices for rain. Brahmanaspati does everything which
is otherwise ascribed to other gods; he becomes identical with
Indra, as victor in the struggle. Brahmanaspati is the infinite
cosmic power of the divine spirit which is active in the man ait
prayer. It is a quite remarkable hypostatization or personif-
cation of prayer, a remarkable view of the essence of prayer. It

is comparable with what was taught in the Gnostic circles of
Hellenistic philosophy about the divine source of man's prayer.
It is not I who pray, but the divine within me. Prayer is a gift of
God, a communication of divine power. Brahmanaspati is that
divine energy by means of which all the gods possess power.
Prayer is a god. It is remarkable in this connection that Brahmanaspati is a figure in the practical religion, a god who is worshipped
active in the man (priest) who prays, but also outside him as the
highest cosmic ruler.

Ludwig Feuerbach (1804–1872) tried to give a psychological
answer to the question of how prayer originated and how it can
be explained.[4] His basic thesis is that man's desire, need and
hope are what have created the gods; what man praises, glories
in or desires is for him "god" (and therefore all ideas of deity are
anthropomorphic). Whatever man rejects are considered to be
hostile powers, "demonic beings." God is a projection of the
human mind; God is created in the image of man, and not vice
versa; theology is anthropology. The gods are "Wish beings"
(*Wünschwesen*), "the wishes of men which are thought to be real;
that is, whishes changed into real beings." Prayer is an act by
means of which man tries to fulfill his wish, but the fulfilment
of a wish, as long as it remains a wish, is an illusion. Religion,
therefore, which is the objectivizing of man's own essence, "is
worthless illusion." If he loses his religion, man loses nothing,
since there is no new reality hidden for him in religion. This is
indeed a remarkable sample of a psychological explanation which
is extraordinarily unpsychological and in conflict with the experience of all ages. What leads man to represent his wish as a
fulfilled wish? To put it even more forcibly, how can he come
to feel dependent on a god who is merely a projection of his own
wish and thus is his own creation? These are psychological
riddles, not explanations. To say that men have always needed
"illusions" in order to dare to live is a witticism which points
only to a lack of real "wit" (in its old meaning of intelligence).
Who is to decide what an illusion is? And what weighs more
heavenly, a thousand years' experience or a theory about the
origin of religion?

CHAPTER 23

THE OATH AND THE CURSE

A. THE OATH

There have been many phenomenological treatments of the oath and the curse. Some encyclopedias are excellent for orientation: Hastings, *Encyclopedia of Religion and Ethics;* and *Die Religion in Geschichte und Gegenwart.* There are also a few older monographs, for instance, Rudolf Hirzel's *Der Eid, ein Beitrag zu seiner Geschichte* (1902), which is concise and good. There are also many treatments of the oath in particular religions, those of the Greeks, Romans, and Semites (Johs. Pedersen, *Der Eid bei den Semiten* [1914], 242 pages). I shall only touch on certain points which seem to me to be instructive.

Let me first mention instances in which it may well be questioned whether the oath is a religious act. The Teutons swore by their own beards, hair, teeth, hands, domestic animals, weapons, ships, etc. The ordinary explanation of this is that swearing by these objects and not by God implies that they are not religious oaths, but stem from the times when the Teutons "believed only in their own power." But then it must still be asked how that power was conceived. As a tutelary spirit, perhaps? And the objects – the hearth, the hand, the weapon, etc. – perhaps as bearers of supernatural energy? We simply cannot say with any certainty, and therefore we should not speak too quickly about the non-religious character of this act. There were Greeks and Romans who swore by the lance or the sword, and the Scythians did the same.[1] But since these weapons were emblems of the war god, the oath was sworn by the sign of the power in which success was sought. These people invoked the foundation and guarantee of their own existence and gave that as a pledge. There are, indeed, numerous instances which prove that whith the oath the entire life, the individual's existence, is given as a

"guarantee" of trustworthiness. At the initiation of the king,
the Brahman priest has the king swear the following oath:
"If I deceive you (in the promises to the priests), all the merits
of my sacrifices will belong to you, as well as other merits gained
by gifts to the gods during my whole life, all my good deeds
(i.e., merit for salvation), my life and my offspring." The proof
that his word is true, then, is this direct link with the highest
human value, with what is absolute for him and in him. The oath
is therefore not, as it is usually conceived, in the first place a
curse directed against the one who swears it in case he perjures
himself. Its purpose is not negative, but rather positive: his
utterance is inseparably bound to the foundation of life. Therefore it was probably always a religious act. This is true in Rome
of the oath sworn by the Genius (*per genium* = *mehercle*) and
by Juno conceived as the female genius (*per Junonem* = *ejuno*);
i.e., by one's own vital spirit, which was worshipped as a divine
being. This means that the sworn word is uttered, not by a
finite man, but by an infinite man, who is aware of the divine
being, the mystical reality of life. The stability of the word is
identical with the stability of divine reality, which continues to
exist forever. Swearing by one's life, by one's genius, is swearing
by a divine being. The Egyptian *ankh*, "oath," means literally
an "utterance of life," quite in the sense of the oath sworn by
a genius. The oldest oath formula reads, "as truly as God lives
for me." This means, as the variations make clear (cf. *Wörterbuch*, 1.202, and Gardiner's *Grammar*, § 218): "as truly as God
is my life (= my Genius)," to which is sometimes added, "and
loves me."

Probably this is the character of the religious oath everywhere. In the Vedas, "Varuna, and the cattle and water" are
invoked as witnesses. Like Varuna and the sacred waters, the
cattle signify the foundation of human existence. The oath thus
has a positive meaning, and not a negative one. In later times
in India the warrior swears by his horses and weapons, the citizen
by his livestock, grain, and gold, the Brahman by "Truth,"
the girl by her wish to gain a stalwart husband. All these things
by which oaths are sworn are instances of vital concerns, except
for "Truth," which is not an instance, but the divine reality
itself, which is the self-sufficient ground of all things. Even

today the Indian may swear an oath with the water of the Ganges in his hand, something which is a positive representative of divine life. The Greeks used the oath sworn by Mother Earth and by women bearing children, who, like the Genius, represent the self-subsistent vital energy of man. The oath sworn by the gods of the universal cosmic order is very characteristic: the word of the man who takes this oath is then in harmony with the universal order, the stability and intransiency which include the stability or sureness of the word.[2] Thus in the Avesta the oath is sworn by the seven Amesha spentas, "the immortal guardians of life." They are the cosmic rulers, the representatives of the seven (and thus of all) powers ot life: fire, living beings, metals, earth, plants, bodies of water, and also Ahura Mazda himself. They are the "unanimous ones," the "good rulers, who live forever and are forever fresh and powerful."

The number seven in the oath is also found in the Hebrew verb, *shābha‘* "to swear." That this really means seven can be seen from Genesis 21 : 28, where Abraham gives seven lambs to Abimelech as a proof of the truth of Abraham's word. Seven is totality, the number of the all-encompassing order. So too, to say something seven (or seventy) times, means that it is a statement which refers, not to finite reality, but tot the totality of being.[3] From the most ancient times, the Greeks swore by "the three gods," without mentioning any particular names, and this practice was according to the laws of Solon. Or they repeated three times the oath sworn by Zeus.[4] The explanation of this is quite certain: what the number seven was for the Semites and Egyptians the number three was for the Greeks: the sign of totality, especially in the context of cosmic order and universal law. The oath is linked to the gods of the cosmic order: the three Moirai, goddesses of fate, and the three at Delphi, the goddesses of destiny, who reveal the cosmic order in the oracle. And with the Greeks it is just as clear as with the Semites (especially the Babylonians) and the Egyptians that the totality (or gods of the totality) of three or seven signifies the divine reality in which opposites are united into absolute life. This is the reality of the other world, of the realm of the dead conceived as the world of absolute life. Therefore there is a triple Hecate, the goddess of the souls of the dead, the triple Cerberus,

or "prophet," inspired by the spirit (*mania*) of the divinity, and so too is he who swears an oath.

Yet the oath which the gods swore by the Styx is known not only from its occurrence in the myths. The oath sworn by the *Palikoi* (Palici) is of the same nature. They were the twin sons of Zeus, probably akin to the Dioscuri. They were worshipped only in Sicily in the region of Syracuse. Their temple was near the *Stagnum Palicorum*, a crater lake which was notorious because of the deadly character of its water and the sulphurous vapours which rose from it.[7] It was "immeasurably deep" and "horrible to behold"; it was, indeed, conceived as an earthly Styx water. The temple there was known especially as the place where the most sacred oath was sworn. The man taking the oath went down into the water and there swore the oath. That this water actually represented the water of the realm of the dead is clear from the fact that the temple was an asylum for slaves, who were there inviolable. The slaves, servants of the gods of the under-world (the Lares and Saturn) were there on their own sacred territory. The water of life was deadly because, like the Styx, it was the water of absolute life.

All of these facts (the swearing of oaths by Demeter, by the Styx, etc.) definitely establish the positive significance of the oath. This positive aim is even intended when the Ancients speak of the "terrible" character of taking an oath; it is the same "terror" as is present at the initiation into the Eleusinian Mysteries, where there was certainly no question of any threat, but indeed the following of a path with fear and trembling before salvation was attained. Zeus Horkios, with lightning in his hand, is the "most terrible of all the gods." As god of the earth, *katachthonios*, he is, like Themis, a god of absolute life. With his lightning and rain he makes the earth fertile, but with his lightning he also kills and consecrates to absolute life, the order of the earth's life. These are the terrors of taking an oath. The rationalism of the Classical "Enlightenment" was the first to see in the terrifying Zeus Horkios a threatening god and to equate his "sanction "with a punishment.

In Antiquity, "to take an oath" meant in most cases to conclude a pact between two parties or two nations; individual oaths were seldom taken. By means of the oath an absolute solidarity was created which excluded all selfish intentions; a relationship came into being which was incorporated into the stable divine order. Abraham swears a covenant with Abimelech (Genesis 21 : 22 ff.), and Isaac later does the same (Genesis 26 : 31). The covenant between Yahweh and Israel (Deuteronomy 29 : 12 ff.) is also a sworn pact between two parties that has nothing to do with the finite world. In Rome the ceremonial at the concluding of a sworn covenant clearly shows that the covenant was concluded in the other world. The leader of the embassy of the twenty *fetiales* was made a "father" (*pater patratus*) by being touched on the head by a piece of grass sod (cf. the custom of the Silesian Poles mentioned above) and by wearing the *herbae sacrae* or *verbenae*, blades of grass, as a sign of the earth's life. In his sacral nature the father possessed the creative power of the earth, which was at work in the realm of the dead; it was there that the secret of his essential being belonged, and so it was there that he had to take his oath. Moreover, he held a flint in his hand, the *silex*, Jupiter's lightning stone. For Jupiter makes the treaty a divine reality; he sanctifies it by his lethal lightning; i.e., by initiating it into the state of absolute life, just as the sacrificial animal is killed with the stone. This is *foedus ferire*, "to slay the treaty"; Jupiter Fulgur is Jupiter Fidius. We may compare the Greek term *horkia pista temnein*, "to slaughter," literally "to kill the stable (*pista*) sworn pace (*Horkia*)," and thus to make it absolute by killing the sacrificial animal. Theognis (1139, quoted in J. C. Bolkestein, *Hosios en Eusebēs*, p. 8) says, *Horkoi d'ouketi pistoi en anthrōpoisi dikaioi*, "and there are no longer any trustworthy oaths or rules of justice among men." So too, the Hebrew term *kārath berīth* which means "to cut a covenant," not only means to create a sphere of sacredness at the concluding of the covenant, but also "to kill" the pact, just as the sacrificial animal is killed (i.e., made sacred) at the concluding of the pact. When Jupiter *foedus fulmine sancit*, "consecrates the treaty by a thunderbolt," he removes it into a world of divine life and imperishable existence. Faithfulness is, then, not an ethical, but a religious concept; it is to join the order of constant life which belongs in the other world. The faithful one who keeps his oath is taken up into the cosmic order of abiding life. The covenant also has this signifi-

cance in the Avesta religion. Mithra, who together with Ahura
Mazda heads the gods, means "covenant, faithfulness," not only
in the ethical, but more especially in the religious sense, which
is to say, in the cosmic sense. It is the stability which is the mark
of the cosmic order, the order of the universe's life. The Greek
Themis, goddess of the justice and order which is expressed in
the institutions of Zeus, was a goddess of the earth. The stability
and trustworthiness of the *themistes* was the stability of the
earth's order of life.

This is also the religious background of *fides* in the sense of
"belief": the believer is taken up into the mystery of divine
life. He is an initiate just as is he who is initiated into the Eleusinian Mysteries. The ethic is a religious ethic; it is a divine
reality, also conceived as a cosmic reality.

The swearing of an oath is thus comparable to the initiation
into the Mysteries. It is performed in the other world as a religio-
magical act, and yet the parties to it, like the initiates, nevertheless remain in this world. It is different when the oath is
broken. He who has sworn an oath lives in this world in a state
of sacredness, just as does an initiate. The oath concerns definite
human relationships, namely the obligations imposed by the
treaty. If the oath is broken, these human relationships are
disregarded, and the man who has broken his oath has broken
his tie with society. But he cannot shake off the sacredness which
he has taken upon himself: that is a relation to God and not to
men. He remains sacred, but now outside the life of society.
He has put himself in the realm of absolute sacredness, the other
world: "God has then taken him to Himself." The breaker of the
oath destroys the earthly relation of the oath, and he actualizes
the oath's divine character, which is its supra-ethical and supra-
social character. He has sinned against society, not against God.
The god of absolute life is not bound by human treaties; the cosmic
order is not ethical in the human sense. He who breaks an oath
acts supra-ethically and supra-rationally; he acts as one insane,
that is, as one who has left the finite world. Well, then, he must
leave this world: he is struck by lightning. He is not "punished,"
but made sacred in the absolute sense; therefore not as the initiate in the Mysteries. It is known that criminals who were struck
by the lightning of Jupiter or Zeus were after their death wor-

shipped as sacred beings, just because of their death by lightning. The worship of the unfaithful Vestal virgin Tarpeia, who was put to death, can be explained in the same way. This worship was a fact which was cited by the Church Fathers as a proof of the inferiority of the Ancient religions. She was buried alive, which was definitely not a "punishment, " but rather a consecration; she was consecrated to the god of the underworld, whose consort the Romans believed her to be. By her unfaithfulness she had shown the courage to actualize her sacral tie with the god (represented by a human lover); by being buried alive she was delivered to her consort in the underworld.

Because of its religious rather than ethical character, perjury was not punished by the state; in Rome only the disgrace of the deed was openly established. The perjurer, who has put himself outside human kind, is *sacer*. Therefore the oath formula reads, "If I break the oath, may Jupiter and the other gods separate me from my fatherland, from safety, and from all prosperity" (*patria me expertem faxint*). He is outlawed by the state and is then placed outside the laws and the human order of life. It is true it was sometimes said that he was "punished" by the gods, or that the "punishment" was left to the gods. Humanly speaking that was true, but people also knew that *sacer* had nothing to do with human justice or injustice. Just like *sanctus, sacer* is a positive religious concept: "sanctified or "made sacred." This makes evident the clear supra-ethical character of the oath.

Naturally there is a contradiction present here in the concepception of the oath. By means of the oath an ethical value, the trustworthiness of a man's word, is incorporated into the absolute order of life, which order is then taken to be reliable in the ethical sense, whereas in a deeper sense it is not always ethically reliable, but is rather supra-ethical, since God Himself is of course not bound to ethical laws. It is the same contradiction as that present in the initiation into the Mysteries, for instance those at Eleusis, to which it is also actually closely akin. How can the man who has been initiated into the Mysteries share in absolute, divine life and yet maintain his own earthly existence? This actually is the contradiction which characterizes every religious relation; it eludes any conceptual understanding, but it is nevertheless a reality which is lived and experienced. The contradiction lies in divine sanction being attached to human behaviour (in the case of the oath: to the human order of life). But it is quite understandable that he who abandons human behaviour keeps only the divine sacredness. Whoever does that has – like the insane person – in full reality accepted infinite life.

All over Europe popular belief knows of many means to ward off the effects of perjury. They are the mystical and magical perjury ceremonies for the benefit of criminals.[8] A common type of such a rite is immediately to divert the false oath as if it were an evil spirit. One may, for instance, hold his left arm behind his back with one or more fingers extended downwards; the perjury then shoots immediately to the ground as if it were going down a lightning rod. In Thuringia it is said in such cases that the perjurer "swears into the ground." Another means is to open a window at the place where one took the false oath: this oath then flies out the window. If one intends to swear a false oath among the Jews, he takes care to do so on an old copy of the Torah covered with dirt. Since the law has really not been touched, the perjury is harmless.[9]

These are instances of superstition which have developed from faith, or which are a dead religious belief. The form or clothing of the religious belief continues to exist, whereas the content, the religious apprehension, has disappeared. The form is the conviction that an oath, in contrast with a simple agreement or promise, creates an extraordinary and dangerous state of affairs. In content the oath is a sacred act, closely akin to initiation into absolute life. The form of the religious belief can continue to exist when the content has disappeared. Such dead religious belief is the object of magic or quasirational acts; "one can do something with it."

B. THE CURSE

After what we have just said we need not enter into an extensive discussion of the curse as a religious act. A curse is directed against a person who violates a sacred institution, and thus corresponds to the negative aspect of the oath (which is of secondary significance). In most cases it is not uttered after a deed has been done, but in view of a possible action, and it is

thus a threat. A very common curse is against any who move
a boundary stone. The boundaries of the territory of a family,
city, or country are sacred, because they mark off sacred territories; i.e., territories belonging to various gods. In Greece and
Rome, boundaries were consecrated to the gods of the soil. The
Babylonians considered the earthly boundaries to be reflections
of heavenly boundaries and relationships; the boundaries of
Niniveh were inscribed in the heavens. The Roman *templum*
is similar to this; a city and even a camp were *templa*, marked off
according to heavenly relationships. Earthly localities reflected
heavenly relationships; the boundaries were not determined by
human caprice. The curse was also directed against the destruction of monuments, which testified to the activity of the gods
and were intended to last forever. Among the Arabs, the curse
was uttered against any who did not carry out the provisions
of a will. A "testament" was conceived as a decision or choice,
or as a witness[10]. All laws of human society can thus be conceived
as divine regulations and are then absolutely binding. But their
transgression is then also a supra-ethical act, and can therefore
not be punished. He who is *sacer* is left to God – that is the curse.

CHAPTER 24

ORDEALS

The "Ordeal" is a divine act of justice which is represented and actualized by the outwardly observable sacred rite. Its affinity with the oath and the curse is clear; the Sanskrit word *shapatha* means ordeal as well as oath and curse. By means of the ordeal it is decided whether an act or an utterance accords with the order of life, which is something only God knows. Hirzel believes that the ordeal, "May God make manifest my righteousness or unrighteousness," is the source of the oath.[1] This is not true; both are independent acts. It is mistaken to think that the observable religious rite, in this case the ordeal, must have come earlier than the more spiritual rite. Neither one is more understandable than the other.

The forms of the ordeal are extremely diverse. We understand best the forms which are not elicited. Pausanias gives an example when he discusses the temple of the Eumenides (Erinyes) which Orestes founded at Cerynea.[2] If someone laden with blood guilt or otherwise polluted entered this temple to see the goddesses, it was said that he immediately went mad. The Eumenides or Erinyes are spirits of the dead and are of a demonic nature: they can be either salutary or lethal, and they engender madness, because madness is the order of the other world. The ordeal at Cerynea thus means that the Erinyes point out the murderer by taking him into their own realm and making him sacred in the most absolute sense. All mad men, including the Hebrew prophets, were "saints." This act, too, has therefore nothing to do with "punishment." Madness is identical with death. But even as a judicial institution, "capital punishment" is not punishment in the ordinary sense of the word. Every punishment is relative and a matter of degree, but death is absolute. And so it is that

in capital punishment all moral indignation is translated into
the feeling expressed in the phrase, "May God have mercy on
your soul." In an ordeal such as the one at Cerynea, God judges
in the very nature of the case, about life and death, and not, as
does a human court, about greater or lesser degrees of guilt.

It frequently turns out that ordeals are undertaken in cases
of very unusual offences, when someone is suspected of having
detached himself from this world by performing some inhuman
deed, such as murder. In many cases a person suspected of perjury is tried by ordeal. In Greece the river Horkos, a branch of
the Peneius, flowed through Thessalonia; it was thought to
come from the Styx and therefore to be especially sacred. The
waters of the two rivers did not mix. Whoever was suspected of
perjury was thrown into this river, and if he was guilty, he drowned. This ordeal was also undertaken at other Styx rivers.[3] Hesiod
describes the same ordeal when he speaks of the gods swearing
an oath by the Styx. When a dispute arises among the immortals
and one of them lies, water is fetched from the Styx. When the
one who has committed perjury pours out a libation of this
Styx water, he falls for a full year into deep sleep and is separated from the gods for nine years.[4] Hypnos, sleep, is identical
to Thanatos, death; both signify a state of sojourn in the other
world. This ordeal of the gods is conceived in quite human terms,
with Zeus as the judge who has the water brought from the Styx.

Ordeal by water is very common. In these cases water represents deity; the sacredness of water is presupposed. Water
is "sacred" as the possessor of self-subsistent vital energy, and
therefore in cases of ordeal by water there is often some mention
of the water which comes from the underworld. Water is either
sacred as such or can be made sacred by certain ritual acts,
and can then be the suitable means for determining an ordeal.
The instance in Numbers 5 : 11 is well known. The woman whose
uprightness is on trial must drink water which has been mixed
with the dust of the tabernacle. This "sacred" water – in this
case intentionally made sacred – in which divine energy works,
will destroy her with dropsy if she speaks untruth.

The idea present in such cases is that sacred water kills the
person who violates the order of life; such a person has detached
himself from the finite world and put himself in the order of the

other, the infinite world. This is demonstrated and actualized by the water: it makes him sacred and takes him to itself, in the same way in which Jupiter or Zeus kills (makes sacred) the guilty person (not only the one guilty of perjury). This is not "punishment" – the offender has already made himself sacred; i.e., he has had the courage to leave this world.

But sometimes another view underlies the ordeal by water, and in these cases the ordeal is interpreted in the opposite way, though with just as religious a meaning. Whoever is guilty is not received by the sacred water, whereas the righteous person is so received. The ordeal is undertaken in the same way as in the cases already mentioned. The suspect is cast into the water; if he is guilty, he floats, but if he is innocent, he does not (which does not mean that he drowns). The water refuses to take the guilty person unto itself, because it is sacred and represents the order of life. In these cases sacredness is conceived in the same way as at initiation into the Mysteries, for instance those at Eleusis. Man can be made sacred in this life, or be an initiate who shares in divine life, which means that even in this life he possesses immortality. The ordeal is therefore just as much a religious act when conceived in this way as when it is interpreted in the entirely opposite sense.

This ordeal by water is frequently used at the trials of witches. The witch and the sorcerer have linked themselves to the other world in a fashion which abolishes human society. Witchcraft cannot be demonstrated by ordinary investigation; god alone can judge, and the sacred water is the means. When someone has been bewitched in Hadramaut (South Arabia), even at the present time, all women suspected of witchcraft are brought to a lake or to the sea and thrown into the water with a stone tied to their back: whoever remains afloat is guilty. This method was often used in Europe during the period when there were trials for witchcraft. Tylor reports that this was still customary in England in the seventeenth century.[5] The suspects were tied hand and foot, etc. A chronicler relates as irrefutable proof of guilt that the woman floated on the water like a goose and that she was dry as soon as she stepped out of the water. King James I (1603–1625) declares that "God has appointed for a supernatural sign of the monstrous impietie of witches, that the water shall refuse to receive them in her bosom that have shaken off them the sacred water of baptism." [6] Baptism is indeed an initiation. *Innoxii submergentur aqua, culpabiles supernatant*, is also ancient Germanic law, which however had already been abandoned as superstition in the ninth century. The statement of King James I proves that for him this was not a superstition. In Phoenicia and Syria,[7] we hear once again of the water of a river Styx. The gifts of Palmyra to Aphaka were entrusted to the sacred water, and the next year they were cast up again by whirlpools; by this ordeal the fall of Palmyra was predicted.

The same conception of the sacredness of the water which wards off offences is evident in what Pausanias tells about the little river Helicon in Boeotia. The river flows under the earth for four kilometers and then reappears. Originally it also flowed this distance above ground, but when the women who had killed Orpheus wanted to cleanse their hands in the Helicon, the river withdrew underground; it would not receive them.[8]

The custom of various peoples of holding court near a spring presupposes that an oracle can be given by the water. Genesis 14 : 7 speaks of '*ēn mishpāṭ*, the "well of justice," as the name of Kadesh (between Canaan and Egypt, south of Judah). It also appears in Numbers 27 : 14 and Deut. 32 : 51 as *mē meribhath kādēsh* the "water of dispute of Kadesh," "because Israel had disputed with Yahweh there" – we know, of course, that Moses had produced the spring with his staff. But it is probable, as Robertson Smith [9] says, that its meaning was originally the same as "Spring of Justice" of Kadesh; that is, it indicated the place where disputes were settled. The idea in the ordeal by water is that the spring reveals from the depths to the judges the law of the underworld (the realm of the dead), which is to say, the law of life. Every judicial act at a spring is related to the idea of the judgment or ordeal by water.

In the Avesta there appear the expressions, the "knowing water," and the water "which knows the lie."

Ordeals also take place by means of other sacred objects, by fire, for example. Whoever walks unharmed through fire is innocent, like the innocent man who does not drown. The Persians placed "red-hot metal on the heart," which felt to the innocent man like a pleasant warmth, but to the guilty man as a consuming fire. Later the metal was replaced by boiling milk. Among the Teutons, suspects had to walk over red-hot plow-shares. The plow was a sacred object in the cultus. When agri-culture was a mystery, as it was at Eleusis, it served to cause the earth to come to life again. It was related to resurrection, just as the customs of New Year and spring serve the prosperity of the fields and of men. And it was not only red-hot for the sake of the ordeal; in general, the plow must bring warmth. Related to this is also the ritual immersion of the plow, a custom which is still encountered at the present time. Ritual plowing was beneficial for animals and men. People jumped between red-hot plows.

In the course of time, and especially through change in religion, the religious character of the many forms of "ordeals" has prac-tically disappeared. These "ordeals" witness to a religious idea and have certainly developed out of genuine belief. They have thus changed from belief to superstition. They are convictions and practices which have continued to live among the people until quite recently, or even up to the present time, customs which exists in a Christian world although they have had a non-Christian origin. A good example, which happens to be entirely explicable, is a custom which can rightly be termed an "ordeal." [10] In order to learn the identity of a witch, the bit of a bridle is placed under the sill of the church door; if the witch crosses this sill, she will neigh. The assumption is that the witch possesses the nature of a horse, and therefore begins to neigh when she discovers another horse.

This clue to a witch's identity is based on a very ancient re-ligious belief. According to Ancient belief, the horse is a chthonic being. There is a widespread belief that the soul of a dead man appears in the form of a horse. (Cf. the white horses at Rosmers-holm, H. Ibsen.) The head of a horse is often drawn on the reliefs on Greek tombs. Since this is also done on the graves of women, this horsehead does not signify the horse of the warrior. The horsehead on the relief is actually identical with the horse of Poseidon, from the underworld (Poseidon and Demeter are also depicted as stallion and mare), or of Hades *Klytopōlos*. In Nor-wegian popular belief, the devil has one leg with a horse's hoof. "There comes the horse-hoof to light" is the Norwegian equiva-

lent of the Dutch, "monkey from the sleeve," and the English,
"Now the cloven hoof is showing." The explanation of this is
that the devil, too, is a chthonic being, and that he is therefore
also depicted with Pan's goat's foot. The witch, who is linked
with hell (the underworld), therefore has the nature of the horse
(the devil). There is a completely parallel example from Greek
antiquity. According to Hippocrates, Poseidon causes the insane
man to neigh like a horse. The church door proves that the consciousness of the religious character of the belief, the character
of the ordeal, has not disappeared. Among religious people there
are still many such magical popular customs, which have developed from religious belief, but it is sometimes difficult to
determine to what extent this belief is still present.

Then there is a large category of customs which are ordeals
at least in a broader sense, in which the verdict is determined by
means of an apparently accidental phenomenon, in which a
supernatural order is seen. Tylor and Bang also mention a
popular belief as to how to catch a thief.[11] A key is allowed to
dangle from a string while Psalm 50 is read aloud. The thief is
indicated by the direction in which the key swings when verse
18 is read: "When thou sowest a thief, then thou consentedst with
him." The oscillating motion appears to be entirely mechanical
and unspiritual, but this is really not the case, according to
those who take part in this practice. It is precisely what is
apparently accidental and irrational which is divinely determined.
The sacred text indicates the divine determination of the
accidental event. In most such cases there is not, as here in the
sacred text, simply an indication of a divine kind of activity;
Tyche and Bona or Mala Fortuna, the "chance," are seen as
divine beings. This is true in casting lots, which is actually an
ordeal or divine judgment, or in the casting of dice before the
image of a god (Gruppe, 982). According to Hirzel, Cicero speaks
of *Deorum Judicium*, to which *Sortis religio* delivers the one who
has drawn the lot.[12] We may compare with this what Plato
says in the *Laws:* people let a bundle of sticks fall and judge
according to the direction in which most of them come to lie.
It is precisely in the accidental that the divine law is seen, the
order grounded in the inscrutability of the divine governance
and omniscience. It is an entirely religious idea that there is

nothing which happens by chance. But whether such an act actually has a religious character is difficult to determine from its outward form. The important question is always: what meaning or significance does the person performing the act ascribe to it? It is certain that Tyche is a goddess, but is it an ordeal, a divine judgment, to decide something by counting buttons? Even that is possible!

CHAPTER 25

RITUAL PURIFICATION

"Purification" is in various religions a ritual term, whose meaning cannot be indicated by any better word. But it is true here, as so often, that its meaning does not correspond to any of our concepts, because the religious rite as such has become largely alien to our modern life and thought. It is certainly quite wrong to consider purification or cleansing in our sense of the word, which is an outward act, as the simple source of this custom. It is therefore just as wrong to conceive of the stains or impurities which are washed off in a material sense, "as if ritual impurity was originally something outward that stuck to the body." The "primitive" is then spoken of as a crudely sensuous conception of something which we consider spiritual. This explanation seems simple, but in reality it is quite incomprehensible that a man by an ordinary washing can remove a spiritual stain which is considered a ritual impurity. If this is a "primitive" rite, then primitive is only a name for something which is completely incomprehensible. If people would recognize this, they would not talk so lightly about the "primitive" and would certainly not introduce this term as an explanation.

Actually every ritual purification is an act which is difficult for us to understand and which we can only understand by a process of approximation. Ritual "Purification" presupposes that something evil has gained control of a man or an object, but is this something spiritual or material, or neither, or both together? Here is a common instance. Someone has become sick; a demon has gained control of him. By means of ritual purification he can become well, but the sickness which is here thought to be present is a mysterious reality. That is what it is for us, too, when we stop to think about it. Besides being visible and tangible, it is also invisible and incomprehensible in its nature. In so many cases, even we have to say that the illness comes and goes according to its own will and law. When ritual purification is required, a fatal spiritual and material influence is assumed to be present, the activity of a "demon." This can be expelled by means of ritual "purification," but what is spiritual can only be fought by spiritual means. It is thus not a profane cleansing, and if the emphasis is placed on its external effect of cleansing, the real meaning has certainly been departed from. Ritual purification is an outward, material act, which at the same time is spiritually active; it is thus an act whose effects range farther than is evident from the observable results. To this extent it is a magical act. Certainly it is not an entirely simple act which is easy to understand. "Purification" as well as "pollution" is of both spiritual and material nature.

The religious meaning of the purification is difficult for us to grasp. In our modern usage we are also acquainted with the "stain" or "taint," but in a metaphorical sense: "free of foreign taints" and "this casts a stain on his name." But this is not the meaning of the ritual act in worship, either; it does not remove such stains. It can be safely said that only those who themselves perform or undergo ritual purification know its religious meaning; for instance the meaning of holy water for the Roman Catholic. And if he speaks about it, he will speak in credal terms of a reality which for non-believers is not a reality at all. We, too, are among the outsiders who only by approximation can grasp the meaning.

We shall note a few examples of ritual purification.[1] Even at the present time the Brahman still prays in the morning, "O water of the sea, of the rivers, of the pools, of the springs, mercifully hear my prayer and vow ... may I find refuge with you in time of misfortune and forgiveness for all my sins ... cleanse me of my sins, and all other men of theirs!" Hereupon he dips a bunch of grass in the water and then sprinkles his head with it – his transgressions are then washed off and he is cleansed. The prayer makes it impossible to doubt the religious character of this magical act, which is of an essentially spiritual nature. Invoking water proves that water possesses a supernatural, divine power, and use is made of this power by means of the religio-magical act. If we call the washing away of sins a symbolic act, we at least bring out strongly its spiritual character. It is obvious that the stains of sins are only removable by a spiritual-material means, such as water. By bathing and washing with certain ceremonies the Creek Indians remove all transgressions which have been committed in the preceding year; this "bathing" and "washing" is certainly of a very special kind. Now we certainly ought not say that this is really just a rinsing. It is much better to call it "the symbol of the spiritual, supernatural, sacramental act." The same is true when there are no prayers or other accompanying ceremonies. Thus the Roman stepped over a fire after a funeral and sprinkled himself with water; water and fire remove the state of death, the "pollution." Such instances lead us to surmise the direction in which we must seek the explanation of ritual purification. People quite rightly see in the elements of life – fire and water – powers just as mystical as those of the sphere of death in which they have been, for no one can escape some sense of this reality. The important thing in both cases is the spiritual and imperceptible reality. We should conceive of "purity," not only as the negative concept of "absence of impurities," but just as much or even more as "being aright and full of splendour," for purity is the splendour of life; in religious language this is called, "to be holy."

The meaning of ritual purification is sometimes clearly evident by the regulations concerning the means of purification. Not any kind of water is suitable. Its effect depends on its degree of sacredness. Thus the water of the Ganges is the most excellent water for purification. The Ganges "flows through the heavens, the earth, and the underworld," which means that it is by the power of the Ganges that the universe lives. Every river and spring creates and sustains life; they are sacred "water of life," but it is the Ganges, above all, which bears the divine life of the cosmos. This is the characteristic of the water of purification in all the Ancient religions. It is not the water of the laundry or the tap, which in theory would cleanse the best. It is rather the divine, sacred water which is linked with the universal order of life. Thus the Greek stream or spring at Mycene is called the *Eleutherion*, the water "which brings salvation," and it was used "for ritual purifications and in the sacrifices of the Mysteries." ² In Babylonia Eridu's water of purification is called *Apsu*. It is Ea's creation water and comes from the underworld; it is thus in a special sense water of life. There was also the belief that a particular springwater only possessed purifying power at "sacred times": on certain days of the week (Thursday) and certain hours (midnight). We are therefore a long way from anything simple or easy to understand.

Frequently the water is deliberately made sacred, or its sacredness is heightened for purposes of purification. In India the water for lustration is consecrated by reading five particular hymns from the Atharva Veda. Or it is mixed with magical material possessing mana, such as salt. This is not done because brine cleanses better in the ordinary sense of the word. According to Numbers 19, touching a corpse requires purification by water in which the ash of a red cow is mixed. This cow is not here slaughtered as a sacrifice; the instance is evidently quite analogous to the brine. At an Indian wedding the remains of the sacrifice are put into water, which is then sprinkled on the bridal pair. This is clearly done to give them vital energy.

All these prescriptions point in a definite direction: the water used in ritual purifications is water of life; whether by origin or by consecration, it is the water which bestows life, and it is thus a means of purification which grants a positive vital power. In most ritual purifications the negative and positive effects are thought to go together. But in this case ritual purification is a "sacrament." In Babylonia, purity achieved by means of water is equated with purity resulting from the use of wine, honey, butter (milk), and salt: each one furnishes its own peculiar power. In the Avesta religion, grain is considered a means of purification. Grain puts to flight the spirits of the dead during the sowing, growth, and harvesting of the crops; its action is thus apotropaeic, but quite clearly because of its positive vital power. The Avesta gives another instance which is especially clear, even if it is not very elevating. The cow is the sacred animal, and the typical purification for removing the spirit of death utilizes the cow's urine. Purification is sacramental, not cathartic-apotropaeic. In Egypt, the liquid which is offered to the gods as a "means of purification" is the fluid which has come out of the body while it is being embalmed.³

The offering of incense, too, is the presentation of divine life in the form of divine fragrance.[4]

Other cases in which the positive, sacramental character of purification stands entirely in the foreground are the *Taurobolia* in the worship of Mithra and the *Kriobolia* in the worship of Attis. In these ceremonies the initiates are sprinkled with blood of the god's sacred animal. This is certainly a "purification," but it is not in this case a cleansing off of certain dangerous influences resulting from conscious or unconscious offences. It is initiation into imperishable life by means of the blood of the bull or the ram, both of which are representatives of divine life. In these ceremonies an impartation of divine life certainly takes place. The sacred rites in the Ancient Mysteries were certainly to a large extent such "purification ceremonies" with a positive effect. Eleusis, too, knew *halade mystai*. But this sacramental impartation of divine life in the purification of the Mysteries means at the same time a termination of the finitude of a man's previous condition; the old man is discarded. This previous condition is sometimes conceived as sin; the initiates are cleansed of sins, "sin" being taken here in the religious, not in the ethical sense. The initiate is saved from death (the negative effect), for to "sin" is the same as to transgress the divine law, the law of abiding and eternal life. Sin is death. There is only one possibility of "punishment" for sin, and that is death. It is self-evident that this negative effect of sin comes along with the positive effect, namely initiation into infinite life by means of the purification of the Mysteries.

The terms for "ritual purification" in some religions show that an act with a positive effect is meant. In the cultus of the Avesta, purification assumes an extraordinarily important place. The word in the Avesta for purification is *Yaozh-dā*. *Yaozh* is the cognate of the Latin *jus*, with the meaning of order. The Sanskrit *yosh* is "welfare" and *dā* is equivalent to our verb "do" or perform. (Bartholomae translates *Yaozhdā* as *heil machen*, which is thus to strengthen life, and this is what grain does.) The Hebrew word, *ṭāhar*, to "purify" or "cleanse" is only used in the ritual sense never in the sense of "to wash off."

It is not only by means of the divine sacrificial blood which ritually actualizes life that this quite sacramental purification takes place, a purification with the meaning of initiation into divine life. In various religions, including ancient Christianity, it is water which purifies, as the bearer of divine, spontaneous, and eternal life. This is true, for example, in the most familiar form of sacramental purification and initiation, water baptism. Since this subject has already been treated (in Cosmology and Anthropology), I should here only like to point out its ambivalent character: apotropaeic (negative exorcism) and positive (sanctification, and initiation into the Mysteries). Both are clearly distinguished and connected in the ancient Christian church.[5]

The first is liberation from the devil, and from the demons and their works; life in "sin" is transgression of the divine law. The sin which is "forgiven" by baptism is in the oldest liturgies conceived as *miasma*. It is removed by the baptismal water; this is the exorcism, but is naturally not a simple washing. The Coptic ritual reads:

> We pray to Thee, O Lord, for this servant ... may all *virtus contraria* be removed by this water and this oil. May every *magia* (calamitous influence), sorcery (demonic action whereby man is led astray from the finite and infinite law of life), and idolatry be destroyed.

Thus by means of baptism the devil is expelled.

But besides this negative effect of baptism there is the sanctification by the Holy Spirit in the baptismal water. Tertullian [6] says that water is *Divini Spiritus sedes;* the baptismal water is creative; it is indeed the water of Creation in the beginning. The *genus* (kind) is the same; only the *species* (appearance) is different. For this reason the Church Fathers called baptismal water the water of Osiris, i.e., the water of life, the Nile. There was indeed every reason for this comparison, for like Asclepius, Osiris was drowned in that water to rise again from it. With or by means of Osiris, man, too, rises from the dead, the reason why the dead man in Egypt is always called "Osiris ... (the man's own name)." And the Christian baptism by immersion is a dying with Christ in order to arise with him.

In the Christian church before the middle of the third century (thus in the time of Tertullian, who died in 240), there was no express consecration of baptismal water. The *Didache* (from about 100 A.D.) speaks only of "living" baptismal water, i.e., running water. Baptismal water should be running, because the

Ancient idea of "living water" (which is any water with creative power) continues in the impression made by running water. For this reason it was called in the *Didache*, living water. It is only later that we find rites for the express consecration of baptismal water, which correspond to the consecration of water for other purposes. The Roman Catholic Church formulates this as follows: "May the Holy Spirit descend into the water and through rebirth recreate man as a new being."

Baptismal water as a positive and negative means of purification is therefore both a material and a spiritual reality. It is God's dwellingplace; Tertullian calls it *Divini Spiritus sedes*. Apsu, the water of purification and of creation, is the dwelling place of Ea. God reveals Himself in His dwelling place; it is a sacred place. It is thus the revelation of God, or – God Himself. Osiris is not the god of the Nile; no, he *is* the Nile. In this idea we have an expression of the Ancient sense of nature, a sense which is difficult for us to share. But the basic thought is, certainly, that whoever is purified with water dies in order to rise again: divine life is revealed in and through death. In Egypt it is said that the dead man dies with the god of the dead, Osiris, in order to arise from the dead with him. The resurrection of Osiris is frequently depicted by having the figure of the god stand upright.

This view leads directly to the Ancient conception of expiation which was practically effected by sacred rites. The concept "expiation" presupposes a previous offence. If the *virtus contraria* (the *miasma* mentioned in discussing baptism) is a result of a certain particular transgression, the guilty person needs "expiation." The ritual purification becomes an act of expiation, sometimes linked to an expiatory sacrifice for sin or guilt, as in the Old Testament and elsewhere. The thought behind this practice is the same as the attitude towards perjury; by his transgression the guilty person has removed himself from the world of the living and violated society's order of life. He has had the courage to go into the other world, the world of absolute life. Expiation consists in his being released from his death. The rite by which this takes place is comparable with the initiation into the Mysteries, such as those at Eleusis: the divine death is carried out in the sinner, the death out of which comes resurrection, and so he returns among the living. By means of the sacred death which is ritually portrayed, his resurrection is assured. His offence is "expiated"; it is terminated.

A typical instance of this is the purification of Orestes after he has murdered his mother, Clytaemnestra. After the murder, the Erinye of Clytaemnestra has him in her grasp, which is to say that although he continues to live in this world, he has been drawn into the sphere of death. He has put himself outside the order of life by spilling the blood of his family, which is his own blood; his life has been cut off. Haunted by the Erinye, who is a spirit from the realm of the dead, he wanders about without finding peace; in other words, he is mad. Then he flees to Delphi to be purified by Apollo. There he sits down by the omphalos, the divine tomb, the realm of the dead, where life arises as it did at the beginning of time. Apollo purifies him there by means of a pig sacrifice, which is an expiatory sacrifice to the powers of the realm of the dead. This means that the mystery of death is carried out in him, for sacrifice is always a state of mystery: the offering, whether plant or animal, is killed in order to ac-tualize absolute life in the offering, which normally is the earth's life. At the omphalos Orestes reaches death which can restore life to him – both the positive and negative elements are quite clear here. Delphi is precisely the place for purification or ex-piation, whenever the demonic powers of death have gained control of man during drought, famine, or plague. For at Delphi the powers of the realm of the dead are worshipped, those powers which command absolute life. It is for this reason that the oracle, too, is there, which is the revelation of the cosmic law of life. Purification is therefore expiation; it is an act of dying in order to make the mystery of resurrection occur.

So too, the purification of Hercules after he has murdered his children and his guest Iphitus is by means of a sacrifice, but in this case one of a quite different nature. He must expiate the murder by serving in a foreign land. Employed by Eurystheus, he must serve Omphale, the Lydian queen. This means that he must go to the other world: Eurystheus is Hades, the Omphale is comparable to Persephone. The atoning purifi-cation takes place in death, and it signifies resurrection. The servant of the god of the underworld performs the work of that

god; he carries out the will and power of that god, and his service
is victory over death. This is expiation and purification of his
mortal sin.

Expiation presupposes a transgression, not in the ethical, but
in the religio-ethical sense. The transgression which puts man
outside of life is an infinite one. The expiation is not achieved
by means of good deeds and integrity, but by self-sacrifice, by
the abolition of one's own existence – something entirely different
from good works. Ethics becomes religion as soon as the infinite
character of ethical life asserts itself and determines the person's
attitude. The infinite, which includes both the moral offence and
its abolition, is a dying to the finite. This is expiation in the religious sense. The same thought is expressed in the baptismal formula about purification by water: "to be buried with Christ (the Egyptians said, to drown with Osiris) in order to arise with Christ."

We meet here with the same type of purification as we find
in the Mithra Mysteries. In them the purification is accomplished
by the blood of the bull which represents the life of the cosmos:
man dies with the god in order to rise again with him.

The character of ritual purification is always the same: it is
impartation of divine life. One more example is the sacrifice of
incense, which also occurs in the Old Testament. In Egypt and
Israel, the smoke of burnt incense purifies a chamber (in a temple,
for example) or an object (such as Israel's ark). And just as in
the case of the washing with water, purification takes place not
because incense has a decontaminating effect, but because it is
the bearer of divine life. The Ancients believed that the divine
being revealed itself in the pleasant fragrance.[7] The Greeks
speak of an "ambrosian fragrance" (odmē ambrosiē),[8] and the
Egyptians speak of the "divine fragrance of incense." Burning
incense means in the cultus the supplying of divine energy;
the sacrifice of incense actualizes the divine presence. Anointing
with sweet smelling oil or ointment is likewise an impartation of
divine power: Demeter anoints Demophon to make him immortal and holds him in the power of the fire. God reveals Himself in sweet smelling fragrance. The anointing of the king is
both "purifying" and divinizing. In the Egyptian liturgy ointment is sacrificed to the gods; this corresponds entirely to the
sacrifice of incense.

CHAPTER 26

SACRAMENTS

The term "sacrament" has a remarkable history. It was taken over in early Christianity from Roman religion, taken over, indeed, with complete awareness of the meaning which it had there. The Roman concept *sacramentum* was found suitable for expressing a Christian idea.

The ending *-mentum* after a verb root indicates the object or act in which the concept contained in the verb is revealed or actualized. It is the bearer and representative of the concept of the verb: *medicamentum* (*medicor*), *ornamentum* (*orno*), *pigmentum* (*pingo*, to paint), *monumentum* (*moneo*, to commemorate) *detrimentum* (lessening, damage, from *detero*, to wear out or break down). Thus *sacramentum* is the means whereby sacredness, the state of being *sacer*, is actualized. For the Romans it was a technical term with a very special meaning: the oath sworn on the military standard by Roman soldiers. The early Christians knew this very well, yet they nevertheless took over the term. But how could an oath on a military standard be called *sacramentum*, and what meaning did the Christians attach to the sacred oath on the standard, the *sacramentum*?

The answer to the first question is to be found in the religious character of Ancient war. War served to maintain the divine order of life against its assailants. Every enemy who threatened the state represented the typical enemy of divine order: uncertainty and unreliability, something on which nothing could be built, deceit and death. Every war was therefore a holy war, God's war for the defense of the order of abiding life. The Roman way of declaring war shows this clearly: Jupiter Fidius, the god of reliability and firm agreements, declares war through the *fetiales* (the *pater patratus*). It is a *pium* (*justum*, or *purum*) *bellum;* only

when the Romans were sure that they would be fighting to uphold the divine order did they dare to begin a war. Livy [1] reports
that in the second war with the Samnites, the Roman consuls
after the defeat in the Caudine passes offered to the Senate to
surrender themselves to the Samnites so that nothing would prevent a *justum piumque bellum de integro ineatur*. Only when the
divine commandments had been observed (the obligation undertaken in the declaration of war) could the war begin again. The
Roman general was therefore subject to priestly authority or
was himself a priest. Josephus says that his tent was "just like
a temple" (*naōi paraplēsios*), with the altar in front of it. The
camp was set out according to the prescriptions of the augurs
with the same two-axis orientation which was used in founding
a city: north-south the *cardo*, and east-west the *limes decumanus*.
As *triumphator* the general represented Jupiter himself; the
triumph was an entirely religious act, the triumphal arch representing the cosmic gate, etc. Therefore the *sacramentum* is the
oath whereby the soldier binds himself to the divine order of
eternal life and dedicates himself to upholding it. The oath on
the standard is initiation into the service of God. The Roman
oath, as has already been said, is always a mysterious act which
was consummated in the other world, and by it one is taken up
into the order of that world.

This was also the meaning of *sacramentum* for other Ancient
peoples. Cumont reports that the subjects of the Asiatic *Diadochoi*
(who "took over" the power of Alexander) consecrated their
entire life – words, deeds and thoughts – to their king by the
sacramentum of the oath on the standard. They were thereby
taken up into the sacred community of the state, like the soldiers
in the army. The army was the organized nation, which guaran-
teed the maintenance of order, and thereby of abiding life.[2]

The same meaning, or one closely akin to it, was possessed by
the *sacramentum* in the mystery religions. There too it was an
initiation into divine life, with deliberate application of the idea
of military service. According to Apuleius, the priest of the
Isis mysteries says to Lucius, "Inscribe yourself in this sacred
army (*sanctae huic militae*), whose sacrament (the soldier's oath,
cuius sacramento) you will later be asked to take." [3] In the Mithra
mysteries there were seven degrees of initiation.[4] The initiation

into the third degree, that of *miles* (soldier), took place by means of the *sacramentum* and by branding (*sphragis*) with a red-hot iron. This brand was also applied to the Roman soldier as a ceremony of initiation.[5] This proves that the military custom had not lost its religious character. The *miles* also refused to have the wreath which was offered to him placed upon his head; he wanted to wear it only around his shoulders: "Mithra is my only wreath," he said. Nor might he later ever wear a wreath, the sign of divine triumph and resurrection: Mithra had become his triumphant commander.

It is indeed remarkable that initiation into military service is so closely akin to initiation into the Mysteries. In both cases the *sacramentum* or soldier's oath had the meaning we have described. It cannot even be said which one of the two was the prototype for the other. For the Ancient peoples war was a sacred rite and the most serious act of religion. It contained the possibility of death, which was always considered the highest form of initiation.

To our minds the connection between religion and military service has entirely disappeared, because "war" has lost all religious meaning. In the time of early Christianity, however, the religious meaning of the soldier's oath was still felt, and the general still performed the traditional religious rites, and it is in this sense that *sacramentum* also became a Christian term. Life was a *militia Christi*.[6] Christ is the general, the *Imperator;* baptism, and especially the oath taken at the time of baptism, was the *sacramentum* whereby one was initiated as a *miles Christi*. Among Christians, too, (Minucius Felix in the third century is one instance) there is the prohibition against ever wearing a wreath, since this sign of triumph and resurrection may properly be given only to Christ.[7] According to Tertullian, who about the year 200 introduced the term *sacramentum* into Christian terminology, *sacramentum* is identical with *mystērion*, initiation into the order of divine life, a "mystery," like the sacrament of Roman soldiers.[8] Other military terms were also taken over: [9] *castra Christi, unitas sacramenti*. There was also the "stigma," the *sphragis*, with which the neophyte was "sealed." The sign of the cross was made on his head and chest, as it is still done in the Lutheran Church. (Cumont presumes that the sign was originally made with a red-hot iron). Early Christian baptism was a three-fold sacrament: immersion in water, sealing (*sphragis*,), and the utterance of the Holy Name above the baptismal candidate.

This contact of Christianity with Ancient religion, the mystery religions, and the Ancient conception of military service is worthy of our continued attention. It sheds light on the religious values in the Ancient religions – even when we keep in mind the different ideas about the person of the general: the Roman *Imperator*, Mithra, and Christ. The sacrament is always a *mystērion*, an initiation, as in all the mystery religions. It is certainly a misunderstanding to relate the *sacramentum* solely, or almost so, to the Mithra religion.[10]

The various "sacramental rites" in the Ancient religions are always acts whereby the believer is taken up into a vital fellowship with God. In many cases this takes place through the sacred meal, at which the sacrificial animal, which is the representative of God, is eaten in common; this is a direct initiation into the life of the god. Julian calls this sacrifice a "mystical" sacrifice (*sacramentum – mystērion*).

The sacramental meal was also observed by the Ancient Mexicans.[11] They made an image of the god Huitzilopochtli out of dough and honey, presumably because he was the god of vegetation. In 1590 de Acosta reports that all the participants had wreaths of corn stalks and that the image sat in a hut made of corn. Around the image stood other objects of dough; they were the bones and the flesh of Huitzilopochtli. The image and the other objects were killed with a lance, after which they were divided and eaten; the King received the heart. De Acosta relates that "with tears they received the flesh and bones of their god, with a fear and emotion remarkable to behold." This was called, "the killing of Huitzilopochtli in order that his body might be eaten." Before the sacred rite there was a fast.

There are numerous instances of the spirit of the grain being sacramentally eaten in bread or beer. The sacramental eating of bread and water or wine also occurs in the worship of Mithra.[12] This is often done by the god himself, as the last act of his life. It is uncertain whether there is a Christian influence at this point, since we only know this custom from the third century A.D. The sacrament of the bread and water of eternal life forms the close of his life. But in the worship of Mithra this meal of the god is also the meal of the believer, who we know shares the life of his god. Justin and Tertullian state that "sacred formulae are uttered to consecrate this food." This mystery was only for those initiated into the higher degrees (called *metechontes* because the name for the fourth grade was "the lion"). In the Avesta religion, only the priest drinks the Haoma juice. At this most sacred sacrament and mystical sacrifice, this mixture of wine, water and milk gives life to the gods of the universe. Unlike the sacrifice of the mass in the Roman Catholic Church, all the members of the congregation are here supposed to be present.

CHAPTER 27

SACRIFICE

The best known conception of the essence and aim of sacrifice, and one which is still very widely held, is the "ethnographic theory of sacrifice." It was set forth in exemplary fashion by Tylor.[1] The clarity of his presentation and the simplicity of his explanation are the reasons why his view is still the prevailing one.

The plan of his presentation is as follows: he first tries to investigate what sacrifice was originally, and he uses ethnographic materials for this purpose; then he seeks to determine what sacrifice has become. All investigators of the origin of sacrifice give the same answer to his first question: sacrifice is originally a quite comprehensible act, just as comprehensible as the other relations between superiors and subordinates among men. God is the great Lord who must be served by deed, by the sacrifice which is offered. To the second question Tylor answers that in the course of religious history the intended goal as well as the act itself have been more or less altered by the special and more spiritual conceptions concerning the essence of deity and of man. They are also often put in a haze of mysticism, but they nevertheless always remain alterations of the original idea. His quarrel with most theologians is that they only pay attention to the altered spiritual conceptions and disdain to understand these mystical ceremonies in the light of the ethnographic data, although they are "the simple and rational interpretation."

Tylor distinguishes between three different motives in the origin of sacrifice: gift, homage and abnegation. The "Gift" is an ordinary present to the gods, which is done with the (more or less conscious) feeling that the giver thus brings the receiver into a relation of dependence. This is the primitive meaning of the

gift (according to Tylor): the giver obligates the receiver and so
is superior to him. Van der Leeuw, too, makes use of this basic
idea of the motive for sacrifice. Homage is honour which is manifested by bringing tribute. Abnegation is the motive for the gifts
which are not made to enrich others, but to impoverish oneself.
This is a need which has also always existed in ordinary society:
he who can give up his own possessions strengthens his feeling
of superiority and causes others to believe in it. These are, according to Tylor, the rational sources of the various types of
sacrificial acts, however shrouded they sometimes may be.

The popular view still assumes that the basis of the explanation
is to be found in the simple origin, which is then thought to have
been discovered among primitive peoples. This is the ethnographic interpretation. It has already been shown why it is
an illusion to hold that ethnographic religious data are easy to
understand. Tylor believes that the idea *do ut des* (I give so that
thou wilt give) is at the basis of every sacrifice, even the sacrifice
of homage or abnegation. There is certainly no mystery in this
idea.

On the West coast of Africa, the Negroes sacrifice to the sea a
jar of palm oil, a bag of rice, a piece of cotton cloth, or a bottle
of brandy, so that the sea will be calm the next day. This is,
like the horse sacrifice that Hannibal offers to Poseidon, the
prototype of sacrifice. Now we should not say, "Anyone can
understand that sort of thing," but should rather recognize that
this conception of the African Negroes is not at all comprehensible to us. Such a practice is related as an amusing example
of naïvety, and is told in a ponderous, scholarly tone, but those
people do this in complete earnest! Now it is precisely this which
needs explanation. We have a great deal of difficulty in putting
ourselves in the state of mind of those Africans; they see with
different eyes than we; the sea is for them a different reality than
it is for us. It is foolish to say that their action is easy to understand. Hannibal's act is actually easier for us to understand, for
the Ancients have provided us with extensive information about
Poseidon. He is a divine person of whose character we can form
at least an approximate notion, and we know why horses belonged to him. And as far as the "understandable principle"
do ut des is concerned, it is certain that this view is present in

every sacrifice. But – a god is never a man, and an immaterial being cannot give or receive an object in the same way that a man can.

Tylor says that "primitive man does not think about the question of how his sacrifice is received." [2] This is probably true, but it is precisely this which we cannot understand. "Only the ethnologist asks about this." That, too, is true: he asks, and he gets no answer. Sometimes, to be sure, interpretations of the natives themselves are cited; they then prove to be very ordinary: "The spirit really accepts the gift, just as a man would," etc. We may, however, not forget in this connection that in all religions, not excepting Christianity, the believers often give rationalistic explanations of their own religious ideas and rites. This happens especially when they are questioned about them or themselves begin to reflect on them. The explanations which they give then do not correspond in the least to their real religious attitude, because that cannot be grasped by any interpretation. The believer can then say and also believe that he is precisely describing his attitude – but it is nevertheless true that the religious reality is always inexpressible. He is a rationalist in good faith, but we deceive ourselves if we think that his religion is rational.

The sacrificial act does not become more comprehensible if we get fairly well thought out answers to the questions of how the sacrifice is received. "The god takes over only the "soul," "life," essence, air, or fragrance of the sacrifice." [3] This may be true, but to say this is, in any event, to deny the simple character of the sacrificial act. For what man takes over the soul of a gift?

It should not be forgotten that the relation between man and deity is different from the relation of one to another, and everywhere and always, it is a relation of a mystical kind. There is no thought here of a simple exchange of services. The believer always knows that the god can and may do what he wishes and that man, in the final analysis, is powerless. This is the religious feeling, or at least an element of it, in religious sacrifice. It is for this reason that it is so wrong to say that the sacrificer is only doing what he might do for another man. If it is said that he acts as he would towards a despotic prince, the comparison is sometimes fitting, since the prince is often a divine being, and it is therefore conceivable that the gift gains the character of a sacrifice, and that an irrational return gift is expected, in the form of health, prosperity, or the like.

What Tylor neglects is the nature of holiness, which causes every sacrifice to be seen as a religious and not a profane act. Sacrifice is always a sacred and therefore a mystical act, because of the relation between man and deity (or spirit). The offering, at the moment at which it is offered, is not an ordinary gift, but rather always a gift which corresponds to the essence of the god. And this essence is actualized in religio-magical fashion by the sacrifice. The offering becomes a sacred object at the instant that it is sacrificed. In those cases where the relations are at all clear to us, we shall see how this quality of sacredness is expressed.

There are two works on sacrifice, which although they do not inform us completely about it, are really excellent and have become classics. One is Robertson Smith's treatment of the subject which presents the totemistic theory of sacrifice.[4] The other is Hubert and Mauss,[5] which is based especially on Indian and Hebrew data. They present important expositions of the religious motives which can be recognized in sacrificial rites. Several years later comes a large volume by Alfred Loisy.[6] It seems to me that this is not a work of great originality. In design it is comparable with the work of Heiler,[7] but without that respect for the subject which is so striking with Heiler.

A. THE OFFERING

What is sacrificed? Both very broad and very particular specifications of offerings are encountered, and both are equally characteristic. Babylonian texts give the following specifications:[8] "I bring (as a sacrifice) to Marduk (Esagila) the riches of the four regions of the earth, the abundance of the seas, the luxuriant growth of the mountains and plains." In another text it is said, "food and drink and all the produce of the land." A remarkable Babylonian description of these offerings is as "the children of Anu (the sky god)." This means all the things which Anu protects and keeps alive as well as the things which he has brought forth ("who has created all things"). We may compare with this the statement that "every man is a child of his god," which is to say that he is brought forth by his individual god and stands under his protection. This individual god is something like the individual genius who enables man to live. Man's life is a divine energy which animates and protects him.

This idea is applied to the offering: what has been created by God and lives by the power of God, or manifests divine life, may serve as an offering to God. We may safely consider this as a very broad, yet very significant definition of the sacrificial "offering." It is truly an important contribution to explaining the essence of the offering: life from God is a divine gift, which by means of the sacrificial rite is given back to God. Sacrifice is the recognition and actualization of divine life in the world. The finite, perishable, and accidental character of the offering is overlooked; it is made sacred by the sacrifice, because it was potentially sacred. Sacrifice is *sacrificium*, making sacred. It is not certain whether *sacri-ficium* originally meant "making sacred"; it may also have had the general meaning of "sacred act." (Cf. *artificium*, which meant artistic act, art, or skill.) But in that case it would be strange that only sacrifice was called *sacrificium*, and not other sacred acts, such as invocation or prayer, the celebration of a religious festival, etc.

This meaning of the term enables us to explain a number of particulars, for instance why the Babylonians repeatedly sacrifice twelve (sometimes twenty-four or thirty-six) loaves of bread to Anu, Ellil, or Ea. They correspond to the twelve signs of the zodiac. The offering is thus related to the entire sphere of the god's power, of his universal governance and the life of the cosmos. By means of this sacrifice the universal character of divine life is recognized and dramatized in a religio-magical way.

In Egypt there is the same idea of sacrifice. The very ancient Shabaka text discusses Creation (the origin of life) by the Word.[9] According to this text, Ptah is the creator, and thus the earth's life. The first creatures are the spirits of life, the Ka's, divine vital energies which are comparable with the Genius and the Juno. The Ka's make "all foodstuffs and all offerings"; they themselves *are* the "foodstuffs." Offerings are foodstuffs conceived as the original bearers of divine life. In sacrifice, the divine life which is present in the empirical world is offered to the gods and returned to them. As a sacrifice to Ptah, the loaves of bread are depicted on his altar. They are the life which has been created by Ptah himself, the substance by means of which the gods live. This same thought is also put in a different way: every offering, whether food, drink, ointment, or something else, can be called the "eye of Horus," and again and again is so named. This is only understandable when we know that the "eye "means the seat of life. Horus frequently stands for deity in general, so that the term "eye of Horus" means "divine life." The sacrificial act is therefore the consecration of the offering, the act of conveying it into the divine world where it belongs. It is the actualizing of its imperishable nature, the perpetuation and strengthening of life on earth, of the resurrection of life.

The same idea is involved in the Egyptian sacrifice of Ma-a-t to the gods; the king passes the sign of Ma-a-t to the god. Ma-a-t is the divine order on the basis of which man and cosmos exist. Thus it is universal life which is the offering to God; the divine essence of the sacrifice is recognized and actualized because it is presented to God. The Ma-a-t sacrifice is the last of a series of particular sacrifices; it sums up all that has preceded it.[10]

But these ideas are also present in other religions. In the Avesta religion the Haoma offering is the only sacrifice, but it is not simply a primitive survival. This rite is rather extremely characteristic of the entire religion of the Avesta. The same or a similar drink is the most important offering in Vedic religion. This Soma is the juice of a particular plant, which probably was intoxicating. Haoma and Soma are the "water of life" in the universal sense, the typical bearers of divine life. They are comparable with Horus' eye and the offering of Ma-a-t. The entire sacrificial book of the Avesta, the *Yasna*, consists of the ritual of the Haoma sacrifice, and the entire ninth book of the Rig Veda is devoted to the Soma sacrifice.

The primary religious meaning of these offerings is unambiguous: they are the perceptible bearers of divine life. The offering is a confession of faith, a participation and cooperation in divine life. Here we have very ancient religious formulations of what the believers themselves (rather than we) understood by "offering," for in these cases the offering represents all offerings. The formulations are not answers to questions which have been asked, and they have thus been written without a rationalistic intention. This is an historical and reliable starting point for a good understanding of other offerings. The origins which lie even further back are not historical, and looking for them is just speculation; they do not interest us at all. Only a person who does not know or understand reality inquires about such fictions as "origins."

The particular offerings are all particular illustrations of the principal theme. A libation, for example, is one of the common offerings; water is poured out before the god or upon the altar. This sacrifice really illustrates very clearly how nonsensical is the theory that a sacrifice is an ordinary gift – even a gift in the primitive sense. The water offering is based on the idea of the sacred water of life which possesses creative energy and autonomous life, but not in the broad or universal sense of Haoma and Soma. But it is indeed considered to be the bearer of the life of plants and of the earth's life in general, and further as the drink by means of which the gods live in the same way that men do; or rather, the drink *in* which the gods live. Water is their life, and therefore it is presented to them as an offering, and its sacred essence is actualized. It is thus that the water sacrifice to Osiris on the island of Philae is to be understood: Osiris is the Nile. Water as a sacrificial offering is water which is consecrated (*sacrificium*) as water of life – comparable with the food which in the food sacrifice is "food of life," often conceived as the bearer of the earth's life.

The libation is frequently a part of the cult of the dead. In those instances where the meaning is more precisely indicated, it turns out that the water of life is meant. In Egypt, the water of Osiris is called the cool, fresh water "which gives eternal youth." [11] The common explanation, that souls are always thirsty ("the thirsty souls"), is a rationalistic explanation of the libation in the cult of the dead. Why should souls be so thirsty?

Other particular offerings are the various animal sacrifices. The meaning of the bull is sometimes indicated very clearly. The sacred bull is "the bull of the earth," the representative of the mystical, self-renewing, and creative life of the earth. At the Bouphonia at Athens bulls were led around the altar for Zeus Chthonios; the bull which ate any of the grain on the altar was sacrificed. According to the myth, at the first Bouphonia the direct result of this bull sacrifice was famine, which only stopped after repeated sacrifices. This is certainly striking, but it is nevertheless quite understandable if we pay careful attention to the meaning of the offering. The bull of the earth's fertility had been sacrificed (killed), and thereby the earth's life was killed, and this death caused the famine. But the bull was dead in order soon to rise again. In the Roman religion, too, the sacrificial bull is the representative of the earth's life. Its power lies in its horns, which, as in Crete and Egypt, are called the "horns of the earth." The horns of the sacrificial bull and its forehead between the horns are decorated with ribbons (*infula, tainia*) in a way which shows that the bull is initiated, just as the *mystēs* at Eleusis is initiated by means of the *tainia*. They correspond to the sign in the hand of the person who offers the sacrifice to the earth gods ( ). In the Mithra religion, too, the bull is a sacrificial offering; there it is the cosmogonic bull conceived as the bearer of universal life. Gestating cows (*fordae boves*) were sacrificed to the earth goddess Tellus; the same idea is present here.

It is a standard rule in all religions that the animal or object is sacrificed to the god which it represents. Wild animals are sacrificed to Artemis and horses to Helios; they are their "sacred animals." The connection between the offering and the god is also evident from the sacrifice of the first fruits of the harvest, in which the god of vegetation reveals himself.[12] The particular offerings illustrate the character of the general offerings. That in which divine life is revealed is given back to God; by means of these things He lives, just as a person lives by food and drink, because he lives in them. The divine nature of life on earth is by means of sacrifice recognized, actualized, and established. By sacrifice the life of nature and man is assured (which means that God's life is assured, too). This is *sacri-ficium*, the consecration. The offering is sacrificed because its divine nature is recognized. The offering is an object which is conceived *sub specie aeterni* by the religious sense of nature; it is a testimony of faith.

Now the fact that the offering is really sacred has led to peculiar but very characteristic views, namely that the sacred is "impure" and unfit for common use. It is, then, primarily the "unclean" animal which is used as an offering. The Syrians considered the fish unclean because it was the sacred animal of Atargatis.[13] Her nature was present in the fish, who was therefore conceived as the lord of the sea and thus of the realm of the dead. Fish were unclean and might not ordinarily be eaten, but fish were sacrificed every day to Atargatis and after that eaten by the priests in a mystical, sacred meal (comparable to the Lord's Supper). In this way they came to share in the divine power. But more about this later. The (unclean) dog, too, who was the animal of the underworld, was sacrificed to Hecate, the goddess of the underworld, and even eaten. This is still in accord with the nature of the ordinary offering. But the relation between the offering and God becomes remarkable when it is said – and rightly said – that the offering represents the god's enemy. For this means that God's enemies are sacrificed to him.

It is not surprising that later interpreters, for instance Greeks such as Plutarch who write about Egyptian religion, explain this as a sacrifice of vengeance: the enemies are punished. Nowhere has there ever been a sacrifice of vengeance. According to Reinach,[14] the Syrians believed that the wild boar is unclean; it is the enemy of Aphrodite (and Adonis) because it had killed Adonis. But once a year boars were sacrificed to Aphrodite. Nevertheless, this was not a "sacrifice of vengeance." The believers knew better. Adonis is the dying and newly arising god of vegetation; he has to die. The wild boar is the death aspect of Adonis. The dual nature of the god of absolute life causes him to be conceived as a pair of gods, Adonis-boar, one of whom "kills" the other. The death of Adonis is remembered in the cultus with wailing; death is conceived as a hostile power. But in reality, the "murderer" is none other than the god himself. The boar sacrifice to Aphrodite is a mystery sacrifice, in which the offering is the representative of the god who had died. Death is offered to the god as his divine being; death is consecrated into absolute life. Thus the mystery of death is consummated. At Harran in Syria, the pig is not only sacrificed, but also eaten at the sacrificial meal; this is the mystery meal to transfer the *virtus* (potency) of the divine death to the believers.[15]

Thus it is frequently said that the offering is the enemy of the god. Plutarch [16] says that "among the Egyptians the offering is *ou philon tois theois, alla tounontion* (enemy); it consists of the bodies of animals into which the souls of ungodly and unrighteous men are transformed." And he writes in chapter eight, "they consider the pig *anieron* (unholy); whoever eats of its meat becomes a leper.[17] Only on certain special occasions, such as at full moon, is the pig sacrificed and eaten." The pig and also the black cow are the animals of Seth, who has killed Osiris. When they are nevertheless sacrificed to Osiris, Plutarch calls this revenge on Seth. This is not the case. Seth has killed his brother Osiris, but death belongs to the essence of Osiris, since he is god of absolute life. Osiris-Seth or Horus-Seth is a double god, just like Adonis-Boar. In the Egyptian texts, too, we read, "I sacrifice to your enemy" (*ou philon theois*), but that the word "enemy" should be taken in the mystical sense is evident from the sequel to this sacrifice. The hide of the black cow which has been sacrificed was put around the image of Osiris, in order that Osiris might come to life out of the hide. This is ritually portrayed by taking the image out of the hide. Seth was then forced to deliver the god who had been killed, i.e., to cause him to rise again from the dead. The "enemy" Seth, was also a god who was worshipped, though, to be sure, one of a demonic nature. This is something different from an "evil spirit," which is simply kept at a distance. Demonic nature implies that the god is characterized by death, which even when it signifies absolute life, is feared by men.

The instances in which the offering is preferably a ritually unclean (and thus sacred) object, such as the fish for Atargatis and the swine for Adonis-Aphrodite, may be relatively few, but they nevertheless show very clearly the irrational and religious character of sacrifice. There isn't a thought of "gifts" in the ordinary sense of the word. Precisely that which is dangerous for man is offered to the god, and this is that which represents divine life and not ordinary human life. The infinite character of divine reality transcends the finite character of human life and translates human life into a higher, divine dimension.

This irrational character of the relation between giver and receiver is also sometimes especially clearly expressed in the opposite relation, namely when the gods are presenting gifts. We

should remember in this connection the remarkable myth of
Pandora. Like Kore, the consort of Hades, she is the earth
goddess who brings to men all the "gifts of the earth": the riches
of the earth in vegetation, grain, etc. But Pandora "deceives"
men; she brings as much misfortune and death to men as she
does life. The meaning of this myth is that all the gifts of the
earth are characterized by the divine life of the earth, by absolute
life. Divine gifts which manifest the characteristic mark of a god
are always sacred and thus dangerous gifts. Prometheus knows
this; he does not accept the divine gifts, but sends them back
to the gods. In the case of Pandora's gifts, men speak of deceit,
because they are so shortsighted as to misjudge the true nature
of life. When death reveals itself, they cry that they have been
deceived; they had not intended to accept death along with life.
They do not want death, although it is necessarily linked with
life.

Applying this notion to sacrificial offerings, we see that all
divine gifts, like those of Pandora, which are presented as offerings, are sacred and dangerous for men. Ritual prescriptions
are repeatedly given concerning the precautions to be taken when
for instance, sacrificial meat is to be eaten, so that eating this
non-profane food would induce no misfortune. This is also true
in Hebrew religion. In short, the mystical nature of the offering
is present not only in cases when people speak (from the human
standpoint) of "enemies of the gods." These instances only
illustrate in especially lucid fashion what is true of every offering.
"All gifts" (which is what *Pan-dora* means) of the gods are
bearers of absolute life, and therefore also bearers of death. The
myth of Pandora was, however, always mistakenly interpreted
by the rationalistic Greeks to mean that woman had brought
misfortune into the world.

The Egyptian sacrifice of the cosmic and human order of life,
the Ma-a-t sacrifice, is also in this sense a mystical sacrifice, for
Ma-a-t belongs, in the first place, among the gods in the underworld, the earth gods, Osiris, Ptah, and Min. Ma-a-t is herself the
goddess of the earth, i.e., of death and life together.

B. THE ALTAR AND THE SACRIFICIAL IMPLEMENTS

Everywhere we encounter the idea that the altar is a sacred object. It is quite remarkable that it is said in Exodus 29 : 36 f. that the altar is "most holy"; "whatever touches the altar shall become holy." A person who thus becomes "holy" must be ritually cleansed before he can return into ordinary life. Every day (or during seven days) the altar must be cleansed by a sacrifice of atonement, and it must be anointed: its holiness must be actualized. The sacredness of the altar is evidently of the same character as that of the offering; the altar did not become sacred just because it was utilized in the cultus. It was not a "table" or a stone object put down in or near the temple, on which the offerings were placed. The altar was taken up in the cultus because, as a bearer of divine life, it was sacred. It is the place where the god of the gifts is present; it is there that he gets back his gifts as offerings, and it is there that ritual sanctity is realized. When the offerings are some of the products of the earth, as is usually the case, the altar is the image of the place where the earth lives, where the god of the earth is at work. Therefore the altar is sacred or holy, just as the temple is sacred, since it is the place within which and in which God reveals himself, the image of God's actual dwellingplace.

The table form of the altar seldom occurs; when it is reported it is the symbol of the divine site of the offering. (Cf. the stone in the altar of the Roman Catholic Church.) In the grottoes of Pan the altar is not a table but a low, circular pile of stones or an ordinary stone; it is only a mound, a rise in the earth (*eschara*), but "rise" means here the "place where the earth lives." In this altar the god of the earth is present; he is also worshipped in a grotto. The altar is thus a temple in the temple or in the grotto. Such double representations or symbolizations of an important reality, one within the other, occur frequently.

This form of altar is also very common among the Semites, and sometimes its religious meaning is clearly indicated. Before the Arabs were converted to Islam, their altar was a crude stone set on end, a pillar, or pile of stones. Next to this altar the sacrificial animal was slaughtered; the animal's blood was spread on the altar, as it was in the temple of Yahweh. It was called

noṣb, and like the Hebrew *masseba* was an "upright stone."
This altarstone or stonepile was God's dwellingplace, for it was
there that the earth lived, or the Baal of the earth.[18] The upright position indicates life or resurrection. Jacob sets up a stone
at the place where God reveals Himself to him (Genesis 28 : 22);
he anoints it and calls it *Beth-el*, God's house. The stone is thus
a temple, and by his anointing it, it becomes an "altar." Later
he sets up an altar at the same place (Genesis 35 : 1, 7). Evidently
"God's dwellingplace" is this upright stone or altar. (Cf. the
baitylos, which means upright stone.) Nothing is said of an ordinary temple in the form of a real house. To the ancient Semitic
way of thinking, temple and altar are identical. The typical altar
is the earth altar, the rise in the earth where the god of the earth's
gifts lives. Thus according to Exodus 20 : 25f, the altar must
be made of earth or of unhewn stones, crude stone, in order to
represent the earth itself. This is therefore like the Greek altar
in the grotto. It can thus be explained why the ancient Hebrew
site of sacrifice was on the *bāmā* ("high place"). The prophets
protested against the worship of the god of the earth, not against
the large number of places of worship, but against the idea of
the "high place" in the earth which is involved in this worship.
The ark of Yahweh is also such a "high place," although the
unique exemplar of its type. In the prophetic proclamation the
symbolism of the earth disappears.

In this connection we should also note the horns which were
attached to the altar to indicate its character. We find them in
Israel, Crete, Greece, and Rome, In Israel they were probably
bulls' horns; this was certainly the case in Crete. In Greece and
Rome they were usually rams' horns. The horns of the Cretan
earth bull indicate the power of the earth god. (Cf. the representation of Yahweh in the form of a bull.) In Egypt, the expression, "horns of the earth," was actually used to refer to the
extreme points of south, north, east, and west. The ram and the
goat have the same meaning; Hermes Charidotes is also called
kriophoros, he who brings the earth's blessing. On the island of
Delos there stood the *bōmos keratōn* or *keratinos*, an altar built
wholly of goats' horns, which was considered to be one of the
seven wonders of the world. Twice for seven days Theseus had
performed the *geranos* dance around it. The altar was dedicated

to Ariadne, the chthonic Aphrodite, who had rescued Theseus from the Labyrinth. Like the labyrinth with the Minotaur, it was an image of the realm of the dead, out of which the rescue had really taken place. By means of the horns, the altar was identified with the living earth.

Sometimes the altar gained a cosmic significance in the broadest sense. In such cases it is an image of the universe, within which and in which divine life is revealed. Perhaps the largest altar which has ever been built is the Great Round Altar in China, near Peking. It is built up into three terraces, which represent the sky god, the heavenly bodies (sun, moon, and planets) and possibly the earth gods. The difference between temple and altar has here practically disappeared. We already have seen how the "temple" sometimes could be identical with the "god"; now it becomes apparent that the altar is sometimes identical with the god. Besides the upright stone (the *baitylos* or *masseba*), near Aleppo a very large and ancient altar has been found of Zeus *Bomos*.[19] There is also inscribed on it in Aramaic, Zeus *Madbachos*.

The many fire altars also have a meaning similar to that of the altars of the earth. The best known is the altar of Vesta or Hestia. In Vesta's temple on the Forum in Rome is the hearth where the earth's life is revealed as the energy of fire. (*Vesta Terra est*). The offering is the fire in this hearth; Vesta lives in and through this fire, and along with her lives the Roman people. Her altar or hearth is her temple, her real dwellingplace; it is there that her life is religiously realized by the maintenance of the fire.

Sometimes the cosmic significance of the altar fire is indicated in a peculiar but very lucid fashion. At Hierapolis, in Syria, on the upper course of the Euphrates, a fire burned on an altar which was so built in the middle of a pool that it seemed to be floating on the water.[20] The idea of the floating fire island occurs among many Ancient peoples. It is the point on earth which first appeared out of the waters of Creation, the point at which light arose. The fire on that altar was the life of the world. Delos, too, a small island of the Cyclades, was once, according to tradition, a floating island.[21] The myth relates that the divine child Apollo was born there. (Apollo is here like the Egyptian Horus, who was born on the floating island of Chemnis near

Buto.) Delos rose up out of the sea so that Leto could bring
Apollo into the world there. According to another tradition it
was already a floating island. Part of the cultus on Delos was
the maintenance of the eternally burning fire on the altar. The
inhabitants of Lemnos, in the northern Aegean, renewed the
fire on their island annually by bringing fire from Delos. During
the nine days in which the ship was away to get the fire, all the
fires on Lemnos were extinguished; when the ship returned
bringing the new fire, "a new life" began.

Pliny also tells of a floating island.[22] In the land of the Sa-
bines is the Lake of Cutilia (*Lacus Cutiliae*) on which there was a
floating island, where – according to Varro – "the navel of Italy"
(*Italiae umbilicus*) was located. According to Macrobius, Hades
was worshipped there. The earth itself is also a floating island; it
floats on the cosmic waters; the earth is a boat.[23], [24]

Yet the most important fire altars in Antiquity are the altar
of Agni in India and the altar of Atar in the Avesta religion;
both are conceived entirely in cosmic terms.

The altar is often linked with the grave. This is usually thought
to be "very simple and easy to understand," and it is explained
on the basis of the worship of the dead: the dead man receives
his food at the place where he is buried, and thus the grave becomes an altar. Sacrifices to the dead give the impression of
being much simpler than sacrifices to the gods. The sacrifice to
the dead is food for the dead man, who like the living man needs
food. As the dwelling of the dead man, the grave is comparable
with the dwelling of the living man. Thus the grave becomes an
altar and the altar to the dead is a grave. No other affinity is
supposed between grave and altar than that between dining
room and dining table. Yet it can be said with complete certainty
that this was not the conception of the believers; it is a modern
rationalistic explanation of an Ancient religious custom.

Like all sacrifices, the sacrifice to the dead is a religious rite,
but, moreover, it is closely related to the religious meaning of
burial in the earth. The idea held was that man lives the life of the
earth and dies the death of the earth; the secret of human life
is the secret of the earth's life. This is true for the dead as well
as for the living. By his burial the dead man is fully initiated
into the earth's life. Like the earth, he dies, and like the earth,

he triumphs over death and rises again with the earth. It is in
this light that the Ancient sacrifice to the dead should be understood. It is all too often forgotten that a sacrifice to the dead is
not the same thing as a meal of the sort which we have. The
sacrifice to the dead is a sacrifice to the gods of the earth. For
in the offering, the earth's life is offered to the gods or to men
and actualized in religio-magical fashion. Thereby the life of the
dead is actualized just as is the life of the earth gods.

In Egypt the typical sacrifice as far back as the Old Kingdom
was the inedible papyrus reed, which, however, was the typical
bearer of plant life: the reed marsh was paradise. The grave was
not a house in the ordinary sense, but the image of the realm of
the dead in which the dead man leads the divine life of the earth.
The place on or near the grave where the offering is received is
also divine, just like the offering itself. In this respect the sacrifice to the dead is quite comparable to the sacrifice to the gods
on the altar: in both cases the sacrifice is offered at the place
where the earth lives.

The Greek data are especially clear: the grave marker is used
itself as an altar to the dead. It is set above the place where the
dead person lies buried, and it represents the spot where the
earth, and with it the dead person, lives. The grave altar is
therefore the same as the altar for the god of the earth. The most
familiar grave marker is the *tumulus*, a mound of earth above
the grave. Why was a *tumulus* built there? Homer says that it is
as a *sēma*, a remembrance, and this is also our modern idea of the
significance of the tombstone. This is an entirely rationalistic
explanation without the slightest religious basis. The Ancient
Greek conception, however, was a religious one: the dead man
lives in the *tumulus*, just as the god of the earth lives in it. By
means of the mound of earth, the grave is made into the spot
where the earth lives. The sacrifice to the dead was offered there,
and was thus quite like the sacrifice to the god of the earth at
his horned altar. This cosmic significance of the grave mound
is evident from the fact that it is quite identical in form with the
hill of Creation, the omphalos of the earth, where life arose in the
beginning of time, and it is thus the typical site of the rising of
life in the cosmic sense. Moreover, the omphalos was also a grave,
namely the divine grave of Python or Dionysus (for instance at

Delphi). The snake is often drawn around the omphalos; it is the earth spirit, whether the dead man or Python.

Roscher [25] mentions another familiar grave marker, which again is a grave altar, a terraced mound, comparable to the *tumulus*, on which a stone (the tombstone or *stēlē*) is set up – it is thus a sort of double grave marker. The *stēlē* (from *stellō*, *histēmi*, to stand upright) is, like the *masseba*, a sign of the living earth god and his altar. Like Jacob's *masseba*, this *stele* was anointed. It was thus a sacred object ,and not only set up as a memorial. In the grave marker and the *tumulus*, the dead man lives the life of the earth. The fact that the grave stele often has the ordinary altar form, that of a low, broad, and upright stone, proves that it was indeed an altar to the dead, at which, as at the *masseba*, sacrifice was offered.

So we see that the grave-altar or altar-grave of the dead man does not differ from the altar of the earth god. At the side where the earth lives, her products, her life, are given back to her, the divine provider. They are recognized as divine gifts, and their divine nature (and therewith also the life of the dead man) are actualized. Moreover, the dead, the ancestors, are the givers of the earth's blessings, of the fertility of the earth. It is the blessing of offspring which is here particularly in mind: human fertility, too, is a revelation of the earth's life. The Greek goddess of birth, Eileithyia, is an earth goddess. So we see even more clearly how close the sacrifice to the dead is to the sacrifice to the god of the earth. Offering a sacrifice to the dead is not the same thing as what we understand by "feeding," although the idea behind it is precisely that by means of this sacrifice the life of the dead man is actualized. When the sacrifice to the dead is performed in a *bothros*, a hollow, or in the opening of the *pithos*, we discern once again the idea of the site of resurrection.[26] In the same way *Pylos*, the gate of Hades, was considered to be the site of newly arising life.

During the Roman Empire a special form of grave altar was used: the fire altar for the "consecration" of the Emperor who had died. It is frequently engraved on the coins which were issued after an emperor's death. The horns on it prove that it is an earth altar, and thus the site where the earth lives. The earth's life is actualized here by means of the fire sacrifice, just as it is in Vesta's hearth. But this site of the earth's life of fire is the tomb of the emperor, and this point is accentuated still further by the door which is engraved on the altar. In the fire the emperor thus obtains the divine life of the earth. Therefore the inscription is *Consecratio* (viz., of the emperor). The fire altar is thus the place where the emperor obtains the eternal, divine life of the earth. In other cases this altar has the form of a building in steps, a *rogus* or pyre, with the door of the tomb on one of the levels. On top of this altar lies the body of the emperor, which is there completely consumed. Like the step-shaped *tumulus* among the Greeks, this altar represents the "earth mountain." [27]

We shall now briefly note the analogous notion of the (grave) altar in the Roman Catholic Church.[28] At the present time in the Roman Catholic Church, the altar must be of stone, or at least contain a stone. In simple altars this stone is set in the center of the wooden altar board. The *sepulcrum*, an opening in the stone, must contain relics of a martyr. When the altar is consecrated, the bishop closes this opening. This altar-grave, for this is what it is, is repeatedly rubbed with ointment; it is sacred. The stone is the image of Christ and the altar is the dwellingplace of the holy martyr to whom the church is dedicated. The sacrifice of the mass is performed only above the relics of the martyr, who represents the Christ who has died. This usage seems to have begun, however, only in the fourth century.[29] Before that time there were *martyria*, grave-churches, but these were only outside the cities and never located in the basilicas of the cities. About the end of the fourth century, the grave of the saint became the most important treasure in the city churches. First it was still separated from the altar, but very soon the altar became the treasury for relics. The oldest Christian altar was an ordinary *mensa*, a table with four (or sometimes three) legs. Now the altar became a real altar-grave or grave-altar. The grave of the saint in the altar is the *confessio* (cf. *martyreō*, testify or confess). *Confessio* is thus metaphorically the site of witness or confession, the place where the religious relation is brought about.

The idea of the sanctity of the altar in the Roman Catholic Church is undoubtedly related to the mass conversion to Christianity in the fourth century. The Ancient conception was that

the (grave-) altar represented the place where the life of earth
and men rises anew. The grave-altar is the place where the dead
man has attained divine life, and where he seeks to further
abiding life among men. This Ancient idea is elaborated in Christian fashion. As among the Ancient peoples, the altar became
the image of the grave (cf. the stone with the *sepulcrum*), where
the mystery of divine life is actualized. The sacrifice of the mass
on the altar is the *sacri-ficium* (making sacred) of the incarnate
Christ, of Christ in his visible form. Bread, the bearer of divine
life, is the body of Christ. The sacrificial act is the consecration
of the bread on the site of the divine life of the earth and of men
(in this case, of the saints who have died with Christ). The Ancient cultus has been transformed into Christian cultus. In spite
of the altar stone the cosmic orientation has been removed.
This is how historical "borrowing" takes place. That which is
borrowed is always, in its new context, something new and
original.

The saints were consecrated by their death and have attained
divine life, just as according to Greek belief, every dead person
in the sacred tombstone or grave-altar (*tumulus* or *stēlē*) became
a sharer in the divine life of the earth, and he brought to men
the earth's divine life, fertility and prosperity.

This alteration in the earliest Christian conception of the altar,
the table for the Lord's Supper, certainly points out the religious
value of the Ancient idea of the altar.

The Basin for Libations

Not only the altar but also various sacrificial implements
illustrate the religious meaning of sacrifice, which proves to be
anything but an ordinary meal given to the god or to the dead
man. Two kinds of sacrificial implements are the most common:
the water basin for the libation and the basket for the vegetation
sacrifice. Both are containers in which offerings are presented.
Sometimes, however, they are very clearly made into "symbols"
which manifest the divine nature of the offerings. That is to say,
they come from God and are given back to Him; God lives in the
offerings.

Especially in the Greek religion there is a large amount of

data concerning the basin for libations. It is noteworthy that the *phiale* is not always an ordinary sacrificial basin. Sometimes it is portrayed in the hands of the gods (Pluto, Dionysus, Triptolemus, Hera, Athene, Demeter, and Themis). A little silver image of Dionysus (or possibly of Pluto) with a *phiale* in one hand and a horn of plenty in the other makes it quite certain that they are symbols of water and vegetation, which is to say, of the divine life of the earth, in which God reveals Himself. Water is thought of here as a divine element of life, "water of life" in the cosmic sense. The *phiale* also has a related meaning in the ordinary libations made by men. Its form is in many cases very peculiar. There is a large round bump in the center of the dish, which is certainly not there for artistic or practical reasons. (There are many examples of this in the Leiden Museum of Antiquities.) The Ancients called these quite rightly "omphalos basins." Omphalos means navel, the navel of the earth. There is only one possible explanation of why an omphalos stands in the water of the libation. It is the *omphalos tēs thalassēs* (Homer), the "earth mountain" which arose from the waters of Creation, the site of the rising of the world's life. This form of the *omphalos phiale* thus serves in a special way to indicate and actualize the divine nature of water as an offering. This is not ordinary water; as a libation it is returned to the god or the dead man. Through the water the god or the dead man lives, just as he does in the offering of food, which is divine food.

We see again how far removed the "quenching the thirsty souls or gods" is from an ordinary meal, at least from a meal in our sense of the word. The sacrifice of food and drink cannot be conceived as a primitive cultic rite, as was done by the Hebrew prophets and is done by our rationalistic historians of religion. They belong to a completely different period than Antiquity, and they are entirely lacking in sympathetic historical understanding. Either they abhor all alien ideas as such, or they contrive a pity for them as something primitive and childish. Just let these haughty interpreters of offerings try to explain the *omphalos* sacrificial basin! They have never yet succeeded in doing so, but if they should do so, they would be liberated from the false notion that sacrifices of food and drink were ordinary meals.

The sacrificial basin for water, the *phialē*, is an emblem of many gods and thereby manifests in the ordinary cultus the character of the libation, because water is a divine being. The "Water of Life" bears, however, divine insight as well as creative power. The divine wisdom dwells in the water which causes life to rise anew. The oracle dispensing Themis on the three-legged stool holds a *phialē* or a branch in her hand. By drinking the water from the Castalian spring, the Pythia (or Themis) at Delphi became inspired and was able to give oracles. The cosmic water from the spring (coming from the underworld) is the dwellingplace of the divine wisdom or order of life, which is revealed in the oracle. The basin contains a divine element; the water in it is from the gods. For this reason it is offered to the gods, and for the same reason it is their emblem.

The Sacrificial Basket

The basket has the same significance in food sacrifices that the basin has in libations. The basket, too, sometimes has a very peculiar and special form, in order to represent what is the natural and real bearer of the offerings, the living earth.

The simplest form of sacrificial basket is a "tray" on which the sacrificial food is put. In India there is the *barhis* or *vedi*, which is a mat of grass or straw. *Barhis* is etymologically related to the Avestan (ancient Persian) word *barsman*, a bundle of plants which represents vegetation or the earth's life, and which therefore is a sacred object in the Haoma sacrifice. The *barhis*, which is spread out on the ground so that offerings may be placed on it, also represents plant life. It is the sole altar for sacrificial meals; the gods descend to it in order to receive the offerings.[30] The same ideas occur in Egypt. ▱▱▱ (offering) is bread on a mat of papyrus reed. There is also ▱▱▱, the mat by itself, or ▱▱▱, a roll of papyrus, but without any bread on it. Such "tablecloths" were never used at ordinary meals.

The actual sacrificial basket is in Egyptian ▱▱▱ , an ordinary basket for sacrifices, in which the offerings are sometimes depicted. Yet like the offerings themselves, the basket is sacred, since it is the image of the true home of offerings, and thus of the living earth, their home in the depths of the earth, where they are produced. Only in this way can we explain the sometimes quite irrational symbolic contexts in which ⌣ appears. Osiris arises from ⌣ . The king who presents offerings to the god is sometimes portrayed kneeling on ⌣ (sic!) but also on ▢▢▢ , which makes possible a rational explanation. It is as if people wished to express the idea that the king performs the creative activities of the earth. At the site where the earth lives, he brings the life of the earth to God. There he recognizes and actualizes the divine nature of the offering. Here the religious meaning of sacrifice is indicated as clearly as possible by such a common sacrificial implement as the basket for the offerings. This is here not a "symbol," but a quite realistic illustration of the supernatural, mystical act which is performed with it. Because the offering represents the earth's life, ⌣ also means festival or resurrection. Thus it can also be explained why as early as the Old Kingdom the king's throne rests on a "rocker," the ⌣ . The throne is itself the rise in the earth to whose top the king climbs when he ascends his throne. The ⌣ underneath is a doubling of the "symbolism." Let no one say that this is an artificial alteration of something so understandable as the basket for sacrifices, for both the sacrificial basin and the sacrifice have a cosmic meaning. This basket or container occurs in the earliest period of the Old Kingdom. The basket is also depicted as ⌣ , meaning the sacred boat of the earth.

The same ideas can be found among the Greeks. The *kaneon* or *kanoun*, the reed basket carried on the head or arm, has this form: ⌣ . This basket, like the *phialē*, is sometimes to be seen in the hands of gods, of Artemis, for instance. In any case it is the image of the living earth. As a rule the basket very clearly has horns on both sides and a mound in the middle. It is noteworthy, however, that this mound is never drawn as an offering of fruit or grain, although "mound" corresponds in meaning to "offerings." A variation is the basket with three horn-shaped handles. This, too, must have a symbolic religious meaning, for how is one to take hold of a basket with three handles? The basket is triple, because the Greeks usually connected the number three with the underworld, just as the Semites

and the Egyptians with the numbers three and seven. In Egypt
there was a triple water vase; it signifies the basket or vase of
the earth. Therefore the sacrificial basket is by itself a sacred
object, even if it contains no offerings at all. It is the earth itself
and brings forth the offerings. And for this reason, again quite
like the *phialē*, it is the emblem of the gods of the earth's life.
It is very closely akin to Demeter's basket-chest, the *kistē
mystikē*, which also was sacred as such, irrespective of its contents. The ark of Yahweh, too, was not a sacrificial object, but
it was the Hebrew's sign of the earth. Yet the ancient Hebrews
were similarly unconcerned about the contents of the ark; it
was very probably empty.

   Thus the sacrificial implements illustrate the religious meaning
of sacrifice just as clearly, and in the same way, as the altar
itself. All these objects instruct us more reliably than most
modern theories, which explain sacrifice as a gift to the gods.
The form and use of the altar and sacrificial implements manifest
the cosmic nature of sacrifice. By means of the sacrifice, the
abiding divine life of the cosmos, of the earth, and of men in
particular, is recognized and actualized. What comes from God
is given back to God. The religio-magical act of sacrifice expresses
faith in God's life. This sacred rite is just as supra-rational as
faith itself.

C. THE SACRIFICIAL ACT

   We need turn only briefly to the act of sacrifice and the way
in which the sacrifice is offered.

   Sacri-ficium was the consecration (or making sacred) of the
offering, whereby the finite phenomenon of an empirical object
that represents divine life was placed in the infinite sphere where
it essentially belonged. It was the actualization of the permanent
and autonomous (and thus divine) being of the object. This
can take place by means of sacrifices in which there is no shedding
of blood. In these sacrifices the consecration occurs by offering
(Latin *offerre*) the ritual to God. This is the case with libations,
and sacrifices of milk, vegetable produce, such as grain and meal,
and ritually prepared cakes and loaves of bread. There were
also sacrifices involving the shedding of blood. The consecration

took place by the killing of the offering, whether a sacred sacrificial animal or sometimes a plant offering. Death is a state of infinite being, or in a more positive sense, of absoluteness, of divinity. Therefore every act of slaughter, especially for the Semites, is an act of sanctification (*sacrificatio*), which must take place according to the proper rites. The Romans believed that Jupiter made men sacred by his lethal lightning. He consecrates a covenant, for instance, by "killing" it: *foedus fulmine sancit* or *foedus ferire*. Thus he actualizes the absolute and divine character of the covenant. A treaty can be concluded because the sacrificial animal, which represents the earth's life (the life which animates the treaty), is killed with Jupiter's stone (*fulgur*).

This consecration or sanctification may be achieved by the agency of the man who is offering the sacrifice. Nevertheless, it remains a divine act, for only God can make life absolute or grant absolute life. Killing the sacrificial animal has, we know, not only the negative effect of taking life, but also an equally strong positive effect, because God actualizes absolute life. Jupiter himself performs this double act of sacrifice when he kills someone with his lightning. The person who had been struck by lightning, whether because of a sin, or for any other reason, was considered a consecrated man and was worshipped as a hero. For this reason the man offering sacrifice performs a superhuman, religio-magical act by killing his offering.

This divine character of sacrifice may also be expressed as follows: the means whereby the sacrificial killing is done is itself divine. It is frequently evident that the way in which the sacrificial death takes place is of essential significance, and that it serves to make clear the divine character of the act. In some vegetation sacrifices this is unmistakable. The last sheaf of grain, in which the "grain spirit" or "rice mother" is situated, is burned. It is thus killed and sanctified by fire, for the grain grows by means of the divine energy of the earth's fire (Cf. Hephaestus.) Sometimes a figure in human form was burned, a figure which was made entirely of flowers and branches. After that the charred remains were buried all over the fields. Sometimes the intention of the act is even more clearly indicated. The offering is first immersed in water and "drowned," and thereupon consumed by fire. Water, too, is a vital element of

the earth. Fields, woods, and pastures live by means of warmth
and water. The sacrifice is killed and thus made sacred by fire
and water, and is thus transferred into the world of absolute
life.

The way in which the offering is destroyed or consecrated
indicates the nature of the god to whom it is dedicated. At
Gades (Cadiz), there was no image of the god in the temple of
Hercules, but an eternal fire burned upon the altar. At the festival of Hercules, his image was burned there. Nilsson [31] reports
that a pyre was made in front of Artemis in Achaia and in front
of Atargatis, the Syrian Astarte, at Hierapolis near the Euphrates. People not only placed all sorts of fruits on this pyre, but
also edible birds, wild boar, deer, and wolf and bear cubs. All of
these things were consumed by the fire. As in the case of the
grain sacrifice, there is here a consecration by means of the
essential element of these goddesses, the earth's fire. Frazer
(IV, 339, Adonis-Attis-Osiris) also tells of a sacrifice to the god
of the growing grain: shovels, spades, and other agricultural implements are "put to death." They are thus considered to be the
divine means whereby the grain is induced to grow, for agriculture is also a mystery, a divine activity.

The sacred and quite special character of the killing of the
sacrificial animal is also indicated in another way. Killing the
sacrificial offering often has fatal results, such as disaster,
decline, or death. In these cases, the sacrifice means a defeat for
the sacrificer; he takes to flight. Thus the legend of the Athenian
Bouphonia, at which the bull of vegetation was sacrificed,
relates that the *bouphonos* took to flight when he had offered this
sacrifice for the first time. Famine broke out and the sacrifice
had to be made again with new and peculiar ceremonies. Killing
the sacrificial animal is, indeed, necessary for the consecration,
but divine death, too, is an actual death, with all its terrors, and
it is feared as the defeat and downfall of everything that is
known as life. The initiation into the Eleusinian Mysteries is the
most terrible consecration that man can undergo. When Kore
is abducted by Hades, there is famine on the earth. Consecration
by death thus has also a negative side, namely the abolition of
finite life, even though this is done in order to attain absolute
life. This flight, connected with famine and decline, does not

occur because God is enraged with the killing of what is sacred. This is not *hybris* – an act of finite man whereby he achieves his own downfall, but an act whereby absolute and divine life is actualized. Pandora, too, brings gifts which are feared. It is quite clear that slaughtering the sacrificial animal is a mystical act, which because of its sanctity is fatal for finite man.

D. THE AIM OF SACRIFICE

Sacrifices with Positive Effect

There are two kinds of sacrifices. There are those with the positive aim of actualizing in nature and among men abiding and self-subsistent divine life, and there are sacrifices with a negative goal, "atoning sacrifices" or "peace offerings" to ward off a dangerous sanctity and thus to cause the ill to cease.

Many examples have already been given of sacrifices for the perpetuation and strengthening of cosmic life. There are all the libations and vegetation sacrifices, and the great comprehensive sacrifices of Ma-a-t, Soma (Haoma), and the Avestan fire sacrifice. But now we shall consider positive sacrifice in the special interest of men.

The idea behind these sacrifices is that the divine life which is actualized by the sacrificial rite is imparted to man. Thus in a sense, the offering represents men; it sanctifies their life, or rather – a ritual link is joined between the offering and men.

The Roman sacrificer puts on the *filum*, made *ex lana hostiae*, from the wool of the sacrificial animal. In this instance the sheep represents various kinds of animals used for sacrifice, including the cow and the pig. It is thus that the offering and the man who brings it are bound together. The sacrifice is offered for the welfare of men. The sacrificer represents the men for whom he offers the sacrifice. He and the people he represents are consecrated. Thus a mystical link is made between the sacrificer, the offering which is sacrificed, and the deity.

The priest's *pileus*, a hat or cap made from the hide of the sacrificed animal, also had this meaning. The symbolism of the hat is also involved here: whoever sacrifices *capite velato*, with his head covered or hidden, is withdrawn from the visible world.

The most common way in which the connection between the offering and man is made recognizable is, however, the sacrificial meal. It is for this reason that Robertson Smith [32] says that the typical and original sacrifice is the communal sacrifice, i.e., the sacred rite whereby the abiding life of the tribe or community is actualized. Originally the sacrificial animal is the "totem" of the tribe (the sacred animal which is considered the bearer of the tribe's life) and thus the god of the tribe. Survivals of this notion of the totem animal in historical times are the unclean animals which may only be killed and eaten in the prescribed ritual manner, such as the pig, the dog, the fish, the horse, the dove, etc. The term "totem" is borrowed from the language of certain North American Indian tribes, among whom this form of religion was first observed. Later it was discovered among the inhabitants of Central and Southern Australia and among other primitive peoples. The tribal animal is ritually killed and thereafter eaten in a common meal. The participants in such a sacred (sacrificial) meal take the divine substance into themselves. Thereby they actualize and strengthen the divine nature of their tribal life; this is a communal sacrifice. It could be said that the god of the tribe or people is sacrificed and consecrated. By means of the sacred meal, people come to share in divine life. It is thus a sacrifice with an entirely positive effect and is in the direct interest of men. Its purpose is not to strengthen the divine life of the cosmos, but directly to aid man, and it therefore differs from the libation, which is in the interests of vegetation, and thus only indirectly in the interests of men.

In the main, this conception of Robertson Smith's about sacrifice is correct, aside from the unprovable and purely theoretical elements of his view, which include his totem theory, which is that every tribe, especially among the Semites, once worshipped a particular kind of totem animal as its special god, felt itself closely akin to this animal, even considering it to be its tribal ancestor. Equally disputable is his theory that the communal sacrifice, including the sacrificial meal for strengthening the tribe's life, is the original sacrifice, and all other sacrifices, such as the "burnt offering" (*holokauston* or *'ōlā*) must be secondary and have only become possible when the belief in a totem was weakened by higher civilization and agricultural life.

The religious significance of the sacrificial meal was first recognized by Robertson Smith, who saw that it was the cultic rite whereby the religious character of the society was repeatedly actualized; the social order was a sacred community. The family or gens, the *phratria* or curia, the *phylē* or tribus, the *polis* or civitas, – all of these were sacramental units with a special cultus, such as the *sacra gentilia*. They also all had their sacred meals, such as the *phyletika deipna*, whereby the sacred unity of these groups was sacramentally constituted and perpetuated. Thus the Athenian community was founded at the first *bouphonia* sacrificial meal. The Ancients believed that the communal meal signified a communion of life. When agreements were concluded, it was here again eating and drinking together which constituted the unity. According to the right of hospitality, the guest was also included in this fellowship; he could claim inviolability. Indeed every meal was a mystical renewal of life. By means of the sacred communal meal, all those participating came to share in the divine life of the consecrated sacrificial animal. Like the Roman *filum* or *pileus*, the sacrificial meal linked the sacrificer, the sacrificial offering, and God. It transferred the divine power of the offering to man.

When we bear this in mind, we can understand why the Hebrews considered the sacrificial meat to be a sacred, divine substance, in which man could share – provided he observed the ritual laws," so that eating the food may cause no misfortune." In Leviticus 7 : 15–20, it is prescribed that sacrificial meat must be eaten on the day it is slaughtered; sometimes it is still permissable to eat it the next day, but the third day it must be burned with fire. Anyone who eats of this meat after it has become "unclean" will be cast out from his people.

In contrast with Tylor's work, this book of Robertson Smith's, although published in 1888–'89, is still of value, especially because of his theory of the mystical character of sacrifice. It is one of the classic works on Ancient religions, admirable in its clarity and simplicity of presentation.

The positive aim of sacrifice, as far as man is concerned, is communion of life with God. But it is not only by means of the sacrificial meal that this is achieved, as Robertson Smith believes. The entire act of sacrifice, *sacrificium*, means a participation in divine life. It is a religio-magical or mystical act which takes place outside the finite realm. The sacrificer (i.e., the one who offers the sacrifice, and not solely the priest), leaves the finite world, or "he steps out of the world of men and into the world of the gods." [33] This is an actual theoretical formulation of the meaning of participation in divine life at the sacrificial meal.

In the *Brāhmanas* this idea is presented at great length, especially when the preparation for sacrifice is described, what is called the *dīkshā*, the "dedication" of the sacrificer. This preparation, too, is part of the sacrificial act, and it is even made an essential element in it. The person who is planning to offer a sacrifice goes to the Brahman (the priest) with the words, "I, [states his name] wish to reach (or win) heaven [i.e., to pass out of this finite world] and to offer a sacrifice." First he must perform a number of rites whereby he brings about his separation from the finite sphere. He cuts his hair, his beard, and his nails. Oldenberg explains this in his *Religion des Veda* as the removal of the dead part in order to be able to enter absolute, divine life. Then there come the ritual purifications, with the same negative aim. Even rebirth is represented in the *dīkshā;* the sacrificer becomes a new man. A hut is built for him which is called the "mother's womb," and he sits in this wrapped in a black antelope's hide. This signifies the realm of the dead from which he will be reborn. In the same way, the Egyptian who would attain the resurrection of Osiris must be wrapped in the hide of a bull, thus taking the place of Kheper. There in the hut, entirely isolated, he is born to new life when the sacrifice begins. He has become a divine being. "For no one will I stand up, not even for the king." The entire period of several months he has fasted and lived solely on milk. "When there is nothing more (when he is thin), he is clean for the sacrifice." He then lives in a state of hypersensitivity, in ecstasy; the gods have then "entered him." It is understandable that *dīkshā* (or *tapas*) gives the sacrificer supernatural power. Only now is he ready and fit for offering the visible offerings; "he is taken up among the gods." The sacrificial animal is now killed and the sacred meal takes place. This means that one has now entered into a relation to God and has left the finite world. The idea at the basis of this *dkīshā* preparation is that he who offers a sacrifice must first sacrifice himself. He must die, as the sacrificial animal dies. After the sacrifice, he takes off the *dīkshā* with the words, "I have carried out my vow ... once again I become a man; I descend from the world of the gods to the world of men." [34]

This preparatory initiation to the sacrificial rite thus indicates clearly the entirely positive aim of the sacrifice, which is to gain a share in divine life. In many religions such preparation is prescribed. In Israel it is especially the priest who is subject to such regulations. The ritual laws governing the sacrifice on the great Day of Atonement are so numerous and so stringent that they may well be compared with the *dīkshā*. According to Leviticus 16 and the Talmud, the priest must separate himself from his family seven days before the festival and observe all sorts of laws of purification, especially on the day just beforehand, and keep awake at night. An extraordinary sanctity is required for this festival. The Greeks performed the preparatory initiation for the sacrifice by having the sacrificer don the wreath. This wreath is the sign of his sacredness, the sign of victory, in the religious sense, over transiency and the powers of death. A dead person is wreathed with the same significance. In Egypt there is "the wreath of righteousness," i.e., of the divine order of life or immortality. (Cf. II Timothy 4 : 8, "the crown of righteousness," *tēs dikaiosunēs stephanos.*)

The positive effect of the sacrificial rite thus concerns human life, not the life of nature; it is man's sacramental participation in abiding, divine life. The various communal sacrifices with a sacrificial meal are certainly of this type. The different groups in society are religious units, which as such are time and again freshly established and actualized. Another example of this type of sacrifice is the so-called "oath sacrifice," which is offered at the conclusion of a covenant; this was the only connection in which oath sacrifices occurred among the Ancient peoples. In concluding a covenant the allies swear faithfulness to one another by means of the oath sacrifice. A sacred mutual relationship is hereby brought into existence which is independent of all fortuitous circumstances. The treaty is then embodied in the divine order of the cosmos and transformed into an absolute relationship. It is quite clear that this oath sacrifice displays the characteristic feature of the social sacrifice, in which a group of men (here the two parties or allies) are constituted into a religious unity. The oath sacrifice moves the treaty from this world into the other, absolute world. It can be said that offering an oath sacrifice is the same as the *sacrificere*, the sacrificing of the treaty (*foedus ferire*, *kārath berīth*). A treaty is a social reality par excellence.

Sacrifices with Negative Effect

The common term for sacrifices which have the aim of causing a misfortune to cease is "sin offering" (*hattā'th*) or "peace offering' (sacrifice of atonement). Both terms, but especially the former, are misleading. For we then unconsciously think of sacrifices occasioned by a particular offence for which pardon, forgiveness of sins, or remission of punishment is asked by means of the sacrifice. Such a motive can, to be sure, be the occasion of such a sacrifice, but it is only a particular application of the idea which is at the basis of every "peace offering," and even then the "sin" which must be atoned is not what we mean by sin.

The "sin offering" is essentially a sacrifice to cause misfortune to cease. In many cases the cause of the misfortune is unknown. God causes calamity without giving any justification of His action. Crop failure or sickness strikes a people even when it is not conscious of any offence; the divine motive remains unknown. Man confronts a sovereign god who, humanly speaking, acts at his own pleasure and caprice. The conception of the "demonic god" is not foreign to any religion. Man's finite life can be obstructed by God, or even abolished and destroyed. Gods leads man into death, out of finite life into infinite life. If God sanctifies man in a fashion which cannot be united with ordinary life, this is not a punishment for crimes and offences. The sacrifice of atonement serves to dispel this state of sanctity. This is the negative aim of all atoning sacrifices. Hubert and Mauss rightly speak of the sacrifice of "desacralization." It can be said, to be sure, that this sacrifice "causes the divine wrath to cease," provided we do not relate "wrath" directly to human transgression. Job was righteous, and nevertheless he was the object of divine wrath. Wrath in this context means simply: the feared Holiness of God.

How is this sanctity abolished or warded off by a sacrifice?

The answer is this: even when God grants sanctification by
means of sacrifice, it is this divine activity as such which is
recognized, accepted, and actualized (*sacrificium*). The special
feature of the sacrifice of atonement is that the sacrifice is offered
with the religious consciousness, the faith, that the misfortune
caused by God is not simply misfortune, and that death is not
simply death. Divine life or the divine will may mean death for
man, but it is a death which brings with it absolute life. Death
is conquered in newly arising life. The misfortune itself is sanctified by the act of sacrifice and is thereby no longer simply a
misfortune. Like every sacrifrice, the "peace offering" is an act of
faith, an act of confession. Not only that which sustains and
furthers human life, but also that which obstructs it, is the work
of God. The term "sin offering" or "peace offering" is correct,
provided we interpret it in the Ancient sense of "sin," which is
closely akin to the Ancient meaning of "misfortune"; that is,
the state of death. To sin was to put oneself outside the laws of
finite life. God can also make a man a sinner by plunging him
into disaster.

A good example of the atoning sacrifice to dispel divine wrath
is the *Ver sacrum* to Mars. Mars is the god of victory, both of
cosmic and of human life. He is the god of spring (March). At
times of great distress and misfortune people promise that they
will sacrifice to him everything which is born the following
spring (thus all those things in which Mars reveals himself.)
Children, however, are not killed. But when they grow up, they
are taken across the border to seek a new home: banishment
is death. Thus they were dedicated to Mars.[35] This "offering"
of young colonists was laden with the divine curse, which had
been revealed in wrath and misfortune, but not in the sense of
divine disapproval which we attach to it. They had been made
sacred by the god and therewith were taken out of the finite
world. This fact was actualized by their banishment. The divine
character of the misfortune was recognized and thereupon realized
by means of the cultic rite. It was said that children were guided
by woodpeckers and wolves, the animals of Mars. This makes
it evident that these children were not cast-offs. On the contrary,
they were under the special protection and guidance of Mars.
Mars guides through death those who are sacrificed to him. The

colonization, which is the founding of a new city, is their resurrection to new life. The peace offering is here quite clearly an actualization of the divine nature of the misfortune, and this means the actualization of death which is absolute life or resurrection. The demonic Mars is no less God of life than is a beneficent god. But though he is worshipped, he remains the god of life who is feared.

The *pharmakos* sacrifice, in which a man is sacrificed to Apollo, is extremely ancient. A *pharmakon* is a means of healing, and a *pharmakos* is a healer or saviour. When disaster had struck the city, such as crop failure or a contagious disease, the most miserable of all the inhabitants was elected as the so-called *pharmakos*. This man was fed for a long time, sometimes for a whole year, at the expense of the state on "clean foods," which are cheese and figs, gifts of the god of vegetation. After that he was adorned with branches and led outside the city where he was beaten with wild garlic plants and fig branches, and finally killed by stoning and burning. All this was done in order to "cleanse" the city. The religious meaning of these acts is clear: the *pharmakos* represents misfortune or the god of misfortune, the demonic Apollo, who as god of vegetation, is here also the god of crop failure. It is for this reason that he is festooned with branches and fed with clean foods. He has already been made sacred before he is sacrificed; he is the sacred offering in which the demonic god reveals his activity; he is the disaster which has struck men. As the definitive consecration, the *sacrificium*, he is killed by whipping, stoning, and burning. The misfortune itself is thus consecrated, i.e., recognized and actualized as a divine reality. But this indicates that divine death does not mean simply death. By the consecration the misfortune is translated into a higher sphere. Divine death is resurrection. It is also said that "the *pharmakos* takes away misfortune," which means that he is sent away like a scape goat on whom all misfortune and malediction is laden. We see that there is no mention of any offence here. Misfortune comes from the god, here Apollo, who sends both life and death according to his own inscrutable decree. The *pharmakos* peace offering has a negative aim; nevertheless it is clear that a very positive religious belief is at the basis of this sacrifice. In misfortune, too, the god of absolute life reveals himself, the god to whom man entirely surrenders himself. Faith in Apollo is not shaken by calamity.

An especially characteristic instance in the Old Testament is the Naziritic vow, prescribed in Numbers 6. A person takes this vow "to dedicate himself to Yahweh" for a certain period of time. He abstains from wine and strong drink, lets his hair grow, and may not go near a corpse. "All the days of his separation he is holy to Yahweh." In this way he is withdrawn from ordinary life. But on the day that his Naziritic vow ends, he shall offer a "burnt offering" and a "sin offering." Why should be bring a sin offering? (*ḥaṭṭā'th*) He has done nothing wrong. Quite the contrary. No, he has been holy or sacred, by withdrawing from life like a man who has died. He has not been sacred in the negative sense; his sanctity implied that he was filled with divine power, and with this new power he returns to life, as soon as his fatal sanctity is terminated and his term as a Nazirite is ended. By means of the peace offering, in which the sacrificial animal is killed, first his separation from life, but later also his return to life are actualized. This is certainly a sacrifice of desanctification. Yet the Nazirite is not the same as he was before he undertook his vow; he has performed an act which remains significant during the rest of his life; it is meritorious for him. The peace offering at the end of his term as a Nazirite is the sanctification of his return to society as well as of his departure from it. "To be holy to Yahweh" is a death which includes resurrection within itself. The peace offering here signifies the actualizing of the divine character of death, which is separation from human society. This is the meaning of sacrifice, also in cases of ritual or other transgressions. In the same chapter of Numbers it is also said that the Nazirite must offer exactly the same burnt offering and sin offering if he should break his vow during his period as a Nazirite, as, for instance, when someone in his vicinity dies and he is made impure by contact with the body. The sacrifice abolishes the consequences of the transgression. Sanctity and impurity are very closely connected.

A Hebrew peace offering or guilt offering (*ḥaṭṭā'th*) of the same type is described in Leviticus 14 : 1ff, where the certification of healing from leprosy is treated. One of two living "clean" birds is killed above an earthen vessel in which there is "living

water" (RSV "running water"). Thus here again there is a
consecration, a *sacri-ficium* of what is sacred. Death or misfortune
is then brought to this sacred offering. After that the priest dips
the second bird in the blood of the first. Finally he sprinkles the
leper seven times with the bloody water and lets the living bird
fly away. This can only mean that the leper and the living bird
are both made sacred, but in different senses: the man by the
blood mixed with the water of life. This sanctification means
resurrection from death. The clean, living bird is by being
sprinkled with blood made sacred in the absolute sense, and so
it belongs no longer to this world. It is set free and carries away
with it the dangerous sanctity.

We should note that this idea of deity does not exclude the
sense of human guilt towards God. When the sovereign demonic
god opposes human life, man knows that this finite life is condemned by the divine judge (and not by a human one), and he
cannot justify himself or appeal to anything. Before God he is a
guilty and "sinful "being. But this guilt has nothing in common
with ethical guilt. The believer knows that in his insignificance
before God he has no right to life. He knows that his insignificance
does not consist only in his impotence, nor only in his ethical
imperfection, but above all in his state of separation from God,
his lack of sanctity and divine life. Only in this way can the sin
offering be explained. The believer accepts and realizes the
divine opposition to life, in the faith that even the condemnation
of human life does not exclude resurrection.

All the "peace offerings" or "sin offerings" which we have
mentioned were offered at unusual occasions, in times of severe
distress, or at special dedications. Other sacrifices of the same
kind were regularly offered to the sovereign god whose sanctity
was sought, but also feared. We know of many clear examples
of this. There is, for instance, the Ancient Indian bull sacrifice
to the Vedic god Rudra, who is frequently lauded in the Rig
Veda.[36] Rudra was the most feared of all the Ancient Indian
gods, the demonic god of the life of young animals and of men.
Like fire, he destroyed life, but also created it. The colour red
was his characteristic. The handsomest bull of the herd was
sacrificed to him. By feeding this bull certain foods they ritually cleansed it and made it a representative of Rudra, and as

Rudra it was worshipped. After that the bull was sacrificed in the middle of the night outside the village to ward off all misfortune from the cattle, but also to implore Rudra's blessing. It was a typical peace offering which was regularly made. When the aim of the sacrifice was to ward off the sanctity which was feared, its negative character was in the foreground, while the religious background was the belief in Rudra as the god of absolute life. However much he was feared, his sacred touch transformed misfortune into something which was not simply misfortune, for in it the mystery of divine life was actualized. The sacrifice in Greece to the Erinyes-Eumenides, where the sacrificers are dressed in red robes, has the same character as the sacrifice to Rudra.

There is certainly fear present in man's relation to the sovereign god, a fear which has arisen from a sense of one's own impotence and utter insignificance before God. But the man who has humbly recognized his insignificance before God has actually elevated himself above finitude. The Christian expression of this idea is that whoever confesses his guilt is righteous in the eyes of God. The peace offering is not made in order to make good certain transgressions, but in order to consecrate the misfortune. In the divine misfortune which overcomes man, his good fortune and salvation are also present.

After we have become acquainted with sacrificial rites which are either predominantly positive or predominantly negative in character, it is not difficult for us to understand the religious meaning of a number of instances of a somewhat divergent type. The ordinary act of sacrifice presupposes three factors: the man who is sacrificing, the offering which is sacrificed, and God. But in many cases the offering and the deity are so closely akin that the distinction between them has entirely disappeared. Frequently it is the god himself who is sacrificed. We have already pointed out that the offering represents God. When the offering is sacrificed (made sacred), its divine nature is recognized and actualized by the abolition (which mystically understood is a transformation) of its finite nature. This is done by killing it or presenting it to God, in recognition of its divine essence. The bread which is sacrificed is a bearer of divine life and reveals that life. Divine life is actualized, but this means that by means of *sacrificium* the god is made a god, i.e., sacrificed. In the great and famous temple of the vegetation god Melkart, there was no image of the god but only an eternally burning fire. (The same was true in the temple of Hercules at Cadiz.) But once a year a large image of Hercules was made and burned. "No stranger might be present." Thus it was evidently a mystery rite. God Himself was thus sacrificed as the offering and was consecrated by the fire. In this way His divine essence was actualized.

The fire, Hephaestus, was the earth's life which was revealed in vegetation, and which was Melkart or Hercules himself. In the mother city of Cadiz, Tyre, Melkart was annually burned in effigy during his festival, and after his death in the fire, "the awakening of Hercules (Sandan)" is celebrated. This death of consecration was a transition into absolute life, into resurrection. According to Frazer, in Cilician Tarsus Sandan was depicted with a sheaf of grain or a bunch of grapes in his hands, as signs of vegetation. On the coins of Tarsus is engraved a pyre with the god in it, which certainly indicates that that was considered the most characteristic mark of this god.[37]

Some old Germanic customs in connection with the lighting of the Easter fires indicate similar ideas.[38] In these fires a human figure is burned. Sometimes he is called "Judas," but this name gives no clue to the real nature of this figure. According to Mannhardt the figure often consists of unthreshed sheaves of grain, sometimes covered with flowers. It is the grain spirit, the god of vegetation, who is burned and therewith sacrificed and consecrated. This is therefore the same type of sacrifice as the burning of Sandan: the god himself is sacrificed.[39]

The Roman Catholic sacrifice of the mass also displays the same characteristic: on the altar the divine sacrificial death is again and again repeated and actualized. The bread is the body of Christ which is sacrificed and consecrated.

This meaning of the divine sacrificial death is indicated even more clearly when the human sacrificer disappears. The idea behind this rite is that God sacrifices Himself. But at this point the realm of cultus is left behind, and we enter the realm of religious myth or credal formulation.

There is a striking example of this in the Mithra religion, at least in the Mithra Mysteries in the Roman Empire. Even in the Avesta, Mithra is the god who has appeared in our world. He stands alongside Mazda, the high, celestial, and hidden God, but Mithra "leaves the heavens" in order to do battle for the maintenance of Mazda's order of life in the turbulent life of the cosmos. With divine weapons in his hands "he goes out of the shining paradise, climbs into his guilded chariot, drawn by immortal horses" in order to defeat the enemies among demons and men and "in order to attain immortality" (an immortality different from that of Mazda). According to Plutarch he is the *mesitēs*, the mediator "because he stands between Mazda (heaven) and Ahriman (hell)." Mithra is indeed the god in the Roman Empire who unites within himself both infinity and finitude, both life and death. While doing battle he associates with the world "to attain immortality," i.e., to make the world and men immortal. This is his mediation, and the central idea or belief in the Mithra Mysteries (second and third centuries A.D. in the Roman Empire) is that he attains the goal of his mission in the sacrificial death which he voluntarily undergoes.

The Mithra of the Mithra religion in the Roman Empire is described to us as the god of the whole universe; in him the nature of God and the nature of the cosmos are united. He is *sol invictus*, the invincible sun, which reflects both deity and cosmos. But above all he is the god of the earth's life; his most important emblem is the bull of the earth. This bull is quite unmistakably depicted as the life and death of the earth: his tail ends in ears of grain, but his testicles are destroyed by the scorpion. He is the god of death and resurrection, in nature and among men. And in all the temples of Mithra, the most important cultic image is the relief of the bull which is killed or sacrificed by Mithra. It can be said with complete certainty that this signifies Mithra *Tauroctonus:* Mithra who sacrifices himself in order to give divine life to the cosmos and therewith to men. Divine death is victory over death; it is resurrection. This death also is shared by the believers, the worshippers of Mithra, the initiates. The suffering and the terror of death are sometimes clearly expressed in the portrayals of this scene: the face of Mithra killing the bull manifests very great suffering, comparable to the face of the dying Alexander.

In this case, the idea of sacrifice is, as it were, expressed quite

purely: sacrificial death is the actualization of divine life. God
who sacrifices himself is the formulation of the thought behind
every act of sacrifice. It is the actualizing of absolute life, which
can only take place in death.

   Here is another example of a god who sacrifices himself.[40]

   Nine nights I (Odin) hung on the tree, wounded by a spear, dedicated
to Odin, I myself to Myself. I hung on a tree of which no one knows from
which roots it grows ... I sought below and lifted up the runic letters,
and I fell down from the tree.

The tree whose roots no one can show is the cosmic tree Yggdrasill, which is the bearer of eternal life. The roots are hidden
in the realm of the dead; they are at Mimir, the spring of Wisdom,
and the tree of life is the tree of divine knowledge. The tree of
life is Odin, the god of the underworld and wisdom himself.
Sacrifices to him are hung upon the tree, or pierced with a
spear, or both. Here the "I have hung myself upon the tree as a
sacrifice to Myself" is thus a self-consecration, a self-sacrifice;
the offering is the god himself. "Death" on this tree is the actualization of absolute life, of which this tree is the bearer.
In the "sought below and lifted up the runes," rune means
"sign of mystery" or "mystery." The rune possesses magic
power; the magic power of writing corresponds to that of the
word. Whoever writes, whoever "cuts runes" in wood or stone,
translates his thoughts into visible reality; he actualizes his
will. There are many instances of a priest cutting runes in order
to heal someone. The dying Odin thus brings superhuman or
magic power out of the depths ("sought below") up into our
world ("and lifted up the runes"). By means of divine death
men have obtained power over death; they have gained health
and salvation. Sophus Bugge thinks there is a direct influence on
Christianity, thinking of the death of Jesus on the cross. The
cross is indeed sometimes portrayed in the early Church as the
tree of life. Yet this story is entirely in the spirit of the Germanic
belief in Odin. Odin was actually the god of Yggdrasill, and the
tree of life was actually the tree of knowledge, of the knowledge which is first attained in death – the runes come from the
underworld.

LIST OF PUBLICATIONS OF
W. BREDE KRISTENSEN

N.B. Book reviews and articles in newspapers or popular magazines, etc., are not mentioned.

1. Ægypternes Forestillinger om Livet efter Döden i Forbindelse med Guderne Ra og Osiris (Egyptian Ideas about Life after Death in Connection with the Gods Re and Osiris), Kristiania, 1896.
2. Om Udödelighetstroen i Orientens gamle Religioner (Concerning the Belief in Immortality in the Ancient Oriental Religions), in *For Kirke og Kultur* III, 1896, pp. 513–526, 577.
3. Brahma, et Stykke indisk Religionshistorie (Brahma, a Chapter from the History of Indian Religion), Kristiania, 1898.
4. Om Religionernes Inddeling i Naturreligioner og etiske Religioner (Concerning the Classification of Religions into Nature Religions and Ethical Religions).
5. Helvedet (Hell), Samtiden, 1901.
6. Het verband tusschen godsdienst en de zucht tot zelfbehoud (The Connection between Religion and the Urge to Self-Preservation), Leiden, 1901.
7. Dualistische en monistische denkbeelden in den Egyptischen godsdienst (Dualistic and Monistic Ideas in the Egyptian Religion), in *Theologisch Tijdschrift* XXXVIII, 1904, pp. 233–255.
8. Eén of twee boomen in het paradijsverhaal? (One or Two Trees in the Paradise Story?), in *Theologisch Tijdschrift* XLII, 1908, pp. 215–233.
9. De Ruach Elohim vóór de schepping (The Ruach Elohim before Creation), in *Theologisch Tijdschrift* XLIII, 1909, pp. 398 ff.

10. Over de godsdienstige beteekenis van enkele oude wedstrij-
den en spelen (Concerning the Religious Meaning of Some
Ancient Contests and Games), in *Theologisch Tijdschrift*
XLIV, 1910, pp. 1–16.

11. De term „Zoon des Menschen" toegelicht uit de anthropo-
logie der Ouden (Some Light on the term "Son of Man"
from the Anthropology of the Ancients), in *Theologisch
Tijdschrift* XLV, 1911, pp. 1–38.

12. De heilige horens in den oud-Kretensischen godsdienst (The
Sacred Horns in the Ancient Cretan Religion), Kon. Akad.
v. Wet., Amsterdam, 1913.

13. Mysteriereligion i Oldtiden (Mystery Religion in Antiquity),
in *Norsk Theologisk Tidskrift*, 1913, pp. 294–336.

14. Hvad religionshistorisk studium beröber os og gir os (What
Study of the History of Religion Takes from us and what
it Gives us), For Kirke of Kultur, 1914.

15. Over waardeering van historische gegevens (Concerning the
Appraisal of Historical Data), in *Onze Eeuw* 15, 1915,
pp. 415–440.

16. De plaats van het zondvloedverhaal in het Gilgameš-epos
(The Place of the Flood Story in the Gilgamesh Epic),
Kon. Akad. v. Wet., 1915.

17. Over de viering der Osiris-mysterien (Concerning the Celebration of the Osiris Mysteries), Kon. Akad. v. Wet.,
Amsterdam, 1916.

18. De „Primitieven" of wij voorop? (Are We Really ahead
of the "Primitives"?), in *Feestschrift Chantepie de la Saussaye*, 1916, pp. 100–104.

19. Idealen van inzicht bij de volken der oudheid (Ideals of
Wisdom among the Peoples of Antiquity), in *Jaarboek der
Rijksuniversiteit te Leiden*, 1916.

20. Over de Egyptische Sphinx (Concerning the Egyptian
Sphinx) Kon. Akad. v. Wet., Amsterdam, 1917.

21. „Diepte-psychologie"? (Depth Psychology?), in *De Gids* 82,
1918, No. 6.

22. De symboliek van de boot in den Egyptischen Godsdienst
(The Symbolism of the boat in Egyptian Religion), Kon.
Akad. v. Wet., Amsterdam, 1919.

23. Over de wetenschappelijken arbeid van Herman Bavinck

(Concerning the scholarly work of Herman Bavinck), Kon. Akad. v. Wet., Amsterdam, 1922.

24. De loofhut en het loofhuttenfeest in den Egyptischen cultus (The Arbor Booth and the Festival of Booths in the Egyptian Cultus), Kon. Akad. v. Wet., Amsterdam, 1923.

25. De Delphische drievoet (The Delphic Tripod), Kon. Akad. v. Wet., Amsterdam, 1925.

26. Het leven uit den dood. Studiën over Egyptischen en Oud-Griekschen godsdienst (Life out of Death. Studies of Egyptian and Ancient Greek Religion), Haarlem, 1926; Translation of Livet fra Döden, Oslo, 1923.

27. De goddelijke bedrieger (The Divine Deceiver), Kon. Akad. v. Wet., Amsterdam, 1928.

28. De absoluutheid van het Christendom (The Absoluteness of Christianity,) *Eltheto* 82, 1928, pp. 129–140.

29. De goddelijke heraut en het woord van God (The Divine Herald and the Word of God), Kon. Akad. v. Wet., Amsterdam, 1930.

30. Symbool en Werkelijkheid (Symbol and Reality), in *De Gids* 95, 1931, pp. 76–85.

31. De Romeinsche fasces (The Roman Fasces), Kon. Akad. v. Wet., Amstrdan, 1932.

32. De ark van Jahwe (The Ark of Yahveh), Kon. Akad. v. Wet. Amsterdam, 1933.

33. Schleiermachers opvatting van de godsdienstgeschiedenis (Schleiermacher's Conception of the History of Religion), in *Vox Theologica* 5, 1934, pp. 97 ff.

34. De antieke opvatting van dienstbaarheid (The Ancient Conception of Servitude), Kon. Akad. v. Wet., Amsterdam, 1934.

35. Kringloop en totaliteit (Cycle and Totality), Kon. Akad. v. Wet., Amsterdam, 1938.

36. Geschiedenis der Godsdiensten (History of Religions), in *Vox Theologica* 9, 1938.

37. Kosmologische voorstellingen in de vroege oudheid (Cosmological Notions in Early Antiquity), in *Antieke en moderne kosmologie*, Arnhem, 1941.

38. Antieke Wetenschap (Ancient Science), Kon. Akad. v. Wet., Amsterdam, 1940.

39. De rijkdom der aarde in mythe en cultus (The Earth's Riches in Myth and Cultus), Kon. Akad. v. Wet., Amsterdam, 1942.
40. De godsdienstige beteekenis van de gesloten perioden (The Religious Meaning of Fixed and Delimited Periods), in Ex Oriente Lux, Leiden, 1943.
41. Den antikke tragedie og Henrik Ibsens verker (Ancient Tragedy and the Works of Henrik Ibsen), in *Kirke og Kultur*, 1941.
42. Tro eller overtro (Faith or Superstition), Oslo, 1946; Dutch translation, Geloof of bijgeloof?, in *Vox Theologica* XVI, 1946.
43. Het mysterie van Mithra (The Mystery of Mithra), Kon. Akad. v. Wet., Amsterdam, 1946.
44. Het sacrament der uitzending, Missa (The Sacrament of Demission of Dispatch, the Mass), Kon. Akad. v. Wet., Amsterdam, 1949.
45. De dubbele gerechtigheid (Double Righteousness), Kon. Akad. v. Wet., Amsterdam, 1950.
46. Primitiv visdom (Primitive Wisdom), in *Kirke og Kultur*, 1952. Dutch translation: Primitieve wijsheid, Leiden, 1952.
47. De Slangenstaf en het spraakvermogen van Mozes en Aäron (The Snake-Staff and the Speaking Ability of Moses and Aaron), Kon. Akad. v. Wet., Amsterdam, 1953.
48. Religionshistorisk Studium, Oslo, 1954; Dutch translation: Inleiding tot de godsdienstgeschiedenis (An Introduction to the History of Religion), Arnhem, 1955.

COLLECTED ESSAYS

49. Verzamelde bijdragen tot kennis der antieke godsdiensten (Collected Contributions to the Knowledge of the Ancient Religions), Amsterdam, 1947.
50. Symbool en Werkelijkheid (Symbol and Reality), Arnhem, 1954.

NOTES

N.B. References to books of the Bible and of the Avesta are indicated in the text itself.

Abbreviations

A.R.W. – *Archiv für Religionswissenschaft*

Delitzsch – Frie. Delitzsch, *Assyrisches Wörterbuch zur gesamten bisher veröffentlichen Keilschriftliteratur*, 1887–1890.

Dieterich – Albrecht Dieterich, *Mutter Erde. Ein Versuch über Volksreligion*, 3rd ed. 1925

E.R.E. – Hastings ,*Encyclopedia of Religion and Ethics*

Frazer, *G. B.* – J. G. Frazer, *The Golden Bough*

Gruppe – O. Gruppe, *Griechische Mythologie und Religionsgeschichte*, München, 1906

Heitmüller – W. Heitmüller, '*Im Namen Jesu.*' *Eine sprach- und religionsgeschichtliche Untersuchung zum Neuen Testament, speziell zur altchristlichen Taufe*, Göttingen, 1903.

Hesiod, *Th.* – Hesiod, *Theogonia*

Hirzel – Rudolf Hirzel, *Der Eid, Ein Beitrag zu seiner Geschichte*, 1902

Hubert and Mauss – Hubert and Mauss, "Essai sur le sacrifice," in *L'année sociologique* (1897–'98)

Kruyt – A. C. Kruyt, *Het Animisme in den Indischen Archipel*, Den Haag, 1906

Mannhardt – W. Mannhardt, *Wald- und Feldkulte*, 2nd ed., Berlin, 1904–5

Oldenberg – Hermann Oldenberg, *Die Religion des Veda*, 2nd ed. Stuttgart, 1917

Pausanias – Pausanias, *Descriptio Graeciae*

Pedersen, *Isr.* – Johs. Pedersen, *Israel. Its Life and Culture.* 2 vols. London – Copenhagen 1926 (1946)

Pliny – Pliny, *Naturalis Historia*

Plutarch, *De Is.* – Plutarch, *De Iside et Osiride*

Robertson Smith, *Rel. Sem.* – W. Robertson Smith, *Lectures on the Religion of the Semites*, Edinburgh, 1889 (References are to the third edition, London, 1927

Roscher – W. H. Roscher, *Ausführliches Lexikon der griechischen und römischen Mythologie*, Leipzig, 1884–1937.

Samter, *Fam.* – E. Samter, *Familienfeste der Griechen und Römer*, Berlin, 1901

Samter, *Geburt* – E. Samter, *Geburt, Hochzeit und Tod. Beiträge zum vergleichenden Volkskunde*, Leipzig-Berlin, 1911

Spencer and Gillen – B. Spencer and F. J. Gillen, *The Native Tribes of Central Australia*, London, 1889

Tylor – Ed. Tylor, *Primitive Culture*

Usener *G.* – H. Usener, *Götternamen. Versuch einer Lehre von der religiösen Begriffsbildung*, Bonn, 1896

Wellhausen – J. Wellhausen, *Reste Arabischen Heidentums*, Berlin, 1897.

Z.Ae.S. – *Zeitschrift für Aegyptische Sprache und Altertumskunde*, Leipzig.

Zimmern – H. Zimmern. *Beiträge zur Kenntnis der Babylonischen Religion. Die Beschwörungstafeln Surpu*, Leipzig, 1901

CHAPTER 1

1 Rudolf Otto, *Das Heilige. Über das Irrationale in der Idee des Göttlichen und sein Verhältnis zum Rationalen.* (English title: *The Idea of the Holy*), 1917

CHAPTER 2

1 Oldenberg, p. 196
2 *Tao Te Ching*, 63
3 *Ibid.*, 4
4 Herodotus, I, 131
5 Plutarch, *De Is.*, 64–65

CHAPTER 3

1 Tylor, II, pp. 247f.
2 Hesiod, *Th.*, 126ff
3 Delitsch, s.v. burume
4 Pausanias, II, 34, 10
5 Pausanias, II, 4, 6f
6 Athenaeus, *Dipnosophistae*, XV, 693ef
7 P. Stengel, *Die griechischen Kultusaltertümer*, 3. Aufl., München 1920; *A.R.W.*, VIII, 206
8 Roscher, I, 2024
9 Gruppe, 1467 note 5
10 *Guide to the Egyptian Galleries*, ad p. 135 and p. 257
11 J. G. Frazer, *Adonis, Attis, Osiris. Studies in the history of oriental religion*, Londen 1906, II, 361f.; See also Roscher. "Mondgöttin," col. 3152f.
12 Pliny, II, 221
13 Ph. Melanchthon, *Initia Doctriniae Physicae*
14 Mariette, *Denderah* IV, col. 34, 121, 136
15 Plutarch, *De Is.*, 39
16 Plutarch, *De Is.*, 42

CHAPTER 4

1 Dieterich
2 Shabaka stone
3 Homeric Hymn III, 529
4 Oldenberg, 234ff
5 *Iliad*, XXIV, 527f
6 Plutarch, *De facie in orbe lunae*, 26
7 H. Junker, *Das Götterdekret über das Abaton* (Denkschriften der kaiserl. Ak. d. Wiss. in Wien 1913) p. 50–54
8 Sophocles, *Oedipus Coloneus*, 698
9 Pausanias, I, 27, 2
10 Hesiod, Fragment 134
11 Virgil, *Aeneid*, VI, 136ff
12 J. Capart, *Abydos. Le temple de Séti Ier. Étude générale*, Bruxelles 1912, p. 42
13 Tertullian, *De baptismo*, 3–4
14 Pausanias, II, 38, 2
15 Hesiod, *Th.* 346–370
16 *Ibid.*, 389, 397
17 Pausanias, VIII, 18, 4
18 E. Rhode, '*Psyche.*' *Seelenkult und Unsterblichkeitsglaube der Griechen*, 7. und 8. Aufl., Tübingen 1921, p. 390
19 *Iliad*, XIV, 271; XV, 37 and elsewhere.
20 Virgil, *Aeneid*, XII, 816f

21 Plutarch, *De Is.*, 35
22 Zimmern, VIII, 150
23 Hesiod, *Th.*, 358, 886
24 *Odyssey*, XII, 165 ff
25 Pausanias, II, 31, 3
26 *Ibid.*, X, 24, 7
27 Servius, Commentary on the *Aeneid*, VII, 84
28 Robertson Smith, *Rel. Sem.*, 179–181
29 Troels-Lund, *Dagligt Liv i Norden i det 16 Aarhundrede*, København, 1908, VII, 238
30 Tylor, I, 140f.
31 *Z.Ae.S.* LI (1914), 127–135
32 Herodotus II, 90
33 Überweg, *Grundriss der Geschichte der Philosophie*, I, 30
34 Cicero, *De natura deorum*, I, 10
35 Justin Martyr, *Apology*, I, 61, 12
36 G. P. Wetter, *Phōs. Eine Untersuchung über hellenistische Frömmigkeit*, Uppsala-Leipzig, 1915
37 Pausanias, V, 27, 6
38 Ovid, *Fasti*, III, 135–144; Macrobius, *Saturnalia* I, 12, 6
39 Mannhardt

CHAPTER 5

1 Usener, *G.*
2 Herodotus, V, 83–86
3 Usener, *G.*, p. 119
4 *Ibid.*, p. 280
5 *Iliad*, XI, 73ff

CHAPTER 6

1 Th. Hopfner, *Fontes historiae religionis aegyptiacae*, Bonn 1922–25, p. 342
2 Herodotus, II, 65–76
3 Kruyt, 120
4 *Ibid.*, 176
5 S. Reinach, *A.R.W.* X (1907), 56; F. Cumont, *Textes et Monuments figurés relatifs aux mystères de Mythra*. Tome I, Bruxelles 1899, p. 315, note 6
6 Hubert and Mauss, 32
7 Tiresias, in Euripides' *Bacchae*

CHAPTER 7

1 J. G. Frazer, *Totemism*, Edinburgh 1887; *Totemism and Exogamy* (4 vol.), London 1910
2 Robertson Smith, *Rel. Sem.*
3 Spencer and Gillen; A. W. Howitt, *The native tribes of South-east Australia*, London 1904
4 Spencer and Gillen, 202
5 *Ibid.*, 181
6 *Ibid.*, 271, 386
7 *Ibid.*, 159–162

CHAPTER 8

1 R. H. Codrington, *The Melanesians. Studies in their anthropology and folklore*, Oxford 1891
2 Herbert Spencer, *First Principles*

3 Pliny, XXVIII, 39
4 Livy, *Ab urbe condita*, XXXVII, 3
5 Festus, *De significatu verborum* (Ed. Müller), p. 278
6 Gellius, *Noctes atticae*, IV, 9, 8
7 J. G. Frazer, *Lectures on the early history of kingship*, London, 1905
8 Frazer, *G.B.*, III, 131
9 *Ibid.*, III, 134
10 *Ibid.*, III, 102–114
11 A. W. Nieuwenhuis, *Quer durch Borneo. Ergebnisse seiner Reisen in dem Jahre 1894, 1896–97, 1898–1900*, 2 Tle, Leiden 1904–1907, II, 102
12 Herodotus, I, 99
13 N. Söderblom, *Das Werden des Gottesglaubens. Untersuchungen über die Anfänge der Religion*, 2. Aufl., Leipzig 1926, Chapter 7.

CHAPTER 10

1 Pedersen, *Isr.* I, 182–212
2 *Ibid.*, I, 182ff
3 *Ibid.*, I, 77ff
4 O. Weinreich, *Antike Heilungswunder. Untersuchungen zum Wunderglauben der Griechen und Römer*, Giessen 1909, 1–76

CHAPTER 11

1 Pedersen, *Isr.* I. 103ff.

CHAPTER 12

1 Pedersen, *Isr.*, I, 184
2 Herodotus, V, 47
3 Hesiod, *Th.*, 31ff
4 Cicero, *De legibus*, II, 4
5 *Odyssey*, X, 28

CHAPTER 13

1 C. Snouck Hurgronje, *Der Islam* (in: Chantepie de la Saussaye, *Lehrbuch der Religionsgeschichte*, 4. Aufl., Tübingen 1925, p. 739ff); F. Heiler, *Die Bedeutung der Mystik für die Weltreligionen*, München 1919, p. 18
2 Ludwig Feuerbach, *Das Wesen des Christentums; Das Wesen der Religion*
3 Plutarch, *De superstitione*, 10
4 F. Schleiermacher, *Reden über die Religion*

CHAPTER 14

1 C. Fossey, *La magie assyrienne. Etude suivie de textes magiques, transcrits, traduits et commentés*, Paris 1902 pp. 345ff

CHAPTER 15

1 *Lamentation of the pious old man*
2 *Ibid.*
3 Dionysius of Halicarnassus, *Antiquitates romanae*, II, 10
4 Imm. Kant, *Die Religion innerhalb der Grenzen der blossen Vernunft*

CHAPTER 16

1 A. J. Gooszen, *Bijdragen tot de Taal-, Land- en Volkenkunde van Ned. Indië*, LXIX (1914), 366–385
2 Dieterich; Samter, *Geburt*

3 Dieterich, 10
4 *Ibid.*, 28
5 *Odyssey*, XIX, 188
6 Pyramid Text 910
7 Samter, *Geburt*, 22
8 *E.R.E.*, "Birth," p. 637*b*
9 Heitmüller, 276ff
10 *E.R.E.*, "Baptism"
11 Tertullian, *De baptismo*
12 D. Plooij, *Tendentieuse varianten in den text der Evangeliën*. Rede. Leiden 1926, p. 11
13 *Ibid.*, 8ff
14 W. H. Prescott, *The conquest of Mexico, with a preliminary view of the ancient Mexican civilisation*, p. 482
15 S. Bugge, *Studien über die Entstehung der nordischen Götter- und Heldensagen*, München 1889, p. 402ff.
16 *E.R.E.*, "Baptism" p. 369a–372a
17 Heitmüller
18 A. van Gennep, *Les rites de passage*, Paris 1909, pp. 94 ff
19 J. G. F. Riedel, *De sluik- en kroesharige rassen tusschen Celebes en Papua*, Den Haag 1906
20 E. Samter, *Familienfeste der Griechen und Römer*, Berlin 1901, pp. 79ff; H. Diels, *Sibyllinische Blätter*, Berlin 1890, p. 48; G. Anrich, *Das antike Mysterienwesen in seinem Einfluss auf das Christentum*, Göttingen 1894, pp. 233ff
21 Samter, *Familienfeste*, p. 3
22 *Ibid.*, p. 1
23 *Iliad*, XVI, 672
24 W. Caland, *A.R.W.* XVII (1914), 481
25 A. van Gennep, *Les rites de passage*, Paris 1909, p. 211
26 L. Lévy-Bruhl, *Les fonctions mentales dans les sociétés inférieures*, Paris, 1910, pp. 322f
27 Hesiod, *Th.*, 211f

CHAPTER 17

1 *Iliad*, III, 73, 256 (cf 94)
2 Dionysius of Halicarnassus, *Antiquitates romanae*, IV, 14, 3
3 Varro, *De lingua latina*, VI, 23
4 Hesiod, *Poem on the shield of Hercules*, 28f.

CHAPTER 19

1 Pausanias, X, 32, 13ff
2 Virgil, *Aeneid*, VI, 136ff
3 Homeric hymn III, 529f
4 Otto Kern, *Die Religionen der Griechen*, Berlin 1926, I, 82f.
5 Robertson Smith, *Rel. Sem.*, 97
6 Otto Kern, *op. cit.*, 80
7 Pausanias IV, 26; Herodotus V, 42
8 Pausanias I, 40. 6; I, 42. 6
9 A. Jeremias, *Handbuch der altorientalischen Geisteskultur*, II, 113f
10 G. Maspéro, *Histoire ancienne des peuples de l'Orient classique*, Paris 1895–99, I, 637
11 Ovid, *Fasti*, VI, 261ff
12 *Ibid.*, VI, 267
13 J. Benzinger, *Hebräische Archäologie*, p. 395
14 Plutarch, *Symposion*, IV, 6
15 Plutarch, *De Is.*, 20
16 Cf. H. Nissen, *Orientation. Studien zur Geschichte der Religion.* Heft I–III, Berlin 1906–10.

CHAPTER 20

1 A. Jeremias, *Das Alte Testament im Lichte des alten Orients*, p. 39 note 4
2 Troels-Lund, *Dagligt Liv i Norden i det 16 Aarhundrede*, København 1908, VII, 245, 249ff
3 J. Pedersen, *Scepticisme Israélite*, Paris 1931, pp. 34, 37–40
4 Cf. Scheftelowitz, *Die Zeit als Schicksalsgottheit*, p. 58

CHAPTER 21

1 J. von Negelein, in *A.R.W.*, V (1902), 11, 33
2 *Iliad*, XXIII, 72
3 B. D. Eerdmans, *De Godsdienst van Israël*, Huis ter Heide 1930, I, 42 (English edition: *The religion of Israel*, Leiden 1947, p. 27)
4 Shakespeare, *Hamlet*, Act III, scene 2
5 A. Erman und H. Grapow, *Wörterbuch der Aegyptischen Sprache*, IV, 291
6 F. Creuzer, *Symbolik und Mythologie der alten Völker, besonders der Griechen*, Leipzig 1819–23
7 Plutarch, *De Is.*
8 Pyramid Text 2063
9 *Ibid.*, 2066
10 Kruyt, 70
11 *A.R.W.* V (1902), 17
12 *Ibid.* V, (1902), 12
13 *Ibid.* V (1902), 18
14 Kruyt, 69
15 *Ibid.*, 71
16 Frazer, *G.B.*, III, chapter VI
17 *Ibid.*
18 A. Erman, *Die Religion der Aegypter*, 2. Aufl., Berlin 1934, 301ff
19 Heitmüller, 133; Pedersen, *Isr.*, I 245ff
20 Heitmüller, 146
21 *Ibid.*, 155
22 *Ibid.*
23 Origen, *Contra Celsum*

CHAPTER 22

1 F. Heiler, *Das Gebet. Eine religionsgeschichtliche und religions-psychologische Untersuchung*, 1. Aufl. München 1918 ("*Prayer. A study in the history and psychology of religion*")
2 Tylor, II, 364ff
3 F. Martin, *Textes religieux assyriens et babyloniens*, Paris 1900 p. 257; Zimmern, 125
4 L. Feuerbach, *Das Wesen des Christentums; Das Wesen der Religion*

CHAPTER 23

1 *A.R.W.* VIII, Beiheft (1905), 72
2 Dieterich, 54
3 J. Wellhausen, *Reste arabischen Heidentums*, Berlin 1897, p. 186
4 H. Usener, in: *Rhein. Mus.* LVIII (1903), 17ff
5 Jan de Vries, *Der altnordische Rasengang*, p. 133
6 Virgil, *Aeneid*, XII, 817
7 Roscher, III, 1, s.v. "Palikoi", col. 1288 and 1284f.
8 A. Hellwig, in: *A.R.W.* XII (1909), 46ff
9 *A.R.W.* XIII (1910), 155
10 Wellhausen, *op. cit.*, 191f

CHAPTER 24

1 Hirzel, 176–213
2 Pausanias, VII, 25, 7
3 Hirzel, 160f.
4 Hesiod, *Th.*, 775-806
5 Tylor, I, 140ff
6 King James I, *Daemonology*
7 Robertson Smith, *Rel. Sem.*, 178
8 Pausanias, IX, 30, 8
9 Robertson Smith, *Rel. Sem.*, 181
10 A. Chr. Bang, *Norske hexeformularer og magiske opskrifter*, Kristiania 1901–02, p. 210
11 Tylor, I, 128
   Bang, *op. cit.*, 210
12 Hirzel, 187

CHAPTER 25

1 Scheftelowitz, *A.R.W.* XVII (1914), 353ff
2 Pausanias, II, 17, 1
3 Blackman in: *Z.Ae.S.* L. (912) 69f.
4 Bonnet, in: *Z.Ae.S.* LXVII (1931), 22f.
5 Heitmüller, 276ff.
6 Tertullian, *De baptismo*, 3–4
7 Lohmeyer, *Vom göttlichen Wohlgeruch*, Heidelberg 1919. (Sitzb. Heidelb. Ak. d. Wiss. 1919, Abh. 9)
8 Homeric hymn to Dionysus (VII) 36f

CHAPTER 26

1 Livy, IX, 8, 6
2 F. Cumont, *Les Réligions orientales dans le paganisme romain*, 2, XI
3 Apuleius, *Metam.* XI, 15
4 F. Cumont, *Textes et monuments figurés relatifs aux mystères de Mythra*. Tome I, Bruxelles 1899, p. 318
5 G. Anrich, *Das antike Mysterienwesen in seinem Einfluss auf das Christentum*, Göttingen 1894, p. 123^e
6 A. von Harnack, *Mission und Ausbreitung des Christentums*, I, 349ff
7 F. Cumont, *Textes et monuments*, I, 319 note 2
8 *Ibid.*, I, 318, 11
9 Harnack, *Mission* I. 349. 3 en Cumont, *Rel. Or.*, 2, X
10 Dieterich; Gruppe, 1617 note 4
11 Frazer, *G.B.* VIII, 86ff
12 F. Cumont, *Textes et monuments*, I, 175f., 320

CHAPTER 27

1 Tylor, II, 375–410
2 *Ibid.*, II, 376
3 *Ibid.*, II, 318
4 Robertson Smith, *Rel. Sem.*
5 Hubert and Mauss, *Essai sur la nature et la fonction sociale du sacrifice*, in *L'année sociologique*, tome II 1899
6 A. Loisy, *Essai historique sur le sacrifice*, Paris 1920
7 F. Heiler, *Das Gebet*, München 1918
8 Delitzsch, 287 s.v. hisbu

 9 Shabaka stone
10 J. Capart, *L'art egyptien*, I, 72
11 E. Rohde, *Psyche*, II, 390f
12 Oldenberg, 357ff
13 Robertson Smith, *Rel. Sem.* 174
14 S. Reinach, *A.R.W.* X (1907), 55
15 Robertson Smith, *Rel, Sem.*, 290
16 Plutarch, *De superstitione*, 31
17 Cf. Robertson Smith, *Rel. Sem.*, 292 and Plutarch, *De superst.*, 10
18 Robertson Smith, *Rel. Sem.*, 201ff
19 A. B. Cook, *Zeus*, 1914–25, pp. 519ff
20 Gruppe, 813
21 *Ibid.*, 813 note 2 and 841.
22 Pliny, III, 109
23 Macrobius, *Saturnalia*, I, 7, 28
24 Gruppe, 777 note 2
25 Roscher, II col. 1147
26 *Odyssey*, XI, 25
27 *Mitteilungen der Vorderasiatischen Gesellschaft*, XXII, (1896) Fig. V, p. 166
28 Joseph Braun S.J., *Der christliche Altar in seiner geschichtlichen Entwicklung*, 1924–25
29 F. Wieland, *Altar und Altargrab der christlichen Kirchen im 4. Jahrhundert*, Leipzig 1912
30 Oldenberg, 342ff
31 M. P. Nilsson, *Griechische Feste von religiöser Bedeutung mit Ausschluss der attischen*, 1906, 219
32 Robertson Smith, *Rel. Sem.*
33 *Śatapatha Brahmana* I.1.1.4
34 Oldenberg, 409f
35 Strabo, *Geographica*, 250
36 Hubert and Mauss, 93f
37 Frazer, *Adonis, Attis, Osiris*, 44f, 48
38 Mannhardt, I, 521ff
39 *Ibid.*, I, 499
40 The Hymn of the Lofty One, the Havemaal, quoted from van Hamel, *Odin hanging on the Tree*, 1932, pp. 138f

GENERAL INDEX *

abaton (pedon) (Gr.) 357f, 364
Abimelech 429, 432
Abraham (Abram) 205, 247, 265, 429, 432
Absalom 76, 199f
Acca Larentia 350
Achaia 323
Achelous 119
Achilles 32, 125, 315, 430
Acosta (de) 456
Acrocorinthus 65
Acropolis 114f, 156, 191, 254
activity (divine —) 81, 251, 482, 489
Adam 189, 191, 249, 263, 325, 335
Adama (Hebr.) 191
Adapa 125, 264f, 289
Adar 384
Aditi 29
adonai (Hebr.) 414
Adonis 119, 165, 281, 333, 466f
adoption of children 320
Adrastus 430
adulthood 306, 326
   transition to — 316-319
adyton (Gr.) 131
Aea 65, 133
Aeacus 277, 430
Aeëtes 65f
Aegina 147
Aegir-Ran 120
Aeneas 119, 359
aerarium (Lat.) 94
Aeschylus 100, 219, 362
   Agamemnon 218f
   Eumenides 293
   Prometheus Bound 257, 289
affinity 239f, 242, 244, 251ff, 258
Africa (West coast of —) 459
Agamemnon 218, 296
Agni 29, 96, 135, 142f, 269, 340, 472
agora (Gr.) 223, 382

agreement 5, 64 ,74f, 274ff, 342f, 453, 485; see also covenant; treaty
agriculture 91, 96, 135, 185, 232, 237, 243, 441, 482
   gods of — 90, 146, 148
Ahriman 30f, 74f, 120, 153, 241, 263, 273, 387, 495
(Ahura) Mazda 29ff, 34f, 38f, 49, 57, 64, 74f, 89ff, 104f, 108, 120f, 125, 135f, 146f, 149, 153f, 185f, 191, 195f, 198f, 204, 210–214, 224, 234f, 241ff, 263, 269, 273, 280, 309, 344, 423, 429, 433, 495
   Mazda's kingdom 49, 70, 105, 121, 186
   Mazda religion 39, 90, 150f, 210, 214, 269
aigis (Gr.) 151
air 54, 56, 262, 460
akhet (Eg.) 374
akhu (Eg.) 137, 150
Alexander 454, 495
Allatu 124
allegory 249f
alms 97
altar 106f, 389, **469-476,** 480
   — of the city 319
ambassador 324f
ambrosia (Gr.) 66, 115, 125, 142, 196
Amenophis IV 76
Amenti 65, 67, 372
Amesha spentas 429
Ammon-Min 82
Amrtat 196
anabasis (Gr.) 144
Anahita 120f, 123ff, 269
Ananke 65, 312
anathema (plural: anathemata) (Gr.) 390, 397
Anaximenes 134
ancestors 43, 45, 89, 209, 239, 316f, 320f, 324, 345, 350, 363, 474, 484

* This index was prepared by JOH. P. H. G. KIEN drs. theol.

midwife 307
Mikado 184
miles (*Lat.*) 455
— *Christi* (*Lat.*) 242, 455
— of Mithra 75, 242, 455
milk 65, 242, 447, 457, 480
mimēsis (*Gr.*) 27, 389
Mimir 117, 120, 130, 496
Min 82, 106, 468
Minos 277, 430
Minotaur 106, 471
Minucius Felix 455
miracle 28, 148, 251, 423
misfortune 488ff, 492f
Mithra (Mithra religion) 39, 64, 71, 74f,
    90, 106, 131, 137, 153, 160, 242, 246,
    274, 325, 336, 343ff, 348f, 361f, 369,
    433, 448, 455ff, 465, 494f
— Saxigenus 71
— Tauroctonus 71, 495
— Mysteries 57, 71, 74ff, 106, 137,
    242, 245, 310, 325, 336, 362, 387,
    452, 454, 494f
Mitra 425
modern 19f, 359f, 378f, 407, 472; *see also*
    ancient
Mohammed 76, 268, 320
Moira (plural: Moirai) (*Gr.*) 48, 50, 56,
    65, 126, 192, 229, 311f, 333f, 338, 386,
    429
momentary gods 145, **149**
monism 36, 58
monogenēs (*Gr.*) 154
monotheism 76f, 148, 268
months 380, 384
moon (god) 51f, 54, 56, 65, 77-87, 88f,
    147, 167, 262, 377-381, 471
crescent — 81ff
full — 83
new — 81-84, 86, 116, 262, 381
phases (shapes) of the — 78, 82, 86,
    377, 381
waning — 79
moon horns 84
moral conduct 284
— conscience 281
— law 44, 267, 270, 278, 281f, 285,
    287, 298, 300ff
— life 290, 296
— sense 276, 287; *see also* ethics; order
Moria 114f
moros (*Gr.*) 114, 334
Moses 269, 280, 414, 440
mother 22, 306–310, 323, 325; *see also*
    Great Mother
— of the gods 65
— of gods and men 89, 139
Mother Earth 191, 306f, 340, 429

mound 479
mountain 56, 106–109
cosmic — 109, 370f
earth — 106, 121, 370, 475, 477
sacred — 365
mourning 329
Müller (Max) 41, 62, 173
Mummu 127ff
mummy 67, 81, 124, 155, 254, 335, 372,
    392
Mundi Animus (*Lat.*) 208
Muse(s) 49, 55, 130f, 220, 328
music 27f, 55, 221, 311, 328
Mycene 94, 340, 446
mystēs (*Gr.*) 465
Mysteries 28, 46, 64ff, 71, 74, 84, 99, 112,
    124, 137, 141, 168f, 258, 305, 366, 401,
    413, 434, 439, 446, 448ff, 455; *see also*
    Egypt; Eleusis; Greece; Isis; Mithra
mystērion (*Gr.*) 455f
mysterium fascinosum (*tremendum*) (*Lat.*)
    355
mystery 20ff, 29f, 67f, 70f, 73, 83, 92ff,
    96, 99, 102f, 106, 112ff, 116, 118f, 137,
    145, 157, 192f, 197, 206f, 220, 222, 228,
    230, 232f, 236, 265, 285, 306f, 309f,
    316, 319, 324–327, 329f, 335ff, 364,
    367, 376, 384, 390, 404, 413, 433, 441,
    451, 455, 457, 482, 496
— of death 101, 119, 193, 326, 329,
    331, 335, 451, 466
— of life 71, 83, 87f, 107, 159, 194,
    228, 233f, 265, 270, 304, 316, 326,
    343, 476, 493
— of resurrection 362, 395
— of the underworld 361
mystery gods 349, 430
— ideas 71
— religions 7, 47, 159, 197, 245, 323,
    338, 454, 456
— rite 494
— sacrifice 466
mystical ground of being 20f
— power 134
— reality 98, 228
mysticism 64, 85, 245
myth 20, 62, 69f, 118, 140, 153, 189f,
    247f, 251f, 402, 404ff; *see also* creation;
    light; sun; vegetation

Nabunaïd 53, 128
nāḥāsh (*nāḥash*) (*Hebr.*) 103, 161, 339
Naiads 104
Nairyosanha 135, 224f
nāma-rūpa (*Skt.*) 204, 237
name 204, 315f, 410, **411-416**
secret — 169, 316
name pillar 199